Military Justice

Military Justice

The Rights and Duties of Soldiers and Government

Nigel D. White

*Professor of Public International Law, School of Law,
University of Nottingham, UK*

Cheltenham, UK • Northampton, MA, USA

Cover image: Dave Lowe on Unsplash

Published by
Edward Elgar Publishing Limited
The Lypiatts
15 Lansdown Road
Cheltenham
Glos GL50 2JA
UK

Edward Elgar Publishing, Inc.
William Pratt House
9 Dewey Court
Northampton
Massachusetts 01060
USA

A catalogue record for this book
is available from the British Library

Library of Congress Control Number: 2022931024

This book is available electronically in the **Elgar**online
Law subject collection
http://dx.doi.org/10.4337/9781789902808

ISBN 978 1 78990 279 2 (cased)
ISBN 978 1 78990 280 8 (eBook)

Printed and bound in Great Britain by TJ Books Limited, Padstow, Cornwall

Contents

Preface

Issues of military justice permeate public discourse. They range from questions of criminal responsibility arising out of the legacy of internal and external military deployments to Northern Ireland, Afghanistan and Iraq, to wider issues of the extent of the application of human rights law to military operations. While criminal responsibility principally concerns breach of duties owed by soldiers under service law and the law of armed conflict, the application of human rights law involves the duties of the government to both civilians caught up in military operations and to the soldiers involved.

Law plays a central role in framing the activities of the military, but there are heated and sometimes bitter debates about the nature and extent of the applicable law. These range across constitutional matters, including the power of the government to order the deployment of soldiers to controversial wars and the duties of soldiers to obey such orders, to the application of the law of armed conflict such as the power of the military to detain civilians in armed conflict and the duties of soldiers towards detainees. All raise matters of accountability when things go wrong, which may take the form of public inquiries or inquiries by Select Committees or lead to the court martial of soldiers involved in the abuse of detainees.

While military or service law is often narrowly understood and studied as the specific and specialist laws, processes and institutions governing service personnel, this book takes a broader approach and examines military justice from a wider consideration of the rights and duties of government in military operations and the duties and rights of soldiers engaged in such. Moreover, by exploring the relationship between the military and society it is possible to reach a more profound understanding of the rationale for military justice and make the case for both its continuation and for any reforms to it. The military is often viewed as a separate society governed by separate laws. This book demonstrates that this has certainly been true historically and in part remains so, for example when considering the prosecution of disciplinary offences such as desertion before a court martial. However, it is not possible to understand the continuing debates about both the need for a system of military justice, and the need for it to change to reflect wider societal changes, without exploring the place of the military in society and recognising the wider influences of justice and law upon it. For example, the court martial, which is the centrepiece of military justice, has changed dramatically over the years and will continue to change to reflect these wider issues of law and justice. More broadly, by considering the relevance of legal regimes, which ebb and flow in terms of applicability because of changing understandings in the law and the differing situations the military is deployed to, the book shows that military justice is both complex and in a state of flux. Whether this justifies the accusation that the military is increasingly exposed to 'lawfare', meaning that the military is now so bogged down with laws and regulations that it can no longer operate effectively, is one of the issues of justice discussed in this book.

This book is dedicated to the memory of two close friends and colleagues: the Reverend Professor Hilaire McCoubrey (1953–2000) and Professor Robert Cryer (1974–2021). Hilaire brought me into the field of the law governing armed conflict. His knowledge of the area as well as military history and philosophy sowed the early seeds of my interest in military justice. He introduced me to former Judge Advocate General Jeff Blackett, whose work and judgments feature in this book and whose frank and informative talks at the University of Nottingham were inspirational to both students and staff (myself included). Rob's encyclopaedic knowledge of international criminal and international humanitarian law and his forensic legal analysis of these subjects were second to none. Hilaire, Rob and myself taught numerous Law of Armed Conflict (LOAC) courses to lawyers from the Army Legal Services, other services and militaries, mainly at Nottingham University. The formal and informal discussions during those courses, in which the myriad of laws, practices and institutions that shape or form part of the military justice system were debated, must have had a cumulative effect on me over the years, leading to the writing of this book. I would like to think that Hilaire and Rob would appreciate this book but, more importantly, without their friendship and influence it would not have been written. Any mistakes or errors, however, remain my own.

Nigel D. White
The University of Nottingham
August 2021

Abbreviations

1 PARA	1st Battalion Parachute Regiment
AFCS	Armed Forces Compensation Scheme
AP I	Protocol I Additional to the Geneva Conventions of 1949 and Relating to the Protection of Victims of International Armed Conflicts (1977)
AP II	Protocol II Additional to the Geneva Conventions of 1949 and Relating to the Protection of Victims of Non-International Armed Conflicts (1977)
ARIO	Articles on the Responsibility of International Organisations (2011)
ARS	Articles on the Responsibility of States for Internationally Wrongful Acts (2001)
BHD	Bullying, harassment and discrimination
CCRC	Criminal Cases Review Commission
CMAC	Court Martial Appeal Court
CND	Campaign for Nuclear Disarmament
CO	Commanding Officer
CPA	Coalition Provisional Authority
CPS	Crown Prosecution Service
DCO	Defence Council Order
DPP	Director of Public Prosecutions
DUF	Directives on the Use of Force
ECHR	European Convention on Human Rights (1950)
ECtHR	European Court of Human Rights
EHRR	European Human Rights Reports
G8	Group of Eight States
GC I	Geneva Convention for the Amelioration of the Condition of the Wounded and Sick in Armed Forces in the Field (1949)

GC II	Geneva Convention for the Amelioration of the Condition of Wounded, Sick and Shipwrecked Members of the Armed Forces at Sea (1949)
GC III	Geneva Convention Relative to the Treatment of Prisoners of War (1949)
GC IV	Geneva Convention Relative to the Protection of Civilian Persons in Time of War (1949)
GCHQ	Government Communications Headquarters
HC	House of Commons
HL	House of Lords
HRA	Human Rights Act (1998)
HSE	Health and Safety Executive
IAC	International Armed Conflict
IAEA	International Atomic Energy Agency
ICC	International Criminal Court
ICCPR	International Covenant on Civil and Political Rights (1966)
ICJ	International Court of Justice
ICRC	International Committee of the Red Cross
ICTY	International Criminal Tribunal for the Former Yugoslavia
IED	Improvised Explosive Device
IFI	Iraq Fatality Investigations
IHAT	Iraq Historic Allegations Team
IHL	International Humanitarian Law
ILC	International Law Commission
IRA	Irish Republican Army
ISAF	International Security Assistance Force
ISIL	Islamic State
ISOP	Interim Standard Operating Procedures
JAG	Judge Advocate General
KFOR	Kosovo Force
LOAC	Law of Armed Conflict
MACA	Military Aid to Civil Authorities
MCM	Manual for Courts-Martial (US)
MCTC	Military Corrective Training Centre

MINUSCA	United Nations Multidimensional Stabilisation Mission in the Central African Republic
MINUSMA	United Nations Multidimensional Integrated Stabilisation Mission in Mali
MoD	Ministry of Defence
MoU	Memorandum of Understanding
MP	Member of Parliament
NATO	North Atlantic Treaty Organisation
NCO	Non-Commissioned Officer
NIAC	Non-International Armed Conflict
NNWS	Non-Nuclear Weapons States
NPT	Nuclear Non-Proliferation Treaty (1968)
NWS	Nuclear Weapons States
ONUC	United Nations Operation in the Congo
PKO	Peacekeeping Operation
PoW	Prisoner of War
PTSD	Post-Traumatic Stress Disorder
RAF	Royal Air Force
RIAA	Reports on International Arbitrations
RMP	Royal Military Police
RoE	Rules of Engagement
RUC	Royal Ulster Constabulary
SAC	Summary Appeal Court
SAS	Special Air Service
SCC	Service Complaints Commissioner for the Armed Forces
SOFA	Status of Forces Agreement
SOP	Standard Operating Procedure
SPA	Service Prosecuting Authority
SPLI	Service Police Legacy Investigations
TCN	Troop Contributing Nation
UK	United Kingdom
UKSC	United Kingdom Supreme Court
UN	United Nations

UNDPKO	United Nations Department of Peacekeeping Operations
UNEF	United Nations Emergency Force
UNFICYP	United Nations Force in Cyprus
UNMIK	United Nations Mission in Kosovo
UNOSOM	United Nations Operation in Somalia
US	United States
WMD	Weapons of Mass Destruction

Introduction to *Military Justice*

The way soldiers treat those they encounter and the way soldiers are treated define a nation. Whether it is the court martial of a British marine for unlawfully killing a wounded Taliban insurgent in Afghanistan, or a claim against the government for not supplying troops in Iraq with adequate equipment, the British soldier is in the spotlight more than any period since the Second World War. The army, navy and air force are part of the national fabric, the essence of the state, tasked with defending the UK and its national interests. The armed forces have to be able to act effectively but, as the paradigmatic state actors, they are both subject to the rule of law and accountable for its breach. The military is built on strong discipline but that is inevitably stretched and sometimes broken in the face of dangerous and life-threatening tasks, making the application of laws challenging but essential. The traditional view of the soldier as servant of the Crown destined to carry out orders without question is no longer beyond dispute after the conflicts in Afghanistan and Iraq. This has led to a re-evaluation of the relationship between state and soldier, and an on-going and profound debate about how the scales of military justice are balanced and, perhaps, ought to be rebalanced.

This book has expository and exploratory aims. First, it explores the legal frameworks governing military operations and British soldiers in increasingly complex situations. As one of the leading commentators on military law, Gerry Rubin has written: 'the legal governance of the British Armed Forces is wondrously complex'.[1] More specifically, and secondly, this book identifies and clarifies the rights and duties of British soldiers in situations that vary from riots to all-out war, and the rights and duties of the government when deploying armed forces to these situations. More broadly, it will consider how the scales of military justice are balanced between rights and duties of soldier and government. This latter aim necessitates that a more conceptual understanding of justice is brought to bear in order to make a considered judgement on the issue of whether the scales of military justice are in balance or need to be rebalanced.

---

[1]   G.R. Rubin, 'Why Military Law? Some United Kingdom Perspectives' (2007) 26 *University of Queensland Law Journal* 353 at 359.

That intent, namely to place the discussion of the law within a broader framework of justice, is hopefully made clear in the opening substantive chapter, which explores the deeper meaning of military justice by considering its position within the social contract between state and citizen. The constitutional evolution of the social contract in the UK is further explored in Chapter 2, alongside the growing international constraints upon the state. This is followed by an exploration of the legal frameworks within which troops are deployed both internally and externally to the UK in Chapters 3 and 4. Although these chapters show that such deployments are largely issues of the rights and duties of the government, high-level decisions of limited legal relevance to the troops on the ground, the divide is being increasingly eroded by the increasing relevance of international law to both state and soldiers. That erosion is shown in Chapters 5 and 6, which address central concerns of soldiers as to when they can use potentially lethal force, when they can detain individuals on security grounds, and the treatment of such detainees. The government has the responsibility under national and international law to ensure that soldiers have clear rules on the use of force and detention, that they understand them, and are held to account for their violation.

Chapter 7 looks at the court martial as the emblematic means of holding soldiers to account for violations of these rules, but also of military laws designed to reinforce obedience and discipline essential for the success of military operations. The resistance of the military to increasing legalisation of their functions, which it strongly argues inhibits operational effectiveness and its ability to defend the nation and its interests, becomes apparent in this chapter and in Chapter 8. Chapter 8 exposes and analyses the encroachment of human rights law into the system of military justice, especially the court martial and its ability to deliver a fair trial and then, even more controversially, the battlefield, where the inevitable loss of life raises the question of whether the right to life of soldiers and civilians should be protected.

Chapters 4 to 8 will assess the rights and duties of government, and the rights and duties of soldiers. Chapter 9 will assess the scales of military justice but in general will show that historically the rights (powers) of the government have predominated, while its duties were few. In contrast the duties of soldiers were many and their rights few. That balance is changing with the duties of government and the rights of soldiers increasing. Conceptions of justice introduced in Chapter 1 and developed throughout the book are used to assess whether the scales of military justice are in balance, answering questions as to whether the duties of the government have become too onerous, in particular unduly hampering the effectiveness of military operations, but also whether the recognition and protection of the rights of soldiers is an inevitable, and arguably long overdue, development in a democratic state. A comparative perspective is brought into Chapter 9 with the aim of helping to assess whether the scales of military justice in the UK are in balance or need rebalancing either in favour of the soldier or of the state, but the overarching standard will be that of justice. To this end the military justice systems of other states will be referred to, not as providing models for reform, but to understand how they balance the rights and duties of soldiers and state.

Turning to the subject matter of the book, the term 'military' has a relatively clear connotation covering all three services (British Army, Royal Navy and Royal Air Force) but it becomes more opaque when covering, for example, military intelligence.[2] 'Justice' is a much more nebulous concept but it is the concept chosen here, rather than military 'law', which would confine coverage to an exposition of the system of primary and secondary rules applicable to the military.[3] The primary rules of military law contain the legal standards by which military personnel work and are judged, and the secondary rules include the processes and mechanisms of the military justice system, including courts and officials, which provide for clarity, efficiency and enforcement.[4] Matthew Groves and Alison Duxbury confine their understanding of 'military justice' to 'the systems states have put in place to regulate both the disciplinary and criminal offences by members of their armed forces', but admit that the 'justice' element has broader and deeper connotations.[5] Both types of rules, primary and secondary, will be at the centre of the subsequent account, but they will be positioned within a wider consideration of justice. As Hilaire McCoubrey has written:

> 'Justice' is a commonly encountered term of legal rhetoric and to deal 'justly' is held out to be a fundamental aspiration of a legal system. At the same time, the intention which this rhetoric supposedly reflects if often less than clear. In practice a distinction is drawn between 'justice according to the law' and 'justice' as an ideal form of dealing. In the former case little more is meant than the proper operation of a given system, albeit subject to some very basic expectations of due process. In the latter case an external standard is being advanced by reference to which the operation of the legal system may be evaluated.[6]

---

2   MI5 and MI6, plus GCHQ. These services will not be examined in this book.
3   H.L.A. Hart, *The Concept of Law* (Clarendon Press, 1961) 89–96.
4   Ibid.
5   M. Groves and A. Duxbury, 'The Reform of Military Justice' in A. Duxbury and M. Groves (eds), *Military Justice in the Modern Age* (Cambridge University Press, 2016) 1 at 2–5.
6   H. McCoubrey and N.D. White, *Textbook on Jurisprudence* (Blackstone Press, 3rd edn, 1999) 297. See J.E. Penner, *McCoubrey and White's Textbook on Jurisprudence* (Oxford University Press, 4th edn, 2008) 228.

Military justice has been depicted by Eugene Fidell as consisting of 'separate rules for a separate society',[7] albeit one that is influenced and, indeed, connected to the broader legal system (and society) within which it operates.[8] Within the distinct area of law governing the military it is possible to consider both the narrow and wide aspects of justice outlined by McCoubrey.

The book serves two functions. First, to provide an accessible path into a complex subject area. Secondly, to consider a central question about the law governing the armed forces and service personnel – whether the scales of military justice in both the narrow and broad senses are in balance. In the narrower sense, we might consider whether the law provides clear rules for military personnel, which are administered consistently and provide due process to any individual accused of breaching them. In the broader sense, we might consider whether or not the duties of soldiers are too onerous and their rights are too few, something that can only be judged by understanding the nature and functions of armed forces in relation to the state and society (national and international) they serve. Moreover, it is necessary to recognise that the nature and functions of the military may change in response to changes in the broader societal context, in particular changing conceptions of security and of rights.

In a sense, the external concept of justice McCoubrey refers to is not an absolute one, but one that reflects the social contract that governs state and citizen, more specifically those social contracts between state and soldier, and soldier and society, which are expressed in terms of a 'military covenant'. The nature and content of the social contract have vexed political philosophers for many centuries, so it is not possible for it to provide a definitive account of 'justice', but it certainly should be possible to establish the parameters of the debate over military justice and suggest ways forward where there are obvious gaps, shortfalls or failings. The book was completed before the enactment of the Armed Forces Act 2021, and any reforms to the military justice system that it will bring. As the book demonstrates, any such reforms would constitute relatively minor steps in the continued evolution of the military justice system.

---

[7]   E.R. Fidell, *Military Justice: A Very Short Introduction* (Oxford University Press, 2016) 1.
[8]   Groves and Duxbury (2016) 6.

1. Framing military justice

1.1   INTRODUCTION

The introduction to the book defined 'military' to cover all three branches of the armed forces and the term 'soldier' is used throughout this book as a generic term to cover a member of the armed forces. 'Justice' was defined in both a narrow and a broad sense. In a narrow sense, military justice concerns the clear application of military law by specialist institutions to soldiers to enable them to do their jobs within a rule of law framework. If soldiers step outside that framework, they will be subject to swift, firm and fair justice. Thus there are specific service offences applicable to soldiers such as desertion and disobedience to lawful commands, and there are specialist elements of the criminal justice system such as a summary process before commanding officers (COs) for minor offences, courts martial for more serious offences, a separate service prosecuting authority, military detention facilities, and service police. Broader issues of justice are more esoteric and involve the search for standards against which to judge the rules, institutions, effectiveness and overall fairness of the military justice system. This will involve a deeper understanding of the nature and functions of the military, and the relationship between the military on the one hand and the society and country it serves on the other. Such broader standards of justice are contested, reflecting disputes about the nature and function of the military and its relationship to society.

It would be an easier, albeit not straightforward, task simply to judge military justice by external standards provided by the laws and institutions of international society. However, it will be seen that the encroachment of international laws, particularly international human rights law, is part of the reason why Rubin is able to describe the legal regulation of the armed forces as 'wondrously complex',[1] when it might be expected that the military would operate most efficiently under a system of rules that are clear and relatively uncontested. It may be that the internationalisation of military justice can add to the problems of delivering justice in some areas, while providing standards

---

[1]   G.R. Rubin, 'Why Military Law? Some United Kingdom Perspectives' (2007) 26 *University of Queensland Law Journal* 353 at 359.

and improvements to the law in others. That is why it is important to understand the nature and function of the military in society in order to understand what constitutes justice, or at least the parameters of the debate, in the unique environment occupied by the military, rather than simply making judgements by reference to international laws.

To this end, this chapter frames the subject matter in a broad way by exploring some of the theoretical explanations for the emergence of military justice as a distinct set of norms and institutions and its increasingly complex nature. The most relevant lenses are drawn from political theory, namely the monopoly on the use force, and the social contract whereby that monopoly over force is centred in the state. Given that the military embodies the state's monopoly on the use of force these ideas should help develop our understanding of the foundations, not only of the military but also of the specific rules and wider regulatory frameworks applicable to it. A brief legal analysis of modern military law and its increasing internationalisation follows, representing the legal fulcrum around which wider debates occur. This is followed by a broadening discussion, which considers modern civil-military relations and the recent attempts to distil the relationship between soldier and society in a military covenant. The chapter will then end by considering how these factors have combined to move military justice from an autonomous system of norms and institutions towards an increasingly externally juridified system.

1.2   THE SOCIAL CONTRACT AND THE MONOPOLY ON THE USE OF FORCE

The army, navy and air force are part of the national fabric, the essence of the state, tasked with defending the UK and its national interests. The armed forces have to be able to act effectively but, as the paradigmatic state actors,[2] they are both subject to the rule of law and accountable for its breach. The military is built on strong discipline but that can be inevitably stretched and sometimes broken in the face of dangerous and life-threatening tasks, making the application of laws challenging but essential. The traditional view of the soldier as servant of the Crown destined to carry out orders without question is no longer beyond dispute, especially after the conflicts in Afghanistan and Iraq, where broader questions over the aims and legality of the wars overshadow acts of individual heroism or cruelty. This has led to an on-going process of

---

[2]   Under Public International Law, the acts of soldiers while performing their duties are acts of state, even when they act beyond their powers but under cover of state authority: ILC Articles on the Responsibility of States for Internationally Wrongful Acts (2001) Articles 4 and 7. See discussion in Chapter 2.

re-evaluation of the relationship between state and soldier, and a profound debate about how the scales of military justice are balanced and, perhaps, ought to be rebalanced.

The relationship between state and soldier has been at the heart of the UK's evolving constitutional settlement. Many of the country's founding constitutional documents, including the Magna Carta of 1215 and the Bill of Rights 1689, helped shape the modern armed forces.[3] The gradual process of centralisation and monopolisation of the use of force is one account of the history of the evolution of the modern British state. From this perspective the history of the UK shows that the state's monopoly on the use of force was hard won, and that the evolution of the armed forces came about as much from internal conflict as it did from defending the realm from foreign invaders.[4]

Without the state asserting a monopoly on the use of force within its territory, a collection of individuals would live, according to Thomas Hobbes, 'in continual fear and danger of violent death' in a state of nature or anarchy, analogous to a continual state of war where 'the life of man' would be 'solitary, poor, nasty, brutish, and short'.[5] According to Hobbes, the sovereign provides security and, in return, the subjects give up their rights to violent self-help. However, if the sovereign is responsible for, or cannot prevent, insecurity man will revert to the 'conditions of war'.[6] As long as the sovereign provides security, their subjects owe allegiance to the sovereign and accept the monopoly on the use of force. However, while securing the monopoly on the use of force at home, Hobbes states that the sovereign remains in a state of nature with other sovereigns: 'kings and persons of sovereign authority' are 'in the state and posture of gladiators'.[7]

Hobbes' depiction of the social contract whereby the citizens of a state give up the right to use force in return for security was forged in the turmoil of the English Civil Wars of 1642–1651, when the seeds of the modern armed forces were sown in the shape of Cromwell's New Model Army: an army built on harsh discipline. Although Hobbes did not deal with the issue directly, it is possible to extrapolate the position of the military as part of the state in the social contract between sovereign and subject. The military through its soldiers was empowered to use force on behalf of the state but those soldiers gave up their freedoms and rights as citizens at least while they served the state. Writing a century later, Stephen Payne Adye wrote: '[t]he moment …

---

[3] See discussion in Chapter 2.
[4] Ibid.
[5] T. Hobbes, *Leviathan: or the Matter, Form, and Power of a Commonwealth Ecclesiastical and Civil*, edited by M. Oakeshott (Blackwell, 1946) 82–4.
[6] Ibid, 99.
[7] Ibid, 83.

a gentleman enters the service, he waives the Rights and Privileges he might be entitled to as an Englishman'.[8]

In contrast to Hobbes, John Locke's conception of the social contract was conceived in the context of the 'Glorious Revolution' of 1688–1689, which saw the overthrow of James II by William III and Mary II upon terms set by Parliament, including a Bill of Rights. Locke's conceptualisation of the social contract was more liberal in terms of the natural rights to life and property individuals continue to enjoy within a state. According to Locke those rights attain naturally, although the instability of a state of nature leads to the consensual formation of government with legislative and executive functions founded on reason and the law of nature. According to Locke:

> Man leaves the state of nature and enters civil society to secure an impartial and regular interpretation and application of the law of nature; if instead he encounters a sovereign who systematically violates that law, he has gained no advantage over the state of nature.[9]

Indeed, he or she is worse off 'because the sovereign possesses far greater power for harm than a private person in a state of nature'.[10] The sovereign's duty to protect persons and property is reflected in the seminal English case of *Entick v Carrington* of 1765, when Pratt CJ stated that 'the great end for which men entered into society was to secure their property'.[11] Essentially, in Locke's social contract the state and its monopoly on force are founded on the consent of its citizens: 'only consent can morally oblige a man to join his own force to the common executive power of a society to assist it in defending the body politic from internal and external threat'.[12] This suggests that citizens, as holders of inherent rights, do not give up those rights when they join the military, but it does suggest that those rights are conditioned by duties derived from a commitment to defend the realm.

---

[8]   S.P. Adye, *A Treatise on Courts Martial* (1789) cited in A.N. Gilbert, 'Military and Civilian Justice in Eighteenth Century England: An Assessment' (1978) 17 *Journal of British Studies* 41.

[9]   J. Locke, *The Second Treatise of Government: An Essay Concerning the True Original Extent, and End of Civil Government* (Prometheus Books, 1986) chapter 2, section 12, 223.

[10]   D. Germino, *Machiavelli to Marx: Modern Western Political Thought* (University of Chicago Press, 1972) 128.

[11]   *Entick v Carrington* (1765) 19 St Tr 1029 at 1060.

[12]   Germino (1972) 136.

Despite its liberal foundations, the political powers of the state were broadly defined by Locke as:

> A right of making laws with penalties of death, and consequently all less penalties, for the regulating and preserving of property, and in employing the force of the community, in the execution of such laws, and in the defence of the commonwealth from foreign injury.[13]

Furthermore, Locke concedes the need for a strong executive in foreign affairs and in terms of an inherent discretionary prerogative power to 'provide for the public good, in such cases, which, depending upon unforeseen and uncertain occurrences, certain and unalterable laws could not safely direct'.[14] The existence of prerogative powers involving the deployment of armed forces, both in response to internal emergencies and to external threats, remains a cornerstone of the British constitution.[15]

Debates about the precise terms of the social contract between state and citizen have continued from the 17th century to modern times, often revolving around the nature and function of government and the extent of a citizen's rights and freedoms from governmental interference.[16] However, debates are often silently premised on the military being squarely on the 'state' side of the contract as opposed to the 'citizen'. This, in part, explains why the armed forces are governed by a special legal regime setting them apart from other citizens containing rules that are, at the same time, more generous in the amount of force soldiers are allowed to use when compared to citizens, while being much more restrictive on the freedoms soldiers have by subjecting them to much harsher discipline than civilians. According to Hobbes the one prerogative power the sovereign cannot contract away without ceasing to be sovereign is that exercised over the 'militia' or army.[17] The armed forces embody the state's monopoly on the use of force and any loss of sovereign authority over the armed forces represents a descent into a state of nature.

The military establishment embodies the state's monopoly on the use of force. According to Elke Krahmann, the state's internal monopoly on the legitimate use of force dates back to the 17th century and was embodied in the social contract depicted by Thomas Hobbes whereby citizens give

---

[13]   Locke, chapter 1, section 3, 220.
[14]   Ibid, chapter 13, section 158, 277.
[15]   See discussion in Chapters 3 and 4.
[16]   For more recent social contractual conceptions see J. Rawls, *A Theory of Justice* (Oxford University Press, 1971) 198; and R. Nozick, *Anarchy, State and Utopia* (Blackwell, 1974) 15–17.
[17]   Hobbes (1946) 109.

up their right to use force in return for protection by the state.[18] In terms of the external use of force, states more gradually asserted control over forces operating in their name and reduced their dependency in the seventeenth and eighteenth centuries on private violence by mercenaries, privateers and chartered companies.[19] For Hans Morgenthau, a sovereign is the 'centralized power' that exercises 'lawmaking and law-enforcing authority within a certain territory': a power 'superior to the other forces that made themselves felt in that territory'. According to Morgenthau, within a century after the Peace of Westphalia in 1648, the sovereign 'became unchallengeable either from within the territory or without … It had become supreme.'[20] While this may be true of European and other Western states, many other areas of the globe from the 17th century until well into the 20th century were subject to the exercise of sovereignty by colonial powers, accepted by international legal doctrine as articulated by Max Huber in the *Island of Palmas* case of 1928.[21] In the case of the UK, by the 20th century, the state's monopoly over the use of force and its command and control over its forces (both those used internally and those deployed externally in policing the empire and securing British interests) had been established. Max Weber defined the modern state in 1918 as a 'human community that (successfully) claims the monopoly of the legitimate use of physical force within a given territory'.[22]

In sum, the monopoly on the use of force has three elements: the central-isation of force in the state, the successful exercise of that monopoly over internal elements that may threaten the state from within, and a projection of that monopolised force to deter any external forces that threaten it. In the modern era, that monopoly is exercised on a semi-permanent basis over the sovereign territory of the monopolising state, but sovereign powers may be exercised in other states. Aside from its colonial practice, the UK has acted as the sovereign power in a foreign country or part of it, for example, when it was an occupying power in post-Nazi Germany in 1945–1949, and in post-Saddam Iraq in 2003–2004. Whereas in Germany the UK, along with other occupying powers, successfully exercised a monopoly on the use of force, it failed to do this in southern Iraq in 2003. According to Frank Ledwidge, a senior British officer declared with some pride in December 2003 that the British Army was

---

[18]   E. Krahmann, 'Private Security Companies and the State Monopoly on Violence: A Case of Norm Change?' (2009) 88 PRIF-Reports 2.

[19]   J.E. Thomson, *Mercenaries, Pirates and Sovereigns* (Princeton University Press, 1994) 43.

[20]   H. Morgenthau, *Politics Among Nations* (A. Knopf, 1972) 306.

[21]   *Island of Palmas Case* (1928) 2 RIAA 829.

[22]   M. Weber, 'Excerpts from Politics as a Vocation' in C. Lemert (ed.), *Social Theory: The Multicultural and Classic Readings* (Westview, 1999) 111.

the 'biggest and best gang in Basra'.[23] The problem was that it was not the only armed gang and its superiority was soon lost as the country descended into violent chaos. Maintaining a monopoly over the use of force has proved difficult for the UK in military terms in its colonial and post-colonial practice.[24] Furthermore, domestic and, increasingly, international laws have sought to regulate that monopoly to such an extent, some would argue, that the armed forces have been put under 'legal siege',[25] further jeopardising the military and political goals of any troop deployment.

1.3 SERVICE LAW AND THE INTERNATIONALISATION OF MILITARY JUSTICE

The increasingly heard complaint from military and other quarters about excessive legalisation of military matters has recently found support in the Defence Committee of the House of Commons. In its Report of 2019, in which it recommended the adoption of a Statute of Limitations to protect veteran soldiers from prosecution for alleged crimes committed in past conflicts, the Defence Committee stated that it 'was determined to ensure that justice prevails for veterans and for current Service personnel, whilst ensuring that wrongdoing and criminality are appropriately investigated and punished'.[26] While emphasising that 'those who serve in the armed forces are not above the law', the Committee expressed its belief that 'there is something fundamentally wrong when veterans and current Service personnel can be investigated and exonerated, only then to become trapped in an endless cycle of re-investigation', a state of affairs that it warned 'risks undermining not only morale within the Armed Forces, and the potential for future recruitment, but also trust in the rule of law'.[27] In determining the reasons for the emergence of

---

[23] F. Ledwidge, *Losing Small Wars: British Military Failure in Iraq and Afghanistan* (Yale University Press, 2011) 29.

[24] For examples of accounts of British military practice towards the end of empire see: N. Barber, *The War of the Running Dogs: How Malaya Defeated the Communist Guerrillas 1948–60* (Cassell, 1972); D. Anderson, *Histories of the Hanged: Britain's Dirty War in Kenya and the End of Empire* (Phoenix, 2006); M. Bell, *The End of Empire The Cyprus Emergency: A Soldier's Story* (Pen and Sword, 2015).

[25] Admiral Lord Boyce, Chief of Defence Staff, Hansard, HL Deb, Vol 673, Col 1236, 14 July 2005.

[26] House of Commons Defence Committee, 'Drawing a Line: Protecting Veterans by a Statute of Limitations', Seventeenth Report of Session 2017-19, HC 1244, 22 July 2019, 3. The Overseas Operations (Service Personnel and Veterans) Act (2021) that arose out of these recommendations is discussed in Chapter 9.

[27] Ibid.

this apparently open-ended pursuit of justice, the Committee concluded that 'the legal frameworks underpinning the role of the Armed Forces in civil and military operations are becoming increasingly complex and difficult to navigate, particularly in the fog and confusion of conflict'.[28] The Committee points to the increasing extension of human rights law to cover military operations as one of the reasons for this increased complexity,[29] and for contributing to an environment in which there are endless cycles of reinvestigation of alleged past abuses, creating 'almost unlimited potential for retrospective claims'.[30]

Whether this position is over-stated will be returned to in the course of this book, but there is no doubt that the legal frameworks have become complex, especially when considering that the essence of the military function is the ability to act and react quickly, often in situations of violence when armed force is necessary. To apply a broad panoply of laws, some specific, others abstract, to such situations seems counter-intuitive at least when considering the military function, even though in principle all those laws at least have the potential to be applicable. There is a tension, therefore, between the military function and what might be called the legal function, the latter being inherent in a system based on the rule of law, whereby all activities are brought within a legal framework which, once established, deepens and broadens. The rule of law does not produce a set of unchanging and clear rules, rather 'as a human construct built upon aspiration and argumentation, law is by its very nature historically contingent'.[31] The process of legalisation could, in theory, result in an over-application of laws. Such an over-application could occur through the proliferation of laws and legal regimes in the broader society that through litigation and judicial decision-making are extended to cover an increasing segment of military life.

The argument is not that the military should be free from law. In fact there is an undisputed body of accepted laws and institutions that over the years have been developed to regulate military personnel, as a form of self-contained, autonomous or semi-autonomous, legal regime of military justice. As described by the Defence Committee: '[a]ll Service personnel must comply with Service law when on operations', which 'means that they must not only comply with the criminal law of England and Wales, but also with the high standards of behaviour which are distinctive to the Armed Forces'.

---

[28]   Ibid.

[29]   Ibid, 4.

[30]   Ibid, para 3. Citing House of Commons Defence Committee, 'UK Armed Forces Personnel and the Legal Framework for Future Operations', Twelfth Report of Session 2013-14, HC 931, 2 April 2013, paras 127–9.

[31]   J.M. Farrall, *United Nations Sanctions and the Rule of Law* (Cambridge University Press, 2007) 29.

These laws are designed to apply extraterritorially as well as when soldiers are based or deployed within the UK. Thus, soldiers can be punished by summary process or by court martial for both 'criminal conduct offences' (murder, rape, assault etc.),[32] which apply to any member of society, but also for contravening another layer of offences known as 'discipline offences'.[33] Discipline offences, as currently defined by the Armed Forces Act 2006, are aimed at ensuring that the military establishment is a disciplined and effective fighting force, and are uniquely applicable to soldiers. When looking at the proscribed list of behaviours,[34] it appears that the regulation of the military, at least in terms of the behaviour of its soldiers, is detailed and definitive, which raises the question of whether extra layers of legal regulation are necessary. Discipline offences include: assisting an enemy, misconduct on operations, obstructing operations, looting, failure to escape, mutiny, desertion, absence without leave, misconduct towards a superior officer, insubordination (including disobedience to lawful commands), failure to perform any duty, negligent performance of any duty, malingering, conduct prejudicial to good order and discipline, and ill-treatment of subordinates.[35]

In addition to domestic service or military law, there is a specialist area of international law that has been developed over the centuries to apply to military personnel in situations of armed conflict, which the military and political establishment in the UK readily accept is applicable as indicated by the UK's ratification of the relevant treaties and, indeed, the incorporation of a number of breaches of them into UK service law.[36] International humanitarian law, also known as the law of armed conflict (LOAC), has been described by the International Committee of the Red Cross (ICRC) as 'a realistic body of law that finds a balance between military necessity and humanity'.[37] Its acceptance as a legitimate form of international regulation lies in the fact that LOAC recognises the imperative of military necessity while protecting the value of humanity by, for example, protecting civilians as much as is practically achievable in war.

The UK's domestic system of military justice has been influenced, supplemented and qualified by a legal regime (LOAC) agreed between states at the international level, but the process of internationalisation has not stopped there. In addition to LOAC, the other most relevant regimes in this regard are

---

[32] Armed Forces Act (2006) section 42.
[33] Defence Committee Report (2019) paras 15–17.
[34] See further analysis of discipline offences in Chapter 6.
[35] Armed Forces Act (2006) sections 1–41.
[36] Under the Geneva Conventions Act (1957) and the Armed Forces Act (2006) schedule 2.
[37] Defence Committee Report (2019) para 21.

international criminal law and international human rights law. While LOAC contains the basic rules for conducting warfare and protecting civilians and soldiers rendered *hors de combat*,[38] international criminal law identifies certain core crimes including war crimes and thus supplements in part the rules contained in LOAC. These crimes can be prosecuted before UK courts as a result of the International Criminal Court Act 2001 and, under certain conditions, the International Criminal Court (ICC) established by the Rome Statute of 1998. In contrast to UK service law, LOAC and international criminal law, which place duties on soldiers and on government to prosecute breaches of those duties, human rights law defines in part the legal relationship between state and citizens (and other individuals within the jurisdiction of the state) in terms of duties of the state and rights of individuals. In the UK, a central component of human rights law is the 1950 European Convention on Human Rights (ECHR),[39] as incorporated into UK law by the Human Rights Act (HRA) 1998. There is clear evidence that human rights law has improved the protections for soldiers facing military justice for alleged infractions of service law.[40] Furthermore, although human rights law 'has been developed largely for application in times of peace', according to Peter Rowe, 'it was envisaged that it would have some relevance during wartime'.[41] Its potential to apply during wartime has only just begun to be realised. By enabling human rights litigation before domestic courts, the HRA effectively sped up the litigious extension of human rights law to military matters, including combat operations.[42]

In general terms, LOAC imposes duties on states and soldiers, for example to refrain from targeting civilians or to safeguard persons rendered *hors de combat*,[43] obligations that if breached should be enforced against soldiers through national military law including by court martial. These duties have, in a sense, been enhanced by the development of international criminal law including by its proscription and punishment of war crimes, alongside crimes

---

[38]   See generally Geneva Convention Relative to the Treatment of Prisoners of War (GC III, 1949), and Geneva Convention Relative to the Protection of Civilian Persons in Time of War (GC IV, 1949).
[39]   Alongside the International Covenant on Civil and Political Rights 1966.
[40]   C. Gale, 'Disciplinary Uniformity in Uniform – A Success of the Human Rights Act 1998?' (2008) 72 *Journal of Criminal Law* 170.
[41]   P. Rowe, *The Impact of Human Rights Law on Armed Forces* (Cambridge University Press, 2006) 3.
[42]   S. Kemp, *British Justice, War Crimes and Human Rights Violations* (Palgrave Macmillan, 2019) 21.
[43]   See, for example, Protocol I Additional to the Geneva Conventions of 1949 and Relating to the Protection of Victims of International Armed Conflicts (AP I, 1977) Articles 41 and 48.

against humanity, genocide and aggression.[44] LOAC also confers protections on soldiers, but these protections are not in the form of enforceable rights,[45] but rather are underpinned by the principle of reciprocity between states, whereby, for example, states agree by treaty or custom to protect captured or wounded soldiers of the enemy in exchange for the same protections for its own soldiers.[46]

Human rights law, on the other hand, confers rights on individuals which are justiciable and can be enforced against the state. In the UK, human rights law has added to the existing rights and liberties of citizens under constitutional and common law. The question then arises as to whether they apply to the soldier. The perennial question since Cromwell's time has been whether soldiers forfeit the individual rights they would normally enjoy as citizens when they join the armed forces?[47] Furthermore, is the collective entity that is the military, underpinned by a system of justice based on duty and discipline, antithetical to a system of law based on enforceable individual rights? That question has been at the heart of the development of military justice and, while the answer was clear under Cromwell and Wellington, it is not as clear in the 21st century, as the human rights obligations accepted by states in the mid-20th century have gradually and often contentiously intruded into the legal regime governing the military. Rowe concludes that it remains the case 'that as the fundamental purpose of any army is to fight during an armed conflict an individual's needs are treated as subservient to this purpose'.[48] This is particularly so in the case of a volunteer army, which has largely been the case in the UK, in which a volunteer 'could be expected to have joined the armed forces with the knowledge that his interests would have to be subsumed to the greater interests of those armed forces'.[49] However, while volunteers can be deemed to have accepted that military discipline will apply to them and that it will be enforced by the military justice system, Rowe argues that this does not mean that the volunteer has 'waived those of his human rights available to him as a civilian'.[50] The argument for the retention of human rights must be even stronger in the case of a conscript, who has been depicted in European states,

---

[44]   Statute of the International Criminal Court (1998) Article 8.
[45]   Rowe (2006) 2.
[46]   Found in the Geneva Convention for the Amelioration of the Condition of the Wounded and Sick in Armed Forces in the Field (GC I, 1949); Geneva Convention for the Amelioration of the Condition of Wounded, Sick and Shipwrecked Members of the Armed Forces at Sea (GC II, 1949); Geneva Convention Relative to the Treatment of Prisoners of War (GC III, 1949).
[47]   Gilbert (1978) 41.
[48]   Rowe (2006) 6.
[49]   Ibid.
[50]   Ibid, 9–10.

where conscription has remained the norm, as 'the citizen in uniform',[51] but even then there is a recognition that the applicability of such rights must be understood within the 'particular characteristics of military life'.[52]

However, it should be recalled that in the social contract, discussed above, the soldier is normally equated to the state and not to the body of citizens, which makes the application of human rights protections intended for the citizen to the soldier more complex than perhaps reflected in the jurisprudence to date. The issue has been litigated in terms of whether soldiers are within the 'jurisdiction' of the state for human rights purposes,[53] when perhaps the question ought to be when is the soldier a 'citizen or other individual' within the jurisdiction of that state and when are they a part of the 'state'? It is important to note in this regard that while human rights law applies to 'everyone' within a state's jurisdiction meaning that the state has a duty to respect and protect the rights of all,[54] LOAC distinguishes between a soldier (as combatant) whose life can be taken lawfully by the enemy and a civilian or other protected person whose life should be preserved. Human rights law does not discriminate between soldiers and citizens but LOAC, which specifically applies to soldiers in armed conflicts, does.[55]

Overall, soldiers can be said to occupy the interface between individual and state, neither clearly protected by rights accorded to the individual nor clearly free to challenge duties placed on them by the state. In practical military terms, 'in an era of an already complex and often confused battle space, there can be little tolerance for adding complexity and confusion to the rules that war-fighters must apply in the execution of their missions'.[56] However, this does not mean a rejection of the applicability of all human rights law in favour of an exclusive application of LOAC, since 'both areas of law have important and constructive contributions to make so as to establish a secure environment for the enjoyment of fundamental rights'.[57] The military operations in both Afghanistan and Iraq led to serious allegations of unlawful abuse and killings, many of which would constitute violations of human rights law attributable to

---

[51]   Ibid, 13.

[52]   *Engel et al v The Netherlands* (1976) I EHRR 647, para 54 (ECtHR).

[53]   See discussion in Chapter 8.

[54]   European Convention on Human Rights (ECHR, 1950) Article 1.

[55]   S. Darcy, *Judges, Law and War: The Judicial Development of International Humanitarian Law* (Cambridge University Press, 2014) 114–15.

[56]   G. Corn, 'Mixing Apples and Hand Grenades: The Logical Limit of Applying Human Rights Norms to Armed Conflicts' (2010) 1 *International Humanitarian Legal Studies* 52 at 54.

[57]   K. Watkin, 'Controlling the Use of Force: A Role for Human Rights Norms in Contemporary Armed Conflict' (2004) 98 *American Journal of International Law* 1 at 34.

the UK as well as giving rise to individual criminal liability under service law, LOAC and international criminal law.[58] The question of how human rights law should be adapted to the battlespace, and how it operates alongside the more specialist legal regimes, will be discussed in the course of this book.

While the parameters of the internationalisation of military justice remain contested, the idea of the military as a separate society subject to its own rules has been eroded by this development, but not as much as might be thought. LOAC applies to the paradigmatic situation a soldier is deployed to – armed conflict – and so in a sense reinforces the idea of separation by the applicability of a specialist set of rules. International criminal law reinforces this separation by providing for the punishment of war crimes committed in violation of LOAC, although other core crimes – crimes and humanity and genocide – are not limited to armed conflicts. Furthermore, the crime of aggression has the potential to blur the civil-military separation, as decisions to go to war, which may violate the prohibition against aggressive war, are made by political leaders.

Christopher Waters makes an important point that while LOAC 'places limits on the means and methods of warfare, the law remains essentially permissive'.[59] According to the UK's *Manual on the Law of Armed Conflict*, which serves as an operational legal guide to the armed forces, LOAC 'is intended to minimize the suffering caused by armed conflict rather than impede military efficiency'.[60] 'Military necessity' is one of the fundamental principles of LOAC alongside 'humanity', 'distinction' and 'proportionality'.[61] The importance of 'military necessity' to LOAC is reflected in the statement in the *Manual* that 'the use of force in ways which are not otherwise prohibited is legitimate if it is necessary to achieve, as quickly as possible, the complete or partial submission of the enemy'.[62] The prominence of military necessity in LOAC, which is designed to support the efficient prosecution of a war, signifies that utilitarian judgements, weighing up the overall impact of certain actions on soldiers and civilians, will have to be made. Implicit in these judgements is a recognition that the rights of some individuals will inevitably have to be sacrificed.

---

[58] R. Kerr, 'A Force for Good? War, Crime and Legitimacy: The British Army in Iraq' (2008) 24 *Defence & Security Analysis* 401 at 402.

[59] C.P.M. Waters, 'Is the Military Legally Encircled?' (2008) 8 *Defence Studies* 26 at 34.

[60] Ministry of Defence, *Manual on the Law of Armed Conflict* (Oxford University Press, 2004) 21.

[61] But see E. Winter, 'Pillars Not Principles: The Status of Humanity and Military Necessity in the Law of Armed Conflict' (2020) 25 *Journal of Conflict and Security Law* 1.

[62] Ministry of Defence (2004) 22.

1.4   CIVIL-MILITARY RELATIONS

In contrast to UK service law and LOAC, human rights law challenges the idea of separation of the military from civil society, and the tradition that soldiers, as agents of the state, only have duties. Human rights law posits that, when they can be seen as individuals within the jurisdiction of the British state, soldiers have in principle the same rights as civilians, although those rights will have to be interpreted contextually. Furthermore, soldiers have to respect the rights of civilians within the jurisdiction of the British state. This can create dilemmas for soldiers and the state. For example, unlike the permissive LOAC regime for the use of force in armed conflict, which allows British soldiers to use lethal force to kill enemy combatants, under human rights law the use of force is clearly proscribed with very limited exceptions for law enforcement or self-defence purposes.[63]

Arguably, recognising that soldiers have rights undermines the classical social contract, whereby the soldier is firmly a part of the state and not part of the citizenry. Following Hobbes' depiction of the social contract, the military's function is to secure the state's monopoly on force in order to protect the state and its citizens from internal and external threats. Under this conception, the soldier acts as an arm of the state, not as a citizen in uniform. As a distinct organ of state embodying the centralisation of force, the military occupies a unique space necessitating special rules both to constrain and, where necessary, enable the use of force. This reasoning fits in with Samuel Huntingdon's classic depiction of civil-military relations where he argues for an 'autonomous military sphere'.[64]

In contrast to Huntingdon, Morris Janowitz 'argues for a military along the lines of a "constabulary" model whereby the military maintains close links to society'.[65] The social contractual roots of such an argument can be traced back to Locke. Locke's liberal conceptualisation of the social contract, whereby the state's function is to protect the natural rights to life and property of its citizens, seems more compatible with the advent of human rights laws and the idea that soldiers should respect the rights of citizens and other civilians within their power. It does not, however, by itself necessitate the recognition that soldiers themselves have those rights, beyond the idea that the 'inherent' nature of those rights means that they are not subject to the discretion of the state.

---

[63]   ECHR (1950) Article 2(2).
[64]   Waters (2008) 33, citing S.P. Huntingdon, *The Soldier and the State* (Harvard University Press, 1957).
[65]   Waters (2008) 33, citing M. Janowitz, *The Professional Soldier: A Social and Political Portrait* (Free Press, 1964).

Certainly, one of the fundamental tenets of human rights is that they are inherent or inalienable and, furthermore, they belong to each and every person. The Universal Declaration of Human Rights 1948 recognises the 'inherent dignity and of the equal and inalienable rights of all members of the human family', and that 'everyone is entitled to the rights and freedoms set forth in this Declaration, without distinction of any kind'.[66] This would strongly suggest that soldiers share the same rights as civilians in theory, but in the theatre of war the full protection of those rights is not always possible, indeed is unlikely, and they will have to be qualified or pared down, or, some would continue to argue, are simply not applicable. How can a state guarantee the rights of soldiers it has to put in the line of fire? It is certainly true that human rights law has not unduly encroached onto the battlefield until relatively recently, then largely as a result of judicial interpretations of its applicability under treaty law and not as a result of state practice and *opinio juris*: the classical method of developing international law.

Although conceptually there is a relatively clear legal assimilation of soldier and state, the political, social and legal relationships between the state as corporate entity and the soldier as individual, as well as between the state and military as corporate entities, are complex and under-studied from the legal perspective.[67] Pauline Collins considers that 'the normative theory of the civil-military relationship establishes a clear preference for civilian control of the military in order to protect democratic values'. However, Collins considers that most theories concentrate on executive and legislative control of the military, and not on the role of civilian courts in exercising control and accountability.[68] The reluctance of civilian courts to become involved in military matters is gradually breaking down in part due to evolving human rights jurisprudence, but the argument that the military should have its own rules and enforce its own laws remains strong.

Looking specifically at the legal relationship between state and soldier, it remains true to say that in the UK soldiers are not employees of the state; rather they are under its direct command. In recent discussions on the reform of the

---

[66] UN Doc A/RES/217A (1948) preamble and Article 2.
[67] For classic non-legal texts on civil-military relations see Huntingdon (1957); S.E. Finer, *The Man on Horseback: The Role of the Military in Politics* (Pall Mall Press, 1962); Janowitz (1964).
[68] P.T. Collins, *Civil-Military 'Legal' Relations: Where to From Here?* (Brill, 2018) preface.

system of military justice and the annual renewal of the Armed Forces Act in the House of Lords, the Minister of Defence stated:

> If the 2006 [Armed Forces] Act was to expire, the duty of members of the Armed Forces to obey lawful commands, and the powers and procedures under which this duty is enforced, would no longer have effect. Commanding officers and the court martial would have no powers of punishment for failure to obey a lawful command or for other disciplinary or criminal misconduct. Members of the Armed Forces would still owe allegiance to Her Majesty but Parliament would have removed the power of enforcement. Service personnel do not have contracts of employment and so have no duties as employees. Their obligation is essentially a duty to obey lawful commands.[69]

As Gerry Rubin has written: '[i]t is paradoxical that while service personnel are entitled to equal pay by virtue of legislation, they are not entitled to sue for pay, per se, since their service engagement is grounded in the prerogative and at the pleasure of the Sovereign'.[70] The need for regular review of legislation governing the armed forces flows from the 'constitutional requirement under the Bill of Rights that a standing army, and by extension, the Royal Navy and the Royal Air Force, may not be maintained without the consent of Parliament'.[71] Parliament retains control by these means but deployment of forces has historically been in the hands of the executive. In recent years, Parliament has asserted greater authority over decisions concerning major troop deployments. In contrast, challenges before the courts on the basis, for example, that deployments breach international law, have generally failed.[72] However, while reluctant to challenge the government over decisions to deploy troops, civilian courts have tentatively encroached into operational matters during or after deployments when challenges have been made on human rights and other grounds.[73] The legal relationship between state and soldier is no longer constructed solely on the basis of prerogative powers where the duties lie with the soldier, but is developing to impose obligations on the state to respect and protect a soldier's human rights.

---

[69]   Hansard, HL Deb, Col 2280, 20 February 2019 (Earl Howe).
[70]   Rubin (2007) 360.
[71]   Earl Howe (2019).
[72]   See Chapter 4.
[73]   See Chapter 8.

1.5 THE COVENANT BETWEEN SOLDIER AND SOCIETY

In addition to the legal relationship between the state and soldier there is the social and moral relationship between soldier and society, which also appears to be undergoing change. During the two world wars the relationship between the armed forces and society was incredibly strong. Worthy of note in this regard was the formation of new Army units during the First World War – the so-called 'pals' battalions', which were 'raised by exploiting strong links within urban communities'.[74] However, such bonds have been more difficult to sustain in an era of foreign expeditionary wars. This has led to a revitalised debate about the bond that links the armed forces to society, revolving around the idea of the 'military covenant'. The state itself has recently attempted to regulate this relationship. Embodied for the first time in legislation in the Armed Forces Act 2011, the Military Covenant recognises that military personnel have legitimate expectations of support when leaving the service, but it does not recognise that they have enforceable rights. It is arguable that future legislation governing the armed forces, which is regularly renewed and updated, should increase the protection of soldiers' rights,[75] but this was not the intention when the Military Covenant was first posited as an aspect of Army doctrine in 2000:

> Soldiers will be called upon to make personal sacrifices – including the ultimate sacrifice – in the service of the Nation. In putting the needs of the nation and the Army before their own, they forgo some of the rights enjoyed by those outside the Armed Forces. In return, British soldiers must always be able to expect fair treatment, to be valued and respected as individuals, and that they (and their families) will be sustained and rewarded by commensurate terms and conditions of service. In the same way, the unique nature of military land operations means that the Army differs from all other institutions, and must be sustained and provided for accordingly by the nation. This mutual obligation forms the Military Covenant between the nation, the Army and each individual soldier; an unbreakable common bond of identity, loyalty and responsibility which has sustained the Army and its soldiers throughout its history.[76]

---

[74] R. Holmes, *Soldiers* (Harper Press, 2011) 189.
[75] Under the Armed Forces Bill (2021) clause 8, when in force, the Military Covenant will be strengthened by placing further obligations of support for soldiers and veterans on public authorities – Armed Forces Bill (Bill 244) 26 January 2021 – https://www.gov.uk/government/collections/armed-forces-bill-2021. All websites in this publication have been accessed 11 November 2021.
[76] *British Army, Soldiering: The Military Covenant* (Ministry of Defence, 2000).

Anthony Forster points to the 'quasi-religious overtones' of the wording, and contrasts the 'unlimited liability' of soldiers under the Covenant in the sense of the sacrifices they make, with the distinct absence of 'a contractual relationship justiciable in law'.[77] In other words the Covenant recognises the duties of soldiers but it does not contain any enforceable rights; indeed it is premised on those rights (or some of them) being given up by soldiers once they enlist.

Helen McCartney argues that the 2000 document is also an idealised and normative picture of the relationship between the Army and society, arguing that 'British armed forces have never had those deep ties with their society'.[78] McCartney states that the 'two world wars and periods of national service, when the army accepted millions of Britons into its ranks, were aberrations rather than the norm', which is one of much smaller deployments to overseas colonial and post-colonial duties.[79] It is interesting that McCartney sees the Covenant as a recent manifestation of what she calls the civil-military contract, which has persisted between the government and the public on the civil side of the contract and the military on the other. Both the treatment of the military by the government and by the public have come under criticism from commentators and from the Army (but not the other services) for failing to provide adequate support to the military in a myriad of ways ranging from the adequacy of equipment through to the way soldiers in uniform are treated while in public.[80] In 2007, Sir Richard Dannatt, head of the British Army, commented: '[t]he real Covenant is with the population at large, not the government … Soldiers want to be understood and they want to be respected for their commitment. When a young soldier has been fighting in Basra or Helmand, he wants to know that people in his local pub know and understand what he has been doing and why.'[81] McCartney describes this relationship as a moral contract, which even when 'articulated on paper' as a 'covenant', remains in the moral sphere by relying 'on commitment and trust between the parties rather than on a more legalistic and prescriptive contract in which outcomes and behaviour are predetermined; yet its very articulation creates particular expectations'.[82] It seems that the Covenant remains unenforceable in law despite its enshrinement in legislation in 2011.

---

[77]   A. Forster, 'The Military Covenant in British Civil-Military Relations: Letting the Genie out of the Bottle' (2012) 38 *Armed Forces & Society* 273 at 275.

[78]   H. McCartney, 'The Military Covenant and the Civil-Military Contract in Britain' (2010) 86 *International Affairs* 411 at 421.

[79]   Ibid, 421.

[80]   Ibid, 411.

[81]   Quoted in ibid, 420.

[82]   Ibid, 413.

One of the reasons for the decline in public support for the military is the increase in perception of the illegitimacy and possible illegality of the expeditionary wars in Afghanistan and Iraq. McCartney cites a poll taken in 2009, which found that 56 per cent felt that the UK was right to fight for the Falklands, 53 per cent thought that military involvement in Northern Ireland was necessary, 25 per cent supported British involvement in Afghanistan, and only 20 per cent supported the war in Iraq.[83] This in turn has affected that aspect of the Covenant that enshrines the 'unlimited liability' of soldiers, who accept that they may have to give up their right to life in the performance of their duties. Deaths of soldiers during controversial wars raise the question of whether they should be bound to lay down their lives in these conflicts, a perception that is heightened when there are issues of inadequate resources, a lack of sufficient numbers of troops,[84] and inadequate command.[85] The dilemma for soldiers serving in unjust wars is summed up by McCartney: 'if military personnel participate in an "unjust" war they are condemned by civilians, but if they refuse to deploy they are punished by the military'.[86]

Anthony Forster argues that one of the reasons for formulating the Covenant in 2000 was to 'resist the threat of civilianisation' of the Army, by emphasising its uniqueness, necessitating 'distinct military codes and laws, supplemented by norms and values to ensure combat effectiveness'. These include: the 'supremacy of collective over individual rights; the right to have a separate legal system of military discipline; a hierarchical structure based on rank and an obligation to obey orders; and a chain of command'.[87] However, while the Army might have put forward the Military Covenant to claim the sort of relationship with society it would ideally want, it has subsequently become used 'against the both the government and the MoD in a partisan and highly politicized way'.[88] It has also been taken up by organisations representing veterans and service personnel such as the Royal British Legion, and generals wanting more resources from the government.[89] In other words, the nature and effect of the Military Covenant is disputed but has become the fulcrum of the debate over the place, functions, rights and duties of the government, the armed forces, and the individuals who serve in them.

---

[83] Ibid, 415.
[84] Ibid, 418–19.
[85] A. King, 'Military Command in the Last Decade' (2011) 87 *International Affairs* 377 at 378–80.
[86] McCartney (2010) 425.
[87] Forster (2012) 275–6.
[88] Ibid, 277.
[89] Ibid, 279.

The Covenant, as shaped by the Army in 2000, outlined 'an agreed set of principles of justice for soldiers, veterans and their families that are morally rather than legally binding'.[90] In 2011 the Ministry of Defence (MoD) published 'an Enduring Covenant between the People of the United Kingdom, Her Majesty's Government, and all those who serve or have served in the Armed Forces of the Crown and their families'. It stated further that:

> The first duty of Government is the defence of the realm. Our Armed Forces fulfil that responsibility on behalf of the Government, sacrificing some civilian freedoms, facing danger and, sometimes, suffering serious injury or death as a result of their duty. Families also play a vital role in supporting the operational effectiveness of Armed Forces. In return, the whole nation has a moral obligation to the members of the Naval Service, the Army and the Royal Air Force, together with their families. They deserve our respect and support, and fair treatment.[91]

That soldiers are expected to sacrifice their lives if necessary had been more clearly highlighted in an earlier 2010 publication, which stated that 'soldiers may be called upon to make the ultimate sacrifice in the service of the Nation'. Further, that in 'putting the needs of the Nation, their Service and others before their own, they forgo some of the rights and freedoms enjoyed by those outside'.[92]

The Covenant of 2011 lists the 'expectations and aspirations' behind it, including a 'responsibility of care' on the part of the Government involving: establishing 'an environment which is free from bullying, harassment and discrimination'; taking special account of the needs of those under 18 years of age; promoting the health, safety and resilience of servicemen and women; and 'ensuring that they are appropriately prepared, in the judgement of the chain of command, for the requirements of any training activities or operations on which they are to be engaged'.[93] However, the document makes it clear that 'operational matters, including training and equipment, fall outside the scope of the Armed Forces Covenant'.[94] The failure to extend what is after all only a moral commitment to operational matters leaves a significant hole in the state's responsibility for ensuring that a soldier's life is not wasted.

---

[90] R. McGarry, G. Mythen and S. Walklate, 'The Soldier, Human Rights and the Military Covenant: A Permissible State of Exception' (2012) 16 *International Journal of Human Rights* 1183 at 1184.
[91] Ministry of Defence, *The Armed Forces Covenant* (2011) https://assets.publishing.service.gov.uk/government/uploads/system/uploads/attachment_data/file/49469/the_armed_forces_covenant.pdf.
[92] Ministry of Defence, *Army Doctrine Publication: Operations* (Development, Concepts and Doctrine Centre, 2010) para 0230.
[93] *Armed Forces Covenant* (2011) para 6.
[94] Ibid.

Up until section 2 of the Armed Forces Act 2011 came into force, the Military Covenant was said to have existed as an unwritten and not legally binding moral and social agreement between the country and its armed forces. Criticisms that the Covenant was being eroded in the way veterans from Afghanistan and Iraq were not only treated in the country upon their return,[95] but also how they were equipped and supported while on deployment,[96] led to the inclusion of the Military Covenant in the 2011 Act, but this did not produce any justiciable rights. Essentially, section 2 imposes an obligation on the Secretary of State to prepare an annual 'armed forces covenant report' accounting for the provision of education, housing, and healthcare, the operation of inquests and other matters as determined by the Secretary of State. In preparing the report, the Secretary of State must have regard to: 'the unique obligations of, and sacrifices made by, the armed forces'; 'the principle that it is desirable to remove disadvantages arising for service people from membership, or former membership, of the armed forces'; and 'the principle that special provision for service people may be justified by the effects on such people of membership, or former membership, of the armed forces'. In effect, the Act provides a promise to improve the treatment of soldiers but it depends upon Parliament to ensure that the government fulfils its promise. The promise does not extend to military operations. It has been commented that the way the Military Covenant has been defined and enshrined into law signifies that the 'unlimited liability' of British soldiers in the course of their operational duties 'places a soldier's right to life both legally and morally in a state of exception'.[97]

The question of whether the embodiment of the Military Covenant in legislation in the Armed Forces Act 2011 has helped balance the scales of justice is returned to in Chapter 9, but at this point it is already clear that the system of military justice, narrowly conceived, is subject to much broader values and pressures. These concern: the encroachment of civilian values and laws into the military and the Army's own view as to its uniqueness requiring a separate system of military discipline; the 'unlimited liability' of soldiers and the obligations, if any, the Army and the government owe to its soldiers;[98] and, more

---

[95] For example, see statement by David Cameron, leader of the opposition, in March 2008, regarding the treatment of wounded soldiers in NHS hospitals, 'Cameron: Military Covenant Broken' http://news.bbc.co.uk/1/hi/uk_politics/7276924.stm.

[96] For example, see statement by Sir Menzies Campbell MP, in September 2008, on the quality of military equipment, 'Conflicts stretching armed forces beyond resources, says Lib Dem report', *The Guardian*, 26 September 2008 https://www.theguardian.com/uk/2008/sep/26/military.liberaldemocrats.

[97] McGarry, Mythen and Walklate (2012) 1189.

[98] Forster (2012) 280–1.

broadly still, the nature of the social contract between soldier and society. While the social contract is normally conceived as pertaining between state and citizen, the position of the soldiers can be perceived as sitting somewhere between the two – legally they have traditionally been viewed as agents of the state to be commanded at will, but morally (and, increasingly, legally) they are seen as 'citizens in uniform'.[99]

The enshrinement of the Military Covenant in law may have wider legal effects than intended. Even before being entrenched in law in 2011, the Military Covenant was cited by the High Court in 2008 in a case involving the denial to Gurkhas who had served before 1997 of the right to live in Britain, which the Court found to be discriminatory. In support of his judgment, Mr Justice Blake concluded by quoting the Military Covenant as defined in 2000, declaring that '[r]ewarding long and distinguished service by the grant of residence in the country for which the service was performed would, in my judgment, be a vindication and an enhancement of this covenant'.[100] Forster also points to the use of narrative verdicts by coroners to highlight breaches of trust by deploying soldiers to Iraq and Afghanistan with inadequate equipment as examples of the influence of the Military Covenant.[101] In ways not intended by its drafters, the Military Covenant has served to highlight broader issues of justice concerning what should be demanded of soldiers as well as what they should expect in return.

1.6   FROM AUTONOMY TO JURIDIFICATION

A more precise history of the emergence of a separate system of UK military justice is found in Chapter 2, but in general terms Rubin states that the 'period of military law autonomy' was a 'lengthy one stretching for almost a hundred years between the mid-nineteenth and the mid-twentieth centuries'. In this period 'military regulations, the authority of commanders, the awards of courts martial and disputes arising from military obligations overwhelmingly escaped the scrutiny of the civil courts regarding their legality'.[102] Military justice was designed to uphold discipline, maintain good order and control soldiers. It

---

[99]   OSCE, 'Citizens in Uniform: Protecting Human Rights in the Armed Forces', 21 September 2006 https://www.osce.org/odihr/57532.

[100]   *R (Limbu and Others) v Secretary of State for the Home Department* [2008] EWHC 2261 (Admin), para 72. For further litigation involving the Gurkhas see *British Gurkha Society v Ministry of Defence* [2010] EWCA Civ 1098; *British Gurkha Society v United Kingdom*, Application no. 44818/11, 15 September 2016 (ECtHR).

[101]   Forster (2012) 282.

[102]   G. Rubin, 'United Kingdom Military Law: Autonomy, Civilianisation, Juridification' (2002) 65 *Modern Law Review* 38 at 42.

was deliberately swift and often harsh, intentionally avoiding the ponderous nature of the civilian justice system and the accompanying 'fiddle-faddle' of lawyers.[103]

Moreover, legal autonomy reflected the 'very distinctiveness of military life',[104] and the higher standards of discipline and conduct expected and needed for an effective and mobile fighting force. The mobility of the armed forces also justified the development of a separate system of justice that could travel with them and could be delivered on the front line as well as back home in the barracks and camps. Military efficiency was in a sense matched by legal efficiency. When deployed, the armed forces have to achieve certain objectives and while the law should regulate their conduct it should not inhibit military efficiency. Legal efficiency enables quick decisions regarding possible action (for example on targeting) and speedy resolution of any violations. A separate legal system embodies the codes and ethos of the armed forces and reflects the position of the army as sitting between state and society – as an organ of the state tasked with defending the country and its interests but drawn from and based in that society. The reluctance of civilian courts to interfere in matters of military justice for over a century is understandable given their lack of expertise in a system of justice that is intimately linked to the unique functions of the armed forces. This was recognised by the Lewis Committee in 1949:

> The tasks which [a soldier] may be called upon to perform ... and the circumstances under which such tasks may have to be performed, call for a high degree of discipline; and the maintenance of such discipline in turn requires a special code of law to define the soldier's duty and to prescribe punishment for breaches of it. The civil law grants the remedy of damages in a case where a servant leaves his master's employment without proper notice; but such a remedy would hardly avail to prevent deserting from the Forces. Disobedience to the orders of a superior is not, in civil life, normally a criminal offence, but such disobedience in the Forces may be an offence of great gravity, imperilling the lives of many men and calling for exemplary punishment. In order to maintain the efficiency of a fighting force and the discipline upon which such efficiency depends, it has, therefore, always been recognised that a special code of military law is necessary.[105]

This explains why a separate system is required for discipline offences but it is also possible to extend this reasoning to normal criminal conduct offences which, when committed by soldiers, are also subject to the system of military

---

[103] Ibid, citing Field Marshall Lord Wolseley.
[104] Ibid, 39.
[105] Mr Justice Lewis, 'Report of the Army and Air Force Courts-Martial Committee', Cmd 7608 (HMSO, 1949) para 11.

justice.[106] Their commission also reflects a lack of discipline and respect for the code of behaviour and conduct expected of soldiers. In effect, criminal conduct committed by soldiers outside their official capacity is also subject to the specialist system of military justice and disciplinary punishment. Soldiers are not simply being punished for breaching the criminal law of the land, but for behaviour that falls short of what is required from them as members of the armed forces.

According to Rubin the autonomy of the military justice system 'remained the case until the first stirrings of change in the 1960s when the "civilianisation" of military law, that is, the (consensual) incorporation into military law of perceived beneficial civilian legal norms, often drawn from the civilian system of criminal justice, was accepted by government and approved by the armed forces themselves'.[107] This 'social and legal process of convergence between military and civilian law' was not detrimental to military effectiveness.[108] It was an approach taken to enable closer military support for the civilian authorities, for example in Northern Ireland and then in the wider confrontation with terrorism after 9/11.[109]

There is some evidence that the process of civilianisation and the consensual incorporation of civilian norms did include an initial acceptance of some human rights norms, at least before their extraterritorial extension started to change the legal framework governing the external deployment of forces. In fact, a close look at the ECHR reveals that a state party's margin of appreciation is sufficient to accommodate the functions of the military in internal deployments alongside the protection of the rights enshrined in the Convention. For example, the rights to freedom of expression, assembly and association can be restricted by the government where necessary, inter alia, in the interests of national security or for the prevention of crime or disorder.[110] The most fundamental right – to life – allows for state agents to take life not only in self-defence but also where absolutely necessary in effecting arrest, preventing escape from detention, and 'in action lawfully taken for the purpose of quelling a riot or insurrection',[111] a provision which could accommodate some forms of internal deployments. Further support for the view that the ECHR was designed to accommodate the military function is found in the provision allowing for derogation in times of 'war or other public emergency threatening the

---

[106]   J. Blackett, *Rant on the Court Martial and Service Law* (Oxford University Press, 3rd edn, 2009) 24–5.

[107]   Rubin (2002) 38.

[108]   Ibid, 47.

[109]   See discussion in Chapter 3.

[110]   ECHR 1950, Articles 10 and 11.

[111]   Ibid, Article 2.

life of the nation', when the government can derogate from a number of rights and, while it provides that no derogation from the right to life is permitted, it adds the important proviso – 'except in respect of deaths resulting from lawful acts of war'.[112] To some extent, this envisages the extraterritorial extension of the right to life to conflicts but it allows the state to derogate from its application. Besides which, the phrase 'lawful acts of war' might be interpreted to signify that such acts are lawful irrespective of derogation.[113]

Other aspects of human rights law, however, were resisted by the government. Changes to both the court martial and the summary process to accord with human rights conceptions of a fair trial and due process,[114] are the most obvious examples. According to Rubin, civilianisation has given way to 'juridification', which he defines as 'the coercive extension to military society of civilian legal norms through litigation'. This has been driven 'not only from pressures within the European, human rights and international legal order exploring inconsistencies within United Kingdom law but also from unconnected developments within the domestic courts'.[115] The imposition of 'external legal norms … on the armed forces in situations where such legal norms had hitherto been absent',[116] included 'judicial review challenges and habeas corpus applications' in respect of the 'armed forces' disciplinary practices and procedures',[117] and cases brought on the basis of equal opportunities, gender, and sexual orientation. Judgments delivered by the European Court of Human Rights (ECtHR) led 'directly to the lifting in 2000 of the ban on openly gay people serving in the armed forces'.[118] Legislation has also encouraged increased litigation before civil courts outside the enclosed system of military justice. Of particular note is the adoption of Crown Proceedings Armed Forces

---

[112] ECHR (1950) Article 15.
[113] For discussion of derogation under Article 15 see Chapter 8.
[114] See discussion in Chapter 8.
[115] Rubin (2002) 52.
[116] Ibid, 37.
[117] Ibid, 52. Rubin gives the example of Drummer Stephen Jordan 'who, prior to his successful ECHR judgment in March 2000 (Appl No 30280/96) under Articles 5(3) and (5), had obtained his release from detention in December 1995 after instituting habeas corpus proceedings. This was followed in February 1996 by proceedings for compensation resulting in payment (part damages and part out-of-court settlement, it appears) from the Ministry of Defence for the admitted unlawful detention. Similar cases raised by other service personnel (even before travelling to Strasbourg became fashionable) and successfully alleging torts such as unlawful detention, false imprisonment and trespass to the person could be cited, though arguably such proceedings might reflect a reversion to eighteenth century legal principles'.
[118] A. Forster, 'British Judicial Engagement and the Juridification of the Armed Forces' (2012) 88 *International Affairs* 283 at 288. See *Lustig-Prean v United Kingdom* [1999] ECHR 71 and *Smith and Grady v United Kingdom* [1999] ECHR 72.

(Act) 1987, repealing section 10 of the Crown Proceedings Act 1947, which had prevented service personnel from pursuing tort claims against the military. The rationale for repeal was that it was unjust not to allow soldiers the same rights in negligence as other employees.[119]

Rubin sounds a note of caution about over-emphasising the phenomenon of juridification when stating that there remains 'a vast amount of military law that is autonomous – instructions, regulations, standing orders, rules of engagement …'.[120] Forster on the other hand argues that the 'cumulative effect' of the process of juridification 'is a transformation from a "professional soldier" voluntarily eschewing their rights to a "citizen soldier" who is in a unique position, but whose fundamental rights are nonetheless protected'.[121] Whether this has happened in whole or in part will be returned to in Chapter 9.

Furthermore, the legalisation of military matters has, according to other critics, entered a more dangerous stage. According to Groves and Duxbury: 'lawfare' is 'the most recent and weaponised successor to civilianisation' and juridification.[122] 'Lawfare does not refer to the modernisation of military law or military justice *per se* but instead to the suggested adverse effect that the use of law to control the military may have on its ability to fulfil its combat function'. According to these authors 'lawfare was originally used to describe "the use of law as a weapon of war" – invariably by one's adversaries – but is now applied to the more subtle circumstances "where law can create the same or similar *effects* as those ordinarily sought from conventional war-making approaches"'.[123] The idea that law is being used to help the enemy, whether intentionally or not and whether accurate or not, shows the depth of antagonism held in some quarters towards the increasing levels of externally driven legal regulation of the military.[124] Much of the criticism is directed at the ECHR, reflected in this statement found in a Policy Exchange Report of 2015: '[t]he British military is now thoroughly entangled in the net of human rights law – often to the benefit of our country's adversaries. The British armed forces remain the most accomplished in Europe; but they suffer courtroom

---

[119]   Hansard, HC Deb, Vol 110, Col 567, 13 February 1987 (Churchill).

[120]   Rubin (2002) 54.

[121]   Forster (2012) 296.

[122]   M. Groves and A. Duxbury, 'The reform of military justice' in A. Duxbury and M. Groves (eds), *Military Justice in the Modern Age* (Cambridge University Press, 2016) 4.

[123]   Ibid, 5 citing C.J. Dunlap, 'Does Lawfare Need an Apologia?' (2012) 43 *Case Western Reserve Journal of International Law* 146 (emphasis original).

[124]   See T. Tugendhat and L. Croft, 'The Fog of Law: An Introduction to the Legal Erosion of British Fighting Power' (Policy Exchange Report, 2013).

defeat after courtroom defeat in London and Strasbourg.'[125] Such sentiments also reflect a profound concern that legalisation has broken the prior synthesis between military and legal efficiency, so that the military function and the legal function are pulling in different, sometimes opposite, directions.

1.7 CONCLUSION

The aspects of justice discussed in this chapter are explored more fully in the course of the book and, in particular, will be returned to in the final chapter. This will include an assessment of whether the scales of military justice have shifted from a position where the rights and powers of the government predominate over its duties, whereas the duties of soldiers are many and their rights few. This chapter has started to identify that the balance is changing, with both the duties of government and the rights of soldiers increasing to reflect a changing conception of justice. As Groves and Duxbury state:

> The evolving conception of 'lawfare' makes clear that no single term can adequately capture the different forces that operate within and without military justice. However, the very notion of lawfare highlights that the 'justice' component of 'military justice' is contested.[126]

Justice is not only a standard by which we judge a system of law; it is in itself a contested concept. In the context of military justice, at its narrowest, justice amounts to the application of military law by military courts and structures to military personnel. In these conditions, military efficiency is supported by legal efficiency. At its broadest, justice challenges the predominance of military and legal efficiency and its intimately related components of obedience, discipline, duty and collective will, not only by stressing the individual rights of soldiers and civilians but also by reassessing the place of the military and the soldier in the society and state they serve. In other words, justice reflects, as well as influences, the changing relationship between soldier and society.

---

[125] R. Etkins, J. Morgan and T. Tugendhat, 'Clearing the Fog of Law: Saving Our Armed Forces from Defeat by Judicial Diktat' (Policy Exchange Report, 2015).
[126] Groves and Duxbury (2016) 5.

2. Constitutional laws and the armed forces

2.1 INTRODUCTION

The first half of this chapter traces the domestic constitutional evolution of the armed forces of the UK. The purpose is not simply to expose the constitutional framework that has developed around the armed forces, but to understand the intrinsic relationship between the military and the state through a legal examination of the evolution of the British state and the role of the military in that endeavour. This chapter builds on the theoretical construction of the social contractual relationships surrounding the armed forces undertaken in Chapter 1. The founding constitutional documents of the UK have shaped the modern armed forces and reflect the paradigm that a state is built on a monopoly on the use of force. This means that the legitimacy of the state is dependent upon it successfully controlling violence within its borders, providing security to its citizens, and protecting the nation from external threats. The history of the UK shows that this monopoly was hard won, and that the shaping of the armed forces came about as much from internal conflict as it did from defence of the realm from foreign invaders.

The international legal frameworks and institutions governing the use of force by the state to tackle external threats are the subject of the second half of this chapter. These legal frameworks seek to regulate the use of force by states and although constitutional in a weaker sense than the domestic public laws surrounding the military,[1] they remain the main normative constraints on a state's freedom to use force in international relations in the state of nature that would otherwise exist between states. These international laws and institutions help to shape the nature and functions of the British armed forces, in the form of constraints and as sources of empowerment.

---

[1] J. Crawford, 'The Charter of the United Nations as a Constitution' in H. Fox (ed.), *The Changing Constitution of the United Nations* (British Institute of International and Comparative Law, 1997) 3 at 8.

Although distinct constitutional regimes,[2] both national and international legal frameworks consist of key constitutional settlements achieved at transformative points in history, which were embodied in charters and other foundational constitutional documents. These documents are then developed by what can be termed customary constitutional law,[3] whereby through interpretation and consistent practice, the abstract constitutional normative bones are given flesh. Together these domestic and international frameworks seek to regulate the deployment and use of armed forces, but they represent the apex of the constitutional legal regime governing the state and its armed forces. The central point that connects the two orders is the legal construction of the state internally and externally. Furthermore, the linking point between the two legal frameworks is that the military is legally an element of the state both domestically (reflected in national legal doctrines of combat immunity and Crown immunity), and internationally (reflected in international legal doctrines of act of state, state responsibility, and state immunity), discussed in the final section of the chapter.

Later chapters explore subsidiary sets of laws, both domestic (service law, criminal law, and laws relating to emergencies) and international (LOAC, international criminal law and human rights law) governing the state, the military and military personnel. These laws operate at a sub-constitutional level and traditionally have been the main concern of military justice. Indeed, the UK has incorporated much of the applicable international law into its domestic law by means of the Geneva Conventions Act 1957, the HRA 1998 and the International Criminal Court Act 2001, strengthening the bonds between the relevant national and international laws. This chapter demonstrates that military justice can only be fully understood by placing it within a broader constitutional framework. Later chapters will explore the legal regimes that have been developed within this constitutional framework to regulate the military and soldiers particularly when on operations. This combination of constitutional and operational law governing and regulating the armed forces, constructed from national and international law, is the subject matter of this book.

---

[2]   For the view that national and international legal orders form one continuum see H. Kelsen, *General Theory of Law and State* (Harvard University Press, 1949) 369–70.
[3]   E. Hambro (writing as Pollux), 'The Interpretation of the Charter' (1946) 23 *British Yearbook of International Law* 54.

2.2   NATIONAL CONSTITUTIONAL FRAMEWORK

By focusing on key constitutional moments in the shaping of the UK, this section traces the development of the state's monopoly over the use of force and provides a series of insights into the evolving functions and duties of soldiers and sailors who served and fought for the sovereign and, ultimately, the state. A number of the statutes in this account (and their successors) remain foundation stones of the British constitution, but they also embody stepping stones in the shaping of the British state and its assertion of a monopoly over violence.

2.2.1   The Great Charter and the Beginnings of the Rule of Law

The background to the adoption of the Magna Carta in 1215 involved two brothers: King Richard I (Richard the Lionheart), and his brother John who succeeded him. When John succeeded his brother, he failed to maintain the loyalty of powerful barons, preferring 'to rely on men and measures about which he had no illusions at all: mercenaries, hostages, blackmail and extortion'.[4] After John suffered defeat against France at the Battle of Bouvines in 1214, the barons took advantage of John's weaknesses in order to push back the centralising power of the king, forcing him to sign the Magna Carta.

According to Simon Schama: '[n]o one should read the Magna Carta as if it were some sort of primitive constitution. It was not, as has been aptly said, a charter of liberty but a charter of liberties, in the medieval sense of exemptions: a catalogue of things that the king would not henceforth be permitted to do.'[5] Schama takes his analysis further to explain how the Magna Carta embodied the emergence of the state as a legal and political construct that included the sovereign:

> So, if the Magna Carta was not a birth certificate of freedom it was the death certificate of despotism. It spelled out for the first time, and unequivocally, ... that the law was not simply the will or the whim of the king but was an independent power in its own right, and that kings could be brought to book for violating it – that they should, for example, show due cause why a person's body might be confined (*habeas corpus*) and not just declared to be detained at the inscrutable pleasure of the prince. All this, in turn presupposed something hitherto unimaginable: that there was some sort of English 'state' of which the king was a part (albeit the supreme part) but not the whole.[6]

---

[4]   S. Schama, *A History of Britain: At the Edge of the World 3000 BC – AD 1603* (BBC Books, 2000) 159.

[5]   Ibid.

[6]   Ibid, 162.

The Magna Carta is seen as establishing a rudimentary rule of law in the country, with no one, including the king, being above the law: '[T]he cry has been not that the law should be altered, but that it should be observed, in particular, that it should be observed by the king.'[7] F.W. Maitland described the great charter as not only the 'beginning of English statute law', but as ushering in the 'reign of law',[8] although in doing so a great deal of power was transferred to the barons.

In the Magna Carta, the king granted a number of 'customs and liberties ... for the better ordering of our kingdom, and to allay the discord that has arisen' between the monarch and the barons. To this end, the Charter provided that the barons were to elect 25 of 'their number to keep, and cause to be observed with all their might, the peace and liberties granted and confirmed to them by this charter'.[9] In Radin's view the Magna Carta has become 'an ancient fetish, a sort of medicine bag, pulled out of the dust of the record-room ... and made into the symbol of the struggle against arbitrary power; and that the true effect of the Charter, if any, had been merely the hardening of the privileges of some hundred petty kings'.[10] This view is countered by Maitland's analysis of the Magna Carta as an early assertion of the rule of law by subjecting all including the king to the law, but also through provisions that were aimed at ensuring that officers of the state fairly applied the law. The Magna Carta declared that: '[w]e will appoint as justices, constables, sheriffs, or other officials, only men that know the law of the realm and are minded to keep it well'.[11] Of course, as Maitland remarked: '[i]t was one thing to obtain the charter, it was another to get it observed'.[12]

At the time, the king was dependent upon the barons and other feudal lords to provide soldiers and so, while the Magna Carta did not mention military forces to any significant extent, it was a social contract that was designed to establish security in the country on the basis that it would be underwritten by powerful barons, who would be responsible for securing the peace and upholding the liberties granted in the Charter. The problem of foreign mercenaries was addressed in the Magna Carta and the agreement was to expel all of these soldiers: '[a]s soon as peace is restored, we will remove from the kingdom

---

[7]   F.W. Maitland, *The Constitutional History of England* (Cambridge University Press, 1931) 15.

[8]   Ibid.

[9]   Magna Carta (1215) at https://www.bl.uk/magna-carta/articles/magna-carta -english-translation#, paras 60–1.

[10]   M. Radin, 'The Myth of the Magna Carta' (1947) 60 *Harvard Law Review* 1060 at 1062.

[11]   Magna Carta (1215) para 45.

[12]   Maitland (1931) 16.

all the foreign knights, bowmen, their attendants, and the mercenaries that have come to it, to its harm, with horses and arms'.[13] However, mercenaries were a continuing feature of the underwritten security of the realm for many centuries to come.

In fact, there was no standing army in Britain until after the Glorious Revolution in 1688; before that it was the case that armies were put together for specific purposes. For example, when Edward I commanded a force against Scotland in 1300, his 10,000 strong army consisted of cavalry drawn from members of his royal household, landowners under obligation, contracted knights and men at arms, while the infantry was largely recruited by royal commissioners, and the force was completed by foreign mercenaries.[14] The obligations of the members of the force were primarily to defend the land, but that included prosecuting wars against Wales and Scotland under Henry VI, and France under Henry VIII, a quarter of whose 44,000 army consisted of foreign troops.[15]

2.2.2   The Civil War and Civil-Military Relations

In 1642, the struggle between Charles I and Parliament led to the English Civil War (1642–1651), which saw both sides creating more structured and professional armies, epitomised by the New Model Army of Oliver Cromwell.[16] In describing the Battle of Edgehill – the opening military encounter of the English Civil War – Allan Mallinson comments that 'there had not been a pitched battle on English soil for 130 years. There has not been much of a battle anywhere for an English army in all that time. There was no English army.'[17] King Charles I and Parliament both pulled together scratch armies largely based on poorly trained county militias. After Edgehill, Cromwell realised that 'war could no longer be made in the old feudal way; that there must be system and discipline, and thus (eventually) a regular professional army'.[18]

The New Model Army would not be especially large, however – 22,000 men and 2,300 officers, two-thirds infantry to one-third cavalry (about the number, indeed,

---

[13]   Magna Carta (1215) para 51.

[14]   M. Prestwich, 'The English Medieval Army to 1485' in D.G. Chandler and I. Beckett (eds), *The Oxford History of the British Army* (Oxford University Press, 1994) 1.

[15]   I. Roy, 'Towards the Standing Army 1485–1660' in Chandler and Beckett (1994) 23 at 26.

[16]   Ibid, 42.

[17]   Allan Mallinson, *The Making of the British Army* (Transworld Books, 2009) ch 1.

[18]   Ibid.

of the British infantry today) – but it would be superbly disciplined, equipped and trained. And for the first time a British army would wear a true uniform – red.[19]

The 'Soldier's Catechism' issued as a pamphlet for parliamentarian soldiers in 1644 stated in clear terms the 'justifications' of the soldier for fighting in the war, as well as the 'qualifications' needed of such a soldier. The latter included directions on the proper behaviour of officers to soldiers including the requirement to treat them 'justly', and soldiers to officers including the duty of 'exact' obedience to commands, as well as provisions on tackling mutiny and desertion. In relation to soldiers who 'run away from their colours' they shall 'by Martial Law ... suffer death, and surely, they well deserve it'.[20]

Although in form the New Model Army sowed the seeds of the modern military, its function also raised the 'fundamental and problematic issue' of the 'place of the army in the state'. While the army was professional and disciplined, by 1649 when Charles I was executed, it 'had become thoroughly imbued with puritan zeal, and thus politicized', and 'became the means of imposing a political and religious vision on the civil population'.[21] This led General Monck to declare that the 'army in England has broken up the Parliament, out of a restless ambition to govern themselves ... For my part, I think myself obliged, by the duty of my place, to keep military power in obedience to the civil.'[22] Monck played a pivotal military role in the restoration of the monarchy, but that fundamental doctrine of military obedience to Parliament remained a problem until 1688.

The reduction in the size of the army after the Civil War led to a return to reliance on the militia, although the 'guards' around the monarch formed the professional core of any future army. Although 'controversy constantly broke out between king and parliament as to military matters',[23] the King's Sole Right over the Militia Act 1661 declared that the 'sole supreme government of the militia and of all forces by sea and land is, and by the laws of England ever was, the undoubted right of the king and his predecessors, and that neither house of parliament could pretend to the same'.[24] However, as Maitland relates: 'loyal as the parliament might be, it would not trust even a king with such an engine of tyranny as a standing army'.[25] The legal position of the military in the state remained unclear until 1688. Until that time, the military

---

[19] Ibid.
[20] http://theonomyresources.com/pdfs/the-soldiers-catechism.pdf.
[21] Mallinson (2009) ch 1.
[22] Ibid.
[23] Maitland (1931) 327.
[24] Ibid, 326.
[25] Ibid, 326.

regulated itself through Articles of War, first issued in 1663, which included provisions for court martial of capital offences, but this operated in effect outside of the public law of England;[26] indeed the Petition of Right of 1623 appeared to prohibit commissions of martial law.[27] Nonetheless, after the failed rebellion against James II by the Duke of Monmouth in 1685, there were trials of a number of the rebels by courts martial consisting of 18 officers constituted under the Articles of War.[28]

2.2.3   The Bill of Rights and Parliamentary Authority

While the army was temporarily an organ of state during the Interregnum, it was the case that until the intervention of William of Orange in the 'Glorious Revolution' of 1688, the post-restoration army belonged to the monarch in that it was not recognised in legislation and Parliament did not otherwise formally recognise its existence.[29] The background to the Glorious Revolution and the Bill of Rights 1689 was James II's pro-Catholic tendencies. Although he could not 'force England back to Rome overnight', James II readily reopened formal relations with Rome and allowed the return of Catholic worship and practices into the public realm. It began to appear that he was prepared to challenge everything the Restoration stood for. Whigs and those Tories opposing this trend turned to James' daughter Mary and her husband William of Orange, Prince of the Dutch Republic, who were invited ultimately to depose James and protect Protestantism in the 'Glorious Revolution' of 1688.[30] According to Schama this was in reality an 'invasion' rather than a 'revolution'. It 'took an immense foreign armada of possibly 600 vessels, carrying perhaps 15,000 Dutch and German troops, to bring about the fall of James'.[31]

In 1689, with the throne vacant (James having fled to France), a Convention Parliament met and was divided between a Whig majority in the Commons who wanted William and Mary to become monarchs immediately, and a Tory majority in the Lords who argued for a regency until the death of James. With Dutch troops on the streets of London, William and Mary rejected anything except the Crown, although at their coronation on 11 April 1689 a reading of

---

[26]   Ibid, 327.
[27]   A.V. Dicey, *Introduction to the Study of the Law of the Constitution* (Macmillan, 10th edn, 1959) 295.
[28]   Maitland (1931) 328.
[29]   J. Childs, 'The Restoration Army 1660–1702' in Chandler and Beckett (1994) 46 at 52.
[30]   S. Schama, *A History of Britain: The British Wars 1603–1776* (BBC Books, 2001) 306–11.
[31]   Ibid, 312–13.

the Declaration of Rights passed by the Convention 'solemnized the Crown's commitment to the reforms of the Long Parliament and the Protectorate as a condition of its authority'.[32]

The Bill of Rights contained both a condemnation of the reign of James II and a legal framework for the new monarchy.[33] In terms of the former, the Bill stated that 'the late King James the Second ... did endeavour to subvert and extirpate the Protestant religion and the laws and liberties of this kingdom', including by: 'assuming and exercising a power of dispensing with and suspending of laws and the execution of laws without consent of Parliament'; 'raising and keeping a standing army within this kingdom in time of peace without consent of Parliament, and quartering soldiers contrary to law'; and 'causing several good subjects being Protestants to be disarmed at the same time when papists were both armed and employed contrary to law'.[34] Parliament's rejection of the monarch having a monopoly on armed forces within the kingdom is clear.

The terms of the legal framework set by the Bill of Rights reflected the above strictures, and included declarations that: 'levying money for or to the use of the Crown by pretence of prerogative, without grant of Parliament, for longer time, or in other manner than the same is or shall be granted, is illegal'; 'the raising or keeping a standing army within the kingdom in time of peace, unless it be with consent of Parliament, is against law'; 'the subjects which are Protestants may have arms for their defence suitable to their conditions and as allowed by law'; and that 'for redress of all grievances, and for the amending, strengthening and preserving of the laws, Parliaments ought to be held frequently'.[35] Parliament asserted authority over the armed forces at least in time of peace. Moreover, by seizing the purse strings, Parliament had the potential to control the monarch's prerogative powers even in times of war by refusing to raise the necessary funds.

2.2.4   The Mutiny Acts: Law Governing the Military

Ian Loveland notes that the 1688 revolution 'marked the crossing of a political watershed' with a 'new political contract' being struck between Parliament and the monarchy containing limitations upon prerogative powers. The 'Monarch might still be responsible for governing the country, and she/he could appoint the Ministers who would do the job, but those Ministers would govern the

---

[32]   Ibid, 320–1.
[33]   Bill of Rights (1689) at http://www.law.gmu.edu/assets/files/academics/founders/English_BillofRights.pdf.
[34]   Ibid.
[35]   Ibid.

country according to laws defined by Parliament'.[36] The Bill of Rights made it clear that both the raising of funds for wars and the maintenance of a standing army in peacetime were in the hands of Parliament. The events of 1688–1689 had further impact on establishing a constitutional framework to govern the armed forces, when the refusal of a number of troops to accept William's rule led to the first Mutiny Act of 1689. This provided for trial by court martial for acts of mutiny, desertion and sedition committed by officers and soldiers and, for those found guilty by at least nine out of the 13 officers constituting the court martial, death or such other punishment determined by the court,[37] thereby marking the beginning of codified UK military law. Regular Mutiny Acts were replaced by the forerunner of modern military law, the Army Discipline and Regulation Act 1879, replaced in turn by the Army Act of 1881.

A.V. Dicey explains the importance of the first Mutiny Act of 1689 as enabling Parliament to reconcile the internal threat to it and to the rule of law represented by a standing army on the one hand, and the need to have such an organ at its disposal to be able to defend the state from external threat on the other. As Dicey explained: 'with a standing army the country could not, they feared, escape from despotism; without a standing army the country could not, they were sure, avert invasion'.[38] The Mutiny Act and its successors managed to reconcile this by subjecting members of the standing army to the ordinary laws of the land in addition to obligations under military law specific to them:

> A soldier, whether an officer or a private, in a standing army, or (to use the wider expression of modern Acts) 'a person subject to military law', stands in a two-fold relation: the one is his relation towards his fellow-citizens outside the army; the other is his relation towards the members of the army, and especially towards his military superiors; any man, in short, subject to military law has duties and rights as a citizen as well as duties and rights as a soldier.[39]

Ordinary soldiers who breached discipline were subject to harsh punishments including lashing and the death penalty following rudimentary courts martial, while officers were less likely to appear before courts martial and, when they

---

[36] I. Loveland, *Constitutional Law, Administrative Law and Human Rights* (Butterworths, 3rd edn, 2003) 25.

[37] Maitland (1931) 329.

[38] A.V. Dicey, *Introduction to the Study of the Law of the Constitution* (Macmillan, 10th edn, 1959) 298.

[39] Ibid, 300.

did, they received lesser punishment. As Gilbert notes in his review of the operation of military justice in the 18th century:

> The term 'military justice' conveniently lumps *two* legal systems under a single heading. Procedures might be similar, but officers and common soldiers were not often tried for the same crimes. Desertion was the pre-eminent crime of the rank and file; indeed, there were times when over ninety percent of [General Court Martial] trials were for that offense. Given the status and relatively pleasant conditions provided for officers, desertion among them was virtually nonexistent. If an officer stayed away beyond his allotted time, he would have been tried, if at all, for being absent without leave. The major 'crime' in the officer corps was 'conduct unbecoming an officer and a gentleman', and clearly enlisted men could not be tried for that offense. The overlap between officer and rank and file crime was limited to cases of murder, robbery, and morals offenses in overseas ports. Even those charges might be subsumed under the 'conduct' charge to protect officers from the disgrace of trial for enlisted men's crimes.[40]

The distinction between the ordinary soldier and the officer is one of hierarchy, which empowers the officers to command and obliges the soldiers to obey. Thus, the ordinary soldier bears the heavier burden of legal responsibility. Although the concept of command responsibility, whereby commanders can be criminally responsible for the infractions of soldiers under their command, has grown in the modern era, recent examples of courts martial such as those reviewed in Chapter 7 still appear to focus on the crimes and breaches of service law of ordinary soldiers.

2.2.5 The Transition from Private to Public Armed Forces

The Royal Navy's development was in some ways similar to that of the British Army, although it is the older and 'senior' service, originating in a mixture of the monarch's own ships, supplemented by private ships commissioned for specific purposes. According to Ben Wilson: '[w]hen Henry V died in 1422 his [four great] ships were treated as his private property rather than as part of a royal navy. Many were sold off to pay his debts.' By 1452, Henry VI 'lost control of the Channel thanks to the greatest enemy of the navy: the indebtedness of the Crown' so that '[o]nce again the Crown was reduced to licensing private interests to "keep the seas"'. Until the 17th century 'it was impossible to distinguish between a nation's private merchant marine and its ships of war. The more private ships there were, therefore, the larger the fleet the king could

---

[40] N. Gilbert, 'Military and Civilian Justice in Eighteenth-Century England' (1978) 17 *Journal of British Studies* 41 at 43–4 (emphasis original).

muster to control the sea, win glory abroad and suppress piracy.'[41] Even by the mid-18th century 'Britons flattered themselves that they were a maritime superpower. The reality was different. The bulk of British naval forces were in home waters, ready to defend the country against invasion.'[42] After the destruction of the Franco-Spanish fleet by the Royal Navy under Admiral Horatio Lord Nelson at the Battle of Trafalgar in 1805 'the Navy achieved an aura of invincibility. It was the pillar of national defence and the bedrock of empire.'[43]

The army too was being shaped by external threats. The threat of a French invasion led to the revival of militias by the Militia Act 1757, further by the Defence of the Realm Act 1798, consisting of part-time soldiers based in the counties. These forces, numbering 176,000, would help defend the nation in the event of invasion.[44] During the Napoleonic Wars the regular army's size grew to 250,000, but this was scattered across the empire and one-fifth of this force consisted of foreign soldiers. The Navy's strength climbed to 140,000 in this period.[45] The expenditure of 'blood and treasure' in those conflicts created the need to reduce military spending so that by the time of the Crimean War in the 1850s, Britain only had a force of 25,000 at its disposal. This led to the creation of a supplementary part-time force of volunteers which, by 1862, numbered 160,000, with each county raising its contribution.[46] Following the Territorial and Reserve Forces Act 1907 this volunteer force was reorganised and continued in its modern guise of the Territorial Army.

In 1870, Parliament passed the Army Enlistment Act, which was designed to make military service in the regular army more attractive, with shorter periods of service. In the same year it passed the Foreign Enlistment Act 'to regulate the conduct of Her Majesty's subjects during the existence of hostilities between foreign states with which Her Majesty is at peace'. This Act created offences to punish British subjects joining or recruiting others to join the armed forces of foreign powers at war with a country at peace with Britain. Mercenarism was in decline by 1870 as large numbers of British subjects fighting in a foreign

---

[41]   B. Wilson, *Empire of the Deep: The Rise and Fall of the British Navy* (Weidenfeld and Nicholson, 2013) chs 5, 7.

[42]   Ibid, ch 29.

[43]   Ibid, introduction to Part IV.

[44]   https://www.parliament.uk/about/living-heritage/transformingsociety/private -lives/yourcountry/overview/frenchthreat/.

[45]   D. Gates, 'The Transformation of the Army 1783–1815' in Chandler and Beckett (1994) 132, 138. In 1914 the British Army numbered 247,432 but after four and a half years of war in November 1918 it totalled 3,458,586 – T. Travers, 'The Army and the Challenges of War' in Chandler and Beckett (1994) 211.

[46]   https://www.parliament.uk/about/living-heritage/transformingsociety/private -lives/yourcountry/overview/victorianarmies/.

war was both a threat to Britain's neutrality but also undermined the state's authority to make war. The immediate concern was to maintain neutrality in the Franco-Prussian War of 1870. According to Janice Thomson the 'last instance in which a state raised an army of foreigners was in 1854, when Britain hired 16,500 German, Italian, and Swiss mercenaries for the Crimean war', although none of the troops were used as they arrived too late for the fighting.[47] As with piracy, mercenarism's transition from a well-used tool of states to being proscribed by those same states was not a result of a realisation that these activities were inherently wrong, rather that they had served their purpose and, moreover, their continuation was a challenge to the state's 'monopolizing authority' over its armed forces and their deployment.[48]

Uniquely, for what have now become permanent organs of the state, legislation governing the armed forces was renewed annually until 1955, when it was adjusted to a five yearly cycle. The Mutiny Act was renewed annually until 1879 with modifications to cover breaches of the Crown's Articles of War. Although Parliament had overall authority over the military, prerogative powers continued to be exercised by the monarch and his or her Cabinet of ministers, with those powers gradually being handed over to the Prime Minister and other ministers. It remains the case that Parliament regularly consents to the presence of a standing army, but, until recently at least,[49] does not approve each deployment of those troops.

2.2.6 Emergency Laws for Defence of the Realm

The two world wars led the governments of the day to take vague prerogative powers to tackle states of emergency and embed them in legislation.[50] The Defence of the Realm Act 1914 empowered the government to authorise

---

[47] J.E. Thomson, *Mercenaries, Pirates and Sovereigns* (Princeton University Press, 1994) 84–8.

[48] Ibid, 88.

[49] See discussion in Chapter 4.

[50] C.P. Cotter, 'Constitutionalizing Emergency Powers: The British Experience' (1953) 5 *Stanford Law Review* 382. There have been judicial debates about the existence, nature and extent of a prerogative power to impose 'martial law', whereby military rule may displace the civil law in times of war or insurrection. While the judges tended towards recognition of such a power they characterised 'martial law' as 'no law at all' – *R v Nelson and Brand* (1867), *Ex parte D.F. Marais* (1901-2), *Tilonko v Attorney-General of Natal* (1907) in W.C. Costin and J.S. Watson, *The Law & Working of the Constitution: Documents 1660–1914*: Vol II 1784–1914 (Adam and Charles Black, 1952) 282, 312, 317. On the chequered practice of imposing martial law in the UK see D.L. Keir, *The Constitutional History of Modern Britain 1485–1937* (Adam and Charles Black, 3rd edn, 1947) 110–11, 191–2, 211, 305.

the punishment of individuals contravening regulations designed to prevent persons communicating with, or otherwise assisting, the enemy, effectively extending courts martial to civilians and causing heated debate in the House of Lords. Lord Bryce argued for the restoration of the right of British subjects who were civilians to be tried before the civil courts saying: 'if it were a case of invasion or civil war then, of course, the Courts would not be available; but while the Courts are available surely some further reason must be given to us than has been given for such an extraordinary departure as this from all historical precedent'.[51] The government responded by introducing amending legislation that allowed civilians charged with offences under emergency regulations to be tried by a civil court with a jury or by court martial, although the government reserved the right to revert to compulsory court martial in the event of invasion, as well as detention without trial of individuals of 'hostile origin or associations'.[52] In *R v Halliday* the House of Lords upheld the validity of a detention order, Lord Findlay stating that 'it may be necessary in time of great public danger to entrust great powers' to the executive, and 'that Parliament may do so feeling certain that such powers will be reasonably exercised'.[53]

Emergency powers were continued in legislation in the inter-war period in the face of crippling strikes. At the outbreak of the Second World War, the Emergency Powers (Defence) Act 1939 was introduced. The government was given power to 'make such Regulations ... as appear to be necessary or expedient for securing the public safety, the defence of the realm, the maintenance of public order and the efficient prosecution of any war in which His Majesty may be engaged, and for maintaining supplies and services essential to the life of the community'. Unlike the 1914 Act, the 1939 Act expressly withheld the power to provide for trial by court martial of persons not subject to military law. Regulations allowed for detention if the Secretary of State had 'reasonable cause to believe any person to be of hostile origin or associations or to have been recently concerned in acts prejudicial to the public safety or the defence of the realm ...'. Again the House of Lords refused to uphold a challenge to the exercise of the power of detention in *Liversidge v Anderson*, dismissing the applicant's argument that 'reasonable cause to believe' provided 'an objectively ascertainable – and reviewable – standard'.[54]

---

[51]   Hansard, HL Deb, Vol 18, Col 209, 26 November 2014.
[52]   Cotter (1953) 389.
[53]   *R v Halliday* [1917] AC 260 at 268–9.
[54]   Cotter (1953) 412. But see Lord Atkin's dissent in *Liversidge v Anderson* [1942] AC 208 at 225–6.

2.2.7   National Service and Duty

In terms of ensuring sufficient troops and sailors, press gangs were used with Parliamentary sanction to force men into serving in the Royal Navy and the Army in the 17th and 18th centuries, although they fell into disuse after 1815.[55] Conscription only formally operated in the UK in the periods 1916–1918 by virtue of the Military Service Act 1916, and 1939–1960 by virtue of the National Service (Armed Forces) Act 1939,[56] adopted on the day Britain declared war on Germany. The National Service Act 1948 continued conscription after the war due to on-going military commitments in Germany, Palestine, India and other colonial outposts. 'Traditionally there had always been a suspicion in Britain of a standing conscript army, but in the aftermath of the Second World War there remained military obligations as part of the need to administer the war-torn countries liberated from Nazi rule as well as the normal duties associated with maintaining empire.'[57]

The continuation of national military service in the aftermath of the Second World War, involving deployment to occupied Germany (1945–1955), the Korean War (1950–1953), and countries in the empire including the emergencies in Malaya (1948–1960), Cyprus (1955–1959) and Kenya (1952–1960), was unpopular. In justifying the extension of military service in the face of opposition, Prime Minister Attlee spoke in 1946 about the need for security in the world, which could not be achieved by disarming but by building up 'police forces able to prevent the rise of aggression' in a world where 'new conditions' pertained, which were 'far different from the days before air power and long range projected missiles'.[58] The changing nature of warfare was reflected in a huge expansion in size and function of the RAF during the Second World War, a service which had only been formed in 1918 towards the end of the First World War.

Attlee countered claims that conscription was anti-democratic by pointing out that time spent in the military was not 'wasted' because much of the 'training is technical and it must be training for citizenship as well as defence', and further that the War had drawn 'on the whole of the intelligence of the nation'

---

[55]   For failed attempts by persons impressed into the Navy to challenge that decision see: *R v Broadfoot* (1743), where, according to Foster J, 'the right of impressing mariners for the public service is a prerogative inherent in the Crown'; and *R v Tubbs* (1776) in W.C. Costin and J.S. Watson, *The Law & Working of the Constitution: Documents 1660–1914*: Vol I 1660–1783 (Adam and Charles Black, 1952) 289, 316.

[56]   R. Holmes, *Soldiers* (Harper Press, 2011) 119.

[57]   C. Schindler, *National Service: From Aldershot to Aden, Tales from the Conscripts, 1946–62* (Sphere, 2012) 5.

[58]   Hansard, HC Deb, Vol 430, Cols 42–4, 12 November 1946.

leading to a more democratic military. He concluded that 'there is nothing undemocratic in national service'. 'We are steadily increasing the rights of citizens in this country ... [t]he more rights we can give our people, the better; but rights involve obligation'.[59] Political leaders recognised that conscript soldiers were fulfilling their obligations to the country but were unclear on the effect of this service on their rights. Conscripts had not chosen to give up any or all of their rights, although the act of military service with its discipline and danger inevitably curtailed them. In the case of volunteers, the state could claim that they knew what they were signing up to, and that by agreeing to follow orders to defend monarch and country, they were subjecting themselves to an entirely different set of rules based primarily on duties not rights.

2.2.8   Soldiers' Rights

The question of the rights of soldiers has vexed military leaders. At the time of the Napoleonic Wars, they were divided between humanitarians like Sir John Moore who argued that 'in keeping with the intellectual spirit of the Enlightenment ... soldiers, if accorded dignity, kindness, and education, would be far better motivated than those whipped into obedience'. Most, however, 'favoured the draconian ways of the authoritarian system; troops should be mere automatons, conditioned to fear their own officers more than the enemy and his fire'.[60] The Duke of Wellington, who commanded British forces at the Battle of Waterloo in 1815, was in the latter camp, being of the opinion that the army was largely 'composed of the scum of the earth ... fellows who have enlisted for drink'.[61] In the case of the navy, in the mid-18th century 'naval discipline was in disarray; in many cases the verdicts of courts martial for cowardice or disobeying orders in the 1740s were undone by civilian courts and politicians'.[62] This was the turning point, however, and by the end of that century disloyalty and cowardice in the Royal Navy were punished by courts martial with an increase in the 'number of fixed penalties for specific offences, including those that were punishable only by death'.[63]

In a modern context, we will see that this debate plays out in the form of whether members of the armed forces should be protected by human rights law,[64] or whether they effectively relinquished at least some of this protection when they enlisted. According to Anthony Forster, unchallenged for a long

---

[59]   Ibid.
[60]   Travers (1994) 144.
[61]   Ibid, 145.
[62]   Wilson (2013) ch 28.
[63]   Ibid.
[64]   See Chapter 8.

time was 'a de facto presumption by the British government that citizens voluntarily joining the armed forces accepted some restriction on their human rights, notably the right to life and the curtailment of some of their freedoms and liberties (including the right to a private life), compared with other British citizens'.[65] The harsh military discipline meted out to soldiers during the First World War showed that, at least at that time, the state exercised the power of life or death over members of its armed forces.[66]

The duties of British soldiers were added to by the incorporation of the Geneva Conventions of 1949 into British law, by means of the Geneva Convention Act 1957, which provided that 'any person, whatever his nationality, who, whether in or outside the United Kingdom, commits, aids, abets or procures the commission by any other persons of a grave breach of any of the scheduled conventions ... shall be guilty of an offence'. Later the international crimes of genocide, crimes against humanity and war crimes codified in the Rome Statute of the International Criminal Court 1998 were incorporated by means of the International Criminal Court Act 2001 into UK law. However, unlike the broadening of a soldier's duties under LOAC and international criminal law, the extension of human rights law to soldiers under the HRA 1998, incorporating the rights and freedoms contained in the European Convention, has proved controversial as shall be seen throughout this book.[67]

2.3 INTERNATIONAL CONSTITUTIONAL FRAMEWORK

As the previous sub-section shows, the national constitutional framework is increasingly influenced by developments in international law, especially in LOAC, international criminal law and human rights law developed at various points after 1945. While these have added to the duties and arguably rights of British soldiers, international constitutional moments have helped shape the rights and duties of the British government.

---

[65] A. Forster, 'British Judicial Engagement and the Juridification of the Armed Forces' (2012) 88 *International Affairs* 283 at 285.

[66] See Chapter 7.

[67] S.L. Kemp, *British Justice, War Crimes and Human Rights Violations: The Age of Accountability* (Palgrave Macmillan, 2019) 11–30. See also the Independent Review of the Human Rights Act, established by the government in 2020 https://www.gov.uk/guidance/independent-human-rights-act-review.

2.3.1 Peace of Westphalia 1648 and the Emergence of Sovereign States

In contrast to the domestic constitutional framework of the UK, which began in earnest as early as 1215, international constitutional development starts much later. This reflected a Hobbesian state of nature in international relations until the League of Nations in 1919, despite Grotius' enduring appeal to those jurists arguing for the existence of natural law as well as the law of nations at the international level.[68] According to Neff: '[b]etween independent States ... there was no social contract and no single political society. States, in short, continued to live in a state of nature vis-à-vis one another. But the duty to adhere to contracts still held, and it could enable at least a modicum of order and predictability to emerge', meaning that clear contracts or treaties between sovereign equals were legally binding.[69]

The Peace of Westphalia 1648 involving the Holy Roman Empire, France, Spain, Sweden and the Netherlands has been described by Leo Gross as the 'first great European or world charter'.[70] Furthermore, the treaty has been seen as reflecting a Grotian community of states: 'the Westphalian settlement was an arrangement reached within the framework of the Holy Roman Empire, with certain prerogatives of the imperial government carefully preserved – ie with the older medieval idea of "independent" states being subject, at the same time, to certain higher norms'.[71] Nevertheless, the Treaty of Westphalia contained provisions shoring up the idea of a sovereign independent state, namely: 'territoriality'; the 'right of a state to choose its own religion'; the 'right of non intervention by other states'; 'sovereign authority with regard to foreign policy'; and the 'right of a sovereign state to its domestic policies without foreign interference'. 'This internal and external sovereignty has remained the main characteristic of the territorial or *Westphalian state.*'[72] While not formally part of the Peace of Westphalia, in 17th century Britain the separation of the state from external religious norms and institutions was entrenched, and the distinction between state and monarch, with the monarch being part of the state but not the whole, was being forged. Britain was, and continues to see

---

[68]   S.C. Neff, 'A Short History of International Law' in M.D. Evans (ed.), *International Law* (Oxford University Press, 5th edn, 2018) 3 at 9.

[69]   Ibid, 9.

[70]   L. Gross, 'The Peace of Westphalia 1648–1948' (1948) 42 *American Journal of International Law* 20 at 20.

[71]   Neff (2018) 11.

[72]   B. Reinalda, *Routledge History of International Organizations: From 1815 to the Present Day* (Routledge, 2009) 19.

itself as, a Westphalian state, most recently evidenced by its departure from the European Union in 2020.

2.3.2   Congress of Vienna 1815 and the Advent of Hierarchy

The history of modern international law starts with Napoleon's final defeat at Waterloo in 1815 and the ending of the Napoleonic revolutionary wars. The Final Act of the Congress of Vienna was in some ways a more comprehensive, or at least more effective, settlement of peace in Europe than its successor (the League of Nations), and more adaptable than the United Nations. This was especially so in the way it allowed powerful states to opt out of any collective action when they were unable to support its efforts, while remaining part of the Concert. Characterised alternatively as the embodiment of a balance of power,[73] or a security community,[74] the Concert of Europe was a system of diplomacy, peaceful settlement and, where necessary, enforcement to pre-serve the 'public law and system of Europe'.[75] The rules of the Concert were designed 'to keep the scourge of revolution from breaking out again', with the four victorious powers: Austria, Prussia, Russia and Britain, granting them-selves powers of intervention when necessary.[76] These 'four great powers took the decisions and restored the European balance of power, but this distinction between "great" and "small" was new'. In particular, the UK 'convinced the great powers that they together were the guardians who had the duty to main-tain and improve the balance of power'.[77] The idea of a legalised hierarchy, sitting uneasily with the orthodoxy of sovereign equality in international law, was to be developed by further experiments in international organisations, especially the United Nations.

2.3.3   The Covenant of the League of Nations 1919: A Tentative Step towards Constitution

The first draft of the Covenant emerging from the Commission tasked with producing a draft at the Paris Peace Conference in 1919 was described by its principal advocate US President Woodrow Wilson as a 'living thing' and as

---

[73]   H. Kissinger, *The World Restored: The Politics of Conservatism in a Revolutionary Age* (Grosset and Dunlap, 1964).
[74]   C. Kupchan, *How Enemies become Friends: The Sources of Stable Peace* (Princeton University Press, 2010) 189.
[75]   Neff (2018) 12.
[76]   Ibid, 12.
[77]   Reinalda (2009) 18.

a 'constitution of peace, not as a League of War'.[78] However, he had to return to the Commission in March 1919 to propose pragmatic changes to the draft Covenant in order to try and persuade the US Congress to support the treaty, changes that included a withdrawal clause, an exclusion of matters within a member state's domestic jurisdiction, and a recognition of regional understandings such as the Monroe Doctrine.[79]

Despite these major concessions to state sovereignty, it was true that the drafters of the Covenant had the belief that the legal procedures contained therein would prevent the world stumbling into another cataclysmic conflict of the type that erupted in 1914. The British Prime Minister Lloyd George was of the view that had the League of Nations existed in the summer of 1914 war would not have broken out as Germany would automatically have been called to account before the permanent machinery of the League.[80] The processes of delaying resort to war, the provisions for conciliation, arbitration or reference to the Permanent Court of International Justice, as well as the guarantee against aggression, all included in the Covenant, would have led to a cooling-off period in which statesmen would have resolved their differences.[81] There was recognition, however, that this procedural approach would not stop a government set on a long-term policy of aggression, and, therefore, would prove not to be robust enough for the sort of ideologically driven aggression that started the Second World War.[82] Nevertheless, the League of Nations was a significant step towards a system of collective security, placing particular duties to preserve the peace on the executive body – the Council – in which the UK was a leading member.

2.3.4   The Charter of the United Nations 1945 and Supranationalism

Just as the drafters of the Covenant looked to the causes of war in 1914 for inspiration, so the drafters of the Charter based their thinking on the war that was coming to an end in 1945. The UN was premised on the need to confront the sort of ideological aggression seen in 1939 by a continuation of the 'United Nations', initially formed in 1942 to prosecute war through executive action.[83] This led to the embodiment of the executive in the UN Charter, but

---

[78]   R. Henig, *The League of Nations* (Haus Publishing, 2010) 38.
[79]   M. Macmillan, *Peacemakers: Six Months that Changed the World* (John Murray, 2002) 17.
[80]   Henig (2010) 43.
[81]   Covenant of the League of Nations (1919) Articles 10–16.
[82]   Henig (2010) 44.
[83]   Declaration by the United Nations, 1 January 1942, in R.B. Russell and J.E. Muther, *A History of the United Nations Charter* (Brookings Institute, 1958) appendix C.

such thinking also ensured that its composition reflected the Second World War. The Covenant provided the beginnings of a public order for states in its sparse provisions, while the Charter provided a much more detailed constitutional-institutional blueprint for a peaceful world. The Covenant placed obligations on member states in a cooperative model largely founded on sovereign equality, and while the Charter also does this (indeed sovereign equality is given first place in the Charter's principles),[84] it goes so much further in centralising enforcement powers to impose sanctions and take military measures in the Security Council.

In the post-1945 era, the international constitutional framework governing the use of force by states is built on the UN Charter and the rules and institutions contained therein. The UK as a founder member of the UN, indeed one of the key drafters of the Charter, is subject to those rules but also, due to its position as a permanent member of the Security Council (alongside China, France, Russia and the US), has special privileges. The idea behind the UN was that states' freedom of military action would be confined to self-defence from attack,[85] but that wider security goals would require states to act collectively under the authority of the Security Council.[86] Britain, along with the US and USSR, was instrumental in shaping the organisation. These states placed themselves in a pivotal position as three of the five permanent members of the Security Council, along with France and China. These states each hold a veto over any proposed non-forcible or forcible action to be taken under the authority of the Security Council. In introducing the Charter to the House of Commons, Prime Minister Clement Attlee saw it as embodying the centralisation of force with the Security Council acing as a 'policeman who is called in when there is already a danger of a breach of the peace' but, more broadly, providing collective security, which he described as 'not merely a promise to act when an emergency occurs, but it is active co-operation to prevent emergencies occurring'.[87]

In essence the external aspect of the use of force, which hitherto had been under the monopoly of states, was brought within the framework of the UN Charter, and subject to regulation by the UN Security Council. Article 2(4) prohibited the threat or use of force by states in their international relations. The sovereign right of self-defence remained, the inherent nature of which was recognised in cases such as *Attorney General v Tomline* of 1880, when the Court stated: '[t]here is a duty on the King, by reason of his being King,

---

[84] UN Charter (1945) Article 2(1).
[85] Ibid, Article 51.
[86] Ibid, Article 24.
[87] Hansard, HC Deb, Vol 413, Col 665, 22 August 1945.

to defend the realm, and therefore of course all his realm and every part of his realm'.[88] However, even the right of self-defence, historically a core sovereign right, only persisted according to Article 51 of the UN Charter until the Security Council had 'taken measures necessary to maintain international peace and security'. Nevertheless, the monopoly on the external use of force that states hitherto enjoyed was only formally subjected to the UN Charter, there being no transference of military capability to the UN despite the provisions of Article 43, which envisaged 'special agreements' for the provision of armed forces by member states to be made available to the Security Council. This failure to centralise severely weakened the effectiveness of the post-1945 collective security system.

2.3.5   Mutual Defence and the North Atlantic Treaty 1949

A soldier might feel that fighting alongside allies against a common enemy must mean that the operation is both just and lawful, going back to the colossal efforts of the Allies during the Second World War. Those Allies formed the core of the permanent membership of the Security Council, but the ideal of great power unity was quickly lost. In 1946, former Prime Minister Winston Churchill spoke about an 'iron curtain' descending across Europe, signalling the beginning of the Cold War.[89] In 1948, the Berlin blockade, the communist coup in Czechoslovakia, and the lack of unity in the permanent membership of the UN Security Council, led Western powers to create NATO to defend Western Europe and North America. The preamble to the Washington or North Atlantic Treaty of 1949 declared that the state parties were 'determined to safeguard the freedom, common heritage and civilisation of their peoples, founded on the principles of democracy, individual liberty and the rule of law'.

In appearance at least, the NATO Treaty of 1949 is a form of international contract between state parties whereby, under Article 5, each state party promises to come to the aid of an attacked state party in exchange for the promises of other state parties to come to its defence if attacked. However, the UK position seems to be that this does not create an 'obligation' to come to the defence of other attacked state parties since Article 5 only commits each party to take action 'as it deems necessary'.[90] Furthermore, the treaty is very careful not to tread on the rights and duties of the state parties under the UN

---

[88]   *Attorney General v Tomline* (1880) 14 ChD 66.
[89]   https://winstonchurchill.org/resources/speeches/1946-1963-elder-statesman/the -sinews-of-peace/.
[90]   House of Lords Select Committee on the Constitution, 'Waging War: Parliament's Role and Responsibility', Vol I, 15th Report of Session 2005-06, HL Paper 236-I, 27 July 2006, para 24.

Charter, or the primary responsibility of the Security Council for international peace and security.[91] Indeed, the NATO Treaty seemed to be an institutional embodiment of the collective right to self-defence preserved under Article 51 of the UN Charter.

The type of attack envisaged by the NATO Treaty was by one state or group of states against another, principally by the Soviet Union and its allies against the US and its allies. However, the first time Article 5 of the NATO Treaty was invoked by the North Atlantic Council was on 12 September 2001, after the terrorist attacks on the US of 11 September 2001 (9/11), when planes hijacked by Al-Qaida terrorists flew into the World Trade Center and the Pentagon killing 3,000 civilians.[92] The application of the right of self-defence to respond to attacks by non-state actors such as terrorists has evolved since 9/11, but it remains controversial especially as the action naturally involves using force against a state (where the terrorists are based) as well as the terrorist group.[93] In October 2001, in response to the attacks of 9/11, and stated to be in self-defence under Article 51 of the UN Charter,[94] the US used force in Afghanistan with UK support to destroy Al-Qaida bases but also to remove the Taliban regime that had provided a safe-haven to the terrorist organisation. Prime Minister Tony Blair justified the British deployment as not simply a 'just cause, though this cause is just. It is to protect our country, our people our way of life.' He went on to say that 'if attacked, we will respond. We will defend ourselves … We will see this struggle to the end and to the victory that would mark the victory not of revenge but of justice over the evil of terrorism.'[95] The UK formally justified its action in Afghanistan in terms of self-defence under Article 51 of the UN Charter.[96]

As a leading member of NATO, the UK has helped re-formulate the purposes of the organisation beyond its clear foundation in the right of collective self-defence preserved in Article 51 of the UN Charter.[97] Just as it has helped

---

[91]   NATO Treaty (1949) Article 7.
[92]   NATO 'Council agrees that if it is determined that this attack was directed from abroad against the United States, it shall be regarded as an action covered by Article 5' of the NATO Treaty – NATO Press Release (2001) 124, 12 September 2001.
[93]   For discussion see C.J. Tams, 'The Use of Force against Terrorists' (2009) 20 *European Journal of International Law* 359; K.N. Trapp, 'The Use of Force against Terrorists: A Reply to Christian J. Tams' (2009) 20 *European Journal of International Law* 1049.
[94]   UN Doc S/2001/946 (2001).
[95]   Hansard, HC Deb, Vol 372, Col, 814, 8 October 2001.
[96]   UN Doc S/2001/947 (2001).
[97]   See NATO's 'Strategic Concept' (2010) para 4(b). Available at http://www.nato.int/nato_static_fl2014/assets/pdf/pdf_publications/20120214_strategic-concept-2010-eng.pdf.

push the parameters of the UN collective security system, starting with the deployment of troops to Korea in 1950,[98] to shape a decentralised military option whereby states can act under an authorising resolution of the Security Council, it has pushed against the other exception to the ban on the use of force contained in Article 51 of the UN Charter, to argue that self-defence can be taken in other states to combat terrorism.[99] Moreover, the UK contends that military action can be taken through a collective-defence organisation to address threats to the peace and humanitarian crises as was the case in the NATO bombing campaign over Kosovo in 1999.[100] In effect, contrary to the institutional and normative structures embodied in the UN Charter, this amounts to a claim that NATO has the legitimacy and authority to act when the UN Security Council is deadlocked. Nevertheless, the legality of NATO actions beyond the remit of collective self-defence remains questionable. It also raises the responsibility of the government for wrongful conduct, and the liabilities of political and military leaders as well as soldiers for their involvement in illegal wars.[101]

2.3.6   The 'Grand Bargain' 1968: Legitimating the Ultimate Weapon

When understanding the normative and institutional architecture governing the UK's military, the UN, NATO (and to a lesser extent the EU until UK withdrawal in 2020) all play key roles, but it is also important to include the UK's possession of nuclear weapons and its status as a 'nuclear weapons state' under the Nuclear Non-Proliferation Treaty (NPT) of 1968. The UK decided that it should build a nuclear bomb in 1947, the argument being won by the Foreign Secretary Ernest Bevin who stated that: 'we could not afford to acquiesce in an American monopoly of this new development. Other countries also might well develop atomic weapons. Unless therefore an effective international system could be developed under which the production and use of such weapons would be prohibited, we must develop it ourselves.'[102] The 'central aim' of UK strategy was 'to convince the Soviet leadership that – even without the Americans – the British could mount an unacceptably destructive blow to

---

[98]   N.D. White, *Democracy Goes to War: British Military Deployments under International Law* (Oxford University Press, 2009) 96–104.

[99]   See further, NATO's Policy Guidelines on Counter-Terrorism, 'Aware, Capable and Engaged for a Safer Future', 21 May 2012.

[100]   White (2009) 211–18.

[101]   See Chapter 4.

[102]   R. Braithwaite, *Armageddon and Paranoia: The Nuclear Confrontation* (Profile Books, 2017) 193.

them'.[103] The UK tested its first atomic weapon in October 1952 in Australia, and a thermonuclear warhead ('Yellow Sun') off Christmas Island in 1957.[104] In 1963, the UK, along with the USA and USSR, became parties to the Treaty banning Nuclear Weapons Tests in the Atmosphere (Partial Test Ban Treaty), which was seen as a way of slowing down the nuclear arms race, although it did not prohibit underground testing.[105]

The NPT 1968 is commonly described as a 'grand bargain' between nuclear weapon states (NWS) and non-nuclear weapons states (NNWS).[106] The epithet 'grand bargain' suggests some sort of exchange of rights and duties between these two different groupings of states. NWS are those states that prior to 1 January 1967 had 'manufactured and exploded a nuclear weapon or other nuclear explosive device'.[107] Of the five states that met this criteria, the US, UK, and Russia were original parties to the treaty, while China acceded in 1992 and France in 1993. Essentially, NWS are obliged not to supply nuclear weapons to NNWS,[108] and not to proliferate their own; indeed the obligation in Article VI of the NPT is to 'pursue negotiations in good faith on effective measures relating to the cessation of the nuclear arms race at an early date and to nuclear disarmament, and on a treaty on general and complete disarmament under strict and effective international control'. NNWS, on their side, agreed not to acquire nuclear weapons or to develop them themselves, and subject themselves to supervision and verification by the International Atomic Energy Agency (IAEA) to check that they are not diverting peaceful nuclear technology towards military purposes.[109] 'In exchange for their commitment to forgo what would otherwise be their right, equal to that' of NWS, NNWS insisted on a right not only to acquire 'nuclear technologies for the purpose of civilian power generation', but also a duty on NWS to help in the development of the civilian nuclear programmes in NNWS.[110] In other words, the grand bargain was for NWS to retain their right to nuclear weapons, while NNWS gave up any right to have them. In exchange for this departure from sovereign equality, NWS promised to disarm gradually and to help develop peaceful uses of nuclear technology in NNWS. The NPT has transformed from tempo-

---

[103] Ibid, 193. Ministry of Defence, 'Defence: Outline of Future Policy', Cmnd 124 (HMSO, 1957).
[104] Braithwaite (2017) 197.
[105] The Comprehensive Nuclear Test Ban Treaty of 1996 has been ratified by the UK but has not yet come into force.
[106] D. Joyner, *International Law and the Proliferation of Weapons of Mass Destruction* (Oxford University Press, 2009) 8.
[107] NPT (1968) Article IX.3.
[108] Ibid, Article I.
[109] Ibid, Articles II and III.
[110] Joyner (2009), 9. NPT (1968) Articles IV and V.

rary bargain to permanent fixture. In 1995, on the indefinite extension of the NPT, the NWS gave NNWS parties 'positive and negative security assurances against the use of such weapons'.[111] It remains the case that the obligation on NWS is to disarm, not simply to promise to refrain from using their weapons against NNWS.

It is no coincidence that the five permanent members of the UN Security Council are the NWS at the heart of the NPT grand bargain, supporting the argument that the NPT is something more profound than an ordinary contractual-type treaty, since it extends the inequality between the five permanent members and other states in matters of international security. The UK MoD stated in a 2018 Policy Paper that the UK is committed to maintaining a credible nuclear deterrent consisting of 'the minimum amount of destructive power needed to deter any aggressor', requiring a nuclear deterrent which is 'not vulnerable to pre-emptive action by potential adversaries'. The UK argues that this is necessary as the number of states with nuclear weapons continues to grow and there are risks that 'a major direct nuclear threat to the UK or our NATO allies might re-emerge'. These risks require the maintenance of an 'independent nuclear deterrent to deter the most extreme threats to our national security and way of life, now and in the future'.[112]

Since 1969, in 'Operation Relentless', the Royal Navy has undertaken the task of providing the UK's nuclear deterrent, through the deployment of up to four submarines equipped with missiles carrying nuclear warheads. Currently, the UK has four Vanguard-class nuclear powered submarines that provide the UK's nuclear deterrent, with at least one submarine being on active service at any one time, carrying up to eight Trident missiles with 40 nuclear warheads.[113] Each warhead is capable of destroying a city. The government claims that maintaining Trident is consistent with its obligations under the NPT: '[m]aintaining a minimum nuclear deterrent is fully consistent with all our international legal obligations, including those under' the NPT.[114]

---

[111] *Legality of the Threat or Use of Nuclear Weapons* (1996) ICJ Rep 226 at para 59(c).

[112] Defence Nuclear Organisation/Ministry of Defence, Policy Paper, 'The UK's nuclear deterrent: what you need to know', 19 February 2018 https://www.gov.uk/government/publications/uk-nuclear-deterrence-factsheet/uk-nuclear-deterrence-what-you-need-to-know.

[113] Ibid.

[114] Ibid. In its 2021 Defence Review, the MoD indicated the government's commitment to modernise the UK's nuclear forces by replacing the Vanguard Class submarines with four new Dreadnought Cass submarines, and by replacing (and increasing) the UK's nuclear warheads – MoD, 'Defence in a competitive age' (CP 411, 2021) para 4.13.

Attempts to challenge the legality of nuclear weapons before the International Court of Justice (ICJ) have thus far failed, with an advisory opinion in 1996 suggesting that while there would almost inevitably be a violation of LOAC by the use of such weapons, it remained unclear whether international law would be violated by the use of nuclear weapons when the very survival of the state was at stake.[115] This was followed by the ICJ's dismissal of a case brought by the Marshall Islands against certain NWS (including the UK) claiming that they had failed to fulfil their obligations to disarm under Article VI of the NPT. The case was dismissed on the basis that there was no formal 'dispute' between the UK and the Marshall Islands.[116] The fact remains that while chemical and biological weapons are prohibited per se,[117] the possession of nuclear weapons and their deterrent effects are part of the architecture of peace and security. The NPT, for better or worse, is therefore part of the international constitutional architecture.[118] The UK's position as a recognised nuclear weapons state brings with it a huge moral responsibility, but also a legal one since the use of such weapons would at the very least violate the rules of LOAC prohibiting indiscriminate weapons, which raises the issue of the liability of political leaders and submarine commanders.

2.4 THE MILITARY AS STATE ACTOR

The above account of both national and international constitutional frameworks show that the UK's armed forces are integral to the state's internal and external sovereignty. The armed forces are thus the paradigmatic state actors, a position reinforced by the accepted understandings of the state in national and international law.

---

[115] *Legality of the Threat or Use of Nuclear Weapons* (1996) ICJ Rep 226.

[116] *Obligations Concerning Negotiations Relating to the Cessation of the Nuclear Arms Race and to Nuclear Disarmament (Marshall Islands v United Kingdom)* (2016) ICJ Rep 833.

[117] Convention on the Prohibition of the Development, Production and Stockpiling of Bacteriological (Biological) and Toxin Weapons and on Their Destruction 1972; Convention on the Prohibition of the Development, Production, Stockpiling and Use of Chemical Weapons and on Their Destruction 1993. The UK is a party to both treaties.

[118] But see the Treaty on the Prohibition of Nuclear Weapons 2017. The UK has stated that it will not become a party – see N.D. White, 'Understanding Nuclear Deterrence within the International Constitutional Architecture' in J.L. Black-Branch and D. Fleck (eds), *Nuclear Non-Proliferation in International Law*: Vol V Legal Challenges for Nuclear Security and Deterrence (Springer, 2020) 237 at 247.

2.4.1   UK Law

When British troops are sent overseas both the decision to deploy them and acts carried out by the forces to execute those decisions are potentially covered by the Crown act of state doctrine, which can protect the state from actions brought in tort against the government before domestic civil courts. *Rahmatullah*, decided by the Supreme Court in 2017, in part involved the claimant suing the government for his detention by British armed forces during the conflict in Iraq and for his transfer from UK detention to a US detention facility in Afghanistan.[119] In allowing the government's defence of Crown act of state to claims arising from 'inherently governmental' acts 'committed in the conduct of the foreign relations of the Crown',[120] the Supreme Court pointed out that the law vests in the government 'the power to conduct' the UK's 'international relations, including the deployment of armed force in support of its objectives'.[121]

> In the nature of things, the use of armed force abroad involves acts which would normally be civil wrongs not only under English law but under any system of municipal law. People will be detained or killed. Their property will be damaged or destroyed. It would be incoherent and irrational for the courts to acknowledge the power of the Crown to conduct the United Kingdom's foreign relations and deploy armed forces, and at the same time treat as civil wrongs acts inherent in the exercise of that power.[122]

Lady Hale made it clear that the act of state doctrine was limited in that it did not apply to acts of torture or to the maltreatment of detainees and would not normally apply to the expropriation of property.[123] While these limitations are clearly justified, they are blunted by parts of the judgment that indicate that the Crown act of state doctrine can apply irrespective of the legality of the conduct under international law.[124] Leggat J followed this in *Alseran* when stating that the act of state doctrine 'does not depend on establishing either the allegedly wrongful act or the wider military operation of which the act formed part or the policy decision to engage in that operation was lawful in international law'.[125]

---

[119] *Rahmatullah (No. 2) v Ministry of Defence* [2017] UKSC 1.

[120] Ibid, para 36 (Lady Hale).

[121] Ibid, para 88 (Lord Sumption).

[122] Ibid.

[123] Ibid, para 36 (Lady Hale). See further *Nissan v Attorney General* [1970] AC 179.

[124] A. Sanger, 'Review of Executive Action Abroad: The UK Supreme Court in the International Legal Order' (2019) 68 *International and Comparative Law Quarterly* 35 at 62–3.

[125] *Alseran v Ministry of Defence* [2017] EWHC 3289 (QB) para 56.

However, he considered that acts of torture and maltreatment would be *ultra vires* under English law and therefore could not be covered by the act of state doctrine.[126]

Clearly the courts are struggling to reconcile the traditional view of the sovereign state as exercising hitherto unchallengeable powers when committing troops overseas, with basic axioms of what the government ought to do given the universal condemnation of torture and maltreatment. This is reflected in the judgment of Lady Hale in *Rahmatullah*, who stated that the act of state doctrine should be narrowly construed to a 'very narrow class of acts: in their nature sovereign acts – the sort of things that governments properly do; committed abroad; in the conduct of the foreign policy of the state'.[127] The reluctance to judge what the government may 'properly do' against the standards of international law reflects the ingrained reticence of the courts to entertain claims against the government based in whole or in part on international law.

In *Rahmatullah* the Supreme Court found that the act of state doctrine had not been removed by the Crown Proceedings Act 1947.[128] Traditionally the Crown (or sovereign) has immunity from both civil suit and criminal prosecution brought by its own citizens, while externally state immunity has protected the UK when performing sovereign acts from private suit.[129] As regards Crown immunity, the Crown Proceedings Act of 1947 fundamentally changed the law for civilians with private law claims in tort against the Crown (the state), by lifting the Crown's immunity and granting a right to sue the Crown. Section 10 of the Act, however, provided that neither the Crown nor soldiers could be subject to proceedings in tort for death or personal injury suffered by a member of the armed forces while on duty. This reinforced the perception that soldiers did not have the same rights as civilians. It was not until 1987, in the Crown Proceedings (Armed Forces) Act, that this provision was repealed, although that Act permitted the Secretary of State to revive section 10 when 'necessary or expedient to do so', 'by reason of any imminent national danger or of any great emergency that has arisen', or 'for the purpose of any warlike operations in any part of the world outside' the UK. One of the sponsors of the Act spoke of the need to:

> Rectify an injustice that has become increasingly more glaring – the discrimination between members of the armed forces and the ordinary citizen in seeking damages in cases of injury or death arising from the negligence of others. An ordinary citizen

126 Ibid, paras 71–5.
127 *Rahmatullah (No. 2)* [2017] para 37.
128 Ibid, para 41 (Lady Hale).
129 J. Crawford, *Brownlie's Principles of Public International Law* (Oxford University Press, 8th edn, 2012) 487–91.

or his dependants may sue through the courts and obtain substantial damages, but members of the armed forces are denied that right. This discrimination has given rise to much bitterness and a sense of injustice among those who have served their country loyally and suffered for it, not once, but twice first, in suffering injury or death in the course of their duty and, secondly, in being denied the proper level of compensation that would be their due if they were in any other walk of life.[130]

Recent conflicts in Iraq and Afghanistan, in which claims for negligence have been made,[131] have led to unsuccessful petitions to invoke the executive power to revive section 10.[132] The Policy Exchange Report of 2015 argued that it was a 'profound mistake to allow for such allegations of fault to be judicially investigated', since to 'investigate such allegations inevitably takes any court deep into political and professional military territory where it would be quite inappropriate for a judge to second-guess policy-makers' choices with the benefit of hindsight'. Rather than judicial accountability, the Report argues that such matters are 'overwhelmingly ... for political decision and account-ability'.[133] The presence of section 10 demonstrates that the state remains of the view that soldiers are state actors whose rights can be restricted where necessary in situations of emergency and war, but that Parliament has, for the time being, allowed soldiers some of the same rights in tort as possessed by the ordinary citizen.

Rights to claim in negligence, however, have been restricted by the doctrine of combat immunity, which has been defined as 'a defence or exemption from legal liability that applies to members of the armed forces or the Government, within the context of actual or imminent armed conflict'.[134] The doctrine provides that 'while the armed forces are in the course of actually operating against the enemy, they are under no "actionable" duty of care as defined by common law to avoid causing loss or damage to their fellow soldiers, or indeed anyone who may be affected by what they do'.[135] The doctrine has been limited by court judgments discussed in Chapter 8,[136] but it seems odd that Parliament lifted Crown immunity in 1987 without excluding situations of armed conflict from this reform. Nevertheless, the common law doctrine of combat immunity persists to protect soldiers and the government from claims arising out of

---

[130] Hansard, HC Deb, Vol 110, Col 567, 13 February 1987 (Churchill).
[131] See Chapter 8.
[132] T. Tugendhat and L. Croft, 'The Fog of Law: An Introduction to the Legal Erosion of British Fighting Power' (Policy Exchange, 2013) 11.
[133] R. Etkins, J. Morgan and T. Tugendhat, 'Clearing the Fog of Law: Saving Our Armed Forces from Defeat by Judicial Diktat' (Policy Exchange, 2015) 21–2.
[134] Tugendhat and Croft (2013) 31.
[135] Ibid, citing *Mulcahy v Ministry of Defence* [1996] EWCA Civ 1323.
[136] *Smith v Ministry of Defence* [2013] UKSC 41.

negligent acts occurring in an armed conflict.[137] There are strong arguments for excluding the common law from the battlefield: 'the situations are very often too confused and fleetingly subjective to allow for fair judgment after the event' and, more fundamentally, the possibility of litigation 'leads to a "safety first" attitude amongst commanders at all levels and injects delay, risking the entire undertaking'.[138]

Soldiers are put in extraordinary situations and are expected to perform their duty to the state, but at the same time there is an increasing recognition that even in those situations they have some rights in common law as well as in human rights law (reviewed in Chapter 8), where the government is clearly at fault, but those rights cannot be based on the same standards of care owed to the ordinary citizen. The rebalancing of the scales of justice between government and soldiers is an on-going process that is further reviewed in Chapter 9.

2.4.2 International Law

In June 2010, Prime Minister David Cameron made a speech in Parliament in response to the Saville Report into the events on Bloody Sunday in 1972,[139] when British paratroopers had used lethal force during a civil rights protest in Northern Ireland, killing 14 civilians and wounding others. He stated:

> What happened should never have happened. The families of those who died should not have had to live with the pain and the hurt of that day and with a lifetime of loss. Some members of our armed forces acted wrongly. The government is ultimately responsible for the conduct of our armed forces and for that, on behalf of the government, indeed on behalf of our country, I am deeply sorry.[140]

Whether the Prime Minister was at the time accepting *legal* responsibility for the deaths, injuries, and the suffering of the victims' families, is not clear, but it is the case that under international law, at least, a state is legally responsible for the internationally wrongful acts of its armed forces. Traditionally, in the era when international law solely governed relationships between states that liability would be towards another state, but in the era of human rights law, which governs the relationship between a state and its citizens, that liability extends to internationally wrongful acts against its own citizens. Indeed, a close look at the Prime Minister's words, where he admits that British soldiers had acted 'wrongly', and that the government is 'responsible for the conduct of our

---

[137] Ibid, para 89 (Lord Hope).
[138] Etkins, Morgan and Tugendhat (2015) 36.
[139] See Chapter 3.
[140] Hansard, HC Deb, Vol 511, Col 740, 15 June 2010.

armed forces', strongly indicates an admission of legal liability. However, in the speech he only offers an apology to the families, even though he recognises their 'pain and hurt' and 'lifetime of loss'.

In international law, and in most national legal systems, the armed forces are firmly part of the apparatus of the state: the British Army, Royal Navy and Royal Air Force are organs of the state. In terms of international law, laid down in 2001 by the International Law Commission (ILC) in its Articles on State Responsibility, this means that any internationally wrongful conduct by a soldier, sailor or pilot performed in their capacity as members of the armed forces, is an act of state under international law for which the UK is legally responsible or liable.[141] The Articles clearly establish that a state is responsible for the conduct of its armed forces' personnel when they act in their official capacity even in cases where soldiers are exceeding their authority or contravening instructions.[142] It is also possible that the conduct of other actors working with the military (say private contractors) can be attributed to the state if they are undertaking inherently governmental functions,[143] such as combat, or because they are acting under the instructions or control of the state.[144]

In a deeper sense, the armed forces are a significant part of the state, representing a state's hard-won monopoly over the use of force discussed in Chapter 1. Older international cases have considered this issue in a number of instances. In the *Moses* case, a Mexico–US Claims Commission declared that 'an officer or person in authority represents *pro tanto* his government, which in an international sense is the aggregate of all officers and men in authority'.[145] Officials of the state operate at all levels, from government ministers to police officers and soldiers and when, acting in their public capacity, they undertake 'acts of state'. The ILC makes it clear that 'purely private conduct should not be confused with that of an organ functioning as such but acting *ultra vires* or in breach of the rules governing its operation'. In the latter case, 'the organ is nevertheless acting in the name of the State'.[146] In the *Caire* case, a Mexico–France Commission considered a claim on behalf of a French national shot dead by two Mexican officers who had demanded money from him. The Commission held 'that the two officers, even if they are deemed to have acted outside their competence ... and even if their superiors countermanded an order, have involved the responsibility of the State, since they acted

---

[141] Articles on the Responsibility of States for Internationally Wrongful Acts (2001) (ARS) Article 4.

[142] Ibid, Articles 4 and 7.

[143] Ibid, Article 5.

[144] Ibid, Article 8.

[145] *Moses Case*, Moore, *History and Digest*, Vol III, p 3127, at p 3129 (1871).

[146] Report of the International Law Commission, UN Doc A/56/10 (2001), para 13.

under cover of their status as officers and used means placed at their disposal on account of that status'.[147] As the ILC records, international human rights courts have applied the same rule, citing as an example the Inter-American Court of Human Rights in the *Velásquez Rodríguez* case, when the court made it clear that the conclusion that the human rights convention in question had been breached by Honduras was 'independent of whether the organ or official has contravened provisions of internal law or overstepped the limits of his authority: under international law a State is responsible for the acts of its agents undertaken in their official capacity and for their omissions, even when those agents act outside the sphere of their authority or violate internal law'.[148]

A state's military forces are clearly state actors and so any unlawful acts committed by the armed forces should give rise to the responsibility of the state under international law. In *Nissan v Attorney General*,[149] the UK House of Lords had to adjudicate on the responsibility of British forces in Cyprus in 1963, in particular for the requisitioning of a hotel. The UK government argued that it was not responsible for the actions of the force as it was either an agent of the government of Cyprus or was part of a UN force. The court dismissed both arguments. Lord Reid dismissed the former argument by stating that '[a]ll the circumstances so far as we know them, seem to me to point to the conclusion that in taking the Respondent's hotel the British authorities acted on their own responsibility on behalf of the Crown'. Lord Pearce dismissed the latter argument in the following terms:

> The United Nations is not a super-state nor even a sovereign state. It is a unique legal person or corporation. It is based on the sovereignty of its respective members. But it is not a principal carrying out its policy through states acting as its agents. It is an instrument of collective policy which it enforces by using the sovereignty of its members. In carrying out the policies each member still retains its own sovereignty, just as any sovereign state, acting under its treaty obligations to another state, would normally still retain its sovereignty.[150]

The ILC has also developed Articles on the Responsibility of International Organisations in 2011,[151] which have revived arguments of whether any wrongful act of a British soldier, who is part of a contingent in a UN mandated peacekeeping or peace enforcement operation, is attributable to the UK or

---

[147]   *Caire Claim* (1929) RIAA 516 at 531.

[148]   *Velásquez Rodríguez* case (1988) Inter-American Court of Human Rights, Series C, No 4, para 170.

[149]   *Nissan v Attorney General* [1970] AC 179.

[150]   Ibid.

[151]   Taken note of in UN General Assembly Resolution UN Doc A/RES/66/100 (2011).

the UN. Although UK forces that are part of a UN force remain organs of the British state, according to the 2011 Articles responsibility for wrongful conduct can be attributed to the UN if the organisation is in effective control of that conduct.[152] However, as Lord Morris made clear in *Nissan v Attorney General*: although 'national contingents were under the authority of the United Nations and subject to the instructions of the commander the troops as members of the Force remained in their national service. The British forces continued, therefore, to be soldiers of Her Majesty. Members of the United Nations Force were subject to the exclusive jurisdiction of their respective national states in respect of any criminal offences committed by them in Cyprus.'[153] It follows that the level of control exerted by the UN over national contingents is not normally at the level of effective control of conduct but the applicability of that test is not without debate,[154] particularly as the UN has recognised peacekeeping forces as subsidiary organs of the UN and on that basis accepting in principle that wrongful acts committed by its peacekeepers are attributable to the UN.[155]

Some commentators have argued that to reconcile these apparently divergent positions it is necessary to adopt a presumption of UN responsibility for the wrongful acts of peacekeepers, which can be rebutted by evidence of effective control of the conduct in question by the troop sending state.[156] This type of reasoning has been applied to the actions of the Kosovo Force (KFOR), which is a coalition of willing states acting under a UN Security Council res-

---

[152] Articles on the Responsibility of International Organisations (2011) (ARIO) Article 7.

[153] *Nissan v Attorney General* (1970).

[154] K.M. Larsen, 'Attribution of Conduct in Peace Operations: The "Ultimate Authority and Control" Test' (2008) 19 *European Journal of International Law* 509.

[155] As provided for in ARIO (2011) Article 6. The UN Secretariat stated in February 2004 that a 'UN peacekeeping force established by the Security Council or the General Assembly is a subsidiary organ of the UN'. It stated further that 'as a subsidiary organ of the United Nations, an act of a peacekeeping force is, in principle, imputable to the Organization, and if committed in violation of an international obligation entails the international responsibility of the Organization and its liability in compensation', UN Secretariat, Responsibility of International Organizations: Comments and Observations Received from International Organizations, UN Doc A/CN.4/545, 25 June 2004, para 17.

[156] A. Sari, 'UN Peacekeeping Operations and Article 7 ARIO: The Missing Link' (2012) 9 *International Organizations Law Review* 78; P. Palchetti, 'International Responsibility for Conduct of UN Peace-keeping Forces: The Question of Attribution' in P. Palchetti et al. (eds), *Refining Human Rights Obligations in Conflict Situations* (Asser, 2014) 24; Y. Okada, 'Effective Control Test at the Interface between the Law of International Responsibility and the Law of International Organizations: Managing Concerns over the Attribution of UN Peacekeepers' Conduct to Troop-Contributing Nations' (2019) 32 *Leiden Journal of International Law* 280.

olution in Kosovo initially deployed in 1999.[157] Although more akin to peace enforcement than peacekeeping, which normally indicates lesser control by the UN,[158] the ECtHR in *Behrami* decided that in the circumstances of Kosovo, where the UN was effectively the sovereign power with 'ultimate authority and control' over KFOR, it was responsible through its UN Mission in Kosovo (UNMIK) for the failure to clear unexploded cluster bombs, and not the troop sending state (France) in whose sector the cluster bombs were located.[159] This reasoning was followed in UK jurisprudence in the High Court's judgment in *Kontic*, which arose from claims made by widows of Serb civilians abducted or murdered on the basis that British forces failed to protect them.[160] On the issue of whether the alleged failure was attributable to the UK or to the UN, Irwin J followed the European Court's reasoning in *Behrami* and added that '[e]ssentially, the failure complained of against' the government 'is a much broader failure to create security and peaceful conditions in Kosovo, and/or to create with immediacy and maintain an effective system of policing, detention and prosecution', making it 'much more apt for such failures to be attributable to the UN'.[161]

Despite our natural instincts that an unlawful act, especially one that involves the taking of lives, should give rise to punishment and reparation, international law at least is not so clear, certainly in terms of the responsibility of the state. In terms of redress by the state for its internationally wrongful conduct, the Articles on State Responsibility of 2001 offer a range of options, explained by the ILC on the basis that the prevailing view in international law is that the 'consequences of an internationally wrongful act cannot be limited either to reparation or to a sanction' and, further, that 'in international law, as in any system of law, the wrongful act may give rise to various types of legal relations, depending on the circumstances'.[162] Under the Articles 'reparation for the injury caused by the internationally wrongful act shall take the form of restitution, compensation or satisfaction, either singly or in combination …'.[163] Although the Articles use the language of obligation for restitution, or compensation if full restitution is not possible,[164] there remains the sense, rein-

---

[157] UN Doc S/RES/1244/1999.

[158] Meaning that conduct is normally attributable to the troop sending state rather than the UN – see judgment of the ECtHR in *Al-Jedda v United Kingdom* (2011) 53 EHRR 23 at paras 83, 86.

[159] *Behrami and Saramati v France and Norway* (2007) 45 EHRR SE10, para 135.

[160] *Kontic v Ministry of Defence* [2016] EWHC 2034 (QB).

[161] Ibid, para 134.

[162] Report of the International Law Commission UN Doc A/56/10 (2001) para 3.

[163] ARS (2001) Article 34.

[164] Ibid, Articles 35 and 36.

forced in state practice, that these are negotiable in the case of responsibility to other states, or dependent on political discretion in the case of states' conduct towards their own citizens.

Returning to Prime Minister Cameron's statement as regards responsibility for the death and injuries arising from Bloody Sunday in 1972, this took the form of what the Articles term 'satisfaction', which 'may consist in an acknowledgement of the breach, an expression of regret, a formal apology or other appropriate modality'.[165] However, his statement opened what one MP labelled a 'Pandora's box', and led to claims being made on behalf of the victims, which the MoD agreed to resolve, admitting that the armed forces had 'acted wrongly'.[166] Families of those shot dead, and those who were seriously wounded, were offered £50,000 each in 2013.[167]

Establishing that a state is responsible for the misconduct of its soldiers does not mean that individual service personnel are absolved of legal responsibility themselves. A single act – say the unlawful killing of a civilian by a soldier – gives rise to the responsibility of the soldier (for murder, and if committed in an armed conflict a war crime), as well as the state (potentially for breaches of LOAC, international criminal law or human rights law). While state responsibility may be decided before an international or regional court, individual criminal responsibility is often determined by a national court. Prosecution of soldiers before UK courts involved in the Bloody Sunday killings remains a possibility.[168] The divide between national and international courts, however, is not absolute. National courts can determine state responsibility (though in the UK this is limited by the Crown act of state and combat immunity doctrines under domestic law) and international courts, such as the ICC, can determine individual criminal responsibility. In many instances, however, a court is not involved and victims' lawyers will seek redress from the responsible government itself. Examples of the various forms of accountability and responsibility can be seen throughout this book.

---

[165] Ibid, Article 36.

[166] *BBC News*, 'Government to pay compensation to Bloody Sunday families', 22 September 2011, https://www.bbc.co.uk/news/uk-northern-ireland-15009999.

[167] O. Bowcott, 'Bloody Sunday families offered £50,000 compensation by MoD', *The Guardian*, 14 February 2013 https://www.theguardian.com/uk/2013/feb/14/bloody -sunday-families-offered-50000-compensation.

[168] But see the collapse of the prosecution of Soldiers A and C for a different murder in 1972 – *BBC News*, 'Joe McCann: Trial of two soldiers collapses', 4 May 2021, casting doubts over whether further 'legacy' prosecutions arising from the Troubles in Northern Ireland will succeed https://www.bbc.co.uk/news/uk-northern-ireland -56942056.

2.5   CONCLUSION

The national and international constitutional frameworks enveloping the armed forces share a similarity in that they have emerged in a piecemeal way, building layer upon layer of principle and practice, largely in response to momentous and transformative changes in national and international society. Indeed, both constitutional frameworks are in a way a culmination of practice rather than a means of controlling it, legally reflecting the developing social contract between state and citizen. Having said that, once in place, key constitutional laws play a regulatory role on subsequent state behaviour until the next significant change. The soldier is a small player in this changing tapestry but their legal status very much reflects the wider constitutional frameworks and, as they evolve, or change, so does the soldier's rights as well as duties.

The evolution of the UK's armed forces is inter-twined with the emergence of the state. From being the private armies of monarchs and, briefly, during the Interregnum an arm of government, the armed forces have become part of the establishment, an organ of state whose function is to ensure the state's security from external threats and to provide stability, alongside law enforcement agencies, in times of internal instability. Political judgements as to the executive's use of the armed forces, both internally and externally, have to be finely balanced between the need to maintain (or restore) the state's monopoly over force and its obligations to respect the rights of other states and its own citizens.

This chapter has strengthened the impression, gained from Chapter 1, that soldiers are inevitably legally conceived as part of the state when they are carrying out their duties, but that they remain citizens, albeit citizens whose rights and freedoms have been significantly curtailed. The duties of the state towards its soldiers will be explored further in this book, but to understand these duties it has to be recognised that the state has considerable powers over the deployment of the armed forces. The exercise of these powers and the duties they impose on soldiers, which arguably leave little room for soldiers' rights, are the subject of the next two chapters.

3. Emergency powers and internal deployments

3.1 INTRODUCTION

The plethora of constitutional laws reviewed in Chapter 2, both national and international, strongly suggests that the deployment of armed forces and the use of violence by the state are bounded by law, in other words, are subject to the rule of law. However, the legal source of control over the armed forces lies in the discretionary or prerogative powers of the monarch, which have passed to the government and its ministers and are used in the modern era as the legal basis for deploying troops both internally and externally. One issue for this chapter and the next is whether the dominance of prerogative powers is countered by the limitations of international law, whose influence may be felt in litigation and Parliamentary debates. Another issue to be discussed in Chapters 3 and 4 is the issue of state and individual ministerial legal responsibility that arises if prerogative powers are exercised in disregard of domestic or international law. Moreover, a question for Chapter 4, when considering external deployments is whether the illegal prosecution of a war has any legal significance for soldiers.

The decision to deploy troops, either within the country in response to emergency situations, or externally in response to external threats, engages a number of legal rules and regimes, both national and international, some of which have already been identified in Chapters 1 and 2. This chapter and the next demonstrate that while there are constitutional and legislative constraints on the deployment of the British state's most powerful forms of force and weapons, there remains a large slice of discretionary executive power that can be traced back to the powers of the monarch and the historical struggle to monopolise the use of force. The continued presence and usage of such powers in the 21st century has led to calls for greater legislative and Parliamentary control of external deployments, but less so regarding the internal deployment of troops.

This chapter focuses on the internal use of armed forces and demonstrates that this is not a historical phenomenon but occurs quite regularly in modern Britain. Northern Ireland is a recent example of a sustained deployment of armed forces to a situation that bordered on an armed conflict, and it over-shadows the many other domestic uses of the military in the modern era. Even though more soldiers were killed in Northern Ireland than in many subsequent armed conflicts in which the UK has been involved, the UK government did not recognise the situation in Northern Ireland as an 'armed conflict' to which LOAC would apply, including a right to kill enemy combatants. This meant that soldiers using lethal force in Northern Ireland were to be judged by the ordinary standards of criminal law, and the government responsible for their deployment would increasingly be judged over the period of the 'Troubles' according to international human rights standards. Although there is a legis-lative basis for internal deployments in the Emergency Powers Act 1964 and the Civil Contingencies Act 2004, as with the external deployment of troops (reviewed in Chapter 4), the government prefers to use largely unreviewable prerogative powers, potentially making ministers 'petty kings' in the discre-tionary military powers they can wield.[1]

3.2   TACKLING PROTESTS AND RIOTS

The internal deployment of armed forces in the UK has proved necessary on occasions in order for the state to assert or re-assert its monopoly over the use of force, but also to prevent any threat to the established order. This practice has taken place despite the 'political and legal principle opposing the use of military force to suppress domestic unrest' dating back to the Magna Carta of 1215 and the Bill of Rights 1689.[2]

In the modern state, tackling civil disorder is normally the responsibility of the police. There have existed methods of community policing dating back to King Alfred. After the Norman conquest of 1066 village law enforcement duties were exercised by parish constables, a system which worked reason-ably well in a stable agricultural society.[3] However, the poor working and living conditions caused by the Industrial Revolution, significant population movements, and unrest amongst the working class led to numerous troop

---

[1]   M. Radin, 'The Myth of the Magna Carta' (1947) 60 *Harvard Law Review* 1060 at 1062, describing the consequences of the power conceded to the Barons by King John under the Magna Carta 1215.

[2]   M. Head and S. Mann, *Domestic Deployment of the Armed Forces: Military Powers, Law and Human Rights* (Routledge, 2009) 19.

[3]   S. Casey-Maslen and S. Connolly, *Police Use of Force under International Law* (Cambridge University Press, 2017) 17.

deployments. Michael Head and Scott Mann describe one of the most infamous incidents:

> One of the most notorious mobilisations of the military against civilians was the Peterloo Massacre of 1819. Cavalry troops charged into a crowd of 60–80,000 people gathered at St Peter's Field, Manchester for a public meeting, which had been declared illegal, to demand Parliamentary representation. Shortly after the meeting began, local magistrates called on the military to arrest the speakers on the platform and to disperse the crowd. Mounted soldiers charged into the crowd with sabres drawn, killing 15 people and injuring 400–700, including women and children ... Whereas the arrested speakers were charged with sedition, found guilty and jailed, a test case against four members of the armed forces ended in acquittal, because the court ruled that their actions had been justified to disperse an illegal gathering ... Nine days after the massacre, the Home Secretary, Lord Sidmouth, conveyed to the magistrates the thanks of the Prince Regent for their action in the 'preservation of the public peace' ...[4]

Richard Holmes explains that the affair was 'dubbed the Peterloo Massacre in parody' of the Battle of Waterloo of 1815. He describes the unrest in the nation after the Napoleonic Wars, with yeomen troops being frequently called upon to assist the civil powers in the absence of an organised police force to tackle 'Chartists and Luddites in the towns and the Captain Swing rioters in the countryside', all groups presenting threats to 'the established order'.[5]

Despite legal support for the actions of troops at Peterloo and other similar incidents reviewed in this section, the constitutional basis for using such levels of military force to quell protesters or rioters is quite thin. It can be traced back to 'Charles I's continued claim to prerogative use of troops', which 'helped precipitate the English Revolution and civil war in 1642'.[6] One response to this claim, contained in the Bill of Rights 1689, was to declare the keeping of a standing army without the consent of Parliament as illegal but, as Michael Head states, '[m]ore generally, after the Glorious Revolution of 1688–89, military force was seen as a grave threat to civil government, and its subordination

---

[4]   Head and Mann (2009) 21–2.

[5]   R. Holmes, *Soldiers* (Harper Press, 2011) 103. Chartism was a working class movement started in 1836 with the purpose of improving the political rights and influence of the working class http://www.nationalarchives.gov.uk/education/politics/g7/. The Luddite movement emerged in Nottinghamshire in 1811 and involved destroying machines in factories https://www.nationalarchives.gov.uk/education/politics/g3/. Captain Swing protestors were agricultural labourers who opposed the introduction of threshing machines in 1829–1830 http://www.nationalarchives.gov.uk/education/politics/g5/.

[6]   M. Head, 'Calling out the Troops and the Civil Contingencies Act: Some Questions of Concern' (2010) *Public Law* 340 at 343.

to civilian rule was established as a constitutional priority'.[7] Thus, when the Riot Act was passed in 1714, it 'called for civilian officials and posses (the posse comitatus) to disperse mobs and put down civil unrest, and authorised civilian personnel to use any force necessary to do so, but made no provision for the use of military force'. A 'different act passed the same year authorised the use of militia, but only to deal with "insurrection" or "rebellion" as well as "invasion"'.[8] The Riot Act was read by the magistrates before the use of force at Peterloo in 1819 with devastating effect.

Statements made in cases involving riots seemed to reflect a reluctance on the part of the judiciary to recognise an unqualified right to deploy armed troops during internal unrest. In 1781, Lord Mansfield stated:

> The common law and several statutes have invested justices of the peace with great powers to quell riots, because, if not suppressed, they tend to endanger the constitution of the country; and as they may assemble all the King's subjects, it is clear they may call in the soldiers, who are subjects and may act as such; but this should be done with great caution ... The persons who assisted in the suppression of these tumults are to be considered mere private individuals acting as duty required ... The King's extraordinary prerogative to proclaim martial law (whatever that may be) is clearly out of the question ... The military have been called in – and very wisely called in – not as soldiers, but as civilians.[9]

In the case, the chief London magistrate, Brackley Kennett, was charged with criminal breach of duty for refusing to read the Riot Act and order military intervention to put down the Gordon Riots.[10] For several days anti-Catholic protesters, after being turned away from Parliament, had confronted authorities burning down buildings (including Lord Mansfield's house). Eventually, the king convened the Privy Council, which issued an order for the armed forces to act without waiting for magistrates. Some 15,000 troops moved into London and, as a result, an estimated 285 rioters were killed. For his reluctance to call in the troops, Kennett was convicted and fined £1,000.[11] Lord Mansfield instructed the jury as above, but the case did not call into question the loss of life only the reluctance of civil authorities to use force. Although something of a legal fiction in the case when the military used considerable force, Lord Mansfield's dictum that in internal deployments to tackle riotous assemblies

---

[7]   Ibid.

[8]   Ibid.

[9]   Ibid, 344. The case is recorded in T. Holdcroft, *A Plain and Distinct Narrative of the Late Riots and Disturbances in the Cities of London and Westminster, and the Borough of Southwark* (1780) appendix.

[10]   On the Gordon Riots see A. Babington, *Military Intervention in Britain: From the Gordon Riots to the Gibraltar Incident* (Routledge, 2015) 21–31.

[11]   Head (2010) 344.

soldiers are in the same legal position as citizens, is an idea that persists in modern legal thinking.[12] It also demonstrates a continuing concern about the potential impact of the military in the internal affairs of state.

A more nuanced picture about the amount of force that could be used lawfully to suppress rioters comes from reading *R v Pinney*, a judgment of the Court of the King's Bench relating to the Bristol Riots of 1831.[13] The case concerned the criminal responsibility of the mayor of Bristol in failing to use 'due means' to suppress the rioters, numbering about 5,000, who had attacked persons and property in the city. The judgment of Littledale J was clear that a balance had to be achieved between excessive force and a failure to perform the duty. Furthermore, the headnote states that the 'general duty of a magistrate with regard to rioters is to restrain, and, if necessary, to pursue, arrest and take them'. Nevertheless, it is clear from the judgment of not guilty handed down by the court that in the case the mayor not only called on constables and citizens to help suppress the riot, but in discharging his duty to 'assemble a sufficient force for suppressing the rioters', the mayor had given soldiers under the command of an officer authority to charge at the protesters. Indeed, the judge thought that 'a military officer may act without the authority of the magistrate if he chooses to take the responsibility, but, although that is the strict law, there are few military men who will take upon themselves so to do, except on the most pressing occasions'.[14] Although the case seems to be placing some legal restraints on the use of military force in suppressing rioters, there remained a clear expectation that the military should be used and, indeed, that the military could act if necessary without civilian authority. It is worth bearing in mind that the question before the court was whether the mayor had assembled sufficient forces in the fulfilment of his duties, not whether excessive force was used.

The Bristol Riots of 1831 also led to the trial of individuals who took part in the riots by a Special Commission. Tindal CJ expressed the view that the 'obligation imposed by the law on every subject of the realm' to help the civil magistrate suppress riots extended to soldiers:

> I wish to observe that the law acknowledges no distinction in this respect between the soldier and the private citizen. The soldier is still a citizen, lying under the same obligation, and invested with the same authority, to preserve the peace of the King, as any other subject ... Undoubtedly, the same exercise of discretion which requires the private subject to act in subordination to, and in aid of, the magistrate ought

---

[12]   M. McCormack, 'Supporting the Civil Power: Citizen Soldiers and the Gordon Riots' (2012) 37 *The London Journal* 27.

[13]   *R v Pinney* (1833) in [1824–34] All ER Rep 125.

[14]   Ibid.

to operate in a still stronger degree with a military force. But where the danger is pressing and immediate, where a felony has actually been committed, or cannot otherwise be prevented, and from the circumstances of the case no opportunity is offered of obtaining a requisition from the proper authorities, the military subjects of the King, like his civil subjects may, but are not bound, to do their utmost, of their own authority, to prevent the perpetration of outrage, to put down riot and tumult, and to preserve the lives and property of the people.[15]

Soldiers, like citizens, were under an obligation to aid the civil authorities, but they also possessed discretion to intervene without prior authority in the case of necessity. While the establishment of police forces first in London and then in other cities in the mid-19th century gradually led to the police having primacy in maintaining public order, the armed forces still retained a significant role in supporting the civil authorities. Troops continued to be deployed against protesters and rioters; for example in Liverpool in 1919 four battalions, tanks and HMS *Valiant* were deployed in response to riots.[16] Post-1945 deployments were undertaken largely in response to serious strikes, with the military being used as labour to supply essential services,[17] or more recently in response to terrorist outrages. For example, in February 2003 troops in armoured personnel vehicles were deployed to Heathrow airport as part of a response to security threats in London.[18] In May 2017, following a terrorist attack in Manchester, troop deployment was a measure designed to reassure the public as well as to provide additional security.[19] In 2019, the government had plans in place to deploy 3,500 troops ('Operation Yellowhammer') in the event that Brexit caused significant disruption.[20] In 2020, 20,000 troops were put on standby to provide military assistance to civil authorities to tackle the

---

[15] *Case of the Bristol Rioters* (1832) in W.C. Costin and J.S. Watson, *The Law & Working of the Constitution: Documents 1660–1914*: Vol II 1784–1914 (Adam and Charles Black, 1952) 259.

[16] Head and Mann (2009) 23–5.

[17] Ibid, 26–7.

[18] L. Brooke-Holland, 'Military Aid to the Civil Authorities', House of Commons Library Briefing Paper, No. 08074, 18 August 2017.

[19] 'Troops deployed on British streets after Manchester terror attack', *The Telegraph*, 24 May 2017 http://www.telegraph.co.uk/news/2017/05/24/troops-deployed-british -streets-manchester-terror-attack-pictures/. According to Brooke-Holland, '10,000 military personnel are on standby to assist the civil authorities for significant terrorist incidents at short notice ... Operation Temperer is the name of the standing operational contingency plan and it was activated following the Manchester attack in May 2017, when the Government raised the security threat to critical. Approximately 1,400 Defence personnel were involved, primarily by guarding locations across the country to free up armed police officers.'

[20] *BBC News*, 'Brexit: What does Yellowhammer say about no-deal impact?', 20 September 2019 https://www.bbc.co.uk/news/uk-politics-47652280.

Covid-19 pandemic.[21] The number of internal troop deployments is considerable – in 2016–2017, for example, it occurred on over 80 occasions,[22] while in
2018–2019 the figure was over 120.[23]

3.3   THE LEGAL BASIS OF EMERGENCY POWERS

The legal basis for deploying troops to Northern Ireland appeared to be the
use of prerogative powers by UK Home Secretary James Callaghan,[24] when
a request came from the government of Northern Ireland on 14 August 1969.[25]
This followed a speech by the Prime Minister of the Irish Republic, in which
he called for the deployment of a UN peacekeeping force to Northern Ireland.[26]
An attempt to put this on the agenda of the UN Security Council failed, with
the UK making it clear that the situation was a domestic matter and so should
not be the subject of UN intervention. Furthermore, the UK argued that the
situation did not constitute a threat to international peace as would be required
if the Security Council was to override the principle of non-intervention in
domestic matters embodied in the UN Charter.[27] The UK government saw the
situation as an internal one of serious unrest that did not constitute an armed
conflict, but one still requiring the deployment of the armed forces. Within
hours of the Home Secretary's decision to deploy troops, an advance contingent of 300 British soldiers replaced police officers to patrol cordons emplaced
around the Bogside in the centre of Londonderry.[28]

The military deployment to Northern Ireland (Operation Banner) was
exceptional in that it gradually became a combined police and military operation to apprehend and, if necessary, use force against members of non-state
armed groups, in effect an exercise in the re-assertion of the government's
monopoly over the use of force in the province. Normally, in modern times at
least, military deployments are much more benign in nature. Common tasks
undertaken under the framework of Military Aid to Civil Authorities (MACA)
include 'explosive ordnance disposal, search support to police services' and
'specialist reconnaissance aircraft to locate missing persons or provide spe-

---

[21]   L. Brooke-Holland, 'Coronavirus: Deploying the Armed Forces in the UK',
House of Commons Library Briefing Paper, No. 08704, 20 March 2020.
[22]   Brooke-Holland (2017).
[23]   Brooke-Holland (2020).
[24]   Head and Mann (2009) 90.
[25]   D. McKittrick and D. McVea, *Making Sense of the Troubles: A History of the
Northern Ireland Conflict* (Penguin, 2012) 55.
[26]   BBC, '1969: British troops sent into Northern Ireland' http://news.bbc.co.uk/
onthisday/hi/dates/stories/august/14/newsid_4075000/4075437.stm.
[27]   UN Doc S/PV/1503 (1969); UN Charter (1945) Article 2(7).
[28]   BBC, '1969: British troops sent into Northern Ireland'.

cialist aerial imagery'. 'More general support may be required during times of flooding, or to protect major events, such as G8 or NATO summits', and the 2012 Olympic Games when 18,000 military personnel were deployed. 'Personnel may also be trained in anticipation of industrial action by emergency or essential services.'[29]

Constitutionally speaking the legal basis of the power to deploy troops to confront internal disturbances is said to derive from the Emergency Powers Acts 1920 and 1964,[30] the Civil Contingencies Act 2004, and residual prerogative powers which operate 'above and beyond the Civil Contingencies Act' in that they can be instigated 'without any formal declaration of a state of emergency under the Act'.[31] Michael Head also notes that the MoD itself has identified two further legal basis. First, a 'common law tenet' derived from judicial statements like that of Lord Mansfield cited above in Section 3.2, which demonstrate that 'members of the armed forces have a duty to provide the support normally expected of the ordinary citizen'. Secondly 'Queen's Regulations place an additional duty on military commanders to act on their own responsibility without a request by a civil agency where "in exceptional circumstances, a grave and sudden emergency has arisen, which in the opinion of the Commander demands his immediate intervention to protect life or property"'.[32] In addition, the government has developed emergency powers to tackle specific threats such as terrorism and,[33] more recently, the Coronavirus pandemic,[34] but the power to deploy troops has its basis in the sources identified in this section with the default position being the use of prerogative powers. As summarised by Head and Mann: '[t]aken as a whole, considerable legal powers are said to exist to authorise calling out the troops to deal with a wide variety of alleged threats to society, including civil unrest, industrial

---

[29]   Brooke-Holland (2017).

[30]   The Emergency Powers Act (1964) section 2 enables the 'temporary employment in agricultural work or in other work, being work of national importance, of members of the armed forces'. Clive Walker reports that the Emergency Powers Acts were invoked on 12 occasions in Britain, almost exclusively to deal with the 'impacts of major industrial strikes', with the last occasion being in 1979 in the so-called 'winter of discontent', when there were plans for troop deployment but they were not implemented: C. Walker, 'The Governance of Emergency Arrangements' (2014) 18 *International Journal of Human Rights* 211 at 212.

[31]   Head and Mann (2009) 91. See also Brooke-Holland (2017).

[32]   Head (2010) 341, citing Ministry of Defence, 'Operations in the UK: The Defence Contribution to Resilience' (HMSO, 2005) para 4-2.

[33]   For example: Terrorism Act (2000), Terrorism Act (2006), Counter-Terrorism Act (2008), Counter-Terrorism and Security Act (2015), Counter-Terrorism and Border Security Act (2019).

[34]   Coronavirus Act (2020).

action and acts of terrorism, and these measures have been augmented by the "almost boundless power" that can be asserted under the 2004 Act'.[35]

3.4   EMERGENCY POWERS UNDER THE CIVIL CONTINGENCIES ACT 2004

Part II of the Civil Contingencies Act 2004 details the 'emergency powers' of the executive, and defines 'emergency' as 'an event or situation which threatens serious damage' to human welfare or to the environment in the UK, and 'war, or terrorism, which threatens serious damage to the security' of the country.[36] Emergency regulations may be made by executive order – Orders in Council – or by a senior minister if 'it would not be possible, without serious delay, to arrange for an Order in Council'. Emergency regulations must be prefaced by a statement by the person making the regulations 'specifying the nature of the emergency in respect of which the regulations are made', and declaring that 'the person making the regulations is satisfied that the conditions in section 21 are met'. That person must also be satisfied that the regulations contain only provisions that are proportionate and 'appropriate for the purpose of preventing, controlling or mitigating an aspect or effect of the emergency'. They must also ensure that the 'regulations are compatible with the Convention rights (within the meaning of section 1 of the Human Rights Act 1998)'.[37] The conditions specified in section 21 are that: 'an emergency has occurred, is occurring or is about to occur', and that it is necessary and urgent 'to make provision for the purpose of preventing, controlling or mitigating an aspect or effect of the emergency'. Regulations may override existing legislation, with the exception of the HRA 1998.[38]

The broad powers conferred on ministers are reflected by the range of regulations that may be adopted in response to an emergency.[39] Such emergency regulations can be adopted to protect human life, health or safety, property, supplies of money, food, water, energy or fuel, systems of communication, transport, health services, financial institutions, Parliament and public func-

---

[35]   Head and Mann (2009) 91, citing C. Walker and J. Broderick, *The Civil Contingencies Act 2004: Risk, Resilience and the Law in the United Kingdom* (Oxford University Press, 2006) 251.

[36]   Civil Contingencies Act (2004) section 19(1).

[37]   Ibid, section 20.

[38]   Ibid, section 21.

[39]   Ibid, section 22(1).

tions.[40] The executive powers granted by the 2004 Act are immense.[41] In general '[e]mergency regulations may make provision of any kind that could be made by Act of Parliament or by the exercise of the Royal Prerogative'; in particular, regulations may confer: a function on a Minister of the Crown; a power, or duty, to exercise a discretion; and a power to give directions or orders, whether written or oral. Regulations can provide for the requisition or confiscation of property (with or without compensation), or the destruction of property, animal life or plant life (with or without compensation). Regulations can prohibit or restrict movement, assemblies or travel. A power is conferred to create offences to tackle failures to comply with regulations or obstructing a person in the performance of a function required by the regulations. In addition, there are powers to enable the Defence Council to authorise the deployment of the armed forces and make provision (which may include conferring powers in relation to property) for facilitating that deployment. There is also power to confer jurisdiction on a court or tribunal (which may include a tribunal established by the regulations).[42]

As well as the conditions necessary to invoke emergency regulation found in section 21, section 23 specifies limitations on emergency regulations, effectively a combination of self-limitation and some clear legal restrictions. The person making regulations must be satisfied that they are appropriate for tackling the emergency, and that 'the effect of the provision is in due proportion to that aspect or effect of the emergency'. Emergency regulations must 'specify the Parts of the United Kingdom or regions in relation to which the regulations have effect'. Emergency regulations may not require a person to provide military service or prohibit participation in a strike or other industrial action. Emergency regulations may not create an offence that is punishable with imprisonment for a period exceeding three months or alter procedures in relation to criminal proceedings. Emergency regulations may not amend the 2004 Act or the HRA 1998.[43] One further important limitation is that emergency regulations shall lapse after 30 days, although new regulations may then be adopted for a further 30 days.[44] This limitation appears to have motivated the government to put forward a new piece of primary legislation to tackle the Covid-19 outbreak of 2020 in the shape of the Coronavirus Act containing

---

[40] Ibid, section 22(2).
[41] Though apparently insufficient to tackle the Covid-19 pandemic of 2020–2021, which necessitated the adoption of the Coronavirus Act (2020) giving the government separate extensive emergency powers.
[42] Civil Contingencies Act (2004) section 22(3).
[43] Ibid, section 23.
[44] Ibid, section 26. See also section 27 providing for Parliamentary scrutiny of emergency regulations.

powers to tackle the pandemic and adopted for a two year period.[45] Blick and Walker go further arguing that the Coronavirus Act 2020 is more neglectful of constitutionalism than the Civil Contingencies Act 2004, in that Parliamentary scrutiny of regulations is reduced.[46] Furthermore, there is no express recognition in the 2020 Act of the primacy of the HRA 1998, which there is under the 2004 Act.[47] Blick and Walker conclude that 'an uphill struggle now looms to control the Coronavirus state'.[48]

Clive Walker writes that 'in the face of calamity and disaster the Civil Contingencies Act 2004 has emerged as the principal legal response in the UK, although a considerable amount of additional "sectoral" laws have also emerged to handle specific crises' such as the threat of terrorism especially after the attacks on London of 7 July 2005,[49] and the Coronavirus pandemic of 2020–2022.[50] Concerns about the breadth of the definition of 'emergency' in Article 19 of the Civil Contingencies Act are offset to some extent by the requirements of duration, seriousness, necessity and geographical proportionality,[51] and by the fact that the primary piece of legislation that is exempt from the overriding effect of emergency regulations is the HRA 1998. Apart from the 1998 Act, '[e]ven statutes regarded as essential to civil liberties and basic constitutional rights, such as the Magna Carta 1297, the Bill of Rights 1688, the Parliament Acts 1911–49 and the Representation of the People Act 1983, can be swept aside'.[52] Walker states that there is an almost unlimited power

---

[45]   Coronavirus Act (2020) section 89. See also the Health Protection (Coronavirus) Restrictions 2020 adopted pursuant to the Public Health (Control of Disease) Act (1984) – discussed in *Dolan v Secretary of State for Health* [2020] EWCA 1605. There is no mention of a power to call on the military in legislation adopted in response to Coronavirus, so presumably MACA requests for military assistance to help tackle the pandemic were made with ministerial approval under prerogative powers. For MACA requests see https://www.gov.uk/guidance/covid-support-force-the-mods-continued -contribution-to-the-coronavirus-response. See statement by the Minister for the Armed Forces, Hansard, HCWS170, Vol 673, 19 March 2020 (Heappey) – 'Defence is committed to assisting HMG by ensuring that there are effective and proportionate contingency plans in place to mitigate the potential impact that the *covid-19* coronavirus outbreak might have on the welfare, health and security of UK citizens and economic stability of the UK. Defence is taking prudent steps to ensure that we can provide support to other Government Departments when requested.'

[46]   A. Blick and C. Walker, 'Why Did Government Not Use the Civil Contingencies Act?' *The Law Society Gazette*, 2 April 2020.

[47]   Civil Contingencies Act (2004) section 30.

[48]   Blick and Walker (2020).

[49]   Walker (2014) 212.

[50]   But see Blick and Walker (2020), who doubt the 'sectoral' nature of the Coronavirus Act (2020).

[51]   Civil Contingencies Act (2004) sections, 23, 24 and 26.

[52]   Head (2010) 348.

in section 22(1) of the 2004 Act to issue emergency regulations, which the executive views as appropriate for the purpose of preventing, controlling or mitigating any aspect or effect of the emergency.[53] Despite these extensive powers, the government insisted on legislating for a separate and even more broad-ranging set of powers in the Coronavirus Act 2020.[54]

Furthermore, the protections provided by the HRA 1998 can be pared down by derogations following a declaration of state of emergency under Article 15 of the ECHR. Detention under the 2004 Act would have to be compatible with Article 5 of the ECHR (right to liberty and security), in particular the entitlement of a detained person 'to take proceedings by which the lawfulness of his detention shall be decided speedily by a court and his release ordered if the detention is not lawful'.[55] However, derogation from this Article is allowed under Article 15 of the ECHR in states of emergency that threaten the life of the nation.[56] Although there are no specific powers of arrest or detention without trial in the 2004 Act, the 'Act's sponsors refused to rule out such detention, which the courts have in the past been prepared to accept, even in peacetime civil emergencies'.[57] It is notable that there has been no derogation from the ECHR during the Coronavirus pandemic,[58] even though regulations adopted to control the pandemic and protect the right to life have impacted on other rights and liberties.[59]

3.5 CIVILIAN-MILITARY RELATIONS IN EMERGENCIES

Despite all the political capital expended on adopting such a sweeping piece of legislation, Part II of the Civil Contingencies Act 2004 has not been invoked due the relative success of Part I, and the presence of residual prerogative

---

[53] Walker (2014) 213.
[54] Hansard, HC, Vol 674, Col 132, 23 March 2020 (Mordaunt).
[55] ECHR (1950) Article 5(4).
[56] See UK derogation from Article 5 to detain suspected terrorists after the attacks of 11 September 2001. While the ECtHR agreed with the UK government that there was a state of emergency, it found the measures were disproportionate by unjustifiably discriminating between nationals and non-nationals: *A and Others v The United Kingdom*, Appl No 3445/05, 19 February 2009.
[57] Head (2010) 350.
[58] See express powers of detention in the Coronavirus Act (2020) section 51 and schedule 21. ECHR (1950) Article 5(1)(e) allows for 'the lawful detention of persons for the prevention of the spreading of infectious diseases'.
[59] House of Commons, House of Lords, Joint Committee on Human Rights, 'The Government's response to COVID-19: Human Rights Implications', HC 265, HL paper 125, 21 September 2020, para 14.

powers that enable ministers to act quickly in the face of emergencies with little accountability.[60] There is also the political fear of a public backlash over the use of such sweeping emergency powers including troop deployment.[61] Walker also argues that the top-down approach of Part II of the Act 'does not fit with the preferred late modern approaches of governance', which are generally based on partnership between different actors, both public and private. While Part I of the Act operates in this way, Part II does not.[62]

Part I of the 2004 Act, which contains the same definition of emergency as Part II,[63] addresses the responsibilities and roles of emergency responders, and provides for responses at the local level. Unlike Part II, Part I of the 2004 Act does not mention the deployment of armed forces as it is directed at civil authorities. However, the deployment of the military in these situations occurs under different legal bases as detailed in a MoD publication of 2017, which outlines how 'Defence contributes to the nation's resilience and security, both routinely and when facing crises as part of an integrated approach to civil contingency'.[64] Under 'military aid to the civil authorities (MACA)', civil authorities take the lead and the MoD plays a supporting role, 'providing niche capabilities, or more generalist support when the civil authorities' capacity/ capability is overwhelmed by an incident, when directed to do so, or when preparing for major national events'.

The MoD states that 'MACA activity is frequent, and occurs across the UK'. Examples given include: providing 'widespread and general support during flooding events across the UK on a number of occasions over the last decade'; supplying 'security for large-scale, pre-planned events of international and national significance' including the London Olympic Games in 2012; assisting UK citizens stranded overseas; providing support 'in response to events not necessarily defined as a risk in the National Risk Assessment,[65] but where

---

[60] Although there has been some judicial paring back of the Royal Prerogative, starting with the House of Lords' judgment in the GCHQ case (*Council of the Civil Service Unions v Minister for the Civil Service* [1985] AC 374) – see A. Blick, 'Emergency Powers and the Withering of the Royal Prerogative' (2014) 18 *The International Journal of Human Rights* 195 at 210.

[61] Walker (2014) 218–19.

[62] Ibid, 219.

[63] Civil Contingencies Act (2004) section 1.

[64] MoD, 'UK Operations: The Defence Contribution to Resilience and Security', Joint Doctrine Publication JDP 02, 3rd edn, February 2017 https://www.gov.uk/government/uploads/system/uploads/attachment_data/file/591639/20170207_JDP02_Resilience_web.pdf.

[65] The National Risk Register of Civil Emergencies, 2015 Edition, March 2015, 19–41 describes three types of hazard and threat: 'natural hazards' – human disease, animal disease, severe weather and flooding; 'major accidents' – major industrial acci-

military support is appropriate, such as providing assistance following the collapse of Didcot Power Station in 2016'.[66] The primacy of civil authorities is reiterated throughout the document, but the significant supporting role of the military, involving the exercise of considerable discretion by local commanders, is made clear:

> Civil authorities and emergency services are required to provide the first response when reacting to crises, emergencies and/or major incidents within the UK. Notwithstanding this, other government departments … or civil authorities are able to request military assistance from the Ministry of Defence … Routinely, such requests will require ministerial authorisation. However, in very exceptional circumstances, for example, grave and sudden emergencies, when there is an urgent need to protect life, alleviate distress and/or protect significant property, a local commander is empowered to deploy assets to deal with the situation without recourse to additional ministerial authority.[67]

Under Part I of the Civil Contingencies Act 2004, the army is neither a category 1 responder (which would, for example be the emergency services) nor a category 2 responder (which would, for example, be the health and safety executive). Nevertheless, it 'should be fully involved with cooperating in emergency preparedness work in a supporting role'.[68] The ancient Parliamentary fear of troops being used to usurp democracy is addressed in the MoD's doctrine, when it states that the 'strategic objectives that underpin the UK Government's response to an emergency' are to: 'protect human life and, as far as possible, property and the environment, and alleviate suffering'; 'support the continuity of everyday activity and restore disrupted services at the earliest opportunity'; and, most relevantly, to 'uphold the rule of law and the democratic process'.[69] The MoD and the armed forces have responsibility to 'defend and contribute to the security and resilience of the UK and its Overseas Territories'. Specifically, this includes 'deterring attacks; defending our airspace, territorial waters and cyber space; countering terrorism at home and abroad; supporting UK civil authorities in strengthening resilience'; and helping in responding to natural disasters, accidents and terrorist attacks. Defence should conduct its UK 'fixed tasks' under MACA, namely 'those tasks that have resources permanently assigned to them, for example, explosive ordnance disposal;

---

dents, major transport accidents, widespread electricity failure, disruptive industrial action and widespread public disorder; 'terrorist and other malicious attacks' – terrorist attacks on crowded places, infrastructure, transport systems, unconventional terrorist attacks and cyber security. See JDP 02 (2017) para 1.17.

[66]   JDP 02 (2017) para 1.1.
[67]   Ibid, para 1.2.
[68]   Ibid, para 1.4.
[69]   Ibid, para 1.5.

and support to UK counter-terrorism operations (including counter-chemical, biological, radiological and nuclear capability)'.[70] The MoD makes a clear distinction between situations where there is military primacy and those where there is civilian primacy:

> There is a distinction between defending the UK from external military threats and responding to the internal and domestic hazards and threats identified in the National Risk Assessment. The Ministry of Defence … will act as lead government department for defending the UK from any external military threat, with other government departments acting in a supporting role. Conversely, Defence will routinely act in a supporting role to other departments in responding to internal and domestic resilience and security challenges.[71]

This, of course, is premised on the government having ultimate authority and responsibility for defending the country from external attack or threat through the exercise of prerogative powers, with the government being accountable to Parliament for its decisions and for decisions made under its name by the military.[72] Furthermore, all 'MACA operations must be conducted within the law. Service personnel are subject to Service discipline (the Armed Forces Act 2006) and military command at all times. Failure to comply with the law may result in criminal charges against an individual, and/or civil proceedings being brought against the MOD.'[73]

The MoD doctrine identifies three possible legal bases for MACA: 'the Royal Prerogative for military tasks where support is supplied in addition to civil authorities' capabilities'; 'a Defence Council Order (DCO) under the Emergency Powers Act 1964' for 'civilian tasks where support is supplied instead of civil authorities' capabilities'; or 'emergency regulations made under Part 2 of the Civil Contingencies Act 2004'.[74] According to the MoD 'service personnel can deploy under the Royal Prerogative for "military" work'.[75] There is no legal definition or test for 'military work' rather, according to the MoD, 'it is an assessment based on knowledge and experience', and is the 'type of work that is usually, but not exclusively, requested by law enforcement agencies'.[76] Presumably, the deployment of troops at the London Olympics was undertaken under the Royal Prerogative, although there was no express invocation of the power in December 2011 when the number of troops

---

[70]   Ibid, para 1.10.
[71]   Ibid, para 2.4.
[72]   Ibid, para 2.11.
[73]   Ibid, para 2.13.
[74]   Ibid, para 2.14.
[75]   Ibid, para 2.15.
[76]   Ibid.

had to be increased significantly due to the inability of a private security con-tractor – G4S – to provide enough personnel.[77] In a written answer, the Defence Secretary Philip Hammond stated that the 'safety and security operation for the games remains police-led', but that troops would deliver a 'range of military support to the police and other civil and Olympic authorities'. Naval, air force and ground based air defence systems would also be deployed.[78]

For 'non-military tasks, the mechanism of a DCO is used to authorise the deployment of military resources'.[79] A DCO 'is made using powers in Section 2 of the Emergency Powers Act 1964', which enable 'the temporary employ-ment in agricultural work or in other work, being urgent work of national importance, of members of the armed forces of the Crown'. Key points for the DCO are that: 'it requires ministerial authorisation and should be signed by two members of the Defence Council on the same day'; 'the work must be both urgent and of national importance'; and 'the Defence Council provides governance and decides whether the task is of an urgent and nationally impor-tant nature'.[80] These provisions generally ensure civilian control of internal military deployments but there are chinks in civilian political control and major gaps in judicial control. The first gap in civilian control is identified by the MoD in the form of the one 'standing DCO, dated 17 January 1983, which is used when there is an imminent threat to life, a need to alleviate distress, or to protect significant property'. In these circumstances, 'local commanders may provide immediate assistance without recourse to higher authority'. The 1983 DCO approves the employment of military personnel for 'urgent work of national importance, such work as is considered by the local commander, at the time when the work needs to be performed, to be urgently necessary for the purposes of the alleviation of distress and preservation and safeguarding of lives and property in time of disaster'.[81] 'After initiating a response, command-ers must inform the chain of command as soon as practicable.'[82]

The second gap, in which the military can take action without civilian authority and oversight, is under the Queen's Regulations for the Armed Forces.[83] These 'provide an authority for military commanders to act on their

[77] R. Booth, N. Hopkins and S. Laville, 'London 2012: frustration and pride as mil-itary steps in to clear up G4S mess', *The Guardian*, 20 July 2012.

[78] Hansard, HC, Col 116WS, 15 December 2011.

[79] JDP 02 (2017) para 2.16.

[80] Ibid.

[81] Ibid, para 2.17.

[82] Ibid.

[83] Ibid, para 2.20. The Queen's Regulations for the Royal Navy J4801–4802, and J4805–4806; The Queen's Regulations for the Army J11.001–010; and The Queen's Regulations to the Royal Air Force J852.

own responsibility without a request by the civil authorities'. This applies where: 'in very exceptional circumstances, a grave and sudden emergency has arisen'; and 'in the opinion of the local commander, the situation demands immediate intervention to save life, alleviate distress and protect significant property'.[84] The MoD states that '[u]sing military personnel armed with weapons for MACA operations will always be an exception', requiring an explicit statement as to 'whether the use of personal weapons or specialist equipment is authorised and, if so, whether guidance cards and specific rules of engagement are to be applied'.[85]

As to judicial accountability, the traditional approach was embodied in the statement of King James I, who declared that the 'absolute Royal Prerogative of the Crown' was 'no Subject for the tongue of a Lawyer'.[86] However, the courts have, in recent times, asserted some authority over the Royal Prerogative. Since the *GCHQ* case in 1984,[87] the courts have shown a greater willingness to examine the content of the power and the 'way in which the prerogative is exercised'.[88] However, there is nothing systematic about the approach of the judiciary: it depends on the cases presented to the courts and the willingness of judges to overcome their traditional reluctance to review the exercise of executive powers in security or defence matters.

The assumption was that Part II of the Civil Contingencies Act 2004 would largely supplant the exercise of prerogative powers, although it was clear from the surrounding debates that it was not intended to replace them.[89] However, that assumption seems to be rebutted in practice, whereby Part II has not been utilised although a significant number of troop deployments have occurred, a number of which are the result of the exercise of prerogative powers. The main reason for preserving prerogative powers seems to be one of effectiveness, enabling ministers to respond rapidly to emergencies, disasters and security threats.[90] It might be speculated that other reasons include the avoidance of a formal declaration of a state of emergency, and that the exercise of such powers largely escape not only political accountability to Parliament (though questions may be asked and emergency debates held), but also accountability before the courts. The exercise of statutory emergency powers under the 2004 Act by the executive might lead to legal challenges by those adversely affected

---

[84]   JDP 02 (2017) para 2.20.
[85]   Ibid, para 2.21.
[86]   Blick (2014) 198.
[87]   *Council of Civil Service Unions v Minister for the Civil Service* [1985] AC 374.
[88]   Blick (2014) 197.
[89]   Ibid, 207.
[90]   Ministry of Justice, 'Review of the Executive Royal Prerogative Powers: Final Report' (2009) 30–4.

by regulations adopted under it, including by mounting challenges under the HRA 1998. In contrast, the exercise of emergency powers under the prerogative leaves such individuals the choice of mounting a more speculative legal challenge in the hope that the courts might be willing to consider the impact of prerogative powers, wielded for reasons of safety and security of the public, on their rights.

3.6   THE USE OF FORCE IN EMERGENCY SITUATIONS

The deployment of troops to the streets of the UK in the face of terrorist threats, riots or other civil emergencies raises many political, ethical and legal problems and, in a number of ways, returns us to the issue of the state's monopoly on the use of force and how it can legitimately be maintained. Specifically, the question as to what levels of force and other methods of coercion can be utilised by soldiers engaged in domestic deployments is one that is not easy to answer. According to Michael Head: '[c]alled-out military personnel have been given no specific statutory powers, but the Ministry of Defence guidelines assert substantial common law powers, including to use lethal force and make arrests'.[91] Furthermore, the MoD 'states that soldiers must act within the law and have no special legal powers beyond those of the ordinary citizen. Nevertheless, they "may use reasonable force to prevent crime, including in self-defence"'.[92] As regards the power of arrest, Head summarises MoD doctrine: '[a]lthough service personnel "should not normally" make arrests, "in certain circumstances there may be no other option"'. The MoD's position is that soldiers can arrest people even to prevent a breach of the peace, which is defined as an 'occasion where a person causes harm or appears likely to cause harm to persons or property, or acts in a manner likely to provoke violence to others'. MoD 'guidelines state that force is lawful if the immediate object is to prevent crime (including public order offences), arrest offenders, self-defence or the defence of others'.[93]

From the soldier's perspective the problem with these vague standards is that they reference the sort of limitations that might operate in a civilian law enforcement context. While numerous civilian support operations undertaken by the armed forces involve unarmed soldiers, if the soldier is armed then it will be with the sort of lethal weaponry not normally carried by police officers; moreover part of a soldier's training will be to kill in combat. Furthermore,

---

[91]   Head (2010) 355.
[92]   Ibid, citing MoD (2005) paras 4-3, 4A-1.
[93]   Head (2010) 355, citing MoD (2005) paras 4-3, 4A-1.

as indicated by Head: '[m]ilitary law provides that troops must obey lawful commands. Secret rules of engagement will be approved by ministers. These may purport to authorise or even require the application of lethal force, as they did in Northern Ireland.'[94] A soldier has limited powers to use lethal force in domestic emergencies, but he will be faced with making judgements about when to use such force including how to interpret rules of engagement (RoE) and, indeed, whether to obey orders given to him to use lethal force. To expect a soldier to make these calculations in dangerous situations requiring split-second decision-making is asking a great deal, but as the Northern Ireland situation shows, this was the reality for soldiers.

3.7   SOLDIERS IN SITUATIONS OF CIVIL DISORDER: THE 'TROUBLES' IN NORTHERN IRELAND

In modern times within the UK the most significant troop deployment has been to Northern Ireland in 'Operation Banner', starting in 1969. The context is described by Nevin Aiken:

> Since the partition of the island of Ireland in 1921, Northern Ireland has suffered from a protracted and seemingly intractable conflict, with communities of (largely Roman Catholic) Irish 'nationalists' engaged in a long-standing struggle with both (largely Protestant) pro-British 'unionists' and the security forces of the British state. The worst period of violence between these groups occurred between the early 1970s and the late 1990s in a period known as the 'Troubles'. During this time over 3,500 people were killed, the vast majority by armed 'Republican' and 'Loyalist' paramilitary groups who claimed to represent local nationalist and unionist communities. The violence of the Troubles was finally brought to an end by the historic peace process of the late 1990s. However, even after the signing of the landmark Belfast Agreement in 1998, Northern Ireland has remained a society deeply divided by a polarised political climate, entrenched social segregation, and intercommunal animosity, prejudice, and mistrust. These divisions are still sustained, at least in part, by ongoing tensions between nationalists and unionists related to the legacy of unresolved human rights abuses associated with the violence of the Troubles.[95]

The initial aim of Operation Banner was to restore law and order in response to outbreaks of violence between the two communities. However, 'thirty years later, the troops were still there, though their duties had shifted from "public order" to "counter-terrorism"'.[96] From keeping the peace between the Catholic

---

[94]   Head (2010) 355.
[95]   N.T. Aiken, 'The Bloody Sunday Inquiry: Transitional Justice and Postconflict Reconciliation in Northern Ireland' (2015) 14 *Journal of Human Rights* 101 at 101.
[96]   Head and Mann (2009) 31.

minority and the Protestant loyalist majority, the army found itself facing the Provisional Irish Republican Army (IRA) as armed resistance was accelerated by ill-fated military actions, in particular the 'Bloody Sunday' killing of unarmed civilians by soldiers of the Parachute Regiment in January 1972. This incident has been subject to two public inquiries reviewed below. To date, there have been no criminal convictions of soldiers involved in that incident. More broadly, there have been a limited number of prosecutions of members of the armed forces for criminal offences committed in Northern Ireland.[97]

Even though more soldiers were killed in Northern Ireland than many subsequent armed conflicts in which the UK has been involved, the UK government did not recognise the situation in Northern Ireland as an 'armed conflict' to which LOAC would apply,[98] including a right to kill enemy combatants.[99] This meant that soldiers using lethal force were to be judged by the ordinary standards of common law and criminal law,[100] and the government responsible for their deployment would increasingly be judged over the period of the 'Troubles' according to international human rights standards. Serious criminal offences committed by soldiers during the violence were tried before ordinary criminal courts, not by courts martial.[101] Looking at the limited judicial consideration of uses of lethal force by soldiers deployed in Northern Ireland, the legal restraints identified seem to be unclear and unevenly applied, reflecting the fact that the courts tried to take account of the difficult position in which soldiers found themselves. In other words, the courts tried to interpret the duties of the soldiers in a context specific way, recognising that although the situation fell short of an armed conflict, the use of lethal force by soldiers in the face of unremitting violence was a reality.

In a House of Lords' judgment of 1976 involving a reference on a point of law by the Attorney General, their Lordships considered the issue before them to be one of fact and not of law, and so was one for the original court to decide (where the accused soldier was found not guilty).[102] The discussion, however, is illuminating. The reference asked 'whether a soldier commits a crime when

---

[97] Ibid, 31. See further discussion in this chapter in Section 3.9 below.

[98] A. Bianchi and Y. Naqvi, *International Humanitarian Law and Terrorism* (Hart, 2011) 36.

[99] See further Chapter 5.

[100] P. Rowe, *The Impact of Human Rights Law on Armed Forces* (Cambridge University Press, 2006) 213. Rowe also notes that a 'large number' of British soldiers in Northern Ireland 'were disciplined for committing military offences while on duty which did not amount to criminal offences' and were either dealt with by the CO or by court martial.

[101] Ibid, 103.

[102] *Reference under s48A of the Criminal Appeal (Northern Ireland) Act 1968 (No. 1 of 1975)* [1976] 2 All ER 937.

… he fires to kill or seriously wound an unarmed person because he reasonably believes that the person is a member of a proscribed organisation (in this case the Provisional IRA) who is seeking to run away, and the soldier's shot kills him'. The facts showed that the soldier had shot dead an entirely innocent man who was running away after being told to 'halt'. The soldier was part of a patrol in a rural area where soldiers were under a real threat of surprise attacks by members of the IRA. It also seemed to be the case that the soldier was under extreme pressure and did not intend to kill but acted instinctively when faced with a person who he believed to be a member of the IRA, but the issue remains that the man was unarmed and was running away.[103] Given that the deceased was fleeing Lord Diplock dismissed self-defence as a possible basis, but was of the view that to be lawful the shooting must have occurred in the performance of the soldier's duty to prevent crime or in the exercise of his statutory right to stop and question the deceased.[104] Lord Diplock then went on to discuss the rights and duties of soldiers in Northern Ireland:

> There is little authority in English law concerning the rights and duties of a member of the armed forces of the Crown when acting in aid of the civil power; and what little authority there is relates almost entirely to the duties of soldiers when troops are called on to assist in controlling a riotous assembly. Where used for such temporary purposes it may not be inaccurate to describe the legal rights and duties of a soldier as being no more than those of an ordinary citizen in uniform. But such a description is in my view misleading in the circumstances in which the army is currently employed in aid of the civil power in Northern Ireland. In some parts of the province there has existed for some years now a state of armed and clandestinely organised insurrection against the lawful government of Her Majesty by persons seeking to gain political ends by violent means, that is by committing murder and other crimes of violence against persons and property. Due to the efforts of the army and police to suppress it the insurrection has been sporadic in its manifestations but, as events have repeatedly shown, if vigilance is relaxed the violence erupts again. In theory it may be the duty of every citizen when an arrestable offence is about to be committed in his presence to take whatever reasonable measures are available to him to prevent the commission of the crime; but the duty is one of imperfect obligation and does not place him under any obligation to do anything by which he would expose himself to risk of personal injury, nor is he under any duty to search for criminals or seek out crime. In contrast to this a soldier who is employed in aid of the civil power in Northern Ireland is under a duty, enforceable under military law, to search for criminals if so ordered by his superior officer and to risk his own life should this be necessary in preventing terrorist acts. For the performance of this duty he is armed with a firearm, a self-loading rifle, from which a bullet, if it hits the human body, is almost certain to cause serious injury if not death.[105]

---

[103]   Ibid, 946.
[104]   Ibid, 947.
[105]   Ibid, 948.

Far from being a citizen aiding the civil authorities, soldiers are tasked with enforcing the laws but, moreover, his or her duty can be described not simply as following orders but, by their presence and actions (including patrolling and manning check points), providing security and keeping the peace. The depiction given by Lord Mansfield and others judges in the older cases on riotous assemblies of a soldier as a citizen was clearly a legal fiction in those cases, but in the circumstances of Northern Ireland it was recognised by the judiciary as no longer relevant. As with the cases of riot, when soldiers are sent into situations of disorder and violence then force above the level normally deployed by law enforcement officers will be used. Lord Diplock then considered what this might mean for a jury tasked with considering on the facts whether the use of lethal force was reasonable:

> The jury would have also to consider how the circumstances in which the accused had to make his decision whether or not to use force, and the shortness of the time available to him for reflection, might affect the judgment of a reasonable man. In the facts that are to be assumed for the purposes of the reference there is material on which a jury might take the view that the accused had reasonable grounds for apprehension of imminent danger to himself and other members of the patrol if the deceased were allowed to get away and join armed fellow members of the Provisional IRA who might be lurking in the neighbourhood, and that the time available to the accused to make up his mind what to do was so short that even a reasonable man could only act intuitively. This being so, the jury in approaching the final part of the question should remind themselves that the postulated balancing of risk against risk, harm against harm, by the reasonable man is not undertaken in the calm analytical atmosphere of the court room after counsel with the benefit of hindsight have expounded at length the reasons for and against the kind and degree of force that was used by the accused; but in the brief second or two which the accused had to decide whether to shoot or not and under all the stresses to which he was exposed.[106]

The Court was concerned to make it clear that the situation was not one of normal law enforcement, and that sending in armed troops has inevitable consequences leading to loss of life. There can be little doubt that the Court was leaning towards the soldier, sympathising with his predicament and criticising the lack of a clear legal framework. Effectively, as a guide to behaviour, this judgment condoned the use of lethal force in such circumstances as the soldier found himself, and thus allowed for the use of potentially lethal force beyond self-defence. More broadly, this case reflects 'the difficulty of holding ... members of the armed forces legally accountable ... even where deaths occur'. Between 1970 and 1979, the army killed 186 people in Northern Ireland, 26 soldiers were prosecuted, and 13 convicted.[107]

---

[106] Ibid.
[107] Head and Mann (2009) 32.

The case of *R v Clegg* embodied the legal uncertainties and wider pressures surrounding the prosecution of soldiers. The case involved a soldier from the Parachute regiment manning a roadblock outside Belfast as part of a patrol tasked with catching joyriders (although there is some doubt as to whether the purpose had been properly explained to Private Clegg). Faced with a car being driven at the roadblock with full headlights on, Private Clegg fired three shots into the windscreen and then a fourth shot, which he claimed was fired into the side of the car as it passed. The bullet hit the rear seat passenger Karen Reilly in the back killing her. The judge accepted his defence that he fired the first three shots in self-defence and in defence of another soldier but, on the evidence, rejected the same argument for the fourth shot, as it was found that the car and the danger had already passed.[108] Furthermore, there was no suggestion that Private Clegg thought that the driver was a terrorist, or that if the driver had escaped he would go on to commit terrorist offences, thereby distinguishing it from the *Reference* case discussed above.

In dismissing his appeal against a conviction of murder, the House of Lords highlighted several facets of the case, which reflected on the position of soldiers deployed to Northern Ireland. First, the Court highlighted the 'yellow card' given to soldiers containing instructions for opening fire in Northern Ireland:

> You may only open fire against a person: (a). if he is committing or about to commit an act LIKELY TO ENDANGER LIFE, AND THERE IS NO OTHER WAY TO PREVENT THE DANGER. The following are some examples of acts where life could be endangered, dependent always upon the circumstances: (1) firing or being about to fire a weapon. (2) planting, detonating or throwing an explosive device (including a petrol bomb). (3) deliberately driving a vehicle at a person and there is no other way of stopping him. (b). if you know that he has just killed or injured any person by such means and he does not surrender if challenged and THERE IS NO OTHER WAY TO MAKE AN ARREST.[109]

The Court of Appeal had suggested that the wording of (b) be changed to more specifically include serious as opposed to any injury. Although it was agreed in the case that the 'yellow card' had no legal force, it still should have been designed to keep soldiers within the law and that, in the case of Private Clegg, he had stepped beyond the 'yellow card' and the law.

The second facet of the case concerned an opinion from the Court of Appeal that because Private Clegg had not killed Karen Reilly 'from an evil motive but because his duties as a soldier' had placed him in a situation where 'armed with a high velocity rifle, he reacted wrongly to a situation which suddenly

---

[108] *R v Clegg* [1995] 1 All ER 334.
[109] Ibid, 339.

confronted him in the course of his duties', the law should reflect this with a conviction of manslaughter not murder.[110] Again there was sympathy from the judiciary for the position of soldiers on duty in the Troubles. In this regard, Lord Lloyd said that:

> In most cases of a person acting in self-defence, or a police officer arresting an offender, there is a choice as to the degree of force to be used, even if it is a choice which has to be exercised on the spur of the moment, without time for measured reflection. But in the case of a soldier in Northern Ireland, in the circumstances in which Pte Clegg found himself, there is no scope for graduated force. The only choice lay between firing a high-velocity rifle which, if aimed accurately, was almost certain to kill or injure, and doing nothing at all.[111]

However, the House of Lords abstained from law-making in that the 'reduction of what would otherwise be murder to manslaughter in a particular class as cases can only be decided by Parliament'.[112] Although the case stands as determining that firing at a fleeing vehicle containing joyriders was an excessive use of force and, if causing death, constituted murder, Private Clegg's conviction for murder was eventually overturned. An appeal against conviction revealed that the 'evidence upon which the conviction has to stand is frail and gives rise to an element of doubt in our minds whether it has been sufficiently clearly proved that the appellant did discharge a shot' after the car had passed his position.[113]

The leeway given to soldiers to use lethal force was demonstrated in the case of *Kelly v UK* (1993) before the European Commission on Human Rights. The applicant's son was a 17-year-old driver of a car that had caused damage to police vehicles at a checkpoint, and had endangered the lives of soldiers there by driving at them after being told to stop and despite attempts to stop the car by breaking the driver's window with a rifle butt. The soldiers then shot at the car as it passed the checkpoint once more, and the driver was killed. The applicant brought a case against the MoD for assault, battery and negligence on the basis that the death of his son was the result of excessive and unjustifiable force. The High Court judge 'found that the soldiers had formed a genuine belief that the occupants of the car were terrorists making a determined attempt to escape from the checkpoint and that the use of force to prevent that escape was justified in the prevention of crime, i.e. further terrorist activities'.[114] As with the above cases the judge reasoned that as they were soldiers with high

---

[110] Ibid, 340.
[111] Ibid, 345.
[112] Ibid, 347.
[113] *R v Clegg* [2000] NI 305 329.
[114] *Kelly v United Kingdom*, Appl No 17579/90, 13 January 1993.

powered riles determined to stop a car then the use of potentially lethal force
was almost inevitable:

> The method of stopping the car to which the soldiers had resort was to shoot at it
> with their rifles. The modern military rifle is a high powered and accurate weapon,
> and each of the soldiers was aiming at the car in order to hit the driver and so bring
> the vehicle to a halt. If he hit his target, there was a high probability that the shots
> would kill him or inflict serious injury ... It could only be regarded as a reasonable
> action if the risks to the public involved in allowing a car containing terrorists to
> escape outbalance on the scales of reason the danger of inflicting death or serious
> injury to its occupants. In weighing these considerations one has to take account of
> the fact that the only weapons available to the soldiers were their rifles, and they
> either used them to effect or took no action to stop the car. ... The use of a firearm
> must in my view be an expedient of last resort, but when it is brought into service
> that can only usefully be done by shooting at the driver.[115]

In so reasoning the judge dismissed any notion that shooting at the tyres, for
instance, would have been a reasonable response. Again the judicial position
appears to be that when a decision is made to deploy armed soldiers to situations of civil unrest then there are going to be occasions, beyond simple
self-defence, where lethal force can lawfully be used. In effect, because the
case was brought against the government it was raising the question as to
whether the government was responsible for the actions of soldiers it had put
into this position.

The applicant took the case to the European Commission on Human Rights
for violation of the right to life under Article 2 of the ECHR. Article 2(1)
provides that '[e]veryone's right to life shall be protected by law', but also
provides in paragraph 2 that '[d]eprivation of life shall not be regarded as
inflicted in contravention of this Article when it results from the use of force
which is no more than absolutely necessary: (a) in defence of any person from
unlawful violence; (b) in order to effect a lawful arrest or to prevent the escape
of a person lawfully detained; (c) in action lawfully taken for the purpose of
quelling a riot or insurrection'.

The Commission dismissed the application, reasoning that the use of lethal
force was justified as absolutely necessary in effecting a lawful arrest as
specified in Article 2(2)(b), and that it did not need to decide whether lethal
force was necessary to prevent future crime, which is not a separate ground
for taking life under Article 2. The Commission was 'satisfied that shooting in
this case was for the purpose of apprehending the occupants of the stolen car,
who were reasonably believed to be terrorists, in order to prevent them from
carrying out terrorist activities'. The suddenness of the appearance of the car,

---

[115] Ibid.

and the dangers it presented, 'assessed against the background of the events in Northern Ireland which is facing a situation in which terrorist killings have become a feature of life', demonstrated that the use of force was proportionate and absolutely necessary in the circumstances.[116]

The judicial responses to the uses of lethal force by British soldiers in Northern Ireland recognise that such force can be used when absolutely necessary in self-defence, defence of others and in order to apprehend terrorist suspects. Although Article 2(2)(c) was not mentioned in the *Kelly* case it is interesting to note that in the *Reference* case of 1976 Lord Diplock did characterise the Troubles as 'a state of armed and clandestinely organised insurrection against the lawful government'.[117] Moreover, the courts recognised that placing soldiers with powerful weapons in such a situation would inevitably lead to deaths and appeared to interpret the criminal law accordingly.

It has been argued that since the *Kelly v UK* (1993) case ECtHR jurisprudence has moved towards a narrower approach to Article 2,[118] where the use of lethal force can only really be justified in self-defence of soldiers or in defence of others under actual or imminent attack. Both the *McCann* case (reviewed in the next section), and a later separate *Kelly* case of 2001 before the ECtHR, illustrate that although the UK authorities could have employed better procedures to prevent the taking of life, the soldiers on the ground did not violate the right to life per se when shooting IRA members, and that the right of self-defence and defence of others allows for some leeway. In the later *Kelly* case,[119] the security forces were alerted to a possible terrorist attack on a Royal Ulster Constabulary (RUC) station, leading to the positioning of soldiers and RUC officers around the station. Five men emerged from an approaching car and began firing; the soldiers returned fire. A digger believed to be containing explosives was also shot at by the soldiers and exploded. The driver of a nearby car was also shot. In total, nine men were killed; one was a civilian unconnected to the IRA and two of the IRA members were unarmed. The Director of Public Prosecutions (DPP) concluded that there was insufficient evidence to prosecute any of the security forces involved in the shootings.

The 'applicants submitted that the death of their relatives was the result of unnecessary and disproportionate use of force by Special Air Service (SAS) soldiers and that their relatives were the victims of a shoot-to-kill policy operated by' the UK government in Northern Ireland.[120] The ECtHR judgment

---

[116] Ibid.

[117] *Reference* case [1976] 948.

[118] J.A. Hessbrugge, *Human Rights and Personal Self-defense in International Law* (Oxford University Press, 2017) 106–10.

[119] *Kelly and Others v United Kingdom*, Appl No 30054/96, 4 May 2001.

[120] Ibid, para 83.

concerned the state's duty to undertake an effective investigation when lethal force had been used. It examined whether the UK had complied with the procedural aspects of Article 2 of the ECHR and found a number of shortcomings in transparency and effectiveness of the investigation,[121] signifying a breach of Article 2, and entitling the applicants to damages of £10,000 each. The applicants had also argued that the failure to attempt to arrest the deceased men was a violation of their due process rights under Article 6 of the ECHR, in that they were denied a fair trial.[122] The Court dismissed this contention, as well as the claim of discrimination under Article 14. According to the Court, the fact that a disproportionate number of Catholics had been killed by security forces did not, of itself, show discriminatory practice.[123]

3.8   THE DUTIES OF GOVERNMENT WHEN DEPLOYING TROOPS

The gradual encroachment of human rights jurisprudence into cases arising from the Troubles effectively shifted the spotlight onto the government and its use of armed soldiers in a situation that fell short of armed conflict. In the *McCann* case,[124] the authorities were aware of a planned IRA attack in Gibraltar, involving the detonation of a car bomb. SAS soldiers shot dead three IRA suspects in the belief that they were about to detonate the bomb. The ECtHR stated that it should be borne in mind that the UK authorities had received information that there would be a terrorist attack in Gibraltar, which 'presented them with a fundamental dilemma': 'on the one hand, they were required to have regard to their duty to protect the lives of the people in Gibraltar including their own military personnel and, on the other, to have minimum resort to the use of lethal force against those suspected of posing this threat in the light of the obligations flowing from both domestic and international law'.[125] The authorities were 'confronted by an active service unit of the IRA composed of persons who had been convicted of bombing offences and a known explosives expert'. Furthermore, the IRA, 'judged by its actions in

---

[121] Ibid, para 136.
[122] Ibid, para 141.
[123] Ibid, para 148.
[124] *McCann and Others v The United Kingdom*, Appl No 18984/91, 27 September 1995.
[125] Ibid, para 192.

the past, had demonstrated a disregard for human life, including that of its own members'.[126] The Court went on:

> Against this background, in determining whether the force used was compatible with Article 2 ..., the Court must carefully scrutinise ... not only whether the force used by the soldiers was strictly proportionate to the aim of protecting persons against unlawful violence but also whether the anti-terrorist operation was planned and controlled by the authorities so as to minimise, to the greatest extent possible, recourse to lethal force.[127]

On the first question regarding the actions of the soldiers, the Court accepted that although it turned out to be the case that the suspects were not about to detonate a bomb, 'the soldiers honestly believed, in the light of the information that they had been given ... that it was necessary to shoot the suspects in order to prevent them from detonating a bomb and causing serious loss of life ... the actions which they took, in obedience to superior orders, were thus perceived by them as absolutely necessary in order to safeguard innocent lives'.[128] While the actions of the soldiers did not violate Article 2,[129] the inadequacies in planning and preparation by state authorities did amount to a breach of that provision by the UK. The Court pointed to 'a lack of care' by the authorities 'in the control and organisation of the arrest operation'.[130] It concluded that:

> having regard to the decision not to prevent the suspects from travelling into Gibraltar, to the failure of the authorities to make sufficient allowances for the possibility that their intelligence assessments might, in some respects at least, be erroneous and to the automatic recourse to lethal force when the soldiers opened fire, the Court is not persuaded that the killing of the three terrorists constituted the use of force which was no more than absolutely necessary in defence of persons from unlawful violence within the meaning of Article 2 para. 2 (a) ... of the Convention.[131]

Louise Doswald-Beck analyses the *McCann* judgment in the following terms: '[t]he European Court found that the shootings by the soldiers were not a violation' of the right to life under Article 2 of the ECHR, 'but there was a violation of the right to life by the United Kingdom because sufficient precautions had

---

[126] Ibid, para 193.
[127] Ibid, para 194.
[128] Ibid, para 200.
[129] Ibid.
[130] Ibid, para 212.
[131] Ibid, para 213.

not been taken to avoid the death of the suspects'.[132] The ruling questioned the UK's decision to use the military in place of police forces in times of peace, especially as these were special forces from the SAS Regiment, and therefore highly trained combatants. The Court stated that the soldiers' 'action in this vital respect lacks the degree of caution in the use of firearms to be expected from law enforcement personnel in a democratic society, even when dealing with dangerous terrorist suspects, and stands in marked contrast to the standard of care reflected in the instructions in the use of firearms by the police which had been drawn to their attention and which emphasised the legal responsibilities of the individual officer in the light of conditions prevailing at the moment of engagement'.[133]

The RoE for the SAS soldiers recited by the Court in *McCann* were as follows:

Use of force
4. You and your men will not use force unless requested to do so by the senior police officer(s) designated by the Gibraltar Police Commissioner; or unless it is necessary to do so in order to protect life. You and your men are not then to use more force than is necessary in order to protect life …

Opening fire
5. You and your men may only open fire against a person if you or they have reasonable grounds for believing that he/she is currently committing, or is about to commit, an action which is likely to endanger your or their lives, or the life of any other person, and if there is no other way to prevent this.

Firing without warning
6. You and your men may fire without warning if the giving of a warning or any delay in firing could lead to death or injury to you or them or any other person, or if the giving of a warning is clearly impracticable.

Warning before firing
7. If the circumstances in paragraph 6 do not apply, a warning is necessary before firing. The warning is to be as clear as possible and is to include a direction to surrender and a clear warning that fire will be opened if the direction is not obeyed.[134]

These rules appear to be in line with the provisions of the ECHR on the basis of self-defence and defence of others under Article 2(2)(a), except for the part of paragraph 4 of the RoE, which state that force can only be used where 'nec-

---

[132] L. Doswald-Beck, *Human Rights in Times of Conflict and Terrorism* (Oxford University Press, 2011) 165.

[133] *McCann* (1995) para 212.

[134] Ibid, para 14.

essary' to protect life, which seems to give a greater margin for interpretation than the phrase 'absolutely necessary' in Article 2(2) of the ECHR.

On the day after the shootings in Gibraltar, in the House of Commons, the Foreign Secretary, Geoffrey Howe, stated that:

> Had a bomb exploded in the area, not only the 50 soldiers involved in the parade, but a large number of civilians might well have been killed or injured. It is estimated that casualties could well have run into three figures. There is no doubt whatever that, as a result of yesterday's events, a dreadful terrorist act has been prevented. The three people killed were actively involved in the planning and attempted execution of that act. I am sure that the whole House will share with me the sense of relief and satisfaction that it has been averted.[135]

The questions raised by Eric Heffer MP constituted the solitary voice of dissent in the House:

> As someone who has always opposed terrorism, whether of the IRA or anyone else, and who still condemns terrorism and who, like everybody else in the House, would have been affronted if people had been killed in Gibraltar, can I ask the Foreign Secretary to explain why those three people who, although accepted as members of an active service unit of the IRA, were shot and killed when it was admitted that they were not carrying guns and had not planted any bombs in Gibraltar? Can the right hon. and learned Gentleman explain why that happened and how that can help us in the fight against terrorism? Will that not help terrorism?[136]

The ECtHR judgment seven years after this debate 'generated political furore' in the House of Commons, with many MPs and members of the government condemning the judgment that found that the UK had violated Article 2 in killing active IRA terrorists.[137] The unwillingness of the government to accept its shortcomings in the *McCann* case is also reflected in its approach to wider issues of justice and accountability in Northern Ireland. In a sense, while the government has been very protective of soldiers and criticises attempts to investigate allegations against them arising from the Troubles, it is at the same time reluctant to accept its responsibility for any failures that may have arisen by placing soldiers in a violent and dangerous situation where lethal uses of force were too commonplace.

---

[135]   Hansard, HC, Vol 129, Cols 21–5, 7 March 1988.
[136]   Ibid.
[137]   P. Cumper, 'When the State Kills' (1995) 4 *Nottingham Law Journal* 207 at 207. See further S. Palmer, 'Death on the Rock and the European Convention on Human Rights' (1996) 55 *Cambridge Law Journal* 1.

3.9   JUSTICE AND ACCOUNTABILITY IN NORTHERN IRELAND

The Belfast Agreement, commonly known as the Good Friday Agreement, was signed by the British and Irish Governments as well as the political parties in Northern Ireland on 10 April 1998, after multi-party negotiations. It provided, inter alia: for the decommissioning of arms of all paramilitary organisations under supervision of an Independent Commission; an early return to normal security arrangements including a reduction of the numbers and role of the armed forces deployed in Northern Ireland to levels compatible with a normal peaceful society; the removal of emergency powers in Northern Ireland;[138] the affirmation of civil rights and religious liberties of everyone in the community; and the creation of a democratically elected Assembly as well as an Executive Authority.[139]

By 2014, there were 1,800 troops in Northern Ireland compared to 27,000 at the height of the Troubles.[140] In assessing the contribution of the armed forces to peace, Frank Ledwidge analyses the early period after deployment in 1969 when troops were seen by the minority community as 'agents of a deeply unpopular government that had no interest in protecting or assisting them', a perception fuelled by internment (between 1971 and 1975), and incidents including Bloody Sunday that indicated military primacy over the police. He contrasts this with the later period when the army's expertise in confronting the IRA had improved dramatically, and it worked to support rather than supplant the police to play a key role in bringing the parties to the negotiating table.[141] The effects of the army's failures in the early years of Operation Banner deepened the divisions in the province and extended the Troubles. A crucial early incident is related by David McKittrick and David McVea:

> In early July [1970] came the Falls Road curfew, which can be seen as a final poisoning of the initially good relationship between Catholics and British troops. Following a confrontation between soldiers and locals, a large area of the Lower Falls district was sealed off by the army for several days while soldiers were sent in to conduct rigorous house-to-house searches. The exercise entailed ordering perhaps 20,000 people not to leave their homes. The searches uncovered more than

---

[138] The Emergency Powers Act (Northern Ireland) (1926) as amended by the Emergency Powers (Amendment) Act (Northern Ireland) (1964) was finally repealed by the Civil Contingencies Act (2004) schedule 2, part 2, para 12.

[139] https://www.gov.uk/government/publications/the-belfast-agreement.

[140] *BBC News*, 'Number of soldiers in Northern Ireland lowest since 1969', 24 October 2014, https://www.bbc.co.uk/news/uk-northern-ireland-29763562.

[141] F. Ledwidge, *Losing Small Wars: British Military Failure in Iraq and Afghanistan* (Yale University, 2012) 162–3.

one hundred weapons but in the process considerable damage was done to hundreds of households as soldiers prised up floorboards and ransacked rooms. In addition to such personal indignities there were four deaths all caused by the army: three men were shot dead by troops while a fourth was crushed by a military vehicle. None of those killed had any IRA or other extreme connections. The sense that the army was being deployed against the general Catholic population was compounded when troops brought in two Unionist ministers to tour the area in armoured cars.[142]

As stated by Andrew Mumford 'political panic found recourse in a military solution'. The 'army was sent in and reacted with a tactical repertoire and a level of force that it had come to know throughout its colonial experiences'.[143] Occasions when unarmed civilians were killed, and unsubstantiated allegations of 'shoot-to-kill' levelled against the SAS after those troops were introduced in 1976, 'severely undermined the belief that the British army was adhering to its own Yellow Card principles'.[144] 'Nevertheless, the army was anxious to absolve itself of culpability by pointing to the highly pressured, split second decision-making that its soldiers were required to make in kinetic engagements with insurgents and wrapped itself in the centuries-old moral risk of warfare – either kill or be killed.' However, 'in retrospect, the army was willing to concede, as the Chief of General Staff's end of Operation Banner report states, that on occasion the army failed to "discriminate between those perpetrating the violence and the remainder of the community"'.[145]

This certainly seemed to be the case in the most notorious loss of life at the hands of soldiers: Bloody Sunday, which involved the shooting dead of 14 Catholic civilians by British paratroopers during an anti-internment march in Derry on 30 January 1972. At the time 'the British government claimed that 1st Para had opened fire in self-defence against armed "gunmen and bombers" suspected to be associated with the PIRA who had sought to take advantage of nationalists' illegal rioting to launch a sustained shooting and nail bombing attack against Army forces'.[146] The Widgery Inquiry into the incident, which reported quickly in 1972, 'largely exonerated the soldiers of 1st Para of wrongful action during the incident, concluding that ultimate responsibility for Bloody Sunday rested with those who organised the illegal civil rights march

---

[142] D. McKittrick and D. McVea, *Making Sense of the Troubles: A History of the Northern Ireland Conflict* (Penguin, 2012) 61.

[143] A. Mumford, *The Counter-Insurgency Myth: The British Experience of Irregular Warfare* (Routledge, 2012) 96.

[144] Ibid, 107.

[145] Ibid, 107, citing Ministry of Defence, 'Operation Banner: An Analysis of Military Operations in Northern Ireland', Report prepared under the direction of the Chief of General Staff, Army Code 71842, July 2006, para 216.

[146] Aiken (2015) 137.

and noting that the soldiers involved had justifiably opened fire only after coming under sustained shooting and bombing attacks by armed republican assailants'.[147] According to Barcat, '[w]hile Widgery did acknowledge in his report that some soldiers had acted in a manner that "bordered on the reckless", he still insisted that most of the blame lay with the organisers of the march for creating a "highly dangerous situation", and added that there was a "strong suspicion" that some of the victims had been handling firearms or bombs – an unbearable conclusion for the victims' families'.[148] In effect, according to Aiken: '[t]aken together, Bloody Sunday and Widgery marked a watershed moment in the Troubles, leading directly to both an upsurge in nationalist recruitment to armed republican paramilitary organisations and an exponential increase in acts of intercommunal violence'.[149]

A clear failure to uncover the truth and to provide forms of accountability that would draw a line under Bloody Sunday led to a second inquiry, which was launched after the Good Friday Peace Agreement of 1998. In announcing the Inquiry, Prime Minister Tony Blair made it clear 'that the aim of the inquiry is not to accuse individuals or institutions, or to invite fresh recriminations, but to establish the truth about what happened on that day, so far as that can be achieved at 26 years' distance'.[150] An inquiry into one incident involving the loss of life, albeit an appalling one, was unlikely to provide a form of transitional justice in Northern Ireland in the sense of processes 'aimed at helping a society come to terms with previous large-scale human rights abuses in order to ensure accountability for wrongdoing, and achieve justice and reconciliation for victims'.[151] The absence of a truth commission with a general remit over the Troubles in Northern Ireland was, according to Aiken 'due to the policy of "constructive ambiguity" underpinning the peace process, which recognized that, while there might be a shared commitment to bringing an end to violence in the country, no consensus existed between nationalists and unionists as to what the future constitutional status of Northern Ireland should be or even whether the Troubles should rightfully be regarded as a civil

---

[147] Ibid, 104.

[148] C. Barcat, 'The Bloody Sunday Inquiry and the Saville Report: Declaring Innocence, Attributing Blame, and the Limitations of Public Inquiries' (2012) 45 *Irish Law Review* 34 at 34, citing Rt Hon. Lord Widgery, 'Report of the Tribunal appointed to inquire into the events on Sunday, 30th January 1972, which led to the loss of life in connection with the procession in Londonderry on that day' (HMSO, 1972) 98.

[149] Aiken (2015) 104–5.

[150] Hansard, HC, Cols 501–3, 29 January 1998.

[151] C. Lawther, *Truth, Denial and Transition: Northern Ireland and the Contested Past* (Routledge, 2014) 129.

conflict or as criminal terrorism'.[152] Nevertheless, as regards one of the most controversial events, the Bloody Sunday Inquiry served 'as a mechanism of truth recovery' and was able 'to establish a new – and less divisive – "shared truth" surrounding the controversial events of Bloody Sunday, a truth that has now largely been accepted among both nationalist and unionist communities in Northern Ireland'.[153]

In contrast to the rapidly produced whitewash in the Widgery Report, the Saville Inquiry meticulously unearthed and examined the evidence and finally reported in 2010.[154] Its findings were indeed very critical of the paratroopers: simply put they were not justified in firing into the crowd. The Inquiry found that 'there was a serious and widespread loss of fire discipline among the soldiers' who lost 'their self-control ... forgetting or ignoring their instructions and training and failing to satisfy themselves that they had identified targets posing a threat of causing death or serious injury'.[155] On the basic issue the Report was crystal clear:

> The firing by soldiers of 1 PARA on Bloody Sunday caused the deaths of 13 people and injury to a similar number, none of whom was posing a threat of causing death or serious injury. What happened on Bloody Sunday strengthened the Provisional IRA, increased nationalist resentment and hostility towards the Army and exacerbated the violent conflict of the years that followed. Bloody Sunday was a tragedy for the bereaved and the wounded, and a catastrophe for the people of Northern Ireland.[156]

Although the Inquiry was not able to grant immunity from prosecution to those who provided statements before it, there was 'an undertaking given by the British Attorney General' that 'no oral or written evidence collected by the Inquiry could be used as the basis for future criminal proceedings'.[157] According to Blom-Cooper the Saville Inquiry 'emphatically rejected the notion that it was its function to determine rights and obligations of any nature', rather 'its task was to do its best to discover what happened on that day and to report the results of its investigation'.[158] While the Saville Report's

---

[152] Aiken (2015) 102. But see 'Troubles proceedings: Mandela-style truth process may be set up: Initiative, first used in South Africa, would give witnesses immunity from prosecution', *The Guardian*, 23 October 2019.

[153] Aiken (2015) 109.

[154] L. Blom-Cooper, 'What went wrong on Bloody Sunday: A critique of the Saville Inquiry' (2010) *Public Law* 61 at 62.

[155] Lord Saville, 'Report of the Bloody Sunday Inquiry', Vol 1, 15 June 2010, 99–100.

[156] Ibid, 100.

[157] Aiken (2015) 106.

[158] Blom-Cooper (2010) 67.

detailed exposition of the facts provided a legitimate version of the truth, it failed to hold the government or soldiers to account in any legal sense for their actions, although the possibility of prosecution of soldiers persists.[159] However, the unequivocal finding that the soldiers were totally unjustified in using lethal force had consequences for the government, who could no longer evade its responsibility for the conduct of its soldiers. This was recognised in Prime Minister David Cameron's response to the Saville Report: '[t]he government is ultimately responsible for the conduct of our armed forces and for that, on behalf of the government, indeed on behalf of our country, I am deeply sorry'.[160]

Beyond that the government was largely exonerated, with Lord Saville refusing to accept allegations about the failure of the authorities to adequately plan for such an operation, including a failure to consider whether paratroopers were the most appropriate force for such a situation: in other words it refused to accept the sort of reasoning utilised in the *McCann* judgment. Concerns were raised by some of those representing the families that 'politicians in both the United Kingdom and Northern Ireland Governments, as well as the military authorities, had planned not simply to stop the civil rights march and to mount an arrest operation against rioters ... but rather to use 1 PARA for the purpose of carrying out some action, which they knew would involve the deliberate use of unwarranted lethal force or which they sanctioned with reckless disregard as to whether such force was used'. On this 'basis it was submitted that the civil and military authorities bore responsibility for the deaths and injuries on Bloody Sunday'. Lord Saville dismissed these allegations, which 'were based on one of two propositions, either that what happened on Bloody Sunday was intended and planned by the authorities, or that it was foreseen by the authorities as likely to happen. We are of the view that neither of these propositions can be sustained.'[161]

Furthermore, the Report did 'not accept that the Army had illegally taken over control of security from the police. The Army and the police worked together in deciding how to deal with matters of security.'[162] These findings effectively exonerated the authorities from allegations of failures in planning the military operation, whether deliberate or careless. This, combined with the Inquiry's failure to deliver 'meaningful accountability for the individual

---

[159] 'One soldier to be prosecuted for murder and attempted murder over Bloody Sunday killings: "Soldier F" to be prosecuted for murder and attempted murder over 1972 killings in Derry', *The Guardian*, 14 March 2019.

[160] *BBC News*, 'Bloody Sunday: PM David Cameron's full statement', 15 June 2010 http://www.bbc.co.uk/news/10322295. For further discussion see Chapter 2.

[161] Saville Report (2010) 90–1.

[162] Ibid, 92.

soldiers of 1st Para involved in the Bloody Sunday shootings',[163] means that justice has not been achieved either for the arbitrary loss of life on Bloody Sunday or more broadly during the Troubles, although a small number of 'legacy prosecutions' remain to be concluded.[164] Aiken concludes: '[w]hile a degree of closure has been brought to some specific events like Bloody Sunday through Northern Ireland's current "piecemeal" approach to the past, there still remain hundreds of highly controversial deaths related to other incidents of Troubles era violence in Northern Ireland for which crucial elements of truth and justice have still not been provided'.[165] According to Ni Aolain the 'large number of lethal force (and other) cases ... strengthen the argument for some group accountability forum', which would 'clarify and acknowledge the past' and 'respond to the needs and interests of the victims', as well as 'outline institutional responsibility and facilitate accountability'.[166] What is clear is that both 'justice' and 'truth' must be provided if any society is to move from conflict towards sustainable peace.

---

[163] Aiken (2015) 112.

[164] See the case of *R v Soldier A and Soldier C* [2020] NICC 6, in which the two defendants involved in the killing of a member of the IRA in 1972, unsuccessfully argued for a stay of the proceedings against them on charges of murder on a number of grounds including: the significant passing of time since the alleged offence, the lack of forensic evidence, the inadequacy of the investigation at the time, the death of witnesses, and repeated statements that there would be no prosecution. Maguire J in the Crown Court of Northern Ireland dismissed the application and allowed the case to proceed to trial. This case is cited as one of four 'legacy prosecutions' of soldiers arising from the Troubles in Northern Ireland in S. O'Neill, 'Troubles veteran faces trial over 1974 shooting', *The Times*, 6 June 2020. The four cases are: (i) Soldier F faces trial for murder and attempted murder during Bloody Sunday 1972; (ii) Soldiers A and C due to stand trial in November 2020 for murder of Joe McCann, an IRA member shot dead in Belfast in 1972; (iii) Dennis Hutchings (former British soldier) faces trial for attempted murder of John Pat Cunningham who was shot dead in County Tyrone in 1974; (iv) David Holden (former British soldier) has been charged with manslaughter of Aidan McAnespie who was shot dead at any army checkpoint in County Tyrone in 1988. The trial of Soldiers A and C (ii) collapsed leading to doubts about further legacy prosecutions: R. Carroll, 'Trial of ex-soldiers over 1972 killing of Official IRA member collapses: Two army veterans acquitted of Joe McCann's murder after judge ruled some evidence inadmissible', *The Guardian*, 4 May 2021.

[165] Aiken (2015) 118.

[166] F. Ni Aolain, 'Truth Telling, Accountability and the Right to Life in Northern Ireland' (2002) 5 *European Human Rights Law Review* 572 at 589. See further C. Campbell and F. Ni Aolain, 'The Frontiers of Legal Analysis: Reframing the Transition in Northern Ireland' (2003) 66 *Modern Law Review* 317.

3.10   CONCLUSION

The deployment of troops in Operation Banner illustrates the problem of introducing soldiers trained to fight wars into an emergency situation, which at least from the UK government's point of view did not amount to a war or an armed conflict. Even in an armed conflict potentially lethal force should not be used against civilians, although some collateral deaths and damage are accepted. However, in situations short of that such force should only be used as a last resort within a law enforcement paradigm as recognised in human rights treaties and in the widely authoritative UN's Basic Code of Conduct for Law Enforcement Officials, Principle 9 of which states:

> Law enforcement officials shall not use firearms against persons except in self-defence or defence of others against the imminent threat of death or serious injury, to prevent the perpetration of a particularly serious crime involving grave threat to life, to arrest a person presenting such a danger and resisting their authority, or to prevent his or her escape, and only when less extreme means are insufficient to achieve these objectives. In any event, intentional lethal use of firearms may only be made when strictly unavoidable in order to protect life.[167]

The court judgments examined in this chapter seem to accept that soldiers are operating within a law enforcement framework when they are deployed to dangerous and violent situations in peacetime. However, there is a lack of clarity in this jurisprudence especially as to the degree to which the context should be taken into account, especially the ever-present danger to soldiers in situations of armed clandestine violence. Without greater clarification of the rights and duties of British soldiers in violent situations there is a danger of further unnecessary loss of civilian life in future deployments.

The case law shows the courts acknowledging that the deployment of soldiers armed with lethal weaponry will result in greater loss of life than would be the case if normal law enforcement methods and personnel were deployed. The idea of the soldier as citizen, which was developed in early jurisprudence involving riotous assemblies, is inappropriate in most modern violent internal situations. Private Clegg was a soldier serving with the Parachute regiment, the British Army's elite airborne assault infantry, as were the soldiers involved in Bloody Sunday. The SAS, the army's special forces, were involved in both *Kelly* (2001) and *McCann*. It might be posited that armed police officers, properly trained in law enforcement, might not have used force in some or all of the circumstances of the cases discussed above. However, it probably has to be

---

[167] Basic Principles on the Use of Force and Firearms by Law Enforcement Officials, UN Doc A/CONF.144/28/Rev.1 (1990).

acknowledged that the monopoly over the use of force in Northern Ireland was only going to be effectively reasserted by the deployment of the armed forces. A clearer legal framework for these operations based on service, criminal and human rights laws remains to be fully enunciated.

This raises the issue discussed in *McCann* concerning the planning and execution of military operations, especially the need to take measures to protect the right to life. This should at the very least make the government wary of deploying soldiers to tackle violence, whether characterised as potentially violent protests, riots, insurrections, or armed struggles short of armed conflict. Furthermore, there should be clear planning, preparation and control over the military by civil authorities. Armed soldiers should be used as a last resort, particularly as their deployment is a recognition that the government has at least temporarily lost its monopoly over the use of force. In any event, the government cannot escape its legal responsibility for the misconduct of its soldiers.

4. Prerogative powers and external deployments

4.1 INTRODUCTION

In the previous chapter covering the internal deployment of troops, domestic law dominates in the shape of ancient public powers, criminal laws and a growing body of emergency legislation, much of it permitting executive regulatory and operational measures. Despite centuries of practice and the widespread use of the military to address internal problems and threats, there remains a lack of clarity as to the legal position of the soldier when faced with riots, insurrections and situations of civil unrest. The idea of a soldier as a citizen in uniform in these situations was shown to be untenable even though still present in legal thinking. The problems of interpreting the right of self-defence, as well as understanding when potentially lethal force was allowable in effecting arrest, preventing escape or crime are particularly problematic when soldiers are faced with an on-going armed threat. Furthermore, the degree of discretion found at operational level was exceeded at governmental level where the executive was seen to prefer prerogative powers to deploy troops. However, this broad legal framework was seen to be under external scrutiny from a human rights angle, which challenged both operational and governmental levels of decision-making. Moreover, external standards of justice are increasingly being levelled against deployments, past and present, exemplified by the calls for broader transitional justice in Northern Ireland.

In this chapter the analysis turns to external troop deployments in a variety of situations ranging from peacekeeping in Cyprus to combat in Korea and, more recently, in Afghanistan and Iraq. Given the gravity of sending troops abroad, especially combat forces, the reader might expect to see a stronger legal framework, but domestically at least it remains dominated by prerogative powers and executive decision-making on the basis that this is necessary for the effective prosecution of any military campaign, although there has been an increase in Parliamentary involvement. Domestically, the 'prerogative' nature of the decision to go to war has meant that legally speaking it belongs to the Crown, which nowadays means the executive branch of government. In the UK this is the Cabinet, or often a small group within the Cabinet known as the 'War Cabinet'.[1] Politically, however, for the government of the day it is often important to have Parliament on its side, particularly if it has decided to prosecute a controversial war that may become unpopular over time.

By its very nature, the sending of armed forces overseas to confront another state's forces or non-state armed groups operating within another state engages international law. Debates over the legality of British interventions have become increasingly prevalent in Parliament and more broadly in the populace. The government appeals to international law to garner support for and bolster the legitimacy of its military interventions, but in so doing it opens itself up to counter-arguments about the legal basis of the war. Since 1945, the UK has shown itself to be one of the most active countries in terms of deploying its armed forces overseas. In reality, a number of its post-1945 military interventions do not fully accord with the rules of international law, but the UK uses its privileged position in the UN and its membership of NATO to protect or legitimate its actions. The UK has also used its formal status as a recognised 'nuclear weapons state' under the NPT of 1968 to maintain a submarine-based independent nuclear deterrent (Trident) which, by its very nature, is deployed in international waters. The nuclear deterrent is designed to protect Britain's vital interests, as well as being deployable alongside US nuclear weapons. Although the UK has not used this ultimate weapon of mass destruction it remains ready to do so in certain circumstances, which raise difficult questions about the legality of such potential uses and the relationship between civilian and military authorities.

The justice as well as the legality of wars of choice, as opposed to wars of necessity, leads to pressure for accountability as well as raising the issue of the legal responsibility of the government, political and military leaders. It also leads to some service personnel questioning their duty to obey orders to deploy to what they might consider to be an illegal war.

4.2   PREROGATIVE WAR POWERS

A.V. Dicey defined prerogative powers as 'historically and as a matter of actual fact nothing else than the residue of the discretionary or arbitrary authority, which, at any given time, is in the hands of the Crown'.[2] The presence and exercise of prerogative power has two serious consequences for the rule of law and democratic accountability. First, 'while Parliamentary approval is

---

[1]   C. Seymore-Ure, 'War Cabinets in Limited Wars: Korea, Suez and the Falklands' (1984) 62 *Public Administration* 181 at 182.

[2]   A.V. Dicey, *Introduction to the Study of the Law of the Constitution* (Macmillan, 10th edn, 1959) 424–5.

not generally needed before action is taken, Ministers [remain] responsible to Parliament for their policies and decisions'.[3] Second, the courts are reticent to encroach on the competence of the executive by claiming a power to review the decisions of the Crown on the disposition and use of the UK's armed forces,[4] although there has been a gradual judicial encroachment in other areas of the prerogative since 1985.[5] Given that prerogative powers by-pass normal methods of democratic control, there is pressure in the modern era to re-evaluate the balance between the necessity of facilitating the effective prosecution of war and the demands of democratic accountability. There is certainly a strong view that the deployment of troops and the waging of war, or more generally 'the exercise of the physical might of the modern state', should be subject to greater democratic control.[6] In contrast, there are strongly held views that greater Parliamentary control will undermine military effectiveness. General Houghton, Chief of Defence Staff from 2013–2016, argued that 'successful military operational activity, particularly at the outset, relies on secrecy, security and surprise', elements that would clearly be undermined by open debate in Parliament.[7] Nevertheless, the increased relevance of international law in domestic political and public debates, especially concerning the legality of 'wars of choice' involving decisions as to whether to become militarily involved in foreign conflicts as opposed to 'wars of necessity' involving instant responses to imminent or actual attacks against the UK,[8] has increased the pressure for greater democratic accountability for decisions that may lead to on-going military commitments to wars fought overseas.

The weaknesses of the British constitution on matters of overseas troop deployments have been exposed by recent conflicts. It is true that the Bill of Rights of 1689 asserted Parliamentary authority over the armed forces when it proscribed the 'raising or keeping of a standing army within the Kingdom in time of peace, unless it be with the consent of Parliament'.[9] However, the purpose of that part of the Bill was to prevent monarchs establishing their

---

[3]   A.W. Bradley and K.D. Ewing, *Constitutional and Administrative Law* (Longman, 14th edn, 2007) 323.

[4]   *China Navigation Co Ltd v Attorney General* [1932] 2 KB 197; *Chandler v Director of Public Prosecutions* [1964] AC 736. See P Rowe, *Defence: The Legal Implications* (Brassey's, 1987) 3.

[5]   *Council of Civil Service Unions v Minister for the Civil Service* [1985] AC 374.

[6]   Bradley and Ewing (2007) 343.

[7]   'Any new Parliamentary convention authorising armed conflict will undermine military effectiveness former Defence Chief says', *The Telegraph*, 6 February 2019.

[8]   House of Lords Select Committee on the Constitution, 'Waging War: Parliament's Role and Responsibility, Volume I', Session 2005-6, HL Paper 236-I, 27 July 2006, para 22.

[9]   See discussion in Chapter 2.

own army. Parliamentary authority was asserted over the standing army, not over each deployment. The Parliamentary power to withdraw authority for the maintenance of an army is not a realistic control in the modern age. Although regular legislation is required to renew Parliamentary authority, it is usually adopted as a matter of course.[10]

The orthodox approach to the exercise of prerogative powers in the areas of foreign affairs and the disposition of armed forces was starkly demonstrated by an exchange in the House of Commons in 1982, when attempts were made to negotiate peace in the period between the Argentinian invasion of the Falklands/Malvinas and the arrival of a British task force to re-take the islands. The leader of the opposition, Neil Kinnock, claimed that the House of Commons had 'the right to make judgment on this matter before any decision is taken by the Government that would enlarge the conflict'. In response, the Prime Minister, Margaret Thatcher, declared that 'it is an inherent jurisdiction of the Government to negotiate and reach decisions. Afterwards the House of Commons can pass judgment on the Government.'[11] There remains the question of whether this untrammelled use of executive power has been qualified by a constitutional convention that arguably started to emerge in the decision-making process that led to the invasion of Iraq in 2003, allowing for Parliamentary debate and possibly voting before the troops are finally deployed in combat. A convention is generally understood to be a 'practice which is politically binding on all involved, but not legally binding'.[12]

Subject to this possible development, the formal method by which the lower House passes judgement on the government can vary and can take the form of either an unamendable procedural motion which may be voted upon or, occasionally, by an amendable substantive vote. The type of vote depends on the political judgement of the government and is not one dictated by legal requirements. For example, there were substantive votes in the House of Commons over the Korean War 1950, Suez Crisis in 1956 and the Gulf Conflict of 1991, but not in the Falklands War 1982 or Kosovo conflict in 1999.[13] The debates prior to the invasion of Iraq in 2003 culminated in a substantive vote in the House of Commons on 18 March, two days before the start of the invasion. On the other hand, there was no prior vote in Parliament concerning

---

[10]   S. De Smith and R. Brazier, *Constitutional and Administrative Law* (Penguin, 8th edn, 1998) 217.
[11]   Hansard, HC, Vol 23, Cols 597–8, 11 May 1982.
[12]   HL Select Committee on the Constitution, 'The Pre-emption of Parliament', Session 2012-13, HL 165, 1 May 2013, para 25.
[13]   HC Foreign Affairs Committee, Fourth Report 1999–2000, HC 28-I, 7 June 2000, para 166.

the deployment of British troops to Afghanistan in 2001.[14] The emergence of a possible convention requiring prior Parliamentary involvement starting with the debate and vote on the invasion of Iraq in 2003 was supported in the Public Administration Select Committee's report of 2004,[15] but the existence, let alone the exact nature, of this convention is unclear as the debates over Libya 2011 and Syria 2013 show. Parliamentary debate and voting occurred after the deployment of the RAF to enforce a no-fly zone and defend civilians in Libya in 2011 in the face of an imminent attack on Benghazi by the government forces of Colonel Gaddafi.[16] However, in deciding whether to respond to chemical weapons attacks on civilians in Syria by the regime of President Assad in 2013, the government's proposal to launch airstrikes was voted down by Parliament and the government of David Cameron did not proceed with the airstrikes.[17] Parliamentary approval was sought and gained by Prime Minister Cameron to use force against the Islamic State in Iraq in 2014,[18] and then for the extension of the operation to Syria in 2015.[19] In contrast, in April 2018 Prime Minister Theresa May launched airstrikes on Syria in response to further usage of chemical weapons by the Assad regime, without seeking Parliamentary approval.[20] Recent practice seems too uneven

---

[14]   HC Research Paper 08/88, 'Parliamentary Approval for Deploying the Armed Forces: An Introduction to the Issues', 27 November 2008, 14.

[15]   House of Commons Public Administration Committee, 'Taming the Prerogative: Strengthening Ministerial Accountability to Parliament', HC 422, 16 March 2004.

[16]   Graham Allen MP raised the issue on the 21 March in a substantive debate two days after force had been used by the UK when stating that this 'House is not taking any decisions: the Government have already taken a decision and have graciously allowed us a debate today. Does he agree that if we are to ensure that we stay properly informed … we need to resolve the question of the House's rights in respect of when this country goes to war?' Foreign Secretary William Hague responded that 'We will … enshrine in law for the future the necessity of consulting Parliament on military action' (Hansard, HC, Vol 525, Cols 739, 799, 21 March 2011).

[17]   Hansard, HC, Vol 566, Cols 1555–6, 29 August 2013. Prime Minister Cameron concluded the debate by saying that 'I strongly believe in the need for a tough response to the use of chemical weapons, but I also believe in respecting the will of this House of Commons. It is very clear tonight that, while the House has not passed a motion, the British Parliament, reflecting the views of the British people, does not want to see British military action. I get that, and the Government will act accordingly.'

[18]   Hansard, HC, Vol 585, Col 1255, 26 September 2014.

[19]   Hansard, HC, Vol 603, Col 323, 2 December 2015.

[20]   Hansard, HC, Vol 639, Col 101, 16 April 2018. Jeremy Corbyn, leader of the opposition, stated 'Members on all sides are therefore rightly concerned that no such [Parliamentary] approval was sought by the Government prior to the air strikes against Syrian Government installations, to which the UK was a party last Friday night, alongside the USA and France. Indeed, this House was not only denied a vote, but did not even have the opportunity to question the Government in advance on the legal and

to amount to a convention. Furthermore, although there have been attempts to embody a convention requiring a vote in Parliament prior to deployment in the form of a non-statutory War Powers Resolution, this has not been adopted by Parliament.[21] At most, the Prime Minister has to decide whether it would be better for political reasons or for reasons of legitimacy to ask Parliament for approval knowing there is an expectation in Westminster that 'wars of choice' involving British forces in combat should be debated and voted on in Parliament prior to deployment.[22]

Before the emergence of an uneven and imperfectly constituted convention to consult and persuade Parliament beforehand, the democratic deficit in the British political system as regards decisions to deploy troops overseas was so severe that it might be questioned as to whether the position was different from that which surrounded the monarch in the 14th and 15th centuries. Maitland portrays the monarch of that time as 'the ruler of the nation, the commander of its armies and its fleets', advised not by Parliament (which did exist in a very early form) but by the King's Council, the members of which 'can be dismissed by the king whenever he pleases; they are sworn to advise the king according to the best of their cunning and discretion'. Furthermore, the 'function of the council … is to advise the king upon every exercise of the royal power'.[23] The monarch's Royal Prerogative powers to make peace and war, specifically to command his subjects to furnish ships, men and stores as

---

evidential basis for their participation in this action, on their new strategy in regard to Syrian intervention.' In contrast Iain Duncan Smith MP stated that 'I am in favour of the House being consulted, but the House also has to give a little leeway to the Executive when it comes to moments such as last week, when it was quite clear that urgent action needed to be taken. Urgent action is based on deep intelligence and if it is not taken quickly, there could well be further consequences later.' Hansard, HC, Vol 639, Col 121, 16 April 2018.

[21] UK Ministry of Justice, 'The Governance of Britain – Draft Constitutional Renewal Bill', Command Paper 7342 (March 2008), annex A. See further Ministry of Justice, 'The Governance of Britain: Review of the Executive Royal Prerogative Powers': Final Report, 15 October 2009, 15.

[22] The practice of consulting Parliament was embedded in the Government's Cabinet Manual in 2011 to acknowledge a convention that before troops were committed the House of Commons 'should have the opportunity to debate the matter' except in emergency situations: House of Commons Political and Constitutional Reform Committee, 'Parliament's Role in Conflict Decisions: An Update', Eighth Report of Session 2013–14, September 2013, para 4. See generally J. Strong, 'The War Powers of the British Parliament: What Has Been Established and What Remains Unclear?' (2018) 20 *The British Journal of Politics and International Relations* 19.

[23] F.W. Maitland, *The Constitutional History of England* (Cambridge University Press, 1931) 197–9.

they thought fit, were recognised in the 17th-century case of *R v Hampden*.[24] Even in the context of a strengthening constitutional role for Parliament, the depiction of the monarch as the military commander of the nation persisted into the 18th and 19th centuries, with Blackstone describing the king as the 'generalissimo, or the first in military command, within the kingdom';[25] while Chitty stated that as 'representative of his people, and executive magistrate, the King possesses' the 'exclusive right to make war or peace, either within or out of his dominions'.[26]

It would be easy to compare the modern Prime Minister and ministerial colleagues in formal or informal War Cabinets to the monarch and his Council as described by Maitland, but it is not necessarily as straightforward as that. Indeed, although medieval monarchs had untrammelled war powers in principle, pressure from Parliament, their subjects (soldiers and civilians), and the treasury meant that in political terms waging war was not as simple as might appear from the constitutional framework. In modern times, there are similar pressures, although the British constitutional legal framework remains weak as recounted by the House of Lords' Constitution Committee in its 2006 report:

> In summary, the deployment power's status as a prerogative power means that there are few restrictions to its use, other than those that have arisen from precedent or convention. Parliament has no formal role in approving deployments, although governments have usually kept Parliament informed about the decision to use force and the progress of military campaigns ... While the armed forces are technically subject to statutory control because legislative authority is needed for the Crown to maintain a standing army in time of peace, their use is for the Government alone to decide. Generally speaking, however, the deployment power is one to which no statutory or legal standards can be applied, and the courts have been reluctant to use arguments based on international law as a standard for assessing the legality of government decisions.[27]

One important consequence of the absence of justiciable legal standards against which to judge government decisions to deploy troops is the constitutional position that military actions undertaken as a result are 'legal as a matter of domestic law'.[28] This has served as an effective shield for soldiers against

---

[24]   *R v Hampden* (1637) 3 State Tr 826.
[25]   Sir William Blackstone, *Commentaries on the Law of England*: Vol 1 (1800) 239–40.
[26]   J. Chitty, *A Treatise on the Law of the Prerogative of the Crown: And the Relative Rights and Duties of the Subject* (Butterworths, 1820) 43.
[27]   HL Select Committee on the Constitution (2006) para 16.
[28]   Ibid, para 28.

different forms of legal liability, but also obliges them to follow orders flowing from the decision to deploy. This was made clear in the same report:

> This in turn means that acts by individual members of the armed forces, of whatever rank, in the execution of a deployment order are themselves lawful. A serviceman is protected from legal liability for the discharge of his orders: a killing in action in the course of the conflict will be justifiable homicide not murder; certain detentions will be lawful and not amount to false imprisonment. This also means, however, that it is not open to a member of the armed forces to rely on domestic law to refuse to obey an order consequent upon a deployment, because such orders are lawful. The present position holds out certainty for troops about their individual liability in conflict situations.[29]

The Constitution Committee recognised that the actions of soldiers will still be judged against the standards of LOAC and international criminal law,[30] which have been incorporated into British domestic law,[31] but not by the *jus ad bellum* governing the legality of using force, which has not been incorporated and, in any case, is the source of obligations for the state not for soldiers.[32] However, this position does not capture the concerns of the military expressed at the time of the decision to invade Iraq in 2003, and after the incorporation of the crime of aggression into the Rome Statute in 2018.[33]

The lack of national legal standards against which to judge political decisions to deploy troops explains the absence of judicial review by British courts, which operate within the framework of domestic constitutional law. Certainly, in the context of decisions to deploy troops, Sedley's comments that the constitution is 'merely descriptive: it offers an account of how the country has come to be governed; and, importantly, in doing so it confers legitimacy on the arrangements it describes. But if we ask what the governing principles are from which these arrangements and this legitimacy derive, we find ourselves listening to the sound of silence.'[34] Furthermore, while there has been an undoubted increase in the penetration of international law into domestic legal systems and courts,[35] the reality is that such standards have not been used by UK courts to

---

[29] Ibid, para 28.
[30] Ibid, para 32.
[31] Geneva Conventions Act (1957), International Criminal Court Act (2001).
[32] The United Nations Act (1946) provides for the implementation of decisions of the UN Security Council on non-forcible measures (i.e. sanctions) into the domestic legal order.
[33] Discussed in Section 4.5 below.
[34] S. Sedley, 'The Sound of Silence: Constitutional Law without a Constitution' (1994) 110 *Law Quarterly Review* 270.
[35] A. Sanger, 'Review of Executive Action Abroad: The UK Supreme Court in the International Legal Order' (2019) 68 *International and Comparative Law Quarterly* 35.

judge decisions to deploy troops,[36] even though the government will expressly rely on international law in the form of advice from the Attorney General to prosecute the war or military action. Nonetheless, in an era of globalisation it is true to say that 'national democratic politics cannot be understood without reference to international forces',[37] no more so than in decisions to deploy combat troops to foreign lands. It must not be forgotten that since 1945 Britain has become part of a wider international institutional and legal order, which affects its ability to wage war.

4.3   INTERNATIONAL LAW AND ACCOUNTABILITY

With British constitutional law providing little by way of legal limitation on the prerogative powers of the government to deploy troops overseas, the spotlight turns to international law and institutions as a means of restricting decisions of the government. Methods of enforcement at the international level are limited, particularly bearing in mind that the UK possesses the power of veto in potentially the most effective executive organ dealing with matters of peace and security – the UN Security Council.[38] Furthermore, for a case to be brought against a state before the ICJ by another state it has to be demonstrated that both states have given consent.[39] In addition, although the UK has accepted the jurisdiction of the ICC as regards war crimes, crimes against humanity and genocide, it has chosen not to be subject to the jurisdiction of the ICC as regards the crime of aggression.[40] The effect of this is to shield political and military leaders from potential individual criminal responsibility for decisions to go to war that may potentially constitute the international crime of aggression.

Despite these built-in protections from the jurisdiction of international institutions, there was some early evidence that the UK was prepared to use both the Security Council and the ICJ to resolve inter-state disputes involving the threat or use of force. In 1946, a dispute arose between Albania and the UK following damage and loss of life caused by mines to British warships in the Corfu Channel. The Security Council recommended that both states refer their dispute to the ICJ, with the UK abstaining on the vote in accordance with the Charter's provisions on voting.[41] Following this, both parties agreed to

---

[36]   Discussed in Section 4.4 below.
[37]   S. Marks, *The Riddle of All Constitutions* (Oxford University Press, 2000) 100.
[38]   UN Charter (1945) Article 27(3).
[39]   Statute of the International Court of Justice (1945) Article 36.
[40]   Discussed in Section 4.5 below.
[41]   UN Doc S/RES/22 (1947).

submit two questions to the Court concerning Albania's international liability for the damage caused by the mine explosions, and whether the UK had, in turn, violated international law by its subsequent heavily armed minesweeping operation. On the second issue, the UK challenged the international legal rules governing the use of force by claiming that its minesweeping operation, taken in response to the loss of its ships, threatened neither the territorial integrity nor the political independence of Albania and therefore did not breach the UN Charter. The Court dismissed the UK's argument and characterised its action as an unlawful form of forceful intervention, but found for Britain on the issue of the destruction of the warships.[42] Although older forms of waging war (gunboat diplomacy, armed reprisals, punitive expeditions, humanitarian interventions ...) had been outlawed in the post-1945 era as they violated the prohibition on inter-state force in the UN Charter,[43] Britain was still prepared to use a form of gunboat diplomacy in the Corfu Channel in 1946, moreover arguing that it was lawful for it to do so.

The *Corfu Channel Case* of 1949 turned out to be a rare instance in which the UK was involved in litigation before the ICJ on matters of force at least.[44] Given the aforementioned protections from the jurisdiction of international institutions and the limited role of domestic courts (reviewed in the next section), the question is whether international law has any role in restraining executive decision-making, or in influencing key Parliamentary votes at the national level. The Corfu Channel incident itself was not propitious in this regard. Although the UK as well as Albania had been found to be in breach of international law by the ICJ, the government was only concerned with the task of recovering compensation from Albania, something that was finally achieved in 1996.[45]

Nevertheless, Parliamentary debates on major troop deployments have regularly included significant discussions about the international legal bases of military actions involving British forces. The question remains as to whether these laws and debates serve to curb the propensity towards conflict, which in

---

[42]   *Corfu Channel Case* (1949) ICJ Rep 4 at 6, 17–22, 35.

[43]   UN Charter (1945) Article 2(4). See C. Henderson, *The Use of Force and International Law* (Cambridge University Press, 2018) 50–7.

[44]   Serbia brought a case against several NATO members in relation to their bombing campaign in the Kosovo conflict of 1999. The case was brought under the Convention on the Prevention and Punishment of the Crime of Genocide (1948) and was dismissed by the ICJ on the basis that Serbia did not have access to it at the time – *Case Concerning Legality of Use of Force (Serbia and Montenegro v UK)* (2004) ICJ Rep 1307.

[45]   In 1992, the parties to the case announced that they had settled their differences and in 1996 the Albanian Government settled the British claim for compensation by paying US$ 2 million – Hansard, HC, Vol 284, Col 224WA, 31 October 1996.

turn reduces the exposure of military personnel to engagement in illegal wars. In 1956, the UK, together with France, launched what was arguably a punitive expedition to secure the Suez Canal against Egyptian nationalisation. The government argued that it was lawful as a form of protection of UK nationals and property,[46] against the advice of the government's law officers, forcing Prime Minister Anthony Eden to declare 'lawyers are always against us doing anything. For God's sake keep them out of it. This is a political affair.'[47] As the operation developed and the wider conspiracy (with Israel) revealed, there was increasing Parliamentary criticism of the government's policy. Although it narrowly survived votes in the House of Commons,[48] the mounting criticism (especially by the US) of the intervention and its legality, contributed to the government's decision to withdraw and agree to the deployment of an impartial UN peacekeeping force.

While the protection of nationals and property was an unconvincing justification for the Suez operation, humanitarian intervention to protect the Albanian population of Kosovo in 1999 was seemingly convincing enough, although the government had to continually reassure the House of Commons that the bombing campaign was justified and above all was working.[49] Interestingly, a year after the bombing campaign the House of Commons Foreign Affairs Select Committee expressed the view that it was illegal though morally justified,[50] when at the time of the bombing the vast majority of the House of Commons were convinced by the argument that humanitarian intervention in support of Security Council resolutions was both morally and legally justified. There was plenty of debate in Parliament and in the country at large, but no opportunity was fashioned to reflect this in a formal vote in the House of Commons in support of the bombing campaign.[51]

---

[46]   The Lord Chancellor (Viscount Kilmuir) justified the intervention in the House of Lords as being one of 'self-defence [which] includes a situation in which the lives of a State's nationals abroad are threatened and it is necessary to intervene on that territory for their protection' – Hansard, HL, Vol 199, Cols 1349–50, 1 November 1956.

[47]   On 16 October 1956 at a meeting of ministers – cited in A. Nutting, *No End of a Lesson: The Story of Suez* (Constable, 1967) 95. On the legal advice given in 1956, see G. Marston, 'Armed Intervention in the 1956 Suez Canal Crisis: Legal Advice Tendered to the British Government' (1988) 37 *International and Comparative Law Quarterly* 807.

[48]   Hansard, HC, Vol 558, Cols 311–12, 13 September 1956; Vol 558, Col 1378, 30 October 1956.

[49]   N.D. White, *Democracy Goes to War: British Military Deployments under International Law* (Oxford University Press, 2009) 225–34.

[50]   House of Commons Foreign Affairs Select Committee, 'Kosovo', Fourth Report 1999–2000, HC 28-I, 7 June 2000, paras 124–44.

[51]   White (2009) 232–5.

The deployment of military forces for combat not only raises the question of whether the decision to go to war is compliant with the *jus ad bellum*, but also whether the subsequent conduct of the war accords with the *jus in bello* or LOAC. The Kosovo bombing campaign raised difficult issues of targeting under LOAC.[52] Two controversial targeting decisions made by NATO serve to illustrate the problems faced by commanders in applying the law. The targeting of the bridge over Grdelica Gorge on 12 April 1999, when a train carrying civilians was crossing the bridge, was justified because the bridge and railway were part of Serbia's supply network. In a report prepared by the International Criminal Tribunal for the Former Yugoslavia (ICTY) Prosecutor's Committee it was determined that the bridge was a legitimate target although the train was not. Since it was the bridge that was targeted by NATO, not the train, the attack was lawful.[53] If indeed this is the clear legal position, the legitimacy of the strike must still be doubted given the presence of the train. More controversially on 23 April 1999, NATO attacked the Serbian TV and Radio Station (RTS) causing loss of life, justifying its strike on the basis of the dual use of the Station for military communications as well as civilian broadcasting, although this was overshadowed by its claim that RTS was inciting the commission of crimes by Serbian forces. The question is whether the strike could deliver a definite military advantage that outweighed the potential civilian deaths.[54] Chapter 5 includes a further discussion of this incident, in particular the attempt by the families of the victims of the attack on the TV station to bring a claim for violation of the right to life under the ECHR.[55]

In the modern era, the UK has a track record of relying on controversial legal justifications for its military interventions. For example, the airstrikes against Syria in April 2018, which were undertaken in response to the use

---

[52] The Foreign Secretary Robin Cook stated that '[w]e have tried hard to avoid civilian casualties, but it simply is not possible to conduct a military campaign of the intensity that is needed while at the same time guaranteeing that no civilians will be killed. To pretend otherwise would be dishonest. NATO forces have worked around the clock trying to save the lives of refugees by providing them with shelter and food. We are therefore deeply concerned if any refugees have perished as a result of NATO action, and if there has been a misjudgment, we deeply regret it' – Hansard, HC, Vol 329, Col 577, 19 April 1999.

[53] ICTY, 'Final Report to the Prosecutor by the Committee Established to Review the NATO Bombing Campaign against the Federal Republic of Yugoslavia' (2000) para 62. See also the Committee's discussion of NATO's attack on the Djakovica convoy on 14 April 1999 when civilian tractors and other vehicles were destroyed with loss of life. The Committee decided that there was insufficient recklessness for war crimes charges (para 70).

[54] G. Aldrich, 'Yugoslavia's Television Studios as Military Objectives' (1999) 1 *International Law Forum* 149–50.

[55] *Bankovic v Belgium*, Appl No 52207/99, 12 December 2001.

of chemical weapons by the Assad regime, had all the hallmarks of a punitive reprisal for a violation of international law.[56] Protection of nationals,
humanitarian intervention and reprisals are part of the legal armoury of the
UK, but they are all prima facie violations of the prohibition on the use of
force in Article 2(4) of the UN Charter. Moreover, problematic *jus ad bellum*
justifications are followed in some instances by potential violations of the
jus in bello or LOAC, especially regarding targeting.[57] While the UN Charter
prohibits the threat or use of force, it clearly preserves the inherent right of
states to defend themselves from armed attack, as well as permitting them to
take military enforcement action under UN Security Council authority given
under Chapter VII in response to threats to the peace, breaches of the peace or
acts of aggression.[58]

The UK relied on more solid legal grounds of self-defence in taking military action against Argentina in 1982 to remove its invading forces from the
Falkland or Malvinas Islands over which the UK exercised sovereignty. There
was no question of any significant criticism of the (often brutal) military campaign in Parliament or in the country, nor more profoundly the British right
to the islands. The Argentinian invasion deepened the House of Commons'
will not only to defend the islands, but also not to negotiate on the issue of
its sovereignty. Only the sinking of the Argentinian warship, the *General
Belgrano*, outside an exclusion zone imposed by the UK proved to be a thorny

---

[56]   The government justified its airstrikes in the following terms: '... 2. The Syrian
regime has been killing its own people for seven years. Its use of chemical weapons,
which has exacerbated the human suffering, is a serious crime of international concern,
as a breach of the customary international law prohibition on the use of chemical
weapons, and amounts to a war crime and a crime against humanity. 3. The UK is permitted under international law, on an exceptional basis, to take measures in order to
alleviate overwhelming humanitarian suffering. The legal basis for the use of force is
humanitarian intervention, which requires three conditions to be met: (i) there is convincing evidence, generally accepted by the international community as a whole, of
extreme humanitarian distress on a large scale, requiring immediate and urgent relief;
(ii) it must be objectively clear that there is no practicable alternative to the use of force
if lives are to be saved; and (iii) the proposed use of force must be necessary and proportionate to the aim of relief of humanitarian suffering and must be strictly limited in time
and in scope to this aim (i.e. the minimum necessary to achieve that end and for no other
purpose). 4. The UK considers that military action met the requirements of humanitarian intervention in the circumstances of the present case ....' 'Syria action – UK government legal position', 14 April 2018 https://www.gov.uk/government/publications/
syria-action-uk-government-legal-position/syria-action-uk-government-legal-position.
[57]   On the LOAC rules regarding targeting see D. Turns, 'Targets' in N.D. White
and C. Henderson (eds), *Research Handbook on International Conflict and Security
Law* (Edward Elgar, 2013) 342.
[58]   UN Charter (1945) Articles 2(4), 39, 42 and 51.

issue that undermined Parliament's conviction that this was not only a war conducted in accordance with international law but was, above all, a just war.[59] No vote in the House of Commons was taken on the issue of the prosecution of the war despite heavy losses, and none was really necessary given bipartisan support. In 1985, after lingering disputes about the necessity and legality of the sinking of the *Belgrano*, the government won a vote in Parliament endorsing its decision.[60] Although this did not absolve the commander of the submarine who fired the missile from any criminal liability under LOAC, it is generally argued that the *Belgrano* was a legitimate military target. Turns states that 'all combatants in an armed conflict are by definition lawful targets who may in principle be attacked at any time and in any place' and, given that the *Belgrano* was an Argentinian naval vessel (military target) and its crew were members of the Argentinian navy (combatants), the attack was 'perfectly lawful'.[61] It is the case that there is no violation of the fundamental LOAC principle of distinction by attacking such a target but might it be the case that question marks can be raised when considering the other principles underpinning LOAC – those of military necessity, humanity and proportionality?

The justification of self-defence and the need to eliminate a substantial terrorist threat also proved sufficient for the government to carry the support of the House of Commons in the war in Afghanistan launched in October 2001 in response to the attacks on the US of 9 September 2001 ('9/11') by Al-Qaeda. The claim of self-defence was not as clear-cut as in the case of the Falklands, in that it was exercised collectively alongside the US and was directed at a state where the terrorist organisation responsible for the attack was based. However, the numerous debates on 9/11 and Afghanistan in the House of Commons did not reveal any significant dissent and there were no concerted challenges or votes on the matter. In 2001, Prime Minister Tony Blair spoke about defending civilised beliefs against the terrorist threat and acting in a just cause.[62] The presence of British troops from 2001 until their substantial withdrawal in 2014 was justified by the government as being necessary to prevent Afghanistan from becoming once again a source of terrorist attacks. This was despite the fact that the legal basis for the presence of British troops had changed from that of self-defence, to acting under Chapter VII authorisation from the Security Council with the consent of the government of Afghanistan.[63] Compliance

---

[59]   W. Little, 'Anglo-Argentine Relations and the Management of the Falklands Question' in P. Byrd (ed.), *British Foreign Policy under Thatcher* (Philip Allan, 1988) 138.
[60]   Hansard, HC, Vol 73, Cols 732–836, 18 February 1985.
[61]   Turns (2013) 348.
[62]   Hansard, HC, Vol 372, Col 814, 8 October 2001.
[63]   Starting with UN Doc S/RES/1386 (2001).

by British troops with the rules of LOAC while deployed to Afghanistan is considered in Chapters 5 and 6.

A controversial combination of self-defence and Security Council approval was used by the UK to extend its military action against the Islamic State (ISIL) terrorist group from Iraq to Syria in 2015. In response to terrorist attacks on targets in France and elsewhere, the Security Council adopted Resolution 2249, which called 'upon Member States that have the capacity to do so to take all necessary measures, in compliance with international law, in particular with the United Nations Charter, as well as international human rights, refugee and humanitarian law, on the territory under the control of ISIL also known as Da'esh, in Syria and Iraq, to redouble and coordinate their efforts to prevent and suppress terrorist acts committed' by those groups.[64] Prime Minister David Cameron relied on the right of collective self-defence of Iraq to extend RAF airstrikes, pointing to the need to defeat Islamic State in both Iraq and Syria, but bolstered this by reference to Resolution 2249.[65]

Chapter VII authority from the Security Council proved sufficient to carry the government's decisions to go to war both in Korea in 1950 and the Gulf in 1991, although in both the deployment of troops to aid South Korea and Kuwait alongside the US had already been made on the basis of collective self-defence. Thus, in Korea troops had already been sent when a substantive vote was held in the House of Commons,[66] whereas in the case of Kuwait in 1990–1991, the long interval between the invasion by Iraq and the use of force to liberate Kuwait meant that the opposition in the House of Commons had greater opportunities to test the government on its strategy, including the legal

---

[64]   UN Doc S/RES/2249 (2015) para 5.

[65]   'Let me turn to the question of legality ... the clear legal basis for military action against ISIL in Syria ... is founded on the right of self-defence as recognised in article 51 of the United Nations Charter. The right of self-defence may be exercised individually where it is necessary to the UK's own defence, and of course collectively in the defence of our friends and allies. The main basis of the global coalition's actions against ISIL in Syria is the collective self-defence of Iraq. Iraq has a legitimate Government – one that we support and help. There is a solid basis of evidence on which to conclude, first, that there is a direct link between the presence and activities of ISIL in Syria and its ongoing attack on Iraq, and secondly, that the Assad regime is unwilling and/or unable to take action necessary to prevent ISIL's continuing attack on Iraq, or indeed attacks on us. It is also clear that ISIL's campaign against the UK and our allies has reached the level of an "armed attack", such that force may lawfully be used in self-defence to prevent further atrocities being committed by ISIL. This is further underscored by the unanimous adoption of UN Security Council resolution 2249 ... The whole world came together, including all five members of the Security Council, to agree this resolution unanimously ....' Hansard, HC, Vol 602, Cols 1490–1, 26 November 2015.

[66]   Hansard, HC, Vol 477, Cols 485–90, 5 July 1950. See also UN Doc S/RES/83 (1950).

basis of the operation. This in part succeeded in persuading the government to help secure a Security Council resolution (Resolution 678 of November 1990), at least as an 'additional' legal basis to that of collective self-defence. The government readily won a procedural vote in September 1990 and another immediately before the hostilities on 15 January 1991, though a substantive vote was not held until four days after hostilities had commenced on 17 January.[67]

Although the UK, through its contribution of troops and its position as a permanent member of the Security Council, helped shape the development of coalitions of the willing acting under Security Council authority, it stretched that loose system beyond breaking point in 2003 when it joined the US in invading Iraq. The main reason for the invasion was the failure of Iraq to disarm in accordance with Security Council Resolution 687 adopted following the conflict in 1991. The inadequacies of Resolution 1441 agreed in November 2002, and the frightening prospect of supporting an American doctrine of pre-emptive defence, led to much greater Parliamentary and public pressure on the government in the lead-up to the war. This criticism was maintained after the initial success of the invasion in removing Saddam from power gave way to a brutal and intractable insurgency. This pressure culminated in the announcement of an Inquiry into Iraq in June 2009. When it reported in 2016, the Inquiry revealed that the legal advice given to the government was by no means as unequivocal as was made public at the time.[68] In March 2003, a substantive vote in the House of Commons was held two days before the invasion and was won relatively easily by the government. The House was persuaded by the release of a sanitised version of the Attorney General's advice stating that there was a clear legal basis for the invasion in the original Security Council authorisation to use force against Iraq in Resolution 678 of 1990, which was said to be 'revived' by Iraq's failure to comply with Security Council resolutions adopted after the conflict ended in 1991.[69] Subsequent evidence given to

---

[67] Hansard, HC, Vol 177, Col 883, 7 September 1990; Hansard, HC, Vol 183, Col 743, 15 January 1991; Hansard, HC, Vol 185, Col 31, 21 January 1991.

[68] J. Chilcot, 'Report of the Iraq Inquiry: Executive Summary', HC 264, 6 July 2016, 119–20; Attorney General's Advice released on 17 March 2003 in Hansard, HL, Vol 646, WA2-3, 17 March 2003.

[69] Hansard, HC, Vol 401, Cols 760–4, 18 March 2003, when Prime Minister Tony Blair relied on the Attorney General's Advice in proposing a substantive vote. The Attorney General's full advice of 7 March 2003 was not released until 28 April 2005, in which he concluded that 'if the matter ever came before a court', that court 'may well' conclude that Resolution 1441 did require a 'further Council decision in order to revive the authorization in' Resolution 678; 'Full text: Iraq legal advice', *The Guardian*, 28 April 2005 http://www.guardian.co.uk/politics/2005/apr/28/election2005.uk.

the Iraq Inquiry showed that the Attorney General was initially of the opinion that on balance the invasion was to occur without UN authority.[70]

Even when a clear authorisation is given by the Security Council, the use of force that follows can be problematic in both *jus ad bellum* and *jus in bello* terms. In 2011, in the face of brutal repression in Libya by the government of Colonel Gaddafi, the UK government strove to operate more clearly within the parameters of the UN Charter than it did in Iraq in 2003. Together with France and the US, the UK secured Resolution 1973 authorising necessary measures under Chapter VII to enforce a no-fly zone over Libya and to 'protect civilians and civilian populated areas under threat of attack'.[71] Resolution 1973 was narrowly adopted by 10 votes in favour and five abstentions (Brazil, China, Germany, India and Russia). The abstaining states expressed concern about the interpretation of the broad mandate given to NATO states. Negative votes, including the vetoes of China and Russia, seemed to be avoided because of the imminent nature of the attack on the rebel stronghold of Benghazi, and the need to prevent core international crimes from being committed.[72] However, the aerial use of force by NATO in March–April 2011 seemed to be increasingly directed at supporting the rebels and in several respects went beyond the protection of civilians as mandated by Resolution 1973. What started out in appearance at least as an application of an emerging 'responsibility to protect' doctrine,[73] seemed by mid-June to be heading towards another instance of regime change with all the problems that entailed.

In the House of Commons, Prime Minister David Cameron informed the House about the implementation of Resolution 1973, and spoke about the urgency of the situation due to the imminent attack on Benghazi where Gaddafi had threatened to show no mercy.[74] Furthermore, the Prime Minister informed the House that the Cabinet had been given clear legal advice from the Attorney General, which he summarised for the House in terms that Resolution 1973 was a Chapter VII resolution clearly authorising necessary measures to protect civilians and enforce a no-fly zone, and such a Resolution was a legally recognised basis on which to deploy and use force.[75] However, that legal advice did not anticipate the problems of mission creep and the subsequent interpretation of Resolution 1973. The House of Commons supported the

---

[70] Chilcot (2016) 199–20.
[71] UN Doc S/RES/1973 (2011).
[72] UN Doc S/PV/6498 (2011).
[73] The doctrine of Responsibility to Protect (R2P) was encapsulated in the UN's World Summit Outcome Document of 2005 – UN Doc A/RES/60/1 (2005) paras 138–9.
[74] Hansard, HC, Vol 525, Col 611, 18 March 2011.
[75] Ibid, Col 613.

government's decision to launch airstrikes in Libya in a vote held after the air campaign had started,[76] and therefore could not provide any challenge to that decision, only *ex post facto* scrutiny. The House of Commons can only play a valedictory role if it is consulted after the decision to deploy has been made and the armed forces are in action. Another lesson from Iraq that does not seem to have been accepted by the government in the Libyan crisis was that the full advice given by the Attorney General on the international legal basis of the operation should be made available to the House of Commons and not just to the Cabinet in order to enable MPs to make an informed decision.

In the modern era, the UK has a track record of relying on controversial legal justifications for its military interventions. While the UN Charter prohibits the threat or use of force, it allows states to defend themselves from armed attack as well as to take military enforcement action under UN Security Council authority given under Chapter VII. This has led to the UK straining to apply these exceptions, for example as regards Security Council authority in Iraq in 2003 and self-defence in Syria in 2015. In addition, the UK has regularly resorted to alleged customary rights to use force, most controversially it is probably the only state to have consistently claimed, in recent decades at least, the right of humanitarian intervention, for example in Kosovo in 1999 and Syria in 2018. Given the controversial nature of a number of its deployments, various forms of accountability might be expected to follow. The most prevalent is political accountability and there is plenty of evidence that international law plays a significant role in Parliamentary debates on wars and post-conflict situations but the actual decision to deploy troops is, despite the debates and occasional votes held in the House of Commons, a governmental issue. Parliament has not been prepared to challenge the government even when the legal basis of the war is clearly suspect, with the exception of Syria in 2013. Public inquiries such as the one held into the invasion of Iraq provide accountability for decisions made but are not tasked with making legal determinations.[77] While international law

---

[76] Hansard, HC, Vol 525, Cols 739, 799, 21 March 2011.

[77] In announcing the establishment of the Iraq Inquiry in 2009 Prime Minister Gordon Brown stated: 'With the last British combat troops about to return home from Iraq, now is the right time to ensure that we have a proper process in place to enable us to learn the lessons of the complex and often controversial events of the last six years. I am today announcing the establishment of an independent Privy Counsellor committee of inquiry which will consider the period from summer 2001, before military operations began in March 2003, and our subsequent involvement in Iraq right up to the end of July this year. The Inquiry is essential because it will ensure that, by learning lessons, we strengthen the health of our democracy, our diplomacy and our military … No Inquiry has looked at such a long period, and no Inquiry has the powers to look in so much breadth … the Iraq Inquiry will look at the run-up to conflict, the conflict itself

on the use of force by states has limited traction in Parliament and in public inquiries, it has even less before domestic courts.

4.4   CHALLENGES BEFORE THE COURTS

According to Rosara Joseph the 'courts have refused to intervene in the exercise of the war prerogative, but have been more ready to intervene in cases involving the exercise of powers incidental to the war prerogative'.[78] Attempts have been made by litigants to indirectly impugn decisions to go to war, for example in the *Jones* case reviewed below, but have been rebuffed.[79] The dismissal of the challenge by the Campaign for Nuclear Disarmament (CND) as to the legality of the decision to go to war against Iraq in 2003 is typical of the deference of the courts towards the prerogative power to deploy troops. The *CND* case was brought in the lead-up to the invasion of Iraq, a period when there was intensive debate about the need for a clear authorising resolution from the Security Council before any force was used by the UK. As stated in the leading judgment by Brown LJ, '[w]hat the applicants ... seek by this judicial review application is solely declaratory relief, an advisory declaration as to the true meaning of Resolution 1441 and more particularly as to whether it authorises States to take military action in the event of non-compliance by Iraq with its terms'.[80] CND argued that Resolution 1441 of 2002 did not contain such an authorisation. 'In short, the court is being invited to declare that the UK Government would be acting in breach of international law were it to take military action against Iraq without a further Resolution.' Brown LJ was clearly sceptical of the claim when stating that: '[i]t is, to say the least, a novel and ambitious claim'.[81] He dismissed the case on three main grounds. First, on the basis that the court had 'no jurisdiction to declare the true interpretation of an international instrument which has not been incorporated into English domestic law and which it is unnecessary to interpret for the purposes of determining a person's rights or duties under domestic law'. Secondly, the 'court will in any event decline to embark upon the determination of an issue if to do so would be damaging to the public interest in the field of international relations, national security or defence' rendering the application 'non-justiciable'.

---

and the reconstruction, so that we can learn lessons in each and every area.' Chilcot (2016) 2.

[78]   R. Joseph, *The War Prerogative: History, Reform and Constitutional Design* (Oxford University Press, 2013) 1.

[79]   *R v Jones* [2006] UKHL 16, paras 29–30.

[80]   *Campaign for Nuclear Disarmament v The Prime Minister of the United Kingdom* [2002] EWHC 2777 (Admin) para 2.

[81]   Ibid, para 2.

Finally, '[e]ven were this claim not barred by either of the above considerations, I would still reject it on the ground that advisory declarations should
not be made save for demonstrably good reason. Here there is none. There is
no sound basis for believing the government to have been wrongly advised as
to the true position in international law. Nor, in any event, could there be any
question here of declaring illegal whatever decision or action may hereafter
be taken in the light of the United Kingdom's understanding of its position in
international law'.[82] The refusal of the courts to scrutinise the decisions of government in the light of the international rules on the use of force is reflected in
Brown LJ's dismissal of CND's 'fanciful' contention that the UK government
was in danger of 'going to war under a mistake of law'. The judge declared that
it was most unlikely that the government made a mistake on the law since 'it
has access to the best advice, not only from law officers but also from a number
of specialists in the field'.[83] Despite this certainty, there have been unresolved
question marks over the legality of the invasion of Iraq in 2003 despite litigation before the courts and a very expensive public inquiry.

Other attempts to gain judicial recognition of the illegality of the invasion
of Iraq in 2003 were also unsuccessful. While the courts have accepted that
the HRA 1998 is applicable in some circumstances to civilians and soldiers in
Iraq,[84] they have been unwilling to accept claims under the Act that amount to
questioning the legality of the invasion. In the *Gentle* case before the House
of Lords, the applicants were 'the mothers of two young men, both aged 19,
who lost their lives while serving in the British army in Iraq. Fusilier Gordon
Campbell Gentle was serving with the 1st Battalion The Royal Highland
Fusiliers when he was killed by a roadside bomb on 28 June 2004. Trooper
David Jeffrey Clarke was serving with the Queen's Royal Lancers when he
was killed by "friendly fire" on 25 March 2003.'[85] Lord Bingham summarised
their case:

> Article 2 of the Convention imposes a duty on member states to protect life. This
> duty extends to the lives of soldiers. Armed conflict exposes soldiers to the risk
> of death. Therefore a state should take timely steps to obtain reliable legal advice
> before committing its troops to armed conflict. Had the UK done this before invad-
> ing Iraq in March 2003, it would arguably not have invaded. Had it not invaded,
> Fusilier Gentle and Trooper Clarke would not have been killed.[86]

---

[82]   Ibid, para 47.
[83]   Ibid, para 44.
[84]   See Chapter 8.
[85]   *R (Gentle) v The Prime Minister* [2008] UKHL 20, para 1.
[86]   Ibid, para 3.

It was not the logic of this argument that was fatal to the claim but the fact that Article 2 should not be read as a 'generalised provision protective of life' and had 'never been held to apply to the process of deciding upon the lawfulness of resort to arms' even though decisions to go to war resulted in loss of life.[87] Lord Bingham did feel it necessary to justify his decision further saying that 'the lawfulness of military action has no bearing on the risk of fatalities', citing the effectiveness (from Japan's perspective) of its attack on Pearl Harbour in December 1941, which was illegal but minimised Japanese casualties.[88] This seems to disregard the essence of the claim that a decision not to launch the attack because it was unlawful would have resulted in no casualties.

Baroness Hale was critical of the Attorney General's advice on the legality of the invasion of Iraq in 2003, and expressed great sympathy with the mothers of dead soldiers, but ultimately decided against their claims.[89] An understanding of the right to life as protected by the ECHR was crucial, with Lady Hale stating: 'I cannot reasonably foresee that Strasbourg would construct out of article 2 a duty not to send soldiers to fight in an unlawful war. The lawfulness of war is an issue between states, not between individuals or between individuals and the state.'[90] Lady Hale reinforced this interpretation by expressing the underlying judicial deference to the executive in decisions to go to war:

> A further reason not to spell such a duty out of article 2 is that it would require both the domestic courts of this country, and the European Court of Human Rights in Strasbourg, to rule upon the legality of the use of force against Iraq in international law. This is beyond our competence. The state that goes to war cannot and should not be the judge of whether or not the war was lawful in international law. That question can only be authoritatively decided, not by us or by Strasbourg, but by the international institutions which police the international treaties governing the law of war.[91]

Those international institutions, namely the Security Council, the ICJ and the ICC have singularly failed to hold the UK to account for any of its international interventions, with the exception of the relatively mild judicial admonition of its intervention in the *Corfu Channel Case* in 1949.

However, with the exercise of the prerogative in other areas of executive action increasingly coming within the purview of the courts, judicial scrutiny of decisions to go to war may be closer than is commonly thought. Leading constitutional lawyers have written that 'the need for military effectiveness in

---

[87]   Ibid, paras 6–7.
[88]   Ibid, para 8.
[89]   Ibid, paras 53–58.
[90]   Ibid, para 57.
[91]   Ibid, para 58.

the defence of the realm does not mean … that the law of judicial review has no role to play in this as in other areas of governmental activity'.[92] Although the transformation of the Appellate Committee of the House of Lords into the Supreme Court in October 2009 was in many ways simply a change of name, it may embolden the Court to take on the most difficult challenge for a constitutional court by taking an opportunity to review a controversial decision to go to war. The Supreme Court has been willing to review the legality of non-forcible measures imposed as a result of a Security Council decision in the *Ahmed* case of 2010, the first case heard by the Supreme Court when it declared that certain aspects of their implementation in the domestic legal order were *ultra vires*.[93] However, obligations to impose sanctions against states, groups and individuals imposed by the Security Council under Article 41 of the UN Charter are incorporated into UK law by executive orders under the United Nations Act 1946. In contrast, military actions whether undertaken as a result of a Security Council authorisation or on the basis of customary rights, are not seen as creating rights and duties justiciable in domestic courts. This is illustrated by the case of *R v Jones* discussed below along with the government's refusal to accept the jurisdiction of the ICC over the crime of aggression, which can be seen as part of a concerted effort to keep claims about the legality of its military actions out of the courts.

4.5   INDIVIDUAL RESPONSIBILITY FOR AGGRESSION

The *CND* and *Gentle* cases were brought against the UK government, in effect amounting to claims that the state was legally responsible for violating international law prohibiting the aggressive use of force. They failed, according to Lady Hale in the *Gentle* case, because that is an issue for international institutions that have jurisdiction over inter-state uses of force and not for domestic courts. However, apart from the *Corfu Channel Case* decided by the ICJ in 1949, that responsibility remains untested at the international level. With the development of international criminal law, particularly the establishment of the ICC in 1998 with jurisdiction over war crimes, crimes against humanity, genocide and aggression,[94] attention has turned to the issue of whether individuals (political and military leaders, commanders and soldiers) can be held

---

[92]   Bradley and Ewing (2007) 348.
[93]   *Her Majesty's Treasury v Mohammed Jabar Ahmed and Others* [2010] UKSC 2, para 61 (Lord Hope).
[94]   Rome Statute of the International Criminal Court (1998) Article 5(1).

criminally responsible for violations of the *jus ad bellum* by committing the crime of aggression.

After 1945, the traditional responsibility of the state for violations of international law was slowly supplemented by the concept of individual criminal responsibility following the judgment of the Nuremberg International Military Tribunal in 1946. The defendants at Nuremberg had argued that 'international law is concerned with the actions of sovereign States, and provides no punishment for individuals; and further, that where the act in question is an act of State, those who carry it out are not personally responsible, but are protected by the doctrine of the sovereignty of the State'. The Tribunal's response was to declare that: '[c]rimes against international law are committed by men, not by abstract entities, and only by punishing individuals who commit such crimes can the provisions of international law be enforced'.[95] Criminal responsibility for war crimes is addressed in Chapters 5 and 6, while the issue of the crime of aggression (what were called 'crimes against peace' at Nuremberg) is considered here.

Soldiers are expected to follow orders, including orders to quell insurrections at home or to deploy to foreign lands to fight the forces of other states, insurgents or other armed groups, irrespective of the wider political and legal debates. However, international criminal law, which focuses on serious violations of the *jus ad bellum* and *jus in bello*, is making slow inroads into the soldier's obedience to the nation state, making the legality of the military operation in terms of deployment and conduct of increasing concern to commanders and soldiers alike. The international legality of any external troop deployment or use of force may seem to be largely a matter for governmental decision, although there will be lively debates in Parliament and various expressions of public opinion in polls and demonstrations, both peaceful and violent. However, it is also of vital concern to British military personnel. They need to be reassured that their actions are lawful (and hopefully just) if morale is to be maintained, but it is also becoming increasingly realised that there are potential, albeit still remote, issues of legal responsibility too.

This was illustrated in the build-up to the Iraq War in 2003, the legal basis of which was disputed as there was no clear UN Security Council authority to militarily enforce the disarmament provisions that had been imposed by that organ on Iraq at the end of the Gulf War in 1991.[96] The Chief of Defence Staff, Admiral Boyce, insisted that he needed a clear statement of the legality

---

[95]   *Trial of the Major War Criminals before the International Military Tribunal,* Nuremberg, 14 November 1945–1 October 1946, 223.
[96]   See UN Doc S/RES/687 (1991); UN Doc S/RES/1441 (2002).

of the operation from the Attorney General.[97] This was just one aspect of the pressure upon the Attorney General to change his initial legal advice to the government, which was that there was a reasonable case in favour of the invasion but one that might not survive judicial scrutiny, to his statement made on the eve of conflict in 2003 that the action was clearly lawful as it could be based on the authority to use force given by the Security Council in 1990.[98] Admiral Boyce gave evidence to the Iraq Inquiry in 2009 expressing the view that becoming a party to the Rome Statute on the International Criminal Court 1998 meant that his 'constituency … of soldiers, sailors and airmen … had to be told that what they were doing was legal'.[99] He did not go so far as to state that the advent of the Rome Statute would give rise to the liability of soldiers if they followed an order from their military and political leaders to prosecute an illegal war, but there certainly seemed to be a view, shared by the Attorney General himself, that there was a risk of such.[100] Furthermore, if the order was unlawful then there arose the possibility of soldiers refusing to obey such on the basis that they may be prosecuted before national or international criminal courts for the international crime of aggression committed pursuant to an order of government or military superior. Under the Rome Statute, soldiers cannot use superior orders as a defence to a charge of committing an international crime unless they can prove that they were under a legal obligation under domestic law to obey the orders, that they did not know the order was unlawful and, furthermore, that the order was not manifestly unlawful.[101]

The contention that the Attorney General was wrong and that an ordinary soldier cannot be prosecuted for the crime of aggression is put strongly by Peter Rowe: 'a British soldier faced no risk at all of liability for the crimes of murder or aggression under English law when he crossed the start line to take part in military operations against Iraq or at any other time during the involvement of British armed forces in that country'. According to Rowe, the soldier's concern should be to avoid committing violations of military law, including LOAC: '[w]hat he did face was liability for his actions in dealing with civilians and civilian detainees where these amounted to offences under English criminal law (including war crimes) or under military law'.[102] For Rowe, this

---

[97]   J. Chilcot, 'The Report of the Iraq Inquiry', 6 July 2016, Vol 5, section 5: 'Advice on the Legal Basis for Military Action', November 2002 to March 2003, para 699.

[98]   Ibid, para 93.

[99]   Ibid, paras 702–3.

[100]   Ibid, para 707.

[101]   Rome Statute of the International Criminal Court (1998) Article 33.

[102]   P. Rowe, 'The criminal liability of a British soldier merely for participating in the Iraq war 2003: a response to the Chilcot evidence' (2010) 10 *Criminal Law Review* 752 at 759.

signified that a soldier would not be prosecuted for the crime of aggression, and further that his duty to obey orders to deploy was undiminished:

> The obligation on a soldier to obey only lawful commands must be understood to mean that he must disobey only orders which, if carried out, would subject him to criminal responsibility under English law or under international law. The crime of aggression is likely to retain its characteristic of being a policy makers' crime. The ordinary soldier will never be responsible for this crime and therefore he should not be able to claim this as a justification for disobeying a lawful command.[103]

Rowe states further that it would be inappropriate to charge any British soldiers with the crime of aggression 'except, perhaps, those individuals at the very pinnacle of the military chain of command'.[104]

Following this reasoning, an order to deploy troops in an operation amounting to an unlawful use of force may constitute the crime of aggression within the meaning of the Rome Statute, and may give rise to the liability of senior military personnel as well as the political leaders who made that decision. Aggression is defined under the Rome Statute as 'the planning, preparation, initiation or execution, by a person in a position effectively to exercise control over or to direct the political or military action of a State, of an act of aggression which by its character, gravity and scale, constitutes a manifest violation of the Charter of the United Nations'.[105] Aggression did not become active as a crime within the ICC's jurisdiction until 2018 when a definition of aggression was finally agreed and, therefore, did not apply to the 2003 invasion of Iraq. Furthermore, the UK has not ratified the crime of aggression amendment to the Rome Statute but, by so refusing, it lays itself open to accusations that it has done so because its practice of using force against other states has been legally problematic.

In 2017, when deciding not to ratify the changes to the Rome Statute that activated the jurisdiction of the ICC over the crime of aggression, the UK argued that aggression was best dealt with by the Security Council rather by the ICC. It further argued that prosecutions for aggression by the ICC should be limited to nationals from those states that have ratified the amendment to the Statute on the crime of aggression.[106] The latter contention was accepted by the state parties to the Rome Statute in a resolution of 2017, which stated that in the cases of state referrals and *proprio motu* investigations the 'Court shall not exercise its jurisdiction regarding a crime of aggression when committed

---

[103] Ibid, 760.

[104] Ibid, 756.

[105] Rome Statute of the International Criminal Court (1998) Article 8(1)bis.

[106] G. Robertson, 'At last, a law that could have stopped Blair and Bush invading Iraq', *The Guardian*, 16 July 2018.

by a national or on the territory of a State Party that has not ratified or accepted these amendments'.[107] This leaves open the possibility of referral of cases of aggression by the Security Council.[108] However, as a permanent member of the Security Council the UK is able to prevent referral of situations involving its soldiers and civilians by the use of the veto. The UK's obstructive attitude towards the crime of aggression in 2017 belies its initial enthusiasm for the Court in 1998 when aggression was included as a crime but remained inactive until the state parties agreed on a definition.

The Nuremberg judgment of 1946 declared that 'to initiate a war of aggression ... is the supreme international crime'.[109] The principles of international law recognised by the Tribunal and the judgment itself were affirmed by the UN General Assembly in 1946.[110] There is little doubt that the prohibition of aggression is a fundamental rule of international law, and gives rise to both state and individual criminal responsibility, but the UK courts have made it clear that it has not become part of UK law. In *R v Jones*, decided by the House of Lords in 2006, the accused's defence to a charge of criminal damage to military equipment after breaking into an RAF base on 13 March 2003, was that she was trying to prevent the commission of a greater crime of aggression against Iraq. This contention was dismissed by the House of Lords in reasoning that *in abstracto* almost seems the reverse of the Nuremberg principle that international crimes are committed by individuals not by abstract entities (states):

> A charge of aggression, if laid against an individual in a domestic court, would involve determination of his responsibility as a leader but would presuppose commission of the crime by his own state or a foreign state. Thus resolution of the charge would (unless the issue had been decided by the Security Council or some other third party) call for a decision on the culpability in going to war either of Her Majesty's Government or a foreign government, or perhaps both if the states had gone to war as allies. But there are well-established rules that the courts will be very slow to review the exercise of prerogative powers in relation to the conduct of foreign affairs and the deployment of the armed services, and very slow to adjudicate upon rights arising out of transactions entered into between sovereign states on the plane of international law.[111]

While recognising the crime of aggression existed in customary international law, the House of Lords stated that it was not a crime in English law. Without

---

[107] Resolution ICC-ASP/16/Res.5, 14 December 2017.
[108] Rome Statute of the International Criminal Court (1998) Article 13(b).
[109] *Trial of the Major War Criminals before the International Military Tribunal*, 186.
[110] UN Doc A/RES/95(I) (1946).
[111] *R v Jones* [2006] UKHL 16 at para 30 (Lord Bingham).

commenting on the legality or otherwise of the invasion of Iraq, Lord Bingham made it clear that the courts are reluctant to review the exercise of prerogative powers over foreign affairs and the deployment of the armed services. In addition to respecting the role of the executive, Lord Bingham stated that decisions as to what conduct should be criminalised was for Parliament not for the courts.[112]

In his evidence to the Iraq Inquiry in 2010, the former Attorney General Lord Goldsmith stated that a resort for force against Iraq in 2003 without a 'credible legal base would be to advocate the commission of a crime of aggression and would expose members of the armed forces to charges of murder'.[113] In 2003, prior to the invasion of Iraq, the Attorney General expressed the fear that there was a remote chance of prosecution of military and civilian personnel for the crime of aggression, which as a crime under international law 'automatically forms part of domestic law'.[114] The Court in *Jones* blocked the 'automatic' incorporation of the crime of aggression under customary international law into UK law, while the government has blocked the treaty crime of aggression from becoming part of UK law by not ratifying the amendment to the Rome Statute that activated the crime in 2018.

There remains little or no prospect of the ICC or a UK court trying political or military leaders for aggression. Similarly, military personnel should escape prosecution for aggression if captured in another state that has accepted the jurisdiction of the ICC over aggression, as the agreement of state parties in 2017 confines such prosecution to nationals from states ratifying the amendment on aggression. However, it cannot be ruled out that a state that has not ratified the Rome Statute may prosecute captured British soldiers relying on the Nuremberg precedent that international crimes give rise to universal jurisdiction under customary international law and, as such, can be tried in any court. In the oft-cited *Eichmann* case of 1961, the Israeli court asserted Israel's 'right to punish' the defendant, who was accused of crimes against humanity committed against Jews as a result of his part in the 'Final Solution'. This right was derived from two sources: 'a universal source (pertaining to the whole of mankind), which vests the right to prosecute and punish crimes of this order in every State within the family of nations, and a specific or national source, which gives the victim nation the right to try any who assault its existence'.[115]

---

[112]   Ibid, paras 29–30.
[113]   Cited in Rowe (2010) 752.
[114]   'Full text: Iraq legal advice', para 34, *The Guardian*, 28 April 2005 http://www.guardian.co.uk/politics/2005/apr/28/election2005.uk.
[115]   *Attorney-General of the Government of Israel v Eichmann* (1961) 36 ILR 5 at para 30.

Overall, the chances of an ordinary British soldier being prosecuted for his or her involvement in an illegal war remains remote. Article 8bis of the Rome Statute makes it clear that such crimes, at least for the purposes of the Statute, are committed by persons who exercise control or direct the political actions of a state. However, the presence of a recognised international crime of aggression, in both the Rome Statute and under customary international law, is an increasingly relevant norm for the ordinary soldier. They may not wish to fight in aggressive wars and, moreover, they may claim that they have an obligation not to fight in these situations, irrespective of an order to so do from their military superiors. However, such soldiers will be prosecuted under UK military law for disobeying orders, which are at least lawful under domestic law, and this will be more pressing on their decision-making than the abstract crime of aggression. When weighing national obligations against international ones, soldiers will probably decide on purely pragmatic grounds not to disobey orders solely on the basis that there is a remote international norm prohibiting aggression, the parameters of which confine it to the highest levels of political and military leadership. Furthermore, it remains the case that the legality of the invasion of Iraq in 2003 remains disputed even after an extensive public inquiry, so soldiers in similar situations cannot be certain that what they are being ordered to do is unlawful, particularly when the Attorney General has testified to the legality of the action.

4.6 A RIGHT TO (SELECTIVE) CONSCIENTIOUS OBJECTION?

The analysis in the preceding section demonstrates that ordinary British soldiers are not going to be prosecuted for the crime of aggression before the ICC or a UK court. However, does this mean that they are obliged to obey an order to deploy to an overseas conflict which does not appear to be taken in self-defence or under UN Security Council authority? Such uses of force are prima facie breaches of the fundamental rule of international law prohibiting the use of force by states. While Peter Rowe is adamant that 'a soldier must disobey an order which would impose criminal liability on him under international law', for example an order to attack civilian targets, nevertheless he is obliged to obey orders given to him that do not impose criminal liability even though they are contrary to international law.[116] An order to take part in an aggressive war does not impose criminal liability on a soldier (except perhaps for those at the top of the chain of command) and, following Rowe's logic,

---

[116] Rowe (2010) 758.

should be obeyed even though it is a breach of international law, indeed is potentially an order to commit a serious international crime.

Clearly, it would be detrimental to military discipline if soldiers could question orders on the basis that the war or use of force was, in their view and probably in the view of others, illegal. However, aggression is an international crime, albeit one that does not extend in application to the lower ranks of the armed forces, and as Rowe admits the soldier's duty is to obey commands that do not breach domestic or international law.[117] The argument that soldiers must obey orders, which breach international law but will not give rise to criminal liability, seems to be in contradiction or at least sits uneasily with that duty to obey lawful orders. The problem for soldiers relying on the illegality of the war as a reason for refusing to obey an order to deploy to such a war is that, as has been seen, many of the conflicts the UK has been involved in involve controversy about their legal basis (for example Suez 1956, Kosovo 1999 and Iraq 2003), with very few clear judicial or impartial determinations that the UK has breached international law. That is probably the real reason why soldiers should obey an order to deploy to such a war. From the soldiers' perspective, they are more likely to face a court martial for refusal to obey an order lawfully made under domestic law than they are to be prosecuted for the international crime of aggression.

Furthermore, a court martial is not going to accept arguments relating to the legality of the war when that war was authorised by the government and endorsed by Parliament and is therefore lawful under the British constitution. Rowe concludes that: '[i]n these situations it is much better for a State to take the line that a belief by a soldier that the military activities of his State infringe international law ... should be reflected through machinery to deal with conscientious objection to service in a particular theatre of operations'.[118] However, it appears that there is no right of selective conscientious objection in an army of volunteers, although conscientious objection has been allowed during times of conscription in the two world wars.[119] Article 9 of the ECHR guarantees the right to freedom of conscience, thought and religion but 'it is a qualified right ... meaning that the state may place limitations upon its

---

[117]   Ibid, 757.
[118]   Ibid, 759.
[119]   Military Service Act (1916) section 2; National Service (Armed Forces) Act (1939) section 5. See G. Wilson, 'Selective Conscientious Objection in the Aftermath of Iraq: Reconsidering Objection to a Specific War' (2008) 12 *The International Journal of Human Rights* 665 at 669–70. See, more broadly, L. Toomey, 'The Right to Conscientious Objection to Military Service: Recent Jurisprudence of the United Nations Working Group on Arbitrary Detention' (2019) 19 *Human Rights Law Review* 787.

exercise in the pursuit of wider interests'.[120] In particular Article 9(2) states that the right 'shall be subject only to such limitations as are prescribed by law and are necessary in a democratic society in the interests of public safety, for the protection of public order, health or morals, or for the protection of the rights and freedoms of others'.

The exercise of the margin of appreciation given to the state under the ECHR is reflected in the way the courts have dismissed claims to conscientious objection. In *Khan* (2004), the RAF Summary Appeal Court dismissed the defendant's argument against his conviction for being absent without leave after failing to appear for duty in the build-up to the invasion of Iraq in 2003. The Court did not accept his defence of conscientious objection, and dismissed his argument based on a violation of Article 9 of the ECHR.[121] In *Lyons* (2011), the defendant challenged his conviction for disobeying a lawful command prior to deployment to Afghanistan on the basis that he should be treated as a conscientious objector who believed the UK's involvement to be wrong.[122] The defendant had applied in accordance with Navy procedure to be discharged from the service on the grounds of conscientious objection, but that application had been dismissed by the Navy and his appeal to the Advisory Committee on Conscientious Objectors failed.[123] The Court Martial Appeal Court (CMAC) dismissed his appeal, including the claim that his rights under Article 9 of the ECHR had been violated. The Court accepted that the procedure for dealing with claims of conscientious objection satisfied 'the requirements of being prescribed by law and being necessary in a democratic society in the interests of public safety, the protection of public order and the protection of others'. The Court emphasised that 'a person who voluntarily enters military service undertakes serious responsibilities potentially involving the lives and service of others', signifying that the person has to accept commands even while applying for recognition as a conscientious objector: 'otherwise he could immediately escape from the responsibilities which he had voluntarily accepted, regardless of the consequent risk to others and regardless of whether or not his claim was well founded'.[124]

The soldier's dilemma when faced with an order that they consider to be unlawful is neatly captured by Baroness Hale in the *Gentle* case:

This places the individual British service man or woman in a very difficult position. If he or she obeys the order and it is not in fact lawful, then he or she could in theory

---

[120] Wilson (2008) 671.
[121] *Khan v Royal Air Force Summary Appeal Court* [2004] EWHC 2230 (Admin).
[122] *Lyons v R* [2011] EWCA Crim 2808.
[123] Ibid, para 21.
[124] Ibid, para 31.

face prosecution for the illegal act. Under the ICC Statute, the more sceptical he or she is about the legality of the order, the less possible it might be to rely on a defence of superior orders: see article 33. If he or she disobeys the order and it is in fact lawful, then he or she will probably face a court martial for disobeying it. A state which expects its soldiers to obey their orders irrespective of their own views on the lawfulness of those orders should, it seems to me, owe a correlative duty to its soldiers to ensure that those orders are lawful. Operationally it is obvious that the burden should lie on the person giving rather than the person receiving the orders.[125]

At this point in *Gentle* Lady Hale was discussing the case of Flight Lieutenant Kendall-Smith, who refused to deploy to Iraq in 2005, and was court martialled for refusing to obey a lawful command. The prosecution accepted that for it to succeed the order to deploy to Iraq must have been lawful under both domestic law and international law. The Judge Advocate ruled that by the time of the order to redeploy in 2005 the UK's military action in Iraq had received an authorisation from the UN Security Council in 2004,[126] thereby making it lawful. In any case the judge made it clear that the defendant's own belief in the illegality of the war was not a defence and that his duty was to obey the order as long as it was not obviously contrary to law.[127] According to Gary Wilson:

> Although not specifically ruling on any plea of conscientious objection, some aspects of the court martial's judgment imply that Kendall-Smith's stance, whereby he refused to be deployed to a conflict on the basis of his belief that it was unlawful, would not find favour in UK law. The court martial ruled that the question of the legality or otherwise of the action in Iraq was not for him to answer, and that once advice had been given by the Attorney-General to the government that the planned UK action was lawful this must be accepted. Military forces were not permitted to 'go behind' such advice. Although it was accepted that Kendall-Smith had acted on moral grounds in disobeying the orders given to him, much emphasis was placed upon the importance for military discipline of the obedience of orders. It was expressly stated that military officers cannot pick and choose which orders they will obey, but must rather follow all of them. The obvious implication to be drawn from the court martial's ruling in the case of Malcolm Kendall-Smith is that selective conscientious objection has no basis as grounds for a refusal to be deployed within a specific military operation.[128]

The question remains as to whether this is a sustainable position in law. The crime of aggression in international law is one that gives rise to individual responsibility. If British soldiers internalise the norm criminalising aggressive

---

[125] *Gentle* [2008] para 50.
[126] UN Doc S/RES/1546 (2004).
[127] Case summarised by Lady Hale in *Gentle* [2008] para 50.
[128] Wilson (2008) 668.

wars, they have an obligation not to be involved in such actions. The fact that none of the organs of state (the executive, Parliament, and the courts) respects the obligations that flow from that criminalisation is deeply problematic. If the crime of aggression is a primary rule that guides the behaviour of military personnel,[129] the secondary rules of the legal system, containing what Hart called 'the means of social control', should reflect that and ensure compliance with those obligations.[130] In identifying the heart of a legal system as a union of primary and secondary rules Hart was referring to the primary rules of obligation within a legal order which reflect fundamental norms against violence, and the secondary rules which essentially help identify, shape and enforce those rules.[131] These primary rules are mainly found in national laws but they will increasingly incorporate rules derived from international norms. At this point in time, the UK has accepted that war crimes, crimes against humanity and genocide are crimes that can be prosecuted within the UK's legal order,[132] but has resisted the incorporation of the crime of aggression. However, more broadly, the UK cannot prevent the blurring of the boundaries between national and international law, which means that the latter is increasingly becoming relevant in decision-making as there are a number of international rules that control the use of violence by individuals as well as states. These rules are relevant for political and military leaders in their decision-making and, at some point in the future, they may be applied by the courts. An ordinary soldier fighting in a foreign war is subject to national military law, but his actions in a foreign state are judged by the rules of international law. Furthermore, once soldiers demonstrate an 'internal aspect' to those rules, meaning they evaluate their conduct and the conduct of others by reference to them,[133] their legitimate expectation is that the government should not order them to violate those rules but, if it does, soldiers should have a lawful reason to disobey those orders.

4.7   CONCLUSION

The external deployment of troops is decided upon by the executive and debated in Parliament at least partially in terms of the legality of state action under the *jus ad bellum*. Rudimentary political accountability is not matched by any legal accountability before the courts. Furthermore, the presumption of the legality of external military operations, which permeates both political and legal scrutiny, leads to a complacent attitude of the UK government and

---

[129] H.L.A. Hart, *The Concept of Law* (Clarendon, 3rd edn, 2012) 90.
[130] Ibid, 170.
[131] Ibid, 91–9.
[132] International Criminal Court Act (2001).
[133] Hart (2012), 89.

military that commanders and soldiers are acting lawfully when they follow orders to deploy to Britain's wars. The illegality or, at the very least, the legally problematic nature of certain external troop deployments, should lead to commanders and soldiers questioning the lawfulness of the order to deploy. The Attorney General's legal advice to the government should clearly indicate the legal basis of the use of force, and if that is something other than self-defence or the authorisation of the Security Council, the government should permit selective conscientious objection.

The judgment of the House of Lords in *Jones* (2006) that the crime of aggression under customary international law is not part of UK law seemed to fly in the face of the spirit of the judgment of the International Military Tribunal at Nuremberg. Furthermore, a political decision by the UK government in 2017 not to ratify the amendment to the Rome Statute on the crime of aggression is unconvincingly holding at bay the rising expectation of greater accountability for conducing aggressive wars. It is disappointing to see that both the government and the courts have acted to protect the state and its leaders from judicial scrutiny. While it might be expected that the government will want to protect itself from legal claims, the cooperation of the courts in this endeavour shows undue deference to the executive and a serious weakness in the rule of law. The contention that judicial encroachment in this area will restrict the freedoms of a sovereign state on the international stage highlights the very problem. States do not have complete freedom of action under international law. A clear judgment on the illegality of the proposed invasion of Iraq in 2003, for instance, might have stopped what was a violation of a fundamental rule of international law as well as a massive miscalculation as to the consequences of such action. Furthermore, it is unlikely that such judicialisation would prevent 'wars of necessity' as opposed to 'wars of choice', thereby allowing the state to defend itself and its citizens as well as fulfil its collective security obligations, while helping to prevent it becoming involved in further dubious expeditionary interventions.

5.   The use of lethal force

5.1   INTRODUCTION

The soldier in combat benefits from combatant privilege for the use of lethal force against enemy soldiers and military targets, but they are also under a duty to protect civilians and civilian property. In war, although soldiers have combatant privilege for lawful acts of killing, they remain restricted in how they fight by LOAC and arguably in certain circumstances by human rights law. From commanders and soldiers using white phosphorus to create the fog of war, to pilots involved in bombing campaigns from 30,000 feet, to submarine commanders considering launching missiles possibly with nuclear warheads – they are all under a variety of duties under LOAC. Furthermore, in peacekeeping operations and in emergencies (discussed in Chapter 3) the use of potentially lethal force is restricted by peacekeeping doctrine and law enforcement paradigms, particularly as the influence of international human rights law deepens. Some modern means of warfare can present problems as to the identification of the applicable legal framework. For example, the use of armed drones in conflict or on the edges of conflict raises questions under the law restricting the use of force between states (*jus ad bellum*), LOAC and international human rights law, potentially producing conflicting answers.

The variety of contexts within which military personnel operate causes legal complexities as explained by Andrew Carswell:

> A NATO platoon commander deployed to Afghanistan is expected to be well-acquainted with the law of targeting, and will understand the principles of proportionality and precaution by virtue of his standard law of armed conflict training. He will appreciate that if Taliban soldiers engage his patrol with small arms and rocket propelled grenades from within a village, his troops are required to ensure that any incidental loss to the civilian population or its infrastructure resulting from their armed reaction is not excessive in relation to the direct military advantage anticipated. If that same officer is ordered six months later to quell a peacetime domestic riot in his home country and applies the principles of IHL [LOAC], he might be inclined to order his subordinates to resort to their rifles against violent agitators, all the while diligently avoiding collateral damage to bystanders. In the absence of an imminent threat to the life of his troops or another person, that decision would represent a fundamental breach of international human rights law. In most countries it would also land him before a court martial for charges up to and

including murder. Accordingly, the importance of context – and mission-specific training – the appropriateness of which is contingent upon the legal classification of the conflict – cannot be over-stated.[1]

The soldier's duty to respect the law has to be matched by the government's duty to ensure that they are prepared, not just in terms of equipment but in terms of training in the relevant laws both domestic and international, and in the adoption of RoE that reflect those laws. RoE 'specify the circumstances in which armed force may be used by a military unit and its permissible extent and degree'.[2] RoE 'provide as clearly as possible the parameters within which armed military personnel assigned to a peacekeeping operation may use force'.[3] In this way, it has been argued that RoE are more important for soldiers than high-level documents and decisions, such as a UN Security Council resolution authorising the use of force by states or by peacekeeping forces, in determining the actual level and extent of force used by military personnel.[4] Despite their operational importance, RoE are usually not 'regarded as legal instruments in their own right, but rather they reflect the law and thus are intended to ensure that military forces act within the law. The "law" in question may comprise both national and international law.'[5] While RoE are meant to be straightforward, thereby enabling soldiers to act and react quickly to situations, the law informing those RoE is complex. This is because of problems in LOAC itself, for example, regarding the classification of conflicts, understandings of 'combatant' and 'civilian', and issues of collateral loss of life. Although the increasing application of international human rights law has added to the complexity, the simple solution offered by the critics of 'lawfare', namely a return to the sole application of LOAC to soldiers in conflict, would only strip away a limited amount of legal regulation.

---

[1]   A.J. Carswell, 'Classifying the Conflict: A Soldier's Dilemma' (2009) 91 *International Review of the Red Cross* 143 at 146.

[2]   H. McCoubrey and N.D. White, *The Blue Helmets: Legal Regulation of United Nations Military Operations* (Dartmouth, 1996) 146.

[3]   R. Zacklin, 'The Use of Force in Peacekeeping Operations' in N. Blokker and N. Schrijver (eds), *The Security Council and the Use of Force* (Martinus Nijhoff, 2005) 100.

[4]   P. Rowe, 'The United Nations Rules of Engagement and the British Soldier in Bosnia' (1994) *International and Comparative Law Quarterly* 947.

[5]   D. Stephens, 'The Lawful Use of Force by Peacekeeping Forces: The Tactical Imperative' (2005) 12 *International Peacekeeping* 163.

5.2 THE PRINCIPLES GOVERNING THE USE OF FORCE IN ARMED CONFLICT

Before reaching the operational level and the use of RoE, it is important to understand the basic principles underlying LOAC as these set the broad framework within which soldiers may use lethal force in combat. As outlined by David Turns, LOAC 'regulates the conduct of hostilities – including the use of weaponry – and the protection of victims in situations of both international and non-international armed conflict', and it 'applies to all armed conflicts, however they are characterized, and applies to all parties in a conflict, irrespective of the legality of the resort to armed force'.[6] The detailed rules of LOAC are based upon a number of core principles: distinction, military necessity, proportionality and humanity,[7] and are underpinned by duties on both the government and the soldier.

Modern LOAC is premised upon there being a distinction between combatants and other legitimate military targets on the one hand, and civilian and civilian targets on the other.[8] The problem is that in modern conflicts, whether internal or international, there is considerable crossover from civilians to combatants, for example where an individual may be a civilian by day and an insurgent by night. In 2009, the ICRC tried to update the law by giving guidance on when civilians should be considered as taking part in hostilities (and therefore losing their protected status). The guidance states that:

> For the purposes of the principle of distinction in international armed conflict, all persons who are neither members of the armed forces of a party to the conflict nor participants in a levee en masse are civilians and, therefore, entitled to protection against direct attack unless and for such time as they take a direct part in hostilities.[9]

---

⁶ D. Turns, 'Law of Armed Conflict (International Humanitarian Law)' in M. Evans (ed.), *International Law* (Oxford University Press, 5th edn, 2018) 840 at 843.

⁷ UK Ministry of Defence, *The Manual of the Law of Armed Conflict* (Oxford University Press, 2004) 21–6.

⁸ See, for example, Additional Protocol (AP) I (1977) Article 48, which states that 'the Parties to the conflict shall at all times distinguish between the civilian population and combatants and between civilian objects and military objectives and accordingly shall direct their operations only against military objectives'. See further detailed rules in AP I (1977) Articles 52–6. For non-international armed conflicts see AP II (1977) Articles 13–18.

⁹ ICRC, 'Interpretive Guidance on the Notion of Direct Participation in Hostilities under International Humanitarian Law', adopted by the ICRC Assembly on 26 February 2009, Recommendation I. A 'levee en masse' consists of 'inhabitants of non-occupied territory, who on the approach of the enemy, spontaneously take up arms to resist the invading force, without having had time to form themselves into regular

In relation to non-international armed conflicts the ICRC guidance states:

> For the purposes of the principle of distinction in non-international armed conflict, all persons who are not members of the State armed forces or organized armed groups of a party to the conflict are civilians and, therefore, entitled to protection against direct attack unless and for such time as they take a direct part in hostilities. In non-international armed conflict, organized armed groups constitute the armed forces of a non-State party to the conflict and consists only of individuals whose continuous function is to take a direct part in hostilities ('continuous combat function').[10]

This constitutes a valid and necessary clarification for the application of the principle of distinction in non-international armed conflicts (NIACs), although the introduction of 'continuous combat function' does not necessarily solve the problems of applying LOAC in modern warfare. These were identified by Francis Lieber, author of the Lieber Code of 1863 during the American Civil War. Lieber pointed out that insurgents will generally deliberately operate in the zone between civilians, who may occasionally participate in hostilities (for example when defending family or group), and full time rebel soldiers.[11] British soldiers faced with an insurgency have to make fine judgements when engaging an elusive enemy who may well not be wearing any type of uniform, striving at all times to distinguish between fighters and civilians in circumstances requiring split-second decision-making. Applying the principle of distinction 'was an easy enough task when battles were fought by organized armies on discrete (mostly rural) battlefields, largely denuded of their civilian inhabitants; however, the proliferation of irregular forces in modern warfare, which is also frequently conducted in an urban environment where the civilian population remains present, has made distinction exceedingly difficult in practice'.[12] Hence, the immediate concern of soldiers is to have clear RoE rather than be concerned with the complexities of LOAC, and other potentially applicable legal regimes.

Targeting also raises problems of distinction. The basic rule is that only military objectives may be attacked.[13] According to Additional Protocol I of

---

armed units, provided they carry arms openly and respect the laws and customs of war' – GC III (1949) Article 4.

[10] Ibid, Recommendation II.

[11] F. Lieber, 'Guerrilla Parties Considered with Reference to the Laws and Usages if War', in Hartigan, *Lieber's Code and the Law* (Chicago, 1983) 41.

[12] Turns (2018) 852.

[13] AP I (1977) Article 52(1). See generally, W. Boothby, 'Does the Law of Targeting Meet 21st Century Needs?' in C. Harvey, J. Summers and N.D. White (eds), *Contemporary Challenges to the Laws of War: Essays in Honour of Peter Rowe* (Cambridge University Press, 2014); A.P.V. Rogers, 'What is a Legitimate Military

1977, 'military objectives are limited to those objects which by their nature, location, purpose or use make an effective contribution to military action and whose total or partial destruction, capture or neutralization, in the circumstances ruling at the time, offers a definite military advantage'.[14] This leaves plenty of scope for interpretation and lists have been made including within them soldiers, tanks, roads and bridges.[15] However, while soldiers and tanks are inherently legitimate targets, roads and bridges are only legitimate targets if they are making a contribution to military action and their destruction offers a definite military advantage.

These issues have not disappeared with the advent of more surgical and accurate means and methods of warfare. In fact, in a number of recent conflicts the desire by militarily advanced states to conduct 'zero casualty warfare' by means of aerial bombing campaigns,[16] has resulted in a number of problematic targeting decisions.[17]

In the attack on Afghanistan in 2001, it was estimated that between October and December nearly 4,000 civilians had been killed as a result of the bombing campaign conducted by US and UK forces.[18] However, Robert Cryer points to the lack of evidence of deliberate targeting of civilians; rather they were the result of mistakes about the location of military targets or were the 'unintentional side-effect of attacks on military targets'.[19] He points to the standard of criminality identified by the Prosecutor of the ICTY in relation to the Kosovo campaign, where it was stated that the 'mens rea for the offence' of targeting civilians was 'intention or recklessness, not simply negligence'.[20] A lack of care in identifying military targets and avoiding civilian casualties will not lead to liability under international criminal law.[21] However, under LOAC the requirement for the conduct of military operations is that 'constant care shall

---

Target?' in R. Burchill, N.D. White and J. Morris (eds), *International Conflict and Security Law: Essays in Memory of Hilaire McCoubrey* (Cambridge University Press, 2005) 160.

[14]   AP I (1977) Article 52(2).

[15]   A.P.V. Rogers, *Law on the Battlefield* (Manchester University Press, 2nd edn, 2004) 83–5.

[16]   A.P.V. Rogers, 'Zero Casualty Warfare' (2000) 837 *International Review of the Red Cross* 165.

[17]   Examples from the NATO campaign in Kosovo 1999 are discussed in Chapter 4.

[18]   R. Cryer, 'The Fine Art of Friendship: The *Jus in Bello* in Afghanistan' (2002) 7 *Journal of Conflict and Security Law* 37 at 48.

[19]   Ibid.

[20]   'Final Report to the Prosecutor by the Committee Established to Review the NATO Bombing Campaign against the FRY', PR/P.I.S/510-E, 13 June 2000, para 28.

[21]   Rome Statute of the International Criminal Court (1998) Article 8(2)(b)(iv), which states that '[i]ntentionally launching an attack in the knowledge that such attack will cause incidental loss of life or injury to civilians ... which would be clearly exces-

be taken to spare the civilian population',[22] suggesting a lower standard of culpability than intent or recklessness. Nevertheless, precautionary measures only require an attack to be cancelled 'if it becomes apparent that the objective is not a military one or that the attack may be expected to cause incidental loss of civilian life … which would be excessive in relation to the concrete and direct military advantage anticipated',[23] which allows for considerable discretion on the part of commanders. 'In effect, the law accepts that at least *some* civilian casualties and/or *some* damage to civilian objects will be inevitable in most military operations, however carefully conducted'.[24] A higher standard of care would probably be required under international human rights law if the type of reasoning found in the *McCann* case concerning the need for care in planning and execution of an operation to protect the right to life was deemed applicable to situations of armed conflict.[25]

In many ways, the essence of international *humanitarian* law or LOAC is its insistence on humanity in warfare, commencing in the modern era with Henri Dunant's witnessing of the suffering of the wounded after the Battle of Solferino of 1859. The principle of humanity is embodied in the Martens Clause located in the preamble to Hague Convention IV of 1907,[26] which provided that 'in cases not included in the Regulations … inhabitants and … belligerents remain under the protection of the rules and principles of the law of nations, as they result from the usages established among civilised peoples, from the laws of humanity, and the dictates of public conscience'.[27] According to the UK *Manual* 'humanity forbids the infliction of suffering, injury, or destruction not actually necessary for the accomplishment of legitimate purposes'.[28]

LOAC is at its most developed in its protection of the wounded, at least in relation to international armed conflicts (IACs).[29] Provisions in the First Geneva Convention 1949 include the requirement that all possible measures be taken to search for and collect the wounded and sick,[30] and any prioritisa-

---

sive in relation to the concrete and direct overall military advantage anticipated', is a war crime.
[22] AP I (1977) Article 57(1).
[23] AP I (1977) Article 57(2)(b).
[24] Turns (2018) 857 (emphasis original).
[25] *McCann and Others v The United Kingdom*, Appl No 18984/91, 27 September 1995, para 194, discussed in Chapter 4.
[26] On the origins of the Martens clause see Rogers (2004) 27, 7.
[27] See also AP I (1977) Article 1(2); and AP II (1977) preamble.
[28] UK MoD (2004) 23.
[29] GC I (1949) Article 12.
[30] Ibid, Article 15.

tion in treatment must be by medical need,[31] in accordance with 'generally accepted medical standards'.[32] There are similar duties imposed by the Second Geneva Convention 1949 in relation to wounded, sick and shipwrecked at sea. These include the positive duty to search and rescue survivors,[33] which does not oblige the commander of the searching vessel to risk his or her ship. The presence of other enemy naval vessels was the reason why the British submarine – HMS *Conqueror* – did not attempt the rescue of Argentinian sailors shipwrecked by the *Conqueror's* torpedo attack on the Argentinian cruiser *General Belgrano* during the Falklands/Malvinas conflict of 1982.[34]

The laws of humanity and the dictates of public conscience are conditioned by military necessity. This has already been seen in the rules that allow for incidental civilian losses and those that can be interpreted as allowing submarine commanders not to expose themselves unnecessarily to attack by surfacing to rescue survivors. When looking overall at the purposes of LOAC, the UK *Manual* states that 'it is intended to minimize the suffering caused by armed conflict rather than impede military efficiency'.[35] However, the point has been made that military necessity does not override the rules of LOAC, rather it is confined by that law, which takes account of other principles such as humanity, distinction and proportionality.[36] This was recognised in one of the early modern expositions of the law, the Lieber Code of 1863, which defined military necessity as 'those measures which are indispensable to securing the ends of the war and which are lawful according to the modern law and usages of war'. The Regulations Respecting the Laws and Customs of War on Land annexed to the Fourth Hague Convention of 1907 made it clear that the 'right of belligerents to adopt means of injuring the enemy is not unlimited', and specifically forbade poisoned weapons, as well as the employment of arms, projectiles or material calculated to cause unnecessary suffering (Articles 22 and 23). Similar rules are found in Additional Protocol I of 1977, which also prohibits methods or means of warfare intended or expected 'to cause widespread, long-term and severe damage to the natural environment'.[37] The Protocol also

---

[31] Ibid, Article 12.
[32] AP I (1977) Article 11.
[33] GC II (1949) Article 18.
[34] See generally House of Commons Foreign Affairs Committee, 'Events Surrounding the Weekend of 1–2 May 1982', Third Report 1984-5, HC 261-I, 16 July 1984; L. Freeman, *The Official History of the Falklands Campaign*: Vol II War and Diplomacy (Routledge, 2005) chs 6, 21, 49.
[35] UK MoD (2004) 21.
[36] Ibid, 23.
[37] AP I (1977) Article 35.

imposes a duty on state parties to determine whether new weapons would be prohibited under the Protocol or other relevant rules of international law.[38]

The question is whether these rules, which largely depend upon reciprocity to induce compliance by states, are strong enough to prevent the development of weapons that cause unnecessary suffering of combatants and those civilians that may be 'incidentally' affected. White phosphorus is an example of a weapon developed and deployed by Israel in Gaza in 2008–2009, and the US in Fallujah (Iraq) in 2004 principally in order to create a fog of war behind which troops could advance. In the latter instance, however, the US admitted that it had been used as an incendiary weapon against enemy combatants, arguing that it was not a banned chemical weapon.[39] The substance's burning effects on individuals caught under it led, in part, to the finding in the Goldstone Report into Gaza of 2009 that 'in a number of cases Israel failed to take feasible precautions required by customary law reflected in article 57(2) (a)(ii) of Additional Protocol I to avoid or minimize incidental loss of civilian life, injury to civilians and damage to civilian objects'. It found that the 'firing of white phosphorus shells over the UNRWA compound in Gaza City is one of such cases in which precautions were not taken in the choice of weapons and methods in the attack, and these facts were compounded by reckless disregard for the consequences'.[40] UK forces reportedly used white phosphorus against military targets in the Falklands/Malvinas War of 1982,[41] and Iraq in 2005 to create smokescreens to protect its soldiers when in action.[42] The MoD *Manual* categorises white phosphorus alongside napalm and flamethrowers, the uses of which are 'governed by the unnecessary suffering principle so that they should not be used directly against personnel but against armoured vehicles, bunkers and built-up emplacements, even though personnel inside may be burnt'. The *Manual* goes on to state that white phosphorus is specifically 'designed to set fire to targets such as fuel and ammunition dumps or for use to create smoke, and ... should not be used directly against personnel'.[43]

Another controversial weapon used by the Royal Air Force in Kosovo 1999, Afghanistan 2001 and Iraq 2003, is the cluster bomb.[44] 'After the bombs

---

[38]   AP I (1977) Article 36.
[39]   *BBC News*, 'UK used white phosphorus in Iraq', 16 November 2005 http://news .bbc.co.uk/1/hi/uk_politics/4441822.stm.
[40]   UN, 'Report of the UN Fact-Finding Mission on the Gaza Conflict', UN Doc A/ HRC/12/48 (2009) para 1919.
[41]   'Tim Collins trained troops to fight with white phosphorus', *The Daily Telegraph*, 20 November 2005.
[42]   *BBC News*, 'UK used white phosphorus in Iraq', 16 November 2005.
[43]   UK MoD (2004) 112.
[44]   On the latter see 'British use of cluster bombs condemned', *The Guardian*, 4 April 2003.

have been released, the bomblets are scattered in an area approximately 200 x 400 metres',[45] 5–10 per cent of which will be 'duds' and present an on-going threat to civilians lives during and after the conflict.[46] The Foreign Affairs Committee, examining the use of such weapons in Kosovo, was of the view that the use of cluster bombs 'in an urban environment where civilians live may well fall foul of the prohibition on indiscriminate weapons'.[47] Their use and transfer were finally prohibited for state parties to the Convention on Cluster Munitions of 2008, which came into force in 2010, with the UK ratifying the treaty in that year.

According to the UK *Manual* the 'principle of proportionality is a link between the principles of military necessity and humanity. It is most evident in connection with the reduction of incidental damage caused by military operations.'[48] Included in the prohibition of indiscriminate attacks in Additional Protocol I, namely those that do not discriminate between military and civilian objectives,[49] are attacks which 'may be expected to cause incidental loss of civilian life, injury to civilians, damage to civilian objects, or a combination thereof, which would be excessive in relation to the concrete and direct military advantage anticipated'.[50] These rules would prohibit the sort of area bombing that the Allies launched against German cities such as Dresden towards the end of the Second World War, which was arguably unlawful at the time, since it is inherently indiscriminate and disproportionate.[51] However, they would not rule out the more precise destruction of a munitions factory killing civilian workers and probably killing or injuring civilians living in the surrounding area if the military advantages were deemed, by a reasonable commander, to outweigh the civilian losses.[52]

The need for objective standards that can be applied to this balancing act was evident on a massive scale in the use of nuclear weapons by the US against Hiroshima and Nagasaki in Japan in 1945, which brought an end to the war thereby saving significant losses to US and Japanese forces, but at a massive cost in terms of loss of civilian lives and poisoning of the environment. It seems perverse, however, to balance the lives of civilians who are meant to

---

[45]   Cryer (2002) 60.

[46]   See the claim made under the ECHR in *Behrami and Saramati v France, Germany and Norway*, Appl Nos 71412/01 and 78166/01, 2 May 2007.

[47]   House of Commons Foreign Affairs Committee, 'Kosovo', Fourth Report 1999–2000 (HC 28-I), 7 June 2000, para 150.

[48]   UK MoD (2004) 25.

[49]   AP I (1977) Article 51(4).

[50]   Ibid, Article 51(5)(b).

[51]   Ibid, Article 51(5)(a).

[52]   UK MoD (2004) 25.

be protected against those of soldiers who are not (at least while they remain as combatants). Given that indiscriminate attacks on civilians are now clearly prohibited, it is not permissible to point to the military advantages of the effects of undermining the overall war effort of the enemy by the use of such devastating weapons.

Unlike chemical weapons, the possession or even use of nuclear weapons is not specifically prohibited by international law.[53] However, the indiscriminate effects of such weapons signifies that their use is unlawful. In the *Nuclear Weapons* opinion of 1996, the ICJ ultimately remained equivocal on the legality of the use of nuclear weapons in the extreme circumstance of when the 'very survival of the state was at stake'. However, the Court did state that normally the 'threat or use of nuclear weapons would generally be contrary to the rules of international law applicable in armed conflict, and in particular the principles and rules of humanitarian law'.[54] In the end game of trying to ensure the survival of the state by using nuclear weapons, states may well have joined in a suicide pact where international law has ceased to be relevant. However, it is curious that the ICJ, as the ultimate guardian of international law, recognised this. Unsurprisingly, the MoD in its *Manual* relies on the ICJ's equivocation to state that 'the threshold for the use of nuclear weapons is clearly a high one', meaning that the UK 'would only consider using nuclear weapons in self-defence, including the defence of its NATO allies, and even then only in extreme circumstances'.[55]

Although purporting to be a very restricted set of conditions for the use of the most destructive weapon the UK possesses, the disputed nature of the right of individual and collective self-defence,[56] and the open-ended nature of 'extreme circumstances', lead to the conclusion that the UK's doctrine on nuclear weapons could result in their use in possible breach of the *jus ad bellum* and in clear breach of the rules of LOAC prohibiting the use of indiscriminate weapons. Additional Protocol I of 1977 prohibits the use of weapons that 'cause superfluous injury or unnecessary suffering' as well as methods or means of warfare which are 'intended, or may be expected, to cause widespread, long-term and severe damage to the natural environment'.[57] The ICJ pointed to the modern version of the Martens Clause in Additional Protocol I,[58] to support its statement that LOAC 'at a very early stage, prohibited certain

---

[53]   Ibid, 117.
[54]   *Legality of the Threat or Use of Nuclear Weapons* (1996) ICJ Rep 226, para 105.
[55]   UK MoD (2004) 117. See discussion of UK's possession of nuclear weapons in Chapter 2.
[56]   See discussion in Chapter 4.
[57]   API (1977) Articles 35(1), 35(2), 55.
[58]   API (1977) Article 1(2).

types of weapons either because of their indiscriminate effect on combatants and civilians or because of the unnecessary suffering caused to combatants, that is to say, a harm greater than that unavoidable to achieve legitimate military objectives'.[59] While this seems to amount in effect to a prohibition on the use of nuclear weapons, the UK made it clear at the time that Protocol I was adopted that its view was that the rules 'apply exclusively to conventional weapons without prejudice to any other rules of international law applicable to other types of weapons. In particular, the rules so introduced do not have any effect on and do not regulate or prohibit the use of nuclear weapons.'[60] The UK's approach to the use of nuclear weapons appears contrary to both LOAC and international criminal law. The Rome Statute includes as a war crime: '[i]ntentionally launching an attack in the knowledge that such an attack will cause incidental loss of life or injury to civilians or damage to civilian objects or widespread, long-term and severe damage to the natural environment which would be clearly excessive in relation to the concrete and direct overall military advantage anticipated'.[61] Political and military leaders, as well as UK nuclear submarine commanders,[62] are under duties not to use nuclear weapons if they are likely (and the likelihood is very high) to breach the provisions of LOAC and international criminal law.

5.3   TYPOLOGIES OF ARMED CONFLICT

LOAC is premised on the continuing validity of a distinction between IACs and NIACs. The rights and duties of the different actors in a war: states, political leaders, commanders and soldiers, vary depending upon the type of armed conflict. Despite some convergence driven by the jurisprudence of the international criminal tribunals in the 1990s,[63] and the development of customary rules,[64] the treaty regime governing IACs is more extensive (basically the four Geneva Conventions of 1949 and Additional Protocol I of 1977) than for NIACs (basically Common Article 3 found in all four Geneva Conventions

---

[59]   *Nuclear Weapons* (1996) para 78.
[60]   UK MoD (2004) 117.
[61]   Rome Statute of the International Criminal Court (1998) Article 8(2)(b)(iv).
[62]   On the discretion given to nuclear submarine commanders in 'letters of last resort' to use nuclear weapons if contact has been lost with the government, see N. Ritchie, *A Nuclear Weapons-Free World? Britain, Trident and the Challenges Ahead* (Palgrave Macmillan, 2012) 51–73.
[63]   S. Darcy, *Judges, Law and War: The Judicial Development of International Humanitarian Law* (Cambridge University Press, 2014) 38–67.
[64]   For authoritative analysis of the customary rules applicable in both IACs and NIACs see J-M. Henckaerts and L. Doswald-Beck, *Customary International Humanitarian Law*: Vol I: Rules (Cambridge University Press, 2005).

of 1949 and Additional Protocol II of 1977). The reason is not one of logic but of history where states have seen greater benefit in ensuring reciprocal obligations in IACs than having their hands tied in dealing with internal rebellions. After all is said and done, states remain the principal law-makers in the international legal system.

In the 19th century, once a state of war existed between states the law of peace was replaced by the law of war, which contained '[r]ules primarily concerned with the rights and obligations of belligerents concerning their subjects, armies and property, and gradually started including some rudimentary rules on the means of warfare'.[65] 'War' as a legal concept ultimately failed to fulfil its purpose of establishing a clear legal regime to govern hostilities since full-scale hostilities might exist between two states without there being a war because neither state recognised a state of war, or a war might be declared by both states but no fighting ensued. Thus, war as a legal concept gave way to a factual threshold ('armed conflict') and the collapse of the formal distinction between law of war and law of peace. The introduction of a factual test has led to a new set of problems.

Nowadays the legal regimes governing war (or armed conflict) and peace overlap, with it being recognised that human rights law, for instance, continues to apply during armed conflict,[66] although the precise relationship between the rules of what has been called the *lex specialis* governing warfare (LOAC), and the *lex generalis* applying during war and peace is evolving.[67] One area of relative clarity is in the area of the right to life where the normal restrictions on the use of lethal force contained in human rights law give way to those permissive rules that allow combatants to use lethal force against legitimate targets, for example to kill enemy soldiers during an IAC.[68]

There is, unfortunately, no definition of 'armed conflict' in the conventions or Protocols. The most utilised definition, covering both IACs (between states)

---

[65]   M. Milanovic and V. Hadzi-Vidanovic, 'A Taxonomy of Armed Conflict' in N.D. White and C. Henderson (eds), *Research Handbook on International Conflict and Security Law* (Elgar, 2013) 256 at 259.

[66]   As recognised by the ICJ in its advisory opinions on: *Legality of the Threat or Use of Nuclear Weapons* (1996) para 25; and *Legal Consequences of the Construction of a Wall in the Occupied Palestinian Territory* (2004) ICJ Rep 136, paras 102–6.

[67]   I. Scobbie, 'Principle or Pragmatics? The Relationship between Human Rights Law and the Law of Armed Conflict' (2009) 14 *Journal of Conflict and Security Law* 449; M. Milanovic, 'A Norm Conflict Perspective on the Relationship between International Humanitarian Law and Human Rights Law' (2009) 14 *Journal of Conflict and Security Law* 459.

[68]   C. Garraway, 'To Kill or Not to Kill? Dilemmas on the Use of Force' (2009) 14 *Journal of Conflict and Security Law* 499.

and NIACs (between a state and an armed group or between armed groups), has been stated by the ICTY in the *Tadić* case:

> An armed conflict exists whenever there is a resort to armed force between States or protracted armed violence between governmental authorities and organized armed groups or between such groups within a State. International humanitarian law applies from the initiation of such armed conflicts and extends beyond the cessation of hostilities until a general conclusion of peace is reached; or, in the case of internal armed conflicts, a peaceful settlement is achieved. Until that moment, international humanitarian law continues to apply in the whole territory of the warring States or, in the case of internal conflicts, the whole territory under the control of a party, whether or not actual combat takes place there.[69]

This would suggest that any use of force between states would trigger the laws of armed conflict, although a threshold of intensity is often argued for,[70] while for a NIAC to exist within a state or between a state and a non-state actor then there must be 'protracted armed violence'. For instance, in Syria the ICRC recognised that a NIAC existed between the government and armed groups in July 2012, when violence had been intensifying for over a year before that starting in March 2011.[71]

According to Additional Protocol II of 1977 'situations of internal disturbances and tensions, such as riots, isolated and sporadic acts of violence and other acts of similar nature' do not amount to 'armed conflicts',[72] meaning that the laws of armed conflict found in Protocol II do not apply to such situations. However, domestic criminal law, human rights law, and aspects of international criminal law remain applicable. Often a government will categorise extensive internal violence as something less than armed conflict in order not to admit it has lost control, and so as not to give credence to a rebellion. For instance, France treated the Algerian insurgency as an internal disturbance in the period 1954–1956; and the UK dealt with the 'Troubles' in Northern Ireland from the late 1960s as an internal disturbance. Confusingly, Additional Protocol II of 1977 contains different criteria for armed groups in NIACs than that stated in the later *Tadić* case, which only required that the armed group be 'organised'. To be operative Protocol II requires the existence of an armed conflict taking place 'in the territory of a High Contracting Party between its

---

[69] *Prosecutor v Tadić*, IT-94-1-AR72, 2 October 1995, para 70.

[70] See International Law Association, 'Final Report on the Meaning of Armed Conflict in International Law' (The Hague Conference, 2010).

[71] 'Syria: ICRC and Syrian Arab Red Crescent maintain aid effort amid increasing fighting', ICRC Operational Update, 17 July 2012 https://www.icrc.org/en/doc/resources/documents/update/2012/syria-update-2012-07-17.htm.

[72] AP II (1977) Article 1(2).

armed forces and dissident armed forces or other armed groups which, under responsible command, exercise such control over a part of its territory as to enable them to carry out sustained and concerted military operations and to implement this Protocol'.[73] Further adding to the confusion is the blurring between international and internal conflicts found in Protocol I, which extends the IAC category to 'armed conflicts in which peoples are fighting against colonial domination and alien occupation and against racist regimes in the exercise of their right to self-determination'.[74]

The complexities of the legal classification of armed conflicts do not end there for it is entirely feasible that hostilities will actually involve a mixture of conflicts. Such 'mixed conflicts' were recognised in the *Tadić* case:

> It is indisputable that an armed conflict is international if it takes place between two or more States. In addition, in a case of an internal armed conflict breaking out on the territory of a State, it may become international (or, depending upon the circumstances, be international in character alongside an internal armed conflict) if (i) another State intervenes in that conflict through its troops or alternatively if (ii) some of the participants in the internal armed conflict act on behalf of that other State.[75]

The initial conflict in Afghanistan in 2001 was mixed, involving: a NIAC between the *de facto* Taliban government and Northern Alliance rebels; an IAC between US/UK forces and the Taliban; and arguably a NIAC between the US and Al-Qaeda. With the defeat of the Taliban, the conflict between the International Security Assistance Force (ISAF) (a NATO-led force acting under the authority of the Security Council) and the Taliban became non-international as the Taliban became the insurgents facing government and ISAF forces present in Afghanistan in a supporting role with the agreement of the government.[76] The conflict in Libya in 2011 was also mixed involving a NIAC between the rebels and the government of Gaddafi, and an IAC between the government and NATO states.[77] The result is an unduly complex LOAC regime of different sets of applicable legal rules depending upon the type of conflict, compounded by the fact that other regimes such as international human rights law, international criminal law, refugee law and general principles of international law continue to apply, making compliance for governments, commanders and soldiers difficult. Arguably, the accusations

---

[73]   AP II (1977) Article 1(1).
[74]   AP I (1977) Article 1(4).
[75]   *Prosecutor v Tadić*, IT-94-1-A, 15 July 1999, para 84.
[76]   Cryer (2002) 37.
[77]   K.A. Johnston, 'Transformations of Conflict Status in Libya' (2012) 17 *Journal of Conflict and Security Law* 81.

of the excessive legalisation of warfare, which have recently been levelled at judges for contemplating the application of human rights law in armed conflicts,[78] should have been directed at the very set of rules such critics point to as the only relevant ones,[79] namely those contained in LOAC. LOAC appears far more complex than appropriate for the primordial conditions of war, where snap decisions and actions have to be taken which affect the lives and welfare of civilians and soldiers. Instead of a clear and straightforward iteration of 'do's and don'ts', what we have is a labyrinthine legal regime for warfare. This puts great weight on the RoE, which must cut through the legal knots without exposing soldiers to criminal liability.

It is the category of NIACs, arguably the most significant in modern warfare, which is the most difficult and problematic. Historically it relates to internal conflicts, but has been applied by the US Supreme Court, for example,[80] to transnational conflicts between states and non-state actors (such as international terrorist groups). On the other hand, the Israeli Supreme Court decided that the transnational nature of such terrorist conflicts meant that they should be viewed as international for the purposes of LOAC.[81] There appears to be a lack of clarity as LOAC, codified in 1949 and supplemented in 1977, struggles to keep pace with modern conflicts.[82] In relation to internal conflicts a useful summary of the applicable law is provided by the UK MoD in the *Manual of the Law of Armed Conflict*:

> The application of the law of armed conflict to internal hostilities thus depends upon a number of factors. In the first place, it does not apply at all unless an armed conflict exists. If an armed conflict exists, the provisions of Common Article 3 apply. Should the dissidents achieve a degree of success and exercise the necessary control over a part of the territory, the provisions of Additional Protocol II come into force. Finally, if the conflict is a recognized as a conflict falling within Additional Protocol I, Article 1(4), it becomes subject to the Geneva Conventions and Protocol I.[83]

Common Article 3 of the Geneva Conventions of 1949 applies 'in the case of armed conflicts not of an international character occurring in the territory' of

---

[78] R. Etkins, J. Morgan and T. Tugendhat, 'Clearing the Fog of Law: Saving Our Armed Forces from Defeat by Judicial Diktat' (Policy Exchange Report, 2015) 7.

[79] M. Warren, 'The "Fog of Law": The Law of Armed Conflict in Operation Iraqi Freedom' (2010) 86 *International Law Studies* 167.

[80] *Hamdam v Rumsfeld*, 548 U.S. 557 (2006).

[81] *The Public Committee against Torture in Israel v Government of Israel*, HCJ 769/02, 13 December 2006.

[82] For useful discussion see L. Moir, 'It's a Bird! It's a Plane! It's a Non-International Armed Conflict: Cross Border Hostilities between States and Non-State Actors', in Harvey, Summers and White (2014).

[83] UK MoD (2004) 33.

a state and provides for basic protections for 'persons taking no active part in the hostilities'.[84] It is argued that customary law on NIACs provides a greater level of protection,[85] but it does not, for instance, provide for prisoner of war (PoW) status for captured fighters, nor for detention of civilians on the grounds of security. Furthermore, although civilians should be safeguarded in NIACs, issues such as collateral damage are much more opaque where rebel factions will often not distinguish themselves sufficiently from the civilian population.

The complexities of classification of armed conflicts has led David Turns to comment:

> The technicalities of the definitions of international and non-international armed conflicts makes it difficult to know when to treat irregular opponents as legitimate combatants, civilians directly participating in hostilities, 'dissident armed forces' under Protocol II, a national liberation movement under Protocol I, or common criminals engaged in violence and entitled to no specific protections under [LOAC]. This has led to an increase in the importance of governmental determinations as to the classification of armed conflicts in which regular forces are engaged and as to the applicable scope of application of [LOAC].[86]

Turns summarises the UK government's approach to the 'Troubles' in Northern Ireland, in which it 'consistently denied that there was an armed conflict of any kind in Northern Ireland – and specifically denied the entitlement of captured IRA members to POW status, preferring to regulate their activity under national law and to regard them as nothing more than common criminals'. In contrast, the IRA 'sought to claim that it was acting in pursuit of Irish self-determination, to "liberate" Northern Ireland from "illegal British occupation", and was thus engaged in an international armed conflict against the UK', leading to it demanding PoW status for captured IRA members.[87]

The advantages to the UK government, particularly in delegitimating IRA actions by categorising them as forms of terrorism as opposed to any form of armed struggle for freedom, outweighed the limitations this placed on British soldiers who had to operate within RoE crafted under a law enforcement paradigm as opposed to the permissive rules of LOAC. Besides which, a decision by the government to fight a fully fledged war against the IRA would potentially have led to a greater spiralling of violence than actually occurred. Clearly, the rules of LOAC relevant to IACs were applied by the UK in 2003 during the invasion stage of the conflict in Iraq. However, that legal clarity

---

[84]   GC I, II, III, IV (1949) Common Article 3(1).
[85]   Henckaerts and Doswald-Beck (2005).
[86]   Turns (2018) 850.
[87]   Ibid, 848.

dissipated as the nature of the conflict changed. Again, Turns provides an accurate summary of this descent into factual and legal chaos:

> The spectrum of conflict is well illustrated by the case of Iraq since 2003; after an initial phase of international armed conflict (March–April 2003) to which the fullest extent of LOAC applied, there followed a period of belligerent occupation (April 2003–June 2004) during which certain parts of [LOAC] (notably Geneva Convention IV) continued to be applied. After the formal end of occupation, however, the legal position became substantially less clear in that Coalition forces were operating extraterritorially against non-State actors; this resulted in the haphazard application of an ad hoc hodgepodge of rules cobbled together from the laws relating to international and non-international armed conflicts, supplemented by a dose of human rights law and overshadowed by the significance of UN Security Council resolutions regarding the rights of foreign forces in Iraq.[88]

While the initial invasion occurred within a relatively clear legal framework for the application of overwhelming force by the US and UK, the second phase of belligerent occupation became more problematic. Belligerent occupation is the 'occupation of enemy territory, that is, when a belligerent in an armed conflict is in control of some of the adversary's territory and is directly responsible for administering the territory'.[89] After the invasion of Iraq in March 2003, the law of belligerent occupation located principally in the Hague Regulations 1907 and the Fourth Geneva Convention 1949, was applied by the US and the UK. These states formed the Coalition Provisional Authority (CPA) that administered Iraq until mid-2004 when power was handed over to the interim Iraqi government. The occupation of Iraq was recognised by the Security Council in Resolution 1483 of 2003.

It is clear that specific aspects of the law of occupation were utilised by the CPA, for example as a legal basis upon which to detain thousands of Iraqis deemed to be security threats.[90] However, there are manifest problems in applying the law of occupation to a situation of regime change and subsequent state building involving the removal of the Baathist regime of Saddam Hussein, and its replacement by an interim and then an elected government. The basic premise underpinning the law of belligerent occupation is that sovereignty does not pass to the occupant, meaning that the occupying state cannot treat the territory as its own. The occupants administer the territory until withdrawal. This is reflected in the Hague Regulations of 1907, which state that the 'authority of the legitimate power having passed into the hands of the occu-

---

[88]   Ibid, 851.
[89]   UK MoD (2004) 274. See generally Y. Dinstein, *The International Law of Belligerent Occupation* (Cambridge University Press, 2009).
[90]   GC IV (1949) Articles 41–3.

pant, the latter shall take all the measures in his power to restore, and ensure, as far as possible, public order and safety, while respecting, unless absolutely prevented', the laws in force in the country.[91] This provision is difficult to apply in the case of long-term occupations such as Israel's occupation of the Palestinian territories. An Israeli court has stated that in long administrations an occupant must ensure growth, change and development, so an occupant is entitled to develop industry, commerce, agriculture, health and welfare.[92]

In the occupation of Iraq, it is clear that the CPA went beyond the administration of the territory to act as the sovereign power, for example in the privatisation of public utilities.[93] Furthermore, the policy of lustration involving the removal from power of members of the former regime – the so-called 'de-Ba'athification' of Iraq by the CPA in 2003 – seems at odds with the law, although it follows the example of the de-Nazification of Germany after the Second World War.[94] It follows from the Hague Regulations that, as far as possible, administrative life should go on as uninterrupted, and, furthermore, there are provisions in the Fourth Geneva Convention preventing the alteration of the status of judges and public officials, although public officials can be removed from their posts if they do not wish to work for the occupant.[95]

In order to overcome the limitations of the laws of belligerent occupation, which it should be borne in mind did not prevent nor were seen as a reason to prevent the reconstruction of Japan and Germany after the Second World War, the occupiers of Iraq secured the adoption of Security Council Resolution 1483. This Resolution not only endorsed the military presence and occupation of Iraq by the US and UK, it also empowered the CPA under Chapter VII of the UN Charter: 'to advance efforts to restore and establish national and local institutions for representative governance, including working together to facilitate a process leading to an internationally recognized, representative government of Iraq'; and to facilitate the 'reconstruction of key infrastructure, in cooperation with other international organizations'.[96] In effect, the law of occupation was supplemented by a layer of abstract and general authorisations agreed in the highly politically charged forum of the Security Council.

---

[91]   Regulations Respecting the Laws and Customs of War on Land, annexed to Hague Convention IV Respecting the Laws and Customs of War on Land (1907) Article 43.
[92]   *Co-operative Society Case* (1984) 14 *Israel Year Book of Human Rights* 30.
[93]   C. McCarthy, 'The Paradox of the International Law of Military Occupation' (2005) 10 *Journal of Conflict and Security Law* 43 at 51–5.
[94]   Ibid, 54.
[95]   GC IV (1949) Article 54.
[96]   UN Doc S/RES/1483 (2003) para 8.

The difficulties in identifying with clarity the applicable legal regime for complex asymmetrical conflicts have serious consequences for the armed forces at the operational level where clarity and precision are needed. Of direct relevance to soldiers is the understanding of LOAC laid out in the MoD's *Manual on the Law of Armed Conflict* also known as the *Joint Service Manual*, the purpose of which is 'to enable all concerned to apply the law of armed conflict when conducing operations and when training or planning for them'.[97] The importance of this document to both the military and the government is reflected in the judgment of the UK Supreme Court in *Rahmatullah* of 2012,[98] which involved a Pakistani citizen taken into custody by British forces in Iraq in 2004. He was transferred to US forces in accordance with a memorandum of understanding (MoU) between the UK and the US. However, the evidence was that the US would not comply with the requirements of the Fourth Geneva Convention, which forbids the forcible transfer of protected persons from occupied territory,[99] obliging the UK to request the return of Rahmatullah.[100] Rahmatullah was detained during the occupation period in Iraq in 2003–2004 and, therefore, was entitled to the protections applicable during an IAC and, in particular, those contained in the Fourth Geneva Convention. Once that occupation ended, and the conflict changed to a NIAC, 'the same individuals would have to look for their protection under Common Article 3 of the 1949 Conventions and Additional Protocol II, 1977, customary international law and English Law (including the Human Rights Act 1998)'.[101] As the discussion of detention in Chapter 6 demonstrates, the precise extent of those protections for detainees are less than clear.

5.4 COMBATANT PRIVILEGE AND IMMUNITY

According to Peter Rowe 'it is not entirely clear whether [LOAC] gives the soldier any "rights" under it'. Rowe goes on to say that the structure of LOAC primarily imposes obligations upon states, although soldiers can benefit from these, by, for example, being entitled to be treated as PoWs if captured during an IAC. Rowe states further that 'those who infringe' the laws 'may be per-

---

[97]   UK MoD (2004) vii.
[98]   *Secretary of State for Foreign and Commonwealth Affairs v Rahmatullah* [2012] UKSC 48 para 34 (Lord Kerr).
[99]   GC IV (1949) Article 49.
[100]   *Rahmatullah* [2012] paras 38–40.
[101]   P. Rowe, *Legal Accountability and Britain's Wars 2000–2015* (Routledge, 2016) 206.

sonally liable',[102] meaning that LOAC can give rise to duties on individuals. The Geneva Conventions of 1949 were based on the idea of soldiers being the beneficiaries of reciprocal duties agreed by the state parties,[103] after all states are the complete international legal persons bearing rights and duties and, until the advent of the human rights era, individuals were not endowed with any rights as subjects of international law. Although all four Geneva Conventions of 1949 state that soldiers 'may in no circumstances renounce in part or in entirety the rights secured to them' found in the Conventions,[104] those rights are incomplete and largely unenforceable.[105]

In that sense a British soldier who is captured by the enemy in an IAC has an unenforceable right to PoW status and the accompanying benefits of the developed regime that governs PoWs. As made clear in the MoD's *Manual* of 2004: '[i]t should always be remembered that prisoners of war are not convicted criminals in need of corrective training or punishment. They are members of the armed forces who, until capture, were simply doing their duty.'[106] The protections that state parties should secure to PoWs on capture include: humane treatment; care if wounded or sick; clothing and personal property (after being disarmed and searched); evacuation from the combat area as soon as possible; and protection from the use of lethal force except when necessary as a final measure to prevent escape.[107] PoWs must normally be removed to camps that are healthy, hygienic and clear of danger.[108] Freedom of religious worship should be guaranteed by the detaining power.[109] A PoW is bound to give his service number, rank, full name and date of birth, in order to establish his identity. Beyond that, PoWs cannot be forced to disclose tactical or strategic information even though the detaining power can ask such questions in what is called 'humane interrogation procedures' in the MoD's *Manual*.[110] This

---

[102] P. Rowe, *The Impact of Human Rights Law on Armed Forces* (Oxford University Press, 2006) 2.

[103] See, for example, GC IV (1949) Article 47, which states that protected persons shall 'not be deprived of the benefits of the present Convention'.

[104] GC I (1949) Article 7; GC II (1949) Article 7; GC III (1949) Article 7; GC IV (1949) Article 8. See also GC I (1949) Article 6; GC II (1949) Article 6; GC III (1949) Articles 6 and 78; GC IV (1949) Articles 7 and 78.

[105] Unless a human rights' court or body incorporates them in its understandings of individual human rights during an armed conflict. See further T. Meron, 'The Humanization of Humanitarian Law' (2000) 94 *American Journal of International Law* 239.

[106] UK MoD (2004) 141.

[107] Ibid, 151–3.

[108] Ibid, 158.

[109] GC III (1949) Article 34.

[110] UK MoD (2004) 156–7.

summary highlights some of the benefits guaranteed to PoWs by LOAC, especially in the Third Geneva Convention 1949 (Articles 1–77) and Additional Protocol I of 1977 (Articles 43–7), but they also illustrate that soldiers are not viewed as criminals as long as they act within the rules of LOAC.

Mirroring the dual approach to penal proceedings in the UK military justice system, PoWs can be subject to disciplinary action of up to 30 days confinement by the camp commandant for minor offences (including for failed escape attempts);[111] while PoWs are answerable before independent and impartial military courts for more serious offences.[112] However, a PoW can only be tried and sentenced for an act that was an offence either under the law of the detaining power or the international law in force at the time of its commission,[113] the obvious example being war crimes committed as a combatant during the armed conflict. There is no combatant privilege in these cases, although any accused PoW has a number of rights in this context, including: not to be subject to moral or physical coercion in order to gain a confession; to be assisted by a fellow PoW; to be defended by a qualified advocate or counsel of his own choice; to call witnesses; to have the services of a competent interpreter; and to be given details of the charges against him and any relevant documents in good time before the opening of the trial.[114]

There can be no individual criminal responsibility for PoWs who, before capture, have killed in lawful acts of war committed during an IAC. 'Combatant privilege' is a phrase used to capture those lawful acts of war, which do not involve criminal responsibility and thereby are covered by 'combatant immunity'. Jens Ohlin defines combatant privilege as 'the right of all lawful combatants to kill enemy soldiers without criminal liability'.[115] During an IAC, a British soldier will normally meet the definition of a lawful combatant contained in Additional Protocol I of 1977.[116] Rowe explains combatant immunity by giving two examples. First, 'a British soldier kills an enemy combatant during the course of an international armed conflict', which 'is permitted by [LOAC] and there could be no charge of murder against him'. In the second example, 'he kills an enemy combatant who has surrendered', which is prohibited by LOAC meaning that the 'soldier would be guilty of murder'.[117]

---

[111] GC III (1949) Article 91.
[112] Ibid, Article 84.
[113] Ibid, Article 99.
[114] Ibid, Articles 99 and 105.
[115] J.D. Ohlin, 'The Combatant's Privilege in Asymmetric and Covert Armed Conflict' (2015) 40 *Yale Journal of International Law* 337 at 338.
[116] Rowe (2016) 135; AP I (1977) Article 43(2).
[117] Rowe (2016) 136.

Emily Crawford explains that in an IAC soldiers have both privileges and immunity due to their status as combatants and, if captured, as PoWs:

> The common factor in both combatant and POW status is their 'non-criminality'. A legitimate combatant is provided with immunity from prosecution for his warlike acts provided he obeys the laws of armed conflict and complies with the criteria for designation as a lawful combatant. A combatant who falls into the hands of an adverse party is entitled to treatment as a POW. POW detention is preventive detention only, designed to remove the combatant from the field of battle, and to prevent his return to hostilities. The non-punitive nature of POW detention is reflected in the rights and privileges that POWs enjoy, such as restrictions on the kind of work they are required to do. All these rules regulating the treatment of combatants and POWs are reflective of the non-criminal status of the participants.[118]

The existence of combatant immunity and privilege, which are logically drawn from the provisions of LOAC governing IACs, is doubted in NIACs to the point that Rowe believes it to be non-existent, certainly for insurgents, given that combatant status (and consequently PoW status) are confined to state forces, and then state forces within IACs. He concludes by saying that a 'British soldier who had taken part in the non-international armed conflicts in Iraq and Afghanistan was not entitled under' LOAC 'to be treated as a prisoner of war if captured by insurgents, but both he and the insurgents, will have been bound by Common Article 3 to the Geneva Conventions'.[119] The 'standard view is that the very legal concept of "combatant" is a creature of international armed conflicts and the international laws that regulate them', meaning that NIACs 'have no combatants at all – only government troops and rebels'. In such wars 'government troops are authorized to commit killings by their own domestic law, while rebels are not' meaning that 'government troops will not be prosecuted at the conclusion of the civil war while vanquished rebels could be prosecuted for their belligerent acts against the government'.[120] The absence of combatant immunity or privilege in NIACs seems to be the preponderant position,[121] although there are strong arguments against this position at least in internationalised NIACs in which British troops are fighting alongside government troops.[122] UK case law reflects this lack of clarity.

In *Gul* in 2013, the appellant had been convicted of terrorism offences in the UK after he distributed videos of attacks by Al-Qaeda, the Taliban and other

---

[118] E. Crawford, *The Treatment of Combatants and Insurgents under the Law of Armed Conflict* (Oxford University Press, 2010) 78.

[119] Rowe (2016) 137.

[120] Ohlin (2015) 342.

[121] Crawford (2010) 78.

[122] See, for example, Ohlin (2015).

proscribed groups on Coalition forces in Afghanistan and Iraq.[123] A central contention of his appeal was that while the definition of terrorism in UK legislation was very wide and capable of extending to insurgent attacks undertaken in other countries,[124] the definition should be read down in the light of the provisions of LOAC, which did not proscribe such attacks on military targets in a NIAC.[125] The UK Supreme Court was very critical of the wide definition of terrorism adopted by the UK, which gave unbounded discretion to police and prosecutors but, given the lack of an agreed definition of terrorism at the international level, the Court felt that the UK's freedom to legislate on terrorism was not limited by any proscriptions of international law.[126] This included Parliament's decision not to exclude from the definition of terrorism lawful acts covered by the provisions of LOAC committed during an armed conflict.[127] Again, the Supreme Court was critical of not making such exclusions, pointing out that other countries had done so and, moreover, an independent report by David Anderson QC had pointed out that there was a danger that UK forces engaged in armed operations overseas could be caught by the definition of terrorism.[128]

There was some unsatisfactory discussion of the notion of combatant immunity during the case, including the statement by the trial judge that 'the use of force by Coalition forces' in Afghanistan and Iraq was 'not terrorism' as such forces enjoyed 'combat immunity ... unless they commit crimes such as torture or war crimes'. The jury asked whether there was 'combatant exemption from what would otherwise be a terrorist attack' when insurgents used IEDs against Coalition forces. The judge answered that in his view such an attack would be covered by the definition of terrorism in the Terrorism Act 2000, but that the jury must decide for themselves.[129] The position of the trial judge seemed to be that while UK troops enjoyed combatant immunity the insurgents did not, leaving the ground clear for the acts of insurgents to be categorised as terrorism and acts undertaken in support of them, such as those of the appellant, as terrorism-related offences. The Supreme Court concentrated on whether the UK could categorise insurgent attacks as criminal even though they might not be seen as such under the rules of LOAC. In deciding that, despite the problems in adopting such a wide definition of terrorism, insurgent

---

[123]   *R v Gul (Mohammed)* [2013] UKSC 64.
[124]   See Terrorism Act (2000) section 1(4)(d).
[125]   *Gul* [2013] para 8.
[126]   Ibid, para 56.
[127]   Ibid, para 39.
[128]   Ibid, para 61.
[129]   Ibid, paras 5 and 6.

attacks could be included within it,[130] the Supreme Court seemed to prefer the view that combatant immunity did not exist in a NIAC. However, while clear that combatant immunity did not extend to insurgents,[131] it was ambiguous on whether it extended to UK forces. The Court cited Emily Crawford that 'international law does not immunize participation in non-international armed conflict', and that there is 'nothing in the customary international law that replicates … combatant immunity for persons who participate in' NIACs,[132] which, by itself, suggests that immunity does not extend to any participants in a NIAC (including UK forces).

There is clearer support for the unequal application of combatant immunity in *Keyu*, when the High Court stated, obiter, that the 'British Army … may well have had combatant immunity under customary law',[133] during what was a NIAC involving British forces and Communist insurgents in Malaya in 1948. The case, which involved the alleged murder of 24 unarmed civilians by a Scots Guards' patrol in the village of Batang Kali, gave rise to a claim that the UK government was required to hold a public inquiry into the allegations. However, the claim was dismissed by the UK Supreme Court on grounds of lack of jurisdiction.[134] The notion that a state's armed forces have combatant immunity while insurgents do not in a NIAC is disputed, with most jurists arguing that it does not exist for either side.[135] The closest the rules of LOAC on NIACs come to combatant immunity is to 'encourage post-war amnesties for those who have participated in the armed conflict'.[136]

However, even if combatant immunity for British soldiers engaged in a NIAC was to be clearly recognised by a British court, such immunity does not extend to wilful acts of murder against unarmed civilians as occurred in Batang Kali in 1948. Such acts are prohibited by LOAC and would constitute war crimes. Indeed, the only clear immunity that persists in an internal armed conflict is civilian immunity,[137] implicitly recognised in Common Article 3 of

---

[130]   Ibid, para 28.

[131]   Ibid, para 50.

[132]   Ibid. Crawford (2010) 78–9. See also S. Sivakumaran, *The Law of Non-International Armed Conflicts* (Oxford University Press, 2012) 515.

[133]   *Keyu v Secretary of State for Foreign Affairs* [2012] EWHC 2445 (Admin) at para 120.

[134]   *Keyu v Secretary of State for Foreign Affairs* [2015] UKSC 69.

[135]   A.P.V. Rogers, *Law on the Battlefield* (Manchester University Press, 2nd edn, 2004) 224: 'The law of armed conflict does not allow for combatant or prisoner-of-war status in internal armed conflict unless either belligerency has been recognized or the parties have agreed, or decided, to accord that status or apply the law of armed conflict in full.'

[136]   Crawford (2010) 79; AP II (1977) Article 6(5).

[137]   Rogers (2004) 225.

the Geneva Conventions, which prohibits violence to the life of persons not taking part in hostilities, and explicitly recognised in Article 13 of Additional Protocol II 1977. Intentionally attacking civilians in an internal armed conflict is a war crime under the Rome Statute of 1998.[138]

Common Article 3 provides limited protection to a British soldier involved in a NIAC, namely if rendered '*hors de combat* by sickness, wounds, detention, or any other cause': they 'shall in all circumstances be treated humanely, without any adverse distinction'; shall 'not to be subject to murder, mutilation, cruel treatment, torture, humiliating or degrading treatment'; or be taken hostage; or be subject to the 'passing of sentences and the carrying out of execution without previous judgement pronounced by a regularly constituted court, affording all the judicial guarantees which are recognized as indispensable by civilized peoples'. If Protocol II 1977 is applicable to a NIAC,[139] then there are more detailed rights to humane treatment for British soldiers captured or detained by insurgents,[140] covering internment,[141] and penal prosecutions for criminal offences related to the armed conflict. The latter must be undertaken before an independent and impartial court where essential guarantees include: a right to be informed of the alleged offence; 'all necessary rights and means of defence'; a presumption of innocence; a limitation to existing criminal offences; and freedom from self-implication.[142]

UK armed forces in a foreign state with the agreement of the government to fight an insurgency may benefit from a Status of Forces Agreement (SOFA) between the UK and the host state that grants exclusive criminal jurisdiction to the UK, providing a degree of immunity from prosecution before the courts of the host state, but not by any court established by the insurgents,[143] nor, arguably, by courts established by a new government following a successful insurgency.[144] There are a number of examples of courts established by armed

---

[138] Rome Statute (1998) Article 8(2)(c)–(e).
[139] The UK signed the Protocol in 1977 and ratified it in 1998, but, for example, Iraq is not a party and Afghanistan only ratified it in 2009.
[140] AP II (1977) Article 4.
[141] Ibid, Article 5.
[142] Ibid, Article 6.
[143] S. Sivakumaran, 'Courts of Armed Opposition Groups: Fair Trials or Summary Justice' (2009) 7 *Journal of International Criminal Justice* 489. See further, P.S. Gejji 'Can Insurgent Courts be Legitimate within International Humanitarian Law?' (2012–2013) 91 *Texas Law Review* 1525; *On the establishment of Courts in Non-International Armed Conflict by Non-State actors*, Stockholm District Court Judgment of 16 February 2017 in (2018) 16 *Journal of International Criminal Justice* 403.
[144] See, however, the principle that a new revolutionary government is bound by the existing obligations of the state which, arguably, might include any SOFA agreed by

opposition groups, mainly to deliver justice in the areas under their control, but also to enforce compliance with LOAC by their own fighters as well as captured government personnel.[145] Although there may be doubts about the legitimacy of 'domestic' laws promulgated by insurgents, the enforcement of LOAC through properly constituted courts established by them is in principle to be supported, as it helps to avoid unpalatable alternatives such as summary executions.[146] The issue then becomes as to whether those courts are independent, impartial and uphold the accused's right to a fair trial as required by LOAC and human rights law.

Understandably, the focus of debate on the lack of combatant status in NIACs has been on the insurgents: 'states view members of non-state armed groups against which they are in conflict as criminals or traitors, and, increasingly, terrorists, thus making it extremely unlikely that combatant immunity would be granted in advance and as a matter of course'.[147] The reason for the absence of combatant immunity in NIACs is the assumption that government forces will benefit from the protection of domestic laws while the insurgents run the risk of prosecution for acts committed during the conflict even if they abide by the principles of distinction, humanity and proportionality that remain applicable in NIACs. The government might decide not to prosecute captured insurgents, for example for taking up arms against the state or for the murder of government soldiers, in order not to inflame the conflict and to induce compliance by the insurgents with LOAC. However, that decision is not obligatory under LOAC. Nevertheless, the downside for states is that government troops captured by the insurgents do not enjoy combatant immunity, and British troops coming to the aid of a beleaguered government run the same risk.

5.5   THE RIGHT TO LIFE IN ARMED CONFLICT

The formal distinction between 'war' and 'peace', whereby each constituted an autonomous legal order, supposedly disappeared with the move towards regulating 'armed conflict' as opposed to 'war' in the Geneva Conventions of 1949. However, this simply led to a different form of the separation thesis, usually taking the form of an unconvincing argument that an 'armed conflict' triggers the *lex specialis* of LOAC, which has precedence over the *lex generalis* that operates in normal peacetime, including the provisions of international human

---

the host state and the UK: Note, 'Revolutions, Treaties, and State Succession' (1967) 76 *The Yale Law Journal* 1669.

[145] Sivakumaran (2009) 510.

[146] Ibid, 512.

[147] Sivakumaran (2012) 514.

rights law.[148] This method has been accepted by the ICJ, but only to the limited extent of interpreting the right not to be arbitrarily deprived of life under human rights law,[149] which the Court accepted as being applicable in principle during hostilities.[150] The Court stated that the 'test of what is an arbitrary deprivation of life, however, then falls to be determined by the *lex specialis*, namely the law applicable in armed conflict which is designed to regulate the conduct of hostilities'.[151] The Court was of the opinion that the right to life was therefore not to be 'deduced from the terms' of the human rights treaty itself, but from the provisions of LOAC. Whether this displacement provides a complete understanding of the right to life in armed conflict will be returned to in Chapter 8 but, even if that is case, it only addresses one potential area of norm conflict between LOAC and human rights law.

This approach does not fully exclude human rights law for it only applies when there is a conflict between the norms of LOAC and human rights law, and is based on a flimsy assumption that the *lex specialis/generalis* distinction, originating in Roman Law, should be applied to the interface between LOAC and human rights law.[152] Rather than relying on such legal artifices, Carswell points to the different rationales of LOAC and human rights law to explain their largely separate fields of operation:

> In contrast to [human rights law], which was developed to civilize the relationship between governments and the individuals within their power, IHL [LOAC] was born on the battlefield. It governs the exceptional circumstance of armed conflict, limiting means and methods of warfare to those that are necessary to weaken the enemy force, and providing protection for individuals who are not, or are no longer, taking part in hostilities.[153]

However, even within this explanation, there are grounds for overlap. By sending troops to conflict zones around the world, the UK government may be setting in train actions that result in the assertion of jurisdiction by organs and agents of the state over individuals within their power, thereby triggering its

---

[148] B. Bowring, 'Fragmentation, *Lex Specialis* and the Tension in the Jurisprudence of the European Convention of Human Rights' (2009) 14 *Journal of Conflict and Security Law* 485.

[149] Under the International Covenant on Civil and Political Rights (1966) Article 6.

[150] *Nuclear Weapons* (1996) para 25.

[151] Ibid.

[152] M. Milanovic, 'The Lost Origins of *lex specialis*: Rethinking the Relationship between Human Rights and International Humanitarian Law' in J. Ohlin (ed.), *Theoretical Boundaries of Armed Conflict and Human Rights* (Cambridge University Press, 2016) 78.

[153] Carswell (2009) 148.

human rights obligations as well as its obligations under LOAC.[154] It may be that in complying with the permissive rules of LOAC, for example on the use of force or detention, the government (through its armed forces and soldiers) will be violating its more proscriptive obligations under human rights law.[155]

Another reason why there has been a partial collapsing of the wall between the distinctive regimes of LOAC and human rights law is pointed out by Charles Garraway:

> As 'war' and 'peace' increasingly morph into a spectrum of violence where … it is difficult to identify the boundaries between the various levels of violence, there has been a battle for legal supremacy between those from the [LOAC] end who wish to see the definition of 'armed conflict' extended down to as low a level of violence as possible so as to extend the protections given by 'Geneva law', dealing with the protection of victims of war, as widely as possible, and those from the [human rights law] perspective who insist that human rights is the foundational law, the *lex generalis*, and that [LOAC], as the *lex specialis*, must be secondary. With each of these bodies of law claiming priority, what happens when they disagree?[156]

In some situations, especially during the emergency situation in Northern Ireland, the UK government deliberately avoided accepting the application of LOAC but, by so doing, could not escape the scrutiny of human rights law, especially under the ECHR.[157]

A final reason as to why both LOAC and human rights law both remain applicable in armed conflict situations is that the obligations have a different focus. Although the UK government is bound by LOAC and by human rights law, the duties under LOAC are directly applicable to the soldier reflected in their incorporation into UK law in the Geneva Conventions Act 1957, while under human rights law the obligations are principally on the state. Having said that, the government has to ensure that it, and its organs and agents, do not violate human rights law as well as LOAC, and that obligation will include prosecution of soldiers under national military law and international criminal

---

[154] See further discussion in Chapter 8. The extraterritorial extension of the Human Rights Act (1998) will be reviewed as part of the Independent Review of the Human Rights Act, established by the government in 2020 https://www.gov.uk/guidance/independent-human-rights-act-review.

[155] For a discussion of how the ECtHR has inconsistently interpreted the standards governing the right to life under Article 2 of the ECHR in the light of the standards of LOAC see S. Wallace, *The Application of the European Convention on Human Rights to Military Operations* (Cambridge University Press, 2019) 73–93.

[156] House of Commons Defence Committee, 'UK Armed Forces Personnel and the Legal Framework for Future Operations', Twelfth Report of Session 2013-14, HC 931, 2 April 2013, para 22 (Charles Garraway).

[157] See further Chapter 3.

law. Furthermore, international criminal law, which enhances the enforcement of the proscription of war crimes, imposes duties on individuals, although the state has obligations to investigate and prosecute. It follows that according to Hemming:

> The standards of conduct mandated by the criminal law are not affected by the application or non-application of the ECHR. If they comply with the criminal and disciplinary law that applies to them at all times, Service personnel can have high confidence in the legal security of their personal positions. They cannot be held personally liable in proceedings based on the HRA [Human Rights Act]. In so far as the HRA created new legal remedies, they concern the liability of the UK Government (not individuals) for alleged breaches by UK public authorities of the UK's international law obligations under the ECHR. This important point is not always made clear. No claim based on the HRA has ever been brought against any individual member of HM Forces because it is not legally possible to do so.[158]

5.6 DRONE STRIKES

New remote methods of using military force challenge the dynamics of which legal regime applies to frame the use of armed force. In this new paradigm, soldiers are not engaged in direct combat with the enemy or in defending themselves from imminent attack by terrorists, instead it can involve the calculated decision as to when to launch a lethal drone strike with no physical danger to the operator.[159] Nonetheless, when the UK is engaged in an armed conflict against a state or an organised armed group within a state the simple fact of membership of the enemy state's military or membership of the armed group will justify the use of force, including drone strikes, against enemy combatants or fighters.[160] Outside of armed conflict, there has to be a legal basis for using force in or against another state under the *jus ad bellum*, principally either acting in self-defence in the face of an imminent armed attack, or acting under the authority of the Security Council responding to a threat to international peace.[161]

---

[158] Defence Committee (2013) para 31 (Martin Hemming).

[159] On the development of fully autonomous weapons systems, including drones, see E. Winter, 'The Compatibility of Autonomous Weapons with the Principle of Distinction in the Law of Armed Conflict' (2020) 69 *International and Comparative Law Quarterly Review* 845; E. Winter, 'The Compatibility of the Use of Autonomous Weapons with the Principle of Precaution in the Law of Armed Conflict' (2020) 58 *Military Law and the Law of War Review* 240.

[160] See, for example, AP I (1977) Articles 48 and 52(2), whereby 'attacks shall be limited strictly to military objectives'. Military objectives include 'combatant members of the enemy armed forces ...': UK MoD (2004) 54.

[161] UN Charter (1945) Articles 42 and 51.

As well as *jus ad bellum* concerns, the use of lethal force by remotely operated drones raises issues of compliance with and liability under the *jus in bello* or LOAC. Questions as to whether drone operators, or indeed GCHQ employees who are ordered to pass intelligence to the US for its drone strikes, enjoy combatant immunity from charges of murder or abetting murder, have not been dealt with by the courts. The *Noor Khan* case involved the issue of intelligence sharing with the US for the purpose of identifying targets for US drone strikes against Al-Qaeda in Pakistan. The claimant argued that there was 'no armed conflict in Pakistan, as it is recognised under international law, still less an international armed conflict, and thus GCHQ employees were not entitled to combatant immunity'.[162] However, the application for judicial review was dismissed on the basis that the courts 'would not even consider, let alone resolve, the question of the legality of United States' drone strikes'.[163]

Furthermore, there is a contested issue of compliance with other rules of international law that potentially apply when lethal force is being used or contemplated overseas, principally the right to life under international human rights law.[164] The UK government does not appear to accept the application of the ECHR to the use of force by armed drones, stating that any use of military force abroad only triggers the application of LOAC. This was criticised in a report of the Joint Committee on Human Rights Report in 2016:

> In our view, the Secretary of State's position that the Law of War applies to the use of lethal force abroad outside of armed conflict, and that compliance with the Law of War satisfies any obligations which apply under human rights law, is based on a misunderstanding of the legal frameworks that apply outside of armed conflict. In an armed conflict, it is correct to say that compliance with the Law of War is likely to meet the State's human rights law obligations, because in situations of armed conflict those obligations are interpreted in the light of humanitarian law. Outside of armed conflict, however, the conventional view, up to now, has been that the Law of War, by definition, does not apply. We recommend that the Government, in its response to our Report, clarifies its position as to the law which applies when it uses lethal force outside of armed conflict.[165]

Bearing in mind that under LOAC attacking a military objective can lawfully result in civilian loss of life if the military advantage outweighs those losses,[166]

---

[162] *R (Noor Khan) v Secretary of State for Foreign and Commonwealth Affairs* [2012] EWHC 3728, para 2 (Moses LJ).

[163] Ibid, para 14.

[164] ECHR (1950) Article 2; ICCPR (1966) Article 6.

[165] House of Lords, House of Commons Joint Committee on Human Rights, 'The Government's Policy on the Use of Drones for Targeted Killing', Second Report of Session 2015-16, HL Paper 141, HC 574, 10 May 2016, para 3.55.

[166] AP I (1977) Article 50(5)(b).

while under human rights law such losses would prima facie constitute an arbitrary deprivation of life and a violation of Article 2 of the ECHR, the government position that only LOAC is applicable to drone strikes allows for their lawful usage even though there may be a risk of civilian casualties.

At the time of its Report in 2016, the Joint Committee was of the view that the remote use of force by drones constituted the assertion of jurisdiction by the UK for the purposes of Article 1 of the ECHR. The Committee stated that in the:

> Current state of the case-law, the use of lethal force abroad by a drone strike is sufficient to bring the victim within the jurisdiction of the UK: in the recent case of *Al-Saadoon v Secretary of State for Defence* [2015], the High Court held that 'whenever and wherever a state which is a contracting party to the [ECHR] purports to exercise legal authority or uses physical force, it must do so in a way that does not violate Convention rights.' The judge found it difficult to imagine a clearer example of physical control over an individual than when the State uses lethal force against them ...[167]

However, in 2016 the Court of Appeal reversed that aspect of *Al-Saadoon* when it considered the implications of the jurisprudence of the ECtHR on whether an extraterritorial use of lethal force by a state constituted an assertion of jurisdiction over the targeted individuals for the purposes of Article 1 of the ECHR.[168]

The case law of the ECtHR on this issue has shown some movement but not to the extent that the use of force per se amounts to the assertion of jurisdiction. In the *Bankovic* case, the applicants argued before the ECtHR that NATO states had violated the right to life of individuals when attacking the Serbian television studios in Belgrade during the Kosovo bombing campaign in 1999. As summarised by David Turns, the ECtHR found that the victims were not within the jurisdiction of the attacking states within the terms of Article 1 of the ECHR inter alia because 'bombing an area from 30,000 feet did not amount to having "effective control" of that area for the purposes of applying human rights obligations'.[169] In a more expansive judgment on the application of the ECHR to the UK in relation to its operations in Iraq, the ECtHR in *Al-Skeini* decided that civilians killed by UK forces in Iraq were protected under the ECHR whether they were killed in detention or on the streets. Given the nature of the occupation of Iraq in 2003–2004, entailing the exercise of public powers by British forces, those Iraqi civilians were within the jurisdiction of the UK.

---

[167] Joint Committee Report (2016) para 3.58.
[168] *Al-Saadoon v Secretary of State for Defence* [2016] EWCA Civ 811.
[169] Turns (2018) 842. *Bankovic v Belgium*, Appl No 52207/99, 12 December 2001; (2001) 11 BHRC 435, paras 67–73.

The ECtHR took the opportunity in *Al-Skeini* to rationalise its case law on jurisdiction, first to situations where a contracting state's agents had effective control over an area in another state and, second, to situations where state agents exercised authority and control over individuals.[170]

In the light of this, in *Al-Saadoon* before the Court of Appeal, Lloyd-Jones LJ concluded that the assertion of jurisdiction 'required a greater degree of power and control than represented by the use of lethal or potentially lethal force alone. In other words, I believe that the intention of the Strasbourg court was to require that there be an element of control of the individual prior to the use of lethal force'. Further he stated that '[i]f the logical consequence of the principle stated in *Al-Skeini* is that any use of extra-territorial violence is within the acting state's jurisdiction for this purpose, I believe that that is a conclusion which must be drawn by the Strasbourg court and not by a national court'.[171]

Thus the issue of whether the right to life would be violated by the use of force delivered by an armed drone, unless it was absolutely necessary in self-defence or on the other grounds specified in the ECHR,[172] remains unclear until the ECtHR finally addresses the issue of whether the use of force per se amounts to the assertion of jurisdiction.[173] The law is unclear but at the least the application of such force must engage the potential responsibility of the government for violation of the ECHR.[174] Also, assuming that LOAC does not apply because the drone strike is undertaken outside of an armed conflict, the individual drone operator firing a missile at a suspected terrorist outside of armed conflict may be charged under military law with the criminal offence of murder if it was established that there was no imminent attack by the terrorist, or that the attack killed civilians and the relevant *mens rea* was proven.[175]

Human rights law increases the weight of legal duties on the government including procedural ones to investigate potential violations of the right to life. However, the judgment in *Al-Sweady* drew a distinction between insurgents killed on the battlefield when Articles 1 and 2 of the ECHR, including the

---

[170] *Al-Skeini and Others v The United Kingdom*, Appl No 55721/07, 7 July 2011, paras 133–49.

[171] *Al-Saadoon* [2016] paras 69–70.

[172] ECHR (1950) Article 2(2).

[173] For the view that the use of force amounts to an assertion of jurisdiction for the purposes of the application of human rights law see the Inter-American Court of Human Rights judgment in *Armando Alejandre Jr, Carlos Costa, Mario de la Pena and Pablo Morales v Cuba (Brothers to the Rescue)*, Case 11.589, Report No 86/99, 28 September 1999, para 25.

[174] For discussion of the killing of Reyaad Khan in Syria in 2015 by a UK drone strike, see N.D. White, 'The Joint Committee, Drone Strikes and Self-Defence: Caught in No Man's Land?' (2016) 3 *Journal on the Use of Force and International Law* 210.

[175] Under the Armed Forces Act (2006) section 42.

obligation to investigate, would not be engaged, and those killed in detention, when they would be applicable.[176] The government will have to incorporate procedural and substantive obligations designed to uphold human rights law into military law to ensure it meets its human rights obligations, but human rights law does not directly impose obligations on soldiers. If the government wants to try and 'manage' its human rights obligations during an armed conflict, there is the possibility that it could derogate from some of its treaty duties, even when deploying to overseas conflicts.[177] These are issues that will be returned to in Chapter 6 when discussing detention. The focus in this chapter is on the dispute about applicable legal regimes and potentially conflicting norms when British soldiers and armed forces are placed in situations that, by their very nature, challenge neat distinctions between war/armed conflict and peace. The use of armed drones within and outside armed conflict is illustrative of the problem, but similar legal contestation emerges in many types of overseas troop deployments, none more so than when the UK deploys a contingent to form part of a UN peacekeeping mission.

5.7 THE USE OF FORCE IN PEACEKEEPING

The temptation is to reach for the MoD's *Manual on the Law of Armed Conflict* as the applicable legal framework for the use of force in peacekeeping on the basis that it is a military operation, and military operations should be governed by LOAC. However, it has been shown in Chapter 3 that there are numerous domestic deployments that are not governed by LOAC, and the same is true for some overseas deployments. Although it is a military operation, peacekeeping sits uncomfortably between a law enforcement operation normally undertaken by civilian police, and a combat operation undertaken by soldiers. In a typical unstable post-conflict situation to which peacekeepers are deployed the levels of violence far exceed those normally encountered by civilian police but fall short of the protracted armed violence between organised armed groups that characterises a NIAC.

---

[176] *R (Al-Sweady) v Secretary of State for Defence* [2009] EWHC 2287 (Admin) para 2 (Scott Baker LJ). On the question whether the Iraq Historic Allegation Team (IHAT), set up by the government in 2010 to investigate allegations of abuse of Iraqi civilians by UK armed forces in the period 2003–2009, fulfilled the UK's procedural obligations under the ECHR see *R (Mousa) v Secretary of State for Defence* [2011] EWCA Civ 1334; and *R (Ali Zaki Mousa) v Secretary of State for Defence* [2013] EWHC 1412.

[177] ECHR (1950) Article 15.

The precarious position occupied by a peacekeeper is captured by the adage that 'peacekeeping is not a soldier's job, but only a soldier can do it'.[178] At its inception in 1956, when the first UN Emergency Force (UNEF I) was deployed in the aftermath of the intervention in Suez (in part involving UK forces),[179] and for many UN operations thereafter, peacekeeping forces have not been deployed as combat operations. The UN mandate given to a peacekeeping operation does not normally place it in a combat situation, in contrast to a mandate given by the Security Council to coalitions of states to enforce the peace (peace enforcement as opposed to peacekeeping), for example against Iraq in 1991,[180] or Libya in 2011.[181] Those mandates lead to armed conflict between states acting under the resolution and the enemy state, whether it be Iraq or Libya, and the application of LOAC to regulate the use of force by armed forces.

Historically, the acceptability of a peacekeeping operation to the states and actors involved lies in the fact that it usually has limited objectives. Traditionally this means helping to maintain a cease-fire and a separation of the belligerents, not by means of enforcement but by consent and cooperation. Hence, peacekeeping is stated by the UN General Assembly Special Committee on Peacekeeping to be based on a trinity of principles, namely consent, impartiality, and restricting the use of force to self-defence.[182] The limitation on the use of force was established in the basic principles guiding UNEF I. In the Secretary General's 'Summary Study' of UNEF in 1958, he stated that while there was some margin for judgement on the level of force to be used by peacekeepers, they were not combat operations and were limited to the right of self-defence. He warned that 'a wide interpretation of the right of self-defence might well blur the distinction between [peacekeeping] operations … and combat operations, which would require a decision under Chapter VII of the Charter'. A 'reasonable definition' of self-defence in peacekeeping operations meant that soldiers 'engaged in the operation may never take the initiative in the use of armed force, but are entitled to respond with force to an attack with arms, including attempts to use force to make them withdraw

---

[178] C.C. Moskos, *Peace Soldiers: The Sociology of a United Nations Military Force* (University of Chicago Press, 1976) 139.

[179] Because of vetoes by the UK and France in the Security Council, UNEF I was mandated by the UN General Assembly – UN Doc A/RES/1000/ES-1 (1956). UNEF I remains exceptional in this regard.

[180] UN Doc S/RES/678 (1990).

[181] UN Doc S/RES/1973 (2011).

[182] UN Special Committee on Peacekeeping, 'Comprehensive review of the whole question of peacekeeping operations in all their aspects', UN Doc A/56/767 (2003) para 46.

from positions they occupy under orders from the Commander, acting under the authority of the Assembly and within the scope of its resolutions'.[183] The essence of this doctrine is a prohibition on the use of offensive force in which the initiative is taken by peacekeepers, thereby restricting them to defensive and reactive force. Although Findlay points out this was a somewhat retrospective construction of the rules governing UNEF,[184] it became UN doctrine, and was applied, at least initially, even to the UN Operation in the Congo (ONUC), which was deployed in 1960 in very different circumstances to UNEF. UNEF was imaginatively described by Finn Seyersted as 'acting like a plate-glass window', incapable of withstanding any significant assault upon it but nonetheless acting as a 'lightly armed barrier that all see and tend to respect'.[185] The limited use of force doctrine for peacekeepers shaped by and for UNEF I has had a lasting effect on peacekeeping, even though it was challenged by a much broader understanding of self-defence during the later stages of ONUC's deployment in the Congo,[186] and a broadening of the functions of peacekeeping after the Cold War ended.

At its core the limited use of force available to peacekeepers means self-defence, interpreted narrowly to cover a peacekeeper using force in defence of his own life, his 'comrades and any person entrusted in [his] care, as well as defending [his] post, convoy, vehicle or rifle'.[187] Beyond this, there has been a continuing lack of clarity as to whether the force could more broadly 'defend' its mandate. In general, peacekeeping was acceptable during the Cold War because it was kept distinct from enforcement action. Such a limited military operation not only suited the veto-wielding powers in the Security Council, it also met with the approval of the Non-Aligned states resistant to coercive forms of intervention redolent of the colonial era. It is no coincidence that the major troop contributors to peacekeeping forces during the Cold War were smaller volunteer states drawn from outside the five permanent members of the Security Council and their immediate allies, with some exceptions such as the British contribution to the UN Force in Cyprus (UNFICYP) from 1964 to the present day. That force's mandate and operating procedures

---

[183] UN Secretary General, 'Summary study of the experience derived from the establishment and operation of the force', UN Doc A/3943 (1958).

[184] T. Findlay, *The Use of Force in UN Peacekeeping* (Oxford University Press, 2002) 22–3.

[185] F. Seyersted, *United Nations Forces in the Law of Peace and War* (Sijthoff, 1966) 48.

[186] O. Schachter, 'The Uses of Law in International Peace-Keeping' (1964) 50 *Virginia Law Review* 1096 at 1112.

[187] 'General Guidelines for Peace-Keeping Operations', UN Doc UN/210/TC/CG95 (1995).

restricted peacekeepers to self-defence, meaning responses to direct attacks against them.[188] This led to the adoption by UNFICYP and subsequent Cold War peacekeepers of a 'constabulary ethic',[189] and an approach to operations designed not to drag them into an armed conflict with any of the factions or parties.[190]

Despite UN-commissioned reports recommending that more offensive action be taken by peacekeepers,[191] there is a reluctance to move away from the doctrine of self-defence as being the basis for the use of force and weapons by peacekeepers. This remains the core of modern peacekeeping practice. Tsagourias' explanation of why self-defence remains the prevailing doctrine, even with peace operations moving towards having more coercive elements to their mandates, for example to protect civilians, is that it makes them acceptable to the host state and the factions within it.[192] Nevertheless, at the doctrinal level the UN has expanded the concept of self-defence. The Brahimi Report of 2000 achieved this by unequivocally extending self-defence from defence of peacekeepers, to defence of civilians and of the mission.[193] As Tsagourias states, this follows the 'gradual expansion of the meaning of self-defence in PKOs [peacekeeping operations], from individual self-defence inherent to military personnel, to freedom of movement and defence of positions, to the defence of the mandate and the protection of third parties'.[194] This change is reflected in the UN's most recent iteration of peacekeeping principles: the 2008 Capstone Doctrine, which while still distinguishing peacekeeping from enforcement action, states that it is 'widely understood' that peacekeepers 'may use force at the tactical level, with the authorization of the Security Council, if acting in self-defense and defense of the mandate'.[195] However, the reality is that once self-defence is so-expanded it is no longer individual self-defence, but permits a certain amount of proactive force, although still falling short of full peace enforcement under Chapter VII of the UN Charter. Ultimately, if peacekeepers' right to use force was solely based on the inherent

---

[188]   Findlay (2002) 96.

[189]   Moskos (1976) 89.

[190]   Findlay (2002) 99.

[191]   See the Cruz Report 'Improving Security of United Nations Peacekeepers' (UN, 2017).

[192]   N. Tsagourias, 'Consent, Neutrality/Impartiality and the Use of Force in Peacekeeping: Their Constitutional Dimension' (2006) 11 *Journal of Conflict and Security Law* 473.

[193]   Brahimi, 'Report of the Panel on United Nations Peace Operations', UN Doc A/55/305-S/2000/809 (2000) paras 48–51.

[194]   Tsagourias (2006) 473.

[195]   Capstone Doctrine, 'United Nations Peacekeeping Operations: Principles and Guidelines' (UNDPKO, 2008) 31.

right of self-defence there would be no need for the mandate of modern peace operations to contain Chapter VII elements.[196]

The increase in levels of force used by peacekeepers has necessitated a recognition that the principles of LOAC could, in certain circumstances, apply to a peacekeeping operation or at least aspects of it. The Secretary General's Bulletin on the observance by UN forces of international humanitarian law produced in 1999 identifies 'fundamental principles and rules' of LOAC applicable to UN peacekeeping forces deployed under UN command and control, 'when in situations of armed conflict they are actively engaged therein as combatants, to the extent and for the duration of their engagement'.[197] The Bulletin is stated not to affect the status of peacekeepers as non-combatants under the UN's Safety Convention of 1994 as long as they are entitled to the protection given to civilians under LOAC.[198] It follows that a peacekeeper is normally a protected person, a civilian rather than a soldier, and yet when they are actively engaged in hostilities their status (temporarily) changes under LOAC to the other side of the civilian-combatant divide. The Bulletin also makes it clear that the list of applicable LOAC rules is not exhaustive nor does it replace the troop contributing nation's (TCN) national military laws.[199] The Bulletin covers: the protection of civilian populations; means and methods of combat; treatment of civilians and persons *hors de combat*; treatment of detained persons; protection of the wounded, the sick, and medical and relief personnel.[200] Furthermore, violations of the rules of LOAC by military peacekeepers shall be subject to prosecution by their national military courts.[201]

It is evident from UN guidelines and versions of the RoE that are publicly available that peacekeepers are not deployed within a combat paradigm to which LOAC would automatically apply, but the 1999 Bulletin is triggered only if they subsequently engage as combatants in an armed conflict and only for that period of engagement. In UN guidelines on the use of force for peacekeepers of 2017:

'Force' is defined as the use of, or threat to use, physical means to impose one's will. In peacekeeping operations, peacekeepers are authorised to use force in self-defense and to execute their mandated tasks in appropriate situations. Depending upon the mandate, this may include the authorisation to use force for the protection of civilians. The objective of the use of force in peacekeeping operations is to influence and deter, not necessarily to defeat threats seeking to threaten or harm United Nations

---

[196] Tsagourias (2006) 473.
[197] UN Doc ST/SGB/1999/13, para 1.1.
[198] Ibid, para 1.2.
[199] Ibid, section 1.2.
[200] Ibid, sections 5–9.
[201] Ibid, section 4.

personnel or associated personnel or the civilian population. In some cases, the use of force may also be authorized to respond to other threats, including those caused by armed spoilers intending to distract peace processes.[202]

In a sense these guidelines embody a robust 'constabulary ethic' to deter violence, but if the use of force by peacekeepers within this paradigm means that they become engaged in an armed conflict as combatants then LOAC will apply. The legal basis for the use of force by peacekeepers 'resides in the mandate of the peacekeeping mission, as reflected in the relevant resolution(s) adopted by the Security Council. The use of force must be exercised in a manner consistent with the mandate. It may be used in self-defense as well as in situations in which the mission is specifically mandated to use force as listed in the ROE'.[203] The guidelines are quite general on the law applicable to the use of force:

> The use of force in peacekeeping operations must comply with international laws, including applicable international humanitarian law and human rights norms, principles and standards. At all times, the use of force must be consistent with the principles of gradation, necessity, proportionality, legality, distinction, precaution, humanity and accountability. Any force used must be limited in its intensity and duration to what is necessary to achieve the authorized objective and, commensurate with the threat.[204]

This paragraph makes reference to the Secretary General's Bulletin of 1999, which clearly limits the applicability of LOAC to peacekeepers, but the references to the principles of 'necessity', 'proportionality', 'distinction' and 'humanity' come very close to the key principles of LOAC, suggesting it has more general application. Furthermore, the reference to human rights norms remains at the highest level of abstraction, although there are more specific references elsewhere in the guidelines, including the following statement on RoE, which reflects a significant movement away from purely defensive force:

> Mission-specific ROE provide the requisite authority for the use of force. ROE also explain the policy, principles, procedures and responsibilities governing the use of force. These rules are designed to ensure that force application is in compliance with fundamental principles and rules of international law, including international human rights law and international humanitarian law. While remaining predomi-

---

[202] UN DPKO/DFS, 'Guidelines: Use of Force by Military Components in United Nations Peacekeeping Operations', 2016.14, January 2017, para 6.

[203] Ibid, para 7.

[204] Ibid, para 8.

nantly defensive in nature, ROE may permit offensive action, if necessary and as authorized by the Security Council, in order to ensure mandate implementation.[205]

Each mission's RoE govern the use of force by military peacekeepers, and directives on the use of force (DUF) govern the use of force by any police contingent to the mission.[206] Oswald, Durham, and Bates assert that the 'legal foundation for DUF is primarily' human rights law, whereas the legal framework for RoE is a 'combination of' LOAC and human rights law.[207] This analysis raises some concerns. The RoE of such forces should only reflect LOAC if, and only to the extent that, peacekeepers exceptionally become engaged as combatants within an armed conflict, and therefore their normal activities should be framed by human rights law.

Human rights law provides some detail on when potentially lethal force is permitted which would not violate the right to life protected, for example, in Article 2 of the ECHR. According to this provision, during peacetime and situations short of armed conflict potentially lethal force is allowed when absolutely necessary for self-defence (including defence of others), to effect an arrest or prevent escape of a detainee, or in action taken to quell a riot or insurrection. During armed conflict lethal force is permitted in accordance with LOAC, when such force is permitted in actions taken against armed groups. Together, human rights law and LOAC provide peace operations with a legal framework for the use of force. In fragile post-conflict situations, where violence and disorder remain common, the human rights standard is applicable and peacekeepers' force should accord with Article 2. In such conditions, force is primarily defensive, while offensive force would be reserved for situations of armed conflict. In the Cold War, RoE largely reflected the defensive nature of force allowed under human rights law, but modern RoE allow for use of force beyond self-defence by peacekeepers if authorised by the Security Council under Chapter VII of the Charter, for example to protect civilians from imminent threat of physical violence.[208] Those additions might push peacekeepers into an armed conflict situation in order to tackle armed groups

---

[205] Ibid, para 38.
[206] See UNDPKO, 'Guidelines for the Development of Rules of Engagement (ROE) for United Nations Peace-keeping Operations', May 2002, UN Doc MD/FGS/0220.0001, in C.K. Penny, 'Drop That or I'll Shoot … Maybe: International Law and the Use of Deadly Force to Defend Property in UN Peace Operations' (2007) 14 *International Peacekeeping* 365.
[207] B. Oswald, H. Durham, and A. Bates (eds), *Documents on the Law of UN Peace Operations* (Oxford University Press, 2010) 562.
[208] R. McLaughlin, 'Some Rules of Engagement Legacies of the 1999 *Report of the Independent Inquiry into the Actions of the United Nations during the 1994 Genocide in Rwanda*' (2018) 22 *Journal of International Peacekeeping* 311–12, discussing the

that threaten civilians or the peace process and, therefore, have the potential to change the applicable legal framework from human rights law towards LOAC.

Nevertheless, there remain clear differences between the RoE of a modern peace operation and the RoE of UN-authorised military peace enforcement action. This is illustrated by the pocket card given to US troops engaging Iraqi forces in Operation Desert Storm under a UN Security Council mandate in 1991. The RoE open with a general statement that 'all enemy military person-nel and vehicles transporting the enemy or their supplies may be engaged', but then it lists a number of prohibitions upon the use of force against: those enemy combatants that are rendered *hors de combat*; civilians and their property (unless necessary to save US lives); and protected targets such as hospitals and churches unless force is necessary in self-defence.[209] These RoE are clearly based on the levels of force permitted by LOAC.

In the end, however, there can only be a presumption that a peacekeeper is restricted to using force in self-defence or defence of others, while a soldier in a peace enforcement operation has greater permission to use lethal force under the rules of LOAC. In the shifting sands of modern UN mandated and authorised operations it may be the case that a peacekeeper becomes engaged in hostilities and subject to LOAC, while a member of a peace enforcement operation will find themselves in a dangerous situation short of an armed conflict with RoE limited to self-defence. This was the case in *Bici* involving British soldiers on deployment with KFOR, which was a UN-authorised NATO peace enforcement operation deployed to post-conflict Kosovo in 1999. The court found that the soldiers had exceeded the limitations upon them to use force in self-defence when they shot at the occupants of a car, causing death and injury.[210]

Although the UN produces RoE for each mission, the TCNs that send troops for particular operations will also give directives to their contingents to ensure compliance with their respective domestic laws. The existence of dual instruc-tions to troops may, as argued by Stephens, help to explain the gap between the mandating resolution, where the language is increasingly of 'necessary measures', and 'the more prosaic question of legal authority *in situ* which has not been properly resolved and, furthermore, it is at this "tactical level" that the success of the operation is often decided'.[211] Stephens makes clear that the limitations on the UN force commander 'to actually command or even control

---

'Guidelines for the Development of Rules of Engagement (ROE) for United Nations Peacekeeping Operations', 15 May 2002 (MD/FGS/0220.0001).

[209] In A. Roberts and R. Guelff (eds), *Documents on the Laws of War* (Oxford University Press, 3rd edn, 2000) 562–3.

[210] *Bici v Ministry of Defence* [2004] EWHC 786 (QB) para 6.

[211] Stephens (2005) 157.

a participating national contingent', signify that the division between national and international RoE and laws remains a problem within peacekeeping operations.[212] He makes the case that on the issue of command at least, the distinction between UN-authorised CoWs and UN-commanded peacekeeping is less significant than may appear; indeed 'the conditions in which the force is deployed, the weapons carried and, to some extent, its actions all remain subject to single-state discretion'.[213] He explains the 'red card' regularly played by TCN commanders,[214] or what he calls the 'phone home syndrome', not solely as an issue of command but also of law. The national commander of a contingent deployed to a UN force will often have to check the compatibility of any order given by the UN force commander with national law: 'such guidance is usually sought to ensure the compatibility of domestic legal standards with the methods and means prescribed by the operations' command structure through RoE or other "command directives" to achieve the mission's goals'.[215]

As Stephens explains, although UN RoE have moved towards 'defence of mission', such 'broad authorities have been effectively "read down" and have been given a very narrow application by force commanders in the field'. He argues thus such 'reading down' is correct, because national law and RoE that flow from it are applicable, but it restricts the UN force's ability to meet the threats against it.[216] This is supported by Peter Rowe, who asserts that UN RoE have no binding application to UK troops, who are subject to British criminal law.[217] For example, while UN RoE allow the use of lethal force to defend property or civilians in certain circumstances, a TCN's national law may not.[218] This signifies that if a peacekeeper uses lethal force to defend property he or she will be subject to the military discipline of the TCN and not the UN (there being no UN disciplinary system in any case), and may only escape punishment at the discretion of a national court if it accepts the argument that he or she was acting under UN RoE.[219] Stephens concludes by stating that it is a 'fact that most peacekeepers operate under both UN and national-issued RoE and sometimes there is a contradiction between the two'.[220]

---

[212] Ibid, 158, 160.
[213] Ibid.
[214] R. Thakur and D. Banerjee, 'India: Democratic, Poor, Internationalist' in C. Ku and H. Jacobson (eds), *Democratic Accountability and the Use of Force in International Law* (Cambridge University Press, 2003) 198.
[215] Stephens (2005) 160.
[216] Ibid, 163–5.
[217] Rowe (1994) 954.
[218] Stephens (2005) 165.
[219] Ibid, 166.
[220] Ibid, 169.

The intrinsic limitations in a peacekeeping force made up of several TCNs, in which UN command and control is not complete and national RoE exist alongside UN RoE, signify that there is a significant degree of resistance from some TCNs to more forceful peacekeeping. Despite this, the most recent developments in UN peacekeeping push such forces further towards enforcement mandates and, therefore, nearer to LOAC as the default legal framework. Alexander Gilder identifies a deepening of UN peacekeeping support for establishing state authority, through the development by the Security Council of 'stabilisation' mandates. Such mandates not only include a 'robust posture' and 'active patrolling', but also incorporate 'increased logistical capabilities from Western military hardware, the encroachment of a counter-terrorism rhetoric, operations alongside host state forces, and an emphasis on (re)establishing the rule of law',[221] pointing to UN peace operations in the DR Congo, Mali and the Central African Republic. According to the UK's understanding, stabilisation 'is designed to protect and promote legitimate political authority', while the US approach to stabilisation 'is to support the legitimate authority in securing the monopoly on the use of force to enable the authority to protect its population'.[222] The UN's understanding is a diluted mixture of the two, with vaguer, broader connotations.

In the case of the UN Multidimensional Integrated Stabilisation Mission in Mali (MINUSMA), for example, the mission has contingents from Western countries and sophisticated military hardware including short range drones and attack helicopters. According to the Secretary General, MINUSMA has attempted to 'progressively dominate areas adjacent to population centres' in order to prevent incursion by criminals and terrorist groups,[223] and the Security Council has called on MINUSMA to engage in direct operations against asymmetric threats, while maintaining allegiance to the principles of peacekeeping.[224] Clearly, the principle of the limited use of force is being bent out of shape in peacekeeping operations.

Furthermore, as Gilder states: 'the position of the UN as an impartial actor becomes tenuous when the mandates of MINUSCA' (UN Multidimensional Stabilisation Mission in the Central African Republic) and MINUSMA 'expressly call for the missions to assist with the extension of state authority, assist with the redeployment of host state forces, and to conduct joint oper-

---

[221] A. Gilder, 'The Effect of "Stabilization" in the Mandates and Practice of UN Peace Operations' (2019) 66 *Netherlands International Law Review* 47.

[222] Ibid, 50–1.

[223] 'Report of the Secretary-General on the situation in Mali', UN Doc S/2014/403 (2014) para 66.

[224] UN Doc S/RES/2295 (2016).

ations and share intelligence'.[225] Stabilisation involves 'peacebuilding in the power vacuum left behind after displacing armed groups', and is based on the peacekeeping mission establishing the rule of law by helping the host state rebuild its criminal justice system. It may also entail peacekeepers using force as an exceptional and temporary measure to maintain law and order and to fight impunity.[226] The issue is made even more complex by the fact that in addition to MINUSMA in Mali there is a significant French military contingent present with the consent of the government and operating in support of the UN force.[227] The UK sent a contingent of 250 troops to support this French effort in 2019, troops who were clearly prepared for combat and not peacekeeping.[228]

5.8   CONCLUSION

Soldiers embody the state's monopoly on the use of force. They carry lethal weapons and are trained to use them. The complexification and slow juridification of the law surrounding the use of force by service personnel is understandable given the serious consequences of such action but, at the same time, it makes the duties placed upon soldiers and governments more difficult to fulfil. Given the degree of discretion that remains for the government in categorising the type of situation that soldiers are deployed to, it should be clear in its determination as to whether the deployment is to engage in an armed conflict (and then whether it is an IAC or NIAC), emergency situation or peacekeeping. The government should not dissemble for political purposes by, for example, ostensibly deploying troops for peacekeeping purposes when clearly the chances of troops being engaged as combatants in a NIAC are high. Nor should the government overclaim by, for example, stating that every time it uses a drone it is engaging in an armed conflict and, therefore, is only bound by the more permissive rules of LOAC. In other words, the government should avoid seeing the law as a malleable tool that can be fashioned to justify a lethal use of force. Such a view leaves the troops, who ultimately are ordered to fire weapons and take lives, exposed to criminal liability before a court where a judge may well apply the law in a much more objective and impartial manner.

---

[225] Gilder (2019) 64.
[226] For example, S/RES/2149 (2014) re MINUSCA.
[227] See UN Doc S/RES/2164 (2014) para 26.
[228] 'Mali: British troops to join force countering Mali militants', *The Guardian*, 22 July 2019.

6. Detention and abuse

6.1 INTRODUCTION

The tension between LOAC and human rights law is illustrated by the problem of detention of individuals by UK forces during armed conflict. While some rules are clear, for example the detention of PoWs in IACs governed by the Third Geneva Convention of 1949, others are not. This is especially so in the case of detention without charge or trial of individuals deemed to be threats to security in NIACs. The absence of clear LOAC rules on detention in NIACs has led to arguments that it should be governed by human rights law. However, this has been resisted by the UK as it would inhibit operational effectiveness. The UK government argues that the security imperative requires the detainment of possibly significant numbers of individuals in these conflicts and, while they will be treated humanely, conditions are not such that full human rights law guarantees can be delivered. In order to secure its position, it may be that the UK will try to derogate from Article 5 of the ECHR in future military operations to allow for security detention. Furthermore, in situations short of armed conflict the same security imperatives and human rights concerns remain, meaning that detention by peacekeepers is legally problematic, as is internment during states of emergency for similar reasons. In violent, unstable situations it may be necessary to detain individuals who are deemed threats to security although there may well be insufficient evidence to charge them with a criminal offence. Protecting the state, its monopoly on the use of force, and the rights of the majority of citizens, are prioritised over the rights of those detained.

The power of detention is largely an issue for government and engages the state's obligations under LOAC and human rights law. The treatment of detainees also engages the state's obligations in the sense that the government must ensure that systems and structures are in place to ensure humane treatment. Inhumane treatment by military personnel of detainees will engage the responsibility of both the state and individual soldiers. Abuse of Iraqi civilians both in detention and during operations in Iraq has been an issue that has dogged the government and the armed forces since the invasion of Iraq in 2003. Amongst a plethora of methods of accountability that have arisen during this period and its aftermath are two separate public inquiries into instances of abuse (the Baha Mousa and Al-Sweady Inquiries), and the establishment of an independent investigatory process (Iraq Historic Allegations Team (IHAT)). The problem of alleged abuse of Iraqis by British soldiers has resulted in numerous claims, cases and inquiries raising issues of the ability of national and international law and legal institutions to hold soldiers and, more broadly, the armed forces, the MoD and the UK government to account.

Peter Rowe explains a further connection between state and individual responsibility: '[o]ne of the responsibilities that a government has in protecting its own soldiers when they carry out its orders, is to ensure that they are never required to do anything that would be illegal under international law or under English criminal law'.[1] Soldiers need legal certainty, so they are concerned with the 'risks of war not those of trial'. Rowe goes further: 'it is more likely that, if British soldiers break the law, they will do so not because they have been ordered to do so, but because they are uncertain during an armed conflict as to where a particular boundary of illegality lies', giving the example of the treatment of detainees in Iraq and Afghanistan by British soldiers.[2] It may be true that uncertainties over the legal framework governing detention creates a grey area in which abuse occurs, but there is little excuse for individual behaviour that falls far short of treating detainees humanely, most infamously illustrated by the treatment and death of Baha Mousa in a British detention facility in Iraq in 2003.

Detention during an armed conflict of captured insurgents and civilians has become a major problem for British armed forces and has in recent years led to copious amounts of litigation before UK and Strasbourg courts. There are disputes and disagreements at all levels from the power to detain, to the treatment of detainees, and the transfer of them to other states. But the reality is that large-scale detentions during armed conflicts are authorised by the MoD and they are often necessary to bring security, and to restore law and order. Indeed, if the armed forces are not allowed to lawfully detain a suspected insurgent, improvised explosive devices (IED)-maker or civilian who conceals weaponry or otherwise provides support for an insurgency, the incentive to use lethal force is increased, which is contrary to the principle of humanity underpinning both LOAC and human rights law. It has become very difficult for those soldiers and commanders on the ground to operate within a clear lawful framework for detention, and it renders the government open to lawsuits against it.

---

[1]   P. Rowe, *Legal Accountability and Britain's Wars 2000–2015* (Routledge, 2016) 183.
[2]   Ibid.

6.2   THE POWER TO DETAIN IN IACS

As might be expected, given the origins of LOAC, the clearest power to detain relates to enemy combatants captured in an IAC, who are to be detained in humane conditions until the conflict is over. PoWs, although under the power and control of the detaining state, are not being detained without charge or trial in violation of the rights to due process and fair trial under human rights law. While there is no express human rights treaty provision to support this, there is plenty of state practice to establish the legality of detaining PoWs in accordance with the Third Geneva Convention of 1949 for the duration of a conflict, at the end of which they should be released and returned to their home state. States have effectively agreed that this is the applicable law in the circumstances of PoWs. In effect, the combatant immunity, which soldiers have for killing enemy combatants under LOAC, is continued when captured in the sense that PoW status protects them from prosecution for lawful acts of war.[3]

However, there is a more serious conflict between human rights law and LOAC when forces detain individuals in an IAC in the belief they constitute threats to security. Security detainees are not captured regular soldiers or combatants who have a duty to distinguish themselves from the civilian population,[4] and therefore they do not qualify as PoWs, neither are they civilians arrested and charged with crimes who have been placed in detention awaiting trial.[5] Under LOAC applicable to IACs administrative detention or internment should only be used for imperative reasons of security 'if the security of the Detaining Power makes it absolutely necessary'.[6] The Fourth Geneva Convention of 1949 states that any individual who has been interned 'shall be entitled to have such action reconsidered as soon as possible by an appropriate court or administrative board'. If internment is continued then LOAC provides for periodic review by a court or board to give consideration to the case with a view to a favourable decision if circumstances permit.[7] Furthermore, in cases of occupation, internment is allowed if the occupying power 'considers it necessary for imperative reasons of security' under a procedure that shall include a right of appeal to be conducted with the least possible delay. In cases where

---

[3]   GC III (1949) Article 99. See discussion of combatant privilege and immunity in Chapter 5.

[4]   AP I (1977) Article 44(7). See also GC III (1949) Article 4A(2).

[5]   In the case of penal offences relating to the armed conflict, LOAC provides basic rights to the detained person – see AP I (1977) Article 75.

[6]   GC IV (1949) Article 42.

[7]   Ibid, Article 43.

the detention is upheld it shall be subject to periodic review, if possible every six months by a 'competent body'.[8]

In contrast to the rules of LOAC, which grant a permissive power of detention on the vague grounds of threats to security, under human rights law detention is an unlawful deprivation of liberty unless it accords with specified grounds. Article 5 of the ECHR provides that 'everyone has the right to liberty and security of person', and further that liberty can only be deprived by detention on specified grounds, namely: after conviction by a court; for non-compliance with a court order; for the purpose of bringing the detainee before a court on reasonable suspicion of having committed an offence; or for the purpose of preventing the spread of infectious diseases.[9] An individual has the right to be promptly informed of the reasons for his arrest, to be brought promptly before a judge, and is entitled to trial within a reasonable time or to release pending trial.[10] Article 5(4) provides that '[e]veryone who is deprived of his liberty by arrest or detention shall be entitled to take proceedings by which the lawfulness of his detention shall be decided speedily by a court and his release ordered if the detention is not lawful'.[11]

In *Hassan v United Kingdom* in 2014,[12] the 'conflict between the limited permissible grounds for detention under Article 5(1) ECHR, and the more permissive rules under [LOAC] allowing security internment in an international armed conflict was put squarely in issue'.[13] Hassan had been detained by British forces in Iraq for nine days in 2003 when the armed conflict was international in character. He was released when it was found that he was in fact a civilian and no threat to security. Hassan's detention did not fall under any of the grounds listed under Article 5(1) of the ECHR and he had no effective access to a court for the purposes of Article 5(4). The British government relied on the rules of LOAC, which conferred a power to detain for imperative reasons of security, arguing that they either prevailed over human rights law by reason of being *lex specialis*, or that the ECHR had to be interpreted to take account of LOAC as the *lex specialis*.[14] Furthermore, it argued that the practice

---

[8]   Ibid, Article 78.
[9]   ECHR (1950) Article 5(1).
[10] Ibid, Article 5(2)(3).
[11] See also ECHR (1950) Article 5(5), which provides for an enforceable right to compensation in cases of unlawful detention.
[12] *Hassan v United Kingdom*, Appl No 2970/09, 16 September 2014.
[13] S. Borelli, '*Jaloud v Netherlands* and *Hassan v United* Kingdom: Time for a Principles Approach to the Application of the ECHR to Military Action Abroad' (2015) 16 *Questions of International Law* 25 at 35.
[14] *Hassan* (2014) para 89.

of parties to the ECHR involved in such operations was not to derogate from Article 5 under Article 15 of the ECHR.[15]

The question was dealt with by the ECtHR not as one of competing obligations as in *Al-Jedda* (reviewed below), but rather as an issue of interpretation of the UK's obligations under Article 5 of the ECHR in the light of the powers of detention available to it under LOAC.[16] The Court stated that the list of permissible grounds in Article 5(1) ECHR 'does not include internment or preventive detention where there is no intention to bring criminal charges within a reasonable time'.[17] Nevertheless, the Court considered that there were 'important differences of context and purpose between arrest carried out in peacetime and the arrest of a combatant in the course of an armed conflict'. This was clearly evidenced by the detention of PoWs, since they enjoy combatant privilege 'allowing them to participate in hostilities without incurring criminal sanctions',[18] but also the Court's reasoning extended to security detainees where the aim is to remove them as a threat or risk rather than to prosecute them or detain them as PoWs. In effect, consistent practice by parties to the ECHR amounted to an agreement to interpret or even modify the text of the ECHR to allow for detention in an IAC on the basis of the powers contained in the Third and Fourth Geneva Conventions and the protections contained therein, which were 'designed to protect captured combatants and civilians who pose a security threat'.[19]

However, the Court made it clear that 'it can only be in cases of international armed conflict, where the taking of prisoners of war and the detention of civilians who pose a threat to security are accepted features of international humanitarian law, that article 5 could be interpreted as permitting the exercise of such broad powers'.[20] Such an approach did not replace Article 5 of the ECHR with the rules of LOAC, rather the security detention under LOAC was in effect added as another ground for detention in the specific circumstances of an IAC. Such a power had to be exercised lawfully, in particular it should not be arbitrary.[21] The Court interpreted Article 5(4) of the ECHR, which requires access to a court, in the light of Articles 43 and 78 of the Fourth Geneva Convention, which provide that internment 'shall be subject to periodical review, if possible every six months, by a competent body'. This understanding allowed detaining powers to review detention by a 'competent body' rather than a court, as long

---

[15]   Ibid, para 90.
[16]   Ibid, para 99.
[17]   Ibid, para 98.
[18]   Ibid, para 97.
[19]   Ibid, paras 101–2.
[20]   Ibid, para 104.
[21]   Ibid, para 105.

as such a body provided 'sufficient guarantees of impartiality and fair procedure to protect against arbitrariness', and as long as an initial review took place
shortly after the person was taken into detention.[22]

Following from this reasoning, the Court concluded that Hassan's detention
was lawful in that it accorded with the UK's powers of detention under rules of
LOAC applicable to IACs, and that it did not violate Article 5 of the ECHR.[23]
The Court effectively changed direction in this judgment in order to accommodate LOAC rules within a framework of human rights law. *Hassan* is inconsistent with the Court's previous jurisprudence on the exhaustive nature of the
grounds for detention in Article 5 and also on the need to have derogations in
place before any limitations on derogable rights could be considered.[24] Borelli
is heavily critical of the Court's 'willingness to disregard the clear text of the
Convention', which will drag it into difficult questions of LOAC for which
its expertise might be called into question.[25] The other side of this argument,
is that civilian courts are increasingly being accessed by citizens and soldiers
alike for alleged violations of their rights and such cases inevitably should
include a consideration of the rights and duties of individuals and governments
under the applicable law, which includes both human rights law and LOAC.

6.3   THE PRACTICE OF DETENTION IN NIACS

At first sight *Hassan* does not solve the problem of preventive or security
detention in a NIAC, given that the provisions of the Third and Fourth Geneva
Conventions 1949 relied upon in the judgment are only applicable to an IAC.
There are no clear powers of detention under LOAC as regards NIACs, and
yet this is the type of armed conflict in which the UK has been most recently
involved in Afghanistan and Iraq. When faced with such practicalities human
rights jurisprudence has shown some flexibility, showing a concern to make
such practices as internment human rights compliant, not necessarily to outlaw
the practices themselves. The Human Rights Committee, when interpreting the
right to liberty under the International Covenant on Civil and Political Rights
(ICCPR), has stated that:

> To the extent that States parties impose security detention (sometimes known as
> administrative detention or internment) not in contemplation of prosecution on
> a criminal charge, the Committee considers that such detention presents severe
> risks of arbitrary deprivation of liberty. Such detention would normally amount to

---

[22]   Ibid, para 106.
[23]   Ibid, para 109.
[24]   Borelli (2015) 39.
[25]   Ibid, 40–1.

arbitrary detention as other effective measures addressing the threat, including the criminal justice system, would be available. If, under the most exceptional circumstances, a present, direct and imperative threat is invoked to justify the detention of persons considered to present such a threat, the burden of proof lies on States parties to show that the individual poses such a threat and that it cannot be addressed by alternative measures, and that burden increases with the length of the detention. States parties also need to show that detention does not last longer than absolutely necessary, that the overall length of possible detention is limited and that they fully respect the guarantees provided for by article 9 in all cases. Prompt and regular review by a court or other tribunal possessing the same attributes of independence and impartiality as the judiciary is a necessary guarantee for those conditions, as is access to independent legal advice, preferably selected by the detainee, and disclosure to the detainee of, at least, the essence of the evidence on which the decision is taken.[26]

This permits internment for imperative reasons of security in the 'most exceptional circumstances' if the detention is made human rights compliant. Even when adequate processes of review of detention are established in these circumstances, long-term detention for security reasons would remain prohibited by human rights law.

The approach of the ECtHR to preventive detention in NIACs appears to show less flexibility. In the *Al-Jedda* case, the applicant had been interned for imperative reasons of security in a British military facility in Iraq for over three years from October 2004 to December 2007 during the NIAC stage of the deployment. His detention was authorised and reviewed by senior military personnel and by the UK government on the basis of intelligence that was not disclosed to him. He was able to make written submissions to the British authorities but there was no provision for an oral hearing, nor was it intended to bring any criminal charges against him. The UK government had not derogated from Article 5 of the ECHR (on the right to liberty and security of person) and therefore the Court held that preventive detention was not permitted where there was no intention to bring charges within a reasonable time.[27]

Much of the UK government's arguments before the Court in *Al-Jedda* had been to try to establish that the applicant's human rights protections were overridden by obligations arising from a Security Council resolution, and very little effort was spent trying to justify the internment in human rights or LOAC terms. This is probably due to the fact that the detention clearly breached Article 5 ECHR. The ECtHR left open the possibility that the Security Council could expressly override the human rights obligations of member states, but

---

[26]   Human Rights Committee, General Comment No. 35, 'Article 9 (Liberty and security of person)', UN Doc CCPR/C/GC/35, 16 October 2014, para 15.

[27]   *Al-Jedda v UK*, Appl No 27021/08, 7 July 2011, paras 98–9.

that in the case before it the authorising Resolution (1546) could not be read in this way.[28] The result is that the UK could utilise its position as a permanent member of the Security Council to argue for the insertion of a clause in future authorising resolutions to provide for reviewable preventive detention as a 'necessary measure', accompanied by an express statement in the resolution that any inconsistent human rights obligations of states acting under the resolution would be suspended for the duration of the operation.

Heike Krieger's analysis concludes that the ECtHR's judgment in *Al-Jedda* has 'strong consequences on security detention during military operations where international humanitarian law is not directly applicable'. 'Even if in these cases detention is modelled akin to the Geneva Conventions and based on the SC Resolution's mandate to use all necessary means or on the right to self-defence, Article 5 ECHR is not set aside'.[29] Krieger concludes that '[i]f ECHR member States want to establish lawful forms of preventive detention they basically have two ways available: (1) explicit authorization in a Security Council mandate or (2) derogations under Article 15 ECHR'.[30] This still leaves open the question of what standards apply to preventive detention in NIACs, assuming the UK has cleared the hurdles for setting aside the guarantees in Article 5 of the ECHR.

In *Al-Waheed and Serdar Mohammed* (2017),[31] the UK Supreme Court attempted to find a way past *Al-Jedda* by extending the reasoning of the ECtHR in *Hassan* on detention in IACs to NIACs. While subject to potential contradiction by the ECtHR, the Supreme Court's judgment attempts to make a practical framework for detention in NIACs possible and, moreover, one that is human rights compliant, at least in the sense accepted by the ECtHR in *Hassan*. The complexity of the judgment can be seen to reinforce the view held by many in the military and politics that human rights law is making the soldier's job very difficult, if not impossible. However, this disregards the fact that much of the judgment was concerned with the government's right or power to detain, while it was relatively straightforward on the guarantees that should be granted to detainees once they are detained. While the armed forces must be assured that there is a legal basis for detention, their practical concern is for what this means in operational terms. It should also be added that the lack of a clear basis for detention under LOAC adds to the legal uncertainty, making it wrong to place the blame on creeping juridification under human rights law.

---

[28] Ibid, paras 102–9.
[29] H. Krieger, 'After *Al-Jedda*: Detention, Derogation, and an Enduring Dilemma' (2011) 50 *Military Law and the Law of War Review* 419 at 432.
[30] Ibid, 433.
[31] *Al-Waheed and Serdar Mohammed v Ministry of Defence* [2017] UKSC 2.

Al-Waheed and Serdar Mohammed arose out of claims made by detainees in Iraq and Afghanistan alleging unlawful detention and maltreatment by British forces while operating under mandates from the UN Security Council. They represented two of hundreds of such claims. In Lord Sumption's words, British forces 'were required to deal with exceptional levels of violence by organised armed groups. In the course of their operations, prisoners were taken and detained in British military facilities for varying periods of time.'[32] Al-Waheed was captured by British forces in Basra (Iraq) in 2007 during a search that allegedly found IEDs, explosives and weaponry. He was held at a British army detention centre for over six weeks and was then released as there was insufficient evidence to charge him. Serdar Mohammed was captured in Afghanistan in 2010 after a firefight with insurgents. He was allegedly a senior Taliban commander and was detained for three and a half months, before being transferred to Afghan authorities. He was subsequently convicted by the Afghan courts and sentenced to 10 years' imprisonment for offences relating to the insurgency.[33]

Broadly, the appeal raised issues of whether the armed forces had the power to detain the two claimants and, if so, whether Article 5 of the ECHR could be interpreted as allowing for such detention. On the power to detain, although there was some disagreement between the judges, the Supreme Court was of the view that such powers lie in the authority given to the UK forces by the Security Council rather than the existence of a customary right to detain in a NIAC under LOAC. Although the Court was clearly of the opinion that a right of detention was not only widely practised in NIACs but, moreover, was justifiable as it 'mitigates the lethal character of armed conflict and is fundamental in any attempt to introduce humanitarian principles into the conduct of war',[34] there was insufficient *opinio juris* from states including the UK to establish it as a customary rule.[35] Instead, the Court read the mandating resolutions of the Security Council as permitting the power of detention as part of its wider authorisation to contributing states to take 'necessary measures' to bring peace and security to Iraq and Afghanistan, even if they did not oblige the UK to carry out detentions as determined by the ECtHR in *Al-Jedda*.[36] On this basis, the UK had the power, if not the duty, to detain: 'if detention is "imperative" for reasons of security, it must be "necessary" for the performance of the

---

[32]　Ibid, para 1 (Lord Sumption).
[33]　Ibid, paras 3 and 4.
[34]　Ibid, para 15.
[35]　Ibid, para 16.
[36]　Ibid, para 20, citing UN Doc S/RES/1546 (2004) and UN Doc S/RES/1723 (2006) re Iraq; and UN Doc S/RES/1386 (2001) and UN Doc S/RES/1890 (2009) re Afghanistan.

mission'.[37] The importance to the international legal order of Security Council resolutions was emphasised, as was their potential to 'constitute an authority binding in international law to do that which would otherwise be illegal in international law'.[38]

Having established a lawful power to detain, the Court then considered the application of Article 5 ECHR in situations of armed conflict where legitimate military measures necessitate interference with life, liberty and property in conditions that are far from the minimum levels of public and legal order envisaged by the drafters of the ECHR and, moreover, are subject to the universal authority of the Security Council.[39] For the Court, this meant that the grounds of lawful detention listed in Article 5 of the ECHR were not designed for situations of armed conflict and cannot easily be adapted to it; a situation recognised in relation to IACs by the ECtHR in *Hassan*.[40] The UK Supreme Court felt that the ECtHR in *Hassan* had moved beyond its rather rigid position in *Al-Jedda*, towards a more 'fruitful approach' of reconciliation of different sources of law which, in the present case, would mean reconciling the terms of the Convention with those of the Security Council resolutions 'by adapting the former to the situation created by the latter'.[41]

The Supreme Court rejected the contention that the reasoning of the ECtHR in *Hassan* had no application to NIACs. Instead of the power to detain under the Third and Fourth Geneva Conventions that applied in IACs, the power to detain in NIACS derived from Security Council resolutions (meaning there would be no power to detain in NIACs without such an authorising resolution). The reasoning in *Hassan* that the six grounds of detention in peacetime listed in Article 5 needed qualifying because of the context of armed conflict applied equally to NIACs, and the necessity of detention on security grounds was equally present in both types of conflict.[42] While there was no requirement under LOAC governing NIACs, or under the applicable Security Council resolutions, for periodical review of detention by a competent body as there is under LOAC governing IACs, such procedural safeguards represented a practical contextual adaptation of Article 5(4) of the ECHR, where the establishment of a court in an NIAC situation would be equally unrealistic. Legally speaking, this is the weakest part of the judgment, but it is premised on the argument that it would make no sense to insist on review by a court in a NIAC while accepting one by a 'competent body' in an IAC. In any armed conflict,

---

[37] Ibid, para 28.
[38] Ibid, para 25.
[39] Ibid, para 41.
[40] Ibid, para 42.
[41] Ibid, para 50.
[42] Ibid, paras 60–1.

the protection of detainees from arbitrary detention is achieved by 'an initial review of the appropriateness of the detention, followed by regular reviews thereafter, by an impartial body in accordance with a fair procedure'.[43]

In fact, in the case of Serdar Mohammed, the Supreme Court found a breach of Article 5(4) of the ECHR, even as qualified, given that the 'UK Detention Authority was responsible both for authorising detention and then for reviewing its own decision' and, therefore, was not sufficiently impartial. Lord Sumption accepted 'that it may be unrealistic to require military detention in a war zone to be reviewed by a body independent of the army or, more generally, of the executive, especially if reviews are to be conducted with the promptness and frequency required. But it is difficult to conceive that there can be sufficient institutional guarantees of impartiality if the reviewing authority is not independent from those responsible for authorising the detention under review, as it commonly is in the practice of other countries including the United States'.[44] Furthermore, the system of review fell down in not providing for the participation of the detainee, bearing in mind that Article 5(4) protected the detainee's right 'to take proceeding by which the lawfulness of his detention shall be decided'. 'This is not simply a requirement that the authorities should review their own act. It is a right of challenge which must necessarily involve the detainee. Specifically, he must be entitled to challenge the existence of any imperative reasons of security justifying his detention, which was the essential condition for it to be lawful.'[45] Such participation should be premised on the detainee knowing in outline the reasons for his detention and the nature of the review process, and in having some access to the outside world in order to obtain evidence, moreover, that he should be entitled to make representations. However, the right to legal advice was said to be debatable given the context.[46]

Inevitably the Supreme Court's judgment has received criticism that the attempt 'to find a principled basis for the interaction of art. 5 with resolutions of the UN Security Council in the context' of NIACs, goes 'further than any decision of the ICJ' or ECtHR.[47] Furthermore, it is argued that the judgment is problematic for the proposition that in the case of NIACs Security Council resolutions 'can stand in for the role' of the Geneva Conventions for IACs. Furthermore, it is questioned whether a Security Council authorisation to use 'necessary measures', which is essentially a *jus ad bellum* justification, can

---

[43]   Ibid, paras 66–8.
[44]   Ibid, para 105.
[45]   Ibid, para 106.
[46]   Ibid, para 107.
[47]   A. Habteslasie, 'Detention in Times of War: Article 5 of the ECHR, UN Security Council Resolutions and the Supreme Court Decision in *Serdar Mohammed v Ministry of Defence*' (2017) 2 *European Human Rights Law Review* 180 at 191.

be used in a *jus in bello* context, essentially collapsing the normative divide between the two.[48] It would also produce an inconsistency in NIACs, whereby preventive detention would only be allowed in conflicts where there was a mandate from the Security Council authorising necessary measures and not in others, when the imperative to detain will be present in both.

Marco Sassoli has stated that when comparing the LOAC applicable to NIACs 'on procedural guarantees for persons arrested with those of' human rights law, 'the former do not exist while ... the latter are clear and well developed by jurisprudence'. For Sassoli the rules of human rights law 'must therefore prevail' since they 'are more precise and more restrictive'.[49] The principle that when two conflicting rules are applicable to an individuals, they should benefit from the one that provides the greater protection, is clearly legitimate but Sassoli then admits the practical problems presented by such an approach, particularly whether 'it is realistic to expect states and non-state actors, interning possibly thousands, to bring all internees before a court without delay during armed conflict. If it is not, such an obligation risks making it extremely difficult to conduct war effectively and, thus, could lead to less compliance with the rules in the long term, eg summary execution disguised as battlefield killings'.[50] In this light, the solution offered by the Supreme Court, amounting to a practical contextual adaptation of human rights law, could be argued to make sense, although the amount of leeway given to a state in setting up an impartial body to review detentions is of concern. Such a body could fall a long way short of an independent and impartial court concerned with upholding the rule of law rather than protecting the security concerns of the state.

6.4   THE POWER TO DETAIN IN EMERGENCIES

The UK practised internment or detention without trial intermittently in Northern Ireland from 1921 following the partition of the island of Ireland, culminating in the period 1971–1975 during the 'Troubles' in Northern Ireland.[51] As Brice Dickson reports:

> Internment was resorted to when the authorities felt that they could not deal with civil unrest through the 'ordinary' processes of law and order because, for example, they could not gather enough evidence from witnesses or informers ... or they

---

[48]   Ibid, 190.
[49]   M. Sassoli, 'The Role of Human Rights and International Humanitarian Law in New Types of Armed Conflicts', in O. Ben-Naftali (ed.), *International Humanitarian Law and International Human Rights Law* (Oxford University Press, 2011) 92.
[50]   Ibid.
[51]   For background see Chapter 3.

believed that if a person was not interned he or she would almost certainly become involved in the commission of violent acts.[52]

From 1957, the UK government had declared a state of emergency in Northern Ireland under Article 15 of the ECHR, and indicated to the Council of Europe in 1971 that the government had 'found it necessary ... for the protection of life and the security of property and to prevent outbreaks of public disorder, to exercise, to the extent strictly required by the exigencies of the situation, powers of detention and internment'.[53] On invoking the power to intern on 9 August 1971, the authorities targeted 500 men for detention.[54] Under the Detention of Terrorists (NI) Order of 1972, the minister could make an 'interim custody order' permitting detention for 28 days, but during this period the police could request an indefinite 'detention order'. Before granting this request, a Commissioner was required to give the detainee an opportunity for an oral hearing where they would hear the case against them and could be represented by a lawyer. If the Commissioner was satisfied that the detainee was involved in acts of terrorism and that detention was necessary to protect the public, the detainee could appeal to a Detention Appeal Tribunal within three weeks.[55]

In *Ireland v UK* (1978), the ECtHR stated that it was clear from the facts that there was a state of emergency in Northern Ireland and accepted that the UK government was 'reasonably entitled to consider that normal legislation offered insufficient resources for the campaign against terrorism and that recourse to measures outside the scope of the ordinary law, in the shape of extrajudicial deprivation of liberty was called for'.[56] While accepting the derogation from Article 5 of the ECHR (protecting the right to liberty and security of person), the Court found that the five techniques used against IRA suspects held in detention (wall standing, hooding, subjection to noise, deprivation of sleep, and deprivation of food and drink) amounted to inhuman and degrading treatment of the detainees. The Court found that this mistreatment did not cause sufficient suffering so as to amount to torture, but that it did amount to inhuman or degrading treatment in violation of Article 3 of the ECHR.[57] Thus, while derogation protected the UK from scrutiny by the courts for its policy of internment, it did not protect it from accountability for violation of

---

[52]   B. Dickson, 'The Detention of Suspected Terrorists in Northern Ireland and Great Britain' (2009) 43 *University of Richmond Law Review* 927 at 930.
[53]   Ibid, 934.
[54]   Ibid, 931.
[55]   Ibid, 932.
[56]   *Ireland v UK*, Appl No 5310/71, 18 January 1978, para 212.
[57]   Ibid, para 167.

non-derogable rights such as the right to freedom from torture or degrading treatment meted out while an individual was in detention.

A similar outcome in terms of judicial review occurred after the UK government had declared a state of emergency and derogated from Article 5 of the ECHR following the terrorist attacks on the US of 11 September 2001, and then had detained a number of suspected foreign-born terrorists in Belmarsh prison. While the ECtHR agreed with the UK House of Lords,[58] and accepted that there was a public emergency threatening the life of the nation within the meaning of Article 15,[59] it found that the measures were disproportionate in that they unjustifiably discriminated between nationals and non-nationals and, therefore, violated Article 5(1) of the ECHR.[60]

It seems to be the case that when there is a clear state of emergency in the UK, for example caused by terrorist threats or attacks, derogation from Article 5 is permitted. However, accompanying measures such as preventive detention must be proportionate to the threat or, in the words of Article 15(1) of the ECHR, such measures can only derogate from a state's obligations under the ECHR 'to the extent strictly required by the exigencies of the situation'. In external situations of emergency to which British troops might be deployed, for example the British deployment as part of a UN peacekeeping operation in the Cyprus emergency in 1964, it is debatable whether derogation is available as there is no threat to the UK per se (but see discussion in the next section). In discussing derogation from Article 9 of the ICCPR (protecting liberty and security of the person) on the grounds of threat to the life of the nation under Article 4, the Human Rights Committee commented that in armed conflict the rules of LOAC operate to reduce the chances of arbitrary detention but, outside that context, 'the requirements of strict necessity and proportionality constrain any derogating measures involving security detention, which must be limited in duration and accompanied by procedures to prevent arbitrary application ... including review by a court ...'.[61]

Preventive detention on security grounds regularly occurs in peacekeeping operations,[62] and as with detention in NIACs, there is considerable confusion as to whether a power to detain exists and, furthermore, even if such a power is present, as to the standards governing the exercise of that power as well as the treatment of detainees. Given that an express power to detain has rarely

---

[58]   *A v Secretary of State* [2004] UKHL 56.

[59]   *A and Others v The United Kingdom*, Appl No 3455/05, 19 February 2009, para 181.

[60]   Ibid, paras 134, 190.

[61]   Human Rights Committee, GC 35 (2014) para 66.

[62]   B. Oswald, 'Detention by United Nations Peacekeepers: Searching for Definition and Categorisation' (2011) 15 *Journal of International Peacekeeping* 119 at 120.

been granted by the UN Security Council in past peacekeeping mandates,[63] in effect a peacekeeper's power to detain individuals as security threats is implied from the Security Council mandate, a practice reaching back to the first peacekeeping force in 1956.[64] An implied power to detain must be utilised by states contributing contingents to peacekeeping forces in accordance with their obligations under human rights law and, where applicable, LOAC. An argument based on the supremacy of obligations under the UN Charter created by a binding Chapter VII resolution adopted by the Security Council, which might prevail over TCN obligations under human rights law and LOAC,[65] can only succeed in the case of an express power to detain which is clearly intended to override inconsistent obligations under human rights law and LOAC.[66]

Section 8 of the UN Secretary General's Bulletin on the observance by UN forces of international humanitarian law (LOAC) provides for detention subject to the detainees being held in secure and safe premises with hygiene and health safeguards, food and clothing, free from torture or ill-treatment, and preserving the right of the ICRC to visit detainees.[67] However, the Bulletin only applies to UN peacekeeping forces 'when in situations of armed conflict they are actively engaged therein as combatants, to the extent and for the duration of their engagement'.[68] It is the case that most instances of detention by peacekeepers will occur outside of armed conflict, and so the rules of human rights law apply given that by detaining individuals TCNs are asserting jurisdiction over them.

There can be little doubt that peacekeepers need a power to detain when faced with otherwise uncontrollable violence by armed gangs, when there are no grounds for laying a criminal charge but there is evidence, for example by reason of membership of an armed militia, that unless detained the indi-

---

[63] B. Oswald, 'Some Controversies of Detention in Multinational Operations and the Contribution of the Copenhagen Principles' (2013) 95 *International Review of the Red Cross* 707 at 713, where it is stated that by 2013 there had been three express grants of a power to detain to peacekeeping forces: in the Congo in 1961 – to detain 'pending legal action … all foreign military and para-military personnel and political advisors not under United Nations command, and mercenaries' (UN Doc S/RES/169 (1961) para 4); Somalia in 1992 – to arrest and detain all those responsible for carrying out armed attacks against UNOSOM II (UN Doc S/RES/837 (1993) para 5); and Liberia 2006 – to apprehend and detain former President Charles Taylor (UN Doc S/RES/1638 (1995) para 1). See also UN Doc S/RES/2448 (2018), para 40(e)(iii), re MINUSCA in the Central African Republic.

[64] Oswald (2013) 713.

[65] UN Charter (1945) Article 103.

[66] *Al-Jedda* (2011) paras 102–9.

[67] UN Doc ST/SGB/1999/13, section 8.

[68] Ibid, section 1.1.

vidual will be a threat to the security of the operation or civilians.[69] Oswald states that detention on the grounds of security can only be undertaken by military peacekeepers, and then detention can only be for the period that the detainee is deemed to be a security threat.[70] Given the duration of many peacekeeping forces, and the persistent levels of violence they face, such detention could be of a lengthy nature and, under human rights law would prima facie violate the right to liberty and freedom from arbitrary detention. In the Guidelines on the Use of Force by Military Components in United Nations Peacekeeping Operations of 2017, the United Nations Department of Peacekeeping Operations (UNDPKO) stated that: '[i]n the case of United Nations peacekeepers detaining individuals or groups, detention should be conducted in accordance with the relevant Interim SOP [Standard Operating Procedure] on detention operations'. Furthermore, 'detained personnel must be handled humanely in a manner that is consistent with international human rights law, applicable international humanitarian law and international refugee law, and other relevant international norms and standards'.[71]

Wohlfahrt summarises the content of the 'Interim Standard Operating Procedures on Detention in United Nations Peace Operations' (ISOP on Detention) of 2010,[72] described as a 'landmark set of interim procedures for detention in UN peacekeeping operations'.[73] A 'key feature of the ISOP ... is the designation by Heads of Mission of a senior official in the civilian component to monitor, receive reports and coordinate the detention carried out by the Missions' uniformed personnel' – the Detention Focal Point, who is independent of the command and control structure.[74] In addition, there are requirements for record keeping and proper reporting by the CO of the detaining unit to the Detention Focal Point and Head of Mission, and from the Head of Mission to UN headquarters. Wohlfahrt states that 'these measures seek to ensure

---

[69]   UNDPKO/DFS, 'Use of Force by Military Components in United Nations Peacekeeping Operations', Ref 2016.14, January 2017, para 35.

[70]   Oswald (2011) 149.

[71]   UNDPKO (2017) para 42.

[72]   UNDPKO/DFS, 'Interim Standard Operating Procedures on Detention in United Nations Peace Operations', Ref PK/G/2010.6, 25 January 2010.

[73]   S. Wohlfahrt, 'Implementing the Legal Framework relating to the Deprivation of Liberty by Peacekeeping Forces: A Practical Example', International Institute of Humanitarian Law, 6–8 September 2018, 1–2 http://iihl.org/wp-content/uploads/2019/02/WOHLFAHRT-REV.pdf. See further K. Grenfell, 'Detention in United Nations Peace Operations' in G. Rose and B. Oswald (eds), *Detention of Non-State Actors Engaged in Hostilities: The Future Law* (Brill Nijhoff, 2016) 345–51.

[74]   Wohlfahrt (2018) 3.

accountability for all involved, and traceability of actions, while protecting the detainees' integrity and their rights'.[75]

On detainees' rights, the ISOP 'contains a detailed body of rules aimed at ensuring the fundamental rights and the health, the well-being and safety of all detained persons throughout their detention; and also beyond, if handed over to host country authorities'. These include 'access to a medical professional, the provision of clean, dedicated detention facilities, with adequate natural light and airflow and clean bedding, separation of men and women, the availing of water, food and hygiene supplies, the right to contact or be contacted by a family member or relative, and so forth'.[76] The maximum detention period is 72 hours before the detainee should be released or handed over to national authorities. In the case of the latter, the ISOP provides that an assessment must be carried out by the Focal Point, in particular a detainee shall not be handed over 'in situations where there are substantial grounds for believing that there is a real risk that the detained person will be tortured or ill-treated, persecuted, subjected to the death penalty or arbitrarily deprived of life and that, in such cases, detained persons shall be released'.[77]

While the ISOP serves to guarantee the rights of detainees while under UN control, it does not provide for any right of judicial review, beyond the role of the Detention Focal Point. Although said to be 'inspired' by human rights law and LOAC, the ISOP does not seem to pay regard to the 'Body of Principles for the Protection of All Persons under any Form of Detention or Imprisonment' adopted by the UN General Assembly in 1988.[78] Principle 4 states that 'any form of detention or imprisonment and all measures affecting the human rights of a person under any form of detention or imprisonment shall be ordered by, or be subject to the effective control of, a judicial or other authority'. Principle 32 states that 'a detained person or his counsel shall be entitled at any time to take proceedings according to domestic law before a judicial or other authority to challenge the lawfulness of his detention in order to obtain his release without delay, if it is unlawful'. In contrast, the Copenhagen Principles on the handling of detainees in international military operations agreed by a number of states and organisations in 2012 provide that 'a detainee whose liberty has been deprived for security reasons is to, in addition to a prompt initial review, have the decision to detain reconsidered periodically by an impartial and

---

75   Ibid, 4.
76   Ibid, 5.
77   Ibid, 7, citing ISOP (2010) para 80.
78   UN Doc A/RES/43/173 (1988).

objective authority that is authorised to determine the lawfulness and appropriateness of continued detention'.[79]

The initiation by the UN of an impartial Detention Focal Point may meet the Copenhagen standards, though the description provided by Wohlfahrt does not suggest that the Focal Point has the power to review and, furthermore, to overrule a detention. Besides which, the Copenhagen Principles fall short of the requisite human rights standard, at least in as much as that requires access to a judicial body, preferring instead the standards provided by LOAC. The Copenhagen Principles seem to be based on LOAC, which is justifiable in an IAC but, as has been shown above, is disputed in NIACs. In any case, in situations short of armed conflict, a human rights standard is applicable. A peace-keeping force is often deployed to situations short of armed conflict, but if they become engaged in hostilities, it is likely to be in a NIAC. The importance of review by a court or similar body, as provided by human rights law, is that the rule of law is asserted over deprivations of liberty, something that is not inherent in review by an administrative or similar body. This indicates that a human rights gap remains in UN detention policies. Furthermore, there are problems in the implementation of UN policies in practice, with evidence of inadequate detention facilities, under-reporting of detention, inaccurate records, and peacekeepers demonstrating poor knowledge of proper detention procedures.[80]

6.5 DEROGATION FROM HUMAN RIGHTS TREATIES

The UK government announced in 2016 that it would seek to derogate from the ECHR in future deployments. This statement of intent was said to be in response to the extension of the extraterritorial jurisdiction of the ECHR to the battlefield in a series of court judgments over the past decades. The 'intention to derogate from the ECHR, if possible in the circumstances that exist at that time, will protect British troops serving in future conflicts from the kinds of persistent legal claims that have followed recent operations in Iraq and Afghanistan on an industrial scale'.[81] Soldiers will remain under the rule of law given that 'they will continue to operate under a comprehensive legal framework in accordance with ... the law of armed conflict ... and with

---

[79] http://iihl.org/wp-content/uploads/2018/04/Copenhagen-Process-Principles-and-Guidelines.pdf.

[80] Wohlfahrt (2018) 14–15.

[81] GOV.UK, 'Government to protect Armed Forces from persistent legal claims in future overseas operations', 4 October 2016 https://www.gov.uk/government/news/government-to-protect-armed-forces-from-persistent-legal-claims-in-future-overseas-operations.

Service Law, which includes UK criminal law ... regardless of where they are serving'.[82] There are two problems with this declaration of intent: first, the following discussion will show that it is not possible to derogate from the whole of the ECHR, only from derogable rights including those guaranteed under Article 5, and then only to the extent of the threat giving rise to a state of emergency. Blanket derogations are not possible, although complete withdrawal of a state from the ECHR is permitted.[83] Secondly, the persistent human rights claims had been brought against the government not soldiers, in effect meaning that the government's statement was a means of protecting itself from such claims in the future.

One of the arguments that has arisen out of the 'lawfare' debate is that the military would be freed from excessive judicialisation of conflict if the UK was not bound by the ECHR when deploying military operations overseas. Withdrawal from the ECHR would of course be detrimental to everyone in the UK. Instead, one of the biggest critics of 'lawfare', the Policy Exchange, has advocated a kind of aggressive policy of derogation in future overseas military operations, which is based on several elements: a binding duty requiring ministers to derogate; a provision that no derogation may be quashed by UK courts; an amendment to the HRA to limit its extraterritorial application; and the adoption of a 'policy of principled non-compliance with judgments' of the ECtHR. The latter is argued to be justified 'because in extending the reach of European human rights law the Court has brazenly departed from the terms of the ECHR'.[84] This would free up soldiers, their commanders and the government from protecting the human rights of captured combatants and civilians, and from ensuring respect for those rights under areas of British military control. This would in turn reduce the burden of duties upon soldiers when detaining individuals on the grounds of security for instance, although all sides of the debate recognise that the rules of LOAC and UK service law continue to apply. However, such an approach would contemporaneously reduce the rights of British soldiers, for example to expect that appropriate measures are taken by their commanders, the MoD and the government, to ensure their right to life is protected.[85]

A question remains as to whether the UK could take advantage of the derogations clauses in both the ECHR and the ICCPR when deploying troops

---

[82]   Ibid.

[83]   ECHR (1950) Article 58.

[84]   R. Etkins and J. Marionneau, 'Lawfare: Resisting the Judicialisation of War' (Policy Exchange, 2019) 7. The extraterritorial application of the ECHR will be subject to review as part of the Independent Human Rights Act Review established by the government in 2020 https://www.gov.uk/guidance/independent-human-rights-act-review.

[85]   See Chapter 8.

overseas.[86] As Marko Milanovic has written: 'derogations allow states parties to depart from the full extent of their obligations in situations of emergency. But no state has ever derogated from a human rights treaty in an extraterritorial setting. The US did not derogate from the ICCPR with respect to Iraq or Afghanistan, nor did the United Kingdom or any other European state do so under the ECHR'.[87] States like the US and UK have not put forward derogation as an answer to the perceived problem they face when operating overseas; instead they have preferred to argue that human rights obligations do not apply extraterritorially, but that argument is being increasingly lost in judicial fora and treaty bodies.[88] Following from this, Milanovic argues that 'derogations might start looking increasingly appealing to states, especially those which have initially miscalculated in arguing that the treaties do not apply at all, and have avoided derogating from fear that doing so would count as an admission that the treaties do apply'.[89]

Although the legality of extraterritorial derogation is disputed, the possibility exists, and the purpose here will be to understand the legal controversy and then, assuming it would escape censure by the UK courts and the ECtHR, the effects of such on the rights and duties of government and soldiers. Article 15(1) of the ECHR provides that '[i]n times of war or other public emergency threatening the life of the nation any High Contracting Party may take measures derogating from its obligations under this Convention to the extent strictly required by the exigencies of the situation, provided that such measures are not inconsistent with its other obligations under international law'. Article 15(2) states that '[n]o derogation from Article 2, except in respect of deaths resulting from lawful acts of war, or from Articles 3, 4 (paragraph 1) and 7 shall be made under this provision'.[90] Article 4 of the ICCPR is formulated in similar terms, though there are some differences in the minimal non-derogable protections provided in times of emergency under Article 4(2).[91]

---

[86] ECHR (1950) Article 15; ICCPR (1966) Article 4.

[87] M. Milanovic, 'Extraterritorial Derogations from Human Rights Treaties in Armed Conflict' in N. Bhuta (ed.), *The Frontiers of Human Rights: Extraterritoriality and its Challenges* (Oxford University Press, 2016) 55.

[88] Ibid, 56.

[89] Ibid.

[90] The non-derogable rights under the ECHR are those of life under Article 2 (except in relation to lawful acts of war), freedom from torture or to inhuman or degrading treatment or punishment under Article 3, freedom from slavery or servitude under Article 4(1), and freedom from punishment for criminal offences that were not offences at the time of commission under Article 7.

[91] The non-derogable rights under the ICCPR are the right to life (Article 6), freedom from torture or to cruel, inhuman or degrading treatment or punishment (Article 7), freedom from slavery or servitude (Article 8(1) and (2)), freedom from

In considering Article 15 of the ECHR in *Al-Jedda*, Lord Bingham stated that the conditions for declaring a state of emergency, namely the existence of a threat to the life of the nation, would not be 'met when a state had chosen to conduct an overseas peacekeeping operation, however dangerous the conditions, from which it could withdraw'.[92] This was an *obiter* statement as the UK government had not attempted to derogate. The UK Supreme Court has repeated this assertion, albeit in another *obiter* statement, in *Smith v MoD* when it interpreted the phrase 'threatening the life of the nation' in a way that suggests the power to derogate is only available in an exceptional situation of crisis or emergency, which 'affects the whole population and constitutes a threat to the organised life of the community of which the state is composed'.[93] From this the Court concluded that the power of derogation could only be exercised in circumstances far different from those where the UK conducts military operations overseas with a view to eliminating threats to the UK's security.[94] This seems a problematic interpretation given that a war or armed conflict did exist in Iraq (and the British deployment was far removed from 'peacekeeping'). It could also be argued that the armed conflict threatened the life of Iraq, and that the UK was there on the basis of agreement with the government of Iraq to protect that country. While the life of the UK was not threatened that of Iraq was, and the UK was acting not only to protect its own security but to preserve Iraq. A purposive interpretation of Article 15, based on the ECHR as a 'living instrument',[95] should arguably allow the UK to derogate from the ECHR in such circumstances. In *Serdar Mohammed* Leggatt J accepted this argument in the following terms:

> Now that the Convention has been interpreted, however, as having such extraterritorial effect, it seems to me that Article 15 must be interpreted in a way which reflects this. It cannot be right to interpret jurisdiction under Article 1 as encompassing the exercise of power and control by a state on the territory of another state, as the European Court did in the *Al-Skeini* case, unless at the same time Article 15 is interpreted in a way which is consonant with that position and permits derogation to the extent that is strictly required by the exigencies of the situation ... Article 15, like

---

imprisonment for breach of contractual obligation (Article 11), freedom from retrospective punishment for a criminal offence (Article 15), right to recognition as a person before the law (Article 16), and freedom of thought, conscience and religion (Article 18).

[92]   *R (Al-Jedda) v Secretary of State for Defence* [2007] UKHL 58, para 38.
[93]   *Smith and others (FC) v The Ministry of Defence* [2013] UKSC 41, para 59 (Lord Hope).
[94]   Ibid, para 60 (Lord Hope).
[95]   The 'living instrument' idea – that the ECHR should evolve in the light of new conditions – has been used extensively by the ECtHR starting with the case of *Tyrer v UK* [1978] ECHR 2 at para 31.

other provisions in the Convention, can and it seems to me must be 'tailored' to such extraterritorial jurisdiction. This can readily be achieved without any undue violence to the language of Article 15 by interpreting 'war or other public emergency threatening the life of the nation' as including, in the context of an international peacekeeping operation, a war or other emergency threatening the life of the nation on whose territory the relevant acts take place.[96]

Such an approach 'would create a coherent and transparent legal framework for the assessment of human rights obligations in such operations, it would allow troop contributing states to avoid obligations that it would be unrealistic to comply with, and it would in fact lead to an increased level of human rights protection in the area of deployment, since the scope of application of the ECHR would shift from "nothing" to "some"'.[97] However, when *Serdar Mohammed* was appealed to the Supreme Court, that body again repeated its *obiter* view that the nation threatened must be the UK, not Iraq or Afghanistan or a situation of 'armed conflict abroad in which UK armed forces were engaged as part of a peacekeeping force under the auspices of the United Nations'.[98]

Nevertheless, the ICJ held in the *Nuclear Weapons* and *Wall* advisory opinions that 'the protection offered by human rights conventions does not cease in case of armed conflict, save through the effect of provisions for derogation of the kind to be found in Article 4' of the ICCPR.[99] It would be incongruous if the UK could derogate from the ICCPR, but not the ECHR. It must not be forgotten that derogation does not mean that the state invoking it is unbound by human rights law or, indeed, international law. In addition to the presence of non-derogable rights, both the ICCPR and ECHR require that derogating measures are consistent with their other obligations under international law, most obviously those under LOAC. In the case of the ECHR, Article 15 explicitly allows for derogation from the right to life in relation to lawful acts of war, thereby recognising that soldiers can lawfully take lives of enemy combatants.

---

[96] *Serdar Mohammed v Ministry of Defence* [2014] EWHC 1369 (QB) paras 155–6.

[97] K.M. Larsen, *The Human Rights Treaty Obligations of Peacekeepers* (Cambridge University Press, 2012) 313. See also Sassoli (2011) 66; Krieger (2011) 436; R. Wilde, 'The Extraterritorial Application of International Human Rights Law on Civil and Political Rights' in S. Sheeran and N. Rodley (eds), *Routledge Handbook of International Human Rights Law* (Routledge, 2014) 635 at 654–5.

[98] *Al-Waheed and Serdar Mohammed v Ministry of Defence* [2017] UKSC 2 at para 45 (Lord Sumption).

[99] *Legal Consequences of the Construction of a Wall in the Occupied Palestinian Territory* (2004) ICJ Rep 136 at para 106. See also *Legality of the Threat or Use of Nuclear Weapons* (1996) ICJ Rep 226 at para 25.

Finally, derogation can only reduce the guarantees provided by derogable rights to the extent necessary in the exigencies of the situation.

It has been argued that in armed conflict the rules of LOAC prevail over those of human rights law when they conflict on the rather specious basis that the rules of LOAC are *lex specialis* that prevail over the *lex generalis* of human rights law.[100] As Milanovic explains, this understanding 'stems from the rigid classical divide between the law of war and the law of peace (which would certainly have no relevance to NIACs, a concept post-dating that rigid divide), has no support in any formal source of modern international law, is contradicted by the text of the derogation clauses themselves, and has been rejected as such by the ICJ and virtually all other authorities'.[101] The abstract, unsupported and somewhat flimsy nature of such assertions of *lex specialis* would not be necessary if the state were to expressly invoke a derogation from the right to life in the case of lawful acts of war as expressly allowed under the ECHR, and implicitly under the ICCPR. Derogation from Article 5 of the ECHR and Article 9 of the ICCPR, and their proscriptions against arbitrary detention, would permit for security detention, which is often necessary in armed conflict. However, such detention would remain subject to LOAC. The weaknesses of LOAC in relation to detention in NIACs could be remedied by making detention practice as human rights compliant as possible in the constrained circumstances of armed conflict.

When engaging enemy fighters and combatants, soldiers do so because of the status of those individuals, meaning that they cannot be restricted to the limited circumstances where life can be taken by state actors under Article 2 of the ECHR. At the very least, the UK should derogate from the right life for lawful acts of war when entering into an armed conflict overseas. Otherwise, soldiers would be under a lingering possibility of prosecution for unlawful killings at some point in the future, and the UK would be under pressure to accept its legal liability for such deaths, especially if the *lex specialis* argument continues to be eroded as a legal doctrine. The position is that in an armed conflict both regimes apply – LOAC and human rights law – and the UK has to interpret the regimes in a way that respects both sets of obligations. The only way it can do this in the two most relevant areas where the regimes differ greatly – in killing and detention – is to utilise the derogation clauses in human rights treaties in order to allow for preventive detention, and to allow for deaths that are the result of lawful acts of war. If a state refuses to derogate,

---

[100] T. Tugendhat and L. Croft, 'The Fog of Law: An Introduction to the Legal Erosion of British Fighting Power' (Policy Exchange, 2013) 59.
[101] Milanovic (2016) 80.

for political or misplaced legal reasons, then it will 'suffer the consequences of their choice and the application of more stringent human rights scrutiny'.[102]

In the case of detention where the rules of LOAC allow for prolonged detention without trial but human rights law does not at least in the absence of derogation, the UK cannot sustain its argument that human rights law does not apply extraterritorially, and it would be unwise simply to rely on the argument that LOAC rules prevail as they are *lex specialis*. The government would be better advised to derogate from Article 5 of the ECHR to permit preventive detention on the grounds of security if necessary for the duration of the con- flict, but, in so doing, increase the protections given to detainees in the form of robust impartial review of the necessity of on-going detention. This would be an example of the UK interpreting its rights and obligations in a tailored way that respects both LOAC and human rights law, making such derogations more likely to be upheld in the event of challenges before the courts. In a sense, the UK recognised the sense of this approach when it was forced into derogating from Article 5 to allow for preventive internment without charge or trial in the face of a growing security threat in Northern Ireland, a derogation accepted as lawful by the ECtHR.[103] In this situation, the UK had refused to recognise the existence of armed conflict and so the rules of LOAC and the argument of *lex specialis* were unavailable to it, but the same result was achieved by derogation.

The UK Supreme Court's jurisprudence on Article 15 of the ECHR has been influenced by ECtHR case law to the effect that a state of emergency could not be declared in overseas military operations. In particular, in *Lawless v Ireland* the ECtHR stated that a public emergency threatening the life of a nation referred to an 'exceptional situation of crisis or emergency which affects the whole population and constitutes a threat to the organised life of the community of which the state is composed'.[104] Although the statement suggests a dire, almost existential situation, undermining the security of the whole population of the UK, the facts in *Lawless* relating to IRA activity in Ireland and Northern Ireland, involving a number of terrorist attacks, were accepted by the ECtHR as justifying the declaration of a state of emergency. Similarly, the UK was allowed to derogate from the ECHR in response to other IRA actions in Northern Ireland,[105] and in response to Al-Qaeda attacks on the

---

[102] Ibid, 84.

[103] *Ireland v UK* (1978) para 205.

[104] *Lawless v Ireland (No. 3)* Appl No 332/57, 1 July 1961, para 28.

[105] *Ireland v UK* (1978) para 205. See also Concluding Observations of the Human Rights Committee on the United Kingdom, UN Doc CCPR/C/79/Add. 55, 27 July 1995, para 23.

US of 11 September 2001.[106] Neither of these situations appeared to constitute existential threats to the UK affecting the whole nation or population, but the ECtHR's response was that the derogations were justified. Moreover, Article 15 ECHR states that derogations are allowed in situations of 'war or other public emergency threatening the life of the nation' suggesting that 'war' (or in current parlance 'armed conflict') in itself meets the threshold for derogation.

In terms of the protection of the rights of soldiers, the jurisprudence establishing their applicability is not yet firmly established,[107] but it is arguable that derogation is unlikely to affect those rights given that they are largely protected by the UK's positive obligations under human rights treaties to take reasonable measures to ensure that the rights are not violated. Given a situation of armed conflict, there can be no absolute guarantees of the right to life of soldiers. The UK's due diligence obligations can be applied flexibly dependent on the seriousness of the situation and for this reason there is no need to seek derogation from the UK's duties to its soldiers. However, in the case of the negative obligation under Article 2 of the ECHR 'to refrain from intentionally taking human life unless it is absolutely necessary' in the circumstances outlined in that provision (self-defence etc.), derogation 'in respect of deaths resulting from lawful acts of war' would allow LOAC standards to apply to targeting and collateral damage.[108] In the case of detention, the government's obligations under Article 5 would be pared down to allow for reviewable preventive detention, and the duties of soldiers would be focused on the proper treatment of detainees.

6.6   THE MISTREATMENT OF DETAINEES

In an analysis of British-controlled detention in southeast Iraq in the period 2003–2008, Aoife Duffy outlines the type and numbers of detainees: 'the British had three detainee categories: POWs, security internees and criminal detainees'. 'British forces held at least 3,000' PoWs captured during the IAC phase of the conflict, 'and 2,000 security internees, although the latter figure is likely to be a conservative estimate'.[109] Duffy cogently argues that the 'protections and standards for security internees, whether drawn' from LOAC, human rights law, 'military or municipal laws, largely failed in Iraq, and this

---

[106] *A and Others v United Kingdom* (2009) paras 177–81.

[107] See Chapter 8.

[108] Milanovic (2016) 69.

[109] A. Duffy, 'Searching for Accountability: British-controlled Detention in Southeast Iraq, 2003–2008' (2016) 10 *International Journal of Transitional Justice* 410 at 415.

failure is intimately related to detainee mistreatment'.[110] As shown earlier in the chapter, the UK Supreme Court in *Al-Waheed and Serdar Mohammed* made a significant contribution towards clarifying the right to detain and the procedural safeguards to ensure that detention is not arbitrary.[111] However, there remains the pressing issue of the mistreatment of detainees especially during interrogation, and the transfer of detainees to other states in particular to the authorities of the host state, where the transferees may risk unfair trial, mistreatment, or be subjected to the death penalty if convicted.

In the case of *R (Maya Evans)*, the policy of transferring detainees by British forces to Afghan authorities was scrutinised for compliance with Article 3 of the ECHR, and the well-established interpretation of that provision to include a prohibition on the transfer of detainees where there is a real risk of torture or serious mistreatment.[112] The High Court was of the view that 'in the absence of specific safeguards governing the position of detainees transferred by British forces' into the custody of Afghan authorities, the 'scale of torture and serious mistreatment evidenced by the background material would be sufficient to justify the conclusion that transferees were at a real risk of such ill-treatment'.[113] The UK's policy was aimed at not transferring detainees if there was a real risk of torture or serious mistreatment and, to this end, the government had put in place a combination 'of formal safeguards, in the form of assurances' from the Afghan authorities, and measures applicable to the practical operation of the transfer arrangements including access to the transferees when in Afghan custody.[114] The court was of the view that a formal system of assurances by the Afghan authorities was not sufficient by itself, and that only a combination of words and actions would be adequate.[115] The court made a point of referring to the need for the 'existence of an effective system of monitoring', which 'not only provides a check after the event but should serve to encourage compliant behaviour on the part' of the Afghan authorities.[116] In the light of its findings about the operation of the safeguards systems in Afghanistan, the court found that transfer of detainees to certain Afghan facilities was lawful except in the case of the facility in Kabul.[117]

In the case of *Al-Saadoon & Mufdhi*, the applicants had been detained by British forces in Iraq in 2003 on the grounds that they were suspected of being

---

[110] Ibid, 411.
[111] *Al-Waheed and Serdar Mohammed v Ministry of Defence* [2017] UKSC 2.
[112] *R (Maya Evans) v Secretary of State for Defence* [2010] EWHC 1445 at para 237.
[113] Ibid, para 292.
[114] Ibid.
[115] Ibid, para 292.
[116] Ibid, para 299.
[117] Ibid, para 325.

involved in violence against Coalition troops. In 2004, the Royal Military Police concluded that they were involved in the deaths of two British soldiers, and late in 2005 the British authorities decided to transfer them to the Iraqi criminal justice system, which the applicants argued exposed them to the real risk of death by hanging if convicted of murder. Before the ECtHR the government contended that 'in accordance with well-established principles of international law, they had no option to respect Iraqi sovereignty and transfer the applicants, who were Iraqi nationals held on Iraqi territory, to the custody of Iraqi courts when so requested'.[118] The ECtHR rejected this contention and found that the applicants were within the jurisdiction of the UK for the purposes of the application of the legal regime of the ECHR, which included a prohibition on the death penalty (under Protocol 13). The Court made it clear that the UK had failed to explore avenues that would not have exposed the applicants to the death penalty, including gaining assurances from the Iraqi authorities or submitting the applicants to trial before a UK court either in Iraq or the UK.[119] The court concluded that it was the case that 'through the actions and inactions of the United Kingdom authorities the applicants have been subjected ... to the fear of execution by the Iraqi authorities ... causing the applicants psychological suffering' of a nature and degree to constitute inhuman treatment in violation of Article 3 of the ECHR.[120]

It appears from the above cases that the duties of the government to ensure that transfers do not expose detainees to torture or inhuman treatment cannot be easily fulfilled, but require positive measures not only at an inter-governmental level but also by service personnel tasked with ensuring that any practical measures such as monitoring are carried out thoroughly. It is also clear that the British Army, itself, has faced serious allegations of abuse of detainees and other persons while deployed to Iraq in the period 2003–2009.[121] However, as Andrew Williams states, 'amidst all the hyperbole of political and press representation of the affair, there has been remarkably little analysis of the efficacy and limits of public law as a means of holding the state and its officials accountable for its involvement in and response to alleged multiple and potentially systemic violations of fundamental human rights standards. This is surprising given the numerous public law issues that have arisen.'[122]

---

[118] *Al-Saadoon & Mufdhi v United Kingdom*, Appl No 61498/08, 2 March 2010, para 138.

[119] Ibid, paras 141–2.

[120] Ibid, 144.

[121] Duffy (2016).

[122] A. Williams, 'The Iraq Abuse Allegations and the Limits of UK Law' (2018) *Public Law* 461 at 461.

Williams identifies four phases in the struggle to achieve accountability for alleged abuses committed by British troops in Iraq. The first phase is characterised as one of 'jurisdictional denial' by the government and the courts refusing to accept the application of the ECHR to Iraq or at least restricting its impact.[123] In this period, a limited number of courts martial of individual soldiers for abuse occurred.[124] There were examples of convictions following courts martial, including the conviction in 2005 of four soldiers for assault, conduct prejudicial to good order, and disgraceful conduct of a cruel kind, in their mistreatment of looters in Camp Breadbasket in 2003.[125] This was followed in 2007 by the conviction of Corporal Donald Payne for the war crime of inhuman treatment under the International Criminal Court Act 2001.[126]

The second phase of accountability is termed one of 'politically constrained public inquiry',[127] first by Sir William Gage, who reported in 2011 into the death of Baha Mousa in a British detention facility in 2003,[128] and then by Sir Thayne Forces, who reported in 2014 into allegations of unlawful killing and

---

[123] Ibid, 462. The approach of the UK government towards the application of the ECHR ultimately did not prevail. It was found to be in breach of both Articles 3 and 5 of the ECHR in relation to the detention and treatment of Iraqi civilians in *Alseran v Ministry of Defence* [2017] EWHC 3289 (QB), which was the lead case in 600 claims. Leggatt J found that on the balance of probabilities British soldiers had run over the claimant's back (conduct violating Article 3 ECHR), and that he had been unlawfully detained as a PoW (in violation of LOAC and therefore violating Article 5 of the ECHR). See further the earlier case of *Iraqi Civilians v Ministry of Defence* [2014] EWHC 3686 (QB).

[124] In *R v Evans et al* (2005), seven UK soldiers were acquitted of murder and violent disorder after they had used force against the occupants of a vehicle that had avoided a checkpoint. There was insufficient evidence to show that the soldiers had used unlawful levels of force. Furthermore, 'it could neither be proven that any of the soldiers had inflicted the final blow nor that they, in a joint enterprise, had – each, individually – applied or encouraged unlawful force in a joint enterprise' – International Crimes Database http://www.internationalcrimesdatabase.org/Case/988.

[125] The Aitken Report, 'An Investigation into Cases of Deliberate Abuse and Unlawful Killing in Iraq in 2003 and 2004' (Army, 2008) 3.

[126] *R v Payne* (2007) – International Crimes Database http://www.internationalcrim esdatabase.org/Case/811.

[127] Williams (2018) 464.

[128] Sir William Gage, 'The Report of the Baha Mousa Inquiry', 8 September 2011 (HC 1452) https://www.gov.uk/government/publications/the-baha-mousa-public -inquiry-report.

ill-treatment of Iraqi nationals by British troops in Iraq in 2004 (the Al-Sweady Inquiry).[129] According to Williams:

> Although both inquiries considered Army training and standard operating proce-dures regarding detainees, there was no coordination between them. Neither was empowered to consider any cases other than those before them, making impossible attributing responsibility for systemic issues that otherwise might have become apparent. In this respect, the acknowledgement of wrongdoing remained partial and the jurisdiction assumed determined strictly by the executive. This is by no means an unfamiliar critique of public inquiries in general.[130]

In the Al-Sweady Inquiry, which had the wider remit, the allegations investi-gated included murder, torture, mutilation and conduct amounting to inhuman or degrading treatment allegedly perpetrated by British military forces on Iraqi civilians in the summer of 2004.[131] Sir Thayne Forbes concluded that 'certain aspects of the way in which the nine Iraqi detainees, with whom this Inquiry is primarily concerned, were treated during the time they were in British custody during 2004, amounted to actual or possible ill-treatment'.[132] For instance, in examining one period of interrogation of the nine detainees the Inquiry found that various 'less serious' interrogation techniques designed to extract intelligence from detainees had been used by service personnel, and this amounted to ill-treatment measured by LOAC standards.[133] These included: the use of sight restriction; the invasion of personal space; the use of a tent peg to create noise but also to suggest possible violence; shouting and screaming at the detainees; and the application of the bridge, carrot and stick technique, which aimed to build bridges with the detainees by promising them something in return for information while pointing out possible consequences for the family if the detainee was uncooperative. The more serious accusations

---

[129] Sir Thayne Forbes, 'The Report of the Al Sweady Inquiry', 17 December 2014 (HC818-I) https://www.gov.uk/government/publications/al-sweady-inquiry-report.

[130] Williams (2018) 465. See generally E. Ireton, 'How Public is a Public Inquiry?' (2018) *Public Law* 277.

[131] Forbes (2014) para 5.192.

[132] Ibid, para 5.196.

[133] GCs (1949) Common Article 3; GC III (1949) Article 17. In *Hussein v Secretary of State for Defence* [2014] EWCA Civ 1087, the Court of Appeal found that the tech-nique of 'direct challenge' used in interrogation of persons captured during an armed conflict adopted by the MoD in 2012, involving a 'series of statements delivered as a verbal short sharp shock during questioning to encourage the captured person to engage with the questioner', did not constitute ill-treatment under LOAC. For criticism that the Court did not fully consider the practice in the light of human rights law stand-ards see I. Renzulli, 'Hussein v Secretary of State for Defence: What Was Not Said of Shouting as a Lawful Interrogation Technique' (2015) *Public Law* 550.

of physical assaults, direct threats to kill, the firing of shots, and the throwing of objects by the interrogator, were deemed to be based on deliberate lies by the detainees.[134] Thus Sir Thayne concluded that 'the work of this inquiry has established beyond doubt that all of the most serious allegations made against British soldiers involved in what has become known as the "Battle of Danny Boy" and its aftermath and which have been hanging over these soldiers for the last 10 years, have been found to be wholly without foundation, entirely the product of deliberate lies, reckless speculation and ingrained hostility'.[135] He also added the following comment on the 'Battle of Danny Boy', which:

> [c]ommenced with a deadly, planned and co-ordinated armed ambush of British troops on Route 6 on 14 May 2004. That ambush was carried out by a large number of heavily armed Iraqi insurgents, including the nine detainees, who were bent on inflicting as much death, injury and damage upon British forces as they could. Although my terms of reference do not permit me to investigate or comment upon the legality of the conduct of the British soldiers during the resulting battle, it does seem to me that the evidence clearly showed that the British soldiers responded to this deadly ambush with exemplary courage, resolution and professionalism.[136]

The impression is of a limited number of relatively minor infractions by individual soldiers outweighed by the overall professionalism of British troops. However, this perception is undermined by the fact that the British Army still seemed to have systematically used variants of the five techniques that had been outlawed in the 1970s following their use against IRA internees,[137] and also by the more critical Inquiry and report into the death of Baha Mousa, which showed the British Army in a much poorer light.[138]

The third phase of accountability identified by Williams was a 'return to criminal justice', when in 2010 the MoD established the IHAT to 'investigate the mounting claims and fulfil the procedural requirements of the ECHR'.[139] In *Ali Zaki Mousa (No. 2)* the Court found that, despite the creation of IHAT, the government had not completely fulfilled its obligations to investigate potential violations of the right to life under Article 2 of the ECHR. The Court did not accept the claimants' argument that a full public inquiry was needed and instead recommended a judicial inquiry into each case of death of a detainee,

---

[134] Forbes (2014) paras 3.330–3.414, examining the tactical questioning carried out by British service personnel at Camp Abu Naji on 14–15 May 2004.

[135] Ibid, para 5.201.

[136] Ibid, para 5.202.

[137] T. Wood, 'A Few Rotten Apples: A Review of Alleged Detainee Abuse by British Personnel in Iraq Following the Al Sweady Inquiry: Is There Still a Case to Answer?' (2016) 21 *Journal of Conflict and Security Law* 277 at 299.

[138] See Section 6.7 below.

[139] Williams (2018) 467.

leaving IHAT to investigate mistreatment amounting to violations of Article 3 of the ECHR.[140] Following this judgment the Iraq Fatality Investigations (IFI) was established and Sir George Newman was appointed to conduct fatality investigations (he was succeed by Baroness Hallett in 2019).[141] The drowning of 15-year-old Ahmed Jabber Kareem Ali in 2003 after allegedly being forced into the Shat' al-Arab waterway by British soldiers as part of a practice of 'wetting' suspected looters, illustrates the failure of this criminal justice phase as no soldiers involved have been punished. Four soldiers were found not guilty of his manslaughter by court martial in June 2006.[142] In his IFI report into the death of Ahmed Jabbar Kareem Ali of 2016, Sir George Newman found that 'the immediate circumstances which caused his death are clear: the soldiers, having detained him for looting, forced him to enter the canal and left him floundering. He should not have been detained and held in armed and confined custody in a Warrior, he should not have been transported in the Warrior to the canal, he should not have been forced to enter the canal, let alone left there to flounder and drown.'[143] The responsibility of the soldiers, as well as the government for their misconduct, seems clear, making the failure of the military justice system even starker.

According to Williams the fourth phase of accountability for detainee abuse has been one of 'institutional denial' since 2014, during which the government combined a 'general and principled denial of systemic wrongdoing' with a 'demonisation of those lawyers who had brought judicial review or civil compensation claims on behalf of Iraqis', who were characterised as 'left wing activist lawyers establishing an industry of false claims'. This was buttressed by a dismissal of the mechanism designed to get to the truth, IHAT, which was 'simultaneously condemned politically and in the press for giving excessive credence to the claims made and pursuing investigations of ex-service people in reportedly intrusive ways'.[144] IHAT was shut down in 2017 and remaining cases passed to the Service Police Legacy Investigations (SPLI), many of which have been closed.[145] Elizabeth Stubbins Bates considers the closure of these investigations as a failure by the authorities to apply the standards of international law, especially the prohibition of torture, inhuman or degrading treatment under Article 3 of the ECHR. IHAT and the service police imposed

---

[140]   *R (on the application of Ali Zaki Mousa) v Secretary of State for Defence (No. 2)* [2013] EWHC 1412.

[141]   https://www.gov.uk/government/collections/iraq-fatality-investigations.

[142]   Aitken (2008) 3.

[143]   Sir George Newman, 'The Iraq Fatality Investigation: Report into the death of Ahmed Jabbar Kareem Ali' (Cm 9324, September 2016) para 6.2.

[144]   Williams (2018) 468.

[145]   https://www.gov.uk/guidance/service-police-legacy-investigations.

a minimum domestic legal threshold of grievous bodily harm to warrant investigation, which was combined with a dismissal of allegations below that level. This approach not only ignored international law standards, but also effectively turned a blind eye to the possibility of 'official tolerance of repeated acts that might violate Article 3'.[146] Such an approach accords with that of the Al-Sweady Report, which effectively accepted a pattern of what was identified as low-level abuse, while dismissing any serious allegations against British troops. In fact, according to the institutional responses and reports emerging out of Iraq, the case of Baha Mousa stands out as an exceptional case in terms of seriousness. As a record of what happened in Iraq that hardly seems credible.[147]

6.7   THE DEATH OF BAHA MOUSA

One of the premises underpinning the ICC is that of 'complementarity',[148] which signifies that if a national legal system demonstrates a competence and willingness to prosecute offenders, then the ICC is unlikely to assert jurisdiction. The UK has demonstrated its ability and willingness to prosecute soldiers committing crimes in Iraq and Afghanistan, for example in the *Blackman* case.[149] However, on only one occasion has it prosecuted someone expressly under the International Criminal Court Act of 2001. The case of *R v Payne* before a general court martial in 2007 arose out of the detention by members of the Queen's Lancashire regiment of a number of Iraqis after a series of raids on hotels in Basra in 2003.[150] The detainees were forced to adopt stress positions for prolonged periods; they were hooded and handcuffed and denied sleep. One method used to keep the detainees awake was the 'choir', whereby

---

[146]   E. Stubbins Bates, 'Distorted Terminology: the UK's Closure of Investigations into Alleged Torture and Inhuman Treatment in Iraq' (2019) 68 *International and Comparative Law Quarterly* 719 at 739.

[147]   The ICC's Preliminary Report of 2018 into allegations of war crimes as prohibited by the Rome Statute 1998 committed by British forces in Iraq, stated that: 'information available provided a reasonable basis to believe that in the period from 20 March 2003 through 28 July 2009 the UK servicemen committed the following war crimes against at least 61 victims in their custody in the context of armed conflicts in Iraq: wilful killing/murder (article 8(2)(a)(i) or article 8(2)(c)(i)); torture and inhuman/cruel treatment (article 8(2)(a)(ii) or article 8(2)(c)(i)); outrages upon personal dignity (article 8(2)(b)(xxi) or article 8(2)(c)(ii)); rape and other forms of sexual violence (article 8(2)(b)(xxii) or article 8(2)(e)(vi))' – ICC OTP, 'Report on Preliminary Examination Activities', 5 December 2018, para 195. Ultimately, the ICC Prosecutor decided not to proceed – see further Chapter 9.

[148]   Rome Statute (1998) Articles 1 and 17.

[149]   See Chapter 7.

[150]   *R v Payne* (2007).

they were regularly kicked and punched to keep them awake forcing cries, shrieks and groans of pain. One detainee, Baha Mousa, was killed as a result of his mistreatment: a pathologist report indicated that he had 93 injuries on his body. Seven members of the regiment were court martialled. The prosecution alleged that Corporal Payne 'plainly enjoyed conducting what he called the choir ... for the enjoyment and pleasure of those that actually visited the detention facility'.[151]

Payne was cleared of the manslaughter of Baha Mousa and perverting the course of justice but pleaded guilty to inhuman treatment of a protected person under the Fourth Geneva Convention as specified in Article 8(2)(a)(ii) of the Rome Statute. The UK was in occupation of southern Iraq at the time and therefore the rules of LOAC, including the Fourth Geneva Convention applied. The Judge Advocate stated that, while he had previously been a good soldier, 'Corporal Payne obviously fell far short of what his duties required, but real mitigation is to be found in the fact that proper systems were not in place to supervise and check that this kind of crime did not take place'.[152] Payne was sentenced to 12 months' imprisonment and dismissed from the armed forces. Payne became the first member of the British armed forces convicted under the International Criminal Court Act 2001. The other defendants were acquitted, including Colonel Mendonca who, as CO, was acquitted of a charge of negligently performing his duty by failing to take any reasonable steps to ensure that Iraqi civilians being held in a detention centre under his command were not ill-treated, a disciplinary offence under UK service law.[153]

The level of abuse meted out deliberately and systematically to detainees by British soldiers amounted to serious violations of LOAC and international criminal law as well as a breakdown in discipline. There is a clear disconnect between the culpability of the soldiers under international law and service law and the outcomes of the military justice process. Nathan Rasiah explores the reasons for this. First of all, there was the 'usual' problem of regimental amnesia, with soldiers being unwilling to inform on each other or otherwise failing to be credible witnesses. Secondly, the trial showed a common failure to properly address the culpability of those further up the chain of command. As stated by Rasiah: 'the Judge Advocate broadly accepted the defence submission that given the Brigade sanction, Mendonca was entitled to say that he had satisfied himself that the conditioning process did not contravene the Law of Armed Conflict or the Geneva Convention'. This was despite the fact

---

[151] N. Rasiah, 'The Court-martial of Corporal Payne and Others and the Future Landscape of International Criminal Justice' (2009) 7 *Journal of International Criminal Justice* 177 at 181.

[152] *Payne* (2007) transcript, 17.

[153] Armed Forces Act (2006) section 15(2).

that such techniques had been banned by the government since 1972, and had been found to be inhuman and degrading treatment when used by UK forces in Northern Ireland by the ECtHR in 1978.[154] 'At Camp Breadbasket, the conditioning was applied explicitly in order to assist the process of tactical questioning: to obtain information.'[155] Thirdly, there was an unwillingness by prosecutors to use techniques developed in international criminal justice to address systematic criminality, such as participating in a joint criminal enterprise, accessorial and command-based liability.[156]

Perversely, by charging Mendonca and two other officers with negligently performing their duties the prosecution faced a heavier burden of proof than if the charge had been framed under the Rome Statute as incorporated into UK law, whereby a military commander may be criminally responsible if they 'either knew or, owing to the circumstances at the time, should have known that the forces were committing or about to commit a crime under the Statute'.[157] As Rasiah observes: 'the Judge Advocate held that the accused must have actual knowledge of the duty' in order to be convicted of the charge of negligently performing a duty. 'No such requirement exists within the jurisprudence on superior responsibility' under international criminal law: 'the existence of the duty on all superiors is a matter of law, and ignorance of law is generally no defence'.[158] This reinforces the view that 'the court martial is an inherently self-serving institution with a tendency to operate as a damage limitation mechanism, focussing responsibility on the lower ranks, characterizing criminality as the aberrant conduct of a few "bad apples", and failing to call the political and military elite to account for their role in the implementation of the systems that lead to or facilitated the crimes in question'.[159] Rasiah suggests that 'if charges had focussed more squarely on those responsible for sanctioning the use of the conditioning techniques a clearer picture of accountability may have emerged'.[160]

---

[154] Rasiah (2009) 185; *Ireland v UK* (1978).

[155] Ibid, 191.

[156] Ibid, 187–8.

[157] Rome Statute (1998) Article 28(a)(i).

[158] Rasiah (2009) 192; Rome Statute (1998) Article 33(2).

[159] Rasiah (2009) 195. Citing in support the unreported case on *R v Price, Blake and Edwards* at Winchester Crown Court (2008), in which a young soldier had died as a result of 'beasting', a technique involving intense exercise as a punishment for misconduct. The Judge criticised the fact that three NCOs had been charged while their CO, who gave the order, was not (indeed he had been promoted). Moreover, the Judge pointed out that the practice of 'beasting' in the camp must have been known to other officers.

[160] Rasiah (2009) 197.

This raises questions as to whether the government was fulfilling its obligations under the Rome Statute to willingly and genuinely prosecute war crimes,
as well as whether it was fulfilling its procedural and substantive obligations
under Articles 2 and 3 of the ECHR. This unsatisfactory outcome led in
part to the establishment in 2009 of the Baha Mousa Inquiry, chaired by Sir
William Gage, a retired Court of Appeal judge, who reported on 31 December
2011.[161] The Report contained over 70 detailed recommendations, a number
of which related to military doctrine, including a clear prohibition on the use
of the five techniques in any situation of internal and external deployment, in
combat or otherwise; and clearer operating instructions, procedures, training
and responsibilities for handling and questioning detainees.[162] The Summary
of Findings indicates the thoroughness of the Report in examining the roles
of the various soldiers involved, extending beyond the defendants in *Payne*.
It is worth noting that at the outset the Summary stresses the importance of
the operational context in which the death occurred: 'the tempo of operations;
the poor state of the local civilian infrastructure; the daily threat to life from
both civilian unrest and an increasing insurgency; the deaths of fellow service
personnel and incessant oppressive heat', which together 'made huge demands
on soldiers serving in Iraq in 2003'.[163]

In the final violent struggle that led to the death of Baha Mousa, the Report
found that he was not trying to escape, indeed 'his injuries show that he was
being subjected to sustained assaults and it is not at all surprising that he
attempted to free himself from his plasticuffs and remove his hood in order to
try and protect himself'. Further, the Report found that 'Payne acted to punish
Baha Mousa for freeing himself from his plasticuffs, his hood, and for leaving
the middle room', and 'that Payne lost his temper and continued unlawfully
to assault Baha Mousa until it was obvious that he had stopped struggling'.
Already severely weakened by injuries, maintaining stress positions, lack of
food and water, and heat exhaustion, the 'trigger for his death was a violent
assault consisting of punches, being thrown across the room and possibly also
kicks', as well as an unsafe method of restraint. According to Sir William
Gage, it was the combination of Baha Mousa's weakened state and the final
assault that caused his death: 'neither alone was sufficient to kill him'.[164]
Payne 'played a fundamental role' in the final minutes of Baha Mousa's
life, by violently assaulting him, which was a 'contributory cause' of Baha
Mousa's death. Furthermore, his part in the treatment of the detainees leading

---

[161] Sir William Gage, 'The Report of the Baha Mousa Inquiry', Vol III (HC
1452-III) 8 September 2011.
[162] Ibid, Part XVII.
[163] Ibid, 'Summary of Findings', para 5.
[164] Ibid, paras 138–43.

up to Baha Mousa's death is described as a 'dreadful catalogue of unjustified and brutal violence on the defenceless'. Payne was a 'violent bully', whose example was followed by more junior soldiers and who 'bears a very heavy responsibility for the events in question'.[165]

Clearly Payne's criminal responsibility goes beyond his conviction by court martial for inhuman treatment. After reviewing the role of other soldiers, Sir William Gage then considered Colonel Mendonca's responsibility. The Report is generally supportive of Mendonca, by stating that he 'shouldered very considerable responsibilities when leading' the Regiment through a challenging tour of duty in Basra, for which he was awarded the Distinguished Service Order. He 'possessed impressive leadership qualities' and was an 'impressive witness' whose 'evidence was given truthfully and in the main accurately'. The evidence did not support a finding that he knew his soldiers were prone to gratuitous violence and, although he knew that they practised the conditioning of detainees, consisting of hooding, stress positions and deprivation of sleep, he did not know of the abuse and violence against them. Nevertheless, the Report states that Mendonca 'ought to have recognised that a process of enforcing hooding and stress positions involved a very serious risk of a detainee being exposed to inhumane treatment', and that as commanding officer he 'ought to have known what was happening' in the detention facility.[166] This would strongly suggest that prima facie his conduct reached the threshold of command responsibility under international criminal law discussed above.

No further prosecutions arising out of the death of Baha Mousa have been forthcoming.[167] Nevertheless, the Baha Mousa Inquiry, like the Saville Inquiry into Bloody Sunday in Northern Ireland,[168] serves as an accurate record of an atrocious incident in a wider conflict. As stated by Williams, the Report was 'an indictment of those involved in the killing and the interrogation and handling techniques adopted by the Army which were contributory factors in Mousa's death'.[169]

---

[165] Ibid, paras 218–22.

[166] Ibid, paras 238–51.

[167] In September 2018 Colonel (Rtd) Mendonca gave evidence to the House of Commons Defence Select Committee, which was examining how former service personnel could be protected from (re)investigations for acts that occurred a number of years in the past. House of Commons Defence Committee, 'Drawing a Line: Protecting Veterans by a Statute of Limitations', 17th Report of Session 2017-19, HC 1224, 22 July 2019, paras 45–55, 69–77, 147. See further Chapter 9.

[168] See Chapter 3.

[169] Williams (2018) 465.

6.8   CONCLUSION

In addition to a court martial and a public inquiry, the death of Baha Mousa
led to a finding of violation of the right to life under Article 2 ECHR against
the UK government in *Al-Skeini* before the ECtHR.[170] It appears that the tragic
death of one innocent Iraqi civilian has triggered a multi-layered judicial and
non-judicial exercise in responsibility and accountability, but the outcomes of
that exercise is that one man's tragedy is recorded and one man's guilty plea
has been confirmed. As Williams points out: '[n]either judicial review nor
criminal justice processes, nor civil litigation for compensation, have been
disposed towards uncovering whether institutionalised wrongdoing has developed. Despite acknowledged violations of human rights standards the truth
of systemic wrongdoing has not been revealed through public law processes
despite the multiple legal initiatives'.[171] The evidence from ICC investigations
is that abuse by a minority of British soldiers in Iraq was much more widespread than has been uncovered by any of these processes.[172] In making out of
court payments of over £20 million to nearly 1,500 claims from Iraqi nationals
the government recognised its broader culpability at least by its actions, though
the MoD has stated that 'the reason for the settlement of the overwhelming
majority of claims is not ... that the MoD accepts that the claimants were
maltreated'.[173]

The inadequacies of the processes of accountability has led Williams to
suggest that a broader approach to justice is necessary, drawing on the experience of societies making the painful transition from war to peace.

> These too have struggled with the problem of accountability and attribution of
> responsibility for the most serious institutional human rights breaches. Different
> methods have been promoted internationally from truth commissions to boards
> of inquiry and fact-finding missions. Respect for the victims and the right to truth
> in general lie at the heart of such initiatives ... Prosecutions may form part of that
> process but not to the exclusion of unearthing what has taken place and recording
> that information as a memorialisation of wrongdoing and its impact through some
> independent body.[174]

---

[170] *Al-Skeini v United Kingdom* Appl No 55721/07, ECtHR, 7 July 2011. For further
discussion see Chapter 8.
[171] Williams (2018) 480.
[172] ICC OTP, 'Report on Preliminary Examination Activities', 5 December 2018,
para 195. See further Chapter 9.
[173] Forces Net, 'MoD Paid over £20m in Iraq War Compensation Claims', 13
June 2017 https://www.forces.net/news/mod-paid-over-ps20m-iraq-war-compensation
-claims. The report suggests that many payments were made for wrongful imprisonment, and only some for maltreatment while in detention.
[174] Williams (2018) 480.

It may be added that before such accountability approaches can be successful, the confusion surrounding the applicable law need to be removed. The government, MoD and military all prefer to apply service law and LOAC, but they need to incorporate relevant rules of human rights law into their doctrines and practices, especially on detention and ill-treatment where human rights law has much greater specificity than LOAC in situations of NIAC. The presence of a well-developed legal regime in the case of IACs cannot be used to screen the fact that the UK is most often involved in NIACs where both the power to detain and standards of treatment for detainees remain unclear.[175] Furthermore, judicial clarity is needed on whether derogation from some or all of the obligations under Article 5 of the ECHR is possible in external deployments.

Most of the exercises in accountability examined in this chapter have included statements about the dangerous and violent conditions in which soldiers find themselves. In these conditions, clear laws, imposing defined duties on soldiers, translated into clear RoE and operating procedures, are a necessary precondition before there can be legitimate exercises in accountability. The government itself has a duty to ensure that soldiers operate within a clear legal framework, in particular that they 'are never required to do anything that would be illegal under international law or under English criminal law'.[176]

---

[175] L. Doswald-Beck, *Human Rights in Times of Conflict and Terrorism* (Oxford University Press, 2011) 277 – LOAC 'relating to non-international armed conflict does not address in any substantial way administrative or pre-trial detention procedures'. But see Tugendhat and Croft (2013) 37 – 'LOAC allows the detention in humane conditions of those deemed security risks until the end of hostilities'.

[176] Rowe (2016) 183.

7.   The court martial

7.1   INTRODUCTION

This chapter and the next consider the scales of military justice from the perspective of soldiers, by examining how they are held to account for their wrongdoings (Chapter 7), balanced against the reforms and systems put in place to ensure that they are themselves protected from injustice (Chapter 8). Centrally, this chapter covers the discipline of soldiers especially through the court martial system, which provides for the trial of soldiers for breaches of military law before military courts. The chapter considers the rationale for such courts and the problems associated with them, a debate continued in Chapter 8 when considering the right to a fair trial. The court martial is the centrepiece of the military justice system and occasionally, given the gravity of a particular case in front of it, it becomes a showpiece for wider political, public and media debate. The court martial of seven soldiers of the 1st Battalion Queen's Lancashire Regiment for the beatings administered to detainees leading to the unlawful killing of Baha Mousa in September 2003 has been discussed in Chapter 6.[1] The conviction of Corporal Payne for the war crime of inhuman treatment was the outcome of the trial, but the case shone a light on the court martial as a mechanism for delivering justice and it did not stand up well to scrutiny. While a description of that particular court martial as 'disastrous' and often 'farcical' seems extreme,[2] it had all the trappings of a tragedy, with a cast of characters gathered at Bulford Court Martial Centre, Wiltshire in September 2006 as described by Williams:

> Many of the surviving detainees, though not all, would come. Dozens of military personnel from the lowest rank to brigadier would assembly and give their accounts of now distant events. There would be army lawyers, trainers, intelligence officers, members of the Territorial Army who no longer served, staff officers talking about tactics and systems and protocols, medical doctors to interpret injuries and their likely causes, a padre too and a number of Royal Military Police Officers to

---

[1]   *R v Payne* (2007) – International Crimes Database http://www.internationalcrim esdatabase.org/Case/811.
[2]   A.T. Williams, *A Very British Killing: The Death of Baha Mousa* (Vintage, 2013) 273.

introduce evidence. The case would run into hundreds by the time proceedings ended towards spring the following year. And, of course, there were the seven men assigned a special role of 'the accused'. They would sit with their lawyers, remaining silent. Once they confirmed their names and pleas, they would not utter a word: no exclamation, no shout, no interjection. Theirs would be a role without a voice.[3]

The end result of this process was a 12-month sentence for one soldier, raising serious questions over whether the court martial could deliver justice by punishing the guilty and bringing some form of closure to the victims and their families. Overall, the way the case was prosecuted,[4] the demolition of the detainees' evidence by the barristers representing the defendants each taking their turn to cross-examine victims and witnesses,[5] and the acute manifestation of regimental amnesia which pervaded witness accounts by service personnel, produced the appearance of a military justice system as an elaborate exercise in damage limitation. The outcome was that the clear and vicious attacks by Corporal Payne could not be excused, but that a wider finding of guilt would be devastating to the armed forces still bogged down in wars in Iraq and Afghanistan amidst accusations of systemic abuse. It is easy, of course, to construct conspiracy theories, but it may remain the case that the criminal trial of soldiers for war crimes (whether the charges are framed as such or not) is so fraught with evidentiary problems arising from acts committed overseas that proof beyond reasonable doubt is a very difficult threshold to cross.[6]

A stronger message, that soldiers accused of serious breaches will be punished, was sent by the court martial and conviction for murder of Marine A (Sergeant Alexander Blackman), who killed a wounded Taliban fighter during an operation in Afghanistan in 2011. The court martial withstood the tremendous pressure upon it not to convict a combat veteran of the most serious offence under English criminal law. Although Blackman's act perhaps should have been prosecuted as a war crime (killing a fighter who was rendered *hors de combat*), nevertheless his conviction for murder restored some faith in the military justice system. Subsequent appeals, which eventually resulted in the conviction being reduced to manslaughter, could be said to have eroded that faith, but they did shed light on an inherent problem in holding soldiers

---

[3]   Ibid, 198.
[4]   N. Rasiah, 'The Court-martial of Corporal Payne and Others and the Future Landscape of International Criminal Justice' (2009) 7 *Journal of International Criminal Justice* 177.
[5]   See the account of the court martial in Williams (2013), for example, at 202–10, 231–40.
[6]   See the failure (for lack of evidence) to convict seven soldiers for the joint enterprise murder of an Iraqi civilian in *R v Evans et al* (2005) – International Crimes Database http://www.internationalcrimesdatabase.org/Case/988.

to account against the standards of criminal law when they are operating in extraordinary situations, often made worse by the fact that such operations are under-staffed and under-supported. It should not come as a surprise that courts martial not only reflect wider pressures and issues of justice, but also both negative and positive aspects of the unique nature of military service: (misplaced) loyalty, (in)discipline and (un)lawful violence.

7.2   HARD OR HARSH DISCIPLINE?

The constitutional account of the military and military justice in Chapter 2 demonstrated how harsh discipline became the backbone of the success of British armed forces from Cromwell onwards. Courts martial, which were essentially military courts consisting of military officers, emerged as a key element in enforcing discipline against soldiers. The military was clearly a separate society governed by separate laws and institutions. Writing of the experience of British soldiers in the First World War, Richard Holmes explains that:

> When a man joined the army he became subject to a code of discipline enshrined in the annual Army Act and the *King's Regulations for the Army*, a legal code explained by *The Manual of Military Law*. The latter emphasised that 'in all times and in all places, the conduct of officers and soldiers as such is regulated by military law'. It was pervasive and intrusive, and created a wide range of offences which had no civil equivalents.[7]

Discipline was informally meted out by non-commissioned officers (NCOs) to soldiers who fell out of line, but also formally by COs and courts martial. Field General Courts Martial that operated on the Western Front in the First World War consisted of a president not below the rank of captain, and two to four other officers (known as the board). The imposition of the death penalty required unanimity of the board. 'The accused could object to the composition of the court, was entitled to speak in his own defence and could be assisted by a "prisoner's friend"'.[8] The major difference between a Field General Court Martial and a General Court Martial was that the latter included a legally qualified Judge Advocate, who advised the court, although from early 1916 the post of court martial officer drawn from experienced lawyers already serving in the army was introduced to ensure that law and procedure were followed.[9]

Although flogging on active service was abolished in 1881, COs and courts martial could impose a range of punishments, including ones that did not

---

[7]   R. Holmes, *Tommy* (William Collins, 2004) 555.
[8]   Ibid, 561.
[9]   Ibid, 561.

allow the soldier in question to avoid active duty. Field Punishment No.1, for instance, led to a forfeiture of pay, but could also lead to the soldier being kept in handcuffs and attached to a fixed object, such as the wheels of a gun carriage, daily for up to 21 days.[10] This punishment was imposed on over 60,000 occasions during the First World War,[11] and so was much more prevalent than the lasting image of British soldiers being shot by firing squad after being tried by a rudimentary court martial. Those acts of capital punishment constituted a small component of a massive global struggle over territory and empires.[12] The composition of the British Expeditionary Force in France in the First World War reflected the British Empire and Dominions. In August 1917, there were 1,721,056 British troops on the Western Front, but with the addition of contingents from India, Australia, New Zealand, Canada and South Africa, the number of men under British command exceeded 2 million.[13]

Technological developments during the First World War, in terms of artillery, ordinance, chemical weapons, tanks and airpower, or what Richard Holmes calls the 'swiftly accelerating technology of killing',[14] reflected the fact that there had been a 'military revolution' between 1914 and 1918.[15] Soldiers fighting in the trenches were subject to inhuman conditions, constant barrage and increasingly deadly weapons. Desertion was a serious problem for the British Army, with an average of just over 1 per cent of soldiers deserting.[16] In order to convict for desertion, which carried the death penalty, 'the court had to be certain that the defendant was not simply absent without leave but had formed the intention of never returning to his unit'.[17] Lieutenant Eric

---

[10] Ibid, 558.
[11] Ibid, 558.
[12] A. Tooze, *The Deluge: The Great War and the Remaking of the Global Order* (Penguin, 2015) 45.
[13] Holmes (2004) 13. At sea, apart from the extensive use of submarine warfare by Germany against allied shipping, the major naval confrontation was in May 1916 in the Battle of Jutland between the British and German navies. As Adam Tooze writes: 'the result was inconclusive. The fleets slunk back to base, henceforth to exert their influence from offstage as massive, silent reserves of naval power': Tooze (2015) 35. The RAF was created on 1 April 1918, but a significant contribution to the First World War effort had already been made by the Royal Flying Corps (under the command of the British Army) and the Royal Naval Air Service, which were amalgamated to form the new force: I. Philpott, *The Birth of the Royal Air Force* (Pen & Sword, 2013).
[14] Holmes (2004) 371.
[15] Ibid, 375.
[16] Ibid, 564.
[17] Ibid, 564.

Poole was found guilty of desertion by court martial in November 1916. The transcript of his trial contains the following statement attributed to the accused:

> I joined 11th West Yorkshire about the end of May 1916. I had been in the trenches several times before July 1916. About July 9th I went into hospital suffering from shell shock and I was sent down to Etaples. I was there for three weeks and was then sent to the Canadian Convalescent Home at Dieppe. I rejoined the Battalion about Sept 1st when they were in the trenches at Ploegstreep. From there I went with the Battalion to the Somme.
>
> Since I have had shell shock at times I get confused and have great difficulty in making up my mind. I was in this condition on October 5th.
>
> I did not realise the seriousness of not going up to the front line on October 5th. I went to an aid post as I had a slight touch of rheumatism.
>
> I went away about 5pm – I did not leave anyone in charge of the platoon and I did not tell anyone I was going away ...[18]

Two men spoke in his defence, including a Royal Army Medical Corps officer, who argued that the 'mental condition' of the accused had precluded him from intentionally deserting his company.[19] Nevertheless, on the 24 November 1916, the Court sentenced the accused 'to suffer death by being shot'. The death sentence was confirmed after review of the accused's mental condition by a Medical Board, which found that Poole 'was of sound mind and capable of appreciating the nature and quality of his action in absenting himself without leave from his unit on October 5th 1916, and that such act was wrong'. The Board was also of the opinion that 'his mental powers are less than average. He appears dull under cross-examination, and his perception is slow'.

Eric Poole was executed by firing squad on 10 December 2016. The commentary on this case in the National Archives reads: 'Eric Poole was the first British army officer to be sentenced to death and executed during the First World War. Despite the abundant evidence that he was medically unfit to command a platoon as a result of the shell shock, Poole seems to have been at least partially a victim of a political decision. In his diary entry of 6 December 1914 ... [Sir Douglas] Haig [who confirmed Poole's sentence] wrote disingenuously that "it is ... highly important that all ranks should realise that the law is the same for an officer as a private".'[20] Three hundred and six British and Commonwealth soldiers were executed following courts martial in the First World War, although many other death sentences were commuted.[21] Medical

---

[18]   Eric Skeffington Poole, general court martial, Catalogue reference: WO 71/1027 http://www.nationalarchives.gov.uk/pathways/firstworldwar/people/p_poole2.htm.
[19]   http://www.nationalarchives.gov.uk/pathways/firstworldwar/people/poole.htm.
[20]   Ibid.
[21]   Holmes (2004) 569

diagnosis of mental illness caused by combat 'was in its infancy'.[22] Although it was not completely absent from the process that led to the execution of Eric Poole, it was given very little weight. Despite the fact that wider military considerations may have been behind the capital punishments of Eric Poole and others, Richard Holmes concludes that 'it was indeed a hard law, but it was, in general, fairly applied'.[23] Controversy about a soldier's mental health, as well as wider political and military considerations, have not been consigned to military history as the recent courts martial of Alexander Blackman and Danny Nightingale, discussed in this chapter, show.[24]

It is interesting to note that a campaign to gain pardons for the 306 executed soldiers led to the inclusion of a provision in the Armed Forces Act 2006. Section 359 is headed 'pardons for servicemen executed for disciplinary offences: recognition as victims of First World War'. Paragraph 2 states that 'each such person is to be taken to be pardoned under this section in respect of the relevant offence (or relevant offences) for which he was executed', including casting away arms, cowardice, sleeping on post, leaving post, sedition, mutiny, striking a superior officer, disobedience in defiance of authority, and desertion. Paragraph (4), however, makes it clear that the section does not 'affect any conviction or sentence', or 'give rise to any right, entitlement or liability', or 'affect the prerogative of mercy'. It seems that the soldiers were pardoned because they were executed. It was probably the case that some of them were suffering from shell shock, but their convictions and sentences were not quashed as would normally be the case with a pardon. Overall, the pardon seemed symbolic and of a legally dubious character.[25]

How would a modern court martial be different from the one that convicted Lt Poole? There is no death penalty, although the maximum sentence for desertion is life imprisonment if the deserter intended to avoid a period of active service.[26] The accused has the right to legal representation. Although there is a civilian judge, there is a military jury known as the board. Psychiatric evidence is more readily sought and available, but in key cases such as *Findlay* and *Blackman*, it still seems to be problematic. The rules of evidence, criminal

---

[22] Ibid, 565.
[23] Ibid, 569–70.
[24] See L.F. Sparr, 'Combat-Related PTSD in Military Court: A Diagnosis in Search of a Defence' (2015) 39 *International Journal of Law and Psychiatry* 23. One study finds a 'surprisingly low' post-traumatic stress disorder (PTSD) rate of 6% in British combat troops 'despite the high tempo of operations in recent years' – E.J.F. Hunt et al., 'The Mental Health of the UK Armed Forces: Where Facts Meet Fiction' (2014) 5 *European Journal of Psychotraumatology* 1.
[25] See extensive debate on the nature of the pardon in the House of Commons, Hansard, HC Deb, Vol 451, 7 November 2006.
[26] Armed Forces Act (2006) section 8(4).

procedure, rules of the court and due process have generally been brought into line with rules used in civilian criminal trials. There is a right of appeal and there are no field courts martial. Although a full court martial can exceptionally be set up overseas, trials are normally held at military court centres at Catterick or Bulford in the UK, or at Sennelager in Germany. Having said that it is true that the military court system is 'portable', meaning that trials can be held outside of the military court centres: recent examples have included Brunei, Belize, Canada, Cyprus and the US.[27] Thus it remains possible to hold a court martial overseas but the idea is that it would be the same in terms of appearance, process and fairness as the ones conducted at the military court centres in the UK and Germany.

7.3   SERVICE LAW: DISCIPLINARY AND CRIMINAL CONDUCT OFFENCES

It is worth briefly recounting the history of the emergence of laws designed to enforce military discipline.[28] According to *Rant on the Court Martial and Service Law*:

> Until the 17th century, the enforcement of naval and military discipline in the Royal Navy and the British Army was a matter flowing from the prerogative power of the Crown, and the necessity for and legality of these powers were never questioned. From then until 1881, a series of Mutiny Acts began to codify some military offences, and to impose some statutory structures and requirements upon court martial. In 1866 the first Naval Discipline Act was passed and that was followed by the first Army Act in 1881. These Acts fully codified naval and military offences and the constitution and rules of Court Martial ... The RAF adopted the Army system when it was established at the end of the First World War and these systems survived more or less intact until the mid-1950s. In 1955 the Army and Air Force Acts substantially altered some of the rules relating to Court Martial and, particularly, to post-trial review of their findings and sentences. In 1957 the Naval Discipline Act did the same for the Royal Navy processes ...
>
>   As early as 1991 there were calls for the three Service Discipline Acts to be combined into a single Act and a single system of law for the Armed Forces, but the Services resisted change ...
>
>   Nevertheless it became clear that a tri-Service approach to discipline was necessary as joint training and operations became more commonplace. Inconsistencies between the disciplinary and justice regimes in each of the three Services became a source of discontent in joint units. Parliament accepted that this fundamental change was necessary, and the Armed Forces Act 2006 repealed the three Service

---

[27]   https://www.gov.uk/guidance/the-military-court-service.
[28]   For detail see Chapter 2.

Discipline Acts in their entirety and established a single system of Service law when it came into force on 31 October 2009. ...[29]

The Armed Forces Act 2006 was a substantial piece of consolidating legislation. It is only possible to focus here on some of the disciplinary offences that are peculiar to the armed forces and apply to 'persons subject to service law' in the words of the Act. These offences flow from the idea of military discipline. Some offences relate to undermining the effectiveness of military operations, such as 'assisting an enemy' by, for example, intentionally giving information that might be useful to the enemy.[30] The offence of 'misconduct on operations' includes sleeping without reasonable excuse while on guard duty, patrol or on watch,[31] while that of 'obstructing operations' includes intentionally or recklessly acting to put at risk the success of a military action or operation.[32]

Other offences are aimed at curbing the excesses of war, such as 'looting', which includes taking property without lawful excuse from those killed, wounded, captured or detained in a military operation.[33] One particular offence which seems to impose a unique duty on soldiers that cannot be rationalised as either necessary for operational effectiveness or to curb the excesses of war, is the offence of 'failure to escape' when a soldier has been captured by an enemy and fails to take those steps he could reasonably be expected to take to rejoin Her Majesty's forces.[34] Other offences are central to maintaining military discipline such as the offence of taking part in a 'mutiny', defined in part as acting in concert with at least one other person, either with the 'intention of overthrowing or resisting authority' or disobeying 'authority in such circumstances as to subvert discipline'.[35] Gerry Rubin details a number of examples of post-Second World War mutinies by members of the armed forces, who were stuck in remote colonial outposts in poor living conditions with little to do. In recalling the mutiny by the 13th (Lancashire) Parachute Battalion, he writes that the 'mass prosecution of 263 British servicemen in August 1946 at Kluang, Malaya, some sixty or seventy miles north of Singapore' constituted a court martial like no other:

Here was a unit in the Far East, part of a wartime airborne unit now earmarked for closure, enduring conditions in a tented camp subject to tropical rainstorms and

---

[29] J. Blackett, *Rant on the Court Martial and Service Law* (Oxford University Press, 3rd edn, 2009) 7–8.
[30] Armed Forces Act (2006) section 1(1)(b).
[31] Ibid, section 2(4)(a).
[32] Ibid, section 3(1).
[33] Ibid, section 4(1).
[34] Ibid, section 5(2).
[35] Ibid, section 6(2)(a).

where, it was complained, the regime of spit and polish had not diminished in its severity, despite the near impossibility of keeping equipment clean in such circumstances. Dissatisfaction with catering, latrines, sports facilities merely compounded the peculiar sense of those men of the unit who queried why they were there at all. Many were young men between 18 and 21 who had first seen active service, if at all, in the dying days of the war in Germany ... There is, to be sure, little evidence that these men shared the perspective of many of the previous RAF mutineers [in Singapore in January 1946]. The latter, as hostilities-only servicemen with strong trade union traditions, wished simply to resume their pre-war craft occupations. Nevertheless, the terminology of the paratroopers' protest was the same. They were conducting a 'strike', not a mutiny, for the improvement of their living conditions. Yet it was predictable that when the defending officer at the men's subsequent court martial for mutiny used the word 'strike' to describe such conduct by servicemen he was pulled up sharply by the judge advocate. The word 'strike' was not in the Army vocabulary, he was told.[36]

Of the accused, 254 were convicted and sentenced to between three to five years penal servitude and were discharged with ignominy.[37] However, a campaign consisting of a number of petitions presented to Parliament by constituency MPs, and more particularly a report by the Judge Advocate General advising on a number of irregularities in the court martial, led to the Secretary of State quashing the convictions using his prerogative powers.[38]

Other offences central to the enforcement of military discipline include: 'desertion', which involves intending 'to remain permanently absent without leave', or intending to 'avoid a period of active service';[39] and intentionally or negligently being 'absence without leave'.[40] 'Insubordination' is covered by a number of offences including: 'misconduct towards a superior officer', which can be behaviour that 'is threatening or disrespectful';[41] 'disobedience

---

[36]   G. Rubin, *Murder, Mutiny and the Military: British Court Martial Cases 1940–1966* (Francis Bootle Publishers, 2005) 132–3.

[37]   Ibid, 172.

[38]   Ibid, 175–8.

[39]   Armed Forces Act (2006) section 8(2). 'Active service' is defined in section 8(3) as '(a) an action or operation against an enemy; (b) an operation outside the British Islands for the protection of life or property; or (c) the military occupation of a foreign country or territory'. See *R v Mahoney* [1957] 1 WLR 98; *R v Glenton* [2010] EWCA Crim 930; *R v Tointon* [2010] EWCA Crim 1781.

[40]   Armed Forces Act (2006) section 9(2). See *R v Martin (Alan James)* [2007] EWCA Crim 3377; *R v Harris (KA)* [2011] EWCA 1242; *R v Foley* [2012] EWCA Crim 71.

[41]   Armed Forces Act (2006) section 11(2)(a).

to lawful commands';[42] 'contravention of standing orders';[43] and 'using force against a sentry'.[44]

Breach of duties that in civilian life would raise issues of employment or contract law, can be disciplinary offences in military law. A 'person subject to service law commits an offence if, without reasonable excuse', he or she 'fails to attend any duty', or 'fails to perform any duty'.[45] Furthermore, a 'person subject to service law commits an offence if he performs any duty negligently'.[46] Other uniquely military offences include: 'malingering', which includes pretending to have an injury to avoid service;[47] 'unfitness or misconduct through alcohol or drugs';[48] 'disgraceful conduct of a cruel or indecent kind';[49] 'damage to or loss of public or service property';[50] and the very broad offence of 'conduct prejudicial to good order and discipline'.[51] Although the latter offence appears ill-defined, it appears that many defendants prefer to be charged with it rather than criminal offences that may cover the conduct in question, thereby avoiding the 'obvious stigma of a criminal conviction for a substantive offence'.[52] COs might also prefer to deal summarily with criminal conduct under the offence of 'conduct prejudicial to good order and discipline'. In *Dodman* the CMAC clarified the nature of the offence,[53] and in

---

[42]   Ibid, section 12. See *R v Brown (Kirsty Elizabeth)* [2007] EWCA Crim 2632; *R v Lyons* [2011] EWCA Crim 2808; *R v James Brown* [2014] EWCA Crim 1160.

[43]   Armed Forces Act (2006) section 13.

[44]   Ibid, section 14.

[45]   Ibid, section 15(1).

[46]   Ibid, section 15(2). See *R v Price and Bell* [2014] EWCA Crim 229.

[47]   Armed Forces Act (2006) section 16(1). See *R v Cross* [2010] EWCA Crim 3273.

[48]   Armed Forces Act (2006) section 20.

[49]   Ibid, section 23. See the Court Martial *In the cases of Soldier X, Soldier Y and Soldier Z*, 4 June 2013 https://www.judiciary.uk/judgments/sentencing-remarks-court-martial-soldier-x-y-z-04062013/.

[50]   Armed Forces Act (2006) section 24.

[51]   Ibid, section 19. In a memorandum on this offence the JAG states that the 'section is broadly worded so as to enable the Services to enforce the high standards of discipline and conduct necessary to support operational effectiveness. However, the section is not intended to permit the criminalisation of any conduct without limit; an accused person must have known or had reasonable cause to believe that the conduct was prejudicial when he did the act or made the omission' – 'Memorandum 1: Conduct Prejudicial to Good Order and Service Discipline AFA06 Section 19' https://www.judiciary.uk/wp-content/uploads/2015/05/practice-memo-ver-6-1Sep16.pdf.

[52]   A. Paphiti, *Military Justice Handbook: For Court Martial Practitioners* (Authorhouse, 2013) 103.

[53]   *R v Dodman* [1998] 2 Cr App R 338, at para 16 – the 'proof of the offence thus involves the proof of conduct of the accused having the requisite character objectively assessed (the *actus reus*) and the proof that at the material time his state of mind was

Armstrong the same court found that the offence did not violate the principle of legal certainty as found in Article 7 of the ECHR, which states that '[n]o one shall be held guilty of any criminal offence on account of any act or omission which did not constitute a criminal offence under national or international law at the time when it was committed'.[54]

The first forty sections of the Armed Force Act 2006 embody offences that are peculiar to the armed forces and reflect the need to maintain military discipline, requiring an additional layer of offences on top of normal criminal conduct offences (murder, rape, assault etc.) that are made applicable to service personnel wherever they are deployed.[55] Soldiers themselves receive little protection from the service offences apart from the offence of 'ill-treatment of subordinates', which imposes a duty on officers, warrant officers, or NCOs not to commit the offence intentionally or recklessly.[56]

Subsequent Armed Forces Acts of 2011 and 2016 contained minor amendments to the 2006 Act. However, the 2006 Act remains the centrepiece of armed forces' legislation. One of the most important changes wrought by the Armed Forces Act of 2016 is contained in section 14, which repealed section 146 of the Criminal Justice and Public Order Act 1994. Section 146 had provided that homosexual acts were grounds for discharging members of the armed forces, reflecting government policy that homosexuality was incompatible with service in the armed forces. While homosexual acts between consenting adults in private ceased to be a criminal offence by section 1(1) of the Sexual Offences Act 1967, they remained offences under the Army Act 1955, the Air Force Act 1955 and the Naval Discipline Act 1957. Until 2000 service personnel who engaged in homosexual acts were administratively discharged

---

that he either intended to do, or omit to do, the act in question or, if he did not so intend, he was reckless whether he would do or omit to do the act'.

[54] *R v Armstrong* [2012] EWCA Crim 83, paras 34–5. In the case *Ainsworth v United Kingdom*, Appl No 35095/97, 22 October 1998 (European Commission of Human Rights) the applicant, inter alia, challenged his conviction for conduct prejudicial to good order and discipline on the basis that the vague and unforeseeable nature of the offence violated Article 7 of the ECHR. The Commission dismissed this claim, stating that the 'criminal offence in question must be clearly defined in the law and that this requirement is satisfied where the individual can know from the wording of the relevant provision and, if need be, with the assistance of the courts' interpretation of it, what acts and omissions will make him criminally liable'. Furthermore, the Commission considered that the offence, 'read in the light of the detailed and precise provisions of the Standing Orders, satisfied the requirement of foreseeability under Article 7 of the Convention'.

[55] Armed Forces Act (2006) section 42.

[56] Ibid, section 22. See *R v Birch* [2011] EWCA Crim 46; *R v Simm & Tennet* [2016] EWCA Crim 1449.

from the armed forces.[57] That policy was abandoned in 2000 following the case of *Smith and Grady* (1999) before the ECtHR,[58] and finally military law was brought up to date in 2016.

As well as consolidating disciplinary offences, the Armed Forces Act 2006 also serves as a conduit for criminal conduct offences under domestic law, and criminal offences under international law. Schedule 2 of the Armed Forces Act 2006 contains the most serious offences that can be committed by service personnel. Its contents show a mixture of military disciplinary offences such as assisting an enemy, looting, mutiny, desertion, as well as serious offences under the criminal law of England and Wales incorporated into military law by section 42 of the 2006 Act. These include murder, manslaughter, grievous bodily harm, unlawful possession or use of a firearm, robbery, blackmail and offences under the Sexual Offences Act 2003. A number of offences under Schedule 2 are a result of the incorporation of the obligations of the UK under international law into national criminal law, including offences under section 1 of the Geneva Conventions Act 1957, and under sections 51 and 52 of the International Criminal Court Act 2001.

Section 1 of the Geneva Convention Act 1957 establishes that 'any person, whatever his nationality, who, whether in or outside the United Kingdom, commits, or aids abets, or procures the commission by any other person of a grave breach of any of the scheduled conventions ... shall be guilty of an offence'. Grave breaches of LOAC are found in the four Geneva Conventions and the First Protocol.[59] For example, grave breaches of the Fourth Geneva Convention on civilians consist of a number of acts committed against persons or property protected by the Convention. Those most relevant to soldiers and commanders include: wilful killing; torture or inhuman treatment; unlawful confinement; and extensive destruction and appropriation of property, not justified by military necessity, and carried out wantonly and unlawfully.[60] These are duties on solders the breach of which should lead to prosecution under the Geneva Conventions Act 1957, which would fulfil the UK's obligations under the Convention to enact legislation 'to provide effective penal sanctions for persons committing, or ordering to be committed' grave breaches of the Convention.[61]

Section 51 of the International Criminal Court Act 2001 provides that 'it is an offence against the law of England and Wales for a person to commit

---

[57] http://www.legislation.gov.uk/ukpga/2016/21/notes/division/6/index.htm.
[58] *Smith and Grady v United Kingdom* (1999) 29 EHRR 493.
[59] GC I (1949) Article 50; GC II (1949) Article 51; GC III (1949) Article 130; GC IV (1949) Article 147; AP I (1977) Articles 11(4) and 85(2)(3)(4).
[60] GC IV (1949) Article 147.
[61] GC IV (1949) Article 146.

genocide, a crime against humanity or a war crime', including acts committed outside the UK by a 'person subject to UK service jurisdiction'. The purpose here is not to summarise the contents of these different crimes but to recognise that for soldiers at least, the immediate duty on them under international criminal law when on deployment in combat is not to commit a range of acts that constitute war crimes. Soldiers should also be aware of the other offences under international criminal law. A single act, for example the wilful killing of a civilian during an armed conflict, is a war crime, but if committed as 'part of a widespread or systematic attack ... with knowledge of the attack' against a civilian population it constitutes a crime against humanity.[62] If committed 'with intent to destroy, in whole or in part, a national, ethnical, racial or religious group' it will constitute genocide.[63]

The Rome Statute of the International Criminal Court adopted in 1998 developed the scope of war crimes by building on the jurisprudence of the ICTY to recognise the commission of war crimes in NIACs. In IACs, war crimes include grave breaches of the Geneva Conventions,[64] but also other serious violations of the laws and customs applicable such conflicts.[65] In the case of NIACs, the list of war crimes in the Rome Statute is less extensive. It includes serious violations of Common Article 3 of the Geneva Conventions including murder of all kinds, mutilation, cruel treatment, torture, humiliating and degrading treatment 'committed against persons taking no active part in the hostilities, including members of the armed forces who have laid down their arms and those placed *hors de combat*'; and other 'serious violations of the laws and customs applicable' in NIACs such as 'intentionally directing attacks against the civilian population ... or against individuals not taking direct part in hostilities', and 'committing rape, sexual slavery, enforced prostitution and any other form of sexual violence'.[66]

The account above has demonstrated that the range of military offences incorporated in the Armed Forces Act 2006 is extensive. Historically, such military laws have been harshly enforced, especially those peculiar service law offences that have no equivalent in civilian life. One reason for the harsh approach taken to military discipline was to 'strike terror into the hearts of soldiers',[67] so that they obeyed orders even when faced with certain death. In a more modern context, Judge Advocate General Jeff Blackett has written that 'discipline and its enforcement was, and is, a fundamental element of

---

[62] Rome Statute of the International Criminal Court (1998) Article 7(1).
[63] Ibid, Article 6.
[64] Ibid, Article 8(2)(a).
[65] Ibid, Article 8(2)(b).
[66] Ibid, Article 8(2)(c).
[67] Rubin (2005) 19.

command and prerequisite of operational efficiency; an indisciplined group of armed men was never a match for an army with a rigid disciplinary code'.[68] That rigidity can lead to a collective and somewhat uniform view of the soldier. Whatever their individual character, mental or physical condition, they are expected to perform to the same standard. If one soldier fails in their duties (whether due to lack of bravery, physical weakness, mental illness or unwillingness to follow a particular order) and is not punished, then the effectiveness of the operation and the willingness of their comrades to follow orders is undermined. Within this approach to military justice there is not only a presumption against soldiers having individual rights, but also against them having individual weaknesses.

7.4   DISPENSING JUSTICE IN THE MILITARY: SUMMARY HEARINGS AND COURTS MARTIAL

There are practical reasons for having a separate system of military justice. First, 'military offences, such as insubordination, malingering, desertion, and conduct to the prejudice of good order and service discipline' are not offences under civilian criminal law,[69] rather they go directly to the need to maintain discipline if military objectives are to be achieved. In the court martial the centrality of discipline and good order is buttressed by having a jury (known as the board) of military personnel, who 'will be expected to bring their military experience to bear in judging whether the accused was guilty of such a distinctive offence'.[70] However, in addition to military offences, courts martial may also try individuals for civilian criminal conduct offences such as murder, rape, assault etc., where the justifications for a military trial seem diminished. The argument, however, is that such offences also require enforcement by the military justice system, as criminal conduct also undermines the high standards of discipline and trust required of soldiers.[71] This position has recently been emphasised by the CMAC in *Vuliwaciwaci*, where the defendant had pleaded guilty before a court martial to assault, taking a conveyance without consent and aggravated vehicle taking, but appealed against the sentences as manifestly excessive. The CMAC dismissed the appeal and endorsed the view that 'offences within the Military Service community do have a special context because of the trust that is placed on Service personnel'. It stated further that 'Military Service is a vocation and trust in Service personnel is particularly

---

[68]   Blackett (2009) 1.
[69]   Ibid.
[70]   Rubin (2005) 19–20.
[71]   Blackett (2009) 11.

important for those who live in close quarters and are expected to fight along-side each other'.[72]

A second practical reason for having a separate form of military jurisdiction over criminal as well as military offences is that British military law applies to soldiers while operating overseas and it will normally prevail over local law by means of an agreement between the UK and the host state.[73] This protects soldiers from being subjected to harsher (possibly non-human rights compliant) standards and processes before local courts in countries where they are deployed. As such, this may be a stronger justification for retaining court martial jurisdiction over normal criminal offences committed by service personnel, but arguably only for those committed outside the UK. Currently, the court martial has jurisdiction to try any service offence,[74] including criminal conduct offences such as murder,[75] but in the UK the 'civil authorities have primacy of jurisdiction and can insist upon investigation by the civilian police and trial of a Service offender by the civilian courts'.[76]

Field courts martial, such as those that were held on the Western Front in the First World War no longer occur, although it remains possible to conduct courts martial outside the UK. Nonetheless, justice for summary or minor service disciplinary offences as well as some substantive criminal offences can still be meted out by COs both on operations and in military bases in the UK and elsewhere by means of a summary hearing,[77] while serious offences are tried in properly equipped court martial centres. According to a MoD overview of the military justice system: 'Commanders are best placed to understand the Service environment and the implications of breaches of standards by those under their command on operational effectiveness'. As a result 'they are vested with statutory powers that go beyond the provisions generally available to civilian employers'. This, according to the MoD, is because 'the obligations of Service personnel are necessarily far more binding than those of civilian employees'. The 'Summary Hearing powers provide commanding officers (COs) with immediate sanctions to enforce discipline in less serious cases, with the outcome being quickly and readily apparent to the offender, his peers and to any victim'. This, according to the MoD, is 'essential in operational theatres, where operational effectiveness is vital' given that in 'such an environment, breaches of discipline that are not dealt with can be corrosive and undermine

---

72   *R v Vuliwaciwaci* [2020] EWCA Crim 1894, para 7. See further *R v Bailey* [2019] EWCA Crim 372; *R v Bagnall* [2019] EWCA Crim 2458.
 73   Known as the Status of Forces Agreement (SOFA).
 74   Armed Forces Act (2006) section 50.
 75   Ibid, section 42.
 76   Paphiti (2013) 247.
 77   Armed Forces Act (2006) sections 52–4; Paphiti (2013) 174.

team working and morale'.[78] The MoD points out that the 'Court Martial process, fully compliant with the ECHR, is able to dispense justice in the most serious and complex cases'.[79] However, this raises the issue of whether the summary hearing process is compliant with the right to a fair trial.[80]

According to the UK's judiciary website: '[m]inor disciplinary and criminal matters are deal with summarily by the Commanding Officer of the accused', pointing out that the 'vast majority of matters are disposed of in this way, which forms one of the foundations of the disciplinary system of the armed forces'. Protections for the accused are provided by the fact that '[i]n all cases an accused person may elect for trial in the Court Martial rather than appear before their Commanding Officer, or may appeal to the Summary Appeal Court after the event'. The accused, 'if dissatisfied with the outcome of a summary hearing, always has the right of appeal to the Summary Appeal Court, which is conducted by a Judge Advocate accompanied by two officers'.[81] Although the option of trial by court martial and the right of appeal protect the accused to some extent, the summary process is a rudimentary 'non-judicial process',[82] which by its nature cannot be said to be a fair trial before an impartial and independent body. Rubin describes it thus:

> Colloquially known as 'CO's Orders', the procedure is conducted on a more informal basis than is a court martial. The prosecution will be conducted by the unit's adjutant or executive officer and lawyers are not permitted to be present to represent the accused or the CO. Moreover the rules of evidence are not followed. However a record of summary dealing is now meticulously maintained … The accused is required to represent himself, to examine and cross-examine witnesses himself (even to the extent of being obliged, if the need arose, to argue legal points such as, for example, the definition of theft) and to present his own submissions. He may, however, be assisted by an assisting officer who may prompt him. The officer will also present any mitigation in the event of a finding of guilty.[83]

---

[78] Armed Forces Bill Team, 'An Overview of the Service Justice System and the Armed Forces Act' (MoD) https://webarchive.nationalarchives.gov.uk/20111018123424/http://www.mod.uk/NR/rdonlyres/0D289346-3BAA-4446-9164-4600458D1CE9/0/AnOverviewoftheServiceJusticeSystemandtheArmedForcesAct.pdf.

[79] Ibid.

[80] See judgment of ECtHR in *Engel v The Netherlands*, Appl No 5100/71, 8 June 1976.

[81] https://www.judiciary.uk/about-the-judiciary/the-justice-system/jurisdictions/military-jurisdiction/.

[82] Paphiti (2013) 176.

[83] G.R. Rubin, 'Why Military Law? Some United Kingdom Perspectives' (2007) 26 *University of Queensland Law Journal* 353 at 358.

The need to deliver swift justice in order to keep a grip on discipline within any military unit explains why the system of summary justice remains largely untouched, except for the right to opt for a full court martial and the right of appeal. The problem remains as to how long this system can survive scrutiny from a human rights perspective.[84] Rubin gives this analysis:

> The accused has the right to elect trial by court martial rather than by summary dealing. This option is considered to enhance the procedure's compliance with the right to fair trial under Article 6 of ECHR. However, the vast majority of service personnel facing summary dealing prefer to have the matter dealt with quickly, and done and dusted. The creation of the Summary Appeal Court [SAC] in 2000 also sought to ensure that the procedure was in conformity with ECHR, for the court is presided over by a judge advocate with two officer wingmen. Recent decisions of the ECtHR have indeed endorsed the view that the whole package of summary dealing is ECHR-compatible notwithstanding the absence of judicial involvement or legal representation at the first instance hearing. The [SAC] can, of course, quash the finding and/or sentence awarded by a CO at summary dealing and an early study of the record of the court suggests no reluctance on the part of the court to do so, notwithstanding how such decisions might be received by the CO whose award is overturned or by the unit generally.[85]

Under Article 6 of the ECHR individuals facing a criminal charge have the right to 'a fair and public hearing within a reasonable time by an independent

---

84   See further Chapter 8.

85   Rubin (2007) 358. The case law does not fully support this. Although the summary system seems to have been seen by the ECtHR as part of the state's 'margin of appreciation' in *Engel v The Netherlands* (1976), in *Thompson v United Kingdom* (2005) 40 EHRR 11 the ECtHR found a breach of Article 6 and stated (at para 43) that it did not consider that 'any choice by [the applicant] of a summary trial would have constituted a valid waiver of his rights under Article 6 §§ 1 and 3 of the Convention. In this respect, it is recalled that a waiver of a right guaranteed by the Convention – in so far as it is permissible – must not run counter to any important public interest, must be established in an unequivocal manner and requires minimum guarantees commensurate to the waiver's importance'. See also *Bell v United Kingdom*, Appl No 41534/98, 15 November 2005, which found that the summary system violated the independence, impartiality and fairness requirements of Article 6 of the ECHR. In contrast in *Baines v Army Prosecuting Authority* [2005] EWHC 1399 (Admin), the High Court appeared to distinguish the case from *Thompson* and stated (at para 59) that 'an accused soldier can be tried *de novo* by a court-martial or by the SAC and he has a free and unrestrained choice to elect the former rather than summary trial and the latter if a finding is made against him on a summary dealing. In our judgement it follows that an accused soldier who is dealt with summarily for an offence … does enjoy the rights conferred by Art 6' ECHR. For discussion see Paphiti (2013) 11–13. Blackett points out that in *Bell v UK*, the ECtHR was considering the pre-2000 summary system, which had been changed by the Armed Forces Act (2000) to allow for an unfettered right of appeal to the Summary Appeal Court: Blackett (2009) 223.

and impartial tribunal', and the right to legal representation. Both of these are absent from the system of summary justice but it could be argued that the right to opt for trial before a court martial, and the right of appeal to the SAC on finding and/or sentence from summary conviction, cure these defects. In his review of the service justice system in 2018, Judge Lyons doubts whether a decision by the accused not to elect for trial by court martial could amount to a waiver of his or her rights under the ECHR. However, the 'right to elect coupled with the unfettered right to appeal from a summary hearing ... is considered to make the overall summary justice system ECHR compliant'.[86]

While human rights problems remain in the summary process, much has been done in recent years to render the court martial human rights compliant.[87] The court martial 'has global jurisdiction over all service personnel and civilians subject to service discipline (e.g. family members, civilian contractors, teachers, administrative staff when serving abroad) and hears all types of criminal case including murder and serious sexual offences'.[88] Further, in terms of jurisdiction, 'serious matters, including both offences against the civilian criminal law and specifically military disciplinary offences, may be tried in the Court Martial, which is a standing court'. A civilian Judge Advocate 'arraigns each defendant and conducts the trial which is broadly similar to a civilian Crown Court trial in all cases, even when dealing with a minor disciplinary or criminal offence'. One key difference with Crown Court trials is that in a court martial the 'jury, known as the board, comprises between three and seven commissioned officers or Warrant Officers depending on the seriousness of the case'. These lay members of the board receive directions from the Judge Advocate at the outset of the trial 'in relation to their duties and responsibilities (as per a jury) but also specifically in relation to the importance of the independence of their role from any chain of command or other Service influence and the need for all lay members to have an equal voice and vote regardless of disparity in rank'. 'This is required to ensure the Court remains compliant with Article 6 ECHR'.[89] The trial is conducted in a way that for most part is indistinguishable from a normal criminal trial, with argument and evidence presented and tested by lawyers for the prosecution and defence. At the conclusion of the trial the members of the board, having 'listened to the Judge Advocate's directions on the law and summary of the evidence', 'are responsible for finding

---

[86] HHJ Shaun Lyons, 'Service Justice System Review (Part 1)' (MoD, 29 March 2018) 24.
[87] See further Chapter 8.
[88] https://www.judiciary.uk/about-the-judiciary/the-justice-system/jurisdictions/military-jurisdiction.
[89] Ibid. See further Armed Forces Act (2006) sections 154–72 and The Armed Forces (Court Martial) Rules 2009.

defendants guilty or not guilty'. Following a finding or plea of guilty, the board joins the Judge Advocate to decide on sentence, which is again different from the Crown Court. The court martial 'has the same sentencing powers in relation to imprisonment as a Crown Court, including life imprisonment'.[90]

In terms of punishment, penalties for summary offences imposed by the COs can range from detention for 28 days (exceptionally 90 days), reduction in rank, fines, reprimands, and other forms of minor punishments.[91] Maximum sentences that can be imposed by court martial are found under the different offences; for example, this could be imprisonment up to life for mutiny and desertion,[92] or up to 10 years for failure to escape or disobedience to superior commands,[93] while a maximum sentence of two years' imprisonment is stipulated for conduct prejudicial to good order and discipline,[94] and for ill-treatment of a subordinate.[95] Other punishments available to a court martial include dismissal with disgrace from Her Majesty's service, dismissal from Her Majesty's service, detention for a term not exceeding two years, forfeiture of seniority, reduction in rank, fine, service community order or reprimand.[96]

In reviewing the service justice in order to ensure that it 'continues to be necessary, fair and efficient', Judge Shaun Lyons considered that the Armed Forces Act 2006 'has created a robust system for the tri-service administration of justice', although he recognised that improvements could be made by tapping into the experience of the civil criminal justice system.[97] The Report recognises the process of civilianisation of the military justice system making the current system 'more complex than its predecessor systems; it is more "lawyerly" and requires a greater degree of support and advice from legal officers'. This has made the military justice system 'at times more complex than its civilian counterparts', but this has arisen 'in part for good service reasons including the requirement to keep the CO in their central position in the training, morale and discipline of their unit'.[98] It is also necessary to point to the extraterritorial application of service law and the extra layers of international laws as adding to that complexity. The focus on 'discipline and cohesion' in the system is necessary given the reality of a soldier's duty,

---

[90]   https://www.judiciary.uk/about-the-judiciary/the-justice-system/jurisdictions/military-jurisdiction.
[91]   Armed Forces Act (2006) sections 132–3.
[92]   Ibid, sections 6(4), 8(4).
[93]   Ibid, sections 5(4), 12(2).
[94]   Ibid, section 19(3).
[95]   Ibid, section 22(3).
[96]   Ibid, section 164.
[97]   Lyons (2018) 2–3.
[98]   Ibid, 11.

including the 'ultimate duty' to kill and 'to accept that they themselves may be killed'. Discipline and the necessities of military operations signify that soldiers, who voluntarily join the armed forces, 'accept the imposition of wide-ranging restrictions on their freedoms, of disruptions to family life, and of inconveniences on both a daily and long term basis all of which would be unthinkable and unacceptable in most aspects of civilian life'.[99] They subject themselves to the military justice system and its demands for 'a higher standard of general conduct'. Significantly, however, Judge Lyons recognises that soldiers 'remain citizens but are citizens in uniform'.[100]

Although Lyons' review does not directly address the juridification of the armed forces through the incursion of human rights law, the recognition of citizenship implies that human rights law applies to soldiers. However, given the uniquely different functions soldiers perform and as a result the unique legal position they occupy, human rights law will have to apply in a way that balances their rights against their very different and much more onerous duties. While a summary hearing before a CO looks suspect when analysed from a non-contextual human rights perspective, it is fundamental to discipline and maintaining that higher standard of conduct required and accepted by service personnel.[101] The summary process has been connected to the wider military justice systems in ways that have improved the rights of accused soldiers but that have also maintained the pivotal responsibilities of a CO for operational effectiveness and discipline.[102] While further adjustments will probably be made as human rights jurisprudence evolves, it is still true to say that the military justice system is capable of adapting to achieve a fair balance between rights and duties. By so doing the system enhances its legitimacy – a fair system is much more likely to engender obedience and be able to withstand criticism.

One key difference between trial before a court martial and before the Crown Court is that in the former the findings on guilt and sentence are decided by a simple majority of the members. The 'judge has no power to require the board to reach a unanimous verdict and he cannot refuse to accept a majority verdict until a specified period has elapsed'.[103] As recognised in the leading work on the court martial by Jeff Blackett 'this differs sharply from the Crown Court, in which the judge in a jury trial will direct that unanimity is

---

[99]   Ibid, 15.
[100] Ibid.
[101] Ibid, 23.
[102] Ibid, 16. See further P. Rowe, 'A New Court to Protect Human Rights in the Armed Forces of the UK: The Summary Appeal Court' (2003) 8 *Journal of Conflict and Security Law* 201.
[103] Blackett (2009) 114.

required until such time as he is prepared to accept a majority verdict [10:2]'. The same commentary recognises the problem with majority verdicts: '[a]n undisclosed simple majority decision in a serious case where the defendant is at risk of significant custodial sentence might be perceived as being inherently unsafe, since the outcome rests on a knife-edge'. 'This provision is a legacy from the past', driven by the need for swift justice and the desire to avoid a hung jury and the prospect of retrials, but 'represents a significant weakness in the Service justice system in striking contrast' to the Crown Court. Blackett argues that 'the law should be changed to require either a unanimous verdict (as for example, is the case in the Court Martial system in … New Zealand) or at least a significant and disclosed majority'.[104] Blackett concludes his analysis of this weakness by stating that '[p]ending any rectification of this weakness and until the law is changed, and as a matter of good practice and elementary fairness, judges urge boards to strive for a unanimous verdict, reminding them that if they were in the Crown Court they would be required to reach a unanimous verdict unless directed otherwise, and the board should reach a majority verdict only after full and detailed consideration of all the evidence'.[105]

Judge Lyons, in his review of the service justice system in 2018, defended the majority verdict in the court martial as it ensures 'certainty of outcome and removes the possibility of retrials',[106] but recognised the need for adjustment to meet criticisms. To this end he recommended a board of six members in serious cases, with an undisclosed finding by unanimous decision or a majority of 5:1. If this reform were to be adopted, '[i]n future, the Defendant before a six-member Board will know that either six or five members returned a guilty vote. The Defendant will not know the detail nor is there any need that he or she should do so.'[107] Trials of less serious offences before a three member board would continue under the current majority decision-making under these recommendations.[108] A move to qualified majority voting for boards of six or five members is proposed in the Armed Forces Bill under consideration

---

[104]   Ibid.

[105]   Ibid, 115.

[106]   Lyons (2018) 46.

[107]   HH Shaun Lyons, 'Service Justice System Review (Part 2)' (MoD, 29 March 2019) 50.

[108]   Ibid.

by Parliament in 2021.[109] Judge Lyons cites the Court of Appeal judgment in *Twaite* in support of the continuation of majority verdicts. The Court declared:

> There is no reason to conclude that a finding of guilt on a basis of a simple majority is inherently unsafe, or that there is an increased danger that it may be unsafe if, after conviction, the defendant may be sentenced to a substantial term of imprisonment. Equally we can see nothing in a process in which a verdict may be returned by a majority which infringes the right of fair trial, or produces an unsafe conviction.[110]

Nevertheless, comparisons with the protections a defendant receives in a Crown Court trial will be made. An overall rebalancing of the rights and duties of soldiers may suggest that a similar approach be taken in courts martial as regards the weight of the collective decision required for guilt, especially in serious offences. Judge Lyons' recommendations go a long way towards this and will largely be reflected in the law when the Armed Forces Bill 2021 is adopted.

7.5 OVERLAPPING JUSTICE SYSTEMS

A further problem in the case of a defendant convicted of a criminal conduct offence by court martial is that they might feel that they would have had a better chance of being acquitted by a Crown Court jury, not only because of the differences in decision-making but also because such a body might be more sympathetic to their predicament than a military board, where the ethos of maintaining a high level of discipline plays a significant role.[111] This might apply, for instance, in the case of a soldier charged with murdering a wounded insurgent, but it does not necessarily apply across all criminal conduct offences.[112] A recent human rights-based legal action launched by serving female service personnel to try to prevent rape cases being tried by courts martial has pointed to the lower conviction rates for sexual offences before courts martial compared to the criminal justice system.[113] The alarmingly low conviction rate

---

[109] The Armed Forces Bill (2021) clause 2, introduces qualified majority verdicts for boards of six or five lay members. It provides that where there are six lay members of the board, five must agree; where there are five, four must agree; and where there are three, two must agree https://publications.parliament.uk/pa/bills/cbill/58-01/0244/en/200244en.pdf.

[110] *R v Twaite* [2010] EWCA Crim 2973, para 29.

[111] But see A. Lyon, 'Two Swords and Two Standards' (2005) *Criminal Law Review* 850.

[112] S.L. Kemp, *British Justice, War Crimes and Human Rights Violations* (Palgrave Macmillan, 2019) 199.

[113] S. Dulieu, Women launch legal challenge to prevent rape cases being heard in military courts', *The Justice Gap*, 5 May 2020 https://www.thejusticegap.com/women-launch-legal-challenge-to-prevent-rape-cases-being-heard-in-military-courts/.

for rape in the military justice system is an issue that is returned to in Chapters 8 and 9.[114] It is worth noting that in the Service Justice System Review Report by Judge Lyons, the recommendation was that cases of murder, manslaughter and rape allegedly committed by service personnel in the UK should be tried before the Crown Court except when the consent of the Attorney General is given.[115] Judge Lyons justified this recommendation on the grounds that trying such cases in the military justice system 'cannot be said to be for the protection of the individual nor yet for operational effectiveness'. In these serious cases 'service personnel remain citizens' and should be tried before the Crown Court.[116]

This leads to a consideration of the enduring problems of the uneasy division of competence between the court martial and the Crown Court, given the overlap in their jurisdiction over non-military criminal conduct offences. Until 2006 'the most serious criminal offences, homicide and rape, if committed by a person subject to service law whilst in the United Kingdom, were solely the domain of Home Office police forces and the Crown Court'. However, 'pursuant to s. 42 of the Armed Forces Act any offence subject to the law of England and Wales committed by a person subject to service law falls within the non-exclusive jurisdiction of a court martial'.[117] According to Lyon and Farmiloe the 'protocol on criminal jurisdiction within England and Wales gives primacy to civilian jurisdiction but makes provision for either Director [of the Crown Prosecution Service (CPS) and Service Prosecuting Authority (SPA)] to consult the Attorney General'.[118] As Lyon and Farmiloe state 'this seems slightly surprising; if civilian jurisdiction is always to have primacy in cases taking place within England and Wales, there seems little practical point in giving courts martial jurisdiction at all, except to cover the rare situation

---

[114] In the recent unreported court martial case of *R v Christie* (2021), the accused, who was the commander of a Royal Navy vessel, was acquitted of raping a cadet, aged 18. The judge said that Christie's behaviour 'fell far short of that expected of a naval officer' and called into question his ability to continue to serve in the Royal Navy. Christie admitted he had 'abused his power' by sleeping with the cadet but maintained that it was consensual – *Mail Online*, 'Royal Navy ship's captain sobs with relief as he is cleared of raping drink 18-year-old cadet', 25 February 2021.

[115] Lyons (2018) 43.

[116] Ibid, 41.

[117] A. Lyon and G. Farmiloe, 'The New British System of Courts Martial' in A. Duxbury and M. Groves (eds), *Military Justice in the Modern Age* (Cambridge University Press, 2016) 159 at 172.

[118] Ibid, 173. Citing 'Service Prosecuting Authority (SPA) concurrent criminal jurisdiction protocol', signed on 4 November 2011.

where the civilian authorities might decline to prosecute in the case of homicide or rape'.[119]

It might be expected that where criminal conduct cases exclusively involve service personnel, moreover are service specific, the court martial would be the natural place of trial. This does not necessarily appear to be the case. Lyon and Farmiloe give the example of Able Seaman Ryan Donovan who, while on sentry duty on HMS *Astute* in 2011, shot one naval officer and seriously injured another while on board ship in Southampton docks. Civilian dignitaries were present on a visit and, although they were unharmed, this was cited by the CPS as the reason for trying the defendant in the Crown Court, where he pleaded guilty to murder and attempted murder. He was sentenced to life imprisonment with a minimum recommendation of 25 years and 194 days. This was the first homicide covered by the Armed Forces Act and, as Lyon and Farmiloe state, 'it was a homicide on a Royal Navy vessel, perpetrated by a naval rating, causing the death of a naval officer, on duty, whilst the vessel was moored in a British port'. Lyon and Farmiloe state that 'clearly this offence was triable within the court-martial system and possessed an overwhelmingly naval character'. However, the decision was made by the 'CPS to retain primacy and allow the matter to be heard within the civilian jurisdiction'.[120] This raises the question of whether the court martial should continue to have jurisdiction over criminal offences in the modern age, although the arguments are stronger when the offence takes place abroad given the extraterritorial jurisdiction of the military justice system.

Later versions of the protocol on criminal jurisdiction seem to provide greater certainty. The Protocol signed in 11 November 2016 states that 'it is an established principle that where there are overlapping civilian and service jurisdiction … the civilian authorities have precedence'. This general principle though is qualified by other more specific ones, signifying that where offences are alleged to have been committed against civilians by persons subject to service law then the trial should normally be in civilian court, while if the alleged offence does not affect the person or property of civilians it would be for a court martial. Further considerations that may sway the decision towards a court martial is the availability of witnesses (which might suggest a court martial, as it is portable and has extraterritorial jurisdiction) or where 'there is a strong service disciplinary context', one in which 'it is important for the disciplinary aspects of the misconduct to be fully understood and taken into

---

[119] Lyon and Farmiloe (2016) 174.
[120] Ibid, 172–3.

account'.[121] The Protocol on concurrent criminal jurisdiction will require further refinement and precision after the Armed Forces Bill 2021 passes into law.[122]

Moreover, the arguments for retaining the court martial are much stronger when considering the specific service offences outlined above, requiring specialist expertise and understanding. Military offences are unique to soldiers, they are aimed at reinforcing obedience, good order and discipline, and the punishments can be severe. A review of 'court martial results from the military court centres' for 2017 provided by the Military Court Service,[123] shows that a significant proportion of trials were for criminal conduct offences such as rape, sexual assault, grievous and actual bodily harm, fraud, theft, some of which led to sentences of imprisonment for periods of six to 11 years. However, a significant number were for disciplinary offences under military law (or a mixture of offences), for example: negligently performing a duty (punishments included 50–120 days' detention, reduction in rank, reprimand); failure to perform a duty (punishments included three months' detention, reduction in rank); misconduct on operations (11 months' detention); conduct prejudicial to good order and discipline (punishment included three to 10 months' detention, reduction in rank, dismissal from service, service community order, £500 fine); absence without leave (punishments included two to six months' detention, dismissal from service, reduction in rank, service community order); desertion (punishments included three to 12 months' detention, dismissal from service); contravention of standing orders (punishments included service community order, £1,000–2,000 fine, reduction in rank); malingering (11 months' detention); and ill-treatment of a subordinate (punishments included reduction in rank, £1,200 fine).[124]

---

[121] 'Protocol on the exercise of criminal jurisdiction in England and Wales between the Director of Service Prosecutions and the Director of Public Prosecutions and the Ministry of Defence', November 2016. In E. Norton, 'Military Justice: Second Rate Justice' (Liberty Report, 2019) Annex 2.

[122] See the Armed Forces Bill (2021) clause 7, which obliges the respective prosecuting authorities to provide for greater clarity in protocols on concurrent jurisdiction https://www.gov.uk/government/publications/summary-of-the-armed-forces-bill-2021.

[123] https://www.gov.uk/government/publications/court-martial-results-from-the-military-court-centres.

[124] Detention for military offences occurs in military detention centres, while imprisonment for more serious criminal offences in HM prisons. On the detention centre – or Military Corrective Training Centre (MCTC) in Colchester see 'A rare glimpse inside the UK's only "military prison"', *BBC News*, 28 August 2013 https://www.bbc.co.uk/news/uk-23793619. See the case of *R v Jackson* [2004] EWCA Crim 371, in which the defendant, who had been found guilty of two offences of assault occasioning actual body harm, unsuccessfully argued against a sentence of detention in a military correc-

7.6   THE TRIALS OF MARINE A

The facts that led to the prosecution of Sergeant Alexander Blackman or 'Marine A' for murder were given in the CMAC judgment of 2014 on appeal from a court martial at one of the UK's Military Court Centres at Bulford in 2013.[125] They relate to events that occurred in Afghanistan on 15 September 2011 in Helmand province where British forces had been combating a Taliban insurgency, having been deployed to that country since 2001 as part of ISAF authorised by the UN Security Council.[126] Following a Taliban attack on a British command post, an Apache helicopter located one of the insurgents and fired upon him. A Royal Marine patrol led by Marine A undertook a battle damage assessment, located the insurgent and recovered his weapon. It was assumed at headquarters that the insurgent had died from injuries sustained in the helicopter attack, but a year later as part of an unrelated investigation a video recording from the helmet camera of one of the Marines on the patrol was found. It showed Marine A standing over a severely wounded insurgent, and shooting him dead as he lay defenceless on the ground. As a result of this recording Marine A and the other members of the patrol were charged by the SPA with murder, contrary to section 42 of the Armed Forces Act 2006. As Lord Chief Justice Thomas pointed out: 'that section makes it an offence if a person in the armed forces does an act that is punishable by the law of England and Wales or, if done in England and Wales, would be so punishable. The offence of murder or manslaughter committed by a British citizen is punishable by the law of England and Wales wherever committed.'[127]

It is interesting to note at the outset that the charge was one of murder, not the commission of a war crime under the International Criminal Court Act 2001. Although in substance the domestic crime of murder and the war crime of murdering a fighter rendered *hors de combat* overlap,[128] it might be speculated that the choice of charge was driven by a desire of the authorities

---

tive centre on the basis that it would be longer than imprisonment. The Court of Appeal noted (at para 10) that '[i]t seems to us that it should to be borne in mind that a period of detention in a military corrective training centre is to be treated in general terms as less severe a penalty than the same term of imprisonment in a civilian prison'.

[125] *R v Blackman* [2014] EWCA Crim 1029 (Thomas LCJ) paras 1–6.

[126] UN Doc S/RES/1386 (2001).

[127] *R v Blackman* [2014] (Thomas LCJ), para 7, citing *R v Page* [1954] 1 QB 170.

[128] Rome Statute of the International Criminal Court (1998) Article 8(2)(c) includes as war crimes in NIACs 'serious violations of article 3 common to the Four Geneva Conventions ... namely, any of the following acts committed against persons taking no active part in the hostilities, including members of armed forces who have laid down arms and those placed *hors de combat* by sickness, wounds, detention or any other cause: (i) Violence to life and person, in particular murder of all kinds ...'. Marine A's

to avoid a second conviction for war crimes following that of Corporal Payne in relation to the death of Baha Mousa, while still fulfilling the state's obligations under LOAC and the Rome Statute.[129] If the thinking was that a murder trial would attract less media and public attention than a war crimes trial, subsequent events certainly disproved this. Nevertheless, it remains the case that this was an alleged crime committed during an armed conflict by a British soldier against an enemy fighter and, as such, suitable for trial by court martial. Marine A and two other marines were brought before a court martial. The President was a Lieutenant Colonel in the Royal Marines, the Judge Advocate was the Judge Advocate General (Jeff Blackett), and the six other members of the board comprised two other marine officers, three Royal Naval officers and a Royal Naval Warrant Officer. On 8 November 2013, the court martial found Marine A guilty of murder, but acquitted the other two defendants. On 6 December 2013, the Judge Advocate General sentenced the appellant to life imprisonment with a minimum term of 10 years less time in custody, a reduction to the ranks and dismissal with disgrace from the armed forces.[130]

In his sentencing remarks directed at Sergeant Blackman at the court martial in December 2013, Judge Blackett made clear the cold-blooded nature of the killing:

> Although the insurgent may have died from his wounds sustained in the engagement by the Apache, you gave him no chance of survival. You intended to kill him and that shot certainly hastened his death. You then told your patrol they were not to say anything about what had just happened and you acknowledged what you had done by saying that you had just broken the Geneva Convention. The tone and calmness of your voice as you commented after you had shot him were matter of fact and in that respect they were chilling.[131]

Furthermore, the judge addressed the criticisms made in the media and elsewhere that killing enemy combatants should not be a criminal offence.

> That Afghan man, as an injured enemy combatant, was entitled to be treated with dignity, respect and humanity. Some commentators and members of the public have said that you should not have been prosecuted and that you have not committed a crime because it was killing within a conflict. Some also suggest it is legitimate to

---

conduct prima facie fitted this crime – see K. Grady and P. Cooper, 'Homicide: R v Blackman Court Martial Appeal Court' (2017) 7 *Criminal Law Review* 557 at 558–9.

[129] Rome Statute (1998) Articles 17(1)(c) and 20(3).

[130] *R v Blackman* [2014] paras 8–9.

[131] Sentencing remarks by HHJ Jeff Blackett, Judge Advocate General in *R v Sergeant Alexander Wayne Blackman ('Marine A')*, Case Reference: 2012CM00442, 6 December 2013 https://www.judiciary.gov.uk/wp-content/uploads/JCO/Documents/Judgments/r-v-blackman-marine-a-sentencing+remarks.pdf.

kill wounded enemy combatants because, as you said after you shot the insurgent, it is nothing they wouldn't do to British casualties. Those commentators are very wrong: if the British Armed Forces are not assiduous in complying with the laws of armed conflict and international humanitarian law they would become no better than the insurgents and terrorists they are fighting. Hearts and minds will not be won if British service personnel act with brutality and savagery. If they do not comply with the law they will quickly lose the support and confidence of those they seek to protect, as well as the international community. You and all Service personnel learn this throughout your training – you demonstrated that you knew that then, because you tried to cover it up, and you know it now.[132]

Unlike in peacetime when life can only be taken in strict circumstances, principally when absolutely necessary in self-defence and defence of others,[133] under the laws of war or LOAC the killing of the enemy is permitted, but not when they are rendered *hors de combat*.[134] The Judge Advocate General made it clear in the case of Marine A:

This was not an action taken in the heat of battle or immediately after you had been engaged in a fire fight. Nor were you under any immediate threat – the video footage shows that you were in complete control of yourself, standing around for several minutes and not apparently worried that you might be at risk of attack by other insurgents. You treated that Afghan man with contempt and murdered him in cold blood. By so doing you have betrayed your Corps and all British Service personnel who have served in Afghanistan, and you have tarnished their reputation. In one moment you undermined much of the good work done day in and day out by British forces and potentially increased the risk of revenge attacks against your fellow service personnel. You have failed to demonstrate the self discipline and restraint that is required of service personnel on operations, and which sets British troops apart from the enemy they fight.[135]

The judge accepted that Marine A was 'in a tough operational environment where' he was 'legally entitled to use lethal force against the enemy'. However, in the case of a 'very seriously wounded enemy combatant', Marine A was 'obliged to care for him', but instead he 'executed' the man. These strong words were accompanied by a robust declaration of the 'independent and impartial' nature of the court martial, which 'will not be influenced' by the

---

[132] Ibid.
[133] ECHR (1950) Article 2(2).
[134] Rome Statute (1998) Article 8(2)(c)(i).
[135] Sentencing remarks by HHJ Jeff Blackett in *Blackman* (2013).

public debate and media outbursts. He also took the opportunity to explain why the court martial was the most appropriate court to deliver justice:

> Of course sitting in a court room in middle England is a far cry from the brutality of the conflict in Afghanistan, but you have been judged here by a Board made up of Service personnel who understand operational service because they too have experienced it. That is one of the strengths of the Court Martial system ... We have reached an independent decision on the appropriate sentence based on all of the evidence we have heard, your plea of mitigation and the legal framework which we are obliged to apply, together with our collective experience of the law and the context and stresses of operations. Board members have served in all the theatres in which you have served.[136]

Finding Marine A guilty of murder meant that by law the sentence was imprisonment for life, although the Court took account of mitigating factors including the defendant's personal circumstances and the immense pressure he was operating under to determine that the minimum term to be served by the defendant was 10 years before he would be eligible to be considered for parole on licence. The Board noted that 'thousands of other Service personnel have experienced the same or similar stresses'. However, while 'they exercised self-discipline and acted properly and humanely', the defendant did not. The wider implications of the case, particularly the concerns of international criminal justice, were also highlighted by the judge:

> It is also very important that this Court sends out a very strong message that while this sort of offence is extremely rare, if not unique, those Service personnel who commit crimes of murder, or other war crimes or crimes against humanity while on operations will be dealt with severely. This is a message of deterrence but it is also to reassure the international community that allegations of serious crime will be dealt with transparently and appropriately. In our view that message is delivered by sentencing you to imprisonment for life. Setting the minimum term reflects the seriousness of the offence while taking account of the unique and special circumstances of this case and your personal mitigation.

The judge stated that as an 'inevitable consequence of a sentence of life imprisonment' the defendant would 'also be reduced to the ranks and dismissed with disgrace from Her Majesty's Service'.[137]

The Judge Advocate General's sentencing remarks powerfully encapsulate the argument as to why British soldiers must comply with those laws that prohibit the taking of life when faced with enemy fighters who have been rendered *hors de combat*. It might be argued that they fail to take account of challenges

---

[136] Ibid.
[137] Ibid.

to the fundamental basis of the laws of war, which share the characteristics of many areas of international law, namely those of consent and reciprocity.[138] In IACs both sides in a conflict have agreed, by becoming parties to the Geneva Conventions, to apply the rules that prohibit the taking of life of those rendered *hors de combat* on the basis that they know that each other's troops will receive mercy if they are either captured or wounded. This can work well in inter-state conflicts but in asymmetrical NIACs such as in Afghanistan, that reciprocal basis is not present, as pointed out by Marine A in his defence. However, at least for serious breaches of the laws of war, those laws apply irrespective of consent or reciprocity, because the prohibition of war crimes is not simply a typical consensual norm of international law – it is a core crime the prohibition of which is *jus cogens*, part of the peremptory norms of international law that allow for no derogation.[139]

The first appeal in the *Blackman* case in 2014 was against conviction and sentence. The appeal against conviction before the CMAC turned upon the differences between a court martial before a board of serving officers who can decide guilt by majority verdict,[140] and a civilian criminal court: 'it was the appellant's contention that it is a fundamental feature of the system of criminal justice in England and Wales, emblematic of a democracy, that those facing serious criminal charges are entitled to be tried before 12 members of the public and can only be convicted by a majority of at least 10 of the 12'.[141] The appellant clearly felt that he would have had a greater chance of acquittal before an ordinary jury in the Crown Court than before a court martial board. He also argued that a simple majority that was required for conviction in a court martial made the conviction inherently unsafe as it suggested sufficient doubt to defeat the criminal standard of proof of beyond reasonable doubt. Indeed, the appellant relied on a passage from *Rant on the Court Martial and Service Law* (authored by the Judge Advocate General in the *Blackman* case): 'an undisclosed simple majority decision in a serious case where the defendant

---

[138] For a wider discussion of the moral dimension see T.W. Simpson, 'Did Marine A Do Wrong? On Biggar's Lethal Injections' (2015) 28(3) *Studies in Christian Ethics* 287, discussing Marine A's case in the light of the argument in N. Biggar, *In Defence of War* (Oxford University Press, 2013).

[139] B. Broomhall, *International Justice and the International Criminal Court* (Oxford University Press, 2003) 41–51. This categorisation is not undermined by the limitation of the ICC to war crimes when committed 'as part of a plan or policy or as part of a large-scale commission of such crimes': Rome Statute (1998) Article 8(1). See G. Simpson, 'Men and Abstract Entities: Individual Responsibility and Collective Guilt in International Criminal Law' in A. Nollkaemper and H. van der Wilt (eds), *System Criminality in International Law* (Cambridge University Press, 2009) 69 at 90–1.

[140] Armed Forces Act (2006) sections 155 and 160.

[141] *R v Blackman* [2014] para 16.

is at risk of a significant custodial sentence might be perceived as being inherently unsafe, since the outcome rests on a knife-edge'.[142]

The CMAC dismissed this aspect of the appellant's argument on the basis that it had previously decided in *R v Twaite* that simple majority verdicts were compatible with the right to a fair trial under Article 6 of the ECHR.[143] As the Court stated 'when the Strasbourg Court reviewed the system of military discipline in *Engel* … it concluded … that the distinctions between the courts and Courts Martial were justified by the differences between the conditions of military and civil life'. Furthermore, those distinctions 'could not be taken as amounting to discrimination against members of the armed forces. The great advantage of reaching a decision by majority is that it avoids "a hung jury". There are good reasons why, in a system of military justice, it is necessary to avoid "a hung jury" for the ordinary run of offences.'[144]

The CMAC observed that it remained 'open to Parliament to change the requirements of [section 160 of the Armed Forces Act 2006], as the Judge Advocate General himself has suggested, to bring the position into line with the position in the courts, either for all offences or more serious offences. That is a matter for Parliament.'[145] Furthermore, it appeared on the information provided to the Court 'that no question was raised at the outset of these proceedings as to whether it was appropriate for the appellant to be tried by Court Martial or by a court'. The Court noted that the 'question as to whether proceedings should be before a court or a Court Martial is governed by a protocol between the Director of Service Prosecutions, the Director of Public Prosecutions and the Ministry of Defence made in September and October 2011'.[146] The 'protocol makes it clear that where there are overlapping jurisdictions between the Court Martial system of justice and the system of justice in the courts, it is for the Director of Public Prosecutions to decide whether a person should be subject to military justice or be subject to trial in the courts'.[147] The Court simply observed that 'in the case of prosecutions for murder committed overseas by members of HM Armed Forces, careful consideration should be given to the question of which is the more appropriate system, bearing in mind the requirement in the court for a specified majority and any relevance in such a case of the experience of the members of the board that comprises the Court

---

[142] Blackett (2009) para 5.126.
[143] *R v Blackman* [2014] para 18, citing *R v Twaite* [2010] EWCA Crim 2973.
[144] *R v Blackman* [2014] para 22, citing ECtHR in *Engel v The Netherlands*, Appl No 5100/71, 8 June 1976.
[145] *R v Blackman* [2014] para 26.
[146] Ibid, para 28.
[147] Ibid, para 29.

Martial as compared with the court system which gives the responsibility for sentence to the judge alone'.[148]

As regards Sergeant Blackman's appeal against sentence in 2014, the CMAC related a number of grave findings by the court martial against the appellant 'as to deliberate nature of the murder'.[149] The Appeal Court determined that 'those grave findings were made by the Court Martial having heard the evidence'. Furthermore, there was 'sufficient support from the video … and the transcript of the video that preclude us in any way from going behind those findings'.[150] Crucially, the Appeal Court found that it 'was not possible two years after the killing of the insurgent to diagnose whether the appellant was in fact suffering from combat stress disorder, but the circumstances to which we have referred may have meant that any combat stress disorder was undetected'.[151]

The Appeal Court considered the aggravating factors found by the court martial:

> First, although there was not a significant degree of planning or pre-meditation, it was clear from what was recorded on the video that the appellant decided, shortly after he had disarmed the insurgent, that he was going to do something to him which he did not want to be seen by his superiors in headquarters. Secondly, the insurgent was seriously wounded and therefore particularly vulnerable. Third, the appellant's actions put at risk the lives of other British service personnel because his actions would be used to radicalise others and encourage them both to fight the British forces and to act more brutally towards them in retribution or reprisal. Fourth, he was in charge of the patrol and it was incumbent upon him to set the standards. He had abused his position of trust by involving the other members of the patrol in covering up what had been done and lying on his behalf.[152]

The court martial found three mitigating factors:

> First, there was provocation. The cumulative effect of lethal military activity had had an obvious effect. The appellant was also affected by stories that the Taliban had hung a British serviceman's severed limb in a tree. The appellant was in no doubt that the victim of the murder was an insurgent who had been firing at [a command post] moments before he was wounded. Second, the appellant was subject to the stress of operations: this was his sixth operational tour and his second to Afghanistan in under 14 years of service. The constant pressure was enhanced by the reduction of available men in his command, so he had often to undertake more patrols and placed his men in danger more often. The Court Martial also accepted the psychiatric evidence … that it was likely that he was suffering to some degree from combat

---

[148] Ibid, para 30.
[149] Ibid, para 32.
[150] Ibid, para 33.
[151] Ibid, para 40.
[152] Ibid, paras 42–3.

stress disorder. However, it noted that thousands of other service personnel had experienced the same or similar stresses, yet they had exercised self-discipline and had acted both properly and humanely. The appellant had not. Thirdly, there was personal mitigation, particularly his previous good character, his excellent record of service and the effect upon him of the death of his father.[153]

In discussing the sentence handed down by the court martial, the CMAC noted that the sentence of imprisonment for life was an inevitable consequence of the conviction for murder.[154] The Appeal Court largely agreed with the court martial on its reasoning on sentencing, particularly when taking into account 'the operational experience of members of the Court Martial',[155] but put greater emphasis on the stress on Blackman in that it was 'self-evident that armed forces sent to a foreign and hostile land to combat an insurgency will be placed under much greater stress than armed forces sent to fight a regular army'.[156] In addition, 'there was the clear perception amongst HM Armed Forces that the insurgents in Afghanistan committed severe atrocities upon British soldiers'.[157] Further 'in addition to the considerable stress of dealing with an insurgency in such conditions, it is very clear that significant further stress must have been placed upon the appellant because the remote location of his command post', which 'meant that he was not seen regularly by those more senior to him'.[158] For the Appeal Court it was 'clear that in the events surrounding the murder of the insurgent the appellant acted entirely out of character and was suffering from combat stress disorder', which ought to have been accorded greater weight as a mitigating factor.[159] Moreover, the Appeal Court found that 'the particular circumstances did not require an additional term by way of deterrence to the sentence as the Court Martial found'. The Appeal Court was of the view that the 'open and very public way in which the proceedings were conducted overall, the worldwide publicity given to the appellant's conviction, the life sentence imposed on him and the significant minimum term he must in any event serve before any consideration of parole' would be sufficient deterrence.[160] On that basis the Appeal Court concluded that 'although he remains subject to a sentence of imprisonment for life, the minimum term which he must serve before being considered for parole should be reduced to 8 years'.[161]

---

[153] Ibid, paras 45–7.
[154] Ibid, paras 48–9.
[155] Ibid, para 74.
[156] Ibid, para 70.
[157] Ibid, para 71.
[158] Ibid, para 72.
[159] Ibid, para 75.
[160] Ibid, para 76.
[161] Ibid, para 77.

The court martial of Marine A, the publicity surrounding it, and the appeal judgment, all demonstrate how controversial it is for soldiers to be tried for killing enemy fighters in a brutal conflict in which the enemy does not respect the laws of war. A Parliamentary petition to free Sergeant Alexander Blackman received 34,440 signatures. It stated that a 'soldier should never go to prison for killing the enemy in a battlefield situation. Sergeant Alexander Blackman was sent to prison for killing a member of the Taliban in a battle in Afghanistan.'[162] This triggered an unprecedented debate in the House of Commons in September 2015, in which members of the House seemed to encroach on the independence of the courts. Richard Drax MP supported Blackman's continuing objections against his conviction: 'by law, the judge advocate general had a duty to direct the jury on all verdicts reasonably open to them, regardless of whether the prosecution or defence chose to raise them'. He declared that the 'verdicts included the ability for a jury to return a verdict of not guilty of murder but guilty of manslaughter', and that 'possible routes to such a manslaughter verdict included: temporary loss of control after months of cumulative stress' or 'diminished responsibility owing to battlefield fatigue and post-traumatic stress disorder'.[163] This was not a claim based on a wider appeal to justice but on specific points of law and seemed to breach the separation of powers on which the legal system is based. Nevertheless, views expressed in Parliament were part of the momentum to restore the reputation not only of Sergeant Blackman but of the British armed forces who had been sent to fight unwinnable wars.

In 2016, the Criminal Cases Review Commission (CCRC) reviewed the case, with 800 supporters of Alexander Blackman urging the CCRC to determine that there had been a miscarriage of justice. Blackman is quoted as saying: 'I made a split second-mistake. I had been sent to a brutal battlefield to fight for my country in an unpopular war. And yet at the end of my trial, the Establishment lined up to portray me as an evil scumbag because it suited them to do so at the time.'[164] The *Blackman* case returned to the CMAC on a reference by the CCRC in 2017.[165] The mental health of Sergeant Blackman became the focus. The Appeal Court noted at the outset of the appeal that 'no psychiatric report had been obtained before the trial and no psychiatric evidence was called at the trial',[166] but for the purposes of sentence the defence obtained a psychiatric report which concluded that 'the appellant may have

---

[162] https://petition.parliament.uk/petitions/108570.
[163] Hansard, HC Deb, Vol 599, 16 September 2015.
[164] 'Marine A case review wait means delay to justice says supporters', *The Telegraph*, 26 October 2016.
[165] *R v Alexander Wayne Blackman* [2017] EWCA Crim 190.
[166] Ibid, para 3.

been suffering from a combat stress disorder which had gone undetected', which was considered by the court martial as an extenuating factor in relation to punishment.[167] Ultimately, after hearing further expert evidence, the Appeal Court gave much greater weight to Blackman's mental condition, thereby increasing the chances of soldiers in future conflicts having a partial defence of diminished responsibility to charges of murder if they have been suffering from combat stress disorder, which impaired their judgement at the time of the offence.

In its 2017 judgment the CMAC summarised the grounds of the reference from the CCRC, including the fact that 'further psychiatric evidence obtained since the court martial showed that both at the time of the killing and at the time of the court martial, the appellant was suffering from an adjustment disorder, a recognised medical condition. On that basis, there was available to the appellant the partial defence of diminished responsibility so that his conviction for murder should be quashed and either a conviction for manslaughter by reason of diminished responsibility should be substituted or a retrial ordered'.[168] The Appeal Court found that 'each of the psychiatrists was of the view that the adjustment disorder was in the circumstances of this case capable of substantially impairing the appellant's ability to form a rational judgement or exercise self-control',[169] and it was 'common ground between the psychiatrists that the appellant was suffering from an adjustment disorder at the time of the court martial'.[170]

> As this was the first case as far as any of the witnesses were aware in which an adjustment disorder had been associated with the killing of an enemy, a very considerable degree of caution is required. The evidence was that all elite troops (which the Royal Marines are) are trained to withstand stress and to be resilient, particularly when well led. However, as Professor Greenberg stated and we accept, everyone has a breaking point. As he pithily expressed when cross examined by counsel for the prosecution: 'There isn't any such thing as a Rambo-type, Arnold Schwarzenegger soldier who can face all sorts of stressors and appear to be invulnerable. That sort of person only exists in the cinema'.[171]

This represents a significant departure from the approach to military discipline that expects soldiers to behave uniformly, an approach based on the punishment of unlawful actions irrespective of any individual weakness. Following *Blackman*, an individual soldier's mental health should become more of

---

167 Ibid, para 4.
168 Ibid, para 6.
169 Ibid, para 38.
170 Ibid, para 66.
171 Ibid, para 71.

a central concern in dispensing military justice, 101 years after Lieutenant Poole's execution for desertion despite suffering from shell shock at the time. The soldier should now be seen as an individual not simply as a uniform cog in the military machine. This does not exonerate soldiers who commit serious offences, but it allows them the same defences as would be available to any individual. It was clear to the CMAC in 2017 that the 'findings of the Board, particularly in relation to the credibility of the appellant, cannot now be of substantial weight, as the Board had not heard the psychiatric evidence which could have impacted on its judgement'.[172] The Appeal Court found that 'if the expert evidence of the psychiatrists' had been 'before the court martial, we are in no doubt but that the defence of diminished responsibility would have had to have been left to the Board and that it could have affected their decision to convict'.[173] As a result, the verdict was unsafe and the conviction for murder was quashed, and substituted with a verdict of manslaughter by reason of diminished responsibility.[174] Alexander Blackman received a seven year sentence for manslaughter and was dismissed from the service (but not with disgrace),[175] and with time already served was released on 28 April 2017.

Although the outcome of the final appeal in *Blackman* may appear to be the result of political and public pressure, the fact remains that he was convicted of a serious offence despite pressure to completely exonerate him. Moreover, the idea that psychiatric evidence was somehow conjured up to produce a more acceptable outcome ignores the fact that some such evidence was presented at the original court martial but only at the sentencing stage, and furthermore had been uncovered in an internal naval review into the killing of the insurgent by Sergeant Blackman. The Telemeter Report of September 2015 referred to in the 2017 appeal judgment found that there were problems with the chain of command in the area of deployment in Afghanistan, which left Sergeant Blackman isolated and placed under severe strain. The Report's executive summary states that the 'face to face supervision' by the COs 'was insufficient to identify a number of warning signs that could have indicated' that J Company led by Sergeant Blackman were 'showing evidence of moral regression, psychological strain and fatigue'. The Report also said that Sergeant Blackman showed 'poor leadership'.[176] The findings were controversial and led to the MoD stating that the Internal Review 'went beyond the remit of its

---

172   Ibid, para 75.
173   Ibid, para 80.
174   Ibid, para 114.
175   *R v Blackman (Sentence)* [2017] EWCA Crim 325.
176   Royal Navy, 'Telemeter – Internal Review', 7 March 2014 https://www.gov .uk/government/uploads/system/uploads/attachment_data/file/576817/Op_Telemeter _internal_review_-_Executive_summary_and_recommendations_-_Appended.pdf.

original terms of reference' and was 'not sufficiently robust to allow conclusions to be drawn as to the appropriateness of individual operational decision making in the chain of command' so that 'specific criticisms of individuals within the chain of command cannot be relied upon'.[177] Nevertheless, even ignoring the problems in command, the Telemeter Report's depiction of the isolation and stress of individual soldiers in an extremely hostile environment remains uncontested and telling.

It was the case that Sergeant Blackman was, after a court martial and two appeals, found guilty of an unlawful killing. Those cases highlighted the extremely harsh and dangerous conditions in which he operated. However, wider questions of whether the Army, the MoD, and the government bore any responsibility for putting him in a situation where it appears that the soldiers were being stretched well beyond what could reasonably be expected of them, were not answered. Looking more broadly at British involvement in Helmand, Frank Ledwidge points to the lack of sufficient troops on the ground, the failure to secure territory beyond a few hundred metres around bases, and the inability to bring security to ordinary Afghans.[178] The focus of the British Army appears to have been on violently engaging the enemy and killing as many Taliban as possible with a lack of proper regard to civilians caught in the cross-fire.[179] In this context, where maximum violence was the norm, the crime of Sergeant Blackman appears explicable though remaining inexcusable. In the end, the military justice system seems to have come to the right conclusion and, in so doing, destroyed the myth of the British soldier as always being unerringly tough, resilient and disciplined. Moreover, it finally recognised the importance of identifying any operative mental illness if soldiers are called to account for their actions before a court martial.

The *Blackman* appeal judgment of 2017 has been heavily criticised by Heller: 'Blackman's supposed adjustment disorder was based on factors common to every soldier who ever served in a dangerous part of Afghanistan or Iraq'. Heller points out that the expert evidence in the appeal revealed that '1 out of every 12 British soldiers in Afghanistan suffered from the kind of "recognised mental condition"', which, according to the Appeal Court, 'meant that they were almost legally incapable of committing murder. That's terrifying.'[180] Despite sharing a flawed depiction of soldiers as uniform actors, this criticism in a sense reinforces the point that if under-resourced and under-supported

---

[177] Ibid.
[178] F. Ledwidge, *Losing Small Wars: British Military Failure in Iraq and Afghanistan* (Yale University Press, 2012) 94–106.
[179] Ibid, 105.
[180] K.J. Heller, 'Bad Criminal Law in the Alexander Blackman Case', *Opinio Juris*, 31 March 2017.

soldiers are put in extremely dangerous situations it is not surprising that a significant number of them suffer from combat stress that might, if proven by the defence,[181] affect their mental capacity when committing atrocious acts. In the end it might be best to view the *Blackman* trials as a series of attempts 'to match the Court's verdict with the recognised moral justice of the case'.[182]

7.7   COURTS MARTIAL UNDER PUBLIC SCRUTINY

Trials before courts martial have received intense scrutiny from the perspective of human rights law, with a number of judgments from the ECtHR requiring the UK to modify its practices.[183] However, scrutiny of courts martial is not simply judicial. For instance, in addition to the *Blackman* case, which attracted significant public and Parliamentary attention, the court martial of Sergeant Danny Nightingale of the SAS, who pleaded guilty to charges under the Firearms Act 1968 after being caught in unauthorised possession of a firearm and over 300 rounds of ammunition found at his home, also caused a backlash on the basis that this was no way to treat a 'hero'.[184] He was sentenced to 18 months' military detention by court martial in November 2012. The CMAC quashed the original verdict in March 2013 'on the basis that Nightingale had been persuaded improperly to plead guilty by remarks made by the Judge Advocate to his counsel during pre-trial legal argument'.[185] In July 2013 after a retrial, Nightingale was convicted and sentenced to two years' detention, but suspended thereby avoiding prison. Nightingale's application to appeal this judgment was rejected by the CMAC in May 2014 on the ground that there was a 'considerable amount' of evidence to support the conviction, and that the claimed new evidence added 'virtually nothing to the evidence before the court martial'.[186]

In his sentencing remarks in the *Nightingale* retrial by court martial in 2013, Judge Blackett, Judge Advocate General, explained the exceptional circumstances that reduced the starting point of five years imprisonment for such an offence to two years, namely that the defendant was 'an outstanding

---

[181]   Grady and Cooper (2017) 561–2. They conclude that the defence of diminished responsibility would have been available to Blackman if he had been charged with the war crime of murder.

[182]   E. Stuart-Cole, 'Blackman (Marine A): Inculpable or Incapable?' (2017) 81 *Journal of Criminal Law* 262 at 264.

[183]   See Chapter 8.

[184]   Lyon and Farmiloe (2016) 175.

[185]   Ibid, 159; *R v Danny Harold Nightingale* [2013] EWCA Crim 405. See also *R v Nightingale* [2012] EWCA 2734.

[186]   'Danny Nightingale loses new appeal bid', *The Daily Telegraph*, 20 May 2014.

Senior NCO' who had served with distinction in a number of deployments with the SAS. Sergeant Nightingale not only did his duty but he went beyond that by improving the medical care of fellow soldiers suffering traumatic injury by developing the 'Nightingale dressing'. Furthermore, he suffered a brain injury in 2009 resulting in some mental impairment, which may have affected his decision to keep the weapon. Furthermore, Nightingale had no criminal intention.[187]

The Judge Advocate General also took the opportunity in his sentencing remarks to set the record straight about the propriety of the court martial of a distinguished soldier. Judge Blackett criticised the defendant and others for misleading comments made while the case was *sub judice* resulting in 'much uninformed and misinformed public debate', indeed much of what was said 'bordered on contempt' and did not help the 'course of justice'. Nightingale's claims that he was being made a 'scapegoat or the victim of some wider political agenda' were 'absolute nonsense', and the criticism of the Army and the SPA was 'unmerited and totally without foundation'. The defendant was 'simply someone against whom there was a strong prima facie case of serious wrongdoing and, given the dangers to society caused by illegal firearms and their misuse, it was in the public interest to prosecute you'; indeed the SPA 'would have been neglecting its duty if it had not brought this prosecution'. The judge extended his comments to 'those who have been so critical' of the SPA and court martial process, 'particularly those which have made unfounded and uniformed remarks under the cloak of Parliamentary privilege', trusting that they realised 'how inappropriate and wrong their criticisms were'.[188]

Statements in the House of Commons seem particularly problematic as they seek to undermine due process while legal proceedings are underway and, as in the *Blackman* case, breached the separation of powers upon which the constitution is based. In raising the *Nightingale* case before the House of Commons in November 2012 after the original sentence had been handed down, Julian Brazier MP thanked a number of 'gallant Friends' in the House for supporting him in bringing up the case before Parliament, presumably referring to a number of MPs who had served in the armed forces. After giving a version of the facts in the case, Mr Brazier then urged the Solicitor General to 'confirm whether, should an appeal be launched, it will be within his powers to discuss whether or not to oppose the appeal with the Service Prosecuting Authority'. He urged the Solicitor General 'to review the service

---

[187] *R v Sgt Danny Nightingale*, Bulford Military Court Centre, Sentencing Remarks of HHJ Jeff Blackett, Judge Advocate General, 25 July 2013 https://www.judiciary.uk/judgments/r-v-sgtdannynightingale/.

[188] Ibid.

interest case, and allow the planned appeal to go through unopposed'.[189] The Solicitor General responded, quite rightly, that as the defendant had been tried and found guilty, the only path was an appeal, which was a process that should not involve 'politicians telling the independent judiciary – or, indeed, the independent prosecuting authorities – what to do'.[190]

At the same time the Defence Secretary, Philip Hammond, asked the Attorney General, Dominic Grieve, 'for advice in relation to the case of Sergeant Danny Nightingale', and 'to review whether the public interest test had been applied appropriately'. A spokesperson for the Attorney General made it clear that it would be inappropriate for him to review either the decision to prosecute or the sentence handed down – that would be 'a matter for the court martial appeal court, in due course'.[191]

The spotlight shone on the court martial of serving soldiers is wrongly cast in the media, and also in Parliament, as the unjust application of harsh laws to heroes who had fought for Queen and country.[192] It is better to recognise that soldiers, like any individual, can be heroes, criminals or victims.[193] Blackman had served heroically until the unlawful killing of the wounded insurgent, and he was a victim in the sense of being isolated, under-resourced and suffering from combat stress disorder. Nightingale also had an exemplary record until his crime and seemed to continue to serve without his mental impairments being detected. Whether the state had fulfilled its duties to provide adequate resources to soldiers in combat and post-combat is not to be determined by a court martial, but many of the points raised in mitigation are indicative that the government had questions to answer as regards its obligations towards service personnel. Some of those questions and obligations are beginning to be litigated before the courts, in particular in cases brought under the HRA 1998. It will be seen in the next chapter that the first stage of human rights cases concerned the nature of the court martial and whether it can deliver fair trial,

---

[189] Hansard, House of Commons, Vol 553, 20 November 2012. Julian Lewis MP mentioned that he had already raised the issue twice before in the House of Commons before stating that 'when the appeal comes, it should not be opposed, and Sergeant Nightingale should be allowed to resume his career and his life with the honour he so richly deserves'.

[190] Ibid.

[191] '"I can't intervene in SAS sniper case," attorney general tells defence secretary', *The Guardian*, 20 November 2013.

[192] See, for example, on the *Nightingale* case: 'This good soldier deserves to be freed', *Daily Telegraph*, 18 November 2013. A petition asking for his release received over 100,000 signatures.

[193] See Chapter 9. See further H. McCartney, 'Hero, Victim or Villain? The Public Image of the British Soldier and Its Implications for Defense Policy' (2011) 27 *Defense & Security Analysis* 43.

but the second stage of human rights jurisprudence is exploring the obligations of the government to ensure that soldiers who are deployed to dangerous situations are not put at greater risk then necessary.

The balance of rights and duties of soldiers was highlighted once again in September 2018, with the court martial of two soldiers for negligent performance of their duties leading to the death of three SAS reservists on a training exercise held in the Brecon Beacons in extreme temperatures. The defendants were alleged to have breached their duties under service law and that was the point of the trial, but the case also raised the wider question of whether the rights of the three soldiers who lost their lives had been adequately protected. In *R v Cipher 1A and Cipher 1B*,[194] the defendants, both experienced army trainers, were in charge of a test march held on 13 July 2013 'for applicants wishing to be selected for one of the most, if not the most, elite military units in the World'.[195] There were 78 applicants on the test march, a mixture of reservists and regular soldiers. Although most completed the test, some withdrew themselves or were withdrawn on medical grounds by medical staff. Three of the reserve soldiers (Lance Corporal Craig Roberts, Trooper Edward Maher and Corporal James Dunsby) died from hyperthermia.[196]

Judge Blackett noted that although the applicants were fully aware of the high standards required for entry into the SAS, those responsible for running the tests had a 'duty ... to provide a safe training environment, to understand the limits of the applicants' endurance and, if necessary, protect the applicants from putting themselves in jeopardy'. The prosecution case was that the two defendants had 'performed that duty of care negligently',[197] contrary to section 15 of the Armed Forces Act 2006. The prosecution was brought despite the fact that an investigation by the Health and Safety Executive (HSE) had identified wider issues of accountability when it 'concluded that there were serious failings in the planning, assessment, conduct and monitoring of the test week, which were causative of the deaths and ill health suffered'; and further that the MoD had 'accepted that there were systemic failures'.[198] Despite these systemic failures, the prosecution alleged that the 'two defendants performed their duty negligently by: failing to carry out an adequate risk assessment in respect of the exercise; failing to put in place adequate control measures to mitigate the risk of heat illness; and failing to take adequate steps to mitigate

---

[194] *R v Cipher 1A and Cipher 1B*, Ruling on Defence application of No Case to Answer in the Court Martial Sitting at Bulford (MCS 2017CM-03), 18 September 2018.
[195] Ibid, para 1.
[196] Ibid, para 3.
[197] Ibid, para 2.
[198] Ibid, para 4.

the risk of heat illness in response to the temperature and heat casualties that arose during the exercise'.[199]

Before considering whether to stop the case for lack of evidence that the defendants had performed their duties negligently, Judge Blackett took the opportunity to clarify the nature of the charges and the unique nature of the court martial, which has criminal jurisdiction over issues of professional negligence. The judge remarked that 'were this a case before a professional body, dealing with fitness to practice or misconduct leading to employment sanctions, there is no doubt that whether a person is negligent or not should rest with the expert panel of that profession'. However, the judge highlighted the 'hybrid nature' of the court martial in that it 'deals with criminal matters and disciplinary matters, including negligence, and has a range of sanctions which include both criminal and employment', namely up to two years' imprisonment as well as loss of employment or rank. Such criminal penalties are not available to professional bodies. It followed that given this 'hybrid jurisdiction' the 'determination of whether a person has been negligent must, therefore, be supported by evidence, and not be left solely to the professional judgement of the Board members'.[200]

Given the criminal nature of the charges and sanctions available upon conviction it was therefore a fundamentally important prerequisite to have sufficient evidence 'to enable the Board to use their professional judgement when applying the reasonable serviceman test',[201] and it was the judge's job to ensure that was done. This was an important intervention by the judge, ensuring proper due process so that the defendants would not be exposed to conviction on the basis of opinion rather than evidence. The deaths of the three servicemen had attracted much publicity, with the subsequent danger of apportioning blame on the basis that the defendants were in charge of the test that caused the deaths. To their immense credit, some of the families of the victims made it clear before the court martial that they felt that the defendants were being made 'scapegoats' by the MoD.[202]

Judge Blackett explained the offence of negligent performance of a duty in the following terms: 'negligence is a failure to comply with the standards of the reasonable person and that standard is measured against that which is to be expected of the reasonable serviceman having similar training, knowledge and experience of each defendant'. As such this 'is an objective test, but in deciding what level of training knowledge and experience to attribute to the

[199] Ibid, para 5.
[200] Ibid, para 7.
[201] Ibid, para 7.
[202] 'Two SAS soldiers charged over death of reservists on Brecon Beacons test march', *The Telegraph*, 2 November 2017.

reasonable serviceman against whom the defendants are to be judged, the state of the defendant's training knowledge and experience at the time are relevant'.[203] The defence had argued that the 'defendants inherited a system which had never been tested as it was on 13 July 2013 and had no reason to question the methodology as being anything other than tried and tested'. The defence also referred to 'the culture of subservience in which any serviceman in the position of the defendants would have been influenced by their position within the Chain of Command'.[204] On the other hand, the prosecution argued that 'against the background of the systemic failures' identified by the HSE, which had been 'accepted by all of those who operated within this chain of command as the norm, a reasonable serviceman of similar training knowledge and experience as each defendant, would have acted differently' – 'in other words, the defendants' performance fell short of what is reasonable to have expected of them'.[205]

This attempt to argue that the defendants bore a share of the blame for the deaths on the basis that they should have departed from the inherently flawed processes they were required to administer was dismissed by the judge: 'if a person is given no training in a particular activity and does what all others have done before him, and what is done is approved by the chain of command, then it is entirely reasonable for him to continue with that particular practice even if objectively it is subsequently seen by experts as unreasonable'.[206] The defendants were aware of the risks caused by the hot weather in that they had started the exercise earlier than scheduled and provided more water at certain points on the march. Although the risk assessment was objectively inadequate, there was 'no evidence that the defendants did anything different from any one else of similar training and experience'. The judge stated further that if the defendants 'received no training, and they did exactly what everyone else did, and that action was approved by the Chain of Command, then it cannot be said that they were negligent'.[207] After sifting through the arguments of both sides the judge determined that there was 'no evidence of negligent performance of duty when the conduct of these defendants is measured against the reasonable serviceman of similar experience, knowledge and training', meaning that a 'Board properly directed could not properly convict' the defendants, leading

---

[203] *R v Cipher 1A and Cipher 1B* (2018) para 8.
[204] Ibid, para 13.
[205] Ibid, para 9.
[206] Ibid, para 17.
[207] Ibid.

to the judge stopping the case.[208] The judge made the following remarks in a post-script:

> I would like to address the families of the deceased who have sat through this trial with the utmost dignity and respect ... You have waited for a long time for the matter to come to trial. You may have thought that this trial might have helped you to obtain some degree of closure. But this trial was never about attaching sole blame for the deaths of these three young men on these defendants. The allegations of negligent performance of duty were only a small part in the overall failings: the deaths occurred because of the systemic failures within Joint Forces Command. Of course the system is made up of people, but there have been successive people in ... the Chain of Command who have failed to address their minds to the real risks involved in exercising in extreme temperatures, and who have failed to ensure that those delivering the training or invigilating the test were properly trained in all aspects ... These two defendants did the best they could in the circumstances of fewer resources than requested, a lack of even the most basic training in relation to heat illness and risk assessment and within the culture that existed at the time. I offer you all my sincere condolences and hope that you understand the reason for my decision today. I will now ask the Board to come back into court and direct them to find both defendants not guilty.[209]

The final statement, and the case as a whole, shows how a court martial can only address one side of the scales of justice – in this case ensuring that the two soldiers were not punished for systemic failings in training, methods and resources. However, it could not address the injustices that led the deaths of the three soldiers, although the judge valiantly tried to balance those scales to the extent available to him by his condemnatory remarks directed at the chain of command.[210] The wider responsibilities of the Army, the MoD and the government could only have been addressed by a claim that the right to life of the three soldiers had been violated by those systemic failings highlighted by the court martial.[211]

7.8 CONCLUSION

Despite legislative improvements to the court martial found in the Armed Forces Acts 2006 and 2011, Lyon and Farmiloe argue for further reforms: first the 'Judge Advocate should become solely responsible for sentencing as in the

---

[208] Ibid, para 21.

[209] Ibid, paras 22–4.

[210] See further, 'Brecon Beacons deaths: relatives attack failure to prosecute senior officers', *The Guardian*, 18 September 2018: one family stated that the 'acquittal of these two junior officers simply reinforces our long-held belief that those responsible sit at a much higher and corporate level'.

[211] See Chapter 8.

Crown Court'; secondly, where the 'maximum sentence upon conviction is ten years or more, a court comprising a president and eleven members should be required, with a requirement for a minimum 10:2 majority'; thirdly 'Board members should be officers or senior non-commissioned officers to widen the pool of available personnel, with the caveat that Board members must be at least the military rank of the accused'.[212] As stated by Lyon and Farmiloe: '[t]hese recommendations would go some way to eradicating the concerns raised both within the judiciary and in the European Court of Human Rights, and popular misconceptions about the military justice system, without any detrimental effects on good order and discipline'.[213] The Armed Forces Bill before Parliament in 2021 goes some way to meeting these concerns by providing for qualified majority voting, although the boards would remain small (with six, five or three members depending upon the seriousness of the offence).[214]

A Liberty Report of 2019 goes even further by arguing that the court martial currently provides second rate justice, not simply because of the smaller size of the jury (board) and the smaller majority necessary for conviction, but because jurors in civilian criminal courts 'are not required to have any professional or other special knowledge of the defendant's circumstances or the circumstances of the alleged offence'. Liberty points out that 'bankers are not tried by jurors working in the financial sector, lawyers are not tried by a jury of barristers and solicitors and police officers are not tried by a jury of people employed by a police force'.[215] Inconsistency is not a compelling reason by itself,[216] and Liberty's argument fails to recognise not only the unique nature of many of the offences that can be committed by soldiers, but the unique role they have in being tasked with using lethal force and other exceptional powers (such as detention) on behalf of the state.

More broadly, military justice is premised on ensuring that soldiers behave in a disciplined manner, moreover to a higher standard of discipline than expected of other professions. As the Judge Advocate General explained

---

[212] Lyon and Farmiloe (2016) 176.

[213] Ibid, 177.

[214] Armed Forces Bill (2021) clause 2, provides that where there are six lay members of the board, five must agree; where there are five, four must agree; and where there are three, two must agree https://publications.parliament.uk/pa/bills/cbill/58-01/0244/en/200244en.pdf.

[215] Norton (2019) 68.

[216] Interestingly, in the case of *Gunn v Service Prosecuting Authority* [2019] EWCA Crim 1470, the defendant argued that as he served in the RAF he should have been tried by members of his own service not, as happened, by an Army Board. His appeal was dismissed by the Court of Appeal, which stated (at para 37) that while the usual practice of trying a defendant by lay members from his own Service was desirable, it was not mandatory.

in *Cipher 1A and Cipher 1B*, a soldier neglecting his duty is committing a criminal offence, something that is not normally the case in civilian life. Furthermore, it could be argued that the court martial needs to have jurisdiction over ordinary crimes as well as military offences because the commission of those crimes also represents a breakdown in military discipline. This was the position taken by the House of Lords in *R v Spear*, where the appellant argued that criminal, as opposed to military, offences should be tried by civilian criminal courts. In dismissing this argument Lord Rodger made it clear that the 'special status of members of the armed forces means that an act which may be a criminal offence under civilian criminal law also has a disciplinary aspect when committed within a Service environment'.[217]

Violations of criminal laws, especially those prohibiting violence to the person or those limiting the possession or use of firearms, represent challenges to the state's monopoly on the use of force, and when these are committed by the very agents of the state who are tasked with maintaining that monopoly, a specific form accountability is necessary and justified. The court martial embodies a specialist form of accountability, with its mixed jurisdiction of criminal and service offences, ensuring that soldiers are not a threat to society at home or step beyond the bounds of the law while on deployment abroad. The extraterritorial nature of military law, and the fact that it is possible to hold courts martial in other countries, adds to the necessity of having a special form of accountability in order to ensure that the military remains bound by law and by discipline.

Soldiers know that they cannot avoid military justice when they join the armed forces, but they are entitled to a justice system that is firm but fair. The outcome of the trial, appeals and furore in *Blackman* should be that greater care is taken to ensure that any recognised medical disorders of soldiers accused of offences, especially those committed in armed conflict, are uncovered if justice to the individual soldier is to be done. The idea that all soldiers should meet the high standards of discipline required by the military justice system does not mean that those suffering from combat stress disorders that affect their judgement and mental capacity should be punished in the same way as those soldiers able to withstand such immense pressures. Blackman was not innocent – he was found guilty of manslaughter after establishing diminished responsibility. Arguments may be made about the strength of the psychiatric evidence, but that does not detract from the justice of including any such evidence at the outset of the case.

Despite a number of weaknesses, some of which will be remedied in the next Armed Forces Act in 2021, and the undoubted failures in the *Payne* case

---

[217] *R v Spear* [2002] UKHL 31, para 51.

and other cases arising out of Iraq,[218] this chapter has shown that in some recent cases – *Blackman, Nightingale,* and *Cipher 1A and Cipher 1B* – the military justice system has not only delivered justice by upholding the duties of soldiers and punishing them when necessary, it has also served to highlight the unique nature of those duties and the extreme pressures under which soldiers operate both on deployment overseas and sometimes in the UK. Those could only be fully understood by a specialist tribunal. One might hypothesise that had the cases been tried by jury in the Crown Court, with all the surrounding media pressure and debates in Parliament, then 'jury equity' might have led to the failure to convict Blackman and Nightingale and perhaps the conviction of the Ciphers, all of which would have undermined discipline in the military.

Furthermore, the court martial can serve to highlight wider problems of what can reasonably be expected of soldiers, whether these are raised in the case or in surrounding discussions. The court martial is concerned to ensure that those soldiers appearing before it receive justice and a fair trial, and changes have been made over the years in response to ECtHR jurisprudence to ensure that it does.[219] However, the primary purpose of the court martial is to uphold the duties of soldiers. The rights of soldiers beyond the due process rights of those on trial, as well as broader issues of systemic failures in command and support for the armed forces, have to be addressed and protected elsewhere.[220]

---

[218] See discussions in Chapter 6. See also report by Redress, 'UK Army in Iraq: Time to Come Clean on Civilian Torture' (2007) 8–16, which analyses the failings of a number of courts martial arising out of alleged abuse by British soldiers in Iraq https://redress.org/publication/uk-army-in-iraq-time-to-come-clean-on-civilian-torture/.

[219] See Chapter 8.

[220] See Chapters 8 and 9.

8.   Rights and protections of soldiers

8.1   INTRODUCTION

From concentrating on the duties of soldiers and their prosecution for violations of service law in Chapter 7, this chapter turns to the rights and protections
of soldiers both before courts martial and more broadly. The strengthening
of the rights of soldiers before courts martial is discussed as the first stage of
human rights' influence on military justice, ensuring that soldiers receive a fair
trial. The chapter then moves on to consider whether human rights law plays
a role more broadly, by providing basic protections to soldiers across the range
of contexts in which soldiers find themselves: in the barracks, supporting civil
authorities, or on deployments overseas in a peacekeeping or combat capacity.
Particularly regarding external deployments, the traction of human rights law
is tenuous and contested, provoking protestations of the growth 'lawfare'. It is
argued by these critics that military operations are becoming unduly hampered
by the encroachment of laws that recognise the rights of soldiers as opposed to
their duties under service law and LOAC. This chapter explores the growing
recognition that even in combat the basic human rights of soldiers deserve
protection, not in an absolute sense but tailored to the exigencies of the situation they are in. The exploration of soldiers' rights requires a consideration
of the state's duties, especially in the sense of the measures the government is
required to take to fulfil its duties to protect the rights of soldiers deployed to
life-threatening situations.

Sergeant Blackman had the duty to treat a wounded Taliban insurgent
with dignity, his failure to do so led to his prosecution for unlawful killing.
However, much of the discussion surrounding his conviction raised questions
about whether his country had put soldiers like Blackman in a situation that
was likely to lead to loss of discipline due to combat stress affecting even the
most highly trained individual. The question of the existence and extent of the
government's duties towards soldiers is explored in this chapter. This involves
a consideration of duties not only under public law (principally human rights
law) but also in private law (principally tort).

The chapter then turns to the problem of abuse of soldiers by other soldiers
or officers, and examines the service complaints system, which operates
alongside the military justice system and aims to provide non-judicial access

to justice for complainants. Incidents of abuse may be prosecuted under the military justice system as discipline or criminal conduct offences, but the service complaints system allows for a broader sweep of alleged abusive behaviour to be investigated. The growth of soldiers' rights and protections and concomitant government duties is one of the biggest challenges facing the military in the 21st century. It will potentially shape the nature of future military deployments.[1]

8.2   THE RIGHT TO A FAIR TRIAL

Historically courts martial were a crude but effective way of ensuring military discipline was maintained, consisting of rudimentary trials of soldiers by their senior officers with little representation or due process. A gradual process of improvement was followed by an accelerated period of improvement in the human rights era especially after the *Findlay* case in 1997.[2] However, the military was slow to adjust following *Findlay* leading to further adverse judgments from the ECtHR before the reforms of the Armed Forces Act 1996 were implemented.[3] These reforms were aimed at ensuring compliance with Article 6 of the ECHR, which in part provides that any individual charged with committing a criminal offence 'is entitled to a fair and public hearing within a reasonable time by an independent and impartial tribunal established by law'.[4] The military's reluctance to change is described by Lyon and Farmiloe as a 'flawed strategy as service justice was no longer wallowing in military obscurity', testified by the procession of cases before the ECtHR and UK courts.[5]

The process of human rights compliance is not a static one, as shown by the judgment of the ECtHR in *Morris* in 2002, by which time the system of military justice had been adjusted to meet the *Findlay* judgment. In *Morris*, the Court stated that the 1996 Act had 'gone a long way to meeting its concerns in the *Findlay* case', but still found partly in favour of the applicant,[6] necessitating further adjustments to the court martial. Furthermore, while in *Cooper*, an RAF court martial, was found by the ECtHR to be fully compliant,[7] in *Grieves*

---

[1]   See generally J. Gilmore, *The Cosmopolitan Military: Armed Forces and Human Security in the 21st Century* (Springer, 2015).

[2]   *Findlay v United Kingdom*, Appl No 22107/93, 21 January 1997.

[3]   *Coyne v United Kingdom*, Appl No 25942/94, 24 September 1997; *Hood v United Kingdom* (2000) 29 EHRR 365.

[4]   ECHR (1950) Article 6(1).

[5]   A. Lyon and G. Farmiloe, 'The New British System of Court Martial' in A. Duxbury and M. Groves (eds), *Military Justice in the Modern Age* (Cambridge University Press, 2016) 159 at 160–1.

[6]   *Morris v United Kingdom* (2002) 34 EHRR 52 at para 1275.

[7]   *Cooper v United Kingdom* (2004) 39 EHRR 8.

a naval court martial was found to be in violation of Article 6 of the ECHR.[8] This necessitated further radical reform of the military justice system in the Armed Forces Act 2006, which unified the separate military justice systems for each service, and created an independent SPA thereby 'centralising disciplinary review in the hands of the Director of Service Prosecutions, as opposed to the accused's Commanding Officer'.[9] This aspect of the Armed Forces Act 2006 has been criticised by Richards on the grounds that it signifies that the CO 'is now required to play the role of senior police officer', not only making their role 'dramatically more complicated' but also eroding their function 'as the source of military discipline'.[10]

While field courts martial no longer occur, commanders are still able to maintain discipline over troops for summary offences (with a right of appeal since 2000 instituted in response to human rights concerns),[11] while more serious issues are subject to court martial where the rights of the accused are fully protected. Although question marks remain over whether the summary process per se would survive further scrutiny from the ECtHR, there are strong practical arguments for retaining it, reflected in a dissenting opinion in *Bell* in which Judge Maruste stated: 'I consider some discretionary, speedy and summary measures as a necessary and natural part of military service, without which the army would lose part of its effectiveness and operationality'.[12] In *Bell*, the ECtHR found the summary procedure to be non-compliant with Article 6 of the ECHR, but the case involved a consideration of the procedure before the safeguard of an 'unfettered right of all accused person to appeal to the Summary Appeal Court' had been added.[13] The question remains as to whether that right of appeal 'together with a universal right to elect for trial in the Court Martial prior to a commanding officer hearing a case' are sufficient to meet human rights concerns, particularly as human rights doctrine and thinking continues to evolve. Jeff Blackett states that these safeguards are sufficient 'to ensure that the whole summary trial process is compliant with Article 6'. However, he qualifies this slightly by saying that 'this statement of

---

[8] *Grieves v United Kingdom* (2004) 39 EHRR 2. See also UK case of *R v Stow* [2005] EWCA Crim 1157.

[9] Lyon and Farmiloe (2016) 168.

[10] D. Richards, 'The Armed Forces Act 2006 – Civilianising Military Justice?' (2008) 3 *Criminal Law Review* 191 at 192.

[11] Armed Forces Discipline Act (2000), which entered force at the same time as the Human Rights Act (1998), again showing the influence of human rights. See E.R. Fidell, *Military Justice: A Very Short Introduction* (Oxford University Press, 2016) 6. See discussion of summary procedure in Chapter 7.

[12] *Bell v UK*, Appl No 41534/98, 16 January 2007.

[13] J. Blackett, *Rant on the Court Martial and Service Law* (Oxford University Press, 3rd edn, 2009) 223.

principle has not yet been challenged in the European Court of Human Rights and is based on legal advice to the Ministry of Defence'.[14]

Despite a question mark hanging over the summary process, overall the system of military justice has become human rights compliant in response to challenges but it has retained its separate character, successfully resisting pressure to replace courts martial with purely civilian criminal courts. Human rights compliance does not mean one size-fits-all solutions. Courts martial involve jurors who are serving officers and a judge who, although independent, is often of a military legal background. Such experience and perspectives are necessary to bring to the trial an understanding of the military environment and expectations for military conduct, which are often very different to those which pertain in civilian life.

When the court martial system was considered by the House of Lords in *R v Boyd, Hastie and Spear*, Lord Rodger adopted the reasoning of the Vice Chief of Defence Staff: '[t]he fundamental purpose of a military justice system is to foster and promote the discipline and self-control required for the maintenance of the capability to act as an efficient fighting force, that is to say operational effectiveness'.[15] This was seen as justifying the jurisdiction of the court martial over both criminal conduct offences and offences under service law. However, while discipline offences are designed to protect the ethos of a separate military society and justify the military composition of the board in the court martial, criminal conduct offences are crafted to protect the values of the broader society, serious breaches of which should arguably be tried before a jury drawn from that society. It may be that military society can be said to incorporate criminal conduct offences and adapt them for its own protection, but a stronger articulation of this premise is needed if the court martial is to continue to have jurisdiction over criminal conduct offences.[16]

The key ECtHR judgment on courts martial, *Findlay v UK*, is worth looking at in some detail as it shows that justice was not delivered by older forms of the court martial, moreover it demonstrates that human rights compliance is an on-going process and is unlikely to be achieved by one-off reforms. The facts leading up to the commission of offences by Alexander Findlay again showed the stresses soldiers are under, with little apparent relief or help being given to him even after being engaged in brutal warfare. In fact, the psychiatric evidence before the court martial stated that the conduct that led to him being charged was an 'almost inevitable' result of a combination of the stresses

---

[14]   Ibid.

[15]   *R v Boyd, Hastie and Spear, Saunby and Others* [2002] UKHL 31 at para 51.

[16]   See the statement by the Court Martial Appeal Court in *R v Vuliwaciwaci* [2020] EWCA Crim 1894, discussed in Chapter 7.

Findlay was under, all of which were the result of him serving his country. Findlay had joined the Scots Guards in 1980. He was injured during the battle of Mount Tumbledown in the Falklands War of 1982, and he witnessed the death and mutilation of several of his friends. In 1990, after carrying out the offences for which he was charged, he was diagnosed with post-traumatic stress disorder (PTSD) involving flashbacks, nightmares, anxiety, insomnia and outbursts of anger. In 1987, he suffered a back injury while training for deployment to Northern Ireland, which affected his ability to perform duties leading him to suffer further feelings of stress, guilt and depression. During a heavy drinking session after deployment to Northern Ireland, he held members of his unit at gunpoint and threatened to kill himself and some of his colleagues. He fired two shots that were not aimed at anyone and then surrendered his weapon. He was arrested and pleaded guilty to common assault (a criminal conduct offence), conduct prejudicial to good order and discipline (a service offence), and threatening to kill (a criminal conduct offence). The psychiatric report before the court martial had recommended the 'minimum appropriate punishment'.[17]

Before a court martial in 1991, Findlay's solicitor urged the court to take account of his PTSD and the fact that he was unlikely to reoffend. The court was asked to allow him to complete the last remaining months of his service and leave the army with his pension intact, with a minimal endorsement on his record. The court martial sentenced him to two years' imprisonment, reduction in rank and dismissal from the army (causing a reduction in his pension entitlement). No reasons were given by the court martial for the sentence.[18] In 1992, Findlay applied for judicial review of the findings of the court martial on the basis of an excessive sentence and violation of natural justice. The Divisional Court refused leave on the basis that the court martial had been conducted in accordance with the Army Act 1955. Findlay also brought a civil claim in negligence against the military authorities, claiming damages in respect of his back injury and PTSD. In 1994 this was settled by the MoD paying the applicant £100,000 without admission of liability.[19]

Before the case reached the ECtHR, Parliament had enacted the Armed Forces Act 1996 designed in part to bring courts martial into line with the requirements of Article 6(1) of the ECHR. Although the ECtHR noted 'with satisfaction that the United Kingdom authorities have made changes to the court-martial system with a view to ensuring observance of the Convention

---

[17] *Findlay* (1997) paras 6–11.
[18] Ibid, paras 22–3.
[19] Ibid, paras 30–1.

commitments',[20] this did not affect Findlay's case as he was tried before the legislation came into force. In this regard, the ECtHR found that Findlay's 'doubts about the tribunal's independence and impartiality could be objectively justified', specifically the fact that all five members of the court martial appointed by the 'convening officer' were subordinate in rank to him and were ultimately under his command. The fact that the convening officer was also the 'confirming officer', whose decision was necessary to make the judgment of the court martial effective, undermined the independence of the tribunal as it meant that the judgment was subject to a non-judicial authority. The Court stated that 'these fundamental flaws in the court-martial system were not remedied by the presence of safeguards, such as the involvement of the judge advocate, who was not himself a member of the tribunal and whose advice to it was not made public ...'.[21]

The case brought about fundamental changes to a court martial system that had remained largely unaltered for many years: 'most importantly the control of the proceedings at trial was acknowledged to have moved formally from the Service president to the independent judge advocate, whose control of proceedings guaranteed their independence and impartiality'.[22] However, it is not at all clear that Findlay himself received justice after being subject to a punishment that appeared harsh and unjustified (evidenced by the lack of reasons given by the court martial for the punishment). The ECtHR did not award compensation for loss of income of £440,200 claimed by the applicant or for non-pecuniary damage of £50,000 caused by his imprisonment, stating that it was not possible 'to speculate as to what might have occurred had there been no breach of the convention'. In conclusion the ECtHR found that 'a finding of a violation in itself affords the applicant sufficient reparation'.[23]

It might be questioned whether such a remedy would now be viewed as sufficient, moreover whether the court martial's failure to consider fully Findlay's mental health at the time of the commission of the offence would compromise a 'fair trial'. In *Findlay*, the ECtHR concentrated on the 'independent and impartial' aspect of Article 6 of the ECHR but followed the Commission's view that it was not necessary to address the applicant's arguably deeper concerns about whether the court martial met his entitlement to 'a fair and public hearing'.[24]

That there will be further challenges to the fairness of the court martial is evidenced by the *Twaite* case, in which the CMAC dismissed the applicant's

---

[20] Ibid, para 67.
[21] Ibid, paras 75–8.
[22] Blackett (2009) 7.
[23] *Findlay* (1997) para 88.
[24] Ibid, paras 59 and 80.

argument that majority verdicts in a court martial violated his right to a fair trial in Article 6 ECHR on the basis that 'we can see nothing in a process in which a verdict may be returned by a majority which infringes the right to a fair trial, or produces an unsafe conviction. The trial process is intended to be fair, and, as in this case, is demonstrably fair'.[25] The rationale of the court is clear but it does not attempt to explore 'fairness' in a broader, comparative sense and thus will not prevent future challenges as perceptions of fairness change and develop, challenges that can be brought forward in future human rights litigation.[26]

8.3   JUSTICE FOR SOLDIERS: VILLAINS AND VICTIMS

The discussion above was concerned with whether a court martial provides justice for the accused, where a number of sticking points have been identified: the failure of the military justice system to identify and recognise mental illness, the fact that the accused can be convicted by a simple majority by court martial, and can be tried before such courts not only for disciplinary offences unique to the military but also criminal conduct offences. Where criminal conduct offences, such as rape and sexual assault, are committed against other service personnel it can be argued that the court martial should be the trial court, as the offence clearly raises disciplinary concerns as well wider societal ones. Indeed, given that the accused, if found guilty, has acted contrary to both the values of the military and wider society, punishment should at least be the equivalent of that meted out by the civilian criminal justice system. There is a danger that the defendant, if convicted, might receive a harsher punishment by court martial, but this can be defended by the acceptance of the higher standards of behaviour expected upon joining the army. Indeed, by upholding the 'military ethic', which 'exalts obedience' and 'self-sacrifice', the court martial could help 'stigmatize sexual assault and further acculturate service members into law-abiding norms',[27] by punishing offenders and sending out a strong preventive message that such actions not only breach fundamental societal values but also are antithetical to military service.

---

[25]   *R v Twaite* [2010] EWCA Crim 2973, para 29.
[26]   The Armed Forces Bill (2021) clause 2 will remove bare majority verdicts in boards of five or six, instead requiring qualified majorities of 4:1 and 5:1 https://publications.parliament.uk/pa/bills/cbill/58-01/0244/en/200244en.pdf.
[27]   J. Bennett, 'Combating Sexual Assault with the Military Ethic: Exploring Culture, Military Institutions, and Norms-based Preventive Policy' (2018) 44 *Armed Forces and Society* 707.

However, this approach places military values above societal ones, and certainly from the victim's perspective does not achieve justice if the military justice system is incapable of punishing perpetrators with sufficient regularity as to act as a deterrent. The problems within the military justice system are apparent in the case of Corporal Anne-Marie Ellement who committed suicide in 2011, the coroner finding that bullying and an alleged rape were factors in her suicide. She had previously alleged that two soldiers had raped her in a barracks in Germany but military prosecutors did not proceed with the case. The case was reopened and the two soldiers were tried for rape before a court martial in 2016 but were acquitted. The feeling that justice had not been done was reflected in the judge's criticism of the soldiers' conduct as well as the length of time it had taken to bring the case to court. This sense of injustice was compounded by the subsequent apology by the Royal Military Police (RMP) for mistakes it had made in the original investigation of the offence.[28] In the recent unreported court martial case of *R v Christie* (2021), the accused, who was the commander of a Royal Navy vessel, was acquitted of raping a cadet, aged 18. Again, the sense of injustice is evidenced by the judge's remarks that Christie's behaviour 'fell far short of that expected of a naval officer', questioning his ability to continue to serve in the Royal Navy. Christie admitted he had 'abused his power' by sleeping with the cadet after she had consumed a significant amount of alcohol but maintained that it was consensual.[29]

These two examples show that in practice the possibility of harsher punishment by a court martial seems to be outweighed by the fact that, in rape cases at least, the chances of conviction in the military justice system seem less than in the civilian justice system. According to a Liberty Report of 2019: 'outcomes at Court Martial for victims of alleged rape are extremely poor, paling even in comparison with civilian conviction rates, with just 2 of the 48 rape cases that got to trial in Court Martial in 2017 resulting in a conviction'. Furthermore, 'sexist attitudes may be reflected in the very narrow range of persons who are able to be summonsed to sit on court martial boards. It appears that the court martial is not able to deliver justice for a victim of rape.'[30] This is clearly a problematically low rate of conviction, but the problems of securing convictions seem endemic to both military and civilian justice systems.

---

[28] L. Brooke-Holland, 'The Review of the Service Justice System' (House of Commons Library Briefing Paper) 20 January 2021, 14–15.

[29] *Mail Online*, 'Royal Navy ship's captain sobs with relief as he is cleared of raping drunk 18-year-old cadet', 25 February 2021.

[30] E. Norton, *Military Justice: Second-rate Justice (Criminal Justice, complaints and human rights myths in the armed forces)* (Liberty Report, 2019) 17, 58. See also J. Welland, 'Militarised Violences, Basic Training, and the Myths of Asexuality and Discipline' (2013) 39 *Review of International Studies* 881.

In giving evidence to the Select Committee on the Armed Forces Bill in March 2021, former Judge Advocate General Jeff Blackett agreed with the proposition that the trial of rape cases should take place in the court 'where the victim will receive the best justice'.[31] However, he questioned the assumption that this would normally mean the trial of rape cases before the Crown Court, referring to the fact that the proportion of rape allegations referred by the civilian police to the CPS in the civilian system is much lower that the proportion of cases referred to the SPA, so that in the military justice system it was true to say that 'the prosecution rate was much higher, even though the conviction rate was lower'. From the victim's perspective this means that they have a greater chance of seeing a trial of the alleged perpetrator in the military justice system, but the chances of seeing a conviction are lower. According to Judge Blackett the 'real problem' is not the issue of jurisdiction, rather 'it is the law around rape' particularly issues of 'consent or capacity to consent' in cases where both parties are intoxicated and there is insufficient evidence to show that the accused committed the offence of rape certainly to meet the burden of proof required for conviction in criminal trials: beyond reasonable doubt. There is a clear danger, however, that perpetrators know that their chances of conviction are low, and that the victim will be reluctant to go to court with all the negative publicity that attracts with little chance of success. Judge Blackett may be right to say that the problem is not necessarily one of jurisdiction, but the law and its enforcement are clearly not acting as a deterrent to potential rapists.

The hurdles in front of women seeking justice are evidenced by the campaign by three victims of rape or sexual assault while serving in the military to have such cases tried before civilian criminal courts as opposed to courts martial. This campaign was referred to during the debates over the Armed Forces Bill in 2021, when the government was challenged as to why it had not accepted the recommendation made by Shaun Lyons in an independent review of the military justice system that cases of rape, murder and manslaughter should be dealt with by the civilian criminal justice system when committed in the UK.[32] Instead, the Armed Forces Bill 2021, if enacted in its current form, will impose an obligation on the civilian and military prosecuting authorities to arrive at a protocol whereby the appropriate 'route to justice' would be

---

[31]   House of Commons, Select Committee on the Armed Forces Bill, Oral Evidence: Armed Forces Bill, HC 1281, Q147, 11 March 2021 https://committees.parliament.uk/oralevidence/1847/html/.

[32]   D. Sabbagh, 'Fears minister has jeopardised effort to stop military trying UK rape cases: Women accuse Johnny Mercer of backtracking on promise made to campaigners in parliamentary debate', *The Guardian*, 18 February 2021.

agreed.[33] This seems little different to the current arrangements and will not, by itself, provide the justice rightly being sought by women.

There is little doubt that the debates will continue and intensify, particularly in the light of the House of Commons Defence Sub-Committee's inquiry into women and the armed forces, which recognised the problem of sexual offences against female soldiers in its terms of reference.[34] Indeed in a Report of 25 July 2021, the sheer scale of the problem was laid bare in the findings of the report that 62 per cent of female service personnel and veterans surveyed had experienced bullying, harassment and discrimination, behaviours which included sexual assault and other criminal sexual offences. Furthermore, the Report found that in 2021, 'servicewomen were more than ten times as likely as servicemen to experience sexual harassment in the last 12 months'. The Report pointed to the serious problems with how the Service Justice System handles criminal sexual offences – most of which (76 per cent in 2020) involve female victims.[35]

The Report criticised the Armed Forces Bill of 2021 as representing 'a missed opportunity to address critical issues' and recommended that the MoD and the armed forces go further by implementing all aspects of the Wigston Review of 2019. That Review by the MoD led by Air Chief Marshal Wigston had pointed to a number of factors that led to high levels of unacceptable behaviours in the military including 'tight-knit units that perceive themselves as elite; masculine cultures with low gender diversity; rank gradients; age gradients; weak or absent controls, especially after extensive operational periods; and alcohol'.[36] The Defence Committee recommendations of 2021 included removing 'the chain of command entirely from complaints of a sexual nature' and removing rape and sexual assault with penetration from the jurisdiction of the court martial, unless the Attorney General gives consent.[37] These recommendations will have to lead to a reconsideration of the approach to military justice and

---

[33]   The Armed Forces Act (2006) has been extended until the end of 2021, meaning that the Bill has been carried over into the 2021–2022 Parliamentary session https://bills.parliament.uk/bills/2822/news.

[34]   House of Commons Defence Committee, Defence Sub-Committee, 'Women in the Armed Forces: From Recruitment to Civilian Life', opened 1 December 2020   https://committees.parliament.uk/work/856/women-in-the-armed-forces-from-recruitment-to-civilian-life/.

[35]   House of Commons Defence Committee, 'Protecting Those Who Protect Us: Women in the Armed Forces from Recruitment to Civilian Life', Second Report of Session 2021-22, HC 154, 25 July 2021, 4.

[36]   Ministry of Defence, 'Report on Inappropriate Behaviours' (MoD) 15 July 2019, 3. For recommendations see 34–5.

[37]   HC Defence Committee (2021–22) 5.

the issue of concurrent jurisdiction contained in the Armed Forces Bill when it comes up for reconsideration in 2021.

In relation to the service justice system, the Defence Committee's Report of 2021 noted that it was the case that before 2006 service personnel who committed the crimes of murder, manslaughter and rape in the UK were dealt with solely within the system of civilian criminal justice. Since the introduction of concurrent jurisdiction, the Report stated that 'in the UK, when both the perpetrator and victim of a sexual offence are serving personnel, the case is normally heard in the' service justice system.[38] This potentially creates a number of hurdles to the successful prosecution of such cases. While the CO has the duty to refer rape and certain other sexual offences to the service or civilian police, according to the Centre for Military Justice 'some sexual offences may be downgraded to non-sexual offences to enable the CO to deal with them via a Summary hearing (for instance, the downgrading of a sexual assault to a battery)'.[39] Even if investigated as cases of alleged rape or other serious sexual offences, the service justice system review of policing found that 'despite some satisfactory investigations, the Service Police "do not investigate enough serious crimes to be considered proficient"'.[40] This may well mean that the evidence presented to the court martial is not as strong as it should have been, leading to poor conviction rates. Although the Defence Committee noted the concerns surrounding the comparison of conviction rates between the civilian and criminal justice systems, it did highlight the significant disparity in rape conviction rates: between 2015–2020, the five-year average conviction rate for rape in the criminal justice system was 34 per cent, while the rate in the military justice system for the same period was 16 per cent.[41]

In the light of these findings the Defence Committee Report of 2021 supported the recommendations of the Lyons Review by finding that the fact that in cases of UK-based sexual offences both perpetrator and victim are service personnel is not an adequate reason by itself to use the military justice system. It therefore recommended that the jurisdiction of the court martial should no longer include rape and sexual assault, except where the consent of the Attorney General is given.[42] It appears that the debate about this aspect of the Armed Forces Bill remains set to continue. The resolution of the debate may depend upon whether Parliament accepts the understanding of the victim as

---

[38] Ibid, 57.
[39] Ibid, 58.
[40] Ibid, 59, citing Sir Jon Murphy, 'Service System Policing Review (Part 1)', March 2018, para 71.
[41] Ibid, 63.
[42] Ibid, 64.

citizen as stated by Judge Lyons in his review,[43] and supported in the Defence Committee's Report.[44] Both parties involved in a rape case may be soldiers, but the desire to try the case before a court martial is premised on the need to maintain discipline, something which the perpetrator if convicted has manifestly failed to do, whereas from the victim's perspective they have had their rights seriously violated – and those rights belong to them as an individual citizen not by reason of them being a soldier. Irrespective of debates over conviction rates, which could be improved in the military justice system by a better trained and capable service police, the issue is one of justice involving understanding that soldiers can be both villains and victims, and moreover can be both soldiers and citizens. As citizens they have rights that may be pared down in the heat of combat, but there is no reason for any restrictions on their rights when they are on duty in the UK.

8.4   THE RIGHT TO LIFE OF SOLDIERS

Peter Rowe posits that 'it is difficult to conclude that, by the mere fact of joining the armed forces voluntarily, a person has consented to all the treatment to which he is subjected in the armed forces, or that he has waived those of his human rights available to him as a civilian'.[45] However, when considering this statement of principle in the context of the human rights protection to be afforded to soldiers in combat, especially their right to life as entrenched in Article 2 of the ECHR, the issue becomes one of balancing their rights as citizens and with the heavier duties they bear as soldiers. Historically soldiers have been seen as duty bearers who were expected to make the ultimate sacrifice sometimes expressed in the notion of 'unlimited liability',[46] and they or their families had no redress if they lost their life while on operational duty. This is reflected in the rules of LOAC, which provide that soldiers' lives can be taken in armed conflict unless they are rendered *hors de combat*.[47] With the development of justiciable human rights the scales of justice in the form of balancing the rights and duties of soldiers has started to adjust towards soldiers' rights, most clearly seen in the right to a fair trial discussed above but also more tentatively in the operational context. The encroachment of human rights law into the battlefield has provoked allegations of 'juridification', 'legal siege',

---

[43]   HHJ Lyons, 'Service Justice System Review (Part 1)', March 2018, para 7.3.
[44]   HC Defence Committee (2021–22) 58.
[45]   P. Rowe, *The Impact of Human Rights Law on Armed Forces* (Oxford University Press, 2006) 10.
[46]   G.R. Rubin, 'United Kingdom Military Law: Autonomy, Civilianisation, Juridification' (2002) 65 *Modern Law Review* 36 at 44.
[47]   See Common Article 3 of the four Geneva Convention 1949.

'judicial creep', and 'lawfare',[48] meaning that the increasing encroachment of extra layers of soldiers' rights (and the rights of civilians they encounter while on operations) as well as government duties makes the tasks of the military unnecessarily difficult thereby aiding the enemy.[49] Do these arguments mean, in the words of Lord Hope when describing the UK government's position on soldiers' rights, that the 'interests of the state must prevail over the interests of the individual'?[50]

The highpoint of this controversy, thus far, has been the Supreme Court's judgment in 2013 in the case of *Smith v MoD*. The case concerned the deaths and serious injuries to five British soldiers arising out of separate incidents: one during the invasion of Iraq in March 2003, and a second during the insurgency that arose thereafter in 2005–2006. The earlier incident involved the destruction of a Challenger II tank by another such tank in a case of 'friendly fire', killing or injuring the occupants. The later incidents involved lightly armoured 'Snatch' Land Rovers that had been hit by IEDs while on patrol, leading to loss of life and injuries. The 'Challenger claims' were brought in negligence under common law on the basis that there was a failure by the MoD to ensure that the tanks were equipped with the technology and equipment (Combat ID whereby friendly tanks can be identified) that would have prevented the friendly fire. The 'Snatch Land Rover claims' involved a mixture of claims under common law and for violation of Article 2 of the ECHR, on the basis that the MoD had failed to take reasonable measures, such as installing electronic counter-measures on the vehicles. It was argued that such measures were within the scope of the MoD's powers to mitigate the real and immediate risk to the lives of soldiers travelling in Land Rovers. The MoD argued that the Challenger claims should be struck out on the basis of the principle of combat immunity, or on the basis that it would not be 'fair, just or reasonable' to impose a duty of care to protect against such death or injury. The MoD argued that the Snatch Land Rover claims be struck out because the soldiers were not within the jurisdiction of the UK for the purposes of Article 1 of the ECHR and, further, that it did not owe the soldiers a duty under Article 2 at the time of their deaths.[51]

---

[48]   Rubin (2002) 36; T. Tugendhat and L. Croft, 'The Fog of Law: An Introduction to the Legal Erosion of British Fighting Power' (Policy Exchange, 2013) 10.

[49]   See further Chapter 9.

[50]   *Smith and others (FC) v The Ministry of Defence* [2013] UKSC 41, para 83 (Lord Hope).

[51]   Ibid, paras 1–13 (Lord Hope).

8.4.1   Claims in Negligence

While the Snatch Land Rover claims in *Smith v MoD* were primarily brought under human rights law,[52] the Challenger claims were brought in negligence under common law on the basis that the MoD owed soldiers a duty of care to provide adequate equipment and training, and that it had breached this duty in the preparation of the tanks and their crews for combat. Together the Land Rover and Challenger claims concerned the duties a government owes its soldiers under both public law and private law. While the government argued lack of jurisdiction and absence of any duty of protection under the HRA 1998 in the Snatch Land Rover claims, in the Challenger claims it raised the defence of combat immunity. Taken as a whole the government's arguments were that the 'interests of the state must prevail over the interests of the individual'.[53]

According to Peter Rowe 'combat immunity appears to be, as its name suggests, limited to providing immunity from civil claims derived from acts or omissions of members of the armed forces during combat'.[54] It had been successfully relied on by the MoD in the *Mulcahy* case of 1996 concerning a claim arising out of the conflict in Iraq in 1991, when it was alleged that one soldier's negligence in the firing of an artillery round caused injury to another.[55] However, the majority in *Smith v MoD* decided that combat immunity only applied to tortious acts committed during the course of combat, and did not extend to government failings in procurement and training that had occurred before combat. These 'activities are sufficiently far removed from the pressures and risks of active operations against the enemy for it not to be unreasonable to expect a duty of care to be exercised, so long as the standard of care that is imposed has regard to the nature of these activities and to their circumstances'.[56]

---

[52]   Although one of the claimants in the Snatch Land Rover claims also brought an action in negligence at common law – ibid, para 10 (Hope).

[53]   Ibid, para 83 (Hope).

[54]   P. Rowe, *Legal Accountability and Britain's Wars 2000–15* (Routledge, 2016) 112.

[55]   *Mulcahy v Ministry of Defence* [1996] QB 732.

[56]   *Smith v MoD* [2013] para 95 (Hope). See the discussion of combat immunity in the light of the *Smith* case in *Durrheim and Others v Ministry of Defence* [2014] EWHC 1960 (QB), which concerned a number of claims in negligence for personal injury sustained by serving and former service personnel alleging noise induced hearing loss caused by service in the armed forces. Some of the claims arose out of pre-deployment training and others during combat. The fact sensitive nature of the claims meant that the defence of combat immunity was also fact sensitive, but the Judge stated that the 'decision of the Supreme Court is *Smith* is clear on the extent of combat immunity. It applies to active operations against the enemy. For an individual case the issue will be

The outcome of the *Smith* case was to establish in principle that both sets of claims should be tried, in effect requiring the claimants to establish in a fresh trial that the MoD had breached its duty of care in tort in the Challenger Tank claims and its positive obligations under Article 2(1) of the ECHR in the Snatch Land Rover claims. Following the Supreme Court's judgment in 2013, the outcome of the Challenger Tank claims remains unclear. The Chilcot Report, finally published in 2016 after an extensive inquiry into the invasion and subsequent involvement of the UK in Iraq, is equivocal on the failings, if any, in preparing the tanks and crews for combat. The Report's headline on this suggests that there was a problem with missing Combat ID equipment: 'despite public assurances given prior to the invasion that previously identified problems had been resolved, Combat ID equipment was not fitted to all vehicles before the start of operations'.[57] It noted that nine 'blue on blue' (friendly fire) incidents, four of which resulted in the death or injury of UK personnel (including the Challenger Tank incident in the *Smith* case), had occurred during the invasion in 2003. The evidence given to the Inquiry seemed to suggest that due to a temporary misplacing of equipment 32 Challenger tanks were not fitted with combat identification prior to combat operations, but in the Challenger Tank incident that led to loss of life in *Smith* the tanks had been fitted with equipment. However, the Report then indicated that the training packages, which had been created to aid recognition of Coalition vehicles, had arrived 'too late and in too small a quantity to be made widely available', but was not clear on whether training packages had been supplied in the Challenger Tank claims.[58] This suggests that there remains a case to be answered that in preparing the tanks and crews for combat there were potential breaches of the duty of care owed by the state to soldiers. However, there is no evidence of the MoD settling the claims unlike in the Snatch Land Rover claims.

There have been a few reported cases in which soldiers have successfully brought claims for personal injuries against the MoD.[59] Prior to 1987, the

---

whether the act or omission relied upon is within active operations. As to the duty of care and whether that needs to be modified that will depend upon the factual findings which are unique to the individual cases' (para 66). 'Decisions on the provision of protective equipment, training and its adequacy are outside that defence' (para 83). 'The duty of care may extend to where men are being trained whether in pre-deployment or in theatre or when decisions are being made about the fitting of equipment to tanks or other fighting vehicles because in each of these situations there is time to think through the implications' (para 86).

[57] 'The Report of the Iraq Inquiry' (2016) Vol 6, para 566 https://www.gov.uk/government/publications/the-report-of-the-iraq-inquiry.

[58] Ibid, paras 567–74.

[59] *Inglis v Ministry of Defence* [2019] EWHC 1153 (QB), in which the claimant was awarded damages for loss of hearing suffered during his service in the Royal Marines.

Crown Proceedings Act 1947 precluded claims in tort.[60] The effects of section 10 of that Act were summarised by Lord Bingham in *Matthews*:

> Where a member of the armed forces of the Crown while on duty as such kills or injures another member of the armed forces who is either on duty or on some land, premises, ship, aircraft or vehicle used for the purposes of the armed forces, no liability in tort shall arise against the Crown ... The member of the armed forces who actually caused the death or injury was also to be exempt from liability, unless the act or omission causing the death or injury was not connected with the execution of that person's duties as a member of the armed forces. In that respect the effect of the clause was to restrict the common law rights of the injured serviceman.[61]

This severe limitation on a soldier's rights was removed by the Crown Proceedings (Armed Forces) Act 1987, enabling claims to be made in negligence by soldiers or their families against the government as in the *Smith v MoD* case, and by civilians against the MoD for negligent acts or omissions of soldiers.[62] The danger of opening a flood of civil claims arising out of

---

See also *Murphy v Ministry of Defence* [2016] EWHC 003 (QB). But see *R v Ministry of Defence ex parte Walker* [2000] UKHL 22, where the House of Lords upheld the refusal of compensation under an *ex gratia* scheme operated by the MoD for soldiers who were victims of crimes of violence while serving abroad. The Court held that the scheme was not intended to compensate soldiers for injuries caused by warlike conduct, but for injuries caused by the commission of domestic crimes of violence. Walker had been seriously injured by a round fired by a Serbian tank while deployed as part of UNPROFOR – a UN peacekeeping force deployed to Bosnia. Lord Hobhouse dissented on the basis that attacks on peacekeepers were crimes under the UN Convention on the Safety of United Nations Personnel 1994, under which peacekeepers are classified as protected non-combatants. The current Armed Forces Compensation Scheme (AFCS) is more generous: it 'compensates for any injury, illness or death which was caused by service on or after 6 April 2005'. Further, the AFCS 'is designed to provide compensation, irrespective of fault, across the full range of circumstances in which illness, injury or death may arise as a result of service. It does not seek to affect the right to make a civil claim if you think that the injury, illness or death was caused by the Department's negligence' https://www.gov.uk/guidance/armed-forces-compensation-scheme-afcs#overview.

[60]   Crown Proceedings Act (1947) section 10.

[61]   *Matthews v Ministry of Defence* [2003] UKHL 4, para 9 (Lord Bingham). This case involved a claim concerning acts or omissions committed before the 1987 Act – see para 23 (Lord Hoffmann).

[62]   *Bici v Ministry of Defence* [2004] EWHC 786 (QB) para 102, in which the Court held that the claimants, who had been shot and injured by British soldiers in Kosovo as part of a multinational operation under a UN mandate (UN Doc S/RES/1244, 10 June 1999) could succeed in their claim in negligence, and that the defence of combat immunity did not apply, inter alia, because the soldiers were not in a combat situation but rather were performing a 'policing or peacekeeping function'. Interestingly, in *Kontic and Others v Ministry of Defence* [2016] EWHC 2034 (QB), in a claim formulated in human rights law, the Court attributed the failure to protect civilians from vio-

combat situations has led to calls for the Secretary of State to invoke their powers under the 1987 Act to revive Article 10 of the Crown Proceedings Act 1947 in 'respect of all future "warlike operations … outside the United Kingdom"'.[63] There are clear implication for the effectiveness of military operations if soldiers and commanders have to take into account a duty of care to their comrades along with their other and often more pressing duties, but to remove that duty suggests that the government is being careless with the lives of soldiers. However, it should be remembered that the accordance of the same rights to soldiers in tort as enjoyed by other individuals in UK law embodied in the 1987 Act has not removed the defence of combat immunity as recognised by the Court of Appeal in *Mulcahy v Ministry of Defence*.[64] In that case Neill LJ stated:

> It is true that the Secretary of State, by exercising his powers under section 2 of the 1987 Act could have reintroduced the immunity conferred by section 10 of the 1947 Act. But in the absence of this statutory protection one still has to consider the position at common law. It is therefore necessary to consider whether at the relevant time Sergeant Warren owed a duty of care to the plaintiff at common law … The issue to be determined is whether it is fair, just and reasonable that a duty of care should be imposed on one soldier in his conduct towards another when engaging the enemy during hostilities … In order to decide whether it is just, fair and reasonable to impose a duty of care … one should bear in mind the dictum of Lord Peace in *Hedley Byrne & Co. Ltd. v Heller & Partners Ltd.* [1964] AC 465, 536: 'How wide the sphere of the duty of care in negligence is to be laid depends ultimately upon the court's assessment of the demands of society for protection from the carelessness of others' … In the absence of legislative guidance the question of policy has to be resolved by the courts … In my opinion … there is no basis for extending the scope of the duty of care so far.[65]

In effect, while Parliament has removed the barriers to tort claims, the courts have carved out a common law exception (known as 'combat immunity') for acts or omissions occurring in combat. This does not appear to be an example of 'lawfare', rather the reverse, in that the courts are restricting the extent of

---

lence in Kosovo to the UN and not the UK, as British troops were operating under a UN mandate, following the ECtHR decision in *Behrami & Saramati v France and Norway*, Appl No 71412/01, 2 May 2007.
   63   R. Ekins, J. Morgan and T. Tugendhat, 'Clearing the Fog of Law: Saving Our Armed Forces from Defeat by Judicial Diktat' (Policy Exchange Report, 2015) 41, citing the Crown Proceedings (Armed Forces) Act (1987) section 2.
   64   *Mulcahy v Ministry of Defence* [1996] 2 All ER 758.
   65   Ibid, at paras 49–54.

the duty of care in military operations on the grounds that such duties cannot be expected to apply in the unique situation of combat.[66]

8.4.2   ECHR Claims and Jurisdiction

The Snatch Land Rover claims in *Smith v MoD* raised the issue of whether the jurisdiction of the UK for the purposes of human rights law extended extraterritorially, in this case to members of the armed forces serving in Iraq. Article 1 obliges states party to the ECHR to 'secure to everyone within their jurisdiction the rights and freedoms defined in Section 1 of this Convention'.[67] In considering this question in *Smith v MoD* in 2013, the UK Supreme Court had the chance of revising its own narrow approach to extraterritorial jurisdiction found in the *Al-Skeini* case of 2007,[68] when it had found that jurisdiction only extended to protect civilians in detention centres and not to those injured or killed on the streets of Basra. In so deciding in 2007 the House of Lords relied on the ECtHR's jurisprudence going back to the *Bankovic* case, which emphasised territorial jurisdiction.[69]

The finding in *Smith v MoD* in 2013 that the UK did have jurisdiction for ECHR purposes over soldiers operating in combat situations outside their bases is a major step from the earlier case of *R (Catherine Smith) v Oxfordshire Deputy Coroner* of 2010, when the Supreme Court restricted the application

---

[66]   See further *Multiple Claimants v Ministry of Defence* [2003] EWHC 1134 (OB): '[T]he application of [combat] immunity can be resolved by reference to the following propositions.

1.   A soldier does not owe a fellow soldier a duty of care in tort when either (one or other or both) are engaged with an enemy in the course of combat.
2.   The MoD is not under a duty to maintain a safe system of work for service personnel engaged with an enemy in the course of combat.
3.   In relation to both (1) and (2) the term combat has an extended meaning in that:
   a.   the immunity is not limited to the presence of the enemy or the occasions when contact with the enemy has been established. It extends to all active operations against the enemy in which service personnel are exposed to attack or the threat of attack. It covers attack and resistance, advance and retreat, pursuit and avoidance, reconnaissance and engagement.
   b.   the immunity extends to the planning of and preparation for operations in which the armed forces may come under attack or meet armed resistance.
   c.   the immunity will apply to peace-keeping/policing operations in which service personnel are exposed to attack or the threat of attack' (para 2.C.20 per Owen J).

Point 3b is now subject to the Supreme Court's judgment narrowing combat immunity in *Smith* (2013); and point 3c. seems inconsistent with the later judgment in *Bici* (2004).

[67]   ECHR (1950) Article 1.
[68]   *R (Al-Skeini) v Secretary of State for Defence* [2007] UKHL 26.
[69]   *Bankovic v Belgium* (2001) 11 BHRC 435 at para 67.

of the ECHR to soldiers within their bases, following its own jurisprudence in *Al-Skeini*.[70] By 2013, the ECtHR had revisited its approach to jurisdiction in the *Al-Skeini* case of 2011, which in effect extended jurisdiction to those civilians shot by British soldiers in Basra.[71] In fact, according to the Supreme Court in *Smith v MoD*, the case for extending jurisdiction and, therefore, the protections of the ECHR to soldiers wherever they were serving in Iraq was even stronger than for those civilians ill-fatedly encountered by British soldiers on the streets of Basra. As Lord Hope stated: 'British servicemen ... are under the complete control of the UK authorities and are subject exclusively to UK law'.[72] He emphasised this point further in the leading judgment of the Supreme Court in *Smith v MoD*:

> the exercise of jurisdiction ... is a necessary condition for a contracting state to be able to be held responsible for acts or omissions imputable to it which gives rise to an allegation of the infringement of rights and freedoms set forth in the Convention. The significance of this observation in the context of these appeals is that it is not disputed that the United Kingdom has authority and control over its armed forces when serving abroad. It has just as much authority and control over them anywhere as it has when they are serving within the territory of the United Kingdom. They are subject to UK military law without any territorial limit: Armed Forces Act 2006, s 367(1). The extent of day to day control will, of course, vary from time to time when the forces are deployed on active service overseas, especially when troops are in face to face combat with the enemy. But the legal and administrative structure of the control is, necessarily, non-territorial in character.[73]

The change in judicial attitude in the Supreme Court was due to the ECtHR judgment in *Al-Skeini* in 2011, which decided that civilians killed by UK forces in Iraq were protected under the ECHR whether they were killed in detention or on the streets.[74] Given the nature of the British occupation entailing the exercise of public powers by British forces, those Iraqi civilians were within the jurisdiction of the UK. The ECtHR took the opportunity in *Al-Skeini* to rationalise its case law on jurisdiction, first to situations where a contracting state's agents had effective control over an area in another state and, second, to where state agents exercised authority and control over individuals.[75]

This application of jurisdiction under the ECHR to soldiers serving overseas seems to have been accepted by the whole of the Supreme Court in *Smith v*

---

[70] *R (Catherine Smith) v Oxfordshire Assistant Deputy Coroner (Equality and Human Rights Commission intervening)* [2010] UKSC 29.
[71] *Al-Skeini v UK* (2011) 53 EHRR 589.
[72] *Smith v MoD* [2013] para 21 (Hope).
[73] Ibid, para 28 (Hope).
[74] *Al-Skeini v UK* (2011).
[75] *Smith v MoD* [2013] para 31 (Hope).

MoD, and is supported in academic commentary.[76] It would not be possible to draw a distinction between soldiers and civilians who are under the authority and control of the UK except on the grounds that civilians have human rights and soldiers do not (or have been deemed to have given them up when joining the services). Nonetheless, as Lord Hope admitted, no case had yet come before the ECtHR raising the question as to whether the control that contracting states have over their troops when deployed overseas equated to jurisdiction in the sense of Article 1 of the ECHR.[77]

8.4.3   The UK's Positive Obligations under the ECHR

Human rights law requires that a state does not violate the rights of individuals within its jurisdiction (the negative obligation), but also that the state takes measures to ensure that those rights are protected within that jurisdiction (the positive obligation). In the *McCann* case, before the ECtHR, the SAS soldiers' actions in shooting known IRA members in the belief that they were about to detonate a bomb in Gibraltar were not deemed to violate the right to life of those killed, but inadequate planning and prevention by the UK was.[78] It is clear that positive (or due diligence) obligations are obligations of conduct not result, so that the fact that deaths occur does not mean that the obligations are breached if the use of lethal force was absolutely necessary to preserve life and the government had acted diligently in planning and preparing the operation.[79]

Much of the *Smith v MoD* case of 2013 was a debate about the positive obligations of the UK government and military to protect the right to life of its soldiers when deployed to Iraq.[80] LOAC applied in Iraq, first in 2003–2004

---

[76]   S. Wallace, *The Application of the European Convention on Human Rights to Military Operations* (Cambridge University Press, 2019) 101.

[77]   *Smith v MoD* [2013] para 42 (Hope). See below for discussion of the ECtHR judgment in *Miller v the United Kingdom*, Appl No 32001/18, 2 July 2019.

[78]   *McCann v UK* (1996) 21 EHRR 97.

[79]   The ECtHR found that Turkey and Russia violated Article 2 ECHR when conducting security/military operations on their own territory (against the PKK in south-east Turkey and against rebels in Chechnya) due to a lack of proper planning and precautions in the choice of means which meant that not enough had been done to minimise civilian casualties – *Ergi v Turkey* [1998] ECHR 59; *Isayeva, Yusopova and Bazayeva v Russia*, Appl Nos 57947/00, 57948/00, 57949/00, 24 February 2005; *Isayeva v Russia*, Appl No 57950/00, 24 February 2005. Similarly, the Court found that the use of gas by Russian security forces, causing the deaths of 125 hostages held by Chechen separatists in a Russian theatre in 2002, was not a violation of the right to life, though the lack of medical preparation for the immediate aftermath of the use of gas was – *Finogenov and Others v Russia*, Appl Nos 18299/03 and 27311/03, 4 June 2012.

[80]   *Smith v MoD* [2013]. See more generally Wallace (2019) 101–6 on positive obligations.

during the occupation by US and UK forces after the successful invasion of the country, and thereafter during the insurgency against the multinational force (including US and UK troops) present under agreement with the interim government of Iraq. The fighting in this period reached the level of protracted armed violence necessary for a NIAC to exist to which LOAC applied.[81] The applicability of LOAC did not displace human rights law, however. In support of this Lord Hope cited a recommendation of the Parliamentary Assembly of the Council of Europe adopted in 2006,[82] in which 'the point was made that members of the armed forces are citizens in uniform who must enjoy the same fundamental freedoms and same protection of their rights and dignity as any other citizen, within the limits enjoyed by the specific exigencies of military duties'.[83]

Despite the applicability of LOAC to British forces in Iraq, the UK Supreme Court in *Smith v MoD* unanimously agreed that human rights law also applied in that the UK's jurisdiction, in the sense of Article 1 of the ECHR, extended to securing the protection of the right to life under Article 2 for British soldiers. However, the judgment focuses its discussion on the government's obligations under human rights law on issues of preparation for combat and not combat itself and, therefore, in a sense represents a practical way of ensuring that the duties arising under the ECHR and those arising out of LOAC are not in conflict. Certainly, the judgment identified an additional layer of duties on the government when deploying armed forces, but it leaves decisions made in the heat of battle (some of which may cost lives) untouched.

Furthermore, while the *Smith* judgment potentially opens up the government to claims by fallen soldiers' families that lives have been lost in violation of Article 2 of the ECHR, the Supreme Court effectively moved the barriers to success for such claims from the issue of jurisdiction on to the nature of the positive obligations a government owes its soldiers. If those barriers are set

---

[81] *Prosecutor v Tadić* (1996) 105 ILR 419 at 488.

[82] Recommendation 1742 (2006) Parliamentary Assembly, 11 April 2006, paras 1 and 2: '1. The army is the institution which is responsible for protecting the state and defending the community. Combat is its *raison d'être*, the very purpose of its existence, and it is bound by the specific constraints of rules regarding unity, hierarchy, discipline and compliance with orders. 2. The Parliamentary Assembly recalls the many texts which it has adopted with regard to the promotion of human rights in the armed forces and notes their continued relevance and topicality. It considers that members of the armed forces are citizens in uniform who must enjoy the same fundamental freedoms, including those set out in the European Convention on Human Rights … and the revised European Social Charter …, and the same protection of their rights and dignity as any other citizen, within the limits imposed by the specific exigencies of military duties'.

[83] *Smith v MoD* [2013] para 54 (Hope).

quite high (as was the case according to the majority led by Lord Hope in *Smith v MoD*) or are of an absolute impenetrable nature (as argued by the minority led by Lord Mance),[84] then litigation will be either largely unsuccessful or fruitless.

Having established that the UK had jurisdiction over its soldiers in Iraq within the meaning of Article 1 of the ECHR, the Supreme Court in *Smith v MoD* set about examining the extent of the UK's positive obligations to protect the right to life of its soldiers under Article 2 of the ECHR. Here it is important to note that the obligations are not absolute, meaning that they must be assessed in relation to the facts of the case where, as Lord Hope recognised, a balance has to be struck between the competing interests of the individual and of the community as a whole, thereby giving the state a wide margin of appreciation.[85]

While the decision to use Snatch Land Rovers in Iraq was criticised as not affording as much protection as Armoured Personnel Carriers, that decision was not in itself a breach of the UK's positive obligation to protect the lives of its soldiers. The decision to use Snatch Land Rovers was made in fulfilment of the functions of the force (to bring security to Iraq), so the question was whether this exposed soldiers to manifestly unreasonable risk. There was a risk with these vehicles that soldiers might lose their lives as a result of the effects of IEDs but, given the efforts to reduce the chances of loss of life (by the intro-duction of electronic counter-measures for instance), it was the case that some due diligence steps had been taken. There is a question mark over how quickly those measures were installed on Land Rovers and whether they sufficiently mitigated the risk, which were issues for the trial court examining all the relevant facts.[86] It is suggested that the due diligence test does not require the provision of the best equipment available, rather it requires that the equipment provided is more than sufficient for the tasks set. That is the sort of balancing dictated by due diligence standards in that they do not provide for absolute (and very difficult to achieve standards) but are satisfied by reasonable caution and careful preparation. For example, if troops are sent into combat with only light weapons the government has failed in its duty to protect the lives of soldiers. If it sends troops with light weapons on a traditional peacekeeping mission, where fighting has ceased, it has not.

Lord Hope, representing the majority view in *Smith v MoD*, accepted the limitations of positive obligations both at the operational level (where the court must be very slow to question decisions made by commanders), and

---

[84]   Ibid, paras 142–3 (Mance).
[85]   Ibid, para 61 (Hope).
[86]   Ibid, paras 77–8 (Hope).

at the planning level (where allocation of resource is primarily a political decision and not normally appropriate for a court). The law should enter this field with great caution, according to Lord Hope, and the courts should not risk undermining the ability of a state to defend itself or risk democracy itself.[87] Normally for a claim under Article 2 of the ECHR to have a chance of success it must fall into the middle ground between high-level policy decisions and decisions of commanders on the ground: Lord Hope stated:

> [T]he court must avoid imposing positive obligations on the state in connection with the planning for and conduct of military operations in situations of armed conflict which are unrealistic or disproportionate. But it must give effect to those obligations where it would be reasonable to expect the individual to be afforded the protection of the article. It will be easy to find that allegations are beyond the reach of art 2 if the decisions that were or ought to have been taken about training, procurement or the conduct of operations were at a high level of command and closely linked to the exercise of political judgment and issues of policy. So too if they relate to things done or not done when those who might be thought to be responsible for avoiding the risk of death or injury to others were actively engaged in direct contact with the enemy. But finding whether there is room for claims to be brought in the middle ground, so that the wide margin of appreciation which must be given to the authorities or to those actively engaged in armed conflict is fully recognised without depriving the article of content, is much more difficult. No hard and fast rules can be laid down. It will require the exercise of judgment. This can only be done in the light of the facts of each case.[88]

While Lord Mance (for the minority) agreed with Lord Hope that the UK had jurisdiction over soldiers within the terms of Article 1 of the ECHR,[89] he disagreed with the majority that the ECtHR would stretch its jurisprudence to identify positive obligations on contracting states to protect the lives of soldiers when deployed to combat situations.[90] He believed the ECtHR would not 'invade a field which would involve ... extensive and highly sensitive review with the benefit of hindsight' of the UK's 'policies, strategy and tactics relating to the deployment and use of its armed forces in combat'.[91] He warned that the approach of the majority would lead to the 'judicialisation of war',[92] and instead he argued, in effect, that such matters were non-justiciable i.e. not appropriate for judicial decision.

---

[87]   Ibid, paras 64–6 (Hope).
[88]   Ibid, para 76 (Hope).
[89]   Ibid, para 102 (Mance).
[90]   Ibid, paras 142–3 (Mance).
[91]   Ibid, para 146 (Mance).
[92]   Ibid, para 150 (Mance).

Although the UK Supreme Court allowed the case to proceed to trial, where the facts would be the focus, Lord Hope gave a strong steer that the duties implied in Article 2 of the ECHR must not 'impose an unrealistic or disproportionate burden on the authorities', and that meant that a 'very wide measure of discretion ... must be accorded to those' planning the operations and procuring equipment.[93] He thus put the claimants 'on notice', in effect, as to their limited chances of success.[94] This hardly seems to justify the charges of 'legalistic and post-operational questioning' levelled at the majority in *Smith v MoD* in a Policy Exchange Report.[95] Yes, the case does establish (without any dissent) that in principle the ECHR applies to soldiers on deployment to combat situations, but it places clear limits on the chances of claims succeeding. Lawyers advising potential claimants should bear this is mind, although this should not stop cases proceeding where, as with the use of Snatch Land Rovers in Iraq, there are questions to be answered. Claims will help shape the government's obligations and the planning and preparation of future military operations, although an individual claim itself is unlikely to be upheld.

While *Smith v MoD* opened the door to claims brought under human rights law and common law arising out of fatalities and injuries suffered by soldiers, the actual claims before it were sent back for trial, which in the end did not take place. The MoD successfully dragged its feet until, in the case of Snatch Land Rovers at least, the Chilcot Report on the Iraq Inquiry of July 2016 unearthed a great deal of evidence concerning their inadequacy for the roles they were expected to perform in Iraq. For example, General Sir Mike Jackson, Chief of the General Staff 2003–2006, gave evidence to the Iraq Inquiry, stating:

> Snatch Land Rovers were deployed to Iraq because they were available or could be made available as we drew down from Northern Ireland, and without them it would have been completely soft-skinned Land Rovers. That's where the state of the inventory equipment was at that point.
>   The Snatch Land Rover was only designed to give protection from low velocity rounds and shrapnel and it wasn't set out to do anything else, but it was better than a completely unprotected vehicle.[96]

The Inquiry's key findings on this matter were that, between 2003 and 2009, 'UK forces faced gaps in some key capability areas', including 'protected mobility' and that 'delays in providing adequate medium weight Protected

---

[93]   Ibid, paras 78, 81 (Hope).
[94]   Ibid, para 81 (Hope).
[95]   Tugendhat and Croft (2013) 33.
[96]   The Report of the Iraq Inquiry 2016: Vol 11, section 14.1 'Military Equipment (Post-Conflict)', para 171 https://www.gov.uk/government/publications/the-report-of -the-iraq-inquiry.

Patrol Vehicles … should not have been tolerated'. Moreover, as regards the competence of the MoD, the Inquiry found that 'it was not sufficiently clear which person or department within the MOD had responsibility for identifying and articulating credibility gaps'. Furthermore, the MoD 'was slow in responding to the developing threat from' IEDs in Iraq leaving commanders with a limited range of protected mobility options until new vehicles were finally ordered following ministerial intervention in July 2006. Crucially, the Inquiry determined that 'funding was not a direct barrier' to address the gap.[97]

In August 2017, the Defence Secretary stated that the 'government entirely accepts the findings of Sir John Chilcot in the Iraq Inquiry in relation to the Snatch Land Rover'. The minister apologised to the families of British soldiers killed while travelling in Snatch Land Rovers,[98] in particular for the delay in bringing in better protected vehicles that could have saved lives. Furthermore, he indicated that the claims could go forward. Michael Fallon stated that the lessons of Iraq had been learnt and that in the future the 'government must and will ensure that our armed forces are always properly equipped and resourced'.[99]

8.4.4 The UK's Procedural Obligations under the ECHR

It was only after the unearthing of further evidence in the course of the Iraq Inquiry that the government was forced into accepting claims in the Snatch Land Rover cases. Such fulsome inquiries are unlikely to be available to future claimants, although there remains the procedural obligation to investigate. This obligation has been read into Article 2 of the ECHR by the ECtHR on the basis that the substantive obligation to protect the right to life 'would be ineffective in practice if there existed no procedure for reviewing the lawfulness of the use of force by state authorities'.[100] This procedural obligation continues to apply even in 'difficult security situations, including armed conflict'.[101] The obligation requires a state to carry out an investigation that has the following features: 'it must have a sufficient element of public scrutiny of the investiga-

---

[97] The Report of the Iraq Inquiry 2016, Executive Summary, 'Military equipment (Post-conflict)' para 821.

[98] C. Coleman, 'Mother wins MoD apology over Snatch Land Rover death', *BBC News*, 18 August 2017 https://www.bbc.co.uk/news/uk-40958686.

[99] J. Grierson, 'Fallon apologises to families of soldiers killed in Land Rovers in Iraq', *The Guardian*, 18 August 2017 https://www.theguardian.com/politics/2017/aug/18/michael-fallon-apologises-family-dead-soldier-snatch-land-rover-delays?CMP=Share_iOSApp_Other.

[100] *Al-Skeini v UK* (2011) 163.

[101] *Jaloud v The Netherlands*, Appl No 47708/08, 20 November 2014, 163.

tion or its results'; 'it must be conducted by a tribunal that is independent of the state agents who may bear responsibility for the death'; 'the relatives of the deceased must be able to play an appropriate part in it'; and 'it must be prompt and effective'.[102] The latter feature must have the purpose of securing the 'effective implementation of the domestic laws which protect the right to life and ensure the accountability of state agents or bodies for deaths occurring under their responsibility'.[103]

The procedural obligation not only applies when civilians are killed by soldiers,[104] it is also applicable when soldiers themselves are killed. In *Smith v MoD*, the Supreme Court was 'not concerned … with the procedural obligation which is implied into the article in order to make sure that the substantive right is effective in practice' because the Snatch Land Rover claims concerned the substantive obligation under Article 2.[105] However, Lord Hope made it clear that systemic or operational failures of the kind alleged in the case 'ought not to be immune from scrutiny in pursuance of the procedural obligation under art 2 of the Convention'.[106] In the same case, Lord Mance remarked that 'the United Kingdom's performance of its investigatory and procedural duties' concerning soldiers' deaths was 'not in doubt, as attested by the sadly numerous inquests (investigating and recording the circumstances of each death)'.[107]

While there is a significant amount of doctrine and practice on the fulfilment of the Article 2 procedural obligation in cases where state agents including soldiers have killed civilians,[108] the practice and jurisprudence on the fulfilment of the obligation when a soldier is killed is less developed.[109] The

---

[102] *R (Catherine Smith) v Oxfordshire Deputy Coroner* [2010] para 64.

[103] Ibid.

[104] For critical evaluation of this this obligation and its equivalents under LOAC and International Criminal Law see A. Williams, 'War Crimes Allegations and the UK: Towards a Fairer Investigative Process' (2020) 40 *Legal Studies* 301; S.L. Kemp, *British Justice, War Crimes and Human Rights Violations* (Palgrave Macmillan, 2019) 41–142.

[105] *Smith* [2013] para 57 (Hope).

[106] Ibid, para 63 (Hope).

[107] Ibid, para 146 (Mance).

[108] See, for example, J. Chevalier-Watts, 'Effective Investigations under Article 2 of the European Convention on Human Rights: Securing the Right to Life or an Onerous Burden on the State?' (2010) 21 *European Journal of International Law* 701 at 711, discussing the conjoined Northern Ireland ECtHR cases of *Hugh Jordan v United Kingdom*, Appl No 24746/94, 4 May 2001; *Kelly and Others v United Kingdom*, Appl No 30055/96, 4 May 2001; *McKerr v United Kingdom*, Appl No 28883/95, 4 May 2001; and *Shanagan v United Kingdom*, Appl No 37715/97, 4 May 2001 – 'in all four cases the available procedures had not satisfied the requirement of Article 2'.

[109] I.D. Park, *The Right to Life in Armed Conflict* (Oxford University Press, 2018) 190–1.

Supreme Court did discuss the issue at some length in *R (Catherine Smith) v Oxfordshire Deputy Coroner* in 2010, with Lord Philips making the point that '[a]s the bodies of servicemen who die or are killed on active service abroad are brought back to this country, any internal investigation that has taken place will be followed by a public inquest that will satisfy many of the requirements of an article 2 investigation'. However, 'it will often be only in the course of the inquest that it will become apparent that there is an issue as to whether there has been a breach by the State of its positive article 2 obligations' – 'only at that stage will it be appreciated that the exercise in progress is one called for by article 2 and one that must, if possible, satisfy the requirements of that article'.[110] In so finding, the Supreme Court rejected the claimant's argument that the death of a soldier automatically triggered the procedural obligation in Article 2, signifying that the procedural obligation will only be triggered if the initial investigation and inquest reveal a potential breach of the state's positive obligations to protect the right to life.[111]

In practice, the procedural obligation may be less onerous in the case of the deaths of soldiers when compared to the death of civilians at the hands of British soldiers. One reason for this suggested distinction 'is the practical difficulties inherent in investigating the death of other individuals when compared to UK armed forces personnel'.[112] In the case of fallen soldiers 'extraordinary efforts are made to recover the body, which facilitates the possibility of a post-mortem to establish the cause of death', and further 'it is also easier to interview armed forces personnel who witnessed the death of a colleague'.[113] In his review of the practice on this matter Ian Park states that it is 'likely that the use of criminal investigation where necessary, service inquiries, and coroner's inquests are sufficient to comply with the state's procedural right to life obligations in respect of armed forces personnel killed during armed conflict'.[114]

8.5 EXPLORING THE MIDDLE GROUND

The majority judgment in the *Smith v MoD* case was cautious in setting the parameters within which a claim under Article 2 of the ECHR might succeed. At one end of the scale, it ruled out claims based on executive decisions relating to 'training, procurement or the conduct of operations' made 'at a high

---

[110] *R (Catherine Smith) v Oxfordshire Assistant Deputy Coroner* [2010] para 86 (Lord Phillips).
[111] Ibid, paras 82–4.
[112] Park (2018) 191.
[113] Ibid.
[114] Ibid.

level of command and closely linked to the exercise of political judgment and issues of policy' (high level decisions). At the other end of the scale, the court ruled out claims which 'relate to things done or not done when those who might be thought responsible for avoiding the risk of death or injury to others were actively engaged in direct contact with the enemy' (combat decisions).[115] Whether the facts fall within the middle ground between high-level and combat decisions is for the trial judge and, even if they do fall in that ground, that does not by itself mean there is a breach of Article 2 of the ECHR.[116]

This middle ground was explored by the Court of Appeal in the case of *Long* in 2015. Corporal Long was one of six RMPs who were unlawfully killed in June 2003 by members of a crowd at an Iraqi police station in Majar-al-Kabir. His mother brought a claim on the basis that there had not been sufficient investigation into the circumstances of his death in breach of Article 2 of the ECHR. The case turned on whether there was an arguable substantive breach of Article 2 so as to trigger a duty to investigate and, if so, whether the steps taken to investigate the death had discharged that obligation.[117] According to the Court of Appeal: '[a]t its most general level, the positive obligation requires the state to have in place a framework of laws and systems which will, to the greatest extent reasonably practical, protect life'.[118] The issue in the case before it was whether there 'was an arguable breach of the state's positive obligation to safeguard the lives of members of its armed forces'.[119]

The alleged failure on the part of the state was that a month before the deaths of the six soldiers there was an order requiring that all patrols should carry a satellite phone, but that the RMP patrol had not been equipped with one (and that this was not an isolated instance). It was not disputed that if the soldiers had been equipped with a satellite phone their lives might have been saved.[120] The Court of Appeal was clearly of the view that the failure to provide the soldiers with phones was neither a high-level decision nor was it the result of a decision made in the course of combat and so fell within the middle ground. Following that, the issue was whether the circumstances of the case, which fell within the middle ground, disclosed arguable substantive breaches of Article 2. Following Lord Hope in *Smith v MoD*, the Court of Appeal stated that at this point there is still a margin of appreciation for the state engaged in armed conflict and, furthermore, Article 2 should not be interpreted so as to

---

[115] *Smith v MoD* [2013] para 76 (Hope).
[116] Ibid, para 81.
[117] *R (Long) v Secretary of State for Defence* [2015] EWCA Civ 770 paras 1 and 3.
[118] Ibid, para 5.
[119] Ibid, para 6.
[120] Ibid, para 2.

impose a disproportionate burden on the authorities.[121] A case will be outside Article 2 if it involved 'no more than an allegation of individual human error', or a 'combination of events of which the state has no control and for which it cannot be held responsible'.[122] However, a 'case involving dangerous activities undertaken, organised or authorised by the state and which falls within the middle ground may engage article 2 if it is arguable that the death was caused by insufficient state systems, regulations or control'.[123]

The Court of Appeal decided that this was an instance of system failure rather than individual error or isolated lapse within a system provided by the state. The introduction of the practice of not normally providing RMP patrols with satellite phones was not an occasional or sporadic error, but constituted the introduction or at least routine acceptance of a different unsafe practice to the one required; in other words it 'was system failure by the military authorities to permit soldiers routinely to disregard the order'.[124] Furthermore, it was not unreasonable or disproportionate to hold the state responsible for the practice of disregarding the order. The Court of Appeal felt that this was not a difficult case compared to *Smith v MoD*, which involved a challenge to the types of equipment provided to soldiers, given that in *Long* satellite phones were available, and it was reasonable and proportionate to carry out an investigation as to why the order to provide them was ignored.[125] Lord Justice Lewison concluded that it was 'not a condition of the engagement of article 2 that it is shown that, but for the failing or omission on the part of the state, the deaths would not have occurred. It is sufficient to show a failure to take reasonable measures which could have had a real prospect of avoiding the deaths.'[126]

Having established this important point of principle, moreover that Article 2 was engaged by the circumstances of the case, the Court of Appeal dismissed the second part of the appeal on the procedural obligation, by deciding that no further investigation was necessary under Article 2. The Court found that the Army's Board of Inquiry and the Coroner's Inquest had revealed why phones were not provided to the RMP patrol and had determined what went wrong and what lessons were to be learnt.[127] In a way, as with the *Smith v MoD* case, *Long* shows both the value and the limits of claims based on positive obligations under human rights law. They can be used to call the government to account

---

[121] Ibid, para 13.
[122] Ibid, para 15.
[123] Ibid, para 13.
[124] Ibid, paras 25 and 28.
[125] Ibid, para 31.
[126] Ibid, para 32.
[127] Ibid, para 55.

for a narrow range of systemic failings when deploying troops, and it is possible that they may trigger further relief to the claimants.[128]

The tortuous and contested nature of such claims is illustrated by the case of *Pritchard v UK*, involving another RMP soldier, Corporal Dewi Pritchard, who was killed in an ambush in Iraq in August 2003. He was involved in an operation to transport rifles and was driving a non-armoured vehicle ahead of a Land Rover, which was transporting the rifles, when a truck overtook the Land Rover and drew level with the vehicle Pritchard was driving. A man in the back of the truck fired into the driver's side window, killing three soldiers including Corporal Pritchard.[129] The issues raised were whether he was within the jurisdiction of the UK within the meaning of Article 1 of the ECHR, and, if so, whether the MoD had an obligation under Articles 2 and 13 of the ECHR to investigate his death. In 2005, the coroner ruled that the ECHR did not apply to British troops overseas and so no investigation under Article 2 was required. That position on jurisdiction was supported to some extent in the 2010 judgment of the UK Supreme Court in *R (Catherine Smith) v Oxfordshire Assistant Deputy Coroner*,[130] leading to Corporal Prichard's father applying to the ECtHR in 2010.

As noted in the Policy Exchange's Report of 2015, the UK government chose to settle the case in 2014 rather than allow it to proceed in the ECtHR. Although the terms of the settlement only covered the family's legal costs, full access to the original report on Corporal Pritchard's death, as well as a promise to answer any questions his father might have, the Policy Exchange Report criticises the government's decision as it 'seems to concede that the Supreme Court's further extension of the extraterritorial jurisdiction in *Smith v MoD* should not now be challenged in Strasbourg'. According to the Policy Exchange Report 'it would have been preferable to fight *Pritchard* to a hearing, and for the Government to seek to argue that the Supreme Court's *Smith v MoD* judgement was an illegitimate extension of *Al-Skeini*'.[131] The hope expressed in the Policy Exchange Report is that the UK government can persuade the ECtHR that the jurisdiction of the UK under the ECHR does not include soldiers on deployment overseas, but there are clear legal arguments for finding otherwise as articulated by the Supreme Court in *Smith v MoD*.[132] Furthermore, although not finally adjudicated upon the case raised issues of

---

[128] In *Long* it was noted that the claimants had also made a civil claim in negligence and that these claims had been settled – ibid, annex para 29.

[129] *Pritchard v the United Kingdom*, Appl No 1573/11, lodged with the ECtHR on 20 December 2010.

[130] *R (Catherine Smith) v Oxfordshire Assistant Deputy Coroner* [2010].

[131] Ekins, Morgan and Tugendhat (2015) 16.

[132] Wallace (2019) 101.

whether the UK had fulfilled its positive obligation to Corporal Pritchard, specifically whether the decision to send him and others on the operation in an unarmoured vehicle was a systemic failure in the middle ground.

8.6 HOWEVER, THE FINAL SAY WILL BE WITH THE ECтHR

The *Smith v MoD* and *Long* cases show the courts inching towards framing the conditions in which right to life claims can be successfully made when British soldiers are killed. It has to be in the middle ground between high-level and combat decisions in order not to fetter the government's prosecution of the war or the ability of soldiers and commanders to respond to immediate events on the ground. Even if in the middle ground, for a claim to succeed it should not be the result of individual error, nor should it place a disproportionate or unreasonable burden on the government. Many hurdles indeed, but there emerges an increasingly clear path that, at least, reassures soldiers that their lives should not be unduly risked by system failures that could have reasonably been avoided. However, that path has yet to be endorsed at the highest judicial level.

In *Smith v MoD*, Lord Hope seemed unconcerned that the issue of whether soldiers where within the jurisdiction of the state for the purposes of Article 1 of the ECHR had not yet been addressed by the ECtHR. He declared that 'one should not be too troubled by the fact that no case has yet come before the Strasbourg court which required it to consider whether the jurisdiction which states undoubtedly have over their armed forces abroad in both national and international law means that they are within their jurisdiction for the purposes of art 1 of the Convention'.[133] However, it is not as clear-cut as he might think. Of particular note is the ECtHR's recent opportunity to comment on the issue of whether British soldiers on deployment overseas are within the jurisdiction of the UK for the purposes of the application of the ECHR, but the Court avoided the issue.

The case of *Miller v the United Kingdom* decided in July 2019, involved an application by the father of another RMP soldier, Corporal Simon Miller, unlawfully killed in the same incident as *Long* in Iraq in June 2003. Relying on Article 2 of the ECHR, the applicant complained that the investigations into the deaths of the RMP patrol had failed to comply with the procedural duty to conduct an effective investigation leading to the establishment of the facts.[134] Essentially the ECtHR agreed with the Court of Appeal in the *Long* case, namely that the inquiry and inquest amounted to an effective investigation

---

[133] *Smith v MoD* [2013] para 42 (Hope).
[134] *Miller v the United Kingdom*, Appl No 32001/18, 2 July 2019, paras 73–4.

by the UK and, therefore, the application was dismissed as being manifestly ill-founded. The Court dealt briefly with the issue of jurisdiction in the following terms:

> Whilst they occurred during the same time period as the facts in *Al Skeini* …, the circumstances leading to this application do not involve the death of individuals killed in the course of security operations carried out by United Kingdom troops, on the basis of which the Court in *Al Skeini* … considered that exceptionally it was able to establish a jurisdictional link between the deceased and the United Kingdom. The subject of the present case is the deaths of the RMPs, caused by members of a local crowd when the soldiers were carrying out activities as part of the United Kingdom's mission in Iraq to restore and maintain law and order … Accordingly, the Court considers that the question whether there is a jurisdictional link for the purposes of Article 1 of the Convention in the circumstances of the present case is potentially complex. However, it is not necessary to decide the matter as the application is in any event manifestly ill-founded for the reasons set out [regarding the adequacy of the investigations].[135]

The ECtHR effectively side-stepped the issue for the time being, leaving the line of jurisprudence in UK courts flowing from *Smith v MoD* in 2013, which is already having an impact in the national legal order, lacking approval or endorsement at the European level. There was no reference to the *Smith* case in the decision of the Court in *Miller*. It is relevant to consider as to why the ECtHR considered the question of jurisdiction over soldiers to be a 'complex' one. It may be that the Court was thinking that the issue of soldiers' rights has to involve more than just a formal understanding of jurisdiction, to include a consideration of the status of soldiers as citizens who in principle are entitled to the same rights and freedoms as any individuals within the UK's jurisdiction, but who are also subject to unique duties especially when in combat situations. Unusually, critics of the growth of human rights jurisprudence into the field of military operations might take heart from a judgment of the ECtHR. Although the judgment in *Miller* does not end the line of cases developing from *Smith v MoD* it has, for the time being, put a question mark over it.

8.7   ILL-TREATMENT OF SOLDIERS: THE DEEPCUT REVIEW

Human rights jurisprudence is gradually evolving to provide soldiers with some form of protection from manifestly unreasonable decisions or actions of government concerning deployment that affect their right to life under Article 2 of the ECHR. There is no reason why soldiers should not also benefit

---

[135] Ibid, para 78.

from both negative and positive obligations to protect and respect their right to be free of torture or other inhuman or degrading treatment under Article 3 ECHR, but this would probably not be a realistic method to address, moreover to reduce, endemic problems of over-harsh discipline, bullying or sexual misconduct by service personnel. The perpetrators may suffer punishment in summary hearings before COs or by courts martial for the service offence of 'ill-treatment of subordinates' and various criminal conduct offences of assault etc., and there is some evidence of this.[136] The protection of soldiers from abuse in the form of bullying and harassment is unlikely to be directly provided by the increasing recognition that soldiers have enforceable human rights, but in a more general sense the acceptance that soldiers have rights and protections has informed the development of non-judicial remedies and processes of accountability.

Problems of endemic abuse are difficult to tackle in a culture where loyalty to comrades and obedience to orders is integral to the success of military operations. The deaths of trainees at Deepcut barracks in the UK serve to highlight the problem. In the Defence Committee's Report of 2005 into the duty of care owed by the armed forces to recruits, produced amidst allegations of bullying and abuse in the armed services,[137] a former Deepcut recruit is quoted as saying: 'staff crossed the boundaries of discipline into humiliation and control through the use of fear ... A handful of staff members made our training unattainable and not only soul-destroying but, for some, life-destroying. Senior staff stood back and watched the morale plummet, self-harming soar and people die and did nothing.'[138] The Defence Committee highlighted the unwillingness of recruits to complain partly because the approach of the military put 'emphasis on the victim of bullying as a weak individual',[139] and few recruits wanted to admit to being 'weak'.

In considering the legal framework applicable to recruits, the Defence Committee Report of 2005 was primarily concerned with identifying the armed forces' duty of care, which it saw as consisting of a bundle of legislative obligations, combined with a moral obligation to look after service personnel. The MoD's approach to its duty of care was based on judicial standards: 'whether an injury was reasonably foreseeable; the proximity between the person alleged to owe the duty of care and the person claiming it is owed, and

---

[136] See 'Court martial results from the military court centres: January to December 2019', 8 July 2020 https://www.gov.uk/government/publications/court-martial-results -from-the-military-court-centres.

[137] 'The Bullying Culture of the British Army', *The Independent*, 15 March 2005.

[138] House of Commons Defence Committee, 'Duty of Care', Third Report 2004-6 (HC 63) 3 March 2005, para 35.

[139] Ibid, para 309.

whether it would be fair, just and reasonable to impose a duty'.[140] The Report identified the duty of care, as defined by the MoD, as deriving from 'health and safety, equal opportunities and anti-discrimination legislation'. In its review of relevant legislative obligations, the Report made the unqualified statement that 'members of the armed forces are entitled to the protections of the European Convention on Human Rights' as enshrined in the HRA 1998.[141]

The fatalities at Deepcut Barracks led to a review commissioned by the armed forces minister into 'the circumstances surrounding the deaths of four soldiers at Princess Royal Barracks, Deepcut between 1995 and 2002 in light of available material and any representations that might be made in this regard, and to produce a report'.[142] The minister justified the commissioning of an independent review as opposed to a full public inquiry on the basis that a 'review can analyse issues much more quickly than a public inquiry and would not interfere with other current investigations or proceedings'. Furthermore, he stated that it was 'of the highest importance that a balanced and authoritative account of the circumstances surrounding the deaths should be put into the public domain, to sustain public confidence in military training'.[143]

The Review of the circumstances surrounding the deaths of four soldiers at Princess Royal Barracks, Deepcut between 1995 and 2002 (the Deepcut Review),[144] was conducted by Nicholas Blake QC. All four recruits had been on guard duty and all had died from gunshot wounds.[145] In considering whether these deaths demonstrated a failure of the duty of care and a violation of standards set by human rights law, the Deepcut Review stated that in 'the present cases, the Review is concerned with the procedural obligation inherent in Article 2 [ECHR] to enable the families to inquire into whether there was evidence of a failure to protect their children from harm, or self-harm, or any other systemic failure relevant to their deaths'.[146]

In terms of findings the Review found that in the cases of Sean Benton, Cheryl James and Geoff Gray, they appeared to be three young soldiers 'who either did, or may have, inflicted injuries on themselves in the course of undertaking armed guard duties at the Barracks'. It followed from this finding

---

[140]   Ibid, para 20.
[141]   Ibid, paras 22 and 26.
[142]   N. Blake QC, 'The Deepcut Review: A review of the circumstances surround-ing the deaths of four soldiers at Princess Royal Barracks, Deepcut between 1995 and 2002' (HC 795) 29 March 2006, i https://assets.publishing.service.gov.uk/government/uploads/system/uploads/attachment_data/file/228930/0795.pdf.
[143]   Hansard, HC, Col 132 WS, 15 December 2004.
[144]   'The Deepcut Review' (2006).
[145]   Ibid, paras 1.1–1.4.
[146]   Ibid, para 2.68.

that the three recruits 'were neither cases of deaths at the hands of state agents nor deaths in custody, where the state was under a particular duty of care to take reasonable steps to protect the health of a prisoner, including protecting a prisoner from self-harm where a reasonable risk of self-harm was known to the state'. The review was critical of the fact that these young recruits 'had probably died as a result of the discharge of a lethal weapon assigned to them, or accessible by them, in the performance of their guard duties when they were young and had yet to complete Phase 2 of their training'. In addition to systemic weaknesses in training there were issues of harsh discipline in the barracks leading the Inquiry to a tentative conclusion that 'there was, at the least, the possibility of a defective system operated by the state that may have failed to afford adequate protection to life'.[147]

As regards the reports of bullying, the Deepcut Review found that in 'only one of the three deaths reviewed, that of Sean Benton, might bullying or overharsh discipline have played any role in undermining the morale of the trainee', but that there was 'insufficient reliable evidence to conclude that it did so'. It further concluded that there was no evidence that any of the trainees were bullied to death. There was, however, evidence to suggest that 'from 1995 to 2002 a number of trainees at Deepcut had, at various times, experienced, or claim to have experienced, harassment, discrimination and oppressive behaviour from NCOs, as well as from other trainees'.[148] In considering the issue of responsibility for the deaths, the Deepcut Review concluded 'on the balance of probabilities, that the deaths of Sean Benton, Cheryl James and Geoff Gray were self-inflicted and that the opportunity for self-infliction was afforded by the policy of frequently assigning Phase 2 trainees to armed guard duty at Deepcut, unsupervised by experienced soldiers or members of the Military Provost Guard Service'.[149]

The question of why the recruits would kill themselves independently from each other but in very similar circumstances, was left unanswered by the Deepcut Review. The failure to protect the right to life of these young recruits is not explained by limited evidence of bullying and harsh discipline, leaving open the question of whether or not there was endemic abuse in Deepcut Barracks. Inevitably, this would lead to further calls for inquiries and truth-finding by the families and more generally by the public. The fact that the Review found that 'there was reluctance by trainees to complain against NCOs', and that 'those who did complain about a senior NCO were

---

[147] Ibid, paras 2.63–2.64, 2.68.
[148] Ibid, paras 12.23–12.25.
[149] Ibid, para 12.2. The inquest into James Collinson's death was ongoing at the time of the Deepcut Review.

vulnerable to reprisals and received an ineffective response by their immediate superiors',[150] was indicative of a regime that was not only harsh but based on unauthorised and unlawful 'reprisals' against those who had the courage to complain about their maltreatment. That regime was probably part of the explanation of why the recruits died, something that is not reflected in the conclusion of the Inquiry that being on lonely and unsupervised guard duty gave them the opportunity to kill themselves. It is therefore clear that the Review did not meet the standards set for a public inquiry as identified by the House of Lords, as cited in the Deepcut Review:

> The purposes of such an investigation are clear: to ensure so far as possible that the full facts are brought to light; that culpable and discreditable conduct is exposed and brought to public notice; that suspicion of deliberate wrongdoing (if unjustified) is allayed; that dangerous practices and procedures are rectified; and that those who have lost their relative may at least have the satisfaction of knowing that lessons learned from his death may save the lives of others.[151]

In recommending that 'a public inquiry into the immediate or broader circumstances surrounding these deaths is not necessary',[152] the Deepcut Review purported to fulfil the above standards. While the Review was deficient in investigating the facts and causes, it did recommend some changes to the wider system of accountability in the armed forces. The Review's main contribution to the improvement of the overall system of military justice was to highlight the inadequacies of the 'military complaints system and any other measures for independent oversight of the welfare of recruits, trainees and young soldiers',[153] thereby recommending the establishment of an ombudsman for the armed forces.[154]

Demands for a public inquiry into the four deaths persist despite an additional Report by the Army Board of Inquiry published in 2009 supporting the Deepcut Review's findings;[155] and a further coroner's inquest into the death of Cheryl James, at the instigation of her family, which found on 3 June 2016 that she had died as a result of a 'self-inflicted' shot which was fired by Cheryl

---

[150]   Ibid, para 12.27.
[151]   *R (Middleton) v West Somerset Coroner* [2004] UKHL 10 at para 31. Cited in 'The Deepcut Review'(2006) para 2.65.
[152]   'The Deepcut Review' (2006) para 12.140.
[153]   Ibid, para 12.28.
[154]   Ibid, recommendation 26. Also recommended by the Defence Committee: House of Commons Defence Select Committee, 'Duty of Care' (2006) para 122.
[155]   Statement by Bob Ainsworth, Minister of Defence, Hansard, HC Deb, Col 61WS, 14 May 2009.

James in an 'intended and deliberate act'.[156] A fresh inquest opened into the death of Sean Benton in 2017,[157] leading to a criminal investigation by Surrey Police into the circumstances which led to his death, specifically allegations including assault and misconduct in a public office involving an instructor who, according to the findings of the coroner, kicked and punched Private Benton days before his suicide. The coroner at the inquest in June 2018, while confirming the finding of suicide, described a 'toxic culture at the barracks' and said Private Benton 'was frequently the recipient of harsh treatment'.[158]

8.8   THE SERVICE COMPLAINTS OMBUDSMAN

The Deepcut Review recommended that it was 'essential that soldiers and their families have access to an established authority who understands the military and its ways of working, but stands outside of the chain of command, and beyond its influence, in order to ensure that best practice is adhered to'.[159] The pressure for a service ombudsman eventually led to the Service Complaints Ombudsman, which was established by the Armed Forces (Service Complaints and Financial Assistance) Act 2015. The Ombudsman was the successor to the Service Complaints Commissioner for the Armed Forces (SCC), a role established by the Armed Forces Act 2006 as part of significant reforms to the service complaints process. The first Service Complaints Commissioner, Dr Susan Atkins, had reported to Parliament that the Service complaints system was not yet effective, efficient or fair, and that her powers were not strong enough for her to effect the necessary change.[160]

The 'role of the Service Complaints Ombudsman is to provide independent and impartial oversight of the Service complaints process for Service personnel in the United Kingdom'.[161] When the first Services Complaints Ombudsman, Nicola Williams, was appointed in 2015, *The Independent* reported:

> Hundreds of formal complaints are made each year concerning bullying and harassment. Improper behaviour and bullying continue to be the most common grievances, accounting for almost 70 per cent of all complaints in 2014, according to the latest SCC annual report. But the true scale of the problem is far larger: 90 per cent of

---

[156] 'Cheryl James died from "self-inflicted shot", Deepcut inquest rules', *The Guardian*, 3 June 2016.

[157] 'Deepcut inquest to examine bullying claims', *The Guardian*, 16 June 2017.

[158] 'Criminal investigation launched into circumstances which led to soldier's death at Deepcut Barracks', *The Telegraph*, 26 February 2019.

[159] 'The Deepcut Review' (2006) para 12.100.

[160] Service Complaints Ombudsman for the Armed Forces https://www.scoaf.org .uk/about-us/history-and-legislation/.

[161] https://www.scoaf.org.uk/about-us/.

those suffering bullying, harassment or discrimination don't raise a formal complaint, according to the latest Armed Forces Continuous Attitude Survey.[162]

In her first Annual Report of 2016 the Ombudsperson outlined her powers of 'referral and investigation', specifically she can: 'refer a Service person's intention to make a Service complaint to their chain of command'; 'review a decision by the chain of command to not accept a complaint for investigation or to not allow a complaint to proceed to appeal for a further decision'; 'investigate allegations of undue delay in the handling of a Service complaint or Service matter'; 'investigate allegations that there was maladministration in the handling of a Service complaint which has completed the internal system'; and 'investigate the substance (merits) of a Service complaint which has completed the internal system'.[163]

In her third annual report of 2018, the Ombudsman was 'still unable to report that the system is efficient, effective and fair. While there has continued to be improvement and an ongoing commitment to ensuring its success, there are still a number of improvements required across both the internal Service complaints system and my office', pointing in particular to the fact that only 50 per cent of service complaints were resolved by the services within 24 weeks, falling significantly short of the 90 per cent target.[164] Of the 763 admissible Service complaints made in 2018, 25 per cent concerned bullying, harassment and discrimination.[165] The situation had not improved in the 2019 Report, which shows the number of complaints had increased to 1,184, 25 per cent, of which concerned bullying, harassment and discrimination.[166]

In its report into women and the armed forces of July 2021, the Defence Committee expressed concerns about the functioning of the service complaints system and the lack of confidence in it. While the Committee understood 'the importance of the chain of command in the Armed Forces', it was of the view that it was 'not always appropriate' for COs to handle complex bullying, harassment and discrimination (BHD) cases. Indeed, it found 'consistent evidence suggesting that the chain of command is a point of failure in the complaints system'. In order to address this problem, the Defence Committee endorsed

---

[162] 'Nicola Williams: Meet the civilian general putting the armed forces on guard', *The Independent*, 5 September 2015.

[163] Service Complaints Ombudsman for the Armed Forces, Annual Report 2016 https://www.scoaf.org.uk/annual-reports/.

[164] Service Complaints Ombudsman for the Armed Forces, Annual Report 2018 https://www.scoaf.org.uk/annual-reports/.

[165] Ibid, 37.

[166] Service Complaints Ombudsman for the Armed Forces, Annual Report 2019, 50 https://www.scoaf.org.uk/annual-reports/.

the recommendations of the Wigston Review of 2019, which included the creation of a Defence Authority 'to handle complex BHD complaints outside the chain of command'. The Committee made it clear that the 'MoD must establish a central Defence Authority, fulfilling the functions as foreseen in the Wigton Review'. Furthermore, in order to increase the influence of the Service Complaints Ombudsman, the Committee stated unequivocally that the MoD 'must make the recommendations' of the Ombudsman 'binding on the Armed Forces and the MoD itself'.[167]

8.9 CHILD SOLDIERS

One of the issues arising out of the Deepcut Review was the fact that two of the four trainees who died were only 17. The Review admitted that there was a case 'for restricting the recruitment of soldiers into the Army to those who are over 18 on enlistment or commencement of training'. Such a policy would mean that 'problems of access to alcohol or *in loco parentis* welfare obligations to trainees would be replaced by a single duty of care – to protect soldiers from foreseeable harm not inherently connected to their role as soldiers'. The Deepcut Review stated that 'although being over 18 is no guarantee of individual maturity, it is the formal moment of transition from the status of minor to adult'. Furthermore, 'it could be argued that employment in the Army, with its particular features, is inappropriate for minors'.[168]

However, the Army 'was unwilling to lose the capacity to recruit those under 18', and the Deepcut Review agreed that there was 'no doubt that such a move would diminish the present ability of the Army to recruit the numbers it needs to perform the tasks the government asks of it'.[169] The Review was not convinced that such pragmatic arguments about 'manpower needs' of the Army were sufficient by themselves to override the 'best interests of the child', termed a 'principle' which 'should be a prime consideration for all public authorities in the United Kingdom'.[170] Despite recognising the fundamental nature of such a principle, the Review was 'satisfied that a military career is an exciting and challenging career for many young people who otherwise may not have an opportunity to lead structured and fulfilling lives'.[171] Essentially, the argument for retaining the recruitment of 16 and 17 year-olds is that the military provides career opportunities that make up for the failure of government and civilian society to provide sufficient education and training for edu-

---

[167] HC Defence Committee (2021–22) 52–57.
[168] 'The Deepcut Review' (2006) para 12.36.
[169] Ibid, para 12.37.
[170] Ibid, para 2.38.
[171] Ibid.

cationally low achieving children. The Review made this clear: 'to deny these young people the chance to start training for such a career when they are of school-leaving age may deprive them of the opportunity they need to get away from difficult social circumstances and acquire new skills, and social discipline, before it is too late to adapt'. The Review noted that 'although the Army is not designed as an agency to improve the quality of life of young people, it does offer broad opportunities for the acquisition of new skills and career development that schools and colleges may not', and further that 'for many young people the "boarding" experience may provide an effective chance to develop self-discipline and independence'.[172]

On this point, the Deepcut Review concluded that 'unless and until educational opportunity for 16 to 18 year-olds in the United Kingdom becomes so diverse and well-resourced that it provides everyone the opportunity of acquiring better life skills in civilian society, this Review is of the opinion that there is not a sufficient case to prevent the recruitment to the Army of those over 16 but under 18'. There was a 'mutual benefit to individual recruit and the Army alike to continue to permit those of this age to have the chance to start a military career and acquire a range of new skills'. The Review did state, however, that 'such recruitment and training must take place in an appropriate environment where there are sufficient staff skilled in understanding and addressing the particular vulnerabilities of young people in general, as well as being alive to any specific issues any individuals may have'. To this end, it recommended that: 'young people with suitable qualities for a military career should continue to be able to enlist at 16, with a view to fully participating in all aspects of military duties from the age of 18, so long as their training takes place in a suitable environment dedicated to the needs of such young people, and particular care is taken for their welfare'.[173]

It seems that the Army's need for 'manpower', combined with the state's failure to cater for children of all educational abilities, justifies the recruitment of 16- and 17-year-old children. The reasons would not appear to be any different to those that existed in Wellington's time in 1811, as noted by Richard Holmes: 'when the demands of war bit harder, regiments were authorised to enlist up to ten under-16-year-olds per company'.[174] Although the formal recruitment rules governing age for normal enlistment had been restricted to 18–25 year-olds by the end of the 19th century, the presence of child soldiers in the British Army persisted,[175] especially in wartime when the Army's 'appe-

---

[172]   Ibid, para 2.39.
[173]   Ibid, para 2.40.
[174]   Richard Holmes, *Soldiers* (HarperPress, 2011) 273.
[175]   Ibid.

tite for manpower is utterly insatiable'.[176] The difference today is that 16 and 17 year-olds are not normally deployed to combat situations.

In international law, there is a condemnation of the recruitment of child soldiers.[177] However, while the Convention on the Rights of the Child 1989 defines a child as someone under the age of 18 in Article 1, Article 38 states in part that state parties 'shall take all feasible measures to ensure that persons who have not attained the age of fifteen years do not take a direct part in hostilities', and further that 'States Parties shall refrain from recruiting any person who has not attained the age of fifteen years into their armed forces'. Article 3(1) of the Convention declares that 'in all actions concerning children, whether undertaken by public or private social welfare institutions, courts of law, administrative authorities or legislative bodies, the best interests of the child shall be a primary consideration'. In considering the UK's periodic report under the Convention of 2016, the Committee on the Rights of the Child expressed regret that the 'right of the child to have his or her best interests taken as a primary consideration is still not reflected in all legislative and policy matters and judicial decisions affecting children, especially in the area of alternative care, child welfare, immigration, asylum and refugee status, criminal justice and in the armed forces'.[178]

Under an Optional Protocol on the Involvement of Children in Armed Conflict of 2002, Article 1 provides that state parties 'shall take all feasible measures to ensure that members of their armed forces who have not attained the age of 18 years do not take a direct part in hostilities'. In considering the UK's initial report under the Optional Protocol of 2008, the Committee on the Rights of the Child expressed concern about the wide scope of the UK's interpretive declaration on Article 1: 'according to which deployment of persons under 18 to take direct part in hostilities would not be excluded when, inter alia, the exclusion of children before deployment is not practicable or would undermine the operational effectiveness of the operation'. The Committee recommended a revision of this declaration to ensure compliance with Article 1 of the Protocol, but the UK's declaration remains in place.[179]

---

[176] Ibid, 267.
[177] See, for example, M. Happold, *Child Soldiers in International Law* (Manchester University Press, 2005).
[178] Committee on the Rights of the Child, 'Concluding observations on the fifth periodic report of the United Kingdom of Great Britain and Northern Ireland', UN Doc CRC/C/GBR/CO/5, 12 July 2016, para 26.
[179] Committee on the Rights of the Child, Consideration of Reports Submitted by State Parties under Article 8 of the Optional Protocol … Concluding Observations: United Kingdom of Great Britain and Northern Ireland', UN Doc CRC/C/OPAC/GBR/CO/1, 17 October 2008.

Furthermore, the Committee on the Rights of the Child expressed regret that the UK had no plans to raise the recruitment age to 18 and encouraged it to do so. It noted that according to figures provided by the UK, 32 per cent of the total intake of recruits were under the age of 18, and that the active recruitment policy pursued by the armed forces 'may lead to the targeting of those children who come from vulnerable groups'. The Committee also expressed regret that 'armed guarding ... of military establishments may be undertaken by military personnel from the age of 17 years, and that this activity entails, as a minimum, weapon handling training and assessment as well as guidance on the use of force and the rules of engagement'. The Committee encouraged the abolition of the use and handling of all weapons by children 'in line with the spirit of the Optional Protocol'.[180]

The British Army still recruits 16 and 17 year-olds,[181] as a 2014 report in *The Independent* shows:

> More than one in 10 new Army recruits are boy soldiers of just 16 years old, according to the latest figures released by the Ministry of Defence. And more than one in four of all new Army recruits are under 18 – too young to be sent into combat. The figures, released last week, have sparked renewed criticism of the British Army's use of boy soldiers. Following an outcry over the deployment of 17-year-olds to the Gulf War in 1991, and to Kosovo in 1999, the Army amended its rules stopping soldiers under 18 from being sent on operations where there was a possibility of fighting. Despite this, at least 20 soldiers aged 17 are known to have served in Afghanistan and Iraq due to errors by the MoD.[182]

In another news report an MoD spokesperson stated that it continued 'to actively recruit across all age groups', and that as 'part of our duty of care to our recruits, no young person under the age of 18 years may join our armed forces without the formal written consent of their parent or guardian'. The statement concludes that there 'are currently no plans to revisit the government's recruitment policy for under-18s, which is fully compliant with United Nations conventions'.[183] Formally correct, the UK's position on recruiting under-18s does not reflect well on a developed country with relatively small volunteer armed forces.

---

[180] Ibid.

[181] https://apply.army.mod.uk/how-to-join/can-i-join.

[182] 'UK under fire for recruiting an "army of children"', *Independent*, 24 May 2014.

[183] 'Army recruitment at 16 should stop', *BBC News*, 23 April 2013 http://www.bbc .co.uk/news/uk-22259982.

8.10   CONCLUSION

In *Smith v MoD*, all the judges accepted that the UK had jurisdiction over its troops in Iraq for the purposes of the ECHR. This has not yet been confirmed at the level of the ECtHR, but the jurisprudence points in that direction.[184] However, the issue of the extraterritorial application of the ECHR remains politically and legally contentious.[185] Nevertheless, extraterritorial application does not mean that all the rights listed in the ECHR are applicable to UK service personnel operating overseas. In fact, the rights of soldiers that are often in issue are very few: they are principally the right to life under Article 2, to freedom from arbitrary detention under Article 5, to freedom from torture or from inhuman or degrading treatment under Article 3, and to freedom from punishment ungrounded in law in Article 7.

Nevertheless, even with the establishment of ECHR jurisdiction over troops it remains very difficult for claimants to establish that the due diligence obligations of the government towards soldiers to protect their rights have been breached. This is because issues of resource allocation, which lay behind much of the procurement of equipment, are not decisions for judges but are issues for politicians. Such decisions should activate mechanisms of political accountability before Select Committees and, if necessary, by public inquiries. Judicial accountability should only be activated below high-level governmental or military decisions in order to cover systemic acts or omissions that lead to under-equipped or under-resourced troops being deployed to situations where there is a real risk to their lives. Furthermore, such systemic failures must be so unreasonable as to constitute a manifest failure to protect the lives of soldiers. In addition, the exclusion of command decisions from forming the basis of actionable claims under Article 2 of the ECHR, and the common law doctrine of 'combat immunity', both serve to protect acts and omissions occurring during combat from judicial review. Given these parameters it is clear that the right to life of soldiers is protected but not at the expense of operational effectiveness.

The state's duty of care extends to taking reasonable measures to prevent soldiers from being exposed to violence, ill-treatment and unlawful punishment by their superiors or comrades, whether that occurs in barracks, bases,

---

[184]   Park (2018) 192; Wallace (2019) 101.

[185]   The government has established an Independent Human Rights Act Review, which will report in 2021. One of its terms of reference raises the following questions: 'In what circumstances does the HRA apply to acts of public authorities taking place outside the territory of the UK? What are the implications of the current position? Is there a case for change?' https://assets.publishing.service.gov.uk/government/uploads/system/uploads/attachment_data/file/953347/human-rights-review-tor.pdf.

training grounds, or operational situations in the UK or abroad. Harassment, bullying and discrimination evidenced in the reports of the Service Complaints Ombudsman for the Armed Forces do not by themselves signify that the provisions of the ECHR are being breached, or that offences under military law are being committed, although that may be the case with some individual complaints. In any case, the MoD owes its service personnel a duty of care to prevent harm, especially when there is evidence that such mistreatment is endemic. That duty is enhanced in relation to 16- and 17-year-old recruits, not simply because of the on-going and unresolved legacy of Deepcut, but because it is a clear legal duty, which should be a very stringent one considering the exceptional nature of allowing children to join the armed forces. One aspect of the state's responsibility for the ill-treatment of soldiers is to ensure that the perpetrators of abuse are properly investigated and, if appropriate, punished under the relevant provisions of service and criminal law, and in this respect there needs to be a better connection between the service complaints system and the military justice system.[186]

---

[186] For details on the service complaints system see MoD, 'Redress of Individual Grievances: Service Complaints' (JSP 831, 22 January 2016) https://www.gov .uk/government/publications/jsp-831-redress-of-individual-grievances-service -complaints. There is the prospect of a referral to the Service Police if the Deciding Officer considers that a criminal or service disciplinary offence may have been committed – MoD, 'The MoD Bullying and Harassment Complaints Procedures' (JSP 763, 1 July 2013) 23 https://assets.publishing.service.gov.uk/government/uploads/ system/uploads/attachment_data/file/209888/JSP763_1_July_2013.pdf. The Defence Committee stated in 2021 that the MoD 'must update' JSP 763 and 831 as a matter of urgency – HC Defence Committee (2021–22) 56.

9. The scales of military justice

9.1   INTRODUCTION

In general terms the aims of this chapter are to provide an overall assessment of military justice as broadly conceived in this book: at a basic level this involves a summary of the rights and duties of government and the rights and duties of soldiers, along with an account of the standards of justice applicable to the military. Following from this there is a re-evaluation of the social contract underpinning the relationship between the military and society in the modern era and the place of the soldier in that contract. As part of this re-evaluation, the chapter addresses the on-going argument encountered on several occasions throughout the book to the effect that the scales of justice are increasingly favouring the individual (soldiers and civilians affected by military operations) and placing unnecessary burdens on the government and the military establishment. This requires an understanding of the relationship between different legal regimes in order to address the argument that we are witnessing the excessive civilianisation and legalisation of military justice. Much of the blame for this has been attributed, rightly or wrongly, to the creeping impact of human rights law. It has been made clear at relevant points in the book that human rights law has an important role to play in military justice, particularly in ensuring that soldiers and civilians have adequate legal protections. However, it is accepted that there have to be legitimate limitations on applicable human rights protections in the extraordinary operational conditions of military deployments and the need to achieve military objectives. Concerns over the increasing legalisation of the military space are offset by the fact that, despite increased legal scrutiny, the accountability of soldiers and government for violations of human rights and other fundamental laws remains difficult to achieve.

In order to gain a wider contextual understanding of military justice, the chapter includes some analysis of selected jurisprudence from other national military justice systems in terms of the rights and duties of soldiers and government, in order to consider how other states balance the scales of military justice. This will lead to an overall assessment of whether the scales of justice – in terms of the rights and duties of government on the one hand and the rights and duties of soldiers on the other – are in balance or whether further adjustments are necessary.

9.2   RIGHTS AND DUTIES OF GOVERNMENT

In the broad sweep of history, the scales of military justice have largely
been weighted in favour of the government. Although executive powers to
deploy troops within and without the UK have moved from the monarch to
government, they remain prerogative powers, which are largely unreviewable
by the courts. However, the government and its ministers exercising such
powers are accountable to Parliament and the people, who can cast judgment
on the government at general elections. Thus, the decision of the government to deploy soldiers is a largely untrammelled right or power, although
political accountability may well follow particularly when soldiers become
embroiled in intractable conflicts. Internally, prerogative powers have been
supplemented but not replaced by broad sweeping legislative powers currently
under the Emergency Powers Act 1964, the Civil Contingencies Act 2004,
various pieces of counter-terrorism legislation, and the Coronavirus Act 2020,
although the exercise of prerogative powers for the deployment of military
forces remains the norm.

Externally, the government has prerogative powers to deploy troops overseas. Historically, accountability to Parliament has been retrospective but
the controversial invasion of Iraq in 2003 represented the start of the emergence of a possible non-binding Parliamentary convention to consult and
seek approval from the House of Commons at least for major deployments,
although its development has been uneven and seems to be subject to several
unclear exceptions. Under international law, the government has the right to
use military force in the exercise of its right of self-defence and under the
authority of a UN Security Council resolution. Those rights are embodied in
the UN Charter of 1945 and are the only express exceptions to the prohibition
on the threat or use of military force in international law. In practice, the UK
has regularly used force in and against other states and has not always clearly
acted within those exceptions. The UK has claimed a disputed right to undertake humanitarian intervention as well as the right to enforce international
law leading to allegations that it has prosecuted illegal wars. Remarkably, this
was recently evidenced in a House of Commons debate over the Overseas
Operations (Service Personnel and Veterans) Bill in 2020, which when it
came into force in 2021 would, amongst other things, make exceptional the
criminal prosecution of soldiers for many offences allegedly committed while
deployed overseas after the lapse of five years. In defending the Bill from
opposition criticism that it undermined the UK's commitment to international
laws prohibiting war crimes and torture, the Defence Secretary stated that
'much of the mess we are having to come and clean up today is because of your
illegal wars, your events in the past and the way you have run the safety of our

forces'.[1] Simply put, this was a Conservative government minister stating that a previous Labour government had prosecuted illegal wars. Although concern was expressed that such admissions may render the UK open to legal claims,[2] it remains the case that UK courts at least remain averse to adjudicating upon claims founded on government decisions to go to war that allegedly breach international law. Furthermore, the most relevant international court – the ICC – does not have jurisdiction over crimes of aggression allegedly committed by UK leaders.

Although the UK's record of military interventions since 1945 is patchy when judged by the standards of the *jus ad bellum*, it remains the case that the UK continues to be bound by those rules. Given the reluctance of domestic courts to entertain claims against the government based on breach of the *jus ad bellum*, at most it can be argued that the government has an unenforceable duty in domestic law not to send troops to fight in illegal wars.[3] Such matters remain to be settled, if at all, at the inter-governmental level. The lack of governmental liability is balanced to some extent by the prevailing view that soldiers are not exposed to any criminal liability arising from decisions to prosecute controversial wars. Following from this, the position is that there is no right of selective conscientious objection for soldiers believing that they are being deployed to illegal wars. Domestic courts are likely to continue to reject claims against the UK government for prosecuting illegal wars and dismiss claims by soldiers to selective conscientious objection. However, pressure will mount on the UK to accept the jurisdiction of the ICC over the crime of aggression and, once it does this, there will be an expectation that the UK courts will finally scrutinise decisions to go to war made by government ministers and military leaders. This, in turn, might serve to deter the government from prosecuting wars of questionable legality.

Under international criminal law and LOAC, the government has a duty to ensure that its soldiers do not commit war crimes and, if there is a failure to investigate and prosecute such offences, the ICC can take up the case. The gradual extraterritorial extension of human rights law has placed extra burdens on the government, not only to investigate deaths but more broadly to ensure that its soldiers do not violate the basic rights of civilians under their power

---

[1]   Hansard, HC, Vol 680, Col 998, 23 September 2020 (Wallace).

[2]   'Three Labour MPs lose roles after voting against overseas operations bill: Defence secretary Ben Wallace says bill is needed because of Labour's "illegal wars"', *The Guardian*, 23 September 2020.

[3]   In relation to claim under the Human Rights Act, Lady Hale stated that 'I cannot reasonably foresee that Strasbourg would construct out of article 2 a duty not to send soldiers to fight in an unlawful war' – *R (Gentle) v The Prime Minister* [2008] UKHL 20, para 57.

or control. Indeed, the evolutionary nature of human rights law has extended limited rights protection to soldiers themselves although this has yet to be confirmed by the ECtHR and, as its stands in domestic jurisprudence, is limited to a 'middle ground' of decision-making excluding both high-level policy decisions and on-the-ground military decisions.[4] How workable such a limited portal will be remains to be seen, but it at least raises the prospect of judicial scrutiny of systemic failures that result in the potentially life-threatening and, therefore, inexcusable under-equipping or under-resourcing of soldiers. However, it is worth noting that the continuing extension of human rights law is not necessarily unstoppable. The government has established an Independent HRA Review, which will report in 2021. One of the Review's terms of reference raises the following questions: 'In what circumstances does the HRA apply to acts of public authorities taking place outside the territory of the UK? What are the implications of the current position? Is there a case for change?'[5]

9.3   DUTIES AND RIGHTS OF SOLDIERS

Turning to military personnel, historically their duties far outweighed their rights. Soldiers in the First World War were expected to follow orders without question, or be subjected to harsh disciplinary measures including capital courts martial for desertion.[6] There is less coverage of the operation of British military justice in the Second World War, although Gerry Rubin recounts a number of courts martial from that period including that of a mutiny by soldiers from India based on Christmas Island in the face of a Japanese onslaught in 1942.[7] Mark Connelly and Walter Miller record that by the middle of 1942, after a series of defeats for the British armed forces, morale was low and 'many senior officers considered lax discipline to be the root cause'.[8] In response courts martial meted out harsh punishments in terms of incarceration and penal servitude for cowardice and desertion, although the 'abolition of the death penalty for desertion and cowardice in 1930 was regarded as a major blow to military discipline'.[9] Although due process appeared to be observed in these military courts, the evidence taken from a sample of courts martial held in North Africa points to a presumption of guilt and little consideration of the

---

[4]   *Smith and others (FC) v The Ministry of Defence* [2013] UKSC 41.
[5]   See https://www.gov.uk/guidance/independent-human-rights-act-review.
[6]   C.M. Corns and J. Hughes-Wilson, *Blindfold and Alone: British Military Executions in the Great War* (Cassell Military Paperbacks, 2005).
[7]   G.R. Rubin, *Murder, Mutiny and the Military* (Francis Boutle, 2005) 74.
[8]   M. Connelly and W. Miller, 'British Courts Martial in North Africa, 1940–1943' (2004) 15 *Twentieth Century British History* 217 at 218.
[9]   Ibid, 218. See the Army and Air Force Act (1930).

mental health of the defendants. Connelly and Miller conclude their careful examination of a sample of trials:

> The evidence suggests that soldiers were right to harbour doubts about the fairness of courts martial. It also reveals a determination to achieve convictions, which was usually achieved and upheld in some form even when the judge advocate had some qualms about the handling of the case. This determination might well be attributed to the desire to make examples and ensure the visibility of discipline rather than justice. It would be difficult to argue, from the evidence, that all the convictions were fully justified. Nearly two-thirds of those convicted of cowardice claimed to have lost control of themselves, and several had supporting evidence. Given the strains on soldiers, it would be difficult to maintain that none of these claims had validity.[10]

During the Second World War it seemed to be the case that procedural justice, embodied in a voluminous *Manual of Military Law*,[11] was insufficient to achieve a fair balance between the need for discipline on the one hand and assuring substantive justice for the defendants on the other. The failure to take account of PTSD and other mental illnesses is a thread running through military justice and, as recent courts martial show including that of Sergeant Blackman, still presents evidentiary problems for the court martial. While human rights law has certainly shifted the balance between discipline and justice towards the latter, the need to ensure that examples are made of accused soldiers in order to deter indiscipline by other soldiers is still present in the court martial process. Deterrence is a function of criminal justice, even more so in the military justice system, but not at the expense of valid defences or mitigations available to the accused.

Modern UK military law contains a core of discipline offences such as mutiny, desertion, absence without leave, disobedience to lawful orders, and conduct prejudicial to good order and discipline. The opaqueness of the latter offence has been filled by case law and practice, reducing criticisms that military law is simply a tool in the hands of COs, prosecutors and courts. Like UK service law, US military law also contains general offences such as conduct prejudicial to good order and discipline and 'conduct unbecoming an officer and a gentleman' under Articles 133 and 134 of the Uniform Code of Military Conduct. As in the UK, US courts have addressed arguments that such offences are too vague as to breach principles of natural justice and constitutional law. In *Parker v Levy*,[12] the US Supreme Court dismissed this argument, reasoning that 'over the years the bare statutory text had acquired a gloss that made its

---

[10]   Ibid, 241.
[11]   Ibid, 220. See The War Office, *Manual of Military Law* (HMSO, 1940).
[12]   *Parker v Levy*, 417 US 733 (1974).

sweep sufficiently clear to afford the fair notice required by due process'.[13] The US Supreme Court stated that it had been 'long recognised that the military is, by necessity, a specialized society separate from civilian society', which has 'developed laws and traditions of its own'.[14] It is difficult to imagine civilian courts being able to assess disciplinary offences properly, without a significant amount of input from military experts. It follows that in the UK it would be better to keep that expertise over disciplinary offences within a separate military justice system that is human rights law compliant so as to provide accused soldiers with sufficient protections. However, the argument that in order to maintain discipline the military justice system needs to maintain jurisdiction over criminal conduct offences such as murder, rape and assault committed by soldiers does not appear as convincing and will be returned to below.

In addition to numerous duties under UK service law, externally deployed soldiers are subject to an extra layer of duties deriving from various applicable domestic and international laws governing such matters as the use of force and the treatment and detention of disarmed combatants and civilians. These duties are brought within the military justice system under the Geneva Convention Act 1957, the International Criminal Court Act 2001, and the Armed Forces Act 2006.[15] The duties of a soldier in internal deployments to situations of emergency or violence short of armed conflict include restrictions on the use of non-lethal force to situations where the immediate object is to prevent crime including public order offences, to arrest offenders or to prevent escape. Lethal force can be used where absolutely necessary in these situations, which would normally be in self-defence or the defence of others.[16] The same rules apply in external deployments when soldiers are sent to situations short of armed conflict, for example if they are deployed to peacekeeping operations characterised by violence but not armed conflict. Essentially, when in internal or external deployments short of armed conflict, military personnel have to operate within a law enforcement legal framework. Those duties are encapsulated in the widely accepted UN Basic Principles on the Use of Force and Firearms by Law Enforcement Officials 1990.[17]

Under LOAC, soldiers have greater leeway to use lethal force against enemy combatants and civilians taking part in hostilities but, otherwise, must obey the principles of distinction and humanity prohibiting attacks on civilians and those rendered *hors de combat*. Those duties have been supplemented

---

[13]   Fidell (2016) 58. See below note 33.

[14]   *Parker v Levy* (1974).

[15]   Armed Forces Act (2006) section 42 and schedule 2.

[16]   J.A. Hessbruegge, *Human Rights and Personal Self-Defence in International Law* (Oxford University Press, 2017) 233.

[17]   UN Doc A/RES/45/121 (1990).

by further obligations imposed by the strictures of international criminal law, breach of which will constitute war crimes. This gives rise to a further duty on soldiers namely to disobey orders that are clearly unlawful under LOAC and/ or international criminal law. These are basic duties, but they add to a heavy burden of duties on soldiers.

It is true to say that human rights law adds directly to the duties of government and not to soldiers but, because soldiers are the paradigmatic state agents, soldiers have to respect and, where appropriate, protect the rights of civilians they encounter. One of the main difficulties government and soldiers face in this respect is when the use of potentially lethal force amounts to the assertion of jurisdiction over individuals, giving rise to state responsibility for any deaths resulting from an unlawful use of force (for example the shooting dead of an unarmed civilian). The individual criminal responsibility of the soldier would arise whether or not jurisdiction for the purposes of human rights law is asserted, but state responsibility depends on that assertion. While the current state of human rights law is that there has to be an additional level of control by soldiers over the civilian to amount to the assertion of jurisdiction by the UK under the ECHR, this is clearly unsustainable in the long run: rather it represents a transient point in the gradual extension (or possible retraction) of the extraterritorial application of human rights law.[18] However, while this is of concern to the government in understanding its duties under human rights law, for the soldier the unlawful use of force should always give rise to criminal responsibility. The paucity of prosecutions for alleged crimes committed by soldiers in Northern Ireland, Afghanistan and Iraq demonstrates weaknesses in the military justice system, not that soldiers are somehow excused from such acts.

Further uncertainty in the duties of government is found in the applicable framework governing detention, especially in NIACs where human rights law seems to provide a clearer and more robust set of protections than LOAC. Having said that, there is still a need to adapt human rights standards, which operate to govern detention in peacetime, to unstable situations of armed conflict where security detention is commonplace and necessary. The application of human rights law to military operations remains fraught with difficulties. The argument that only LOAC should apply in conditions of armed conflict remains a live one and has been given renewed life by the sustained criticisms from some influential quarters of the legalisation and juridification of warfare. However, from the soldier's perspective, the prohibition on abuse of prisoners

---

[18] See the Independent Human Rights Act Review established by the government, which will report in 2021.

applies irrespective of debates about whether that prohibition derives from human rights law, LOAC or the basic axioms of criminal law.

The rights and protections of soldiers can be listed more briefly, even though they have increased significantly in recent years. Protection from bullying and sexual harassment, which is a serious problem in the armed forces, is partially provided by the service complaints system, by the prosecution of alleged perpetrators of criminal conduct offences such as rape before a court martial in the service justice system, and by the occasional prosecution of the service offence of ill-treatment of subordinates.[19] The deficiencies in these avenues should be of serious concern to the military and the government, and are being addressed by the Defence Sub-Committee's inquiry into women and the armed forces, which has detailed the endemic problem of sexual offences against female soldiers and the high proportion of female complaints of BHD.[20]

Protections, rather than enforceable rights, can also be identified in armed conflict when soldiers captured or rendered *hors de combat* in an IAC should be treated humanely as PoWs under LOAC and wounded soldiers should receive treatment without discrimination. Protections of soldiers in a NIAC are much reduced in particular as regards capture, detention and ill-treatment. It is doubtful whether a captured soldier is better protected under human rights law in a NIAC. If the state in which they find themselves is a party to a human rights treaty such as the ICCPR, the duties arising therefrom, or from their equivalents under customary human rights law, only bind the state and not the usual enemy faced by British soldiers in a NIAC – a non-state armed group. This is partly why it is important to recognise that the UK has duties to protect the basic rights of its soldiers on deployment overseas by reducing the risk of death, serious injury or capture through under-resourcing or under-equipping. Soldiers have to be given the best chance of survival and it is principally their sending state, in practice the British government acting through the MoD and the chain of command, who can do this.

Soldiers have combatant immunity for acts of killing that accord with LOAC but should be prosecuted for unlawful killings. However, in these cases they have the right, derived from basic principles of due process and fair trial, to have any mental illness affecting their judgement on the battlefield to be properly assessed and put before the court martial. The court should take such

---

[19]   Court martial results in 2019 show that there were four cases of charges brought before a court martial of ill-treatment of a subordinate, in three of which the defendant was found not guilty https://www.gov.uk/government/publications/court-martial -results-from-the-military-court-centres.

[20]   House of Commons Defence Committee, 'Protecting those who protect us: Women in the Armed Forces from Recruitment to Civilian Life', Second Report of Session 2021-22, HC 154, 25 July 2021.

evidence into account in deciding on issues such as whether the conduct under scrutiny constitutes murder or manslaughter as well as in determining the sentence to be served. The pervading strong assumption found in courts martial that all soldiers are trained to be resilient in the face of existential violence and that anyone falling short of the high standards of discipline expected of British soldiers should be punished without fear or favour (a collective view of soldiers), is a presumption which over the years has proved hard to rebut. This presumption should be replaced with a recognition of the individuality of soldiers, requiring a genuine inquiry into the defendant's mental health at the time of the offence. Although human rights law has benefited the soldier in recent years by improving the procedural aspects of due process in courts martial, a fair trial does not simply mean that the court is impartial and independent, but also that the whole of the evidence surrounding the conduct in question is considered. The state cannot put soldiers into high-risk situations in inhospitable combat zones and expect all to perform to the highest standards, especially when the government has not provided the resources and equipment to effectively underpin that operation.[21] Unlawful conduct by soldiers cannot be excused but it needs to be fully understood.

9.4   RESTRICTING ACCOUNTABILITY FOR VIOLATIONS

Government decisions to deploy troops remain non-justiciable before domestic courts, but that has not prevented cases being brought against the government and against soldiers for unlawful conduct following deployments. As has been seen in this book, there have been a relatively limited number of successful human rights and negligence claims brought by soldiers and civilians against the government. There have been criminal prosecutions of soldiers for offences committed in Northern Ireland, and trials of soldiers by court martial for offences committed in Iraq and Afghanistan, although such trials appear to provide limited accountability overall, with few convictions.

---

[21]   In the Aitken Report (2008) it was noted that with the collapse of law and order in Iraq after the invasion of that country in 2003 'the British Army was the sole agent of law and order within its area of operations … In May 2003, the same soldiers who had just fought a high-intensity, conventional war were expected to convert, almost overnight, into the only people capable of providing the agencies of government and humanitarian relief for the people of Southern Iraq. Battlegroups (comprising a Lieutenant Colonel and about 500 solders) were allocated areas of responsibilities comprising hundreds of square miles: companies (a Major with about 100 men under command) were given whole towns to run'. British troops 'were very thinly spread on the ground': 'The Aitken Report, 'An Investigation into Cases of Deliberate Abuse and Unlawful Killing in Iraq in 2003 and 2004' (Army) 25 January 2008, paras 8–9.

According to the Aitken Report of 2008, after the invasion of Iraq in March 2003 'over 120,000 members of the Armed Forces' had served in the region. Up to the time the Report was delivered, '229 allegations of criminal activity have been investigated by the Service Police, 20 of which have been dealt with, either by court martial trial or by summary dealing within the chain of command'. Out of these 20, six cases involved allegations of deliberate abuse resulting in the death or injury of Iraqi civilians. Of the four cases involving Iraqi deaths as a result of deliberate abuse, the Army Prosecuting Authority brought charges in three 'yet not one conviction for murder or manslaughter has been recorded'.[22]

In 2014, a RMP investigation (Operation Northmoor) was launched into allegations surrounding detention operations by British forces in Afghanistan between 2005–2013. Six hundred and seventy-five allegations were investigated but no case was referred for prosecution by the SPA.[23] In Northern Ireland, the collapse of the prosecution of Soldiers A and C in May 2021 for the alleged murder of an IRA commander in 1972, has led to doubts being cast over the future success of further legacy prosecutions,[24] as well as government promises to introduce further legislation to protect former soldiers from such prosecutions.[25]

Such legislation covering the actions of soldiers during their domestic deployment to Northern Ireland before the Good Friday Accords of 1998 will build on the Overseas Operations (Service Personnel and Veterans) Act, which after much debate and a number of amendments received Royal Assent

---

[22]   Ibid, paras 2, 3 and 27.
[23]   C. Mills and J. Dawson, 'Overseas Operations (Service Personnel and Veterans) Bill 2019-21', House of Commons Library, Briefing Paper, No 8983, 22 September 2020, 14–16. But see continuing allegations of war crimes by British forces in Afghanistan – 'Rogue SAS Afghanistan execution exposed by email trail', *The Sunday Times*, 2 August 2020. See also 'Australian special forces involved in murder of 39 Afghan civilians, war crimes report alleges: Brereton report finds prisoners were executed to "blood" junior soldiers and unlawful killings were deliberately covered up', *The Guardian*, 19 November 2020.
[24]   R. Carroll, 'Trial of ex-soldiers over 1972 killing of Official IRA member collapses: Two army veterans acquitted of Joe McCann's murder after judge ruled some evidence inadmissible', *The Guardian*, 4 May 2021.
[25]   H. Siddique, 'Bereaved families angry at reports of UK plan to ban Troubles-era prosecutions: Proposals to stop paramilitaries and soldiers from facing charges over incidents before Good Friday peace deal', *The Guardian*, 6 May 2021; B. Quinn, 'UK confirms plans to call time on Troubles prosecutions', *The Guardian*, 14 July 2021, in which it was reported that 'all criminal prosecutions relating to the Troubles and future attempts to take civil actions' will be blocked under proposed legislation, instead a new independent body likened to South Africa's Truth and Reconciliation Commission would be established.

in April 2021.[26] The Act reflects a desire by government to counter the trend towards the juridification of military matters by restricting the accountability of both soldiers and government for alleged violations, although the rationale given by the MoD for the legislation was that 'the uniquely challenging context of overseas military operations, and the exceptional demands and stresses to which Her Majesty's forces are subject on such operations' should be 'taken into account in relation to legal proceedings arising from historical overseas operations'.[27]

The Overseas Operations Act covers criminal allegations in Part 1, while Part 2 covers civil claims. Part 1 includes a strong presumption against prosecution of soldiers for alleged offences committed during overseas operations after the lapse of five years from the date of the alleged offence.[28] After changes to the original Bill sexual offences, torture, crimes against humanity, genocide, and war crimes, but not murder per se, are excluded from the provisions of Part 1.[29] Part 2 purports to narrow the opportunity for claimants to bring civil and HRA claims, not by reducing the primary limitation period for such claims, which remains three years for civil claims and one year for HRA claims, but by providing for an absolute limitation period of six years, after which the courts will no longer have discretion to extend the time period.[30] It is clear that this Part is not only designed to protect individuals from historic civil claims arising out of military operations overseas but applies 'in the same way to all claimants bringing claims connected with overseas operations against the Ministry of Defence, whether they are military personnel ... or local nationals'.[31] While Part 1 reduces the accountability of soldiers for alleged crimes, Part 2 reduces the accountability of the government by partially closing the window for claims brought by soldiers or civilians against the government. In

---

[26] MoD, 'Overseas Operations (Service Personnel and Veterans) Act 2021: Guidance' 30 April 2021 https://www.gov.uk/government/publications/overseas -operations-service-personnel-and-veterans-bill/overseas-operations-service-personnel -and-veterans-act-2021-guidance.

[27] Ibid.

[28] Overseas Operations (Service Personnel and Veterans) Act (2021), section 2: 'it is to be exceptional for a relevant prosecutor making a decision to which that section applies to determine that proceedings should be brought against the person for the offence'.

[29] Ibid, schedule 1 (part 1).

[30] Ibid, section 8, schedule 2 (part 1).

[31] MoD, 'Overseas Operations (Service Personnel and Veterans) Act 2021: Guidance' 30 April 2021.

effect, the Act represents one of the ways in which the government is attempting to counter the increase in litigation against it and soldiers.[32]

9.5   MILITARY OR CIVILIAN JUSTICE?

The impact of human rights law on the military justice system in the UK has been profound, although it has not resulted in that system being subsumed into the civilian criminal justice system. The procedures and structures of military justice have largely been brought into line with criminal justice norms and processes, although the distinctness of the military justice system remains, in particular the summary process and court martial. The rights-pressures on governments more generally could signify that, according to Eugene Fidell, they 'may follow the course charted in Western Europe of largely abandoning military justice in favour of reliance on civilian justice systems, perhaps with some military involvement, as in the Netherlands'. He argues that the 'continued erosion of the powers of command can be anticipated in countries that retain freestanding military justice systems, with prosecutorial discretion shifting to lawyer decision makers (civilian or military)'. He further predicts that 'subject matter jurisdiction could also shrink (and with it, caseloads) if states begin to take seriously the human rights axiom that military justice must be reserved for offenses that have a substantial and direct connection to military service, rather than sweeping in any and all criminal conduct in which military personnel engage'.[33]

Panagiotis Kremmydiotis argues that the continuation of separate military courts is not incompatible with human rights norms, pointing to recent reforms to the military justice systems in New Zealand and Ireland, which 'ensure that accused persons under military jurisdiction enjoy comparable rights to civilians', while maintaining a form of military justice that enables discipline to be maintained.[34] Nevertheless, the momentum of human rights law, deepening and broadening the duties of the UK government towards individuals within its jurisdiction, including its own military personnel, may require further reforms of the military justice system. According to Christina Cerna the 'trend

---

[32]   Service personnel and veterans can continue to access the Armed Forces Compensation Scheme (AFCS), which has a seven-year limit for bringing claims.
[33]   E.R. Fidell, *Military Justice: A Very Short Introduction* (Oxford University Press, 2016) 101. See further F. Rosen, 'The End of Military Justice In Europe: An Agenda for Juridical Civil-military Relations' (2013) 24 *Small Wars & Insurgencies* 335.
[34]   P. Kremmydiotis, 'The Influence of Human Rights Law on the Reform of Military Justice' in A. Duxbury and M. Groves (eds), *Military Justice in the Modern Age* (Cambridge University Press, 2016) 311 at 324.

in international human rights law is to narrow the scope of military jurisdiction whereby it only applies to military officials who have committed military crimes and offences in the line of duty'.[35] This development would suggest that criminal conduct offences committed by UK military personnel should be tried by civilian criminal courts, but this issue is not so clear-cut and will be returned to below.

Suffice to say at this stage that human rights law is the main, but not the only, driver of change in the military justice system, but it has resulted in a shift in the scales of justice from one in which the government is primarily a rights-holder towards it increasingly being a duty-holder as well. The government may slow this shift down by further legislation building on the approach adopted in the Overseas Operations Act, but in so doing it will expose itself to an erosion in the legitimacy of its foreign policy in which it claims to be promoting human rights in other countries while seeking at the same time to protect itself from human rights claims arising from the conduct of its armed forces.

The basic aim of the military justice system is to underpin efficient, well-ordered and highly motivated armed forces. It must be borne in mind that these qualities are essential if the armed forces are to achieve the arduous tasks required of them in a dangerous and volatile world. The military justice system therefore reinforces discipline, good order and obedience by the firm enforcement of military laws that have been crafted over time to reflect those values. The system also supports the nature of military work as a collective enterprise, meaning that to succeed soldiers have to be able to rely on their comrades and commanders to follow and give orders that maximise the chances of success while minimising to an acceptable extent the risks to soldiers. Soldiers fight together and in order to do so effectively, both in terms of achieving military objectives and minimising the risk to life, discipline, good order and obedience are essential. Military justice reinforces the idea of the collective over the individual. It might be thought that these values are antithetical to good morale, but soldiers' lives depend on those values being upheld, and success in their actions depends upon duties performed collectively rather than individual freedoms. Soldiers have to accept that breaches of this code will be met by swift, firm but fair justice, in order to maintain discipline and retain confidence in the actions of their comrades. Military justice has to be harsh enough to deter widespread indiscipline or disobedience, which would be potentially catastrophic in the field, but fair enough to ensure that military personnel are sufficiently protected and, therefore, willing to accept the greater restrictions on their freedom that operate in the military context.

---

[35] C.M. Cerna, 'The Inter-American System and Military Justice' in Duxbury and Groves (2016) 325 at 345.

Civilian courts have supported these distinct values in appeals coming from the separate system of military justice. In what amounted to a robust defence of the Canadian system of military justice, albeit one that still could be improved, the Supreme Court of Canada emphasised the special characteristics of the system, which is 'tailored to the unique needs of the Armed Forces' by means of processes that 'assure the maintenance of discipline, efficiency and morale of the military'.[36] The US Supreme Court has stated that '[t]he military constitutes a specialized community governed by a separate discipline from that of the civilian';[37] and that 'the rights of men in the armed forces must perforce be conditioned to meet certain overriding demands of discipline and duty'.[38]

A soldier's limited freedoms and extensive duties are reflected in unique military offences aimed at preventing and punishing conduct which undermines good order, discipline and obedience to command, and in a military justice system that depends at the operational level on rudimentary summary hearings before a CO for less serious disciplinary infractions, with trial by a military court (court martial) for more serious matters. In order to mitigate the absence of fair trial protections at summary level, the military justice system in the UK has added a right of appeal from summary conviction as well as giving the defendant the right to opt for a court martial rather than a summary hearing. The summary hearing itself remains deficient in terms of due process, but essential in terms of maintaining the CO's control and discipline over their troops. The 'overriding demands of discipline and duty', in the words of the US Supreme Court, signify that the rights of due process that an individual has in summary hearings in the civilian criminal justice system cannot be guaranteed in the military justice system. However, the absence of due process can be mitigated by ensuring that the soldier's rights to choose a trial by court martial or to appeal against summary conviction or sentence are unhampered by pressure to demonstrate obedience to the COs.[39]

There is little doubt that the court martial has been significantly modified over the years since the advent of the ECHR and its gradual encroachment into the military justice system. Nonetheless, the court martial in the UK is still a military court with a board (jury) of military officers but with an independent judge, arriving at verdicts and sentences by an undisclosed majority. The reasons for these unique features still withstand scrutiny when the needs of the

---

[36]   *R v Stillman* 2019 SCC 40, para 2, citing *R v Moriarity* 2015 SCC 55 at para 46.
[37]   *Orloff v Willoughby*, 345 US 83, 345 US 94 (1953).
[38]   *Burns v Wilson*, 346 US 137, 346 US 140 (1953).
[39]   A.E. Tshivhase, 'The Future of Military Summary Trials in the Modern Age' in Duxbury and Groves (2016) 347.

military are borne in mind.[40] The specialist board is essential to maintain the values of the military and to understand the actions of soldiers, and the majority verdict is a product of the need for swift and decisive justice. The majority verdict, however, looks increasingly out of line with civilian criminal courts, particularly when those courts have overlapping jurisdiction over criminal conduct offences committed by soldiers. While undisclosed majorities may be justified in relation to disciplinary offences, which more directly underpin the need for efficiency and discipline, they seem unfair for criminal conduct offences, which, if tried before a Crown Court, would require at least a 10–2 majority verdict for conviction. Given that the boards in courts martial are normally smaller (again for reasons of efficiency) a similar requirement would mean that conviction would require all but one member of the board to find guilt for a conviction. In fact, the Armed Forces Bill of 2021, when enacted, will require qualified majorities for any conviction and sentence.[41]

The above discussion assumes that the court martial continues to retain jurisdiction over criminal conduct offences. In this regard, the Decaux Principles, developed under UN auspices in 2006, recommended limiting the 'functional authority of military courts' in terms of jurisdiction to 'offences of a strictly military nature committed by military personnel'.[42] According to Decaux, this limitation derives from the functional necessity of having a specialist form of justice applicable to field operations, where normal civilian courts are prevented from exercising jurisdiction for practical reasons.[43] This conception would confine the court martial, as well as the broader military justice system, not only to disciplinary offences but only to those committed while on deployment overseas, disregarding the needs of discipline and good order which apply to the armed forces whether at home or abroad.

The argument for restricting the jurisdiction of the court martial to military offences seems to be driven by a presumption that military courts are flawed forms of justice,[44] whose operation should be confined to an irreducible min-

---

[40] P. Rowe, 'How Well Do International Human Rights Bodies Understand Military Courts?' in Duxbury and Groves (2016) 15 at 17.

[41] The Armed Forces Bill (2021) clause 2, introduces qualified majority verdicts for boards of six or five lay members. It provides that where there are six lay members of the board, five must agree; where there are five, four must agree; and where there are three, two must agree https://publications.parliament.uk/pa/bills/cbill/58-01/0244/en/200244en.pdf.

[42] 'Draft Principles Governing the Administration of Justice through Military Tribunals' (Decaux Principles) UN Commission on Human Rights, UN Doc E/CN.4/2006/58, 13 January 2006, principle 8.

[43] Ibid, para 29.

[44] There is certainly evidence that military courts have been used as a repressive form of justice in a number of countries. See for example, UN Commission on Human

imum.[45] If justice equivalent to that delivered by civilian criminal courts can be delivered by military courts when trying criminal conduct offences that presumption is rebutted. However, there are serious problems in ensuring justice for victims of rape and sexual abuse in the military justice system, where conviction rates are considerably lower than in the civilian system of criminal justice.[46] There are strong arguments for trying these cases in the court that gives the best chance of delivering justice to the victim, which may mean within the civilian system.

In contrast to the UK system of military justice, international human rights law has had little impact on the US system of military justice. Although the US has ratified the ICCPR, it has not ratified the Optional Protocol allowing for individual complaints to be filed with the Human Rights Committee, meaning that 'the Covenant remains essentially a dead letter' for the US 'from the standpoint of legal effect'.[47] That aside, Charles Dunlap's explanation of the evolution of the US military justice system mirrors that of other countries including the UK: in particular 'the need to maintain discipline under the enormous stress of combat and the high stakes of war', which impelled the creation of a 'separate and, in many ways, unique justice system'.[48] This has resulted in a 'criminal law process in which military needs sometimes take precedence over certain rights-centred formalisms' of the civilian justice system.[49]

Nonetheless, the US military justice system has also seen a move towards civilianisation and judicialisation, which, according to Dunlap, has resulted in 'modifications that have often proved ill-suited to combat zones'.[50] The purposes of the US military justice system are specified in the US Manual for Courts-Martial (MCM): 'to promote justice, to assist in maintaining good order and discipline in the armed forces, to promote efficiency and effectiveness in the military establishment, and thereby strengthen the national security of the United States'.[51] Despite the increasing effects of civilianisation on the US military justice system, Dunlap argues that the dictum of the Supreme

---

Rights, 'Report of the Special Rapporteur on the independence of judges and lawyers', UN Doc E/CN.4/2005/60, 20 January 2005, paras 38–41.

[45] Decaux Principles (2006), para 29.

[46] See Chapter 8.

[47] Fidell (2016) 97.

[48] C.J. Dunlap, 'Military Justice' in D.M. Kennedy (ed.), *The Modern American Military* (Oxford University Press, 2013) 241.

[49] Ibid, 241.

[50] Ibid, 242.

[51] 'Manual for Courts-Martial United States' (2019 edition) Part I.3 https://jsc .defense.gov/Portals/99/Documents/2019%20MCM%20(Final)%20(20190108).pdf ?ver=2019-01-11-115724-610.

Court in *Reid v Covert* (1957) remains largely true;[52] namely that 'it has not been clearly settled to what extent the *Bill of Rights* and other protective parts of the constitution apply to military trials'.[53]

While the constitutional protections for US soldiers are unclear, the arguably harsher resultant military justice system has not necessarily led to better discipline or increased efficiency in the US when compared to other militaries where soldiers' rights protection is stronger. The My Lai killings in Vietnam in 1968 are the most infamous but as Dunlap relates: 'incidents from the wars in Iraq and Afghanistan indicate an erosion of discipline'.[54] However, he argues that the failures of the military justice system in securing convictions for a number of these incidents may be a result of 'saddling commanders in austere location with adhering to many of the same intricacies of a domestic judicial system'.[55] This raises the question of whether civilianisation prevents convictions, where they seem justified. The answer is likely to be a combination of factors operating alongside the growth of civilian-like protections for soldiers, including the difficulty of securing evidence and reliable witnesses in combat zones. More deeply, the endemic self-protecting nature of a separate military society can be pointed to.[56] This is reflected in regimental amnesia (a form of self-protection for soldiers), and the unwillingness to prosecute commanders on the basis of alleged failures of command responsibility. If the military justice system is to retain its autonomy and avoid being integrated into the wider system of civilian justice, it has to tackle these issues.

An unwillingness to consider command responsibility, particularly when British forces are thin on the ground, is reflected in the Aitken Report of 2008 regarding misconduct of British soldiers in Iraq: '[i]n hindsight, we now know that some soldiers acted outside the law in the way they dealt with local criminals. However, diligent they were, commanders were unable to be everywhere, and so were physically unable to supervise their troops to the extent they should; as a result, when those instances did occur, they were less likely to be spotted and prevented'. The Report paid lip service to command responsibility – 'whilst tasks can be delegated, responsibility for them can never be

---

[52] Dunlap (2013) 246.
[53] *Reid v Covert*, 354 US 1, 37 (1957).
[54] Dunlap (2013) 259.
[55] Ibid, 261.
[56] There is also evidence of the existence of separate groups within the military society, particularly in special forces, which can promote a culture of brutality amongst that sub-society. See, for example, the evidence of war crimes committed by Australian special forces in Afghanistan – Major General Justice Paul Brereton, Inspector-General of the Australian Defence Force, 'Report of Inquiry into Questions of Unlawful Conduct Concerning the Special Operations Task Group in Afghanistan', 19 November 2020.

delegated: that responsibility remains with the commander'. However, with forces being overstretched the 'luxury' of command supervision of troops was often lost: '[w]ith all their other duties, the commanders on the ground cannot reasonably be blamed for failing to identify what may or may not have been a trend'.[57] This disregards the fact that the criminal responsibility of commanders, at least in the context of war crimes, requires that the commander knew or 'should have known' that forces under their command and control were committing such crimes, and that they had failed to take all necessary and reasonable measures to repress their commission.[58] Failure to prosecute commanders weakens the military justice system and its claims to autonomy.

Up to the middle of the 20th century, military regulations, discipline by commanders and the awards of courts martial escaped the scrutiny of the civil courts. The military was indeed an autonomous entity or separate self-governing society and the military justice system helped to strengthen this autonomy. The period of civilianisation that followed, in which the military justice system consensually incorporated many of the standards and processes from the wider civilian criminal justice system, was in a sense inevitable if the armed forces were to retain that autonomy. The uneven application of criminal law to soldiers serving in Northern Ireland demonstrated how difficult it was to continue to see soldiers as citizens in situations of internal violence, but the jurisprudence did at least show that the military was covered by the rule of law. The process of partial integration with the wider justice system, once started, is difficult to stop and is shown by the increasing assertion of rights by soldiers almost as an instinctive response to the increased number of duties being imposed upon them by domestic and international law. This is not confined to the criminal sphere but is also shown by the increasing number of compensation claims made by soldiers for wrongful acts.[59]

According to Eugene Fidell the 'ultimate in civilianization' is the abolition of military courts 'at least in peacetime', giving the examples of Germany and France where criminal cases against military personnel are handled by civilian courts and prosecutors. In the Netherlands, such cases are also adjudicated

---

[57]   Aitken Report (2008) paras 10–12, 37.

[58]   Rome Statute of the International Criminal Court (1998) Article 28.

[59]   These claims have varying degrees of success. See, for example, the failure under the Limitations Act (1980) of the claims of service personnel for illnesses caused by exposure to radiation when witnessing nuclear weapons' tests undertaken by the UK in the Pacific in the 1950s: *Ministry of Defence v AB & Others* [2012] UKSC 9. See also the failure of a claim for damages by a soldier who contracted Q-fever while serving in Afghanistan: *Bass v Ministry of Defence* [2020] EWHC 36 (QB). In contrast, in *Inglis v Ministry of Defence* [2019] EWHC 1153 (QB), a soldier succeeded in a claim for damages for hearing loss suffered while serving in the Royal Marines.

before a specific civilian criminal court in Arnhem. In such cases, a judge is provided by the Dutch military and it provides support to the prosecutors – 'this too is civilianization but not the high-octane variety found in Germany or France'.[60] The focus on the trial forum tends to ignore the more fundamental necessity of having a separate military justice system when on deployment. In these situations, the military justice system is increasingly civilianised, but it remains of necessity a separate portable system.

This need for, and problems of, a portable system of military justice are illustrated in the *Jaloud* case of 2014 before the ECtHR. The applicant alleged that Article 2 of the ECHR protecting the right to life had been violated by the Netherlands, in particular that the investigation into the death of his son had been inadequate.[61] The incident that led to the loss of life involved Dutch soldiers firing at a car that had approached a checkpoint in Iraq, where they formed part of the multinational force operating under UN Security Council mandate.[62] In terms of the extraterritorial application of the ECHR, the Court found that the Netherlands 'exercised its "jurisdiction" within the limits of its … mission and for the purpose of asserting authority and control over persons passing through the checkpoint'.[63] The Court balanced the operational difficulties faced by the Dutch military in Iraq against the rights protected in the ECHR. The ECtHR was 'prepared to make reasonable allowances for the relatively difficult conditions under which the Netherlands military and investigators had to work', including the presence of armed and hostile elements. However, the Court found that the investigation into the death in question failed to meet the standards required by Article 2 in a number of ways: the lack of availability of key documents; the lack of precautions in preventing collusion between soldiers; an inadequate autopsy; and the fact that key material evidence was mislaid. The Court concluded that 'it cannot be found that these failings were inevitable, even in the particularly difficult conditions prevailing in Iraq at the relevant time'.[64]

The Court dismissed the applicants' arguments that alleged deeper systemic weaknesses in the Dutch military justice system, questioning in particular the independence of the military justice system from the regular army in terms of investigation and prosecution.[65] The applicants had argued that the inde-

---

[60] Fidell (2016) 26. See further B. van Hoek, 'Military Criminal Justice in the Netherlands: The 'Civil Swing' of the Military Judicial Order' in Duxbury and Groves (2016) 218.

[61] *Jaloud v The Netherlands*, Appl No 47708/08, 20 November 2014, para 3.

[62] Ibid, paras 12 and 53. See UN Doc S/RES/1483 (2003).

[63] Ibid, para 152.

[64] Ibid, para 228.

[65] Ibid, paras 159, 189–90, 196.

pendence of the system was undermined by the fact that the Royal Military Constabulary Unit in Iraq was under the sole command of the Netherlands' battalion commander and shared living quarters with regular troops, and further by the presence of a serving army officer in the Military Chamber of the Arnhem Military Court of Appeal.[66] The latter argument was dismissed as the military member of the Court was qualified for judicial office and 'his functional independence and impartiality are the same as those of civilian judges'.[67] The former argument, that there appeared to be blurred lines between the military police and regular troops, was dismissed on the grounds of lack of evidence of any impairment of the investigation by the military police.[68] However, if the military is to keep its distinct system of justice, which is essential to maintain its constitutional position as a separate society, then the military justice system has to be at certain key points separate from the military. This may be the culmination of a number of elements: the presence of a civilian judge in charge of the court martial is one, but another is the independence of the investigation and prosecution of the case, and any appearance otherwise should be avoided. The Court arguably missed the opportunity to make these points in *Jaloud* by concentrating on the failings in the case before it rather than some of the worrying systemic weaknesses in the Dutch military justice system. Military justice is no longer hidden in the shadows, and it will be continually evaluated within a wider concept of justice, including comparisons to its civilian counterpart.

9.6   LEGALISATION: 'LAWFARE' OR JUSTICE?

Cases such as *Jaloud* mark the move from consensual civilianisation, in which the military willingly adopts standards and processes found in civilian criminal justice, towards juridification embodying the coercive extension to military society of civilian legal norms through litigation. The pressure to change military law comes from a combination of international and regional courts, but also from litigation before domestic courts. As Anthony Forster states: '[a] rights-based system has replaced self-regulation ... Judicial outcomes are permanently open to new challenge based on different readings of where the proper balance lies'.[69] The dynamic nature of human rights jurisprudence, whereby in each case the court interprets and develops the very broad texts of human rights treaties, not only produces uncertainty in the armed services

---

[66]   Ibid, para 106.
[67]   Ibid, para 196.
[68]   Ibid, para 189.
[69]   A. Forster, 'British Judicial Engagement and the Juridification of the Armed Forces' (2012) 88 *International Affairs* 283 at 299.

where certainty and clarity are not only valued but also necessary, but has also led to allegations of 'lawfare'. The idea that the armed forces are being 'defeated' in legal battles, and that the legal constraints placed on the government, the military and the soldier are effectively helping the enemy, has taken hold.

In a foreword to the first 'Fog of Law' report by the Policy Exchange think-tank in 2013, Moses LJ evocatively wrote: '[n]one have succeeded in defeating the armed forces of the United Kingdom. Napoleon, Falkenhayn and Hitler could not. But where these enemies failed, our own legal institutions threaten to succeed.'[70] In a second report of 2015, the authors state that the 'British military is now thoroughly entangled in the net of human rights law – often to the benefit of our country's adversaries. The British armed forces remain the most accomplished in Europe; but they suffer courtroom defeat after courtroom defeat in London and Strasbourg': constituting a 'new form of judicial imperialism'.[71] Comparing defeat in the courtroom to defeat in battle, especially existential battles involving major military threats to the nation, is a disingenuous artifice, but reflects a deep-rooted predisposition to praise the armed forces and condemn criticisms of them. It also fails to recognise that human rights law may benefit soldiers who put their lives on the line in dangerous situations.

Helen McCartney asks whether the British soldier is hero, victim or villain?[72] Might it be that each soldier has the potential to be all three, and the answer is to prosecute the villain, protect or compensate the victim, and decorate the hero. The first requires a fair trial for the adjudication of clear breaches of duty; the second requires rights, protections and access to justice; and the third requires respect and recognition.

The real risk to soldiers is exposed in the first Policy Exchange Report where the authors argue that the 'juridification' of warfare represents a 'grave danger' to the British armed forces, but then admit that such forces are 'traditionally maintained ... at levels which might easily seem inadequate for the tasks which they are expected to face'. This potential weakness is said to be compensated by the innovation of commanders and soldiers thereby enabling the UK to 'maintain a smaller force' when compared to its rivals and yet one that remains able to 'more than match them on operations'.[73] Furthermore, the

---

[70]   T. Tugendhat and L. Croft, 'The Fog of Law: An Introduction to the Legal Erosion of British Fighting Power' (Policy Exchange, 2013) 7.

[71]   R. Etkins, J. Morgan and T. Tugendhat, 'Clearing the Fog of Law: Saving Our Armed Forces from Defeat by Judicial Diktat' (Policy Exchange, 2015) 7.

[72]   H. McCartney, 'Hero, Victim or Villain? The Public Image of the British Soldier and its Implications for Defence Policy' (2011) 27 *Defense & Security Analysis* 43.

[73]   Tugendhat and Croft (2013) 16.

first report states that '[s]mall militaries must be creative and take calculated risks if they are to prevail': soldiers must be war-fighters and not just professionals, '[b]ut this initiative risks being undermined by juridically-inspired caution'.[74] Another view might be that inadequate military forces are typically deployed by the UK and too much is expected of soldiers in terms of bravery, risk-taking and loss of life or injury – they are being expected to make sacrifices to make up for the failure to maintain an army of the size and equipment needed to fight expeditionary wars. As Max Hastings has stated: 'throughout its history, Britain has repeatedly sought to ignore the importance of mass on the battlefield, despatching inadequate forces to assert moral or strategic principles'.[75] Frank Ledwidge makes the point that 'there is nothing heroic in deploying too small a force to get a job done'. He relates the words of a former CO of the SAS: 'punching above your weight in the military, tactical sense is likely to get you killed'.[76] Deploying too few troops to battle situations unnecessarily endangers the lives of those soldiers.

The 'lawfare' critique recognises that even shorn away of what are argued to be inhibiting and unnecessary legal regimes, the government, military and soldier remain governed by LOAC. LOAC is designed for armed conflict and therefore should be at the core of the regulation of leaders, commanders and soldiers in combat situations. It was crafted as an essentially permissive regime allowing for the extensive use of lethal force embodied in the underpinning principle of 'military necessity', but subject to balancing principles of 'humanity', 'distinction' and 'proportionality', and consequent rules on protecting civilians, wounded soldiers and PoWs. Legal artifices aimed at retaining the exclusivity of LOAC such as assertion that it is the *lex specialis* have been shown to be unconvincing. LOAC will prevail in some instance (such as the taking of the life of an enemy combatant, or in the detention of PoWs), but in others where there are gaps in LOAC (such as detention in NIACS) human rights law prevails or at least influences.[77] In principle, the norms of LOAC and human rights law both apply in armed conflict, meaning that where they cannot be harmonised there is the potential for actions to be compliant with LOAC and yet breach human rights law.

It has been argued in this book that a more profound way of resolving the arguments about applicable laws is to consider the wider issues of justice

---

[74]   Ibid.

[75]   M. Hastings, *Finest Years: Churchill as Warlord 1940–45* (Harper Press, 2010) 129.

[76]   F. Ledwidge, *Losing Small Wars: British Military Failure in Iraq and Afghanistan* (Yale University Press, 2011) 130.

[77]   I. Park, *The Right to Life in Armed Conflict* (Oxford University Press, 2018) 104–5.

within which it is possible to understand the relationships between soldier and government, and soldier and society. For immediate purposes, it suffices to say that the scales of military justice have shifted towards balancing the established duties of obedience and sacrifice (of life and limb) of soldiers with limited rights: to fair trial and due process, but also to freedom from inhuman and degrading treatment, and the right to life. The method of achieving the synthesis of LOAC with human rights law is outlined by the Human Rights Committee in its General Comment on the right to life as protected by Article 6 of the ICCPR:

> Like the rest of the Covenant, article 6 continues to apply also in situations of armed conflict to which the rules of international humanitarian law are applicable, including to the conduct of hostilities. While rules of international humanitarian law may be relevant for the interpretation and application of article 6 when the situation calls for their application, both spheres of law are complementary, not mutually exclusive. Use of lethal force consistent with international humanitarian law and other applicable international law norms is, in general, not arbitrary. By contrast, practices inconsistent with international humanitarian law, entailing a risk to the lives of civilians and other persons protected by international humanitarian law, including the targeting of civilians, civilian objects and objects indispensable to the survival of the civilian population, indiscriminate attacks, failure to apply the principles of precaution and proportionality, and the use of human shields, would also violate article 6 of the Covenant. States parties should, in general, disclose the criteria for attacking with lethal force individuals or objects whose targeting is expected to result in deprivation of life, including the legal basis for specific attacks, the process of identification of military targets and combatants or persons taking a direct part in hostilities, the circumstances in which relevant means and methods of warfare have been used, and whether less harmful alternatives were considered. They must also investigate alleged or suspected violations of article 6 in situations of armed conflict in accordance with the relevant international standards.[78]

The Human Rights Committee's analysis shows that the 'lawfare' artifice, which sets up the argument as a choice between LOAC and human rights law, is a distraction, since logically they both apply (along with other applicable regimes such as refugee law, international environmental law as well as international criminal law). Indeed, although the duties created under both LOAC and human rights law fall on states (as parties to the relevant treaties), they are primarily enforced against soldiers in the case of LOAC and states in the case of human rights law. Under human rights law, the duty to ensure the human rights of individuals falls on the government as does the responsibility for a violation of that duty, for example if soldiers violate the right to life of civilians. Soldiers

---

[78] Human Rights Committee, General Comment 36 on the Right to Life, UN Doc CCPR/C/GC/36, 30 October 2018, para 64.

should, however, be prosecuted following investigations in fulfilment of the procedural obligations required under Article 2 of the ECHR. The purposes of such investigations are to ensure the 'effective implementation of the domestic laws which protect the right to life and ensure the accountability of state agents or bodies for deaths occurring under their responsibility'.[79]

Rather than viewing human rights as antithetical to operational effectiveness, the premise of this book is that ensuring human rights compliance in military operations, whether in conflict or otherwise, is essential for the legitimacy of the operation and, therefore, the longer-term effectiveness of military operations and any peace-building efforts that follow from them. Military operations can be undertaken for different purposes: self-defence; peace enforcement; or peace support, stabilisation and restoration, but the conduct of those operations whether short or long term sets the framework for what follows. It would be very difficult to enforce, keep and build the peace if the military operation is not undertaken in accordance with basic human rights laws. Although LOAC has lost any link to just war doctrine in that it applies equally to both sides irrespective of the stigma of aggression, in wars of choice where a state has opted to intervene militarily in another state, the justice of its cause as well as its conduct will be scrutinised against all applicable standards, not just the *jus ad bellum* and LOAC, but also human rights law.

Furthermore, although LOAC has military necessity built into its framework as a basic principle it also has humanity.[80] Therefore, LOAC is not incompatible with human rights law per se. However, in terms of philosophy LOAC and human rights law are different. LOAC is designed to ensure that war is fought between combatants and that non-combatants are protected as much as possible, while human rights law is designed to protect the rights of individuals from abuse by states and their agents, but also requiring that states ensure that the rights of persons under its jurisdiction are protected. Military necessity is at the heart of LOAC, allowing for proportionate collateral damage, while human rights law can be qualified by the requirements of state security in certain circumstances, including through derogation from certain rights. Thus, state concerns can erode the protection of civilians and individuals under both regimes, although they are not necessarily always the same concerns. Furthermore, while human rights law is subject to significant scrutiny by civilian courts, LOAC in primarily enforced through the UK's military justice system, with the possibility of cases going to the ICC. Ultimately, the ICC's investigations

---

[79]   *R (Catherine Smith) v Secretary of State for Defence* [2010] UKSC 29 at para 64 (Lord Phillips).

[80]   See UK Ministry of Defence, *The Manual of the Law of Armed Conflict* (Oxford University Press, 2004) 21–6.

into war crimes alleged to have been committed by British soldiers in Iraq did not result in any prosecutions before the ICC, but the government and military have been put on notice for any future operations.[81]

Just as the rules of LOAC governing IACs and NIACs have become more sophisticated since the Second World War, so international human rights law has deepened and broadened since the Universal Declaration of Human Rights was adopted in 1948, as the abstract norms in human rights treaties have been applied by courts to concrete cases. It is not possible to retreat from the idea universalised in 1948, that all individuals have inherent rights in times of war and peace. Indeed, it is in times of war that human rights come under the greatest threat and therefore require greater protection. Although the government might seek to push back against human rights being applicable extraterritorially by trying to extend the idea of derogation to overseas situations, as well as trying to limit the extension of the concept of jurisdiction,[82] these may well only delay the increasing extension of human rights law to military operations. Increasingly wars are being fought over the basic rights of citizens and so it would be incongruous to state that human rights law is inapplicable during that conflict. It follows that both civilians and soldiers are entitled in principle to human rights protection, but that can only be the case in practice if it can be established that the state has a duty to protect them in the circumstances. Thus, human rights law does not simply apply as a blanket protection wherever British troops are deployed. There is considerable difference between the ideal of an extensive range of universal *human rights* and the reality of *human rights law*, which recognises limitations upon a state's duty to respect and protect those rights. The practicalities of prosecuting wars signifies that the obligation to protect human rights has to be limited.

The attempted marginalisation of human rights law and the accompanying demonisation of lawyers who have helped bring human rights or civil compensation claims, and the worrying political interference with the military justice process (highlighted by Parliamentary debates on the Blackman case), distract

---

[81]   *BBC News*, 'Court finds UK war crimes but will not take action: The International Criminal Court says it will not take action against the UK, despite finding evidence British troops committed war crimes in Iraq', 9 December 2020 https://www.bbc.co.uk/news/uk-55247033. ICC, Office of the Prosecutor, 'Situation in Iraq/UK: Final Report', 9 December 2020 https://www.icc-cpi.int/itemsDocuments/201209-otp-final-report-iraq-uk-eng.pdf.

[82]   The Independent Human Rights Act Review will report in 2021. One of its terms of reference raises the following questions: 'In what circumstances does the HRA apply to acts of public authorities taking place outside the territory of the UK? What are the implications of the current position? Is there a case for change?' https://assets.publishing.service.gov.uk/government/uploads/system/uploads/attachment_data/file/953347/human-rights-review-tor.pdf.

from a number of wider issues of justice. These include: the inadequacies of the system for uncovering the truth and delivering accountability where there have been allegations of systematic abuses by soldiers; the failure to enforce command responsibility in international criminal law; the continuing blindness of the military justice system in identifying mental illness in soldiers; the failure to protect women in the armed forces from BHD; as well as the weaknesses in the military justice system in addressing the serious and continuing incidence of rape and sexual abuse in the armed forces. It is difficult to see how these issues can be addressed and justice upheld except by greater legalisation accompanied by fair and effective judicial and quasi-judicial processes.

9.7   MILITARY COVENANT OR SOCIAL CONTRACT?

The Lockean idea of a social contract between citizen and state has recently been revived in the military context by the introduction into political and legal debate of the Military Covenant. In terms of content, the Covenant is based on an exchange between soldiers and state, namely that soldiers give up their rights as citizens in return for proper support and treatment, but without giving soldiers legal rights to enforce governmental duties to provide that support and treatment. The net result of the Covenant is that soldiers are required to continue to relinquish civil liberties and human rights inherently belonging to individuals in a society but are being given no clear rights of access to support or treatment in return. The duties on the state seem general and depend upon self-policing, and the duties on the wider society seem to be moral rather than legal – basically comprising of an expectation that soldiers and veterans are shown respect commensurate with the sacrifices they have made. As such, the Military Covenant is clearly a one-sided contract. On the soldiers' side of the bargain their duties are legally grounded and enforceable through the military justice system, while on the government/society side their duties are morally based and largely unenforceable (although the Covenant may be used to buttress claims based on other grounds).

It is true to say that soldiers are state agents meaning that acts done in the performance of their functions are acts of state for the purposes of state responsibility, so that in internal and external deployments military actions which violate the rights of citizens or civilians within the state's jurisdiction give rise to the legal responsibility and liability of the state. In the context of the social contract between state and citizen (and other civilians within the jurisdiction of the state), the soldier is on the state side of the contract. However, that does not mean that a soldier is always to be legally associated with the state. Indeed, Forster concludes that the effect of juridification 'is a transformation from a "professional soldier" voluntarily eschewing their rights to a "citizen soldier" who is in a unique position, but whose fundamental rights are none-theless protected'.[83] Forster, is also falling into the 'either/or' trap. A member of the armed forces can be both professional and citizen soldier reflecting an 'increasingly complex network of subjectivities' enmeshing each individual in wider society.[84]

Although the military remains a much more structured society than the wider society within which it is situated, it is not immune from these changes. Just as a soldier can be a hero, victim and villain, they can be both a state agent and a citizen and as such they should in principle enjoy the same rights as other citizens, but with the qualification that those rights are to be adapted to military exigencies in ways that do not denigrate from their citizenship. This is reflected in a recommendation adopted by the Parliament of the Council of Europe in 2006 entitled 'human rights of members of the armed forces'.[85] In this resolution the Assembly recognised that 'the army is the institution which is responsible for protecting the state and defending the community. Combat is its *raison d'être*, the very purpose of its existence, and it is bound by the specific constraints of rules regarding unity, hierarchy, discipline and compli-ance with orders.' While accepting the unique constraints on the military, the Assembly then declared that it 'considers that members of the armed forces are citizens in uniform who must enjoy the same fundamental freedoms, including those set out in the European Convention on Human Rights ... and the revised European Social Charter ..., and the same protection of their rights and dignity as any other citizen, within the limits imposed by the specific exigencies of military duties'. The Assembly makes the point that 'members of the armed forces cannot be expected to respect humanitarian law and human rights in their operations unless respect for human rights is guaranteed within the army ranks'.[86]

Finally, the Assembly identifies fundamental rights that must be enjoyed by members of the armed forces as citizens: the right to life '(bearing in mind, however, the inherent dangers of the military profession)'; the right to protec-tion against torture and inhuman or degrading treatment or punishment; the prohibition of slavery, servitude, and 'employment in tasks incompatible with their assignment to the national defence service'; 'the right to legal protection in the event of violation of their rights, the right to freedom and safety, and

---

[83]   Forster (2012) 296.

[84]   B. de Sousa Santos, 'The Postmodern Transition: Law and Politics' in A. Sarat and T.K. Kearns (eds), *The Fate of the Law* (Michigan University Press, 1991) 79 at 105.

[85]   Council of Europe, Parliamentary Assembly, Recommendation 1742, 11 April 2006.

[86]   Ibid, paras 1–3.

the right to a fair trial by independent tribunals, as well as the right to appeal';
the prohibition of discrimination; the right to freedom of thought, conscience
and religion; the right to full enjoyment of civic rights, particularly the right to
vote; the right to respect for property; the right to marry and found a family'.
In addition, certain socio-economic rights must be enjoyed by soldiers: the
right to decent and adequate housing/accommodation; the right to receive fair
remuneration and a retirement pension; the right to health protection and work
security; and the right to decent and sufficient nutrition.[87] The contrast between
this substantial framework of rights and the lack of human rights content in
the Military Covenant is stark and reflects a profound distinction between the
soldier as citizen and the soldier as an arm of the state.

The panoply of applicable human rights identified by the Assembly, which
would seem normal in civilian life, seem onerous when applied to military life.
However, there is no reason why the framework should not apply when soldiers are not on deployment in combat zones or crisis situations. The Assembly
recognises that certain rights can be restricted even in these more benign
circumstances: freedom of association, assembly and the right to respect for
private and family life.[88] The challenge for military justice is to more precisely
identify the 'limits' upon protection of these rights 'imposed by the specific
exigencies of military duties'.[89] In some ways that process of delimitation has
only just begun in overseas deployments, not only in terms of the negative
obligation on the state not to violate the human rights of soldiers and civilians
within its jurisdiction, but also in terms of the positive obligations on the state
to protect the lives of soldiers.[90]

In *Smith v MoD* Lord Hope indicated that concerns over the practical consequences for the military and for the government of extending the right to life
to soldiers in situations of combat can be met in ways other than derogation.[91]
He pointed to the 'fair balance' to be 'struck between the competing interests
of the individual and of the community as a whole' when assessing positive
obligations under the ECHR, something that a government can do within the
wide margin of appreciation recognised by the ECtHR. Here Lord Hope points
to the 'competition between the interests of the state and those of the individual', which 'is no less acute where issues arise about the risk to life of soldiers
in the context of military operations conducted on the state's behalf'.[92] The
fact the 'the proper functioning of an army in a modern democracy includes

---

87   Ibid, para 10.
88   Ibid.
89   Ibid, para 3.
90   *Smith and others (FC) v The Ministry of Defence* [2013] UKSC 41.
91   Ibid, para 60 (Hope).
92   Ibid, para 61.

requiring those who serve in it to undertake' potentially 'inherently dangerous' operations, means that deployment per se does not violate the soldier's right to life.[93] The soldier's duty is to follow lawful orders ultimately coming from the government to protect democratic society even if this exposes them to a higher risk of death than a civilian-citizen. However, the social contract between state/society and soldier cannot be construed as removing the rights and protections of a soldier as citizen. Soldiers' duties are far more onerous than the civilian-citizen so that their rights cannot be guaranteed to the same extent, but they are not extinguished. This means that deployments per se do not violate a soldier's right to life even though the risk of death is increased but only as long as they are sent 'as part of an organised military force which is properly equipped and capable of defending itself'.[94]

The unnecessary loss of life caused by deployments of inadequately resourced or staffed military operations can no longer be excused in terms of soldiers bravely dying or being wounded in the line of duty, rather it should be assessed in terms as to whether the failures of government breach its positive obligations to protect life even in extreme circumstances. As made clear by Lord Hope it is neither impossible nor inappropriate to apply the ECHR 'to the relationship between the state and its armed forces as it exists in relation to overseas operations in matters such as, for example, the adequacy of equipment, planning or training'. That relationship cannot simply be one way, whereby the government has all the rights and powers, and service personnel have all the duties. Lord Hope recalls that 'there have been many cases where the death of service personnel indicates a systemic or operational failure on the part of the state, ranging from a failure to provide them with the equipment that was needed to protect life on the one hand to mistakes in the way they are deployed due to bad planning or inadequate appreciation of the risk to be faced on the other'. At the very least such failures should be subject to 'scrutiny in pursuance of the procedural obligation under art 2 of the Convention'.[95] Bearing in mind that the procedural obligation – to investigate as opposed to brushing such incidents under the carpet – is a limited and wholly retrospective protection of a soldier's right to life in circumstances where that life has already been lost, any objections to such minimal protection are morally indefensible if the social contract between state and soldier has any reciprocal content. It is true, as Lord Hope explains, that the substantive right protected under Article 2 is much denuded by the onerous duties placed on soldiers, and by the fact that they are being deployed to situations where opposing forces

---

[93]   Ibid, para 62.
[94]   Ibid, para 62.
[95]   Ibid, para 63.

will want to kill them. Furthermore, Lord Hope recognises that 'situations may develop where it is simply not possible to provide troops in time with all they need to conduct operations with the minimum of casualties'. For this reason, 'a court should be very slow indeed to question operational decisions made on the ground by commanders, whatever their rank or level of seniority'.[96]

As well as a judicial reluctance to inquire into operational decisions on the ground, political decisions about procurement concerning the allocation of finite resources to the three armed services, involving hugely expensive equipment, is not usually appropriate for review by a court.[97] The judicial concern to set clear and limited parameters for the protection of the right to life of soldiers is understandable given that deeper judicial scrutiny would indeed hinder (Lord Hope used the word 'disable') the ability of the 'state to defend itself, or its interests, at home or abroad'.[98] This argument is wholly convincing in the cases of wars of necessity (such as defending the UK from armed attack, which has a clear legal basis in international law), but less so in the case of wars of choice (such as invading a country in order to remove weapons of mass destruction (WMD), which does not have a legal basis in international law unless clearly authorised by the UN Security Council). In terms of the social contract, there is a difference between the state calling on soldiers to do their duty to defend the UK from attack where the country is relying on the military to protect it from existential threats; and ordering them to fight a war in a foreign country because the government, having weighed up the options (including diplomacy, sanctions and other forms of pressure), decides to intervene militarily. It can be argued that in the latter instance, the substantive rights of soldiers may be stronger and they might expect to be better protected. In justifying the narrow parameters where the courts may find violations of the substantive right to life Lord Hope concluded by declaring that the 'world is a dangerous place, and states cannot disable themselves from meeting its challenges. Ultimately democracy itself may be at risk.'[99] While the UK as a democratic state is defended when necessary by the armed forces, democracy has not manifestly been protected by intervening in Afghanistan, Iraq and Libya. Indeed, those interventions have not only led to further chaos by spawning even more violent armed groups, but arguably have weakened rather than strengthened democracy at home.

Following this line of argument, a soldier has a very strong if not absolute duty to defend the state in a war of necessity and the government has

---

[96] Ibid, para 64.
[97] Ibid, para 65.
[98] Ibid, para 66.
[99] Ibid, para 66.

a broad-ranging power to order them to do so. However, in a war of choice, the government should include in its calculations whether the risks to the lives of military personnel (taking into account the degree of danger, the preparedness of the armed forces, the numbers and equipment available) outweigh the risks to its interests. Given that Lord Hope recognises that the substantive right to life of soldiers varies 'according to the context',[100] the delimitation of that context becomes of great importance. Lord Hope confined the context to an evaluation of the situation once troops had been deployed. Further he con-fined the protection of the right to life to the space between high-level policy decisions and operational decisions on the ground. However, this limitation is clearly a judicial device to limit the justiciability of rights, which reflects the courts' historical reluctance to evaluate decisions to deploy troops.

While the limited protection of a soldier's human rights during combat might be expected, there are weaker objections to a more extensive protection of their rights outside that context. Nevertheless, there is clear judicial recogni-tion that military service entails a degree of separation from the normal mores and laws of society. The ECtHR has recognised that states with armed forces will as a consequence have systems of military discipline and, moreover, that they have a margin of appreciation in the design of those systems established to ensure military discipline but with the safeguard of rights protection. In *Engel v The Netherlands*, the ECtHR recognised that 'a system of military discipline ... by its very nature implied the possibility of placing on certain of the rights and freedoms of the members of these forces limitations incapable of being imposed on civilians', but the Court made it clear that the 'existence of such a system ... does not in itself run counter to' the obligations of state parties under the ECHR.[101] The limitations upon the state imposed by the ECHR 'are not identical for servicemen and civilians'.[102]

9.8   THE RATIONALE FOR MILITARY JUSTICE

The Canadian Supreme Court has recently considered the differential treat-ment of soldiers and civilians in terms of their rights as protected by the Canadian Charter of Rights. These judicial reflections were remarkably similar to those that are occurring in the UK, which is not surprising considering the shared legal heritage of the two countries. In *R v Stillman* (2019), the accused members of the Canadian armed forces were charged with service offences and

---

[100]   Ibid, para 64.
[101]   *Engel v The Netherlands*, Appl Nos 5100/71, 5101/71, 5102/71, 5354/72, 5370/72, 8 June 1976, para 57.
[102]   Ibid, para 59.

convicted by courts martial despite asserting their right to be tried by a civilian jury as guaranteed by the Canadian Charter of Rights and Freedoms (section 11(f)).[103] The Canadian Supreme Court, by a majority of five to two, dismissed this argument after engaging in a thorough review of the Canadian military justice system and its intersection with the Canadian Charter. Section 11(f) contains within it a 'military exception' by guaranteeing every person charged with a criminal offence carrying a punishment of at least five years' imprisonment the right to trial by jury 'except in the case of an offence under military law tried before a military tribunal'.[104] The accused had been convicted of civilian criminal offences which, as in the UK system, came within the jurisdiction of the Canadian military justice system as service offences by reason of the National Defence Act 1985 (section 130(1)(a)). They argued that the military exception only covered offences unique to the military such as mutiny and insubordination and was not intended to cover criminal offences such as fraud or sexual offences.[105] The Supreme Court held that when a serious criminal offence is tried as a service offence it qualifies as an offence under military law and therefore comes within the military exception.[106]

In a number of ways, the *Stillman* judgment amounted to a robust defence of the Canadian system of military justice, albeit one that still could be further improved, particularly in the matter of sexual misconduct.[107] The Supreme Court emphasised the special characteristics of a system of military justice 'tailored to the unique needs of the Armed Forces' by means of processes that 'assure the maintenance of discipline, efficiency and morale of the military'.[108] In an earlier judgment, the Canadian Supreme Court had affirmed that these special needs and processes required 'the existence of a parallel system of military law and tribunals, for the purpose of enforcing discipline in the military', when it considered whether the court martial system provided for trial by an independent and impartial tribunal as required by Article 11(d) of the Canadian Charter.[109] In *Stillman* the Supreme Court stated that this parallel system had evolved 'over time from a command-centric model of discipline to a full partner in administering justice alongside the civilian justice system'.[110]

---

[103] *R v Stillman* 2019 SCC 40.
[104] Ibid, para 1.
[105] Ibid, para 6.
[106] Ibid, para 9.
[107] Ibid, para 52, which recognised the ongoing problem of inappropriate sexual conduct identified by Marie Deschamps, 'External Review into Sexual Misconduct and Sexual Harassment in the Canadian Armed Forces' (2015).
[108] Ibid, para 2, citing *R v Moriarity* 2015 SCC 55 at para 46.
[109] *R v Genereux* [1992] 1 SCR 259 at 295.
[110] *Stillman* (2019) para 20.

While the 'purposes of the military justice system have remained consistent over the years, the complexion of the system itself has changed significantly over time in response to developments in law, military life, and society, more broadly'.[111] The Court stated that '[j]ust as the civilian criminal justice system grows and evolves in response to developments in law and society, so too does the military justice system', and further that it saw 'no reason to believe that this growth and evolution will not continue into the future'.[112] The idea of an evolving military justice system, consistent in its purposes but constantly adjusting to changes in society, applies to the UK system of military justice and challenges those who criticise the civilianisation and juridification of military life.

The approach of the Canadian Supreme Court to the issue of justice before it recognised that the right to a jury trial is not an absolute right and, more generally, that rights and their exceptions should be interpreted purposively: 'since a Charter exception can be understood only if the right it qualifies is understood, the court should consider the two together'.[113] According to the Supreme Court the 'right to a jury serves two main purposes'. 'First, at the individual level, it protects the accused by giving him or her the benefit of a trial by his or her peers.' 'Secondly, at the societal level, it provides a vehicle for public education about the criminal justice system and lends the weight of community standards to trial verdicts.'[114] The balancing of the rights of the individual and the needs of society also applies to the military exception that allows for a parallel system of military justice. In this regard, the Court found that in certain respects at least a military panel in a court martial 'is analogous to a jury, and over the years they have become more and more so'.[115] In contrast to the UK, Canadian courts martial have moved away from majority verdicts to requiring the panel to reach their decisions on guilt unanimously. Furthermore, the panel's involvement in sentencing had ceased in 2010, after which it was the judge who was tasked with imposing a sentence after a finding of guilty by the panel.[116] The first change has been mooted in the UK for courts martial boards, while the second may be in order if the court martial is to give the same guarantees as a civilian criminal court. Nevertheless, the Canadian Supreme Court stated that the military panel in a court martial is not a jury, not simply being of much smaller size 'thereby lowering the threshold for a finding of guilt', but because its members are drawn from the military community only.

---

[111] Ibid, para 36.
[112] Ibid, para 53.
[113] Ibid, para 22.
[114] Ibid, para 28.
[115] Ibid, para 67.
[116] Ibid, para 67.

'Thus, the community embodied by a panel is a particular one'.[117] The idea of 'members tried by members' fosters morale within the military by assuring the accused that he will be tried by those who understand military life with its duties and pressures while maintaining a commitment to uphold military law and its values, 'even where the underlying offence is an ordinary civil offence' found in criminal law.[118]

The extraterritorial application of military law and the necessity on occasions to hold a military trial outside Canada at short notice support the separation of military justice system from the ordinary criminal one and, moreover, 'help to explain why it has opted for a unique military panel rather than a jury one'.[119] As the Supreme Court stated: '[t]he military justice system has thus developed an alternative, portable, and efficient solution that can be implemented whenever and wherever needed', which 'in turn contributes to discipline, efficiency, and morale in the military'.[120] The purpose of the 'military exception' contained in section 11(f) of the Charter was thus found by the Court to be to 'recognize and affirm the existence of a separate military justice system tailored to the unique needs of the military, and to preserve the historical reality that jury trials in cases governed by military law have never existed in Canada'.[121]

In rejecting the accused's arguments that normal civilian criminal offences committed by service personnel did not have a sufficient 'military nexus' to be tried as service offences beyond the fact that the defendants were in the military, the Court cited its previous decision in *Moriarity* in 2015, where it had given a number of illustrations of why this is a flawed doctrine. One instance given by Court was of a member of the military committing an assault in a civil context, which 'may call into question that individual's capacity to show discipline in a military environment and to respect military authorities'. An officer engaged in drug trafficking justifies a 'rational connection between the discipline, efficiency and morale of the military and military prosecution for this conduct', while 'a member of the military who has been engaged in fraudulent conduct is less likely to be trusted by his or her peers'. The criminal behaviour in these examples 'relates to discipline, efficiency and morale even when [the soldiers] are not on duty, in uniform, or on a military base'.[122] Furthermore, upholding the fundamental purposes of the military justice system, which differ from those in the civilian justice system, means that the violation of ordi-

---

[117]   Ibid, para 68.
[118]   Ibid, para 70.
[119]   Ibid, para 71.
[120]   Ibid.
[121]   Ibid, para 80.
[122]   *Moriarity* (2015) paras 52–4.

nary criminal offences may warrant more serious punishments.[123] In Canada, as in the UK, the military prosecuting authorities may decide, pursuant to a directive, that certain cases are better tried by ordinary criminal courts, but this does not negate the principle that the military justice system has jurisdiction in instances of ordinary criminal conduct by members of the military, even if it might not be exercised in a particular case.[124] The Court concluded that 'where such an offence is tried before a military tribunal – as was the case for each of the accused persons in this instance – the military exception in s. 11(f) of the *Charter* is engaged', meaning that the accused persons' right to trial by jury had not been violated.[125]

There is undoubted pressure to narrow the jurisdiction of courts martial to service offences only and for them not to have jurisdiction over 'offences that have no relation to military service'.[126] Fidell argues that 'permitting the military to handle these cases unwisely increases the gulf between the armed forces and larger society'.[127] However, in *Solorio v United States*, the US Supreme Court held that the US Constitution did not prevent the court martial of military personnel for civilian criminal offences, which were not service-connected.[128] It is argued in this book that giving courts martial jurisdiction over criminal conduct offences as well as disciplinary offences, while serving the purpose of maintaining the military as a separate society, imposes an obligation on the military justice system to properly and transparently address the criminal conduct of soldiers within the wider society they are meant to serve. Military establishments are in many ways separate from the wider society they serve. However, if the social contract between soldier and society is to be a strong one then society's respect and support for soldiers, including respect for their rights, should be given in exchange for respect by soldiers for the constitutional and criminal laws protecting society. If the military justice system supports this strong social contract, by fairly trying and appropriately punishing soldiers who violate those laws, then its jurisdiction over criminal conduct as well as disciplinary offences is justified: military justice would be enforcing society's values as well as those specific to the military. Importantly, victims should be able to see justice being delivered as they would have done if the trial had been conducted in a civilian criminal court. The onus is on the military justice system to deliver accountability of soldiers for abuses committed,

---

[123] *Stillman* (2019) para 100.
[124] Ibid, para 102.
[125] Ibid.
[126] Fidell (2016) 47.
[127] Ibid, 47.
[128] *Solorio v United States*, 483 US 435 (1987), overruling *O'Callahan v Parker*, 395 US 258 (1969).

whether against detainees in Iraq or against female soldiers in the UK. At the moment it seems to be falling short in this regard.[129]

The right in question in *Stillman* – the right to jury trial in serious criminal cases – is not a universally recognised human right, but it is nonetheless an important constitutional right in common law countries such as Canada and the UK. The reasoning of the Canadian Supreme Court is therefore illuminating in terms of how it carefully analyses the ability of the court martial to provide justice to the accused in the absence of a jury, while upholding the unique values of the military. The continuous evolution of the military justice system to mirror as much as possible the protections and processes of the civilian criminal justice system is fundamental to the Court's acceptance of the continued need to maintain a separate system of military justice with jurisdiction over ordinary criminal conduct offences as well as offences under service law. In this way, the military justice system maintains its connection to the wider system of justice and relevance to changing societal values and conditions.

The Court thus accepted and indeed protected the idea of the military being a separate community, governed by special laws and processes including trial before a panel drawn from that community, but importantly looked to ensure that the system as a whole reflects the values of society. This can be viewed through the lens of a social contract between the members of the military and wider society, whereby soldiers accept the restrictions placed upon them by military justice but in return expect to be protected from unjust or unfair trial and punishment. Although the appeal to the civilian courts by the accused failed in *Stillman*, the judgment served as a check to ensure that the military justice system had adapted to these wider societal values, while still upholding those unique military values of discipline, efficiency and morale. This demonstrates that 'civilianisation' (in the sense of the incorporation of civilian norms) and even 'juridification' (in the sense of scrutiny by civilian courts) of military justice is essential if the system is to continue to retain its legitimacy.[130]

The right to a jury trial is not, unlike the right to life, an absolute right. However, the balancing between societal needs and values, and the rights and protections of the individual including the soldier, unites the judgments in *Stillman* by the Supreme Court of Canada in 2019 and that of *Smith v MoD* in 2013 given by the UK Supreme Court. The social contract – between society and soldier – needs to be borne in mind when restricting the rights of soldiers, rights that are enjoyed by civilians. The fundamental position has to be that

---

[129]   See discussion of abuse in Chapter 6 and protections in Chapter 8.

[130]   See further, C. Waters, 'Democratic Oversight through Courts and Tribunals' in Duxbury and Groves (2016) 36; P. Collins, 'The Civil Courts' Challenge to Military Justice and Its Impact on the Civil-military Relationship' in Duxbury and Groves (2016) 57.

soldiers have such rights, but they cannot always be protected to the same level as civilians. However, it is important to ensure that soldiers' rights are only restricted to the extent necessary to protect discipline, efficiency and morale in the military, and to enable it to fulfil the dangerous tasks it has to perform. Thus, soldiers can be tried by a military court as long as it is a fair trial by an independent and impartial tribunal whose processes and values reflect as much as possible those pertaining more broadly in society, and they can be put in dangerous situations where their life is on the line in defence of society as long as there is adequate planning and they are properly equipped. Their rights are not lost, rather they are protected as much as they can be in the military environment that they have entered. It is not only the duty of government to ensure that this happens, but it is the duty of courts to ensure that the government can be held to account if it falls short.

Support for a social contractual approach to military justice can also be drawn from the seminal US Supreme Court judgment in *Parker v Levy* 1974, when it considered the position of the military in the US constitutional order. The appellant was an army physician, who had been convicted by court martial for disobeying lawful commands, conduct unbecoming an officer and a gentleman, and conduct prejudicial to good order and discipline, contrary to Articles 90, 133 and 134 of the Uniform Military Justice Code. He had refused to establish a training programme for special forces and had made public statements, inter alia, urging black enlisted soldiers not to obey orders to deploy to Vietnam because that group were suffering a disproportionate casualty rate. He also made public comments about special forces personnel being 'killers of peasants' and 'murderers of women and children'.[131] He challenged his conviction, which resulted in being sentenced to three years' hard labour, on the grounds that Articles 133 and 134 of the Uniform Code were void for vagueness under the US Constitution, in particular the due process clause in the Fifth Amendment. Essentially, the appellant's argument was that the military offences of conduct unbecoming an officer and a gentleman and conduct prejudicial to good order and discipline were so vague and broad as not to constitute sufficient warning to military personnel of the sort of conduct that might be prosecuted or indicate the grounds upon which the appellant could challenge such charges. In effect, the offences gave far too much arbitrary discretion to the prosecutor and the court martial, and not enough protection to the soldier charged with such offences. Mr Justice Renquist delivered the Court's opinion

---

[131]   *Parker v Levy* (1974).

by placing the offences in question within the broader context of the role of the military and military justice.

> This Court has long recognized that the military is, by necessity, a specialized society separate from civilian society. We have also recognized that the military has, again by necessity, developed laws and traditions of its own during its long history. The differences between the military and civilian communities result from the fact that 'it is the primary business of armies and navies to fight or be ready to fight wars should the occasion arise'.[132]

That separation of the military from civilian society is essential as it ensures that the military is less able to intervene in the democratic process, but it remains subject to democratic control as part of the executive. Justice Renquist cited previous Supreme Court judgments when it had stated: '[a]n army is not a deliberative body. It is the executive arm. Its law is that of obedience. No question can be left open as to the right to command in the officer or the duty of obedience in the soldier.'[133] As an extension of the executive arm of government the military is clearly part of the state, but the individuals within it are recognised as citizens with rights, albeit ones conditioned by military values: '[t]he military constitutes a specialized community governed by a separate discipline from that of the civilian',[134] so that 'the rights of men in the armed forces must perforce be conditioned to meet certain overriding demands of discipline and duty'.[135]

Discipline, duty and rights conditioned by those demands, all clearly require a separate military code and justify a separate system of military justice. According to Justice Renquist:

> The differences noted by this settled line of authority, first between the military community and the civilian community, and second between military law and civilian law, continue in the present day under the Uniform Code of Military Justice. That Code cannot be equated to a civilian criminal code. It, and the various versions of the Articles of War which have preceded it, regulate aspects of the conduct of members of the military which in the civilian sphere are left unregulated. While a civilian criminal code carves out a relatively small segment of potential conduct and declares it criminal, the Uniform Code of Military Justice essays more varied regulation of a much larger segment of the activities of the more tightly knit military community. In civilian life there is no legal sanction – civil or criminal – for failure

---

[132] *Parker v Levy* (1974) 743, citing *United States ex rel. Toth v Quarles* 350 US 11, 350 US 17 (1955).
[133] *In re Grimley*, 137 US 147, 137 US 153 (1890).
[134] *Orloff v Willoughby* (1953).
[135] *Burns v Wilson* (1953).

to behave as an officer and a gentleman; in the military world, Art. 133 imposes such a sanction on a commissioned officer.[136]

The separation of the military and civilian community in a sense strengthens the social contract between the two. The military has specific purposes and values designed to make it an effective organ for the protection of the civilian community, while the civilian community accepts the autonomy and distinct values of the military. By joining the military individuals have to restrict their freedoms and rights: they, in effect, move partly from one side of the contract to the other, but by so doing they do not relinquish their rights as individuals but accept that they must be curtailed in pursuit of the collective values and discipline of the military: '[w]hile members of the military community enjoy many of the same rights and bear many of the same burdens as do members of the civilian community, within the military community, there is simply not the same autonomy as there is in the larger civilian community'.[137]

Applying this reasoning to the constitutional rights claimed by the appellant in *Parker v Levy*, Justice Renquist stated that, since he 'could have had no reasonable doubt that his public statements' were both 'unbecoming an officer and a gentleman' and 'to the prejudice of good order and discipline in the armed forces', 'his challenge to them as unconstitutionally vague under the Due Process Clause of the Fifth Amendment must fail'.[138] Importantly, however, this did not mean that soldiers had lost their protections under the constitution:

> While the members of the military are not excluded from the protection granted by the First Amendment, the different character of the military community and of the military mission requires a different application of those protections. The fundamental necessity for obedience, and the consequent necessity for imposition of discipline, may render permissible within the military that which would be con-stitutionally impermissible outside it.[139]

In this regard, a judgment of the US Court of Military Appeals was cited by Mr Justice Renquist: '[i]n the armed forces, some restrictions exist for reasons that have no counterpart in the civilian community. Disrespectful and con-temptuous speech, even advocacy of violent change, is tolerable in the civilian community, for it does not directly affect the capacity of the Government to discharge its responsibilities'. In 'military life, however, other considerations must be weighed. The armed forces depend on a command structure that, at

---

[136] *Parker v Levy* (1974) 749.
[137] Ibid, 751.
[138] Ibid, 757.
[139] Ibid, 758.

times must commit men to combat, not only hazarding their lives but ultimately involving the security of the nation itself. Speech that is protected in the civil population may nonetheless undermine the effectiveness of response to command. If it does, it is constitutionally unprotected.'[140] The courts in the cases of *Parker v Levy*, *Smith v MoD* and *R v Stillman* share a belief in the value of a separate military justice system that recognises the unique duties and qualified rights of soldiers.

9.9   CONCLUSION

This concluding chapter has demonstrated that a soldier's rights are not lost when joining the armed services. However, those rights are pared down when compared to those enjoyed by a civilian and, furthermore, this is a result of the social contract between soldier on the one hand and the society and government they serve on the other. Throughout the book it has been argued that soldiers agree to such restrictions in order to serve society most effectively, but in return the government and society owe soldiers a duty to respect and protect them. This chapter has reconsidered the notion of the social contract between state and soldier drawing upon judicial consideration of the rights of soldiers. The rights of the soldier are qualified and limited (but not extinguished) when soldiers are deployed to fight in wars, but their rights have already been conditioned by entering into military service, where they subject themselves to a different legal order based on discipline, order and efficiency. This means that soldiers' rights remain, but they are not always protected in the same way and to the same extent as civilian-citizens, and their duties are more onerous.

Although they give up a great deal when entering into military service, soldiers do not give up their rights. However, in considering the balance between their rights and duties and those of the government (and wider society) they serve, it is clear that their rights, even though conditioned by the dictates of discipline and the exigencies of military necessity when on operational duty, still have to be protected. Otherwise, the soldier's side of the covenant or contract simply comprises legal duties, and the government's side solely consists of rights and powers. While this might have represented the relationship between state and soldier throughout much of the history of the military, it can no longer prevail in the era when individual rights have become entrenched as the basis for democratic government. The government, on its part must not shirk its legal (as well as moral) obligations to the soldier, namely: to respect and protect those rights found in the ECHR in peacetime, and to ensure that it properly assesses the risks to soldiers' fundamental rights during wartime or

---

[140]   *United States v Priest*, 21 CMA 564 at 570 (1972).

deployments to other life-threatening situations, and put in place a clear series of proportionate, preventive and on-going measures to reduce those risks as much as possible in order to fulfil its obligations to protect the rights of soldiers even when deployed to combat zones.

Military justice is no longer a simple matter of a soldier's complete obedience to orders and to the military code, with harsh punishment for transgressions. In order to maintain its legitimacy and its continued separation from civilian justice, military justice has to recognise that, like any individual, members of the armed forces have multiple subjectivities: hero, victim, villain, soldier and citizen. In addition to maintaining discipline, duty and efficiency, the system of military justice should aim to cover, anticipate, and address all of these subjectivities by means of covenants, access to justice, compensation, prosecution, punishment, discipline, duties and rights.

The book has shown that there is a growing recognition of the rights of soldiers, but it is a somewhat precarious development. While the rights of individuals in wider society have been entrenched, rights of soldiers are being recognised more slowly and have been upheld tentatively. Furthermore, there is concerted pressure to restrict and even quash these green shoots, and a number of signs that the government is reasserting its legal superiority by various means: demonising judges and lawyers who oppose it; reasserting untrammelled prerogative powers; legislating to limit its liability; threatening to derogate from human rights; and legislating to restrict scrutiny of unlawful conduct under the guise of protecting soldiers from prosecution. The legitimacy of the military justice system ultimately depends on protecting the rights of soldiers, but also in successfully prosecuting soldiers for breaching their duties whether owed to civilians in foreign countries or fellow soldiers in the barracks back in the UK. There is certainly much work to be done on both these counts.

Despite recent unwelcome developments, a just balance between the rights and duties of government and the duties and rights of soldiers may be achieved if the line of jurisprudence that began with *Smith v Ministry of Defence* in 2013 is allowed to develop into a clear legal framework, which takes account of both operational necessity and the rights and protections of soldiers. Clarity as regards the types of claims that might succeed will prevent speculative claims but will also provide accountability for what was previously a legal black hole, not covered by LOAC. Further protection of the rights of soldiers by reform to the military justice system would close unjustifiable gaps between the standards of justice applied to civilians and soldiers. Bringing decision-making on guilt or innocence and sentencing into line with civilian criminal justice, and improving the prosecution and punishment of rape, sexual and other forms of abuse, are achievable without undermining the system's unique and essential function – to support a disciplined and efficient army. The military is of necessity a separate society, subject to special rules and processes. However, the military remains connected to the wider community by the social contract between soldier and society, which brings with it standards of justice applicable to all.

Index

CHAPTER 1

auxhall Gardens, 1818

In the shadows of the lantern that hung outside their supper house, Fanny registered the dismay on Lord Alverley's face and realised she'd just made the biggest miscalculation of her life.

He shuffled his feet, unable to look her in the eye. "I'm afraid I can't marry you, Miss Brightwell. Forgive me."

The distant strains of the orchestra now playing in Vauxhall Gardens' rotunda competed with his awkward let-down. He cleared his throat and mumbled, "Lady Georgiana has been my intended bride since we were children... I thought you knew that."

Despite her shock, Fanny kept her smile in place. If there was one thing her mother had taught her it was that dignity must be maintained at all times. Even when the unstable ground beneath her daughter's feet brought back Fanny's ever-present fears she was on the verge of being tossed overboard and fed to the sharks.

Her mother would do it, too. Fanny had just failed in her most important mission—make a match that would restore the Brightwells to their former position on society's ladder—and now she

must accept her fate...marriage to that other odious creature who'd got into Lady Brightwell's ear and made her a bargain she couldn't refuse: Her eldest daughter in return for a comfortable lease in Soho with a carriage and two for the baron's widow for the rest of her days.

Carefully she breathed out. She would not cry. But she would not make it easy for him, either. No, there was a limit to how accepting Fanny could be, even for the sake of dignity. Lord Alverley wanted Fanny to forgive him for such a betrayal when her future lay in tatters? Her mother would never forgive *her*.

Clutching the spider-gauze fichu of her daring masquerade costume, Fanny stepped back to avoid his open-armed approach.

He wanted her, but not as his wife. Could he really imagine she'd sacrifice her reputation, and that of her family, to be his *mistress*?

"You deceived me, Alverley." It was true. He'd led her to believe he was in love with her and she'd formed a fondness for him—for her mother's sake— because there'd been precious few other suitors prepared to take a dowerless bride whose father, well-born though Baron Brightwell had been, had married so far beneath him.

"Fanny, wait—" His eyes were beseeching.

Cow's eyes.

She'd thought it from the start, so why had she persisted in this futile courtship? Surely she should have been clever enough to trust her instincts?

But of course she'd persisted because Lord Slyther had been waiting in the wings.

An alternative worse than death.

Grotesque Lord Slyther, with his moist skin and his repulsive breath, had known Fanny was on a doomed mission to find a husband who would satisfy Lady Brightwell's exacting criteria as well as the yearning of Fanny's ridiculously sentimental heart.

Lord, what Brightwell of Fanny's generation could afford to be

sentimental?

She shook her head not trusting herself to speak as she turned away. It wasn't only Alverley's deception that had landed her in this predicament. She had to take responsibility for her own gullibility. The normally careful, calculating Miss Fanny Brightwell had miscalculated, and soon her mother would remind her that Lord Slyther was both just punishment and more than a girl like her could have hoped for.

The tongue-lashing would be almost worse than what was happening right now.

"Fanny, I—"

"Please, leave me, my lord," she managed in something just above a whisper. "I should never have agreed to visit you here, alone. If you have *any* regard for me, you'll say nothing about this if only to preserve my reputation."

"Just one final kiss." His voice was too near her ear when she thought he'd comply and slink into the shadows. The thought of being touched by him, ever again, made her recoil, and as she spun away, her flimsy-soled slippers skidding on the gravel, her ankle gave way beneath her. She felt the brush of leaves, the scratch of branches, and thought of the pitiful sight she would make as her mother vented her fury upon her.

Fanny was to have made the Brightwells' fortunes. She amended this in the split second available for thought. Fanny had begged to be given this last chance before the ghastly alternative that would ensure the Brightwells' survival...

...but Fanny had failed.

The ground rushed to meet her. So! This was to be the final indignity—to land in the dirt at his feet!

She closed her eyes, throwing out her hands and tensing as she anticipated the pain, wishing the price of her failure could be similarly condensed.

Instead, strong, unfamiliar arms scooped her up and an amused voice murmured in her ear, "Young lady, I think you'd be

far safer tucked up in your own bed than consorting with this obviously unsatisfactory gentleman."

Fanny blinked up into a pair of dark eyes that glinted at her through the slits of his demi-mask. Her first instinct was to cleave closer to whomever was prepared to offer rescue from her current nightmarish predicament; then remembering that her instincts had been decidedly off lately and that if she had any chance of getting home before her mother discovered her missing, she made a violent attempt to struggle out of his arms.

The chest against which she was now pinioned seemed to ripple with amusement. To her fascinated horror it was a naked chest, hard and tense beneath the fine linen of his pirate costume. "It seems your companion has bitten off more than he can chew."

For the first time ever, Fanny was robbed of speech. Then she realised with a spurt of anger that this man, fascinating though he was—and no doubt all the more because he was in masquerade—was toying with her. He had no idea of the magnitude of the disaster Fanny now confronted and his levity in the face of her humiliation, still so fresh, swept away the gratitude she might otherwise have felt.

"Put me down," she ground out as Alverley, after a hesitation, stepped forward, saying, "Your intervention, sir, is appreciated…"

When the stranger made no move to set Fanny on her feet, Alverley's voice became diffident. "However, we must rejoin our party. Please…put the lady down."

Was he afraid? For her? Her reputation? Or did Alverley fear for his own safety, since her saviour's piratical costume revealed that this was a man who did not resort to padding to bolster his masculine attributes?

The pirate tightened his hold on Fanny and regarded Alverley critically. "I gained the impression the young lady has no wish for your company, sir."

Fanny was not going to deny it. Having realised the futility of her struggles, she simply gave up. Why not enjoy the intimate

warmth this man radiated for the few minutes it would take him to whisk her out of Alverley's orbit?

Perhaps she shivered, for suddenly the arousing, mellifluous tones of this pirate stranger sounded intimately in her ear. "You are cold, madam, and this man has caused trouble enough. I think it's time we took our leave."

"Sir, I must object!"

It wasn't Fanny who said this but she made no attempt to respond to Alverley who sprang forward as she was swung wide, her bare arm feeling the brush of Alverley's vainly grasping fingers before she was borne into the gloom.

A crowd of revellers rounded the bend, sweeping Alverley into their midst as Fanny was carried in the opposite direction. Still she did not struggle as his shouts faded into the distance.

"I'm surprised you didn't scream?" The stranger's voice was conversational as he rapidly traversed the serpentine walk that led to the river; as if it were a normal occurrence for a pirate to bear a damsel in his arms.

The strong beat of his heart through her fine muslin gown made Fanny's beat all the more erratically, as he went on, "Isn't that what ladies do when they're kidnapped?"

"I thought you were rescuing me." Despite her uncertainty, she found his sardonic humour appealing. She consoled herself with the thought that she need only scream and he would set her back upon her feet. She would be free.

It was not a liberating thought. Free to tell her mother she had misjudged matters? Free to become an object of pity—if not ridicule—to her so-called friends?

She decided to surrender herself to fate for the moment, clinging to him more tightly as he negotiated a hazard upon the footpath. Trying to sound bolder than she felt, she said, "Besides, bringing attention to my predicament might injure my reputation."

"While my attentions won't?" They were by the river now. A

short crossing would take them out of the gardens. Almost disappointed, she acknowledged she'd been in good hands after all. Her rescuer was going to put her in a hackney carriage when they got to the other side.

Lord, what was she thinking? Of course that was what must happen. If she wasn't home before her mother took herself off to bed, Fanny would be marching up the aisle to join Lord Slyther before the week was finished.

Her rescuer signalled to a waiting ferryman by the river's edge who navigated his vessel towards them and then she was deposited upon the bench of the barge. Her pirate rescuer joined her, the corners of his mouth turning up at her obvious embarrassment when he sat so close their thighs touched. Fanny raised her face to the moon and closed her eyes as a cool, gentle breeze caressed her heated skin. Soon she would be home to face an uncomfortable confrontation with her mother. Right now the unknown was far more enticing.

"My Lady of Troy is an enigma," the handsome man beside her murmured, settling closer while he rearranged his sword and scabbard. "Cavalier enough of her reputation to cavort alone with gentlemen in secluded supper boxes and offer no resistance when a better offer comes along, but suddenly so prim."

Fanny's objection was truncated by the jolt of the boat as it pushed off from the river bank, which threw her closer against her companion. Drawing back, she said icily, "I am not from the ranks of the Fashionably Impure, sir." Suddenly she was doubting the wisdom of having accepted his assistance. She glared. "Might I remind you that you tore me from the arms of a serious suitor—"

"—whose marital criteria I believe you failed to meet—?"

"His mama's marital criteria!"

"I beg your pardon." With a chuckle, he flashed her an infuriating smile before issuing instructions to the ferryman. He was a gentleman—his voice, his bearing left her in no doubt about that. He was also a very well built gentleman. But he was amusing

himself at her expense. After the night she'd had, Fanny was in no mood for his lightheartedness.

Yet when he caressed her cheek, the most extraordinary sensations fizzed through her. Though she pressed herself against the side of the river craft in order not to be too close, she couldn't help running her gaze the length of his leather-booted feet and calves, up his long, outstretched legs and lean hips and across the hard, flat chest against which she'd so recently been pressed.

Reluctantly she admired his strong, well-sculpted jaw which had her locking gazes with him when she reached his treacle-brown eyes. She slid her own away in embarrassment. Confident eyes, she thought. Like hers, his demi-mask sufficiently concealed his identity for an *amour* such as this, but the eyes were pools of information and she was satisfied that his conveyed all the attributes she considered essential in a man—humour, decisiveness, confidence and, just briefly, kindness. Perhaps he was not a swaggering 'Johnny-take-all', after all.

The moon was high in the sky now, a golden orb above the revellers in masquerade who promenaded along the river's edge. Others lolled in boats upon the water.

As Fanny's pique dissipated and her good humour returned, she began to shiver. Not from the cold, or the disappointment over the events already played out with Alverley—they were best forgotten—but as a result of the sudden anticipation of what might happen during the next few minutes in the river barge with this handsome stranger…if she was bold enough.

She sucked in a breath as she slid a glance up at her rescuer who was gazing across the river, apparently lost in thought for one brief moment. She wondered what he was thinking. Was he as excited as she? Would he kiss her?

Having experienced her first kiss in Alverley's thin-armed embrace this evening, Fanny wasn't sure such an unsatisfactory mingling of tongues deserved the title kiss when she'd always dreamed of it as a magical, life-changing moment. But an oppor-

tunity had been handed to her on a platter. If Fanny was destined to become the wife of Lord Slyther, the handsome pirate beside her, she decided, would provide the benchmark of comparison.

The voice of reason perched upon her shoulder.

If Mama were ever to find out...

She shuddered. *If anyone at all were ever to find out.*

Yet how would they and what was her crime—if it could ever be laid at her door? In all her nineteen years Fanny had always been played the dutiful daughter, ever mindful of the faith invested in her by the rest of the family to do whatever she could to salvage their sinking fortunes.

Even if that meant sacrificing herself.

She gave herself a figurative—and physical—shake, turning to find her companion studying her, an interested twist to his mouth, a curl of dark hair falling across his forehead.

Byron. That's who he looked like. Mad, bad and dangerous to know. Just what attracted her in a man, if only because it was the antithesis of the man she'd inevitably marry.

"How disappointing. Not a fair Cyprian? So if I offered you five shillings for a quick tumble you'd turn me down?"

She wasn't sure she'd heard him correctly before her suppressed anticipation was swept away by outrage. "How dare you!" Any cautious, properly brought-up young lady would have considered the indignity of Alverley's let-down infinitely preferable to a horribly compromising situation with a stranger. She was a fool!

Fanny scrambled to her feet, causing the small vessel to rock perilously and the riverman to round on them with an angry curse.

"Careful, or you'll drown us all." With another lazy smile her rescuer—or was he to be her ravisher, after all, by the time he was done with her?—tugged at her hand. Clumsily, she landed across his lap, her head thumping against his chest. So hard and broad. So unlike Alverley's.

Arms like steel bands encircled her upper body and knees as he held her tucked against him like a baby.

Fanny realised she had *behaved* like a baby. He'd been teasing her. She pretended to be so worldly but in truth she knew nothing of men—nothing, at least, of handsome men possessed of confidence and humour. Men who could offer her what she wanted—a pocket book that would please her mama, a title her sister and brother could trade upon and...

Wistful longing for the seemingly unobtainable stayed her struggles as she stared up at him and his face fractured in her imagination before reassembling into the incarnation of all she could desire and more—a man who promised excitement and adventure at the very least.

"Many people lose their nerve on the water"—his eyes glinted mere inches above her face with wicked pleasure—"and, while I've neglected to bring along my burnt feathers, a kiss works wonders for warding off the vapours."

Oh, she was tempted, but was this one more miscalculation?

However, a demeaning struggle that might pitch them all into the Thames seemed an extreme reaction, Fanny decided, when this man's close proximity was the antithesis of distasteful.

Yes, the antithesis, she confirmed, her bones going soft as his long, elegant fingers caressed her hair, her throat and shoulders with surprising gentleness, for he had shifted her so her head rested in his lap. She gazed up at his face, with all the glory of the starlit sky behind him, closing her eyes as her companion contoured her décolletage with gentle fingertips, causing her mind to spin with wicked, sensuous thoughts.

She would *never* accept Lord Slyther. Like a patient toad, he was waiting to crawl back out of the wings to repeat his offer of three months ago, revelling in the knowledge that Fanny was cornered.

When the stranger's hand brushed across her breast, she caught her breath.

"The unworldly virgin is out for adventure," her pirate lover murmured, lowering his head to whisper in her ear, "and, if I'm not to be accused of nefarious deeds, I think our encounter should end here."

The desolation of his withdrawal caused her to open her eyes and cry out incautiously, "My companion earlier this evening kissed me and it was horrible." *Why had she said that? Fanny was never incautious.*

In the moonlight his look was enquiring. "If I kiss you, I can't promise it won't be just as horrible."

Longing and desire tore at her like a creature suddenly come to life within her. She reached up and stroked the plane of his cheek, contouring his high cheekbones before resting her forefinger tentatively upon his lower lip. With a glint in his eye, he bit down gently and hot, lustful longing speared through her.

She tried to breathe evenly. "I'm prepared to take that risk."

"In that case, my bold ingénue…" He brought his mouth down to hers, murmuring against her lips, "Let me show you *one* of the things for which I am renowned."

He began gently, brushing his lips against her cheek, nose and lips with featherlight touches that seemed to promise more than they delivered.

She *wanted* more. What harm could come from a kiss with no one the wiser? Tomorrow she would deport herself like a lady and venture forth to do her mother's bidding. She would find herself the husband her mother demanded.

Lord Slyther…

Ugh…

She sucked in the scent of the man who held her—fresh sweat and sandalwood— revelling in the wonderfully suffocating proximity of his body against hers.

Oh, sweet heaven…that's exactly where she was. Heaven, in the arms of a man who had brought her to life—for excitement had never before fizzed through her veins like this.

The gentle lapping of the water and the splash of the oars reminded her that their journey would soon be at an end. So would her sensory adventure—a brief flash of pleasure in an otherwise dried-up existence.

Reaching up her hands, she pulled his face down to deepen the kiss. His dark, tousled hair, his full, poetic mouth, and the sardonic gleam in his treacle eyes made him the consummate lover of her imagination. A lover she could never have.

But she could have a taste.

Again his mouth returned to hers, this time bruising it with an urgency his previously unhurried pace belied. Blood coursed furiously to her extremities as he breached the seam of her lips with his tongue, gently and expertly whipping up her excitement. Murmuring against her lips, his hands skimmed her body, touching, stroking, feeling her into wild sensation through the light gauze of her costume.

It was madness, she knew, and she was powerless against the need unleashed within her. Alverley's betrayal of her hopes was insignificant compared with this sensual gratification. She felt the tension in her whole being stretch, feared she would burn to a cinder or explode in a shower of ashes if he continued—yet her world threatened to return to its barren wilderness if he stopped.

"Is this what you meant by a kiss?" he murmured during a brief interlude before redoubling his efforts.

"Oh...yes..."

But wasn't there more? What were these unsatisfied cravings?

It seemed that the more thoroughly he kissed her, the more her body wanted to feel his...what? Possession of her...?

Self-preservation, like a single dust mote, lodged in her brain, and she gasped her resistance. Miss Fanny Brightwell, who'd spent her life trying to prove that her beauty and virtue put her on a par with all those with handsome dowries, was about to throw it all away like a common doxy for five minutes of self-gratification.

What a little fool...

Her hands were against his chest, palms turned inwards as a prelude to forcible resistance, when another totally unexpected, all-consuming sensation cast aside every objection she'd been about to make.

Obviously mistaking her gasp for permission to move to the next level, he'd transferred his explorations to beneath the hem of her dress and his hands were now skimming the length of her leg, moving lightly above the tops of her stockings, the gentle, rhythmic touch of soft fingertips against the heated, sensitive flesh of her inner thigh making her want to shriek aloud her pleasure.

Instead she jerked out of his arms, upright, her breasts straining against her bodice as she remembered who and where she was: respectable debutante, Miss Fanny Brightwell in a boat alone with a stranger.

"So nearly there and yet not quite," murmured her pirate, as the nose of the barge hit the riverbank with a muted jolt. Not even looking chastened, he made a gallant show of helping to straighten Fanny's clothing before he took her hand and drew her to her feet.

"Aye, we're at t'other side, now," announced the riverman with a sly look as he jumped out to steady the craft.

Fanny rose shakily, as if the foundations of her life had shifted.

And they had, for just now she'd experienced what no unmarried young woman ought to have experienced. Certainly not a respectable one.

As they reached level ground, her pirate lover bent to kiss her lightly on the lips before signalling to a jarvey waiting nearby with his hackney carriage.

A curious blackness had invaded Fanny's mind, where both opportunity and terror seemed to lurk hand in hand. She'd felt excitement like she'd never known— albeit cruelly truncated—but now an even greater horror intruded at the thought of allowing Lord Slyther access to her body like she'd allowed this hand-

some...*stranger*, whom she stumbled against while he held open the door for her.

She had no one to rely upon for support—never had—so it was ridiculous to lean against handsome strangers as if she were some helpless, lovelorn creature. Fanny had always prided herself on her strength. Feminine frailty was the preserve of her younger sister, Antoinette.

"Good night, fair damsel." The pirate made a sweeping bow. "It has been a delightful finale to what had been a lacklustre evening."

There was a painful lump in Fanny's throat that made her eyes sting when she swallowed. Somehow she felt he deserved her gratitude. "Thank you, sir. Tonight you showed me the only excitement I will ever know for very soon I shall be forced to marry a man I do not love."

He helped her into the carriage, his smile disbelieving. "My commiserations, mystery lover," he whispered as he leaned through the window to brush her lips once more with his. "What a sad tale. Nevertheless, I wish you every happiness."

Fanny turned her head. Of course he didn't believe her and she'd been naive to have imagined he felt anything other than satisfaction at his latest conquest.

She rapped on the roof to signal the jarvey's departure. She would not give her address in earshot of her pirate prince. The house her mother had leased for the season was lowly and the danger to her reputation unknown.

Of course she would never see this man again. But what he'd done for her was immeasurable. He'd shown her that she did indeed possess a heart that could flutter with desire when the right man came within her orbit.

The tragedy was that Lord Slyther, for whom she was now definitely destined, was not that man and after tonight her life would never be the same.

CHAPTER 2

$\mathcal{F}$anny tiptoed across the threshold, her heart pounding as much from fear of being discovered by her mother as from the tumultuous events of tonight.

She'd had both the disappointment and the thrill of a lifetime, and at that moment she wasn't sure if she would ever recover from either.

The front door that Mary, her maid, had left unbolted by special arrangement, made little noise as she closed it behind her. All was silent and dark within. If she was lucky, her mother would never even know she'd left the house.

She was not lucky. She felt the stinging slap of her mother's hand across her cheek as she rose from shooting the bolt.

"Little fool!" hissed Lady Brightwell, flinging her daughter into the hallway. "Where have you been? Certainly not playing cards with Miss Brownhill in that scandalous rig-out! Helen of Troy, indeed. It's a gossamer web that leaves nothing to the imagination! Answer me, girl! Have you brought our good name into disrepute?" Lady Brightwell, her thin lips pressed into a bloodless line, hustled her daughter into the dim, candlelit drawing room, slamming the door behind her.

"I told you Mama would find out." Appearing out of the darkness from the other side of the room, Fanny's younger sister resembled a pale ghost in her plain nightrail, her shining, golden hair cascading over her shoulders. "But I swear I didn't tell her."

"Quiet, Antoinette," Lady Brightwell snapped as Fanny shrugged out of her grasp and stalked towards the dining table.

"Courtesy of Alverley, Mama!" she said, tossing a simple silver ring set with a garnet onto the table.

In tense silence, they watched its spiralling progress across the mahogany surface. With a theatrical sigh, Fanny added, "Alas, the ring comes without security. It was merely a sop." She didn't care if her mother slapped her again for her attitude. Pain scoured her heart and lanced her pride. She supposed it would be even more painful if she'd loved Alverley though she'd liked him well enough. Her mother had fiercely counselled her daughters from infancy to hold onto their virtue until marriage and their hearts forever; and indeed Fanny had believed she didn't have a heart until it had started to make all that fuss inside her chest when she'd got close to that piratical stranger. The river crossing had set the stage for more than her first experience of a proper kiss.

Tingles of excitement coursed through her just at the memory but of course, she couldn't be thinking of that. She must relegate her pirate stranger to her past, just like Alverley if she were to carry out her mother's orders.

What choice did she have?

So with a challenging look, she said, "Invite Lord Slyther to call, mother, but do not blame me if he does not make an offer. I've lost my touch, as you can see." She nodded at the ring. "Perhaps you'll have to look to Antoinette to fill the family coffers. Or Bertram." Her voice broke.

She was suddenly desperately weary, though she felt she'd never sleep again—and not because of Alverley's humiliating betrayal.

"Don't be saucy with me, girl." Lady Brightwell pocketed the

ring. "We may be poor but we are respectable. You asked for this chance with Alverley on account of the interest he'd already shown and I had every reason to hope you would fulfil our expectations." Her face looked haggard in the guttering candlelight as she sank into her chair. "Now let us hope Lord Slyther will be as forthcoming in *his* interest as he was three months ago. You know we depend on you, Fanny. Bertram is a wastrel, just like your father was." She fixed her sharp eyes on the last of the glowing coals. "And Antoinette's beauty won't make up for the fact she is a pea goose. She'll likely take her pleasure in a haystack with a footman and ruin us all."

"For goodness' sake, Mama, it's only because of *me* we've been invited to the Earl of Quamby's ball the night after next." Antoinette, warming her hands by the fire, looked up, offended.

"That was luck, not cunning, Antoinette, and I helped him as much as you," Fanny objected, kneeling beside her sister, for the room was freezing and their breath clouded in the guttering light.

"You only returned his walking sticks. It was my screams which frightened away the footpads."

"Girls, girls!" Lady Brightwell admonished wearily.

Antoinette giggled, pushing aside the curtain of her glorious hair as she simpered, "Lord Quamby likes me immensely. I make him laugh."

"I'd rather you made him your husband"—Lady Brightwell's lip curled—"though I fear Lord Quamby is not about to marry anyone. Otherwise I'd relent, Fanny, knowing the aversion you feel for Lord Slyther, and send you after the earl instead."

"I'd infinitely prefer Lord Quamby, with his frightful red wig and his crippled legs and his brilliant wit." Despite herself, Fanny smiled, recalling her last spirited exchange with the eccentric earl who sometimes sent for the Brightwells at the oddest times, merely so Fanny could play cribbage with him—an excuse, Fanny knew, for some lively banter—or when he was in the doldrums

because he'd been required to bail out his detested nephew and heir, George Bramley, once more.

George Bramley. Fanny's lip curled, just like her mother's but with far more reason. Small wonder Lord Quamby detested his nephew, a boorish young man with not one redeeming quality she could think of.

Fanny was always carefully chaperoned during her visits to the earl, though never had she gained the impression he was even slightly interested in her feminine attributes. It was all quite confusing.

Her mother grunted, her shoulders slumping as if she really was preparing for the end. "If Lord Slyther declines my invitation to call, Thursday's ball is your last chance, girls. We've received no further invitations."

Both daughters looked at her. For the first time, their mother appeared weak, her usually hard, flinty tone a mere whisper as she added, "The truth is, unless one of you contracts a good marriage by the end of this season, we have not the funds to maintain the household."

Antoinette gasped. "You mean—"

"I mean that if you girls are determined to be ape-leaders like hatchet-faced Aunt Hester, we'll have no choice but to accept her charity—or else you will both have to seek employment."

~

BUT LORD SLYTHER DID ACCEPT, WITH ALACRITY. THE GLEAM IN HIS eye hinted at victory as he shuffled into the drawing room, puffing at the exertion expended by his bloated body. Fanny and Antoinette had watched from the window as he'd been delivered to the front portico by sedan chair. He'd then been all but manually hoisted up the steps, causing Antoinette to remark happily, "He's unlikely to live long, Fanny. Look at him!"

Fanny did, then covered her face with her hands as she turned back from the window and sank into a chair with a groan. "Oh, Mama, what if he doesn't? He's so repulsive!"

"Doesn't what? Doesn't live long or doesn't offer?" Antoinette asked with another giggle, prompting their mother to snap, "It's of no account whether you find him repulsive, provided he does not find Fanny so. Now, my girl, pinch your cheeks and remember everything I've taught you. Hush!" For his laboured breaths could already be heard from halfway down the passage. "This is our last chance."

Within a few minutes Fanny found herself alone in the drawing room with her erstwhile suitor, abandoned by her mother and siblings at the request of the ageing viscount who had 'something of importance' he wished to say to Miss Brightwell.

Fanny knew what this meant as she put her fingertips briefly to her eyes which suddenly stung with tears. But Fanny never cried. Her mother had taught her how to hide emotion. *If only she'd taught her how to stop feeling.*

And now her whole body seemed suddenly under attack from a plethora of feeling.

There'd been a time when she'd have done anything to evoke the gleam of approval in her mother's eye that had been in evidence before Lady Brightwell had unctuously acceded to Lord Slyther's request for privacy. Now Fanny experienced again that strange feeling in her chest cavity where her heart felt it was beating too rapidly to be healthy only this time it wasn't excitement that was the cause, such as last night's extraordinary interlude, it was panic.

Lord Slyther was about to make her an offer and she should be overjoyed. At the very least, she should take consolation from Antoinette's remark regarding his imminent demise. Until last night she would have—but until then she'd not known the liberties, the intimacies that would become the preserve of her new

husband. Last night, she'd responded to a stranger in the most extraordinary and illogical way. She'd not even seen his face properly, yet her body and her mind had been drawn to him, purely through the timbre of his voice, his manly, musky smell, the strength of him and— undoing her completely—the intimacy of his touch when he'd taken her properly in his arms in the barge and kissed her with both passion and sweetness.

Unconsciously, she touched her finger to her lips, her mind transporting her back to that wondrous moment. Then she clasped her hands together. It was too much to think of that, now. Too much to think of what it might be to feel something other than disgust and aversion to the man who would enjoy husbandly intimacies, conjugal rights. No—in return for the Brightwells retaining their position amongst the ton, Fanny must give herself to this disgusting, odious man mind before her, body and soul.

As she straightened in her spindly, uncomfortable little chair opposite Lord Slyther, striving for the demure pose required, unable to rid her mind of the thrilling events of last night, she nearly wept.

"Come here."

Fanny blinked with surprise. The viscount was leaning forward, indicating with an imperious wave of one bejewelled hand that she should seat herself on the footstool on which he rested his bandaged foot.

From their first meeting at a dinner three months ago, he'd made no secret of his interest in her, and within the week had spoken to Lady Brightwell. In a gesture of unprecedented kindness her mother had not accepted Lord Slyther's proposal upon the instant. This, though, could have been on account of the fact that as the prospective mother-in-law her mother would have known she too, would have to suffer his putrid breath whenever visits were exchanged.

Of course, bargains had of necessity been made, Lord Alverley

being the prize Fanny had failed to obtain. Now Fanny was simply paying her dues.

"You wish me to sit by you, my lord? On the footstool?"

He grunted his agreement.

It was irregular and not very courteous, Fanny thought, as she transferred herself and awkwardly lifted his leg so she could sit down. When he made it clear he wanted her to rub his leg, she gingerly replaced his heavy, swollen limb across her lap. With an effort she managed not to wrinkle her nose at the unpleasant odour of ulcerating flesh, which all the bandaging could not disguise.

Lord Slyther grunted again as he shifted himself more comfortably in his chair. "So, you know why I'm here, and you're prepared, are ye, Miss Brightwell?"

Fanny blushed. She was here, of course, because she was the spoils of a bargain Lady Brightwell had made with Lord Slyther; and she ought not feel so ashamed. She was no different from any other penniless young woman seeking security in a perilous world that offered little to those whom fortune failed to smile upon. Yet most gentlemen making an offer in such circumstances would maintain the charade required by good manners.

She hesitated before saying demurely, just as her mother would have her say, "I do not know what you mean, my Lord." If she'd been able to follow her own inclinations she'd have leapt to her feet, told him there'd been a terrible misunderstanding and she'd decided to join a nunnery.

Becoming a nun would be preferable to marrying Lord Slyther, except that then Antoinette would have to become a governess and there'd be no one to bail out Bertram next time he suffered a gaming loss.

Fanny had always found that if she breathed very slowly and carefully and replayed in her mind exactly the tone in which her mother would have her respond to a would-be suitor, she could

survive the ordeal. There'd been several pleasant enough gentlemen in the past whom she'd have married with little angst—young, immature boys who'd clearly been taken with her at a ball or assembly—but ultimately the marriage proposal for which her mother was angling never quite came.

"I think you know exactly what I mean." He chuckled. "Well, keep up the play acting, my lovely Miss Brightwell. The prospect of tutoring an innocent pleases me...for all you were not so innocent last night."

She gasped and her fingers tingled. The shock blanching her skin white and bloodless would be a testament to her guilt but she said nothing. Then a wonderful thought intruded. Perhaps he no longer wished to marry Fanny after all. Fanny didn't care how he might have known what she'd been up to last night, but if he simply withdrew his offer and Lady Brightwell was none the wiser as to the reasons Fanny would be the happiest young lady in the world.

"It's pleasing to observe genuine contrition for such unladylike behaviour, but you failed, did you not, Miss Brightwell?" He leant forward, bringing his face close to hers, and she smelt the stink of his breath, like there was something rotting within him. Forcing herself not to recoil, she braced herself for his next words.

"You accompanied young Alverley to Vauxhall, alone and unchaperoned, but he did not make you the offer you took such risks for, did he?"

Fanny hung her head, the weight of Lord Slyther's bandaged leg making her thigh hurt—like her heart, her dignity... "Who told you this, my lord?" There was no point denying it and now her brief euphoria was replaced by the knowledge of her stupidity. She had compromised her reputation.

Survival now depended upon knowing what else and how much else he knew.

"Never you mind, my dear. Suffice it to say it was a friend. A

friend I did not know I had until he came to me shortly after your mother's surprise and welcome visit to see me yesterday."

She felt rather than heard him chuckle, his body creating ripples of movement that increased her fear like a rising tide.

"Your friend must dislike me very much." What else could Fanny say? So she had an enemy. Someone who was clearly hoping to ruin her. But why? Surely not a jealous fellow debutante for Fanny had never succeeded where another had failed when it came to the ultimate prize: marriage.

"On the contrary, your friend likes you only too well. Like me, he was vastly put out when the engaging Miss Brightwell felt her beauty and her wit could override her lack of dowry and the scandal of her father, putting her above the likes of…"

"*George Bramley!*" She gasped the name, fury rising within her like trapped steam about to explode.

Lord Slyther gave a grunt of satisfaction. "I'm glad his name immediately came to mind, for I'd like to think there were no others competing for the role of rejected suitor. Ah, but, Miss Brightwell, your misfortune is that you have miscalculated, and my fortune is that it gives me all the bargaining power in the world."

Her already great horror was compounded as she felt his hand upon her neck, gently caressing her skin. Frozen, unable to move as she accepted the truth of his assessment, she trembled as she tried to assimilate his words. Until last night, she had conducted herself with all the decorum required by a chaste innocent, hopeful of contracting a suitable marriage. True, she wasn't decorous by nature, but only the gleam in her eye when a handsome gentleman showed interest would give her away, surely? Not her actions. Her mother had spent her lifetime trying to subdue that reckless, adventurous streak Fanny had inherited from her ill-fated father and, until last night, Fanny could not have been accused of anything that would compromise her reputation.

"It is true, my lord, that I accompanied Lord Alverley to Vaux-

hall, alone, in masquerade," she whispered, "but my virtue is unblemished."

"Surely the boy tried to kiss you." In the firelight she saw Lord Slyther's stained teeth bared with prurient interest before he burst out laughing. "You didn't enjoy it, eh? Well, that's good, because as your future husband it's *my* job to show you how to kiss. Now stand up, Miss Brightwell, if you please, and face me."

Fanny rose, silent while her mind whirled at this new and dreadful situation. Her mother was in the next room with Antoinette. When Fanny emerged with Lord Slyther to announce the news of their engagement, Lady Brightwell would clasp Fanny tenderly to her bosom in perhaps the only gesture of genuine pleasure she'd ever extend towards her eldest daughter—the daughter upon whom she was pinning all her hopes. All the *family's* hopes, Fanny amended silently. Lady Brightwell had made this brutally clear only last night. If neither Fanny nor Antoinette married well by the end of the season the Brightwell family would slide into worse than simply genteel poverty.

If Fanny was not prepared to sacrifice herself to this horror, there would be no more rubbing shoulders with the *haut ton*. No, she'd be rubbing the chilblains of some crotchety old woman to whom she'd be paid companion, while Antoinette tried to teach infants how to count when she could barely count to a hundred herself and their mother lived out her days beholden to her detested cousin, having never forgiven Fanny for failing in her duty.

"Show me your ankles."

Fanny swallowed down her surprised outrage, only raising the skirts of her cerulean blue lutestring gown when he repeated the command in a less cajoling tone.

He relaxed deeper into his chair with a sigh. "Such prettily turned little ankles, Miss Brightwell." He patted his heart. "Indeed, you are going to bring me much pleasure in my dotage. Now let

me *feel* your ankle, if you please. Raise your leg upon the footstool so I may bend forward and caress your pretty little limb."

Fanny shook her head while trying not to cry. Never had she been so demeaned in all her life. "With all due respect, my Lord, I committed no sin greater than conversing alone with Lord Alverley."

"And kissing him."

"One kiss—"

"Your reputation is besmirched, Miss Brightwell, and only I will be prepared to overlook it once it becomes public knowledge. Now, if you please, my dear, raise your little ankle over the arm of my chair so I may stroke it for you while we discuss the terms of this marriage you're in no position to refuse."

This was too much. Pushing back her shoulders, Fanny stared him in the eye and breathed out on a hiss, "I will not."

He laughed, then raised his fat, bejewelled fingers and waggled them at her. "Well, you can play the coy maiden with me now but once we are married…"

It was true. Once they were married he could do whatever he wished to her. She'd be his property.

Dear Lord, what could she do to save herself? Lord Slyther's loathsome touch put him in the league of some wart-ridden toad, crawling, fat and oily to the touch.

"You go too far, sir," she said, her voice shaking. "I wish to leave, now."

Lord Slyther gripped her arm to stop her as she turned and, as if reading her thoughts, said between laboured breaths, "If you call your mother there will be no wedding and your peccadilloes, Miss Brightwell, will be all over town." He pulled her onto his lap. "Now, let me press a kiss to that adorable point just behind your elbow. Yes, you'll have to move closer so I can reach it better. Such sweet flesh." He breathed in after the kiss, Fanny having failed to wriggle away in time.

She was surprised at the surprising strength of his grip. "So

you've already determined the terms of our marriage with my mother?" She shut her eyes as Lord Slyther moved his face forward, bracing for the wetness of his lips against her own then relaxing with a sigh of relief when instead he responded with a satisfied chuckle before answering her question. "At great length, Miss Brightwell. Indeed, she was most forthcoming, offering me first your younger sister, Antoinette, whom she described as much more manageable." He began to stroke her arm. "Less likely to cause me problems. I told her I had eyes only for you. Now raise your chin so I can see your face. That's right, yes…and just what I'd hoped to see. Fear. Innocent creature though you are *now*, I intend to keep you true to your adoring and—as long as you play your cards right—indulgent husband."

Fanny was determined not to him see her cry. She was helpless. Her mother would not come at her screams, she knew that, for her mother had all but sold her to this loathsome creature.

"I also relish the idea of keeping such a bold and beautiful creature as you in check, my dearest Miss Brightwell. Now, raise your skirts a little. I want to satisfy myself that your lovely limbs and wondrous bosom are as soft and well-formed as in my fevered imaginings. No, do not be afraid, Miss Brightwell. I plan to keep some surprises on hold. No doubt you wish to build up your anticipation for our wedding night as much as I do. For now, I wish merely to caress those magnificent mounds of creamy flesh while we discuss some of my stipulations as regards our happy union."

"No, my lord." Fanny scrambled to get away but he snatched at her hand and jerked her back to him so that she landed with a thud across his thighs.

Breathing heavily, her mind screamed out at her lack of options. Escape was not possible. Even for one as bold and clever as she, there was nowhere to turn. Her mother would cast her out, meaning that, without protection, Fanny would have to resort to selling her body for a few shillings—though the whole

business of what *that* was all about was still clouded in obscurity. However, much as she abhorred the idea, common sense told her she was still better off selling herself—for a better price—to Lord Slyther.

"If you please, my Lord, I would request that you keep your hands to yourself until we are married."

With a grunt of laughter, he obediently dropped his hands and made no move to detain her as she rose. "Your final request is granted, Miss Brightwell. Like a good little debutante you know how to behave, but when you are my wife you will know who is master. When we are married, I shall enjoy coaxing from you a little of the fire and passion I know lurks just below the surface. I saw it in your knowing eyes the first time we met, my dear, and so was disappointed you saw fit to take such a gamble and cast a lure at that milksop Alverley when you could have had me three months ago."

"Please, I would like to return to my mother, now." She sounded as defeated as she felt.

"Would you now? Well, not before you rub my poor swollen legs. Your mother assured me you were an excellent nurse." Encased in gold pantaloons, both his legs rested on the footstool she'd earlier vacated. "Kneel down," he ordered.

What should she do?

He saw her indecision and continued his taunting. "Your little act of rashness put the ball back in my court, didn't it, Miss Brightwell? I'm sure you don't want your mother to hear of it. Now, kneel down." He tugged at her wrist and forced her to her knees. "Ah, so you see there's more to me than meets the eye. I hope you're impressed."

The reason for his sudden satisfaction was no doubt the horror on Fanny's face as her gaze moved up his thighs to the tent-like structure growing at the juncture of his legs.

"Meet my Magnificent Member, Miss Brightwell." His eyes gleamed. He seemed suddenly far from infirm. "As you can see,

my Magnificent Member is in far better health than the rest of me. You and he are going to enjoy great sport together."

Fanny tried to rise but he gripped her wrist tightly, ensuring she remained on her knees.

"In my coat pocket I have the special licence that will see us married tomorrow, my pretty." He closed his eyes as if in rapture then raised his eyes to the ceiling. "Only one more night to wait, Miss Brightwell, and then you'll be all mine."

"Tomorrow? Please, Lord Slyther, that is too soon. I…have no wedding dress. I need to prepare."

"The day after that, then—and that's as long as I'm prepared to wait. The anticipation I feel…" He glanced down at his still bulging trousers and amended this to: "that we both feel, is almost too much to bear."

Fanny was almost sick upon the spot.

"Tears, Miss Brighwell?" he enquired as he smoothed the silk over his crotch. "No time to get too carried away when there are appearances to be maintained, eh?" After an initial pained look while he straightened his breeches, his sigh was one of immense satisfaction as he regarded Fanny's slumped shoulders. She covered her face with her hands to hide her distress and tried to stop her body from shaking.

"I am a kind master, Miss Brightwell," he said, his tone fatherly as he patted her shoulder, "who shall govern you appropriately, as will be my duty as your new husband. Provided no whisper regarding unseemly conduct on your part ever comes to my ear, and no suspicions as regards your straying interest lodge in my brain, you shall have all the pretty clothes and indulgences you could wish for. Your mother will have a comfortable abode for the rest of her life and, in view of her willingness to please me as regards the terms of this marriage, her own carriage. I shall also bail out your wastrel brother, Bertram, for we can't have him following in his father's footsteps, can we? Your father owed a lot of money when he died, and it was just as well, some would say,

that he chose the time and method of his death—else there were others prepared to help him along."

She tried to block her ears to Lord Slyther's chuckle but could not. It would haunt her. There was no way out. She was doomed and he spoke nothing but the truth when he insinuated there were no other contenders prepared to overlook the collective Brightwell failings.

He cupped her chin and forced her to look at him.

"So, Miss Brightwell, the day after tomorrow will be the happy day, eh? You can think of nothing to stand in the way of our happiness, I trust, after this very satisfying little discussion? No? Good. Then call your mother through, so we may impart the happy news."

Wearily, unsmiling, she rose, but he stopped her as she had her hand upon the doorknob.

"Appearances, Miss Brightwell"—his voice was warning, his expression evil—"are everything. You will be my *joyful* bride and my *constant* wife."

A green log in the fire hissed. Fanny forced her lips into the required smile, wondering how far it was possible to pretend joy when her soul was all but dead.

"Tomorrow you shall wear my ring—the Slyther ring—to Lord Quamby's ball, where you shall have eyes only for me and my comfort. The morning following that, we shall be married."

Fanny curtsied. "Yes, my Lord."

"One other thing, Miss Brightwell…"

"Yes?"

"If I hear a word to suggest that your behaviour is anything but beyond reproach, and your heart and body are not wholly dedicated to me, then I shall cut off your mother's pension and refuse all assistance to your siblings. You will discover I am not the kind and indulgent husband you thought you'd married. Is that understood?"

Fanny nodded as she felt the boldness of a lifetime drain from

her. Lord Slyther held all the cards. She was powerless to resist. All she could hope for was that salvation would come before she was a dried-up prune of a creature with all her joy in life sucked from her.

Once more she curtsied, before she offered Lord Slyther the response required of a dispirited, subjugated bride-to-be.

Through constricted airways, she forced her words past the threatening tears, "Yes, my Lord."

CHAPTER 3

elix Linley, Lord Fenton, cast his roving eye over the gathering. Now that he was in the market for a wife, after a decade of idle dalliances, he'd never been more spoilt for choice.

And he'd never been more dissatisfied with what was on offer.

His companion, the undiscerning libertine George Bramley, was doing his best to acquaint Fenton with the dazzling debutantes new to society since Fenton's return to England after two years abroad. The truth was that Fenton was too busy reliving his nocturnal adventure at Vauxhall Gardens to pay attention. He far preferred amorous intrigue to a roomful of eligible maidens parading their wares. Scowling at a Titian-haired miss whose smile faltered as she scuttled away, he realised he was comparing them all against a new standard—the exquisite ingénue he'd scooped up from under Alverley's nose. As he watched the redhead's return to the safety of her mama, his resolve hardened. Once he'd paid his respects to Lord Quamby this evening, he'd return to Vauxhall and see if the mysterious creature of the night was parading her far more delectable wares in one of the garden's serpentine walks.

He was certain she was very new to the trade—though her lines had been very polished. *"I am destined to marry a man I do not love."* Ha! What sort of credulous fool did she take him for? Nevertheless, he *had* been a fool not to have snared her when he had the chance. He might be in the market for a wife but enjoying the pleasures offered by an enthusiastic and diverting mistress was a far more enticing prospect.

"And passing by is the Baby Brightwell Beauty," Bramley remarked as a golden-haired debutante crossed his line of vision. "Unleashed this season to rival her sister in the fortune-hunting stakes, she is yet another to beware."

Fenton watched the girl join a bored Corinthian wearing such ridiculously high collar points that the chafing of his neck could be seen from five yards away. Beside him stood a dark-haired girl, partly obscured by her companion's posturing, though he could see she filled out her gold-flecked gown very nicely.

With peculiar grace, she turned, setting off a chain of events that had Bramley thumping Fenton on the back and sympathising. "Ah, the Brightwell Beauty. One glance from her azure blue eyes will damn a man to eternal restlessness. Have nothing to do with her, Fenton. She can only cause you grief."

The young woman had not even glanced at him and already Fenton was in the grip of a maelstrom of powerful emotions, not all of them pleasant, as he watched the girl he'd abducted from Vauxhall Gardens sip her champagne and laugh with her companions. Mesmerised, he feasted his eyes upon her lithe and lovely figure in a gown that was both modest and alluring. Her eyes were most arresting, dancing with liveliness in a heart-shaped face framed with dark ringlets tumbling from the crown of her head. Her cheekbones were high, her mouth a delectable pout of a rosebud he remembered only too well grazing his jawline before he'd plundered it with fierce kisses of his own.

The young woman's hair he remembered as having been

powdered. Now, reflecting the light from a thousand beeswax candles, it had the sheen of a raven's wing.

He tried to master his desire, or at least the effect it was having upon him, shifting position, his discomfort exacerbated by the deepest dismay. He'd assumed the girl he'd carried off from Alverley to be a fair Cyprian—or close enough—yet her presence tonight confirmed her status among the *haut ton*. For all his eccentricity, their illustrious host Lord Quamby did not invite members of the *demi mondaine* to the same entertainments to which he invited his gorgon of a mama.

If he was lucky, the dark-haired beauty would not recognise him. If he wasn't so fortunate he'd be fronting up to a dawn appointment on Hampstead Heath with some irate brother or father.

"Not marriage material, old chap, though that's what she's been angling for the past two seasons."

Bramley's leer aroused Fenton's chivalry. Turning, he said icily, "I well recall Baron Brightwell's fall from grace, and his subsequent exile." The kernel of dislike he'd always felt for Bramley hardened and grew. There was something unpleasantly brutal about the man, despite their loose friendship. "Lord Brightwell's pecuniary embarrassment and the nature of his death are not stains to be borne by his daughters."

Bramley chuckled and scratched his thick nose. "Brightwell's fall from grace has nothing to do with society's low opinion of his daughters." His tone was suggestive.

Ignoring him, Fenton resumed the pleasant occupation of gazing upon Miss Brightwell, and felt again the swell of his manhood. Unconsciously he licked his lips, unable to rid himself of memories of her mouth, captive beneath his, responding with delightful passion. The softness of her curves, the lushness of her body, were branded on his thoughts and it took all his willpower not to groan aloud. What had he done? He'd compromised an innocent! He'd whisked her away from Alverley, thinking it no

more than a game that would teach the silly boy a lesson, and before he knew it he'd been bewitched by his captive.

At first he'd not believed her insinuations about her inexperience, for what *kind* of young woman would allow herself such liberties with a strange man in a boat?

Uncomfortably he realised he'd not put her down when she'd requested. But that had been much earlier. In the boat she'd made it clear she *wanted* him to kiss her.

Thank the Lord it had gone no further than that though if they'd been discovered... He shuddered. He dare not think of it.

Fenton tried to breathe evenly. He'd abducted the girl and, despite their respective disguises and lack of knowledge of one another, they'd discovered some powerful, unexpected chemistry between them.

He closed his eyes in contemplation of her soft arms, cool to the touch, her body radiating a delightful, fragrant mix of sweetness and desire.

Desire!

He jerked his eyes open as he tried to cast his mind back to the worst of what he'd done.

Kissed her. Yes, that's all. She'd not let his hands stray which he'd though coy playacting. Fenton swallowed, hoping it wasn't too soon to feel relief. It was an uncomfortable notion but until he'd intruded on her heated exchange with Alverley—and who knew but that there had been some discreet chaperone hiding in the wings—Miss Brightwell had quite likely had no experience of relations between men and women.

Now she was here, a respectable debutante, and if word got out as to what he'd done he'd be pilloried. It would be no more than he deserved. The thought that he'd compromised an innocent was not something that sat well with him. However, the more he thought about it, the more appealing was the idea of atonement.

He was conscious of the irregular beat of his heart, the

suspended pause as, glancing up, she locked eyes with him. Holding her gaze, he watched the play of emotions flit across her lovely, mobile face. God, she was a beauty. He longed to cross the floor and offer the most abject of apologies.

Except he could not do that. He could say nothing in company that would suggest she was guilty of any impropriety, yet he was screaming inside to whisk her away to some secluded arbour so he could determine her feelings for him after two days of sober reflection.

On the short ferry crossing, he'd been taken aback by the unexpected sizzle of excitement that had been lacking during his numerous encounters with other women. Miss Brightwell was as charmingly refreshing a contradiction as had ever crossed his path.

Just then, her attention was claimed by her companion and Fenton returned reluctantly to Bramley's unflattering monologue.

"...likes to think she's a cut above the rest, though she'll be lucky to snare a rich merchant prepared to overlook her reputation. She's more than willing to make discreet compromises when a fellow makes her a good offer."

Fenton unleashed a cold, level stare upon Bramley, then allowed him to drone on while his thoughts ran their own course. His kiss with Miss Brightwell in the boat had unleashed his desire. Oh, he wanted to teach her so much more...but without compromising her reputation. For the novel notion had popped into his head that it would be rather splendid to take for his wife a woman with whom he'd experienced instant attraction. He'd had plenty of mistresses whose transitory excitement had quickly given way to an air of jaded experience he found quite unpalatable but he was ready for a wife now.

And he wanted one he found pleasing and who responded to him with genuine enthusiasm. At the very least, he would pay his respects to the young woman across the room and set matters in motion. It would be interesting to see where they led.

Yet wasn't there was something about the Brightwell name to which his mother had also taken exception?

Brightwell... Fenton racked his brains to capture the elusive drift of memory. What had his mother's caveat been, following her joy at his admission that he'd decided to find himself a wife?

"Just so long as it's not a Brightwell." Lady Fenton's elegant nose had wrinkled with disgust. "They came back from exile last year, trying to insinuate their way into society. Like pretty, common dandelions dressing themselves up as exotic tulips."

The recollection of his mother's aversion was dampening, but of course no reason not to make up to a beautiful girl this evening. He would discover the truth for himself, and act accordingly.

Unable to drag his eyes away, he watched as the beautiful Brightwells, one so fair, the other so dark, were led into a cotillion. "If you're trying to warn me off, Bramley," he said, coolly, "you've not succeeded."

"I was thinking of your poor mama," Bramley assured him. "Mine had heart palpitations after I paid court to Miss Brightwell. When I learnt more of the young woman's—er—colourful history, and her willingness to meet me halfway in the hopes she'd gain a wedding band, I'm afraid I shared Mama's disgust."

"Why does Quamby invite them if they are so beyond the pale?" Fenton's bored drawl masked the tumult in his breast. Fortunately he knew Bramley was a renowned liar.

His friend had clearly been awaiting an opportunity to elaborate. Adjusting a cufflink below his coat sleeve with exaggerated care, he said, "It's been suggested by some that the lovely Miss Brightwell made it into this world before the church register was signed—"

"Good God, Bramley, that can be verified easily enough without your evil assertions!"

"I have heard it said that Miss Brightwell enjoys her status

purely on account of a little bribery and doctoring of dates in the church register."

Fenton grappled with the ramifications of this. The stain of illegitimacy would be an all but impossible hurdle for a young woman to overcome—if what Bramley said was true.

Reason returned. Miss Brightwell's presence here this evening was proof she was accepted into society and that was good enough for him.

"The Beauty of Blackfriars, as the mother was known in the trade, was an engaging little Ladybird Lord Brightwell whisked off to France with him from some house of ill-repute. You know our good baron's proclivities for spice and scandal." Bramley's nostrils flared. Slanting a look at Fenton, he added, "It's not just the uncertainty of Miss Brightwell's origins, my friend, which need to be investigated if you are serious about paying her attention, for there are other toes you must beware treading upon…"

Fenton curbed the desire for a more forceful response to the smug manner in which Bramley delivered his cautions, as if he were the arbiter of what was morally acceptable. Before he could object, Bramley went on, "Miss Brightwell is very adept at playing the untutored innocent. Just ask Lord Bickling, whom she provided with some much-appreciated nocturnal diversion during his wife's confinement last year."

Bramley lied. And yet…

Fenton watched the Brightwell sisters perform their figures on the dance floor with as much grace as any duke's daughter. Could she be such an actress? He imagined the dark-haired beauty pretending the same innocent enthusiasm she'd shown with him in the ferry as she writhed beneath the fat and leering Bramley and the philandering Lord Bickling.

If Bramley was spouting evil tales with no foundation, he should stop him now—but what if they were true? Was that why his mother had taken so against the Brightwell females? Because they pretended one thing while being quite another?

"Rumour also has it that Lord Slyther has just offered her a *carte blanche.*"

"Lord Slyther! That fat old toad?"

Bramley inclined his head. "You sound sceptical, but I speak the truth. Gout has him laid up in bed this evening, but if you wish to keep Miss Brightwell in your sights you'll discover she's prepared to trade her favours for a little pecuniary respite. All of London knows the creditors are pounding at the door while the brother is under the hatches and *persona non grata* at his club."

During Bramley's denunciation, Fenton's eyes never left the lovely creature who moved with such fluid grace, who spoke to her companions with such animation, and whose every gesture conjured up in him the almost unbearable urge to whisk her away so he could have her all to himself. Again.

This was what he'd hoped to find in a wife. He didn't want some obedient miss who knew nothing of how to whip up his desire or make him feel a man—the very elements that made Miss Brightwell the most desirable contender yet for his lifelong companion.

Though, of course, a companion of any sort would be better than nothing.

"Your fanciful tales, Bramley, are no impediment to my desire to further my acquaintance with Miss Brightwell." He offered his friend a curt smile before realising his error and amending, hurriedly. "I mean, to be introduced to Miss Brightwell."

Desire was at the heart of it. She had bewitched him.

Now, here she was, presented to him on a platter, and he was not going to let her slip away again.

The Earl of Quamby shifted the weight off his withered leg. He gripped Fanny's arm for support as she helped him onto a gilt settee beneath a potted plant with luxuriantly sprouting leaves. In

a thin, rasping voice, he said, "Never have I seen you in greater beauty, my dear Miss Brightwell. But if my instincts are as finely honed as I believe them to be, I'd say the flush on your cheek was due to some fascinating object of the male species amongst us this evening."

Transferring his gaze from the lavish water display before him, complete with leaping goldfish, to the point upon which Fanny's eyes were focused, he added, "Young Alverley didn't come up to scratch, I heard. But then, I did warn you."

Fanny jerked her head around but the Earl's regretful expression did not suggest he'd heard anything else that might reflect badly upon her.

Her relief was short lived. Lord Slyther knew and he was extracting the greatest price she could pay. She fingered the ring that her loathsome future husband had given her. It hung on a chain around her neck and he'd be expecting to see it as a sign of her dutiful submission when he arrived here this evening, though the rumour that gout had laid him up in bed offered a sliver of hope for her temporary deliverance. She shuddered as she recalled the feel of his fingers when he'd fastened it there. It might as well have been a cowbell signifying ownership. How he'd enjoyed her submission.

Antoinette patted her on the shoulder. "Are you thinking of Lord Slyther again, Fanny?" Her sister sounded genuinely sympathetic as the Earl's attention was claimed by one of his handsome young acolytes. "You must not let it upset you. Really, I am quite surprised, for I have never seen you display feeling like this. I'd have had him quite happily."

"Then obviously I am more discerning than you, Antoinette," Fanny sniffed, retreating further behind the potted palm. "Have you not considered what liberties marriage allows a man? Perhaps this is not the place to say it, but beware of offers made by creatures who make your skin crawl, for you're going to have to please them in ways you can't imagine!"

Antoinette offered Fanny a knowing smile. "I am not as naïve as you think, Fanny, and it doesn't bother me one bit. As long as I have a title and the respect I deserve and all the pretty clothes I could want, I don't care what I have to do."

Fanny glanced over her shoulder, fearful that Lord Slyther was advancing upon her at that very moment.

Dear Lord, to imagine the man of her desires was at this moment not ten feet away. She'd not believed it when she'd seen him but though he was dressed now in the height of sartorial elegance, she'd have recognised him anywhere. How could she not? The dark curl that flopped over one brooding eye, the sardonic twist to his sensuous mouth... The recollection of the reactions that mouth had aroused in her made her hot with longing.

And shame.

Yet had not his boldness exceeded hers? Who was he to make her feel she'd been the only one to venture beyond the limits of propriety?

But she'd kissed a stranger in a boat and if he recognised her, what would he think of her?

"Lord Fenton would have been my choice, too." The earl had returned his attention to Fanny once her sister had left her side. "Such a beautiful young man—so perfect in every way." He sighed wistfully. "I'm sure he'd do very well for you, Miss Brightwell. He returned to London only last week after two years travelling the Continent, prostrating the women with his wicked poems and manly attractions. I believe he's mellowed sufficiently for me to introduce you, though I must warn you again, he's an incorrigible rake. Dashed irresistible, nonetheless."

"No!" Fanny ground out, adding in response to his look of enquiry, "That is, I already know he's a rake." The hand that held her champagne coupe trembled. Taking a great leap of faith and desperate to unburden herself now that Antoinette had gone, she said softly, "I believe he is the gentleman who—er—whisked me

away from Alverley several nights ago in the Druid Walk." She took a convulsive sip of champagne before explaining briefly what had happened. "You are the only one to whom I could admit such a thing."

Lord Quamby raised an effete hand to pat a faded red curl into place.

"Masquerades carry that risk," he soothed. "One quite forgets oneself and then one is awfully sorry in the morning. Well, I don't feel that way anymore now, but I remember it when I was young and guilt was my faithful companion. I was convinced I was damned for all those desires of the flesh I could not control. If it's any reassurance, Lord Fenton is a rake who adheres to Rake's Honour."

Fanny closed her eyes briefly. A man who adhered to Rake's Honour would never divulge that which might compromise a lady. It was reassuring that Lord Quamby appeared so confident but what if his confidence was misplaced? "If Lord Fenton uttered one word about what had happened…" She couldn't continue. The thought of losing her reputation on account of her simple, mindless stupidity was too dreadful to contemplate.

"Lord Fenton would never knowingly take liberties with a lady. He may be a rake but he is first and foremost a gentleman. Another thing that may be of interest"—Lord Quamby's tone was contemplative—"he has promised his mama that by season's end he will have found a wife."

Fanny refused to be drawn by his obvious allusion. "If he's marrying to please his mama, he'll have the pick of the company here tonight."

"Why, Miss Brightwell, you are his equal in every way"—her companion cleared his throat—"if we neglect to mention your dissolute father and the daughters' dowries he gambled away."

Fanny's gaze remained fixed on the tousle-haired young man whose poetic good looks would surely win him an earl's daughter with ten thousand a year. And that was discounting the fact that

he was a viscount with a long-established title and vast estates in the north, which he'd inherited two years before.

Lord Fenton.

The mere sight of him heated her blood as much this evening as two nights ago—and would have done so had he been no more than an impecunious poet.

If only he had been!

Intruding upon her lustful fantasies came the reality of Lord Slyther. How could she give herself to such a repulsive creature when she could enjoy a lifetime of bedroom delights with a man like Viscount Fenton—legally? Apart from the fact that she was penniless, she had the credentials that made her Fenton's equal— and it was quite apparent from the heated glances he'd sent her earlier that he felt the same connection. The heated glances after the shocked recognition had caused them both to blush and then smile.

Sucking in a breath through constricted airways, she took another sip of her champagne. Lord Fenton showed interest, most definitely. But within twenty-four hours, if Lord Slyther had his way, she would be married.

Lord Quamby chuckled and said, oblivious to her distress, "I shall enjoy watching the incomparable Miss Fanny Brightwell charm the deliciously dangerous-to-know Lord Fenton from the boughs."

Fanny scanned the room. Lord Slyther intended announcing news of their upcoming nuptials tonight, but still there was no sign of him. If gout had not laid him up in bed perhaps his sedan chair had broken under the weight of him. He lived only two streets away, but he was in such ill health he'd need to be conveyed physically from door to door.

Lord Quamby patted her arm and said, still referring to Lord Fenton. "The dear boy wants a wife with a bit of dash and spirit. Needs one, if you ask me, as a first line of defence against his appalling mama to whom he is devoted but whom I should warn

you"—he grimaced—"is reason alone for you to stay well clear of our dashing viscount."

This he said with a pointed look at his own mama, who was propped up on pillows on a sofa against the far wall. The trailing feather in her purple toque trembled in time to her gentle snoring.

"Your reputation is safe, my dear Miss Brightwell, if only on account of Mama's presence here tonight. Everyone knows that if the venerable dowager duchess is in attendance the company is beyond reproach, though I will admit to enjoying my other entertainments better." The wistful look returned. "Such handsome young men rushing from the stage to dance upon my table. I see a glint of longing in your eye but you'll never be invited. I would not dream of injuring your reputation." He grunted. "Ah, here's my detestable nephew come to pay his respects. Evening Bramley. Trading on your expectations once again, I hear. Your distracted mama called on Monday asking me to bail you out."

Fanny watched the fulminating look cross her erstwhile admirer's face. A thug in gentleman's attire, with his thick nose and close-set eyes, George Bramley had never forgiven her for spurning his advances the previous summer.

A supercilious smile replaced the young man's ill humour. Bowing, he said smoothly, "Evening Uncle; Miss Brightwell. Allow me to introduce my old friend, Lord Fenton."

Fanny inclined her head, her smile brittle as the object of her palpitating heart rose from his bow. Adept in the art of using her fan, she was uncomfortably aware it was of little use in concealing the deep blush that spread upwards from her bosom at the memory of their recent intimacy. A discomfort not eased by the intensity of his gaze and the knowing smile that turned up the corners of his handsome, generous mouth.

The strains of the orchestra tuning up for another cotillion drifted from the next room. Lord Fenton held out his hand.

"Miss Brightwell, would you do me the honour…?"

Her skin prickled under his assessing look as they arranged

themselves in a group of four couples. She felt as exposed as if she were standing, naked, under a blazing sun.

"With your dark hair and proud blue eyes you'd have made the perfect Anne Boleyn at the Vauxhall masquerade," he murmured.

Fanny stared ahead as she prepared for the dance, and wondered how she should respond. So he knew...everything.

"You certainly risked that beautiful neck of yours," he went on, as they performed their figures in the centre of the group before returning to the sidelines. Then, squeezing her hand, he murmured, "I just want to assure you that, as a gentleman, your secret is safe with me."

Reassuring her or taunting her? Was this sport at her expense?

"A great relief, sir," she responded warily as they watched the other dancers go through the motions, "though I believe that in carrying me off forcibly yours was the greater crime. I had become separated from my friends and Lord Alverley was about to help me find them before you took advantage of the situation."

Though she said it with hauteur, the memory of the burning kisses this man had trailed over her throat and across her collarbone made her desperate for more. The other liberties she'd nearly allowed him to make made her want to crawl into a dark hole.

"You're flushed, Miss Brightwell. Perhaps you need air. Shall we step outside?"

So, he was taunting her. "How dare you—?" she began in an angry undertone, but was cut short by the realisation that indeed he was only teasing her.

His deep brown eyes held laughter. "My dear Miss Brightwell, you surely do not imagine I would be so bold as to whisk you away from tonight's company as I did two nights ago?" He grazed the sensitive skin of her forearm with his hand and she shivered as he added, "And for that you have my apology. The truth is that, much as I would like that, I am a gentleman."

She glanced at the nearest couple, afraid their conversation

might be overheard, relieved when he murmured with surprising intensity, "I just wanted to reasure you of that. Whatever happened between us was between you and me...alone."

Holding Lord Fenton's gaze, Fanny executed her dance steps like an automaton. They'd been drilled into her as thoroughly as her need to perform in the marriage mart.

The brittle pride that had armoured her against the damage he could do her—in so many ways—was replaced by a tiny kernel of hope. Lord Fenton was studying Fanny with the greatest interest...and lack of condemnation.

She thought of her impending marriage to Lord Slyther. In twenty-four hours she'd be his possession; his prisoner. And right beside her was a young man who acknowledged that he had feelings for her and that despite her boldness he nevertheless respected her.

A yearning and desperation gathered force within her that was so powerful she thought she might be extinguished. Desperately she needed to explain. "My Lord, in your arms something came over me... I'd never felt it before and"—she kept her eyes trained on his as they linked elbows to dos-à-dos down the centre of the room—"I felt I was in heaven."

Looking decidedly pleased, he put his head close to hers before they separated briefly once more. "Then we shall have to do it again, Miss Brightwell—only this time I promise to proceed in a far more gentlemanly manner."

Was there any clearer way for him to indicate his interest? She was about to respond, to indicate her pleasure and hopefully prolong the boyish charm that had replaced for the moment his rakish self-confidence, but her words were truncated by a gasp. Right before her very eyes she was bearing witness to what threatened to be her sister's greatest impropriety yet.

"Oh, dear Lord," she whispered, clutching the hated ring on its chain, which she had all but forgotten.

"Miss Brightwell?"

When he touched her arm, bare above her gloves, she jerked into sensual awareness, her heart rate speeding up now on more than just Antoinette's account. She pointed. "My sister has this moment disappeared through a door behind that tapestry." Her head swam as she contemplated her mother's fury at the possible repercussions. A fury that would, in this case, be warranted. "Not one second after Mr Bramley," she added, faintly.

"George Bramley knows this is your sister's first ball." She heard concern in Lord Fenton's tone. His dark eyes gentled. "I'm sure he wouldn't—"

"You don't know Bramley if you believe that, sir." She knew she spoke too hotly but her mind was running circles around Antoinette's potential for ruining the entire Brightwell family's prospects.

The squeeze of his hand upon her wrist brought her close to tears. Again he lowered his head to speak softly, his warm breath against her ear spearing tingles of almost unbearable need throughout her entire body.

"The moment this set ends I'll follow them. We need to be discreet. Don't worry, Miss Brightwell—Mr Bramley will not ruin your family's good name under my watch." Pointing to a single door at the end of the saloon that led to the ladies' mending room, he added, "Follow the passage to your right until the last door. I'll meet you in the chamber beyond."

Fighting her impatience, Fanny watched his judicious exit. As soon as she deemed it appropriate, she hurried away to carry out his instructions...right into the path of her chaperone for the evening.

"Lady Harwood, I have two loose buttons that need securing," she gasped. "Please excuse me."

Although Lady Harwood's sponsorship of the Brightwell girls was a discreet arrangement that eased the dowager duchess's pecuniary difficulties and gilded Fanny and Antoinette's

prospects, she took her duties seriously. Holding her lorgnette up to her hooded eyes, she scanned the assembly.

"I trust the ladies' mending room is where we'll find Antoinette." She gave a disapproving sniff. "The girl is too pretty with too little sense to make me easy."

"She accompanied Miss Conyngham to the library, I believe," Fanny lied.

To her relief an old acquaintance chose that fortuitous moment to address the dowager and Fanny was able to slip away.

She was unprepared for the scene that greeted her in the Earl of Quamby's 'chamber beyond'. At first she could see no sign of Antoinette or Bramley. Nor did she immediately seek them out, such was her shock as she pushed open the double doors. The room was clearly for entertaining on a lavish scale, but for a purpose that Fanny could only imagine. Lit now by a series of candles in wall sconces, its lofty proportions disappeared into darkness.

But enough could be seen of the entwined limbs and glazed eyes of the Bacchanalian orgy wall murals reflected in a myriad mirrors that Fanny turned away with a gasp. This was not a room she should enter.

It was only when she heard weeping overlaid by Lord Fenton's stern tones that she forced herself to venture in.

Following the sounds of a heated exchange between two men, punctuated by Antoinette's sobbing, Fanny came upon them by the edge of a sunken area piled high with red and gold silk cushions.

Antoinette sent her sister a baleful look from where she sat hunched on a richly embroidered banquette. Mr Bramley and Lord Fenton angrily faced each other across her.

"I suppose this is your doing," she sniffed.

Instantly, Lord Fenton came to Fanny's defence. "With your best interests at heart, Miss Antoinette." The glower he directed at her younger sister sent a vicarious thrill right through to Fanny's

bones. It was enormously comforting to see the man who'd imprisoned her in his arms two nights before read the two miscreants the riot act regarding the proprieties.

"Good God, Bramley," Fenton railed at him. "Have you no concern for how damaging your rash overtures are to someone of Miss Antoinette's lack of experience?"

Fanny watched, fascinated by the transformation. The sensual mouth and poetic eyes were hard with anger. This man was much more than just a brooding poet with the usual masculine propensity to notch up conquests without regard for consequences. Fanny was awed, as she would be by anyone who could wipe the cynical smirk from Bramley's thuggish face.

Stepping forward, she addressed her sister sternly. "Antoinette, your absence will be noticed unless we return you immediately to the ballroom. Good evening, gentlemen." Nodding coldly to Bramley, she pulled her sister up from her seat.

"No one would have missed us for five minutes longer," Antoinette muttered as Fanny hustled her along the corridor.

"A lot of things that can't be undone are done within five minutes. Are you such a fool, Antoinette," Fanny asked under her breath, "that you would ruin your chances—and quite possibly mine, too—because that knave Bramley sees you as easy prey?"

Antoinette tugged her arm free of Fanny's grip, her mouth sulky, as she stopped in the middle of the passage to face her sister.

"Bramley's next in line to inherit from Lord Quamby and we all know Quamby's never going to produce an heir. Why, Mama would be thrilled."

Fanny shook her head, taking her sister's arm again and hustling her once more along the corridor. "How credulous you are. Bramley is toying with you to avenge himself against me for rejecting his advances last summer. Now, here comes Lady Harwood. If I see you move out of her sight I swear I shall tell Mama *everything*."

She was already turning, barely able to contain her impatience to thank Lord Fenton, when Antoinette gasped, "Oh Fanny, I've lost Lady Harwood's bracelet—"

Fanny felt like throttling her. As their mother had predicted, Antoinette was well on track to doom the Brightwell family's chances.

"Stay there and don't move!" she hissed. "I'll find it. It must have come undone when..."

Now was not the time to put her sister's misdemeanours into words. Seething, Fanny returned to the large, immoral room, hesitating before the double doors. How could she venture, alone, into a room that would shock any well brought up young lady? Indeed, she had been shocked. The scenes had been disturbing.

Disturbingly compelling.

They filled her with strange longings she could not put into words.

Forcing her gaze downwards, she searched the gold laurel leaf pattern of the luxurious carpet for the lost bracelet, seizing upon it with relief. It was a pity, she reflected seconds later as she picked herself up after an undignified tumble down the three steps into the pit, that she had not paid more attention to the hazardous terrain.

Dismay turned to horror as she glanced down, smoothing her hands over her lovely, damaged gown. How could she possibly return to the ball when her skirt had all but been completely ripped from her bodice?

CHAPTER 4

*C*ith a determined squaring of his shoulders, Fenton forced his gaze away from his host's tribute to lust. It was impossible to look upon such scenes and not become prisoner to almost uncontrollable impulses regarding thoughts of the lovely Miss Fanny Brightwell.

Who'd have thought that just a kiss would fire up the desire for so much more? Just those few exchanges on the dance floor had been enough to confirm that his initial interest had not been misplaced.

There was a wary pride to her that he found quite adorable. She thought she was doing such a fine job of appearing impervious to societal opinion but she was clearly desperately aware of its judgement. That's why she was so wary of any allusion to their wicked encounter. Her lapse threatened to confirm all the aspersions anyone might have regarding the Brightwells.

Oh, he liked her pride and he liked her spirit. He liked, too, the fact that despite all the playacting she could not disguise the strong attraction she felt for him.

It was palpable.

And it was mutual.

Fenton let out a sigh of deep contentment. He'd never expected a courtship to go so smoothly. He was attracted to her and she to him. The fact she didn't have much in the way of a dowry was not sufficient to put him off. He'd declared to his mama from the outset that he would marry to please his heart and to provide heirs—not because his pocketbook depended upon it.

Just as well Bramley had fumed off in the other direction and he was alone, Fenton thought wryly as he adjusted his bulging breeches and prepared to return to the ballroom. Miss Brightwell may well have been taken for the next set and he wanted very urgently to commandeer her for the rest of the evening.

He knew he had behaved badly towards her, both two nights ago and with his teasing this evening. The time had come to offer Miss Brightwell the formal apology she deserved. The truth was, he'd not known how to treat her in view of what had transpired between them, while Bramley's assertions...

He shook his head. Bramley was not a man he'd trust above his own instincts and he'd been a fool to concede even a jot of what he'd suggested about Miss Brightwell, as if she were no better than a tuppenny whore! It was sour grapes on Bramley's side, he was sure of it.

No, there was something curiously affecting about Miss Brightwell's combination of boldness and hauteur. If Fenton were to go on instinct alone, he'd venture that Miss Brightwell was only too well aware of her fragile foothold on the society ladder and that every reason she'd given regarding her conduct with Alverley was true.

Yet what else had she said? That she was betrothed to a man she found abhorrent? He needed to discover more. He needed to discover what steps to take to secure her for himself. After the experienced women whose pleasures he'd enjoyed during his two years abroad he was very responsive to Miss Brightwell's charms. The European whores had flattered him, pandered to his every

desire and exhibited the utmost artistry in their ability to raise him to ever greater heights of sexual gratification. He'd taken the Grand Tour to become the cultured man his mother required to take the reins and run the estate when he returned. Any culture he might have acquired had been incidental to the surfeit of lust that had consumed him after discovering how fascinating he was to women. Now it was time to settle down. He realised he was in danger of losing himself to vanity. He'd been given a long leash and he'd taken advantage of his opportunities until he'd felt tethered to nothing.

Now he wanted to return home to Grantham, the family seat for more than three hundred years, and start behaving responsibly. To do that, he needed a wife. Preferably one who would keep him interested and keep him in check.

Miss Brightwell showed every potential of fulfilling both criteria once he'd satisfied himself that Bramley spoke nothing but evil lies and that his mother had no reasonable grounds for her objections.

Shaking his head as he passed a depiction of bedroom sport that was, even to one of his jaded experience, extreme, Fenton was about to return to the entertainment when he was arrested by a short, sharp squeal and the sound of tearing fabric. He turned, his eyes quickly becoming accustomed to the gloom until he caught sight of movement.

After a pregnant silence came a deep sigh followed by Miss Brightwell's dry, unmistakable tones. "Of all the inconvenient times to be disrobed."

A little shocked, Fenton moved closer, following the direction of her voice. He melted into the shadows and watched her in a shaft of light cast by a candle set high on the wall.

She was at the bottom of the pit, sitting amongst a collection of brightly coloured silk cushions, staring with dismay at her gold-flecked skirts. The diaphanous fabric hung limply, torn almost entirely free of her bodice, exposing her chemise. The

sight of the crisp linen undergarment thus revealed—so pristine, yet so shocking—was strangely erotic.

Fenton was torn, too—torn between what a real gentleman ought to do and what, in truth, he *felt* like doing.

The ladies' sewing room was just down the corridor. A real gentleman would hasten there and return with needle and thread to render assistance.

By contrast, he wanted to hurl himself upon her and roll around in that pit of cushions, tearing the rest of her gown from her and running his hands over all her soft, fragrant body with all the passion of a first-time smitten green boy.

Such unadulterated lust was combined, however, with a healthy desire to atone. He looked down at himself and realised that with an erection the size he was sporting he was in no fit state to present himself to any young lady. Therefore, a trip to the ladies' sewing room and the prospect of two minutes' conversation with hatchet-faced Miss Mortimer whose domain it was would hopefully have the required dampening effect.

He turned his footsteps in that direction. He wanted Miss Brightwell but he had no intention of repeating his rash overtures —albeit delicious—of the other night if it should in any way compromise her. She featured in his more long-term plans and he wanted her to know it. Delivering to Miss Brightwell the means to return to the ballroom with her dignity intact might be one way to reassure her that his intentions towards her were honourable.

He was unprepared, upon his return to the pit of cushions, for his crushing disappointment at discovering the object of his desire gone.

Raising his candle, he peered through the gloom, expectant hope returning at a very unladylike exclamation from the darkness beyond what he had at first taken to be a screen.

Drawing nearer, he discovered it was a tent festooned with swathes of red silk woven with elaborate designs in green and

royal purple. About to announce his presence as he searched for the entrance, he was taken aback to discover what could only be a series of peepholes cut into the fabric.

Fenton's mission to the ladies' mending room in the face of almost insurmountable temptation had surely established his credentials as a gentleman. But what gentleman could resist putting his eye to the peephole?

It was spontaneous curiosity, not the conscious intention to spy, that had him gazing upon the incredibly arousing sight of Miss Brightwell, with her hair in disarray, hitching her skirts thigh-high to adjust her garter.

Such a sight would, he felt sure, have robbed far more gentlemanly gentlemen than he of their good manners. Yet good manners demanded that he step away and announce his presence, giving her time to make herself presentable.

Indeed, he was on the point of doing just that—had moved his head away from the peephole and was stepping back—when his practiced eye was caught by a flash of creamy, womanly curves that surely not even the most disciplined of gentleman could resist. Had a marauding tiger been bearing down upon him, Fenton would not have had the power to move.

He returned his eye to the peephole, all concentration focused on the scene before him, all his energy gathering in his loins, like a cannon about to explode. The surface of his skin tingled. With breath fast and shallow he watched the strip of naked flesh lengthen between knee and thigh as she raised her arms to pull off her gown, taking with it the chemise beneath.

He saw slender hips, a triangle of dark hair, creamy, gently rounded belly and a pair of breasts so pert they almost seemed to beckon to him. His own sigh echoed hers as she sank onto an Egyptian sofa with armrests carved in the shape of sphinxes, almost instantly covering her briefly revealed nakedness as she studied the damage done to her gown.

Suddenly he'd never wanted anything, or anyone, so much.

The gold-flecked gossamer fabric and crisp cotton chemise pooled in her lap. Fenton could see her slipper peeking from beneath the chair and willed her to rise and allow the fabric to fall in a shimmer to her feet.

He shifted position, trying to ease his discomfort. Closing his eyes, he tried to control his heathen impulses. He had promised to act the gentleman therefore he should go.

Yet how could he tear himself away from the most seductive, sensuous sight he'd experienced—ever? He realised that even he who prided himself on his self-control was defeated, and stepped forward to return his eye to the peephole.

Miss Brightwell's long, dark hair had come loose from its coiffure and a tendril curled around the rosy peak cresting one of her full, pert breasts, surely the most magnificent bosom he'd ever seen. His vision blurred.

He held his breath. The anticipation was killing him but he dare not reveal his presence or the show would be over—and what would be his reward?

He swallowed. Outrage? Or would she melt into his arms if he promised to restore her dignity?

She shifted a little and he caught a glimpse of naked thigh, a shapely calf encased in its white stocking tied at the knee. He'd seen many a Cyprian in greater undress than this, but the fact that he now gazed upon a lady made the blood sting the surface of his skin. He stifled another groan.

If ever a man was close to the brink of drowning in desire…

It was time to bring matters to a head. In the boat, her responses had shown her desire for a stranger whom she clearly desired considerably more than either Alverley or her intended groom.

He was that man—the man who had made her heart beat fast and furiously during the short ferry crossing.

Now he was back, and he was ready to do far more than just make her heart beat fast and furiously. He wanted Miss Fanny

Brightwell ready to pledge herself to him, heart, body and soul. If her kisses were as sweet as the other night and her body as yielding and pliant, then he intended to woo her right from under the nose of her mystery intended. He would hustle her down the aisle and into his bed as his legal, wedded wife.

Strange what a sense of satisfaction the thought brought to a man who'd feared the shackles of matrimony for his entire life.

"Miss Brightwell?" With conscious devilry, Fenton chose that moment to announce his presence, his intonation suggesting he had not yet ascertained her whereabouts.

Observing her confusion added to his excitement. He'd atone when he handed her needle and thread. Then he'd make her reel from his tender ministrations and he'd show her how exquisite their union could be—without actually taking her virginity. That would be his reward on her wedding night.

"One moment, sir."

The fierce blush that rose from her bosom upwards was enchanting. As was the faint tremble in her voice. Miss Brightwell was not a young lady accustomed to allowing herself to feel at a disadvantage—he'd discovered that much about her.

Now he had to rediscover what she felt like beneath the diaphanous skirts she'd raised so high. The brief sampling of her charms aboard the ferry had been enough to drive him mad to know more. His ungentlemanly spying was driving him to the brink.

~

DEAR LORD, HE MUST NOT SEE HER LIKE THIS, THOUGHT FANNY AS she scrambled into her gown. What on earth had made her eschew undergarments? Vanity, of course. And a desperation to cut more of a dash than anyone else at the ball. Her diaphanous skirts clung far more alluringly to her limbs when dampened. Her chemise provided sufficient modesty. Yet what had possessed her

to remove that as well? She'd hoped to engineer some means of joining the two garments together but now she was completely at a disadvantage.

Anxiety and urgency made her fingers clumsy as she tried to fix the damage. In despair, she glanced up at her reflection in the huge gilt mirror that formed one entire wall of the festooned tent.

How was she to re-fashion her Grecian coiffure when she'd lost most of the necessary hairpins? If that was not bad enough, how could she ever make her reappearance at the ball in a gown so badly damaged?

She was conscious of his presence near the entrance and both longed for and feared his arrival.

"I… I'm not quite ready." Would she ever be?

The insidious knot of self-doubt always lurking beneath the surface grew. It hardened, lodging in her chest cavity, and ground away at the self-assurance she'd polished to a shine. Who did she think she was, parading as a society miss, dangling her brassy powers of attraction before Britain's ten thousand in the hopes of snaring a husband who would benefit the Brightwell family, collectively? A baron's daughter she may be, but she had nothing other than good looks and a reputation still intact—*if* Fenton kept his word—to recommend her. At this moment, even that was imperilled on account of her careless pea goose of a sister. Her feverish attempts at feigning a life of leisure and frivolity in accord with those whose life she sought to share seemed suddenly stupid and pathetic. She'd be a laughing stock if people knew the long hours she plied needle and thread to clothe her sister and herself in the latest splendour.

Desperation at her plight was shredding her insides. Tomorrow she was to marry Lord Slyther, unless…

Unless what? There was not time. Lord Fenton was waiting for her and all she could do was stare into the looking-glass like some unworldly debutante frozen by fear.

Right now, in her hour of need, she could not even find a

threaded needle to save her reputation. Lord Fenton would think her little better than a costermonger when he saw her with her torn skirt and disordered hair. What would he think if he could see into her shrivelled-up little soul?

Her toes curled and her insides cleaved with frustrated longing. Tonight she'd recognised in his eye the mysterious fascination she wielded. She'd wielded the same power over Alverley.

It was true that she'd not wanted Alverley but he'd offered the means of survival. Survival for her and her family.

Lord, but she wanted Fenton. It was too early to call it love—when love was what she aspired above all else—but there was a magnetism between them that defied common sense. Surely that was a good enough beginning to warrant throwing all her efforts into making him want her when the alternative was Lord Slyther?

With an effort, she steadied her breathing. Her mother would be equally satisfied with Lord Fenton. Fenton provided the same opportunities as Lord Slyther. He had lineage, money, prospects enough to offer the entire Brightwell clan. Her mother would be as delighted over a match with Fenton as she was with Lord Slyther. *Wouldn't* she?

Fanny could be a wife worthy of Lord Fenton. Fanny *needed* a man like Lord Fenton. And Fanny *wanted*…Lord Fenton.

Actually wanted him, like she'd never wanted a man. The need to reconnect with him, physically, was so powerfully intense she had to grip the sofa arm to steady herself.

Beware. She closed her eyes and forced reason to prevail. Fenton had the power to make her forget herself. It had happened before and she'd been lucky.

In Fenton she wondered if she'd met her match. She recognised in him qualities that went deeper than the ironic façade he chose to present to the world—for she practiced the same deception. A necessary deception if she were to shield her most vulnerable self from an exacting and judgemental society.

She bit her trembling lip and tried to collect her wits. If she

had time she could work herself into the woman of Fenton's dreams—dreams that would last beyond the here and now…

…if only she had time.

"You may come, Lord Fenton."

She sat heavily upon the sofa and buried her head in her hands. There was no time. No time to insinuate herself into not just his heart, but his soul, his psyche. No time to receive the marriage offer that would save her from Lord Slyther.

The season was winding down. Matches were being made and the capital was emptying—as were the Brightwell coffers. With the parlous state of their finances came desperation. Fanny could not risk refusing Lord Slyther in case Lord Fenton proved as disappointing as Alverley. Her mother would never allow it, for, unless Fanny married a man who not only was prepared to overlook her lack of dowry but would be generous to the rest of her family, they were all lost.

"Miss Brightwell!"

She jerked up her head at his entrance and hope clawed a jagged journey from the soles of her feet to pound in her chest. Framed in the opening of the silken tent, the smile that hovered about Lord Fenton's wide sensuous mouth echoed the salvation in his eyes.

Everything for which she could have hoped was reflected in their depths. Admiration, curiosity—and, above all, desire. Yet while it was his desire upon which she'd pinned her hopes, it was the kindness of his words that gave her the reassurance she needed.

"I've brought needle and thread," he said, offering her the tools to restore her respectability, "which I snatched from the sewing room when I witnessed the unfortunate results of your fall."

She managed to muffle the hysteria that tinged her laugh as she rose and took up the threaded needle.

"I'm not sure I'm in a position to play the seamstress." With a wry look at her jutting bosom, which obscured the seam she must

sew, her hand trembled as she handed the needle back to him. "Perhaps you, Lord Fenton, have hidden talents." Her smile was as unsteady as her shaking hand. What was happening to the cool façade she'd cultivated to such a fine art? Her nipples ached and she was conscious of the sudden heat and moisture between her legs.

She swallowed, barely able to force the words out through dry lips. "I cannot see to sew, but you will be my hero if you can stitch a straight seam."

Lord Fenton took the needle, resting his other hand upon her shoulder. Whether that was to steady her or himself, Fanny wasn't sure, but that was immaterial as her whole body seemed to come alive at his touch. A dull, needy ache started in the pit of her belly as his eyes, full of sympathetic understanding, bored into hers. The usual, calculating gleam of the rake was replaced with something deeper and more sincere that nearly took her breath away.

But it was his lack of skill with a needle that, in fact, did so. At her exclamation of pain they jerked apart.

"My apologies!" he cried, reflexively clasping her wounded breast.

Each froze at the contact. With a soft gasp Fanny swayed and he caught her to him. His touch seared her soul, branded her his, melting her insides into a pool of heated longing. It was apparent he wanted something between them to happen as much as she did. She could feel the bulge of of his manhood pressed against her stomach. Lord Slyther had at least imparted some useful information on the mechanics of intimate relations between men and women. The thought burst into her head that, as God was her witness, she had no intention of allowing Lord Slyther to rend her asunder with his Magnificent Member when the man before her was just as willing to do so—and, oh, so damnably irresistible.

Suspended in an agony of waiting, she watched Lord Fenton's sudden awareness combust into something far more primal, tensed for his response, then wilted as he gathered her in his arms

with a low groan. She had wit only to be thankful for the fact that the needle was no longer between them before she responded— completely, and with every particle of body and soul.

"Oh, my Lord!" The fast and furious pounding of her heart and the urgency of her breathing almost deafened her. Or was that Lord Fenton's breathing? The gaze he trained upon her was rapt. His eyes were glazed. In fact, for a moment he looked like a sleek, handsome wolf contemplating his dinner. Miss Fanny Brightwell? Oh, she was more than ready. Her nipples ached as her mind was tugged ever more insistently into the dangerous swirl of sensation that threatened.

When his mouth came down on hers she was ready and eager as she'd never been with Alverley—as she'd never been with any man. Her heart, pumping ever more furiously, seemed to carry hope, fire and passion through her veins, not the familiar resignation wrought by a man's interest. The body she'd groomed since womanhood, the mind her mother had filled with careful calculation, all for the purpose of snaring a husband, no longer screamed its endless litany of 'caution, as long as you catch him'.

Fanny's mind emptied itself of every last drop of the careful advice with which it had been filled by her mother over a lifetime. As Lord Fenton's hand contoured her from breast to knee, resistance was the furthest thing from her mind. The inner voice of warning that should have pierced her consciousness was stifled by the heady sensations that pumped through her like honey.

"You are exquisite," he murmured against her lips as his hands roamed all over her, making her gasp as they skimmed her waist and thighs, cupping her bottom and pulling her hard against his jutting erection.

And so was he. Lord Slyther's sly insinuations and the forced physicality in which she'd been an unwilling participant the night before had been her first initiation into the underworld of desire. Of the effect desire had on men. There was nothing sly or forced about this contact.

Excitement took on a life of its own as Lord Fenton's mouth, a hot, wet cavern of mystery and delight, became a playground of tangling tongues and panting desire.

A desire that became increasingly mindless in response to her throbbing need as he bent to clasp her knee, hooking her leg over the armrest of the Egyptian sofa. He cupped her face before burying his mouth in her décolletage, his lips probing, his hands massaging until her breast burst free of its confinement and his tongue curled around her nipple.

Delighted, she moaned, arching against him, prickles of excitement shooting from her breast to her lower belly, the apex of her legs now a mass of quivering sensation. When he cupped her mound she cried out with frustration at the intrusion of her clothing against heated skin, an unnecessary layer that kept them apart. For they were destined to be one— she felt it in the basest regions of her mind, body and soul.

"Oh, God!" she gasped as the laving of his tongue heated the tip of her nipple beyond endurance. In an agony of ecstasy she rained kisses upon his crisp, dark curls, unsure whether to push him away or hold him closer.

She thought she had reached the summit of her pleasure, but it was just the beginning, she realised, as he insinuated his hand beneath the hem of her gown. She held her breath, poised on the edge of she knew not what as he trailed gentle, probing fingertips up her leg. He massaged the heated, highly sensitised skin of her inner thigh with agonising slowness.

"You like it?" His voice was hoarse as he stroked the contours of her body with a tenderness at odds with the hard masculine strength of his own. It seemed he had barely the strength needed to groan, "Just say the word, and I'll do whatever pleases you, my love." The tension and effort it clearly cost him to remain gentle only intensified the thrill. He was hers to command and she was enthralled.

Gasping as he gently parted her folds with probing fingers to

resume his secret exploration, she felt as if her soul were on a string he was pulling ever tighter. And tighter. The rhythmic motion was creating needs she had never known she had. She held her breath, digging her fingers into his back and shoulders as he pleasured her, the tension within building to almost unbearable limits.

His breath, husky with need, tickled her ear. "I want you like I've never wanted any woman." Briefly, she closed her eyes as her mind swam into a realm where her life existed on another plane and her body was a temple to this man whose touch unleashed such dangerous, forbidden impulses.

Clenching her jaw in sudden determination that overrode every sensible notion her mother had ever instilled in her, she weighed up her future.

Lord Slyther was a sure bet. She'd marry him tomorrow and perhaps be a widow within the year. Or ten. Meanwhile Fenton would wed another. Fenton, the man she wanted like no other.

She couldn't let it happen…wouldn't let it, whatever the sacrifices she must make. Fanny had never truly desired anything with complete and utter conviction as she desired Fenton as her legal wedded husband in that moment.

Whatever it took, she would…

With shock she realised all that was at stake. It was too much of a risk. She must retreat.

If he were to continue wanting her as much as she wanted him, the key to her happiness lay in sustaining his fascination with her. She couldn't succumb like some common doxy.

She could hear her mother's voice in her head telling her that a graceful retreat would leave him dangling for more. The faint voice of her own sensible self said the same.

So that's what she must do.

But another voice intruded; reminding her that she didn't have time to take risks.

And letting him go with nothing more than a kiss to bind them was too great a risk.

Or was it that her pleasure was mindless and she'd never felt so secure in her powers of attraction?

He hadn't stopped kissing her and now it was starting all over again as his clever fingers played her like a harp and her good intentions were swept away by the intense sensation that started with the throbbing between her legs and built up in every fibre of her body, pulling on her heart strings until they threatened to snap. She was gasping her desire for—what? She could not know and when, with a groan, he dragged his mouth from hers to say, raggedly, he was honour-bound to release her, the idea was suddenly like an end to her world.

"No!" she cried, her hands fumbling for the buttons of his breeches. *Rake's Honour.* He wanted her, and if he took her now she'd be his forever. The powers she exercised tonight would be nothing to those she'd exert to ensure he never regretted it.

His look of shocked delight caused her to drop her hands. Foolish girl! This could be the end of everything. She tried to wriggle out of his embrace but it seemed her brief forwardness had redoubled his enthusiasm.

"You are magnificent, Miss Brightwell," he murmured against her lips as he scooped her up and then lay her on the ground, caging her body with hers. "Say you'll be mine."

Say you'll be mine.

It was too enigmatic to take as a promise of fidelity or honour but Fanny was too overcome by want and need to take heed of the cautions that echoed in her mind. For once her own desires were riding roughshod over the careful teachings of a lifetime.

She felt as if at last she was breaking free, obeying the impulses of her body rather than her mind. It was a glorious and liberating feeling to live in the moment rather than for an uncertain future.

The next few moments passed in a whirlpool of ecstatic sensa-

tion. She did not know how he'd managed it, but her legs were wrapped around his waist as he plundered her mouth like an oasis in a desert. His deft, clever hands swept over her bottom, turning the swollen bud at her very core once more into a quivering mass of sensation. When, groaning, he thrust himself into her, the surprising second of searing pain was immediately swept away by an encore of the first act—wave after wave of blissful, wicked, intense pleasure.

CHAPTER 5

*I*n a daze, Fanny gave herself up to the rocking motion of the carriage as she sat quietly between Lady Harwood and her sister. Antoinette's chatter was a welcome diversion. Clearly, the girl felt no shame or remorse about her conduct with Bramley.

But what of Fanny's own behaviour?

Sinking into her cloak and closing her eyes, she relived the heady passion followed by its sweet aftermath.

The urgency of their physical need had taken them both by surprise. Even now, she was conscious of the throbbing between her legs at the mere thought of him. He'd invaded the very core of her in more ways than one. Lord Fenton was *bound* to her. He'd said as much as he'd cradled her in his arms, whispering sweet endearments while he gently kissed her eyes and lips.

Yet despite his assertions that what they'd shared was the most real and true moment of his life, doubt needled.

How could she have got so carried away? Had she been a fool? A mere conquest?

As Antoinette chattered, Fanny sank deeper into hopelessness. In the morning she would marry Lord Slyther. What choice did

she have? Neither he nor her mother would allow further postponement, so what possible hope had she of eliciting anything from Lord Fenton before it was too late? *Anything* that would give her reason to delay her nuptials for a few more days.

How had she allowed him to take her virtue when she was to marry another?

Well, the answer to that was easy. There was no way Fanny had intended allowing Lord Slyther take her virtue when the man for whom she'd fallen was so willing.

But why hadn't she told Lord Fenton she was to marry Lord Slyther in less than twenty-four hours. That had been a distinct oversight.

After delivering Lady Harwood to her modest lodgings, the carriage deposited the two sisters in front of theirs, but before the jarvey was dismissed Lady Brightwell came hurrying down the front steps dressed in a dark cloak.

"Inside with you, Antoinette—Fanny, we're going to see Lord Slyther." She rubbed her hands together as she waited to be assisted up the step, while Antoinette obediently disappeared through the front door. "He's impatient, Fanny. You did well last night. Perhaps Lord Slyther has the priest and witnesses already waiting." She squeezed Fanny's arm as she settled herself on the carriage seat beside Fanny. "Tonight could be your *wedding* night!"

Fanny didn't know whether to scream, faint or be sick.

"Come, girl, show a little jubilation. You have done well. *Very* well."

Dully, Fanny stared ahead. After a long silence she whispered, "I don't know if I can do this, Mother."

"Whatever is this nonsense, Fanny?" A note of alarm crept into Lady Brightwell's tone. She rapped on the roof for the jarvey to go faster, as if hastening to their destination might stay Fanny's disquieting sentiments. "Lord Slyther is a *viscount*. He is *rich*. He has promised to be *generous*—"

Fanny shuddered. "Provided I become his slave. Oh, Mother,

he made me do the most appalling things the other night." She slumped against the cold window. "You have no idea. I thought I was going to die of shame—"

"Do you imagine you're the only young woman who has had to barter her body to buy a life?" Lady Brightwell's dismay turned to anger. Growing anger. "Would you see us cast into the streets, or forced into a grinding, menial existence because you are not prepared to do what *every* other young woman has to do in order to satisfy a man? Yes, men are disgusting creatures and Lord Slyther is probably worse than most. But he has one redeeming feature, Fanny, that you can't ignore." Directing the full force of her fulminating glare upon Fanny as the carriage drew up in front of Lord Slyther's elegant Mayfair address, she comforted her daughter, "He cannot possibly live long. Then, my dear, your reward will be widowhood and, if you play your cards right in the meantime, a sizeable widow's portion. Now, get out of the carriage and do what you have to do without that long face!"

Terrified, Fanny waited outside Lord Slyther's bedchamber, as instructed. Her mother had been ushered to the drawing room.

As the door opened to admit her she nearly gasped at the foetid sickroom air but managed to retain the pleasant and decorous smile demanded by her mother.

If she could conjure up Lord Fenton's image she might get through this, she counselled herself. Oh, *why* had she not told him about Lord Slyther? He'd been overcome with feeling. It had been more than just lust. He'd shared her feelings of genuine attraction. She'd never have done what she had if she hadn't truly believed that the extraordinary force that had drawn them together wasn't based on something more than that.

Now, as she took in Lord Slyther's satisfied, triumphant look she knew her mother spoke the truth. Only careful calculation was going to get Fanny what she wanted.

She curtsied. "I missed you this evening, my Lord." She made a point of fingering the ring she'd been given, holding it up on its

chain and looking at it proudly. There had been an uncomfortable moment when Lord Fenton had whisked up Fanny's handkerchief, in which the ring had been wrapped, in order to assist with some discreet mopping up. Fortunately for her white muslin, she had not bled—her days as a keen horsewoman during the family's exile in France had seen to that.

When the ring had fallen from the handkerchief into Lord Fenton's lap, along with Lady Harwood's retrieved bracelet, he'd barely glanced at it. Fanny hoped the coat of arms would not be familiar to him; but he'd made no comment as he'd returned the items before resuming his loving comfort in the aftermath of their passion.

Comforting it had been, and it was all Fanny had to sustain herself with, for now Lord Slyther was struggling up on his pillows, his grimace of pain contorting into one of relative pleasure to see her.

"Missed me, eh?" he repeated, patting the mattress at his side. "Come and tell me *how* you missed me, Miss Brightwell. Such pretty words, but empty unless you elaborate."

Fanny had resolved not to shrink from him. His odious person, reeking with decay, and his words, foul and disrespectful, would not find their mark. Tonight, Fanny would do what she had to in order to play for the time she so desperately needed.

Sinking beside him, she briefly stroked the hand he placed upon her thigh before carefully removing it. "My mother is in the next room so you must not take liberties, Lord Slyther."

He let out a crack of laughter. "Got your spirit back, have you? My, but I enjoyed our last little session, teaching precocious Miss Brightwell her place. I see you are not so easily cowed as I'd thought. Good, more sport for me—for you *will* learn how to behave in my company, Miss Brightwell."

Fanny lowered her eyes. He liked her spirit only so he'd have more enjoyment in seeing her cowed? Well, she would not be. Not cowed and certainly not married to him, if she could help it. Her

difficulty was how she should play her behaviour so that he would grant her the few days' delay she needed.

"I am a lady, my Lord, and I will not have my reputation besmirched, even if we are due to wed in the morning. It is late and I am surprised my mother acceded to your unconventional request."

"Your mother is so eager for all I can confer on her daughter and the benefits to herself that she'd accede to anything."

It required no play-acting to look as desolate as she felt. Fanny had always been a dutiful daughter, desperate to achieve whatever her mother demanded, but she did not want to hear the truth laid bare in such a way.

He softened at her expression and said, almost kindly, "Let us pay no heed to your mama. You'll be free of her soon enough and, though you might fear me now, I promise you, I shall be an indulgent husband...provided you are a good girl. Kiss me, Miss Brightwell."

She could not show the aversion she felt, though fortunately it was appropriate to display reluctance at such a great liberty.

"You can kiss me all you like when we are wed, my Lord," she told him, holding her ground.

"I shall enjoy your acquiescence, then, and your dutiful enthusiasm"—he tugged on her arm—"but tonight I will enjoy showing you who is master."

Before she could object further, he jerked her into his arms so that she was across his lap, and plastered his loose lips upon hers. Revulsion swamped her but she refused to reveal her distress. It would only excite him more.

Allowing him sufficient satisfaction before she broke free, she forced her tears into abeyance, saying briskly, almost playfully, "Let us save some surprises for after we are wed. Now, my Lord, your leg looks painful. Allow me to bring you some relief with the unguents I see beside your bed. Shall I remove the dressing and massage it?"

The suggestion took him by surprise. Clearly, even he had thought she'd be reluctant at such an obviously disgusting task, for the weeping sores were evident beneath the bandages.

Holding her breath, forcing her smile to remain unwavering, Fanny unwrapped the stained linen and laid the limb beside her. She'd thought to place it upon her lap but lost courage at the last minute. She couldn't bring herself to come *that* much into contact with it, for she noticed it was worse than on the previous occasion. The suppurating flesh would stain her dress and the stink she'd have to carry home with her was more than she could bear.

Briefly closing her eyes, she wavered between those wonderful memories of being in Lord Fenton's arms and acknowledging that this life of nurse and bedroom mate was nearly upon her. She'd known all her life it was her lot to make sacrifices for the sake of the family so it was foolish to start objecting now.

She'd been trained well. Almost immediately her smile was back in place as she rubbed in the ointment and murmured, "I hope this eases the discomfort a little, my Lord. My grandmother said I was a very good nurse when I used to massage her painful old legs."

Lord Slyther grunted. His eyes were closed and, judging by his expression, he'd all but given himself up to the soothing sensation.

Fanny tried to separate herself from the hateful present and return to the thrilling past. She would not feel shame. Perhaps in the eyes of her mother she'd done a terrible thing but no punishment could take away from her the satisfaction of giving her virginity to a man who set her senses on fire. She'd exercised free will and she'd pleased herself.

Please, dear Lord, don't make it for the last time.

For so long did she gently knead Lord Slyther's white, pestilential flesh and rub ointment into the sores that Fanny hoped he'd gone to sleep. But when she paused to return sensation to her aching hands, he opened his eyes.

"You're more than just the pretty face I thought you, Miss

Brightwell." There was grudging admiration in his tone. "Your grandmother was right—you have a nurse's touch and the sooner we're wed the better."

Fanny accepted the compliment with a gracious nod. "You are kind, my Lord." She knew bullies preyed on weakness so she would have to appear strong, even though the thought of offering herself up to him as required made her want to break down upon the spot.

She put her hand gently upon his ankle. "How long do your gout attacks last, my Lord? Will you be better in the morning? At least able to walk, I mean?"

"Another two or three days in bed, if previous attacks are anything to go by. The parson arrives at ten." He gave her a sly look. "Unless you're willing to wait and I'll send for him now. I have a special licence and I can choose for myself."

"Would it not be better, my Lord, if you were in less pain to enjoy your wedding night"—she lowered her eyes—"so you could be more...yourself?"

He grunted again. "Don't know I can wait that long, Miss Brightwell." He struggled upon his pillows and his hand went out to touch the bare skin above her décolletage. Fingering the ring upon its chain, he hesitated as he added, "Though you are right..."

Fanny's heart lurched at the concession. "In three days' time, my Lord, you would be well enough to stand by my side and"— she swallowed—"be the bridegroom of my desires."

For a second he appeared to consider her suggestion. Suddenly, he jerked forward and pulled her to him, though he immediately released her, despite the fact that she had not squealed. He seemed angry when she straightened, staring wide-eyed, shocked by his surprising strength and his erratic behaviour.

"Three days, then, Miss Brightwell. I see the good sense in a short delay. In the meantime, you can stand up and come to my side. You've had the pleasure of running your hands over my tender flesh. Now it's my turn."

Finally Fanny was permitted to return to the drawing room and rejoin her mother who hissed, "I hope your smile was pleasanter than *that* for Lord Slyther," as she looked up from her tatting.

But Fanny couldn't respond until, once in the carriage, she burst out, "Oh, Mama, the things he did to me. He put his hands—"

"I don't want to hear it," her mother cut in, looking straight ahead as she settled herself. "I'm just sorry he couldn't have waited until tomorrow, when you'll be safely wed."

"The wedding is in three days' time—"

"*Three* days!" Her mother swung round sharply. "What has happened, Fanny? Why three days?" There was panic in her tone before her eyes narrowed with suspicion.

Fanny hurried on. "Lord Slyther's gout is paining him. He'll wed me when he is a little more recovered."

Lady Brightwell rounded on her. "*You* asked for a postponement, didn't you, Fanny? *You* suggested his manliness would be greater for the fact he could at least walk, when all that matters is that it is legally done and you are Lady Slyther. What possessed you, daughter, after everything I have done for you? How *could* you—?"

"Mama, there is a gentleman, a viscount, handsome and rich, who has taken a fancy to me." Now was Fanny's moment and she must not squander it. "I know that with a little time, even three days, perhaps, I can win his regard sufficiently for—"

"Little fool!" Lady Brightwell's anger was accompanied by another of her stinging slaps across her daughter's cheek. "I've heard that one too many times before, Fanny! Lord Alverley, remember? Oh yes, smitten he might have been, but he was young and tied to his mother's apron strings. You couldn't see that, though, could you? Well, what truth have you overlooked this time? You are ruled by your foolish heart, girl. It sweeps away all reason. It'll be the same story with your latest fancy. Mark my

words, he'll tell you he'll fly to the moon to make you his, but when his mama hears her son has fallen in love with a baron's daughter with no fortune—in one night—the same thing will happen. Who is this viscount?"

"Lord Fenton—"

Her mother's wail of anger drowned Fanny's reassurance that Lord Fenton was so unlike Alverley that the comparison was laughable.

"Lord Fenton!" Lady Brightwell nearly choked on the name as she repeated it. "Why, if his mama is still alive—and unless she passed away this last week then she *is*—you can be assured you will *not* be marrying her son. Not while she has breath in her body. Of all the young bucks to pick, you have chosen the worst, Fanny! The one with the *worst* mama, at any rate! What have you *done*?"

It was rare that Lady Brightwell's anger took this despairing form. Usually she was brisk and cold, but now her railing frightened Fanny who cried, "He loves me, Mama, and he's in the market for a wife! Lord Quamby himself told me—"

"Well, you will not make it onto Lord Fenton's list of contenders, Fanny—"

"Mama, do you know what Lord Slyther made me do?" Fanny gripped her mother's arm but Lady Brightwell prised off her fingers, replying, "I don't care! I've had to do nothing less. We've spoken of this before."

The carriage rounded a corner. They were nearly home but it offered no sanctuary. Lady Brightwell would not hear her out.

Desperately, Fanny cried, "You married Papa for love. What can you know of being mauled by a disgusting old man? He kissed me, and put his tongue in my mouth and then he made *me*—"

"If you'd played your cards right, Fanny, he'd be doing it as your husband, not besmirching your reputation. Your position is weak. You are a complete fool, just like your father! Do you think *he* was some handsome young buck I fell head over heels for? He

was charming enough when I wed him, thinking to elevate myself just a little, but it wasn't long before the drink and the gambling ruined him—and *your* chances. A disappointed man, when he's drunk, is a frightening prospect, Fanny. So don't tell me I know nothing of the horrors you've endured. *You* know nothing of horror! I've shielded you, like the best of mothers, and look how you repay me! You are a stupid, ungrateful girl and you will rue this day!"

Hunching back into the corner as the carriage halted in front of their town house, Fanny wiped her streaming eyes. "I'm going to marry Lord Fenton, Mama," she muttered. "You'll see."

CHAPTER 6

*L*ord Fenton peered into the darkness from the comfort of his silk-lined carriage and watched the hired hackney roll up to the front portico of Lord Slyther's residence. His senses seemed to be suffering from a surfeit of feeling—lust, definitely, but something more than that; something sweet and deep and intense he'd never experienced until tonight.

Now another emotion, more difficult to describe, was creeping through his bones.

The cross-eyed jarvey who pulled on the reins was, he was sure, the very one who had conveyed Miss Brightwell, her sister and their chaperone home, not ten minutes ago, though he'd come here directly from the ball.

Two cloaked figures were being ushered through the door.

Fenton's exuberance was checked. It was long after midnight and this was the confirmation he'd been hoping *not* to see.

This was Lord Slyther's London town house. Earlier he was sure he'd seen Lord Slyther's ring. Fenton would not have troubled to discern the crest had it not been for Bramley's words before he'd been properly introduced to the young lady, but it had

struck him as odd that Miss Brightwell had concealed the ring in her handkerchief when earlier she'd been wearing it on a chain around her neck.

Why?

She was surely too lovely for guile. Despite her outward confidence there was an inner fragility that had touched him. He didn't want to think it was an act, just as he didn't want to think of all Bramley's ugly slurs upon Miss Brightwell's character.

They surely couldn't be true? That's why he was here. To reassure himself. Now he didn't know what to think.

Fenton had no doubt that George Bramley had a grievance against the girl. When he'd left to come here after Lord Quamby's ball he'd battled with his conscience. He should trust her, of course. But surely if he intended to make her his wife it was all the more reason to ensure she was…trustworthy?

Narrowing his eyes, he tried to make out the identity of the two cloaked figures that were being ushered into the house. Surely one of them was not *his* Miss Brightwell.

As he'd been unable to verify anything, Fenton scanned the four storeys of the building for any chink through the curtains that might give a clue to what was going on inside. Anxiously? No —*angrily*—for a closer look at the jarvey convinced him it was indeed the same man, and the confident manner with which the younger woman had swept past the parlour maid was Miss Brightwell personified.

The idea appalled him that she could go directly from the ball where she'd given herself to Fenton with such enthusiasm straight to the arms of…who? Her erstwhile secret lover? Given Bramley's lewd talk and the fact Fenton was newly returned to London, perhaps it *was* common knowledge.

There must be some explanation. Miss Brightwell must have a perfectly good reason for being there. Could Lord Slyther be her godfather, who'd requested her presence upon his deathbed?

After Bramley's talk, he doubted it.

He shivered though his blood was boiling by the time the two cloaked figures reappeared nearly an hour later. He saw the older woman hurry into the carriage while the other paused for a moment upon the top step. Straining, Lord Fenton tried to identify the lonely, straight-backed figure as Miss Brightwell. He wanted desperately to be proved wrong but when she raised her lovely, familiar face to the light spilling from the lamps he nearly wept aloud with disappointment.

Miss Brightwell's perfect, high cheekbones cast shadows over her rosebud of a mouth and her dimpled chin as she gazed into the darkness.

Thinking of what? Fenton, or the man who *kept* her? A gamut of unpleasant emotions roiled in his gut. He'd been in the market for a wife and Miss Brightwell had seemed a gift from heaven—a creature who combined everything he desired. He'd had enough of transient pleasures. Spending so much time in the country, as he would from now on, he wanted a wife to please him in bed as much as she did over breakfast and...well, during every other part of the day.

He was about to turn away when he saw her put her hand to her neck; to the chain upon which she kept Lord Slyther's ring. She had secreted it away for the brief duration of their own clandestine tryst, but now she had returned it to its original position. With a sharp tug, she tore the chain from her neck. The ring skittered to the flagstones at her feet.

Lord Fenton watched her stare at it, as if undecided.

Then, slowly, like an old woman, she bent to retrieve it before putting it in her reticule.

IN HIS MAMA'S MAYFAIR DRAWING ROOM THE FOLLOWING MORNING,

Lord Fenton paced between fireplace and window, his thoughts in turmoil. His mindless activity clearly infuriated the dowager who eventually snapped, "What is wrong with you, Fenton! Spit it out, for I cannot keep my mind on my stitching while you're behaving like some lovelorn schoolboy...unless you're dunned and too afraid to tell me."

Fenton stopped by the stuffed mongoose in its glass box atop a round table and managed a wry smile. "I'm not the gambler I used to be, Mama." He let out a deep sigh as he looked out of the window, his gaze taking in a couple in the park across the street. Newlyweds, by the look of them, their fair heads bent towards one another as they discussed something in animated fashion, their bodies suggesting a companionable union.

"So, no, I'm not dunned." Though, to tell the truth, he might be accused of lacking the courage to tell his mother the exact nature of his distraction. Anyone would consider it a gamble to stake his happiness on a bold young woman whom he'd met for the first time when she'd encouraged his all but complete seduction of her. The truth was, despite everything he'd heard and the scene he'd witnessed in the dead of night at Lord Slyther's residence, he still held out hope that Miss Brightwell remained a contender for the position of his viscountess.

He ran his hand around his shirt collar and sighed again. What was the truth behind what he'd seen last night?

Until he'd witnessed Miss Brightwell's nocturnal visit to Lord Slyther, he'd convinced himself that Bramley's spurious words were borne of spite and a need to avenge himself on a woman who more than likely had spurned him.

He'd taken Bramley to task for his heedless behaviour towards Miss Antoinette, but perhaps it had not been so heedless. Perhaps Bramley had every indication that Miss Antoinette was in the market for nefarious activities if so inclined—that, like her elder sister, she was indeed willing to barter her body if the price was right. He had a sudden vision of Miss Fanny Brightwell allowing

Lords Bickling and Slyther the same liberties she'd allowed him the previous night and pain tore through him like a sabre.

Out of the corner of his eye he watched the young couple reach the gates of the park, where the woman stopped and laughed, as though her companion had made a joke. She raised her head, touching the young man's cheek, revealing her age to be at least two decades older than her companion—perhaps mother or aunt.

Fenton nearly laughed out loud. Appearances were not always what they seemed. The observation ignited a spark of hope that made him raise his shoulders and turn towards his mother. No doubt there was some perfectly acceptable reason for Miss Brightwell's nocturnal visit to Lord Slyther. The young woman had been chaperoned and there was every possibility of some family connection that Bramley, with his vulgar talk, had discounted. His imagination had conjured up all manner of lurid possibilities the night before because he'd been tired and had had too much to drink.

Fired up with fresh hope, he said, "Old age must be catching up with me, Mama, for I'll admit to being tempted by the idea of marriage for the very first time in my life."

Hah! What did he care for the opinion of others? It was a gamble he was prepared to take.

He wanted Miss Brightwell and he wanted her for his *wife*. His mouthed stretched in a grin. Lord, the sight of himself in the mirror above the mantelpiece was like gazing into the past—to the eager schoolboy he must once have been, contemplating some great adventure or intrigue.

Marrying Miss Brightwell would be both.

"Why, Fenton! This is news to me. Who is the young lady?" The severe lines around Lady Fenton's mouth softened when she smiled.

"Miss Brightwell."

It was the brittle silence more than the gasp—which could

have been occasioned by the accidental stabbing of her needle into her thumb—that said more than words. Words, however, were quickly forthcoming.

"Miss Brightwell?" His mother looked stricken, disbelieving and furious at the same time before she rose from her chair, her needlework falling at her feet. "*Miss Brightwell!* Oh, dear boy, pray don't break your mama's heart. No, no, it cannot be she who has stolen your heart—"

Fenton made no move towards his mother's open arms. His tone was cool, though his feelings were the very opposite. "Pray tell what might discount her candidacy, Mama? I am aware that her father disgraced himself and that she comes with no dowry, but I love her."

Lady Fenton's ashen face took on the heat of indignation. She clenched her fingers and drew in her breath. For a moment words failed her, before she croaked through bloodless lips, "The girl's mother was a toad-eating upstart who sold herself for a title. A cooper's daughter!"

"She married Lord Brightwell in a union that, while not spectacular, was not ignominious." Fenton's voice rose. "Is there a slur upon the reputations of either Miss Brightwell or her newly fired-off sister?"

"If you were a woman you'd blush at the tactics that Friday-faced miss used to entice Baron Brightwell. Now I hear she's prepared to go to any lengths to snare good matches for her daughters. No doubt she's parading her girls like—like enticing sweetmeats before any old duke or viscount in an attempt to ease the family's financial woes. No, I wouldn't put a little procurement past Lady Brightwell." She all but spat the name.

"Mother!"

"You have no idea, Fenton." His mother's lips were a compressed line. "I went to school with the designing creature. Her father made his fortune through trade. He thought his money could put her on a par with the daughters of baronets, if not

earls." Lady Fenton's lip curled. "No, nothing was too good for little Miss Lottie Lucas as she was then and, believe me, there's *nothing* I wouldn't put past her."

"You went to school with her? I know, too, your father was a friend of the fourth Baron Brightwell. Nothing wrong with the lineage, Mama..."

Lady Fenton's trembling increased. Tugging on the bell rope to demand her vinaigrette in a high, thin voice, she turned to Fenton and muttered, "Nothing wrong with the lineage but everything wrong with your choice, my boy, just remember that!" Her eyes flashed and for a moment Fenton believed she was going to beat him with her clenched fists as she took an unsteady step forward. "Let me warn you, Fenton, if you marry this designing Miss Brightwell I will *never* receive her! Do you hear me? *Never!*"

❧

"WHAT DO YOU THINK OF THESE?" LADY BRIGHTWELL WAVED A PAIR of York tan gloves at her eldest daughter from the other side of the shop. "Without waiting for a response, she said to the assistant, "We'll have two pairs. Fanny, try them on for size...oh, and perhaps the lilac, too. They're very fetching and will brighten up your newest muslin."

There was no time for a new gown but Lady Brightwell was finding far greater enjoyment than Fanny in spending the money Lord Slyther had provided for a few accoutrements for his intended. It was not the August heat that made Fanny feel like a wilting dandelion. It was late afternoon on the day following the Earl of Quamby's ball and she'd heard nothing from...

Closing her eyes and clutching her reticule as she steadied herself against the counter beneath a hanging display of shawls, she forced herself to silently finish the sentence—the man who'd stolen her heart *and* her virtue.

No! The truth, Fanny. The man to whom you've given your heart and your virtue.

So why had Lord Fenton not sought her out? Certainly, she'd not disclosed her address but they had sufficient mutual acquaintances that it would not be difficult to locate her.

She noticed her mother looking oddly at her as she glanced up from perusing a selection of fans.

Fanny forced a smile. "I thought Antoinette and Bertram would be here by now." Rousing herself, she looked around as if for her siblings, when in truth she was hoping beyond hope to see Lord Fenton passing by the window in the midst of Oxford Street. The busy shopping quarter was teeming but she could see no sign of anyone who bore any resemblance either from the back or from the front to the man who made her pulses race— nor anyone who could rival him in looks and presence. With a sigh, she peeled off the gloves she'd just tried, nodding to the shop assistant that she'd take them. "You must watch Antoinette, Mama," she said. "Bertram is not a suitable chaperone, for he'll let her go wherever she chooses. Besides, I've never heard Antoinette profess the desire for a long walk before. I'd wager she's gone to meet someone and is hoping Bertram will make himself scarce."

Fanny's concern was hardly allayed by her normally exacting mother's reply.

"Once you've wed Lord Slyther, my darling, I'll pay more heed to Antoinette—though our troubles will be over then."

For a moment, Fanny was afraid her mother was going to embrace her right there in the shop. At least Lady Brightwell's anger over the postponement had abated. What was a short delay when the day after next Lady Brightwell would see her ambitions realised? Her daughter would be wed to a titled man of fortune.

Lady Brightwell tapped one of the fans, indicating to the assistant that she'd take that, too. Looking extremely satisfied, she said, "I think a treat is in order, Fanny. An ice at Gunter's after your siblings appear, perhaps?"

A treat?

Fanny was in no mood for treating herself after the events of last night. She'd treated herself at Lord Quamby's, treated herself to the heated kisses and the hot and humid embrace of muscled, manly flesh, and now it appeared she'd completely miscalculated.

Yes, miscalculated when it came to giving her mama what she required: a rich and titled son-in-law; and miscalculated when it came to achieving Fanny's heart's desire: a man she desired and believed she could love.

Oh, dear Lord, how could she have been so stupid...

She closed her eyes briefly and concentrated on holding back the nausea. She had only ulcerous sores and limbs of white, marbled fat flanking Lord Slyther's all-too-enthusiastic Magnificent Member to look forward to.

"Are you all right, Fanny?"

Again, Fanny forced a smile.

"You groaned." Her mother took her wrist, the smile that brightened her face so at odds with her usual sour expression. "Later, after we visit Gunter's, we must talk. You're to be married soon and there are some things I need to tell you"—Lady Brightwell rarely spoke so kindly but she did so now, her tone low in their deserted corner of the shop—"about what to expect."

They were near the door, the obsequious shop assistant wrapping their purchases, when Antoinette and Bertram rushed in. Their handsome faces were flushed and showed signs of barely tempered exertion or excitement, very different from the usual languor displayed by world-weary Bertram.

"Mama! Have you heard the news?" Antoinette's eyes were like saucers; Bertram looked green around the gills. It was he who clapped his hand over his sister's mouth, muttering, "Not here, Antoinette. Have you no sense of decorum?" before discreetly ushering his mother further from the curious looks of the assistant. Fanny followed. This was most unlike her brother.

"What news?" Fanny tugged at Bertram's sleeve, for now he

was gaping like a fish, unable to say what Antoinette had been about to say so peremptorily.

"Lord Slyther's dead." Antoinette's voice shook. She looked uncertainly at her mother. "Of a stroke...around midday, I overheard it said."

Relief was Fanny's immediate reaction. Relief that they were in a public place so her mother could not beat her over the head with whatever object came to hand, and relief that salvation had come before it was too late.

Lady Brightwell put her hand to the wall to steady herself. The blood drained from her face while her eyes blazed like they were being stoked by the fires of Hell. Fanny's joy at her reprieve was tempered somewhat by the observation. Her mother was never going to forgive her unless she succeeded with Lord Fenton.

By all the saints in Heaven, though, she was!

"Mama, you need to sit down." Fanny's tone was soothing, as if her first concern was her mother, but when she laid her hand upon her mother's sleeve Lady Brightwell shook it off.

"Stupid girl," she hissed. She drew a staccato breath. Fearfully, her children watched while they formed a barrier to potential interest from other shoppers. Like a spider about to strike, Lady Brightwell glared at Fanny from the shadow of her bonnet as she tossed her tippet around her neck and stepped forward. "Stupid, stupid girl, Fanny! You'd be a widow right now if you'd played your cards right and all our fortunes would be made. But no, you were too precious and too *selfish* to do what was required."

Antoinette and Bertram looked downcast. Shuffling one foot over the flagstones, Antoinette ventured, "I saw Mr Bramley today and he was very attentive. I'm sure he's going to make me an offer and as he *is* the Earl of Quamby's heir—"

"Shut *up*, Antoinette!" Her mother rounded on her. "You understand nothing of the ways of men. You think because you are loose and obliging with your affections that a wedding band will secure the deal?" She shook her fist at her youngest. "They'll

be only too delighted to secure their pleasures without having to negotiate a marriage contract with ticklish family who consider there are better contenders than the Brightwells. You are, there's no getting round the fact"—the substance appeared to drain from her and she slumped against the wall—"not every designing mama's dream."

CHAPTER 7

*L*ady Brightwell was in no mood to accept the various attempts made by her offspring to paint their circumstances more rosily. In the bleak hues she had cast over their futures, 'Fanny's gross selfishness and disregard had ruined those who had sacrificed everything on her account'.

"Fanny will find another brilliant match, Mama," Bertram generously predicted as Lady Brightwell directed her three children—in clipped tones and with a brow as glowering as they'd ever seen—to arrange for a conveyance to take her home.

To Fanny's relief, she had acquiesced in allowing the rest of them to walk, provided they return directly to their dingy residence, but she was in no mood to be mollified by Bertram.

"You're as much a foolish optimist over your sister's prospects as you are over your fortune at the gaming tables, Bertram," Lady Brightwell snapped, slapping away his hand as he solicitously tugged her skirt clear of the door of the hackney.

"Really, Mama, you all but forced the match upon her," he persisted, unperturbed by the set-down.

"Did it never occur to you that your folly is as much a reason why your sisters must accept unpalatable alliances as your father's

impecuniousness is the cause of our distress?" Lady Brightwell slammed the door and glared out of the window before rapping on the roof for the jarvey to take up the reins.

Antoinette had by this stage lost a little of her usual effervescence. "I've never seen Mama quite so angry," she said as the three of them set off along the pavement.

It was a lovely day and Fanny had used the excuse of needing the good air in the hopes of spying Lord Fenton. Her distracted answer obviously needled her sister who said, "Perhaps Mama has good reason to be angry with you after all, Fanny—for all that I sympathise—since you *could* have been married in the morning and a widow by noon if you'd simply done what was required."

"I'd have been a widow before the wedding breakfast was digested," muttered Fanny in disgust, "if Lord Slyther had tried to have his way with me. Ugh." She shuddered. "Then I'd have had to wear widow's weeds for a year and how do you suppose that would have advanced my chances?"

Bertram looked quizzically at her. "Surely it wouldn't have mattered, Fanny, since you'd have inherited a fortune? Lord Slyther had no children. I can see why Mama is down in the mouth."

"Fanny wants to marry Lord Fenton," Antoinette said matter-of-factly. "She thinks he's going to ask her in the next few days. That's why she's not concerned by what's happened to Lord Slyther."

This came as such a shock to Bertram that he dropped the monocle he was using to ogle the passing young ladies.

"Marry Lord Fenton?" He gawped at his sisters as if the idea were preposterous. "My, you've aimed high this time. I mean, after Alverley, surely—"

"Lord Fenton thinks Fanny"—Antoinette giggled behind her hand— "highly desirable." Fanny rounded on her with a glare before she continued. "And, after the way they carried on at Lord Quamby's, I'd say there's every chance he'll make her an offer

before tomorrow is ended. Isn't that what a gentleman *has* to do when he compromises a lady?" Antoinette tossed her pretty head, more concerned with the interest she was receiving from the passing males than her sister's patent horror.

"What are you saying, Antoinette?" Fanny felt about to swoon on the spot.

Antoinette wrapped a ringlet around her finger as she turned her dazzling smile upon her sister. "Just that I saw you and Lord Fenton when you thought you were alone and I realised that you were tricking him into having to make you an offer. That's when I realised that I, too, could be as clever, and why I agreed to slip away with Mr Bramley this morning." She looked smug as she took Bertram's arm. At his look, which was more quizzical than Fanny's scandalised horror, she added gaily, "Mr Bramley isn't nearly as nice as Lord Fenton but he *is* Lord Quamby's heir."

※

WHAT LORD FENTON FELT UPON REFLECTION ON THEIR INCREDIBLE union, Fanny had no idea. Whether he felt tricked—as Antoinette regarded it—or whether he was at that moment pondering his obligations towards Miss Brightwell, he had not yet been galvanised into letting her know his intentions. He owed her *something*, surely—a word of reassurance at the very least? But no word came all that long evening, or even the next morning.

Just before noon, the parlour maid appeared bearing a silver salver on which lay an elegant cream wafer. Fanny cried out with relief as she snatched up the correspondence, but her desperation turned to abject misery as she studied the missive before handing it to her sister.

"From Mr Bramley," she whispered, feeling akin to some pathetic creature slinking into a chair with its tail between its legs.

Gaily, Antoinette scanned the few lines. "Can I go riding with

Mr Bramley in his high-perch phaeton this afternoon, Mama?" she asked.

Her mother did not look up from her stitching. Wearily she said, "I see no harm in it," adding with a sigh, "I see no harm in anything anymore. Once the lease runs out on this place, we're all doomed."

Fanny felt doomed already. Dazed, doomed and undecided as to what course she could take. Two days had not yet passed. She couldn't behave like some eager strumpet and demand her beloved explain himself—not when she couldn't very well explain her own actions.

She hadn't even the heart to reiterate her warning to Antoinette about her suspicions that Bramley was only using her —though she did mutter, "Be wary and don't go off with him alone."

She felt a fool for miscalculating so badly—like a traitor to her family and, worse than that, like she carried a great hole in her heart.

She'd pegged Fenton for a romantic. A man of sincerity. The words he'd whispered in her ear at Lord Quamby's had filled her with hope for the future.

So Antoinette went riding, returning full of glee owing to the admiration she'd received from all quarters. She was flushed and as pretty, Fanny reluctantly conceded, as she'd ever seen her. Antoinette, her pea goose of a sister, was either going to ruin them all or win the marriage Fanny had failed to secure, which would ensure their mother's eternal devotion.

Fanny prostrated herself along the length of the window seat in their bedroom, between bouts of lonely weeping, while the others played backgammon in front of the drawing room fire. She could speak to no one of her distress. She'd taken a gamble on love, having eschewed the solid, albeit unpalatable, offer that would have made them all comfortable and secure...

And she had lost.

Adding to her torment was another night of Antoinette's endless chatter, after the candle had been snuffed out, with tales ever more marvellous as to the great stir Miss Antoinette was making in London society. Fanny stared, eyes glazed, into the darkness of their bedroom, and wondered how a future without the handsome rake Lord Fenton would be even tolerable.

She drifted off to sleep at dawn, after a seemingly eternal night of tossing and turning, and did not awake until noon…to find a letter waiting for her in the drawing room.

CHAPTER 8

*F*enton twitched the ribbons of his high-perch phaeton as he searched the throng of exquisitely attired prom-enaders. He was as restless and uncertain of his reward as he'd been when his horse had taken the lead at St Leger three years before—and won him a purse that had trebled the amount he'd lost the night before.

Gambling! His mother was happy that he'd got over the gambling mania that had ruled his life as a young buck, but not so happy at his choice of the one woman who might keep him inter-ested enough in domesticity not to want to stray from the straight and narrow again. If only he knew his mother would not make his life living hell if he crossed her in choosing a wife she was dead set against. Though, truth to tell, his mother's furious objections were only the start of Fenton's concerns.

Despite his anticipation, he was in a quandary, unable to decide what to *do* though he knew what he *wanted.* He wanted Miss Brightwell to come to him with an unblemished reputation so the whole world—his mother included—could endorse her as his viscountess.

But Miss Brightwell's nocturnal visit to Lord Slyther had

rattled him. While it did not confirm that she was the man's mistress, or that her reputation *was* besmirched, or that she had not been a virgin before she and Fenton had got so gloriously carried away, it posed all sorts of questions. Questions he needed answered before he was willing to proceed along the marriage path.

So, after despatching a note that he'd meet Miss Brightwell in Hyde Park at the fashionable hour, he'd come prepared for every contingency, including a ring in his coat pocket should he decide on the spur of the moment to throw caution to the wind and ask for Miss Brightwell's hand in marriage. That was his preferred course of action, for he'd had enough of dalliance. His Continental Tour had whittled away the mystique of feminine enticements. With the looks, leisure and licence to do whatever he chose, he'd become, quite frankly, bored to tears—until five nights ago when Miss Fanny Brightwell...

At the mere thought of their passionate encounter his heart beat out the maddest, most creative tattoo before settling back into its steady routine. Discreetly, he put his hand to his breeches and took a deep breath. One way or another, he was going to have exclusive rights over the damnably delightful, enigmatic Miss Fanny Brightwell, or he would go mad. Their exquisite encounters had been far too cursory to satisfy a man who liked to spend hours bringing a woman to climax before following, himself, into explosive abandonment.

Fenton shaded his eyes and perused the crowd more closely while he tried to rein in his thoughts.

He glanced anxiously at his time piece. It was well and truly past five o' clock and there was still no sign of her. Further ruminations took his anticipation down a notch. Lord Slyther had died several days previously. Could it be that Miss Brightwell was grieving...for her previous lover?

No, he strenuously would not countenance such a scenario. Miss Brightwell was in love with *him*. Fenton. His certainty that

her enthusiastic reception of his overtures was pure and unfeigned was part of her charm. Miss Brightwell was direct. She was honest and unaffected.

Very different from the eligible maidens of his acquaintance.

Lord, but he *wanted* to make her his wife, though, regardless of what he ultimately settled for, right now he just wanted Miss Fanny Brightwell up here beside him.

He shifted like a schoolboy, unable to contain his restlessness. Three rounds in the ring with Gentleman Jackson the previous afternoon had not achieved the release of pent-up energy for which he'd hoped. He felt like a large cat, coiled tight and ready to spring. Miss Brightwell was the only prey that would satisfy him.

But the niggling doubts persisted. Was she eligible for the role of his wife? Did she even expect to be?

And where *was* she?

Impatience grew as the minutes passed. It had been torture to wait this long—now he could not wait a moment longer. He burnt to hold her in his arms, to be alone with her and to crush his lips against hers. To feel her heated flesh, suckle her magnificent breasts, plunder the slickness of her desire...

"My apologies, Lord Fenton."

The gleam in her lively, blue eyes made him want to gather her up, whisk her to somewhere secluded and repeat in exquisite detail the thrilling rendition of the other night. Trying to temper his schoolboy's grin into something more sophisticated, he extended his hand and pulled her, then her sister, up beside him.

"If you are feeling a little cramped, Miss Antoinette"—he sent the young girl a meaningful look—"Miss Conyngham over there was asking after you. She thought you'd make a pleasant addition to their party." He indicated a knot of people in the middle distance.

"And leave my sister alone with *you*, who are so concerned about the proprieties?" Antoinette's smile was pert.

"It is *because* I am so vigilant about the proprieties that you

escaped the censure that would have been occasioned by Mr Bramley's appalling conduct the other night and we are all able to make the most of this beautiful afternoon." Fenton sent her a cloying smile, which she greeted coolly before availing herself of his assistance in getting down from the carriage.

"As you remind us, we are in your debt, Lord Fenton." Miss Brightwell shifted a little closer after her sister had departed and Fenton reached for her hand. For a moment they were silent as they both stared at it, resting upon her knee. The knowledge of how smooth and shapely that knee was starved him of the air he needed for rational thought. The memory of her impassioned writhing beneath him fuelled his desperation. God, he wanted her.

"It is I who am in yours," he ground out, and heard the hoarseness of his voice. He touched her cheek, gently contouring her high cheekbone with his forefinger before tracing the Cupid's bow of her shapely mouth. "You are exquisite."

Lust or love? He wasn't sure what it was that made him so mad for her but did it matter when he just wanted...*her*?

She trembled beside him. He could see how impossible she found it to disguise that her longing matched his own. It filled him with a sense of power he'd never felt before. Agonised soul-searching had led to the greatest quandary of his entire, lust-filled life, but now he realised the only way to end his torment was to have her...*now*.

In that split second he decided. These were feelings he ought not have for a wife. His mother had always counselled him that a wife should be held up on a pedestal. Virtue and good breeding were the hallmarks of the ideal bride and, regardless of Bramley's tales, Miss Brightwell had given herself too willingly. Besides, if she were to be his wife, he couldn't have her *now*.

Nevertheless, he knew he was reacting too hastily; that he was being dictated to by his base need for instant gratification as he reached down to retrieve the cigar-shaped velvet box from the

wicker basket at his feet. But he couldn't help himself. He handed his gift to her, nearly deafened by the pounding of his heart as he waited for her response.

"Saphires," he murmured as she fingered the stones. "Because I can't stop thinking of them, I bought you something to match your eyes."

Relieved at her obvious delight as she held the delicate sapphire necklace up to the light, he imagined her wearing it— naked. He'd kiss her from the toes upwards, while his gift encircled her graceful neck and the gems in her ears glinted in the candlelight. Hardening yet again, he had to clamp his teeth against the pain, cursing the fact that the public location of their assignation meant he must keep up appearances—and keep his hands to himself.

"And this?" she asked, her look enquiring as she held up the little key on a black velvet ribbon that had also been contained in the box.

His excited determination to savour her charms before the afternoon was over was tempered by the possibility that he might have been too peremptory. Yet what of Lord Slyther's ring about her neck? What had she done in return for that?

He clasped her hand in both of his. "A place where we may meet, my love." Doubt vanished as visions of their future trysts made his vision blur. He was so hungry for her it took every ounce of willpower not to whip up the horses and drive her to some place they could be alone. The way she had looked at him just now indicated she wanted him just as much.

Yes—for the moment he would have her as his mistress. But, perhaps, if they were discreet and her liaison with Lord Slyther did not make it into the public domain, who knew but he might even succeed in persuading his mother to overlook her ineligibility enough to sanction marriage?

He didn't like to think these were the thoughts and actions of a cad. He was simply covering all contingencies. And yes, it

was an unconventional approach, but perhaps the only way forward.

Seeing the troubled look in her eyes as she continued to look from the key to his face, and wanting to reassure her—and himself—he touched her cheek once more.

She did not look happy. She bit her lip and the doubt and concern that it had taken days to exorcise scorched him like a furious furnace.

In the face of her hardening silence, he hurried on. "I understand that your need for discretion, Fanny—if I may call you that—is greater than mine. Certainly, until your younger sister is fired off."

Her limpid love-hungry look, which had fuelled his actions earlier, had evaporated. Dismayed, he leaned towards her but she shrank back. Her next words were like a blow to the solar plexus, knocking all the expectation from him.

"It appears, sir, I acted more rashly than I believed at the time." Her tone was crisp. Replacing the jewels and the little key in their box, she carefully handed back his gift. "My apologies for leading you astray."

Her expression was distant, imperious, as she bade him help her down.

"Please, Fanny, I'm sorry if I—"

The look she sent him made it clear he had no choice but to acquiesce, surrounded as they were by the crowds promenading in Rotten Row.

Unsure of what to say, he watched her leave, realising only now that he wanted her at any price. But her expression was stony with hurt pride, her beautiful blue eyes as cold as flint as she gazed up at him after he'd set her down.

How could he have misread the situation so badly? This was not a woman who had been expecting a *carte blanche*.

Nor, he acknowledged painfully, was she a woman who deserved one.

~

Blinking furiously to hold back her tears, Fanny stepped into the mêlée, searching for some other party she might join so as not to bring attention to her unchaperoned state.

The sun was blinding, her head pounding, every whit of self-confidence and esteem reduced to nothing. She'd made the greatest miscalculation of her life—now she would pay with it. It was not an overstatement. Everything she held dear—position, prestige, respectability, not to mention Lord Fenton's respect—had been reduced to cinders by her one foolish moment of unbridled passion.

"Miss Brightwell! Alone, for goodness sake? Where is your sister?"

The reedy voice that floated down from a dashing purple curricle emblazoned with the arms of the Earl of Quamby belonged to the Earl himself. Startlingly attired in a suit of red and gold, his strawberry blonde curls topped by a matching low-crowned beaver, which he doffed in greeting, the Earl sounded as censorious as her mother.

"Separated in the crowd," Fanny mumbled, shading the face she raised to him so he wouldn't see her tears. She was glad of the fashionable floral profusion beneath the brim of her bonnet that helped to hide her distress.

Trembling, she felt as if she were in the grip of a palsy that threatened the integrity of her seams—as if she might burst apart, spilling her insubstantial stuffing like a roughly used rag doll. Yes, she had been roughly used—but she had no one but herself to blame. She wanted to block her ears to the sound of society's heedless gaiety, which competed with the rumble of carriages and the chirping of birds. It seemed they were all mocking her.

"My dear Miss Brightwell, something has happened to upset you." With a complicated manoeuvring of sticks and props, Lord Quamby inched his way to the edge of his vehicle and held out his

hand. "Come up beside me and tell me your troubles as we drive. I assure you, it is better to be seen alone with me than to be remarked upon, on the promenade, unaccompanied and in tears."

"It no longer matters what I do, since I've no reputation left to speak of," Fanny whispered brokenly as she settled beside him, wishing she could bury her face in her hands but knowing she was currently being observed by everyone within sight. "I soon won't, at any rate."

"Good Lord, has my lovely, canny Fanny followed trouble where she ought not?" Lord Quamby chuckled as he gave her knee a squeeze. Not at all a respectable gesture in public but one that made Fanny feel better, nevertheless. It bridged the great divide in sensation between her mother's cold, brief embraces when Fanny had looked like snaring a title, and the molten reaction of her body to Lord Fenton's hot, fiery kisses and bold sensual exploration.

Blushing at the memory of those passionate interludes, Fanny glanced up to find the Earl's sharp, blue eyes upon her. The expectation that she explain herself was clear.

So she did, giving voice to every thought and feeling that had dictated her actions the other night. The unlikely friendship that had grown up between herself and the Earl since the afternoon she and Antoinette had rescued him from footpads on Hampstead Heath was more real and sustaining than any she had developed with the numerous acquaintances she'd made during her two years in London.

"What fun the old cats will have in sending you to Coventry, my dear." That his voice was matter of fact, even amused, was no surprise or disappointment to Fanny. It was a comfort that Lord Quamby, despite his theatrical temperament, never tried to dress up the truth. "That is, if you do become Lord Fenton's mistress." His right eye twitched as he gazed at her through his lorgnette. "Can't make the fellow out, I must say. Rake's Honour and all that, and you a respectable young lady. Even feel a trifle guilty myself,

since I was so reassuring about the young man seemingly five minutes before he tumbled you in my Arbour of Love." He sighed. "Fact remains, m'dear, you were a foolish girl…and the consequences can't be foretold for some while yet," he added with a pointed look at her belly.

As if she hadn't thought of that.

"Come now, child, it's not the end of the world—though a bruised heart in youth always seems like it." He smiled kindly and tapped his chest. "This old heart has been on fire and doused with cold water more often than I care to remember."

Resting his hand on her arm, he gazed at the passing throng. Many cast them decidedly curious looks. To be taken up so publicly by an earl—even if only for an afternoon ride— might not ease her bruised heart but, after her humiliation at the hands of her dashing and ultimately devastatingly disappointing viscount, it bolstered her courage. Courage she would need, for to be cast from society's embrace would be a bitter pill and one she'd not willingly have swallowed had she considered more deeply the consequences of her actions. She knew she had no one but herself to blame. She knew also that no matter how generously Lord Fenton clothed and housed his new mistress, or showered her family with largesse, Fanny's mother would never forgive her.

Never.

She had lost everything. Fenton, her mother's fair-weather affection, position and security. And all because she'd given into her lustful feelings for Lord Fenton.

Yes, lustful though she'd truly believed it might have been something more than that.

"You still think of your lost love?" Fanny asked, trying to be kind, for she did so like him—but it was hard to find sympathy for another when her own heart was breaking.

"It will be twenty years ago on Friday since my beloved Richard fell into the arms of his Banquo." He sighed.

"Oh," said Fanny, blinking. "I didn't…"

"Of course you didn't," he chuckled. "You're an innocent, despite your worldly air. A worldly innocent with so much to learn. You mistook your Lord Fenton's desire for love. And now Miss Fanny Brightwell is furious at making such a fatal, obvious mistake." He shrugged. "But perhaps it *was* love on his part, for even love can be compromised when the future weighs in. I've no doubt Lord Fenton would have happily made you his wife were it not for the objection of his odious mama. The heir to three estates in the north must marry well—not some dowerless nobody, regardless of her charms."

Fanny rubbed at the stain her tears had made on her York tan gloves and sniffed. "Mama has always been so ambitious for us. Mr Bramley was right when he said I'd be lucky to catch a wealthy tradesman."

"My nephew is jealous."

Fanny shrugged as she twisted her fingers in her lap, for that was true enough. "When Lord Fenton took an interest, I"—her voice trembled—"took a foolish gamble. Mama will die of shame, yet I truly thought that when I returned home following this afternoon's ride she'd think me the cleverest and dearest of daughters."

Lord Quamby sighed. "Meanwhile, perhaps Fenton is kicking himself for serving you so badly, never expecting he'd lose you. I've always thought it strange how far we'll compromise our own happiness to please our mothers." He looked wistful. "My blond Adonis wanted a more public declaration of our love, which of course might have sent us both to the gallows and certainly killed off my poor mama. Now I realise *she* would sooner have killed me. She's sustained herself these past three score years and ten in the fond hope I'll do my duty yet and provide the heir the family so desperately requires."

He gave Fanny an assessing look. It grew even more speculative as he traced the figured gold silk of his red pantaloons with an effete hand. "Miss Brightwell," he said in quite a different tone.

His bright eyes twinkled like a blackbird's, his full, pert little mouth turning up as if it held a wicked surprise. Taking one of her hands between his, he said in his thin, wheezing voice, "Your predicament has just inspired a plan which I believe will see our mothers twitter their joy from the tree tops." The pressure on her hand increased, as if he could barely contain his excitement. "Certainly, if it comes to fruition, Ladies Brightwell and Fenton and the Dowager Duchess Quamby will be celebrating the joyful and entirely satisfactory unions of their respective offspring at their next little witches' coven."

Fanny narrowed her eyes, hope taking root as he began to explain.

CHAPTER 9

"*M*iss Brightwell to see you, my Lord."

The censure Fenton saw in the expression of his butler Brimble suggested Miss Brightwell was alone. Carefully placing his tumbler of brandy on the sideboard, Fenton turned towards the door, hoping his own expression did not reveal the unalloyed joy shining through his disordered thoughts.

He'd spent a sleepless night castigating himself for his lack of finesse. Miss Brightwell had every reason to feel insulted at the direct manner in which he'd proposed to set her up as his mistress, rather than make her an offer of marriage.

He'd been testing the waters, so to speak, and in the end it had been his ungovernable impatience and desire to have her soon—yes, as his mistress—rather than later as his wife that had caused him to give her the bracelet and key as he'd blurted out his clumsy words.

Miss Brightwell had every reason to be insulted. To add insult to injury, he'd referred to their need for discretion to protect her *sister's* reputation. What had he been thinking? Well, that was the problem, he'd been thinking with his little head and that was no

way for a man to conduct himself in the arena of life with a mind to his long-term happiness.

Perhaps it had been pique and confusion over witnessing her nocturnal visit to Lord Slyther that had made him offer her a carte blanche that challenged her pristine reputation, leaving it to her to defend herself.

His mother's strictures were not inconsequential, either. She'd rammed it down his throat that she was not marriage material—said outright that Miss Brightwell was so decidedly unsuitable that she'd never even receive her. Well, his mother was harsh but she was not unjust. She would not have hinted at factors that precluded Miss Brightwell as wifely material had she not had good reason.

Yet the last twenty-four hours had been an agony. He wanted Miss Brightwell at any cost, regardless of any possible misdemeanours, whether or not her reputation was unsullied. He'd given her no chance to defend herself which made him, quite simply, an out and out cad.

But if Miss Brightwell was here, surely it meant she...

"My Lord."

The demure set of her lips and her regal curtsy was a powerful contrast to their heated encounter a few evenings ago. Blood pounded behind his eyes and rushed to his extremities, and he would have put the sofa between them to hide his fierce arousal had she not immediately glided forward and—oh, joy—placed her dainty, gloved hand upon his shoulder and raised her perfect heart-shaped face to his.

It was all the answer he needed. In paying a call unchaperoned upon a bachelor, she was making it clear that she accepted his proposition.

He had been right to have gone about matters as he had, and now vindication swept away the guilt that had weighed him down since she'd regally departed from his carriage twenty-four hours previously. Yes, she had no doubt hoped he would take her for his

wife but the only reason she could be here under such circumstances was if she were guilty of what George Bramley had accused her.

Expectation made him lightheaded. He would have snatched her to him right there and greedily devoured her, except for the proud, vulnerable way she bore herself. What a tragedy he could not make her his wife. She was magnificent, both inside and out, and he wasn't only referring to the regal bearing she projected to the world for he'd sensed her vulnerability beneath the cloak of confidence that was such a large part of her allure. Losing himself inside her had been like losing himself in Heaven.

With a sigh, she brushed her hand across her forehead. "How hot it is in here," she murmured, turning away from him to glance around the room.

She wore a dove grey bonnet adorned with white flowers and a matching pelisse-robe trimmed with white fur that obviously covered her walking dress.

"The hooks are so difficult," she said with another sigh, raising her chin and stepping up to him. "Won't you help me?"

It was only after undoing the third fastening that he realised her daring little ploy. Dear Lord, she wore nothing beneath the fine, woollen garment. No petticoat, no chemise, no stays. He swallowed. No undergarments of any kind. Only neat, half kid boots in green with matching garters to hold up her white silk stockings.

He was on his knees by the time he'd worked loose the final button.

"My God, you are perfection," he managed through constricted airways as he gazed up at her, trembling with the knowledge of all she was offering him.

She smiled as she rested her small, ungloved hand on his head. Groaning softly, he wrapped his arms around her waist and rested his cheek against her smooth, gently rounded belly, sniffing appreciatively. "Musk and ambergris," he murmured.

She giggled and bent down to kiss the top of his head as she shrugged off her pelisse. "Yours for the taking, my Lord," she whispered, giving a provocative wriggle, then arching slightly.

It was all the invitation he needed.

Mesmerised, he gazed up at her from where he still knelt. She was astonishing. The most exquisite confection of womanhood he'd ever encountered in his wanton-woman-filled years as a rake. He couldn't have torn himself from her had the walls of his town house been crashing down about their ears.

He rose up on his knees, and she placed her hands upon his shoulders, throwing back her head and gasping as he took one perfect, pink peak into his mouth.

Her reaction thrilled him. She shuddered. He could feel her trembling to her very core. He was her prince of pleasure, her puppet master, pulling the strings of her passion. He'd never felt so powerful—so privileged—in all his life.

And it would be no one-off encounter. She'd pledged herself to him as surely as if in marriage. Yet she'd taken all the risks. How he adored her for it. How he intended to honour her sacrifice.

Starting with the truth.

"I think I love you, Miss Brightwell," he murmured, burying his face between her full, soft breasts. They were his. She was offering him her all.

She gasped as he began to suckle the other nipple and it nearly drove him to the brink. He could feel her temperature rise, the warmth and moistness of her skin acting on him like a red rag to a rutting bull. Her trembling and the constricted way she managed to reply, "I think I love you, too, Lord Fenton," could not be feigned. She had come back for him because he, of all the men she'd ever enjoyed, was her chosen, consummate lover.

It was time for to return to the other delectable mound of lily-white flesh. Taking the delicate rosebud peak in his mouth, he toyed with it, delighting in her moans and sighs while his fingers tangled in the soft, damp curls at the juncture of her legs. He

couldn't wait to pay a more intimate visit there. He was nearly bursting out of his breeches with the need to do so.

But the time was not yet right. He needed to show her what a generous lover he could be.

When her breath came in short, staccato bursts and he glanced up to see that her eyes were glazed, he paused just long enough to divest himself of his own clothes. Then he was back on his knees wearing only his linen shirt and, he suspected, a grin like the village idiot. This creature had stepped from another sphere into his life, as if a fairy godmother had waved her magic wand and granted him the elixir of love.

He kissed his way up the smooth white silk of her stocking, sucking at the damp, heated flesh above the garter, revelling in her moans—more intense now—and the way her hands fisted in his hair. Her cries of rapture when his tongue found the swollen nub at her centre, slick with desire, nearly undid him.

"More," she whimpered when he released her before sweeping her into his arms and depositing her upon the hearthrug. The impatient grinding of her hips, the thwarted desire that flared in her eyes, were enough to convince him this was no feigned performance.

Still, he was careful not to move too fast. If she was comparing him with past lovers he didn't want to come up wanting.

"What can I do for you, my darling Fanny?" he muttered, pausing in the midst of rolling one rosy red nipple around his tongue. "Just name your desire."

She said nothing for a moment and he watched, mesmerised, as she tore her eyes from his face to rove over his flanks. The flare in their sapphire depths when they reached his manhood suggested she liked what she saw and his tremor of anticipation echoed hers.

Grasping her by her elbows, he raised her so that they were kneeling, facing each other, raw longing surely in each look during this brief hiatus in proceedings.

For a second, she looked uncertain, as if this was new territory. What a consummate actress she was. What a consummate lover! Then, experimentally, she weighed his long, rigid shaft in her hand, gently moulding his balls. He held his breath as she ran her finger round the tip. Lord, it felt good, this prelude to what promised to be the most exquisite pleasure of his life. Lowering her head, she flicked her tongue over the tip of him. He gasped and gripped her shoulders, pushing her back, gasping, "No, I won't last a minute and right now, Miss Fanny Brightwell, I want to brand you as mine, to claim you, body and soul."

No, Fenton was nearly past the brink and this vixen was about to make a fool out of a man known for his sexual endurance.

Cradling her shoulders, he lay her upon the hearthrug and covered her fine-boned body with his, revelling in the moist warmth of her skin and the heart-rending way she looked up at him.

She smiled, her expression full of love and his heart answered, full to bursting with the need to honour her gift to him. She had forsaken her position in society to be with him and he intended that she should never regret her decision.

"Whatever happens, I shall keep you safe," he promised hoarsely, closing his eyes and kissing her lips as he positioned himself at her wet, velvety entrance. Her response, eager and childlike as she dug her little fingers into his flesh and kissed him back, was like a spark to straw.

With a groan, he plunged deep within her, the roaring in his head competing with her cries and the fury of their mingled breathing. She was tight and smooth and slippery and her excitement was as great as his. Miss Fanny Brightwell was the consummate lover, rocking with him and arching against him in their race for the summit. At each thrust he felt he was burying himself ever deeper into her welcoming, molten core, branding her as his.

Forever.

Until at last he came with a gasp of rapture and triumph and

love, because in this woman's arms he'd finally found the fount of happiness.

For several minutes he was unable to move. It was the most stupendous love-making he'd ever experienced and he felt he'd run the race of his life. Exhausted, with eyes still closed, he lazily licked the salty sheen of sweat from her heated skin. Finally, he rolled off her and onto his side, resting his elbow on the rug and cushioning his head on his hand. She looked dazed when he drew her against him but she chuckled happily when he kissed her almost reverently on the forehead and whispered, "I do not take lightly the sacrifices you've made." He looked wonderingly at her. "I am the happiest, most satiated man alive."

With a languid stretch she sighed and snuggled closer, smiling and murmuring, "I've made no sacrifices, my Lord."

He rose to help her dress, understanding her concern as she tensed when she heard the clock chime the hour. He knew what risks she had taken to be with him. She could have chosen respectability with a wealthy merchant. There were enough of them who'd have overlooked her lack of dowry and reputation to wed the bold and beautiful daughter of a disgraced baron. Instead, she'd followed her impulsive desires to be his mistress, to be with *him*.

The fire in the grate hissed and crackled. He could not bear to see her leave.

"I want to see you…be with you every moment of the day," he whispered, securing the last hook beneath her chin which he cupped in his hands. He'd never wanted anything more. No woman had intrigued and excited him like Miss Brighwell. He could imagine them together until the end of their days. Clearing his throat he added, "But you must dictate the terms, for I know you have considerations other than me." He adored the delicate blush that swept her cheeks.

When she lowered her face demurely he could not contain his excitement as he said in a rush, "Tomorrow I must show you the

charming residence in Mayfair I have selected, which I'm sure you'll adore—though I understand it is prudent to wait a while before you install yourself." His impatience to set her up, permanently, as his was killing him.

She touched his cheek and his heart swelled at the tenderness in her eye as she murmured, "Mayfair? How...convenient."

"And I shall provide you with a carriage," he promised, his generosity fuelled by her kindling look.

"Oh, that will not be necessary, as I shall have my own." Leaning in to him, she raised her hand to stroke the curls at the nape of his neck as he tied her bonnet. He was taken aback when, sighing, she added, "My love, I have much to organise during the next few days. I will send a note around when I'm free to see you again."

Free to see you again?

He did not understand her meaning. "Of course we must be discreet but, my darling Fanny, I want to be with you every moment of the day." He was surprised at how anxious he suddenly felt. Had she not considered their coupling the most extraordinarily exciting experience of her life?

He certainly had.

~

Rain slashed against the windowpanes. It was a fitting tribute to his mood. Like a caged beast, Fenton paced the hearthrug, his mind able to turn upon only one thing—Miss Fanny Brightwell. For three days she had been unobtainable, neither at any of the fashionable watering holes or even, when in desperation he'd begun calling in person, at her London lodgings. She'd even sent him a note to tell him she was too busy to see the lodgings he'd secured for her but that she looked forward to their next encounter.

Lord, what did *that* mean?

He turned, heart pumping in hope and expectation at the sound of crashing upon the front door, though it was not a lady-like entrance.

Instead, Bramley thundered past a clearly distressed Brimble and burst into the library. As he removed his hat a great torrent of water splashed from its brim and joined the droplets from his multi-layered coat in a puddle on the Wilton carpet.

"Perhaps, Brimble, you'd divest Mr Bramley of his sodden garments," Fenton said with pointed disapproval to the hovering and clearly enraged butler. The fact that he had hoped it might be Fanny made him even more disinclined to entertain Bramley, who was obviously in one of his moods.

"No time." Bramley sucked in a breath, running a hand through his rain-darkened hair as he fended off Brimble's discreet ministrations. His eyes burned like coals in his pallid face, his agitation clear as he rasped, "You have to come quickly, Fenton. The news is all over town. I heard it just now at my club. Miss Brightwell is betrothed to the Earl of Quamby."

Fenton could only blink. Stupidly, like an owl. Shock robbed him of an intelligent response and left him physically deflated, as if the air had been sucked right out of him. Not just the air but the bones and substance that enabled him to walk tall, like a man. He gripped the sideboard for support. *His* Fanny Brightwell? The woman who'd played his heartstrings not three afternoons before like a bewitching harpist before disappearing in a puff of enchanted smoke?

"I've come directly from my uncle's house, where Quamby confirmed that he and Miss Brightwell are to be married without delay." Bramley's face contorted with malice as he paced. "I believe the betrothal took place three days ago."

"*Three days ago?*" Fenton repeated. He shook his head. It could not be true. A powerful combination of disbelief, wounded pride and devastation swept out the thick, sluggish horror that slowed his responses.

No! *This could not be.* Miss Fanny Brightwell could not do this to him. She could not be allowed to shake up the happy, ordered world that revolved around her making him the most important man in her life.

What was she up to? Three days ago he'd been the happiest man alive. Miss Brightwell had been wrapped in his arms, sighing happily as he rained kisses upon her face. Dear God, she'd been beneath him on this very carpet, moaning in ecstasy as he'd thrust deep inside her. He'd assumed that the giving of her smooth, fragrant, sensual body was her ultimate gift to him. He'd felt like some great, all-powerful God. So what had happened? Had she walked straight from Fenton's embrace into the path of Lord Quamby, who had made her an offer of marriage she couldn't refuse?

"Lord Quamby." The growl came from his very depths. He was vaguely aware that Bramley was at the sideboard helping himself to brandy and, with shaking hands, was trying to replace the glass stopper. Neglecting to consult with his host, or even offer some much-needed fortification, he quickly followed the first shot with another.

"Why have you come to *me?*" Fenton's tone was clipped. Calm and reason were slowly returning.

Bramley slammed down the glass tumbler and turned. His lip curled. "Because Lord Quamby is my uncle and I am his heir. He was never supposed to marry. A woman in his bed is laughable, yet that insinuating little baggage has sneaked right under my guard, wrapped my uncle around her little finger and is about to deny me my inheritance. Antoinette told me all about the pair of you. God knows, I've seen it in the way Miss Brightwell looks at you. She loves you! I wanted to stop that but…right now, you're the only one who can stop *her!*" In several strides he was across the room, seizing Fenton by the arm and propelling him to the door as he called to Brimble for his Lordship's coat.

They found a hackney carriage, though with the rain and

traffic congestion of the fashionable hour it would have been quicker to walk.

The only one who can stop her?

Fenton hunched over in the shabby seat, his mind in turmoil. Three days ago he'd arrogantly thought he held the upper hand. Pain mocked him while gleefully lancing his vulnerable heart. He didn't understand any of it. He'd thought she loved him. Bramley said she did.

Clearly, though, she'd not loved him enough.

Through clenched teeth he said, "It seems the Dowager Duchess of Quamby will see her son marry at any cost if she's prepared to countenance a match with an ineligible. Why not Miss Antoinette? She's just as comely and willing and, unless you've ensured otherwise, her reputation is still intact." He heard the snideness of his tone, an armour against his pain and turmoil. "There's no slur upon *her* past, for all that that happy truth is more due to me than to you. Miss Antoinette has not entertained Bickling and Slyther and God knows who else, although it matters not one jot to me."

There was something jarring in Bramley's stillness. Fenton turned from his angry contemplation of the passing foot traffic as a drift of memory from the ball a little over a week ago floated just out of reach. What *exactly* was it Miss Brightwell had said with regard to Bramley's conduct? It had been derisive, he knew that. He stared at Bramley's profile and racked his brain. Something to the effect that Bramley was unlikely to have much regard for Antoinette's best interests—that in fact Bramley was on a mission to do the precise opposite. At the time, Fenton had been too concerned with seeing to Fanny's best interests to register that her remark indicated more than just a passing association. Yes, he knew they were acquainted and that Bramley had perhaps been put out by Fanny's lack of interest...but was there more to it?

"How well do you really know Miss Brightwell?" With shoul-

ders hunched, Fenton leaned menacingly across the small space between them.

A flash of lightning illuminated Bramley's pallid, sweating brow. As usual, his lip was curled with derision. "She has the airs of a princess"—his voice was rough and ugly— "though she has not a penny to her name."

It was as if a veil had been drawn from across Fenton's eyes, though in truth he'd suspected it before, then discounted it. "She spurned your *suit*"—Fenton thrust out his hand and seized Bramley by the neck cloth—"didn't she? Not just your attentions?"

Bramley wrenched free and threw himself back against the squabs as he hissed, "She told me I had the address of a coster-monger and not to insult her with my persistence."

"You offered *marriage!*"

"Of course I offered marriage," Bramley muttered. His fingers tapped the scratched leather seats as he stared grimly at the rain-soaked streets. "D'you think I'd offer to make her my mistress?" He chewed his lower lip. "Yes, Fenton, I lied about the lovely Miss Fanny Brightwell when I saw the way she looked at you. I did not want to see her compete with all the other pretty, vacuous debu-tantes who parade their wares at Almacks, knowing she was the cream of the crop and could have anyone she wanted." He rasped in a breath, muttering, "Not when *I* wanted her."

Horror and prickles of cold sweat made Fenton shiver. What had he done? He had been taken for a fool, believing Bramley almost without qualification when he'd witnessed Fanny's late-night visit to Lord Slyther's. Believing the whispers of other no-doubt jaded, spurned suitors. Believing his mother's insinuations. Assuming, upon reflection, that Fanny's eagerness for their coupling in the tent at Quamby's ball and the fact that she had not bled were further evidence that she had not been a virgin. And all because it suited him to; that it justified him making her an offer so he could set her up *now* when he was too impatient to wait. He'd thought he could have the best of both worlds, hadn't he?

Right now he hated himself.

Bramley was still talking. It was not soothing to listen to him go on, "And then Lord Slyther made her an offer. Antoinette told me. Miss Brightwell turned me down, but she was prepared to accept *him*. That mountain of pestilence!"

Fenton closed his eyes, mocked by memories that had, until now, sustained him.

He clarified, "Lord Slyther made an offer of *marriage?*" wincing as Bramley muttered viciously, "Given the choice, I daresay she'd have preferred me, but her mama had organised the match and was not about to let her wriggle out of it after her *disappointment* with Alverley."

Fenton tried to breathe evenly through his anger. If ever a virtuous woman deserved revenge, Miss Brightwell did—but to be on the receiving end of her scorn and disgust when he'd imagined a lifetime of her delights was like a cold knife in his heart.

Yet he deserved it!

He turned back to Bramley and hissed, "You suggested I make her my mistress."

Bramley stared through the window. "You'd hardly be so stupid, my dear fellow." He appeared to have trouble breathing as he added, "I wanted to find a way to punish her for turning her nose up at me. I wanted to punish *you* for being to her what I wanted to be." He let out his breath in a burst of sour air. "Now I'd embrace you with open arms if you enticed her away from my uncle. No doubt the designing wench plans to present him with an heir nine months from their wedding day."

Perhaps even earlier than that.

Fenton clenched shut his eyes. Quamby's heir. Fenton's child.

"Good God, Fenton, what's got into you?" Bramley's words ended in a wail of pain as Fenton seized him by the collar and thrust him across the seat.

"I should call you out, here and now!" Fenton snarled as

Bramley struggled beneath him. "Though I'd rather beat your brains to a pulp where you lie, you puling, whining puppy."

~

FANNY, SITTING BETWEEN HER SISTER AND LORD QUAMBY, LOOKED up with a smile as she heard footsteps just outside the saloon.

"Lord Fenton, my Lord," announced Lord Quamby's stately butler from the double doors where his employer was entertaining his future in-laws. With a disdainful sniff he added, "And your nephew, Mr Bramley."

"What a pleasant surprise. Come to pay your respects to the happy pair, no doubt." Lord Quamby patted Fanny's hand, which rested on her primrose silk skirts, before introducing the rest of the party. "Indeed, we are all here to celebrate—joyful mamas and siblings, too." He winked at Antoinette, who cast Bramley a coy but knowing look from beneath lowered lashes.

Fanny ran her eyes over Fenton, hoping the effects of her thundering heart were not visible through the fine fabric of her bodice. She was well satisfied by the wild look in his eye. His neck cloth was in disarray and there was a cut on his cheek. Bramley bore evidence of a bloody nose.

Wonderful, she thought without sarcasm, and her heart swelled. They'd been engaged in fisticuffs.

She'd assumed Fenton would be shocked by the news of her impending nuptials but it appeared that his reaction had surpassed that. So she was more than amenable to his suggestion when he growled, ignoring everyone else in the room, "I'd like to speak to Miss Brightwell. Alone."

Fanny squeezed Lord Quamby's shoulder as she rose, responding to her mother's warning look with a bright, "Lord Fenton and I will take a turn about the room while the rest of you continue. Order up the wedding breakfast as you wish, but don't

plan the wedding tour without me. I've a particular desire to see Venice."

The saloon was a palatial expanse divided into various seating and entertaining arrangements. It was to the large bay window at the far end, with bench seating around its sides, an area partly obscured by a gold velvet tasselled curtain, that Fenton led her.

"What is the meaning of this?" His voice was low and demanding. Fanny could hear the tension. The extent of his obvious suffering made her heart thunder even harder with excited longing and breathless anticipation.

Gripping her by the shoulder, Fenton swung her out of sight behind the curtain.

"My dear Fenton, we must be discreet," Fanny objected mildly, revelling in the look of wounded pride on her beloved's face. The agitation with which he raked his hand through his sooty, tousled curls was heart-warming.

"You're playing with fire, don't you know?" He shook his head, as if the situation was surreal. Which, of course, it was. "You've pledged yourself to *me*, Fanny. You *gave* yourself to me and now…" He began to pace back and forth in front of the window, his breathing laboured as he struggled for words. Swinging round, he glared at her. "If Lord Quamby were to discover what you were doing—" He swallowed and closed his eyes briefly as if the memory were too much to revisit. "What you were doing with me just hours, it would appear, before you accepted his suit, you and your family would be unable to hold your heads up in this town."

"But Fenton, dearest—" She broke off and tilted her head, "I can call you Fenton, can't I, if I'm to be your mistress? No, please, hear me out—it's *because* I told dear Lord Quamby what we'd been doing that he asked me to marry him."

"What!?"

Reaching up on tiptoe, she pressed one finger to his lips, "Hush, Fenton, you sound as if you're about to lose your temper." It was hard to keep up the charade. Her sense of vindication fully

equalled her joy at this confirmation of his true feelings for her. "And please don't interrupt. Lord Quamby knew I'd lost my heart to you. He understood my devastation when you offered to make me your mistress rather than your wife. That was when he suggested that, as it would please his mama enormously if *he* took a wife—"

Seizing her by both elbows he pushed her backwards so that she landed with a thud on the bench seat.

Pinioned beneath his bulk of muscle, Fanny's excitement increased as he loomed over her, his eyes roiling with passion. His chest pressed against her breasts. She could feel the hard bulk of his manly swelling further down, too, and her own body responded with a rush of warmth to her lower belly. She wanted to rip off his clothes and make love to him, right there in the alcove. She saw he was tormented by a similar longing.

With his face barely an inch from hers, he ground out, "Living here, in Mayfair, with a carriage of your own, no doubt?"

Fanny had never seen such tortured workings in a man's expression. She was delighted. "Yes. I thought I'd order one in cerulean blue with two footmen wearing—"

"So when you visited me at my town house you'd already accepted him?"

"Of course, otherwise I'd have gratefully accepted your generous offer of accommodation on the spot rather than dissembling." Stifling the urge to kiss away his scowl, she wriggled out from under him, smiling serenely as she smoothed her skirts. "I was secretly betrothed to Lord Slyther, only I couldn't bear the idea of marriage to him after I met you. So in the hopes of receiving an honourable offer from *you* I delayed the marriage." She sighed. "Then he died just *hours* before our nuptials. You can't imagine how relieved I was— *still* thinking you cared enough for me to make me your wife."

She glared at him before resuming with another smile. "Now, of course, I have the best of both worlds. I shall be a duchess

rather than a viscountess and Lord Quamby, who is very generous, says you and I can be together as much as we wish—provided we are discreet. You shall be my cicisbeo, Fenton darling."

Sweeping aside the curtain she took his arm. "The others will be wondering where we are," she added, as she pulled him out of hiding, proceeding into the room with as much decorum as if they were at a state ball. "How proud you will be, Fenton, when your son becomes an earl instead of a mere viscount."

TWENTY MINUTES LATER, FENTON THREW OPEN THE DOORS TO HIS mother's sunny morning room and strode across the green and gold Aubusson carpet.

His mood was grim but all was not yet lost. Not if Fanny truly loved him—though, Lord knew, she'd done a mighty fine job of humiliating him.

Lacerated he'd been, yet it had done nothing to dampen his desire. Hope flickered uncertainly in his breast.

"I need the Fenton diamonds, Mother."

"Right now, darling?" Arching her plucked eyebrows, Lady Fenton glanced up from her book.

"Yes, right now, Mama." He was in no mood for going through the motions of playing the dutiful son. She knew he could want them for only one thing.

"I plan to propose to Miss Brightwell this afternoon."

"Goodness!" Lady Fenton dropped her book and twisted in her chair by the fire. "You've enticed her from Lord Quamby?" Her face was animated. "Well done, darling!" she cried, holding out her arms. "Come here so I may congratulate you."

He blinked as if to clear his head. "You're pleased?" This day was throwing out more shocks than he believed his poor, ravaged system could take. He stared with disbelief at the curved mouth, usually puckered with disapproval. "But, Mama," he muttered,

"you warned me against Miss Brightwell even *before* I met her. Lord knows, you threatened a veritable schism if I married her. You considered her patently unsuitable a week ago and I can't see what's changed. She still comes with no dowry, her father still killed himself to thumb his nose at the moneylenders and God knows who else was after him—"

"But you've enticed her from the Earl of Quamby. And the girl is a beauty. She has style and finesse. She'll make you a fine wife."

Fenton could only stare. There was not even the suggestion of a slur upon Fanny's reputation. If his mother had heard whispers she'd have said something. Fanny's ineligibility had been the result of something entirely different, as far as his mother was concerned. Something entirely irrelevant. Why, in view of everything he'd learnt in the past couple of hours, Fanny had been the most innocent of debutantes and certainly a virgin when he'd...

He swallowed down his guilt as he finished the sentence... taken her virtue before offering to make her his mistress.

"What does anything matter now you've pulled the rug from under Lord Quamby's feet?" Lady Fenton cut in with a dismissive wave of her hand. She looked grotesquely playful as she patted the footstool by her side in invitation. "Really, Fenton, you make me sound like an old tartar. Besides, at the time I had good reason to warn you, with that detestable mother of hers ready to insinuate herself where she could."

Fenton, who had chosen to remain standing, was silent as he digested this. "You're telling me it was *only* her mother you'd taken against?"

"Lofty little Lottie Lucas, that's right." Lady Fenton looked as if she'd just drunk sour milk. "As I think I mentioned, we were together at Mrs Smedley's Seminary for the Daughters of Gentlemen, in Kensington." For a moment his mother looked like an old and angry parody of Bramley as she clenched her fist. "The whey-faced ape-leader said I smelt of shop because grandfather's fortune came from brewing."

Fenton felt ill. He swayed before forcing his manliness to the fore. So much had happened in just a few short days. He'd taken too much of what he'd heard at face value, leaving him looking like a fool.

Worse, he'd quite possibly ruined all chance of future happiness with the utterly beguiling Miss Brightwell because of Bramley's jealousy and an old grudge held by his mother.

Rising, Lady Fenton warmed her back at the fire as she shook her head. "Curiously, Miss Lucas later asked me to attend her at her wedding to Monty Brightwell. I suppose she was dangling after a generous wedding present."

"You attended Lady Brightwell's wedding?" Fenton swung out of his mother's orbit and began to pace, shaking his head. How much more could he endure?

Lady Fenton clapped her hands and her eyes glittered with excitement once more. "And now you're to steal Miss Brightwell away from the Earl of Quamby, which, upon my word, will set up *that* dowager's bristles nicely. She was ever the schoolmarm. Did I tell you what the old Friday-faced gorgon said to me just after she became Lady Quamby…?"

❦

"LORD FENTON, MY LORD." LORD QUAMBY'S BUTLER RAKED A disapproving eye over the viscount as he passed into the centre of the company. The young man's cravat was still askew, and he'd obviously not attended to the cut on his cheek.

Fanny managed to plaster an expression of careless unconcern upon her face as she looked up from her discussion with Lord Quamby.

So he had come back. Obviously her little charade had worked, and now her future happiness rested upon the next few moments. Her hands felt cold and clammy. She gripped Lord Quamby's arm, her spirits bolstered by his theatrical wink.

"Methinks Miss Brightwell has just snared her viscount," he murmured, giving her hands a quick squeeze. "Don't let him off too easily, my poppet. The more you make him suffer now, the more he'll respect you for it, I promise."

The Dowager Duchess Quamby, who was chatting comfortably with Lady Brightwell over a dish of tea, offered their guest a seat.

Antoinette, looking up from the game of piquet she was playing at a table in front of the fire with Bramley, giggled. "You look very dark and Byronesque, Lord Fenton," she said.

Ignoring her and with the most cursory acknowledgement of the rest of the company, Fenton focused his glowering expression upon Lady Brightwell. "I wish to speak to your daughter. Alone."

Fanny watched her mother exchange disapproving looks with the Earl's mama. Her heart rate increased.

Lord Quamby knew exactly what this was about, and she already had his approbation. But her mother was not going to be pleased.

Interjecting before Lady Brightwell could reply, Fanny ran a languid hand across her brow, and sighed. "I'm positively fagged to death from all that walking about the room we did only an hour ago, Lord Fenton. Surely you can say all that needs to be said in front of present company?"

"I cannot."

"Unpardonable," muttered Lady Brightwell of the man Fanny knew her mother would have embraced with open arms as her daughter's suitor mere days ago. The reflection galvanised her into rising.

"Just three minutes, my Lord," she said with a smile, taking Fenton's arm and strolling with him to the alcove.

Her leisurely progress ended with an unseemly push so that she landed, for the second time that day, with a thud on the window seat obscured by the gold-tasselled curtain. For the

second time that day, Fenton's face loomed over hers as his arms gripped the windowsill on either side of her face.

"Enough of these games—"

Fanny's laugh was part amusement, part indignation. "What games? Lord Quamby asked me to be his wife and you asked me to be your mistress and I have accepted both offers."

"I am here to ask you to marry me, Miss Brightwell." His voice quavered as he thrust at her a much larger, heavier velvet box than the last. "In case you doubt the sincerity of my offer, I hope the Fenton diamonds will convince you." He cleared his throat and, in that second, Fanny saw his vulnerability so much more clearly than the persona of the practiced rake.

Perhaps he had acted as any young buck hearing rumours of her unsuitability, and he'd only been testing the waters. She shouldn't forgive him but he truly did seem to wish to atone.

Fanny gazed with appreciation at his beautiful eyes, smouldering with fire but full of fear; at his strong jaw, clenched with angst; and at his large, strong hands with their delicate long fingers that had stroked her face with such tenderness, and her desire with such finesse. Inside, her heart seemed to flip over.

Goodness, but she wanted him.

And right now it looked as if he truly doubted her answer if he was about to make her the offer for which she longed. Indeed, he looked as fearful but as resolved that he would cross shark-infested waters to have her. An enormous wave of tenderness engulfed her.

Fenton cleared his through. "They have passed through three generations of my family and are worn by the reigning viscountess and now I offer them to you"—he took a breath, adding in a rush that did nothing to conceal the wavering tone —"if you will have me."

Tingles of excitement started in her toes and worked their way upwards, and they weren't on account of the diamonds. Her ploy had worked and, judging by the determined look on Lord

Fenton's face, he was not going to take no for an answer. But if he truly wanted her he would to have to work harder.

She affected a small frown. "You're asking me to sacrifice what is probably my only chance to become a duchess—?"

"I'm asking you to follow your heart. Dear God, Fanny..." He took her seat, settling her across his lap and forcing her head onto his shoulder so he could caress her cheek. "I know you're trying to make me suffer for the humiliation I've caused you, for which I'm truly sorry. But after what we shared..." He shook his head. "Surely you felt it, too?" Cupping her face in his hands he gazed into her eyes. His own looked tortured. Gently he touched his lips to hers.

She shivered, barely able to restrain her answering impulses as he murmured into the gentlest of kisses, "If I have to spend the rest of my life atoning I will, if only to hear you say yes to becoming my wife. Just name your terms, Fanny."

It wasn't the desperation in his voice, reaffirming her power over him, or even his generous offer. It was his kiss that confirmed she could belong to no one else. How could she say no to a man whose touch unleashed feelings of love and tenderness she had never known existed within the heart she had once thought as cold as her mother's? Gently clasping his face, she kissed his lips, his eyes, his cheeks, revelling in the shudders that ran through him. Behind the tasselled gold curtain, her dreams were finally coming true.

"I want my own cerulean blue carriage with four high steppers," she murmured. She wasn't serious and was surprised when he dug his fingers into her shoulders and ground out, "Done."

He was trembling as if he had the ague, their lips barely touching throughout their exchange. His voice was strained. "You can have it in royal purple or scarlet for all I care."

With the tip of her tongue, she traced the line of his mouth. His eyes were still closed, but his senses were clearly alert to her slightest touch. She smiled at his shudders, then whispered, "And

Antoinette must have a dowry." Though Lord Quamby had already discussed taking care of Antoinette's future himself, Fanny knew this was something she had to ensure if she was to placate her mother later that evening.

Still kissing her lightly, though with growing impatience, Fenton agreed to this, also. "And a house for Mama with her own annuity."

He drew back, his eyes widening. Perhaps perceiving her determination, he curbed any objection, saying with a defeated air, "As long as it's not near us."

"Definitely not!" Fanny agreed, stroking his face. "But with three hundred a year she could afford her own carriage and something commodious in Northumbria so she can lord it over her cheeseparing cousin. That would keep her busy and her nose out of our affairs."

"Agreed."

Fanny brought the kiss to a satisfying conclusion. He did not need to know that her shuddering surrender was the culmination of so many fears bound up with the need to please her mother before she could please herself. She wanted to weep her joy, but it was too soon. She remembered Lord Quamby's words and whispered, smiling, "In that case, all seems in order. Shall we inform the rest of the company?"

CHAPTER 10

enton groaned at the sound of tapping and hauled himself into a sitting position, shouting to the impatient servant on the other side of the door that he'd present himself in the saloon presently. He gazed at Fanny, curled up like a kitten beside him. She looked innocent and childlike in her slumber, and his heart swelled. If he wasn't so terrified she would change her mind, he'd have the servant send the parson away until another time.

They'd made love three times since Lord Quamby had granted Fanny an honourable reprieve, but if it had been three hundred it wouldn't have been enough.

She stirred and, with a lascivious chuckle, he traced a line with his finger from the Fenton diamonds at her throat, over the contour of Fanny's right breast, before resting his hand on her belly. The mere touch of her smooth, warm skin stoked the fires of his desire.

"I'm sure you could never have predicted your scheme for revenge would have so unexpectedly pleased our collective mamas, my dear," he murmured as she blinked open sleep-laden eyes. "All I can say is thank you for having saved me the trouble of

finding a dull, suitable bride to please mine, so I could rush off to my mistress." He gave her shoulder a playful squeeze rather than the languorous all-over body massage he'd have preferred as he flung his legs over the side of the bed. Friends and family were waiting for them in the saloon. Now was not the time to slake his lust.

"*When* I could get away," Fanny replied, stretching luxuriantly. "Quamby and I are fierce combatants at whist." She yawned, adding in a voice of feigned boredom, "It's our favourite way to while away the evening together."

Fenton pulled his shirt over his shoulders while Fanny feasted her eyes on his bunched-up muscles. She adored the vulnerable look of his nipples set into such masculine hardness. He paused in his dressing to grin at her. "You mean I haven't *yet* convinced you of the advantages of fornication with me above whist with Quamby? You'd better be sure you know what you want, darling, for the parson is waiting."

Crawling off the bed, Fanny wrapped her arms and one leg around the bedpost. Since she was still naked this provocative move had the desired effect. Fenton stifled a growl and closed his eyes, seemingly in pain as his manhood swelled.

"You'll not convince me of anything until I'm your viscountess," Fanny told him pertly, reaching for her chemise.

Suddenly she stopped, frowning as she clasped her hand to her forehead.

"What is it, darling?" Fenton was at her side in an instant, drawing her against him. "Is everything all right?"

"Oh, Fenton, when I'm your viscountess we can do this any time we wish."

The puzzled concern on his face was adorable. He touched her cheek. "That will be wonderful, won't it?" His tone was uncertain.

Fanny bit her lip. "Oh, Fenton, I'm having second thoughts." She covered her face with her hands, pretending real distress as he gripped her shoulders and put her away from him.

"Second thoughts?" There was no trace of amusement in his voice. "You certainly *appeared* to enjoy our bedroom sport. Have you any complaints? Why, we are not even married, Fanny, and yet we've...we've made love like rabbits *five* times. Are you telling me now that you're dissatisfied with proceedings?"

She dropped her hands. Lord, he appeared so adorably vulnerable with that look of concern that indicated he feared his performance was not up to her exacting standards that she had to suppress a giggle.

"Oh, it was all wonderful, Fenton, truly it was. But I have such a low boredom threshold. I mean, perhaps I'll be bored by the sixth time. It's usually about the sixth time I start to get bored with something and until a few days ago I knew nothing of all this." She shrugged as expressively as she could. "*Will* the sixth be any different or have you demonstrated your entire repertoire?"

"You little wench!" Correctly interpreting the quirk of her lips and arch look he finally realised she was teasing him.

With a squeal she landed on her back upon the bed, looking up into Fenton's burning eyes as he caged her body with his.

"Three minutes!" he muttered as he lowered his face to plunder her mouth, coming up for air to add, "Enough time to give you an experience you won't forget *and* deliver you to the parson with sufficient self-respect so we can both hold our heads up in front of the gathered company."

He lowered his head to kiss her, his erection jutting into her belly, his breathing, fast and furious, heating her ear while his artful fondling between her legs heated her blood.

"Lesson number six," he growled as he raised his head.

She gasped as she received him, bunching the counterpane in her fists and squeezing shut her eyes as he worked his magic. Never before had she felt him so deep. Arching her back to meet him at each thrust, she cried out as her beloved husband-to-be pounded into her, burying himself to the hilt.

"Oh, God!" she moaned as the rhythmic motion of his fingers

upon the slick, swollen nub between her legs heightened each spiral of sensation and his deep thrusting seemed to reach the very core of her.

"Harder! Harder!" she shrieked as he pounded into her and she felt her inner being claw its way to the summit. Higher and higher she climbed, despite knowing she was entering dangerous, unknown territory until she was balancing on the precipice, her senses suspended in an agony of thrilling excitement before a final thrust sent her over the edge.

"Oh, Fenton!" she cried out as her body seemed to combust in a shower of fiery embers. A red haze swirled behind her eyes as she felt Fenton's fingers digging into her upper arms while he continued his thrusting until, with an orgasmic howl, he, too, collapsed, boneless on top of her.

For a moment neither moved nor spoke. The landscape had changed. They were altered, inside and out. Bound forever in that moment, even before they intoned the vows that would unite them inextricably in the eyes of the church.

"That was...exquisite," she whispered, conscious of the wonderful feel of him, inside and out. It took her several minutes to recover her breath sufficiently to add, "I'm convinced."

"And *you're* wonderful." As if he were drawing on his final reserves of strength, Fenton withdrew, drawing her up against his chest and holding her close.

His adoring look lanced her heart and Fanny squeezed his hand. "Let's get ourselves married now, shall we, darling?" she whispered.

He nodded, adding in a rush as he stayed her from rising, "Fanny, I'm so sorry I believed Bramley's unfounded allegations." He buried his face in her hair, adding wryly, "Though I think Bramley will feel he's been served more than his just desserts when he gazes upon the squalling Quamby heir eight months from now and sees his own thuggish nose."

Fanny pulled away to frown at him. "Antoinette is flighty but

I'm sure she never went quite so far before accepting Lord Quamby's suit."

Her frown was obliterated by Fenton's kiss, even as she knew her defence of her sister was completely unfounded.

"She certainly did, and the talk's all over town." Fenton took her hand and helped her off the bed. "It's just fortunate she's been taken up by His Grace and everyone knows that at least if the child she bears isn't her husband-to-be's it will have been foisted on her by Lord Quamby's heir."

Fanny sighed happily. "Mama is so pleased."

"Enough about Antoinette. Here are your stays, madam." Fenton assisted her with her undergarments before helping her into her rose-coloured twilled silk gown. With an appreciative sigh, he stepped back. "And now we'd best hurry and be sure to arrive separately if we are not to be thoroughly chastised by the terrifying dowagers." With a finger beneath her chin he tilted Fanny's head up. "They've been waiting for us in the blue drawing room this half hour, completely unaware that we've both been under the same roof, and as it's my Uncle Roderick marrying us I'd wager he's already cock-eyed."

With a final, proud and proprietary look, he tucked her hand through the crook of his arm and led her to the door. "I shall be paying scrupulous attention to ensure he doesn't inadvertently marry you to Brimble or Mama's pug."

"*Darling* Fenton." She felt overcome by the love and warmth in his smile. He'd shown her what it felt to be adored and appreciated and he'd more than atoned for his brief lack of faith. Bramley would spend the rest of his life paying for *that*—and the odious creature knew it.

Nevertheless, her tone was offhand as she murmured, "Just so long as they can kiss like you, my dearest, I'll be content."

His feigned glower of displeasure and the trembling of his lip as he bit back his amusement made her yearn for his embrace. The urgency of his response had her gasping for air after he'd

released her from another fierce, lusty kiss. No, three rounds on the feather mattress this afternoon alone hadn't quelled in the slightest her appetite for mad, bad and dangerous-to-know Lord Fenton.

"Let Brimble or Mama's pug try and match that!" he growled, caging her hand upon his arm. "I intend to make you the happiest, most *satisfied* wife in all England."

THE END

Would a potential suitor be bolder if he were told the object of his desire had only six months to live?

Sweet, pretty Thea Brightwell's dull, quiet life with her

crotchety aunt is about to be turned upside down by a visit to Bath and a chance encounter with handsome Mr Grayling.

However, the fledgeling affair is quickly nipped in the bud by Thea's aunt who has no intention of losing her unpaid nurse and companion, while Mr Grayling regretfully acknowledges he needs to marry an heiress to restore his family's crumbling fortunes.

Unbeknownst to penniless Thea, she has an unlikely champion in her well-meaning but 'not-too-bright' Cousin Bertram who has decided to play matchmaker.

If the lack of a dowry is the only impediment to Mr Grayling making an offer of marriage, Bertram reasons the gentleman would play a riskier hand if he were told that the damsel he covets were destined for her deathbed within six months?

Crotchety maiden aunts, love letters gone astray, and 'old flames' appearing from the woodwork lead to a most disconcerting outcome!

What Readers are Saying about the series:

"I LOVED beautiful Thea's story and couldn't put it down losing hours of sleep!" ~ ***Amazon reader***

"The unexpected twist at the end made me smile and think...yes that's perfect." ~ ***Amazon reader***

"Nicely written and enjoyable Historical romance with a little steam." ~ ***Amazon reader***

*Note: Due to the respective natures of the various Brightwell heroines, Rogue's Kiss is sensual rather than steamy while Rake's Honour is hot and steamy.

EXTRACT

Sylvester stared after lovely Miss Thea Brightwell in genuine bemusement.

To avoid looking like a fool, he half-heartedly speared a slice of nearly transparent ham from the sad looking display before

him and deposited it on his plate. This was not the way he'd expected matters to proceed.

Surely the scorching looks Miss Brightwell had sent him could not have been misconstrued?

He was sure she'd desired his advances, yet no sooner had he contrived to present himself once more to her when she was no longer in company with the oyster-velvet-clad gorgon, than she'd run off like a frightened rabbit...or a coquette. Which was it? Could she really have been playing games?

"Charming chit, ain't she?" Bertram Brightwell's bluff laugh cut into Sylvester's musings and he turned to raise an eyebrow at the young man who was accompanied by his beautiful sister, the youngest, blonde—not to mention, scandalous—Miss Antoinette, who'd snared an earl and whose supposed antics behind closed doors titillated society.

He'd met Lady Quamby—though he could only think of her as Miss Antoinette—at the earl's birthday celebration earlier that year, just weeks after she'd given birth, in fact. Not that one could tell. The girl was exquisite in pale pink silk with silver trimmings, and her bearing was confident, almost conspiratorial, yet when he glanced over her creamy bared shoulder towards the far corner of the room, where her lovely, chestnut-haired but less flamboyant cousin had just jilted him by the food table, she paled into insignificance.

"More of a charming enigma," Sylvester responded.

"Pray enlarge?" Miss Antoinette's blue eyes danced with mischief. There was nothing maternal about her, he thought. She was as flirtatious as he imagined she must have been before she'd become Lord Quamby's countess. Forcing his gaze away from the more sober but more enticing—to his eyes, at least—Miss Thea Brightwell he tried not to stare, but the stories he'd heard about Quamby's wife were incredible; that the earl gave her complete licence to seek out pleasure discreetly as her reward for silence

regarding his own peccadilloes. Dangerous ones, he understood, that courted the death penalty.

Before he had a chance to respond, Bertram said, with an intense frown, "No telling what a gel will do if she's only got six months to live."

"What?"

It tumbled from Miss Antoinette's lips with an expletive and Sylvester's own as a gasp of dismay. "Six months?"

Miss Antoinette looked shocked. "What are you saying, Bertram?" she demanded.

Bertram sighed heavily. "I overheard Dr Horne telling Cousin Thea the terrible news. Don't you wonder why she looks so sad and won't dance? Her heart cannot be exposed to sudden shocks…although," he looked contemplative, "I did also hear the doctor say that gentle pleasures and mild, controlled excitement might well prolong her life." He cleared his throat, adding, "That is, by a couple of months or so only."

Sylvester shook his head, his horror echoing Miss Antoinette's, who clearly had not been privy to the news of her lovely cousin's imminent demise. "Poor young woman," he murmured. "So lovely and so…"

"Doomed," Bertram supplied with a sigh. "Still," he brightened, "she is to be commended on her stoic acceptance of her miserable lot. Her aunt has brought her to Bath to take the waters but sadly is so concerned for her niece's health, she will allow Miss Bright-well no pleasure whatsoever."

"She would not allow me to even dance with her," Sylvester recalled, the rejection taking on a different hue. "Is she…so reduced in health?"

"Oh, Miss Brightwell would dance a jig if she were allowed. She simply craves something that will draw her out of the unhappy final few months she's been allotted." He shrugged before fixing Sylvester with a long and meaningful stare. "But what chance is there of that?"

Buy Rogue's Kiss here.

READ AN EXTRACT FROM ROGUE'S KISS (BOOK 2)

Devil's Run is Book 3 in the Scandalous Miss Brightwell series.

Miss Eliza Montrose will do anything to be reunited with her son — even if it means marrying a man she does not love.

When Eliza discovers that the boy she was forced to give up after an indiscretion is now a foster child living in the household of the earl of Quamby, she accepts the marriage offer of Lord Quamby's odious nephew, George Bramley, because he also resides at Quamby House.

But when Eliza unexpectedly finds a kindred spirit through a shared love of horses, she must choose between her love for her child and her love for the kind and gentle man who wants to make her his own.

It may, however, take a little help from the scheming Brightwell siblings — Fanny, Antoinette and Bertram — and the outcome of the county's most important horse race, to help Eliza make the right decision.

Get Devil's Run at all retailers here.

SAVE ~ THE SCANDALOUS MISS BRIGHTWELL SERIES BOX SET

Buy the first three romances in the *Scandalous Miss Brightwell* series, and save!

Wicked and lively Fanny and Antoinette Brightwell have made spectacular marriages—despite scandals and the treachery of a disappointed suitor determined to derail their plans and besmirch

their reputations. *So, who better to play matchmaker when a deserving candidate waltzes into their orbit?*

Here are the first three stories in the series. Each can be read as a stand-alone.

However, this is the perfect order:

Rake's Honour
Rogue's Kiss
Devil's Run

ALSO BY BEVERLEY OAKLEY

Do you enjoy intrigue-filled romances with unexpected plot twists?

The Daughters of Sin series follows the intertwining lives and sibling rivalry of Lord Partington's two nobly born - and two illegitimate - daughters as they compete for love during several London Seasons.

With Hetty and Araminta both falling for men on opposing sides of a dastardly plot that is being investigated by Stephen Cranborne, now a secret agent in the Foreign Office, there's lashings of skullduggery and intrigue bound up in the central romance.

And, just in case you're ever worried that someone doesn't get their happy ending, or just desserts – rest assured that they will do, either in their book, or by the end of the series.

What Readers are Saying About the Series:

"...lies, misdeeds, treachery, and romance. What an impressive story! Ms. Oakley has a unique way of telling her stories, bringing unknown heroes/ heroines into the spotlight, as they navigate a world of espionage, and intrigue, all while trying to survive and find their HEA. Magnificent and mesmerizing!" ~ **Amazon reader**

"Full of secrets, murders, intrigues and you feel you know the characters and want to strangle some of them, especially Araminta!!! I have since read all in the series and can't wait for Book 5... This is a series I will read again and again." ~ **Amazon reader**

Below is the order of the books:

Book 1: Her Gilded Prison

Book 2: Dangerous Gentlemen

Book 3: The Mysterious Governess Book 4: Beyond Rubies

Book 5: Lady Unveiled: The Cuckold Conspiracy

She was determined to secure the succession, he was in it for the pleasure. Falling in love was not part of the arrangement.
*** *When dashing twenty-five-year-old Stephen Cranbourne arrives at the estate he will one day inherit, it's expected he will make a match with his beautiful second cousin, Araminta. But while proud, fiery Araminta and her shy, plain sister, Hetty, parade their very different charms before him, it's their mother, Sybil, a lonely and discarded wife, who evokes first his sympathy and then stokes his lustful fires.*

Shy, plain Hetty was the wallflower beneath his notice...until a terrible mistake has one dangerous, delicious rake believing she's the "fair Cyprian" ordered for his pleasure. *** Shy, self-effacing Henrietta knows her place—in her dazzling older sister's shadow. She's a little brown peahen to Araminta's bird of paradise. But when Hetty mistakenly becomes embroiled in the Regency underworld, the innocent debutante finds herself shockingly compromised by the dashing, dangerous Sir Aubrey, the very gentleman her heart desires. And the man Araminta has in her cold, calculating sights. Branded an enemy of the Crown, bitter over the loss of his wife, Sir Aubrey wants only to lose himself in the warm, willing body of the young "prostitute" Hetty. As he tutors her in the art of lovemaking, Aubrey is pleased to find Hetty not only an ardent student, but a bright, witty and charming companion. Despite a spoiled Araminta plotting for a marriage offer and a powerful political enemy damaging his reputation, Aubrey may suffer the greatest betrayal at the hands of the little "concubine" who's managed to breach the stony exterior of his heart.

Two beautiful sisters – one illegitimate, the other nobly born – compete for love amidst the scandal and intrigue of a Regency London Season. Lissa Hazlett lives life in the shadows. The beautiful, illegitimate daughter of Viscount Partington earns her living as an overworked governess while her vain and spoiled half sister, Araminta, enjoys London's social whirl as its most feted debutante. When Lissa's rare talent as a portraitist brings her unexpectedly into the bosom of society – and into the midst of a scandal involving Araminta and suspected English traitor Lord Debenham – she finds an unlikely ally: charming and besotted Ralph Tunley, Lord Debenham's underpaid, enterprising secretary. Ralph can't afford to leave the employ of the villainous viscount much less keep a wife but he can help Lissa cleverly navigate a perilous web of lies that will ensure everyone gets what they deserve. THE MYSTERIOUS GOVERNESS is Book 3 in the Daughters of Sin series but can be read as a stand-alone as it features the sibling rivalry between Viscount Partington's two nobly-born and three illegitimate daughters from a completely different perspective. Book 1: Her Gilded Prison Book 2: Dangerous Gentlemen Book 3: The Mysterious Governess Book 4: Beyond Rubies Heat rating: sensual. The Daughters of Sin series has been described as a Regency-set 'Dynasty'.

Fame. Fortune. And finally a marriage proposal! Book 4 of the Daughters of Sin series introduces Miss Kitty La Bijou, celebrated London actress, mistress to handsome Lord Nash and the unacknowledged illegitimate daughter of Viscount Partington. Having escaped her humble beginnings, Kitty has found fame, fortune and love, but the respectability she craves eludes her. When she stumbles across Araminta, her legitimate half-sister, on the verge of giving birth just seven months after marrying dangerous Viscount Debenham, Kitty realises respectability is no guarantee of character or happiness. But helping Araminta has unwittingly embroiled Kitty in a scandalous deception involving a ruthless brothel madam, a priceless ruby necklace and the future heir to a dazzling fortune. And when Kitty finally receives an offer of marriage she must choose. Respectability or love?

Kitty has the love of the man of her dreams but as London's most acclaimed actress and a member of the demimondaine, she accepts she can never be kind and handsome Lord Silverton's lawful wedded wife. When Kitty comes to the aid of shy, accident-prone and kind-hearted Octavia Mandelton, her sense of justice leads to her making the most difficult decision of her life: Give up the man she loves for the sake of honour. For Octavia is still betrothed to Lord Silverton who'd rescued Kitty in dramatic circumstances only weeks before. Cast adrift, Kitty joins forces with her sister, Lissa, a talented artist posing as a governess in order to bring to justice a dangerous spy, villainous Lord Debenham. Complicating matters is the fact Debenham is married to their half-sister, vain and beautiful Araminta. However, Araminta has a dark secret which only Kitty knows and which she realizes she is duty-bound to expose if she's to achieve justice and win happiness for deserving Lissa and Lissa's enterprising sweetheart, Ralph Tunley, long-suffering secretary to Lord Debenham. All seems set for a happy ending when Kitty tumbles into mortal danger. A danger from which only a truly honorable man can save her. A man like Silverton who must now make the hardest choice of his life if he's to live with his conscience.

Want to read the next two books in the series, and save?
If you've read book 1, you can get Books 2 and 3, discounted in a Box Set.

In Dangerous Gentlemen, Sweet, shy Hetty finds herself in competition with her beautiful, spoiled sister, Araminta, as they both hope for a marriage offer. In The Mysterious Governess, the girls' unacknowledged half-sister, Lissa, a governess, uses her sketching ability to help apprehend a dangerous spy.

NOTE FROM THE AUTHOR

I hope you enjoyed **Rake's Honour** and the snippets from **Rogue's Kiss** and the *Daughters of Sin* stories.

Weaving stories has been in my blood for as long as I can remember but rather than my writing career having been a solitary journey I've been richly rewarded with a wonderful family and a supportive and loving husband.

So, a huge thank you to my loved ones and all the friends who've helped me along the way.

And a huge thank you to you, my readers.

Do stop by my website for the various specials and contests I run from time to time. And feel free to chat any time.

I'm also assembling a Street Team so if you think you might be interested, you can email me at beverley@eikli.com.

And please consider writing a review. It is so appreciated and makes such a big difference to an author's career.

Thanks again and Happy Reading!

ABOUT THE AUTHOR

Beverley was seventeen when she bundled up her first 500+ page romance and sent it to a publisher. Rejection followed swiftly. Drowning one's heroine on the last page, she was informed, was not in line with the expectations of romance readers.

So Beverley became a journalist.

After a whirlwind romance with a handsome Norwegian bush pilot she met in Botswana's beautiful Okavango Delta, Beverley discovered what real romance was all about, saved her heroine

from a watery grave in her next manuscript and published her first romance in 2009.

Since then, she's written more than fifteen sizzling historical romances laced with mystery and intrigue under the name Beverley Oakley.

She also writes psychological historical mysteries, and Colonial-Africa-set romantic suspense, as Beverley Eikli.

With an inspiring view of a Gothic nineteenth-century insane asylum across the road, Beverley lives north of Melbourne with her gorgeous husband, two lovely daughters and a rambunctious Rhodesian Ridgeback called Mombo, named after the safari lodge where she and her husband met.

You can read more at www.beverleyoakley.com

Please get in touch here:

www.beverleyoakley.com
beverley.oakley@gmail.com

AUTHOR'S NOTE ABOUT THE SERIES

Wicked and lively Fanny and Antoinette Brightwell have made spectacular marriages—despite scandals and the treachery of a disappointed suitor determined to derail their plans and besmirch their reputations.

So, who better to play matchmaker when a deserving candidate waltzes into their orbit?

Here are the first three stories in the series, each following on from each other, although each can be read as a stand-alone.

1. **Rake's Honour** (Totally sizzling. Insatiable Fanny is a wild child!)

2. **Rogue's Kiss** (Sensual - not sizzling at all. Sweet and innocent Thea follows the rules.)

3. **Devil's Run** (A bit more sensual than **Rogue's Kiss** but not sizzling like **Rake's Honour**. Eliza has a 'past' and although she's sworn off falling in love, she knows what love is when she stumbles upon it.)

I hope you enjoy reading the series as much as I enjoyed writing about these two scandalous sisters!

65774412R00092

RAKE'S HONOUR

For my wonderful husband, Eivind.

RAKE'S HONOUR

SCANDALOUS MISS BRIGHTWELL SERIES (BOOK 1)

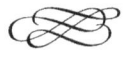

BEVERLEY OAKLEY

LIST OF CONTRIBUTORS

Gerlese Åkerlind	University of Canberra; Australian National University, Canberra, Australia
Paul Atkinson	School of Social Sciences, Cardiff University, Cardiff, UK
Sara Delamont	School of Social Sciences, Cardiff University, Cardiff, UK
Fiona Hallett	Edge Hill University, Ormskirk, UK
Paul Hodge	Discipline of Geography and Environmental Studies, University of Newcastle, Callaghan, Australia
Cecilia Jacobs	Stellenbosch University, Stellenbosch, South Africa
Peter Kandlbinder	Institute for Interactive Media & Learning, University of Technology Sydney, Sydney, Australia
Manfred Lueger	Vienna University of Economics and Business, Vienna, Austria
Mandy Lupton	Queensland University of Technology, Brisbane, Australia
Jo McKenzie	University of Technology, Sydney, Australia
Fee Mozeley	Discipline of Geography and Environmental Studies, University of Newcastle, Callaghan, Australia
Brian Paltridge	Faculty of Education & Social Work, University of Sydney, Sydney, Australia

Louise Ravelli	School of the Arts & Media, University of New South Wales, Sydney, Australia
Farshid Shams	School of Management, University of Bath, Bath, UK
Sue Starfield	The Learning Centre, University of New South Wales, Sydney, Australia
John Struthers	Isle of Man Department of Health, Strang, Isle of Man
Malcolm Tight	Department of Educational Research, Lancaster University, Lancaster, UK
Jonathan Tummons	School of Education, Durham University, Durham, UK
Oliver Vettori	Vienna University of Economics and Business, Vienna, Austria
Sarah Wright	Discipline of Geography and Environmental Studies, University of Newcastle, Callaghan, Australia
Oili-Helena Ylijoki	School of Social Sciences and Humanities, University of Tampere, Tampere, Finland

EDITORIAL INTRODUCTION

This is the second volume in this series that focuses on the critical discussion of aspects of theory and/or method being applied or developed in higher education research. Its aims are to both encourage higher education researchers to give more attention to these issues and to provide a forum for their discussion.

We have taken a rather pragmatic stance regarding what constitutes a theory or a method. Our point of departure was that theory may refer to specific mid-range theories developed within higher education – for example academic literacies, communities of practice, diversity, modes of knowledge, threshold concepts – as well as to broader discipline-based (psychology, management, history, linguistics, public administration, political sciences, sociology, economics) perspectives. The methods considered would include the broad range developed within educational and social research – for example multivariate analyses, documentary analyses, interviews, observation, cross-sectional and longitudinal studies, secondary data analyses – as well as methodologies specifically developed within higher education research (e.g. phenomenography). We think this broad conceptualization, warranted by the rich diversity of approaches in the field of higher education, has allowed contributors more scope to present what they thought was relevant and important.

With recognizing that it may not always be possible to make clear distinctions between theory and method, this volume contains five contributions which feature theory strongly (learning architectures/communities of practice, theories of teaching and learning, theories of time, threshold concepts, variation theory), a larger proportion than in the previous volume.

It is striking to see that most of the contributions to this volume, as with the first one, focus on qualitative methods, with only one focusing explicitly on quantitative methods (fuzzy set analysis) and two paying attention to both qualitative and quantitative methods (both of which illustrate their argument with bibliometric data).

So, if you're interested in contributing to a future volume on *Theory and Method in Higher Education Research*, contributions that examine aspects of theory and/or quantitative methods would be particularly welcome.

Jeroen Huisman
Malcolm Tight
Editors

THEORISING TEACHING AND LEARNING IN HIGHER EDUCATION RESEARCH

Peter Kandlbinder

ABSTRACT

This chapter explores the theorising practices of successful researchers in higher education. The biographical case studies use teaching and learning as their focus to provide four succinct accounts of how the researcher's thinking around their signature concepts evolved over time. They analyse the narrative that surrounds these signature concepts to understand what successful researchers do with their ideas to maximise their symbolic capital in the higher education research field. The researcher's experiences of theorising highlight the contextual factors that have influenced them as they tried to explain how they achieved the outcomes of their research. The chapter concludes with an overview of the beneficial strategies used in these four cases, so potential researchers can appreciate the approaches to theorising that are compatible with higher education research traditions.

Theory and Method in Higher Education Research II
International Perspectives on Higher Education Research, Volume 10, 1–22
ISSN: 1479-3628/doi:10.1108/S1479-3628(2014)0000010006

DATA, THEORY AND THEORISING

Thinking theoretically is a necessary part of any research project. Since Kuhn's (1970) investigation of scientific research practice we have come to see that even the most objectively framed research method is theoretically informed. It is the theories of the research field that help researchers identify their data, and the same theories provide the structure for understanding the meaning of what was learned. Researchers need to come up with explanations for the outcomes of their investigations in order to make their research data comprehensible to others. A key role for theory is to put research findings into a broader framework to allow debates among scholars, in which the veracity of explanations are tested (Popper, 1972).

Research outcomes cannot be expected to stand on their own without the researcher explaining the significance of what was discovered by completing the research project. However, ideas do not spontaneously spring into the minds of researchers. Like many academic tasks, theorising requires more effort than inspiration. Not only is it generally recognised that theorising is important, it is usually acknowledged that it is also difficult (Kettley, 2010). Not only do ideas need to be novel, they need to be compatible with the culture that they address. While personal descriptions of theorising are hard to find, those who describe their method of thinking theoretically describe the process as 'messy, incomplete and non-inductive' (Clegg, 2012, p. 407).

Consequently, there is not a great deal of guidance on theorising available for academics new to higher education research. Most studies of knowledge construction have focussed on the natural sciences (e.g. Knorr-Cetina, 1981; Latour & Woolgar, 1979). Yet, to be proficient in thinking about higher education requires the same learning about the traditions of the field, as well as how to use these traditions to examine research questions important in higher education. This is particularly challenging for academic staff new to higher education teaching and learning, who can struggle to come to terms with a new discipline and sometimes have difficulty seeing the complexity in the field's key concepts (Kandlbinder & Peseta, 2009).

A further complication comes from the reliance on part-time researchers who dabble in higher education research for short intervals in their academic careers (Kandlbinder, 2012). As such, they rely on methods and methodologies from their home disciplines, even when they may not be suitable for researching higher education teaching and learning. They are not necessarily committed to the different ontological, epistemological and methodological assumptions that guide the decisions made by higher education researchers (Tight, 2003). Nor are they aware that certain theoretical perspectives have been found to be more engaging for higher education research, such as ideas around diversity or scholarship (Tight, 2004).

The competing definitions of theory, disciplinary differences in knowledge construction and different traditions in how theory is used combine to make theorising particularly challenging. When it comes to higher education researchers building powerful explanations of teaching and learning in higher education the successful theory building strategies are not obvious. Accordingly, this chapter throws light on how highly respected researchers in higher education teaching and learning developed the theoretical components of their research. The reputation and prestige of each of these researchers was such that their body of work contains a signature concept that addresses a distinctive aspect of academic knowledge (Kandlbinder, 2013a). I will use a detailed analysis of the narrative that surrounds these signature concepts to understand what successful researchers do with their ideas. The aim is to learn from beneficial theorising strategies used by others, so potential researchers in higher education can appreciate which approaches to theorising are compatible with higher education research traditions. The chapter concludes with an overview of, as well as recommendations for, researchers who seek to incorporate these techniques into their own research repertoires.

SIGNATURE CONCEPTS

Signature concepts are a useful analytical framework for understanding how researchers have gone about theorising in the past. A signature concept is different from a key concept since it is the authors in the field who recognise the importance of an idea in a researcher's body of work. A key concept is subjective in the sense that it hinges on individual personal preferences that can change at any particular time. Moreover, a signature concept is associated with a specific researcher, and is objective in that this association is recorded in the references to the concept made in the major journals in the field.

Tight (2003) undertook the first comprehensive study of higher education publications to show that particular journals focus on different segments of the research field. Drawing on Tight's analysis I was able to show that authors in the four dominant non-North American journals of higher education teaching and learning — *Higher Education, Higher Education Research and Development, Studies in Higher Education* and *Teaching in Higher Education* — have a clear preference for some concepts over others (Kandlbinder, 2013a). As such, they are more likely to discuss the idea that students adopt different approaches to learning, and attribute that concept to any one of four researchers. A similar pattern is found in three North American journals of higher education: *Journal of Higher Education, Research in Higher Education* and *Review of Higher Education*. In a review of 17,466 references from 884 articles published in these three journals between 2000 and 2005, I found that authors were most likely to discuss the idea of student persistence and associate this concept with four researchers (Kandlbinder, 2013c).

As well as leaning towards particular concepts for their field, authors attributed particular researchers with developing specific ideas on higher education teaching and learning. The pattern of citation practices in journals located in the non-North American higher education field suggest authors are more likely to turn to seven researchers when discussing matters of teaching and learning. In the North American-based journals the pattern is similar, although it is for a different set of six researchers. Each researcher has produced a significant body of work, and when the citation practices of authors writing about teaching and learning is analysed we find that, on average, the most highly referenced researchers in the field are cited for one publication beyond all others. That publication was largely used to discuss a single concept, albeit for little more than acknowledging its importance in a research tradition. This signature concept shows that particular researchers are strongly associated with specific ideas, even when a variety of researchers across the field discuss the same concept.

I will use a selection from this pool of 13 researchers — Alexander Astin, Ronald Barnett, John Biggs, Noel Entwistle, George Kuh, Ference Marton, Ernest Pascarella, Paul Ramsden, Sheila Slaughter, Edward St. John, William Tierney, Vincent Tinto and Keith Trigwell — identified by authors as providing the signature concepts for the field, to examine the successful strategies for theorising in higher education teaching and learning. This will take the form of a case study analysis proposed by Gruber and Wallace (1999), who suggested analysing the interactive relationship between individuals and the context in which they work. I will begin with Ference Marton, who was the most referenced researcher in the four non-North American journals of higher education teaching and learning (Kandlbinder, 2013a). Marton's signature concept was the idea of a phenomenographic method for analysing variation. The signature concepts in the North American field were published over approximately the same timeframe as the non-North American concepts. Alexander Astin was the most referenced researcher over a comparable five-year sample of the literature, and his signature concept was the idea that student interactions with their institution influence student success at college.

PATHWAYS TO SIGNATURE CONCEPTS BY RESEARCHERS IN HIGHER EDUCATION TEACHING AND LEARNING

Both Marton and Astin began to formulate the ideas that were to become their signature concepts well before the date of their most cited publication. On average it took five publications from a researcher's body of work to account for half of their references in the literature. It is this body of work that will be reviewed here, while recognising that these are not the only articles or book chapters the researchers will have published during this time period. These are simply the publications recognised by hundreds of authors over a decade of writing about higher education teaching and learning as making the greatest contribution to the research field. This intertextual referencing is one way in which the story lines of theorising are constructed by authors, who draw their ideas from texts in an ongoing interplay of reading, thinking and interpretation (Gubrium & Holstein, 2009).

What therefore are subjective in this study are the views on theorization expressed by the researchers at the time of publication. It is in the introduction to their research articles or chapters in books that researchers have a conversation with the field, as they attempt to explain the aims of their research programmes. Swales (1990) found authors use a three-part model in the introduction to research articles to orientate the reader to what is to come later in the article. Lewin, Fine, and Young (2001) established that the first two parts of the introduction are where researchers made the claim for the relevance of the research field and establish the gap for the research. The favoured method used by authors is to stress the importance of the research that is reported in their study, followed by claims to novelty of what was described as they indicate the gap or the addition that will be made to what is known (Swales, 2004).

What is presented below are four short biographical studies of these explanations from the publications that account for half of the references by some of the most referenced researchers in the field. As suggested by

Gruber and Wallace's (1999) case study approach, this reconstructs the meaning of the researcher's experience from their own point of view. The goal is to maintain a focus on the theorisation of the research, while outlining the evolving pattern of interrelationships as the researcher interacted with the wider research field. The convention of explaining the development of an idea leads to the construction of a narrative, which I have set out for the publications that make up half of the researcher's references in the field. Each summary is presented in the sequence in which they were written, with the proportion of their total references indicating a relative level of significance assigned to the publication by authors in the journals sampled.

The development of the ideas that led Ference Marton to prominence in the field are described in the introductory comments made in five publications that begin in 1976 and proceed to 1997. In most cases Marton co-authored these publications, firstly with Roger Säljö (1976), then Gloria Dall'Alba and Liz Beaty (1993), followed by Dai Hounsell and Noel Entwistle (1997) and finally with Shirley Booth (1997). The dotted line in Fig. 1 shows the envelop of analysis in which the first and last of these publications account almost equally for the largest proportion of citations in this series.

The short biographical study of Marton's development of phenomenography is followed by a description of the development of student interaction theory by Alexander Astin. The envelope of analysis constructed

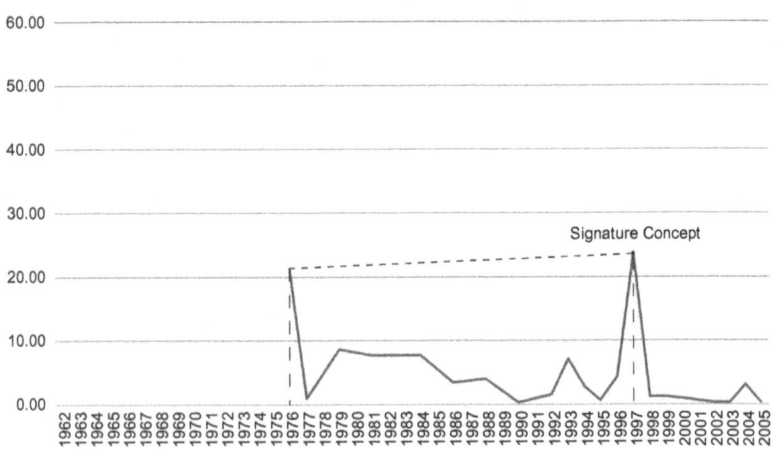

Fig. 1. Percentage of References in Four Non-North American Journals to Publications by Ference Marton.

around Astin's theorising has a different shape to the interaction with the research field that constructed Marton's signature concept. Firstly, Astin is sole author of each of his publications that account for more than half of his references in the three major North American journals of higher education teaching and learning. Secondly, as well as being cited for one fewer publication than Marton, the envelope of theorization described here is somewhat more concentrated, starting in 1977 and proceeding to 1993 (see Fig. 2). This is despite Astin entering into the research literature as early as 1962. Finally, there is not the same launching publication as Marton and Säljö (1976), with Astin's last publication in the series accounting for a third of all his references.

FERENCE MARTON: THEORISING PHENOMENOGRAPHY

Ference Marton was a professor in the Institute of Education at the University of Gothenburg in Sweden when he wrote the first of two publications with Roger Säljö. In their introduction Marton and Säljö (1976) described how their earlier research studies had led them to identify the limitations of previous learning research. They believed learning research

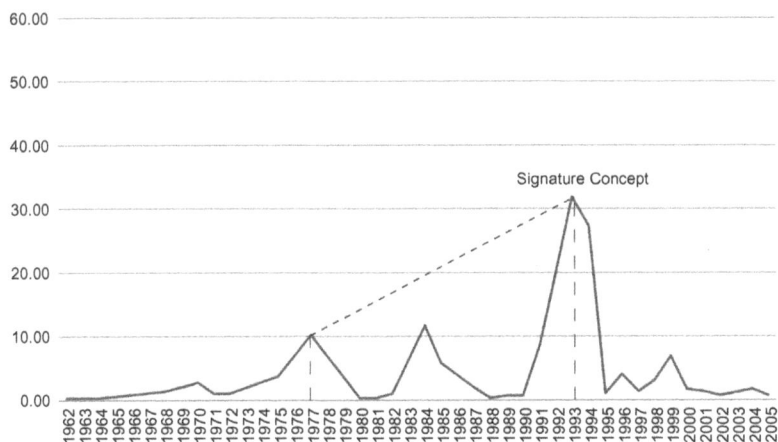

Fig. 2. Percentage of References in Three North American Journals to Publications by Alexander Astin.

focussed too much on the quantitative outcomes of tests. Marton and Säljö wanted to describe what was learned rather than how much was learned. Instead of observing students they asked student volunteers about their process of learning, and found that they described qualitatively different understandings of the same material. Marton and Säljö set out to describe the different processes students used to learn a piece of text, and discovered that they broadly fell into two different approaches that related to the learner's intention for the learning task.

By the time that Marton came to write *Phenomenography* he had begun to make the distinction between first-order and second-order perspectives. A first-order statement is a statement about the world. The second-order statement is about people's ideas about the world. Marton claimed he was only interested in analysing the statements people made about their experiences rather than classifying or judging the people themselves. Instead he wanted to find and systematise forms of thought in terms of how people interpret different aspects of reality. Marton argued that a research programme that aims to describe, analyse and understand what is said about experience rather than experience itself suggests a relatively distinctive field of inquiry, which he labelled 'phenomenography' (Marton, 1981).

Marton et al. (1993) used this distinction of statements about experience to reanalyse an earlier research study by Roger Säljö (1979), which had found five distinctive conceptions of learning. They said they wanted their study to give a more precise characterisation of the differing conceptions of learning, and to identify the relationships between the different conceptions students use when thinking about their learning. They framed Säljö's work within their concept of phenomenography, introducing a distinction between *what* is learned and *how* it is learned.

This newly validated research approach was further confirmed in a compilation of research studies into the qualitative differences in the outcomes of student learning. Rather than focus on individual student differences, three researchers combined to describe how the different ways of understanding a text have come about (Marton, Hounsell, & Entwistle, 1997). This rested on a fundamental assumption that, if the outcome of learning differed between individuals then the process of learning that leads to those different outcomes must also have differed between individuals. Marton et al. (1997) used this opportunity to clarify the kinds of studies that they classified as phenomenography, only recognising those that examined the relationship between the process of learning and the different meanings attributed to learning outcomes.

Finally, Marton provided a detailed explanation of his mature theory in Marton and Booth (1997), with a further shift in focus from descriptions of learning to learning itself. They defined learning as coming to experience aspects of the world in particular ways. What they were interested in was the variation in ways in which people experienced situations and phenomena in their worlds. They broadened their definition of phenomenography to include the research into ways of experiencing things. Marton and Booth (1997) applied this method to the investigation of learning, defined as an increased differentiation and corresponding integration of the whole and its parts to build ever more complex and advanced forms of knowledge.

ALEXANDER ASTIN: THEORISING STUDENT INVOLVEMENT

It took a considerable time for Astin to come to prominence in the U.S. field of higher education teaching and learning. He began by spending 17 years studying the outcomes of students who received scholarships to undertake doctoral degrees. Over that time he came to the realisation that the quality of college graduates largely depended on the abilities and aspirations of students entering universities (Astin, 1977, p. ix). Astin refined his approach for surveying the environmental factors that influenced achievement among the most able students, and applied the same questions of family background, secondary school achievement and educational aspirations to undergraduate students in the first large-scale study of entering freshmen in four year colleges and universities (Astin, 1977). This survey was adopted by the American Council of Education and, over the next 10 years, gradually expanded into an annual national survey of commencing students.

Following the success of his approach for identifying student impact, Astin clarified the features of his theory (1984). Astin explained that he was motivated by a desire for simple theories. For him, student involvement referred to the amount of physical and psychological energy that students devoted to the academic experience. He recognised that there was a growing confusion around the question of student development in higher education, which in part came from the diversity of problems being studied. This diversity resulted in researchers looking at different variables or employing different methodologies to study the same questions. To bring order to the confusion that had emerged from discussions of his own research, Astin turned to dictionary definitions and alternative wording and phrases that captured some of the intended meaning behind his theory of involvement. Unlike Marton, who shied away from categorising students, Astin felt a behavioural component to student involvement was essential, as he wanted to focus on what the individual did, although he did not deny that motivation was an important aspect in students becoming involved in their studies.

Having clarified the key tenets of his theory and its application to educational research, Astin (1991) then applied the theory of student involvement to what he considered to be a significant problem in higher education; the question of students' experiences of assessment. Astin was convinced that a great deal of assessment activity had very little benefit to students or higher education's educational mission. He reviewed his 25 years of data on assessment and concluded that good assessment used much the same approaches as good research, with the ultimate aim of helping university teachers make better decisions in running educational programmes and institutions.

After demonstrating the general utility of his theory of student involvement to answer questions about student experiences of teaching and learning, Astin updated the results of his original study (Astin, 1993). He summarised the theory of student involvement as understanding the environmental effects on student learning. He had found that learning was enhanced by such things as living on campus and full-time attendance, because students tended to invest more time − as well as physical and psychological energy − into the educational experience. Astin (1993) enhanced our understanding of these processes by showing that one of the most powerful sources of student involvement was the peer group. He suggested that there are a number of additional studies that confirmed his findings, and these findings extended well into the post-college years.

ALTERNATIVE TRACKS TO THEORISING SIGNATURE CONCEPTS

Marton and Astin are the two most referenced researchers in the higher education field of teaching and learning. We can see that they both adopted similar strategies to argue against experimental psychology and provide methodological confidence for their alternative research programmes. First, they identified inadequacies of prior research approaches, which they then countered in a detailed explanation of the theoretical basis for an alternative approach to higher education research. This new approach was then tested on previous research to show the validity of the proposed alternative. The results of multiple examples of the alternative approach were then used to provide evidence for a fuller formulation of their mature theory.

To test whether this kind of strategy is a common method to theorising in higher education teaching and learning, I will compare the tactics used by the researchers with the shortest and longest paths in developing a signature concept. I will begin by describing the approach used by Sheila Slaughter, who, of the 13 researchers identified with signature concepts, was the only one principally referenced for a single publication. I will follow this with the pattern of interrelationships described in the introductions to the 12 publications required by Noel Entwistle to account for half of his references in the field of higher education teaching and learning. This was the largest number of publications required by any of the 13 researchers in either the North American and non-North American field of higher education teaching and learning.

SHEILA SLAUGHTER: THEORISING ACADEMIC CAPITALISM

Plainly it is not possible to construct the same narrative of development from a single instance. The publication Sheila Slaughter co-wrote with Larry Leslie accounts for 53% of all of Slaughter's references in the field of higher education teaching and learning (Fig. 3).

To recount Slaughter and Leslie's (1997) own explanation of their research, they began by examining the changing nature of academic work and found that the period of their investigation (1970–1995) was a time of extraordinary change not experienced in higher education since the last quarter of the 19th century. Fuelled by globalising economies, universities were experiencing a large reduction in public funding that was leading to dramatic changes in academic work, including undergraduate teaching. Slaughter and Leslie described their choice of labelling this change as academic capitalism as a deliberate play on words, using capitalism to define a system in which decisions were being influenced by market forces and increased competition for resources. Academic capitalism described a distinctive commodity owned by academic staff who engaged in producing

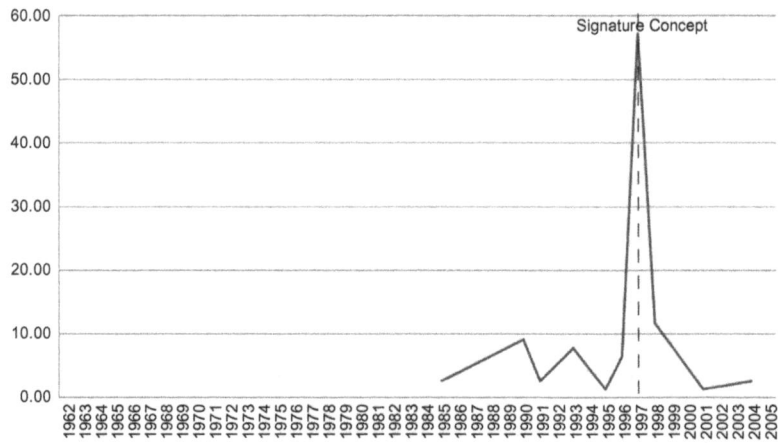

Fig. 3. Percentage of References in Four Non-North American Journals to Publications by Sheila Slaughter.

specialised knowledge for their own benefit, for the benefit of the university they served and for society at large.

NOEL ENTWISTLE: THEORISING STUDENT APPROACHES TO LEARNING

Noel Entwistle rose to prominence in the higher education teaching and learning field shortly after he introduced the Swedish approaches to learning research to a UK audience. Entwistle began writing about learning research in 1981, and his 12 most referenced publications continued on the theme of student approaches to learning until 2003 (Fig. 4). He initially entered the field as a sole author and progressively wrote with other researchers after he had published his signature concept with Paul Ramsden.

Entwistle outlined his break with traditional psychology in 1981. He described the aim of this publication was to bring coherence to a fragmentary set of topics drawn from mainstream psychology, by building a framework with which to understand the learning process (Entwistle, 1981). In so doing, Entwistle outlined many of the main themes of his future research programme, such as the emphasis placed on learning in higher education; looking at learning from the point of view of the learner; awareness of

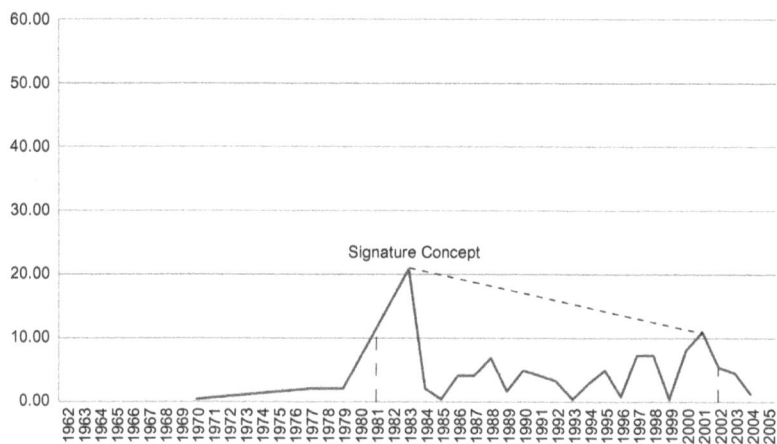

Fig. 4. Percentage of References in Four Non-North American Journals to Publications by Noel Entwistle.

factors associated with success and failure in higher education and showing how theories were related to personal experiences – all of which Entwistle identified as not being fully considered previously.

Entwistle then completed a five-year study to investigate student approaches to learning. The result was the publication most commonly referenced to Entwistle across the four non-North American journals, which was responsible for 20% of his references in the field (Kandlbinder, 2013a). The publication written with Paul Ramsden identified student learning research as examining different conceptions of subject matter and differences in how students tackled learning tasks to determine how these differences arose (Entwistle & Ramsden, 1983). In the process it outlined Entwistle's signature concept that students can adopt a third, strategic approach to learning.

In Entwistle's next significant publication he again attempted to bring together disparate concepts, by providing a survey of important ideas from psychology and matching them with educational issues that had relevance for classroom practice. He selected concepts that portrayed learning from the learner's perspective which also related to classroom realities (Entwistle, 1987). Entwistle (1988) described the theoretical background to an inventory he had devised to determine the organisation of study, active learning processes and motivation for learning. Entwistle then combined with Tait to recap the progress made on student learning research to that point, to argue for a further examination of the relationships between individual perceptions and approaches to learning (Entwistle & Tait, 1990). They argued that there was sufficient consensus on what constituted good teaching, and the reliability of student feedback questionnaires, to use the outcomes from a variety of surveys to demonstrate that different ways of studying are influenced by particular methods of teaching. This was then followed by a re-examination of previous studies that had found an outlier group who adopted different learning strategies than found in earlier studies (Entwistle, Meyer, & Tait, 1991). These outlier students did not follow the usual linkages between approaches to learning and perceptions of the learning environment, but instead demonstrated a random set of associations that resulted in unsuccessful study behaviour.

Entwistle continued this process of reanalysing, reassessing and revisiting parts of original transcripts to support a new direction in his research. Initially teaming up with Ference Marton, Entwistle began to focus on the different ways students described understanding (Entwistle & Marton, 1994). Having demonstrated the utility of this research tradition, Entwistle described the contribution that phenomenography had made to research in higher education (Entwistle, 1997). Then reusing the strategy employed in the approaches to learning research, Entwistle and Entwistle (1997) identified understanding as the desirable outcome of university learning, and argued for clarity on what was meant by this term. Entwistle then continued the exploration into the distinction between memorisation and understanding, which he identified as the outcome of deep approaches to learning (Entwistle, 1998).

Entwistle returned to the question of outliers and the analysis of earlier surveys to see whether passing and failing students answered their earlier questionnaire differently to other students (Entwistle, Tait, & McCune, 2000). Finally, Entwistle and Smith (2002) returned to the development of a conceptual framework to describe classroom learning from models of learning that had their origins in the classroom, and could be used to improve the quality of teaching.

PATTERNS OF THEORISATION IN HIGHER EDUCATION TEACHING AND LEARNING

The four short case studies of developing conceptual understandings of teaching and learning show four different patterns of intertextual engagement by researchers, as they built their reputation in the field of higher education teaching and learning. The idea of travelling along a path is an analytical device to understand the links between ideas – those leading to a signature concept or following from it – which are in a constantly moving field of ideas (Tsoukas, 2009). The path to a signature concept is only obvious in hindsight, and should not be seen as a roadmap to predictable results that others can follow. It simply highlights the contextual factors that have influenced four researchers as they were trying to answer the shifting questions central to their field. The value of these cases is they were derived from researchers' actions as they undertook the difficult task of explaining the outcomes of their research. They are not the remembered processes of theorisation derived from participant interviews.

The explanations used by Marton to introduce his research programme to a wider public in his five most referenced publications describe the methods he used to define which research approaches are consistent with his theory of phenomenography. Marton began by identifying inadequacies in the prior approaches to learning research and proposing an alternative approach, which he continually redefined with each new publication deemed significant by authors in the field. To convince others of the validity of this approach he tested its application on previous research, and defined the kinds of research approaches that did not fit with his definition. He then worked with a group of UK-based colleagues to collect examples that matched his notion of research, until he was able to formulate a detailed description of his mature theory.

By comparison, Entwistle's approach of continually revisiting, reviewing and recapping research created an extended period of influence in the field, without the dramatic entry from virtual obscurity experienced by Ference Marton. Entwistle was cited for publications well before he engaged with the ideas of Marton and the Gothenburg School, which he acknowledged formed the theoretical basis for his research after he began to question the value of traditional psychology to classroom practice. It was 13 years from the first reference in the literature to his publication that was responsible for his signature concept. However, this is arguably the only concept that could be conceived as original to Entwistle's body of work, and instead he placed his energies into refining ideas, pursuing studies of integration and revision throughout his career. Consequently, while his signature concept occurred in the early stages of Entwistle's envelope of influence, it tapered off over his career until the refocus on the conception of understanding lead to a minor resurgence towards the end of the sampled articles.

Alexander Astin had the longest career in researching higher education teaching and learning of the four researchers presented here. He was referenced in the sample of articles for publications written over a 43-year period. Yet, it only required four publications within a 16-year envelope of influence to account for half of the references made to his work in North American higher education journals between 2000 and 2005. In Astin's case, there was a steady accumulation of data about students undertaking university studies, with his last publication in his series also being his most significant. Like Marton, Astin (1993) wanted to study the world as it was to provide a comprehensive portrait of student development in all its complexity. Astin also battled against the methodological limits imposed by psychology, which only recognised the superiority of experiments over correlational studies. Again, like Marton, Astin recognised the impracticality of conducting psychological experiments in the classroom and instead set about showing the validity of making causal inferences from correlational data, much as other fields of science unable to control all input variables in their studies had done. Convincing others of the validity of his approach required showing the inadequacies of prior research methods and verifying his theory on previous research outcomes.

At first glance, Sheila Slaughter appears to be at odds with the other three examples selected to discuss theorisation. Like Marton, she has a major launching publication but, unlike the other researchers, she is then largely uncited for her later work following that early success. Similarly to Entwistle and Astin, Slaughter was being cited for work done more than a decade before the publication of the research that was to result in her signature concept. Nonetheless, it is the unique qualities of Slaughter's case that highlights the importance the research field plays in dictating the directions of theorisation.

From time to time it must be possible to achieve the perfect timing of publishing an idea just when authors in a field are looking for explanations that clarify important changes in their circumstances. Sheila Slaughter appears to have achieved such a confluence of factors with the concept of academic capitalism. Slaughter acknowledges that neither she nor her co-author were the originators of the term, which was first used by Hackett (1990) in relation to academic science. Instead of attributing the importance of the concept to this distinctive term, Slaughter and Leslie (1997) argued that it was the dramatic nature of the changes to academic work that were as great as any that occurred during the industrial revolution. It was the universality of the global changes and the consistency of the institutional responses – regardless of the university system that they had analysed – that created value in the explanation that was being offered.

Still, it is unexpected that this particular research field so strongly adopted a concept that does not obviously address questions of teaching and learning. There was no apparent focus on learning, although Slaughter and Leslie certainly described the effects of economic changes on teaching. By showing that changes in teaching were linked to changes in the economy, Slaughter and Leslie were able to bring in ideas from economics that had previously been considered to be incompatible with theorising teaching and learning. It was through the integration of topics that were often treated as separate that Slaughter and Leslie were able to provide a language for discussing economic forces that resonated with changes that continue to play out in higher education.

In addition, it is unusual for the non-North American field to adopt a signature concept from across the Atlantic. Taking an international view and making cross-sector comparisons allowed others to make sense of changes affecting their own university system, regardless of whether they are located in North American or non-North American countries. Slaughter remains an active contributor to her own field of academic work, and has moved to researching specific examples of academic capitalism, such as the conditions for women in the entrepreneurial university. Moving away from the international perspective means it is unlikely her current studies will resonate so resoundingly with the field of teaching and learning, without another significant shift in the context of higher education. Where Slaughter is cited in reference to higher education teaching and learning, authors continue to prefer the original study on academic capitalism to more recent work.

DOING THEORISING WORK

What distinguishes the successful theorisers discussed above from others in the field is they took a risk to break away from traditional approaches to research, and the field decided these new directions were worth pursuing. It needs to be acknowledged that 58% of the 56,000 references in 1,935 articles only appeared once in the sample of articles reviewed for this study. Stand out performers, like Sheila Slaugher, are rare, and gaining prominence in the field takes many years of effort. Successful researchers, such as Marton, Astin and Entwistle, all produced large volumes of work, of which only a few key examples are discussed above. What these examples show is only two of the four researchers could be described as having a growing reputation in the research field. That is to say that their later publications received a higher proportion of references from authors than their earlier publications. However, it is worth noting that it took Marton 20 years to achieve the same level of recognition for his most referenced work as he received for his launching publication. Similarly, it took Astin 15 years to build on his first major national study, producing a publication judged by authors in the North American journals to have made a significant contribution to the field approximately every four years.

Finding the problem worth solving was the key to the creative actions in my four case studies. For three researchers these were constraints caused by applying the central ideas from their parent discipline to a new domain, which drove them to modify their ideas as they were assimilated into new situations. Understandably, no one likes to waste his or her time on unfruitful pursuits, yet problem situations are ill defined and difficult to recognise in advance, and it is impossible to know which new direction will succeed ahead of time. In the case of the research method that became known as phenomenography, the limits imposed by methodological requirements for experimental research esteemed in psychology lead Marton to study students' statements about their experiences of learning, and thereby to classify different meanings used to describe how students approach learning. This distinctive approach to studying student learning stimulated a significant body of followers who were looking for a straightforward empirical method specific to learning in higher education settings.

If we look at the explanations used by Astin to gain prominence for his ideas in the North American field of higher education teaching and learning (as offered in the introductions to his four most referenced publications), we can see that he developed his theory of student interactions through an ever-expanding generalisation of his research outcomes to increasingly nation-wide contexts. Like Marton, this began by identifying inadequacies of psychology for understanding factors that impact on student success at college. Astin then clarified features of his theory as it was extended into new domains, firstly for graduate students, then undergraduates, followed by assessment and finally nation-wide experiences of higher education. It is the range of these interactions that Astin summarised in his best known publication (1993) which defines his mature theory.

The process of theorisation, as performed by these four cases in higher education teaching and learning, is then a balance between continuous improvement and originality that leads to a continual refinement of ideas that address important questions relevant to the field. In addition to a pro-digious output, building a reputation in the field required a dedication to a single idea for significant periods in these researchers' careers. There has been a continuity of work that has been recognised as a signature concept, even when these researchers may have been working on multiple research projects. Researchers, much like Entwistle, had to be willing to experiment with alternative perspectives to push beyond the limitations imposed by their parent discipline, until they discovered something of value to higher education teaching and learning. In Entwistle's case, he followed finding an alternative research framework with a commitment to convince the field of the validity of this different direction in higher education research. By test-ing the boundaries of a research tradition, and having occasional successes, these researchers acquired an international reputation as contributing to our knowledge of teaching and learning.

FINAL THOUGHTS

In this chapter I have looked into the explanations provided by successful researchers as they negotiated the boundaries of higher education research to create new ideas that would become central to the field of teaching and learning. These are intended as succinct accounts of what they have achieved, and how that compared to a few of their contemporaries also working in the field. Comparing their explanations over time shows that their thinking was evolving along a path that would eventually become recognised as their signature concept. Understanding the influence of tim-ing, scale, persistence and the value of translating ideas from other fields enriches our repertoire for appreciating the many ways that ideas are created.

There is much in these examples that warrants further discussion, espe-cially around individual methods of theorisation. While it may not be pos-sible to generalise from their individual motivations or attributes, there are still many more lessons we can learn from individual experiences. For example, did Astin become better at choosing promising lines of inquiry as he refined his methods of correlational analysis that led to his most refer-enced publication? How was Marton able to launch his earlier research from Sweden into the English-speaking field and retain a foothold, even when the majority of others would have returned to obscurity? What quali-ties enabled Entwistle to lead others to adopt academic ideas well beyond their central site of inception?

The close relationship between publishing and academic reputation suggests that the growth of higher education journals will provide many more opportunities to publish, and, therefore, the potential to include previously excluded groups (Kandlbinder, 2013b). This requires a willingness to integrate new ideas into local situations, and, if we are to gain a clearer understanding of the process of theorisation, we need to continue examining the interplay between individual and contextual factors and the different ways ideas have been received, adapted or resisted by those interested in answering questions about higher education teaching and learning. When the two factors are aligned new ideas can be embraced in spectacular fashion, even where they first appear unrelated to the research field.

REFERENCES

Astin, A. W. (1977). *Four critical years*. San Francisco, CA: Jossey-Bass.

Astin, A. W. (1984). Student involvement: A developmental theory for higher education. *Journal of College Student Personnel, 25*, 297–308.

Astin, A. W. (1991). *Assessment for excellence*. New York, NY: Macmillan.

Astin, A. W. (1993). *What matters in college*. San Francisco, CA: Jossey-Bass.

Clegg, S. (2012). On the problem of theorising: An insider account of research practice. *Higher Education Research & Development, 31*(3), 407–418.

Entwistle, N. (1981). *Styles of learning & teaching: An integrated outline of educational psychology for students, teachers, & lecturers*. New York, NY: Wiley.

Entwistle, N. (1987). *Understanding classroom learning*. London: Hodder & Stoughton.

Entwistle, N. (1988). Motivational factors in students approaches to learning. In R. S. Schmeck (Ed.), *Learning strategies & learning styles* (pp. 21–51). New York, NY: Plenum Press.

Entwistle, N. (1997). Introduction: Phenomenography in higher education. *Research & Development in Higher Education, 16*, 127–134.

Entwistle, N. (1998). Approaches to learning & forms of understanding. In B. Dart & G. Boulton-Lewis (Eds.), *Teaching & learning in higher education* (pp.72–101). Camberwell: Australian Council for Educational Research.

Entwistle, N., & Entwistle, A. C. (1997). Revision & the experience of understanding. In F. Marton, D. J. Hounsell, & N. Entwistle (Eds.), *The experience of learning* (2nd ed.), Edinburgh: Scottish Academic Press.

Entwistle, N., & Marton, F. (1994). Knowledge objects: Understandings constituted through intensive academic study. *British Journal of Educational Psychology, 64*, 161–178.

Entwistle, N., Meyer, J. H. F., & Tait, H. (1991). Student failure: Disintegrated patterns of study strategies & perceptions of the learning environment. *Higher Education, 21*, 249–261.

Entwistle, N., & Ramsden, P. (1983). *Understanding student learning*. London: Croom Helm.

Entwistle, N., & Smith, C. (2002). Personal understanding & target understanding: Mapping influences on the outcomes of learning. *British Journal of Educational Psychology, 72*, 321–342.

Entwistle, N., & Tait, H. (1990). Approaches to learning, evaluation of teaching, & preferences for contrasting academic environments. *Higher Education, 19,* 169–194.

Entwistle, N., Tait, H., & McCune, V. (2000). Patterns of response to an approaches to studying inventory across contrasting groups & contexts. *European Journal of Psychology of Education, XV,* 33–48.

Gruber, H. E., & Wallace, D. B. (1999). The case study method and evolving systems approach for understanding creative people at work. In R. J. Stennberg (Ed.), *Handbook on creativity* (pp. 93–115). Cambridge: Cambridge University Press.

Gubrium, J. F., & Holstein, J. A. (2009). *Analysing narrative reality.* Los Angeles, CA: Sage.

Hackett, E. (1990). Science as a vocation in the 1990s: The changing organisational culture of academic science. *Journal of Higher Education, 61,* 241–77.

Kandlbinder, P. (2012). Recognition and influence: The evolution of higher education research and development. *Higher Education Research and Development, 31*(1), 5–13.

Kandlbinder, P. (2013a). Signature concepts of key researchers in higher education teaching and learning. *Teaching in Higher Education, 18*(1), 1–12.

Kandlbinder, P. (2013b). Signature concepts of women researchers in higher education teaching and learning. *Studies in Higher Education.* doi:10.1080/03075079.2013.801430

Kandlbinder, P. (2013c). *Signature concepts of key researchers in North American higher education teaching and learning.* Manuscript submitted for review.

Kandlbinder, P., & Peseta, T. (2009). Key concepts in graduate certificates in higher education teaching and learning in Australasia and the UK. *International Journal for Academic Development, 14*(1), 19–31.

Kettley, N. (2010). *Theory building in Educational Research.* London: Continuum.

Knorr-Cetina. (1981). *The manufacture of knowledge: An essay on constructivist and contextual nature of science.* Oxford: Pergamonn.

Kuhn, T. S. (1970). *The structure of scientific revolutions.* Chicago, IL: University of Chicago Press.

Latour, B., & Woolgar, S. (1979). *Laboratory life: The social construction of scientific facts.* Beverly Hills, CA: Sage.

Lewin, B. A., Fine, J., & Young, L. (2001). *Expository discourse: A genre-based approach to social science research texts.* London: Continuum.

Marton, F. (1981). Phenomenography: Describing conceptions of the world around us. *Instructional Science, 10,* 177–200.

Marton, F., & Booth, S. (1997). *Learning & awareness.* Mahwah, NJ: Lawrence Erlbaum.

Marton, F., Dall'Alba, G., & Beaty, E. (1993). Conceptions of learning International. *Journal of Educational Research, 19,* 77–300.

Marton, F., Hounsell, D., Entwistle, N. (Eds.) (1997). *The experience of learning* (2nd ed.), Edinburgh: Scottish Academic Press.

Marton, F., & Säljö, R. (1976). On qualitative differences in learning. I. Outcome and process. *British Journal of Educational Psychology, 46,* 4–11.

Popper, K. R. (1972). *Conjectures and refutations: The growth of scientific knowledge* (4th ed.), London: Routledge & Kegan Paul.

Säljö, R. (1979). *Learning in the learner's perspective. I. Some common-sense conceptions.* Reports from the Department of Education, University of Göteborg, No. 76.

Slaughter, S., & Leslie, L. (1997). *Academic capitalism. Politics, policies, and the entrepreneurial university.* Baltimore, MD: Johns Hopkins University Press.

Swales, J. M. (1990). *Genre analysis: English in academic and research settings.* Cambridge: Cambridge University Press.

Swales, J. M. (2004). *Research genres: Explorations and applications.* Cambridge: Cambridge University Press.

Tight, M. (2003). *Researching higher education.* Maidenhead: Open University Press.

Tight, M. (2004). Research into higher education: An a-theoretical community of practice? *Higher Education Research and Development, 23*(4), 395–411.

Tsoukas, H. (2009). A dialogical approach to the creation of new knowledge in organizations. *Organisation Science,* 1–17.

FINDING MEANING IN HIGHER EDUCATION: A SOCIAL HERMENEUTICS APPROACH TO HIGHER EDUCATION RESEARCH

Manfred Lueger and Oliver Vettori

ABSTRACT

Higher education is positively imbued with social meaning. Every academic ritual, scientific routine or scholarly practice carries meanings that go far beyond the situational motives of the actors themselves. Social science hermeneutics, one of the best-known institutionalised paradigms in German-speaking qualitative research, offers a sound methodological basis and various methodical variants in order to approach such latent meaning levels. With its focus on reconstructing the underlying logics, values and norm systems of interaction processes and social structures, social science hermeneutics tackles questions that are highly relevant for understanding contemporary developments in higher education strategy and policy. This chapter introduces readers to key concepts in social science hermeneutics and their potential for higher education research. Based on an overview of the main methodological characteristics, the

Theory and Method in Higher Education Research II
International Perspectives on Higher Education Research, Volume 10, 23–42
Copyright © 2014 by Emerald Group Publishing Limited
All rights of reproduction in any form reserved
ISSN: 1479-3628/doi:10.1108/S1479-3628(2014)0000010007

authors then give an in-depth example of an interpretative process by
providing a step-by-step reconstruction of different levels of meaning.

INTRODUCTION: MEANINGFUL ACADEMIA

Higher education is positively imbued with social meaning. Every academic
ritual, scientific routine or scholarly practice carries meanings that go far
beyond the situational motives of the actors themselves. Lectures and
examinations, peer reviews, conferences and, last but not least, the daily
actions and interactions in higher education institutions can be regarded as
manifestations of the structures of meaning that underlie them — and
which are themselves shaped and changed by these actions and interactions
in fascinating reciprocity. New students, for example, can enter a seminar
room and immediately understand most of the relevant rules and practices
of the social interactions without having received any explicit instructions
beforehand. Parts of that may be a learning result from previous experiences (most secondary school classrooms are not that different), and other
parts will be the result of a keen observation of others. Yet, overall, the
success of the interactions in the seminar room largely depend on the
actors' success in interpreting the situation and the required behavioural
patterns by (usually unknowingly and unintentionally) choosing those
options that appear to be more meaningful and reasonable than others.
Even the architecture of such seminar rooms carries meaning in a way that
some interactions are encouraged and others are precluded. However, this
process is not one-directional: meaning structures are constantly actualised
and changed by the actors themselves. Long gone are the days, where a student booting up his/her laptop during a class was legitimately regarded as a
provocative act of showing disinterest or a display of materialism. It is only
the reconstruction of such meaning structures — that is the stock of knowledge, values, norms and interpretative patterns actors orient themselves at,
and which their (inter)actions are embedded in — that enables us to understand the contextual factors that shape all social processes or structures
and the, often contradictory, social logics they are pervaded with.

This seems highly relevant for the field of higher education research:
every attempt at understanding educational processes leads to questions on
the structural conditions for such processes, on the patterns and rules
which they are following, on the institutions and actors that are involved in
their formation and execution, and on the historical and social contexts

they are embedded in. The meaning dimension is an integral part of all such aspects, be it in the form of objective structures of meaning that are closely interwoven with manifest patterns of action (e.g. Oevermann, 2001), of implicit assumptions that underlie organisational norms and rules (e.g. Schein, 2004), of latent interpretive patterns that enable actors to interact without the need to put every routine into question (e.g. Lüders & Meuser, 1997) or in the form of socio-historical lifeworlds (*Lebenswelten*) as a shared background for our individual or social sense-making (e.g. Berger & Luckmann, 1966; Schütz, 1972).

However, being largely latent and intangible, the meaning dimension of social phenomena can be hardly directly enquired or approached, and thus requires a methodology that enables the researcher to carefully reconstruct the meaning structures from those materials (texts, artefacts, protocols) in which they manifest themselves, without succumbing to speculating or subsuming over-interpretations. Modern social science hermeneutics offers such a methodological framework. As one of the best-known institutionalised paradigms in German-speaking qualitative research, the approach provides a sound methodological basis and connections to various theoretical traditions, such as phenomenology (with its focus on the relation between subjective experiences and the social world in which these experiences occur: cf. Husserl, 1999), institutionalism (from which perspective the typifications of acts and actions and socially shared stocks of knowledge form the basis of social interactions) or modern systems theory (which regards communication as the key element all social systems are built upon: cf. Luhmann, 2013). Having originated in projects related to education and socialisation research, social science hermeneutics is strongly established in the fields of organisation studies and institutional research. On the other hand, the approach is still rather unknown in international higher education research. Yet with its focus on reconstructing the underlying logics, values and norm systems of interaction processes and social structures, social science hermeneutics tackles questions that are highly relevant for understanding contemporary developments in higher education strategy and policy on the organisational and on the field dimension, such as:

• Understanding the emergence and development of contested issues, conflicts and politically imbued discourses within socially complex arenas that involve a great range of actors and different perspectives (e.g. reconstructing the conflicting logics that accompany the emergence of external quality assurance procedures or institutions; or investigating different

levels and patterns of acceptance when it comes to the development and implementation of educational policies);
- Researching the embedding of institutionalised educational arrangements in broader socio-historical contexts (e.g. enquiring into the formal and informal requirements which students from different backgrounds have to meet when entering their studies, and uncovering the strategies which emerge from dealing with such requirements; or examining the conditions for change with regard to formal academic and professional standards and what consequences can arise from such dynamics);
- Reconstructing the underlying assumptions, norms and values that manifest themselves in educational architectures, learning technologies, learning designs, institutional processes and, last but not least, policy and strategy documents (e.g. analysing the institutional logics or value arrangements represented in mission statements; or exploring the ambivalences in higher education institutions' dealings with rankings and certifications);
- Analysing the interplay between different organisational and institutional levels with regard to organisational development and cultural change (e.g. studying the diffusion and translation processes of policy or strategic goals among different actor groups within a university; or researching the dynamics of negotiation processes between different hierarchical levels, formal or informal);
- Inquiring about actors' reality constructions and patterns of perception and evaluating their impact on their interactions and organisational structures (e.g. evaluating study programmes, development projects or policy implementation processes with the help of hermeneutically oriented responsive approaches such as Guba and Lincoln's fourth generation evaluation framework) (Lincoln & Guba, 1985).

Basically, hermeneutic approaches help to understand the dynamics of (higher) education by examining the contexts, lifeworlds and meaning horizons in which educational arrangements are embedded and on which actors' perceptions of realities build.

Methodically, modern social science hermeneutics offers a broad range of data collection methods and interpretative variants to choose from. Following a long and rich history that leads back into the antique, the approach does not only provide a fully developed research framework that integrates various methods of data gathering (i.e. interviews, observations, document analyses, artefact analyses), but pays particular attention to interpretative strategies; an aspect that is often marginalised, with the exceptions of a few other approaches such as grounded theory and conversation analysis.

All in all, however, it is impossible to cover even a couple of these variants within the scope of this chapter (for some excellent overviews on the most established methodological strands, see Garz & Kraimer, 1991; Hitzler & Honer, 1997; Hitzler, Reichertz, & Schröer, 1999; Jung & Müller-Doohm, 1993). The following sections can, however, introduce readers to the main methodological premises and key concepts, describe some parameters that are common to most interpretative variants and demonstrate one concrete example of how to conduct an analysis.

THE METHODOLOGICAL STARTING POINT: COMPREHENDING UNDERSTANDING

Every functioning social system relies on people's ability to understand each other and make their communication and interactions work. In order to (inter)act, people need to recognise other people's actions as meaningful and decipher that meaning: that is read others' activities against the background of their shared lifeworlds. In this way, new actions can tie in with previous ones, creating new meaning – and new options for (mis)understanding. Yet as any action or communication is in principle ambivalent and can signify various things to various actors in various situations, understanding each other is not just an act of comprehending some pre-fixated meaning, but should be regarded as a complex process of constructive interpretation – or rather *re*constructive interpretation, as interpretations can only allude to something that has already happened. Seen through such a lens, our processes of every day understanding turn out to be very complicated, demanding and fragile. Consequently, scientific efforts to understand this every day understanding have a long tradition. *Hermeneutics*, very broadly defined as the science and art of text interpretation, has dedicated itself to such problems since Aristotle and Plato in ancient Greece (cf. Grondin, 1994; Hufnagel, 2000; Joisten, 2009; Kurt, 2004). Stemming from the Greek term *hermeneuein*, which holds various meanings such as 'to explicate', 'to interpret', 'to construe' or 'to translate', it comprised all types of interpretation of written texts, particularly texts in the areas of law, literature and religion.

For a long time, though, the only texts to be hermeneutically analysed were of a sacral nature, in the manner of scriptural interpretations and biblical exegesis (Schleiermacher, 1995; Thiselton, 2009). Yet, despite the focus on theological questions, the problems were associated with any historical text interpretation: how is it possible to gain an adequate understanding of texts that were created under specific, almost inconceivable, socio-historical conditions, and which can only be construed against the background of one's present cultural context? From this question, we can deduce the three centres of reference for any hermeneutic analysis (cf. Grondin, 1994, p. 20f; Kurt, 2004, p. 19f):

• The starting point of any analysis is the manifest information contained within the text, that is the facts as expressed in the written form (text production).
• This goes hand in hand with the question, which meanings manifest themselves in the text, independent from the producer's actual intent (text interpretation).
• Finally, any hermeneutic interpretation has to fulfil the requirement to make all meanings that were reconstructed from the text comprehensible for others (text transformation).

Though initially regarded as a purely theological problem, these aspects soon found their way into a broader philosophical discourse, constituting hermeneutics as a general methodical-systematic *Kunstlehre des Verstehens* ('art of understanding': cf. Schleiermacher, 1995). This approach was further developed by Dilthey (1990), who established a general theory of *Verstehen* (which can be either translated as understanding or comprehension – we will continue to use both terms, depending on which seems to be more fitting for the respective context) across all scientific disciplines.

For Dilthey (1990, p. 278), interpretation would not be possible if every observed phenomenon was completely alien to the observer, and thus did not provide a single starting point for comprehending it (e.g. when trying to read an Arabic text without being able to decipher the letters or being in ignorance of the meaning of the words composed of these letters). On the other hand, interpretation would be completely unnecessary if every observed phenomenon was completely familiar to the observer and its meanings absolutely and objectively fixated. Consequently, every interpretative act has to oscillate between these two extremes. In our daily lives, interpretation is almost unavoidable, as all texts (but also actions or products of actions) offer a range of readings, whose actual selection is strongly dependent on the context of both, the text producer and its recipient, as well as on the situation it is perceived in. This is where herme-neutics comes in, examining the communications and sense-making acts between different actors and aiming at reconstructing the latent structures of meaning that accompany (and frame) communication and action. Hermeneutic approaches aim at comprehending the permanently achieved forms of creating (meaningful) order in the social world.

In order to comprehend the construction of social realities, it is neces-sary to analyse the conditions for their constitution. Husserl (1999, p. 113ff) offers answers to the question of what it is we actually perceive in our daily perceptive routines. Husserl argues that, even though we often only see parts of objects and phenomena, we usually perceive the object as a whole. If we see one side of a house, for example, we usually infer the rest of the house. In a way, the present is always related to the non-present parts. From such a perspective, our consciousness creates typifications that are based on previous experiences, of which a considerable part is shared with other actors: we do not need to observe every detail of a specific higher education course in order to understand how such a course (should) work(s) in principle. In order to explain the patterns that give orientation to actors in the social world, it is thus commendable to reduce observations to their typical core aspects, for example by extrapolating those elements that are structurally constitutive and would be considered as 'normal' across different perspectives. Following this train of thought, such an approach also makes it possible to examine in which aspects different con-structions of reality actually differ from each other, and what practical con-sequences arise from this.

Schütz (1982, p. 122ff) approaches the significance of meaning and con-structed realities from a different, yet equally important, direction. In his work, he emanates from the thesis that perceptions are already existent within coherent meaning structures. In this regard, previous experiences can never be separated from present ones. To a large degree, such experi-ences are gained through interactions and communications with others, and build on already existing socially shared stocks of knowledge and experience. As a consequence, actors create socially meaningful ensembles of different elements (e.g. the various aspects of a higher education course), which are perceived as a whole and get only re-separated if a disruption or dysfunction occurs (e.g. when a student complains about an assignment). Separating the various components of a meaning structure is only possible in analytical contexts, where the complexity can be systematically reduced. One way of approaching the meaning dimension is to separate different observational perspectives and forms of meaning (see also the interpretative model introduced later):

- On the immediate situational level, every actor links specific meaning to his/her actions — yet this is in general not approachable for the researcher or any other actor (it remains anchored in the consciousness of the actor him/herself and may not even be fully understandable to him/herself).
- Subjective meaning is a typified form of this specific meaning, which an actor could normally associate with a certain action (cf. Weber, 1978).
- Objective meaning is a type of meaning that manifests itself in the logic of an action itself, independent of the actor's actual intentions (or subjective meaning, cf. Oevermann, 1993, p. 144).
- Pragmatic meaning is usually related to the situational context in which an action occurs and which makes social interactions possible by mapping the relevant norms, rules and values of a certain social field (cf. Bourdieu, 1995).

Independent from the analytical perspective or the meaning dimension to be analysed, the researcher always has to deal with the consequences of their latent character: social meaning cannot be observed, as the relevant rules and patterns do not have any immediate empirical correlates. Consequently, the meaning structures hermeneutics is interested in have to be inferred and interpreted from the contextual relations in which they manifest themselves. Relatedly, it is important to note, that hermeneutic approaches never look for some objective truth or 'the right interpretation', but rather critically examine whether a specific reconstruction can be regarded as a sustainable and relevant pattern, as well as whether it is able to hold its ground against respective alternatives. In other words: whereas the success of every day actions depends on the assumption of their normality, hermeneutic approaches make this very normality the starting point of critically reflexive research. Therefore, asking questions from different perspectives becomes one of the key elements of any hermeneutic approach (cf. Gadamer, 2004). Such questions are not just directed at the data material, but at the interpretative results, aiming to constantly re-evaluate previous interpretation strands and thus screening the structurally stable ones. This structural stability, however, has its limits, as any interpretation cannot claim validity independent of the specific socio-historic constellations from which it emerged (showing some similarities to the premises of symbolic interactionism as described in Blumer, 1969, p. 2ff).

THE METHODOLOGICAL KEY CHARACTERISTICS: EXTENSITY, DECONSTRUCTION AND SEQUENTIALITY

Initially, most hermeneutic approaches were oriented at the so-called hermeneutic circle. This concept describes the repeated interplay between the interpreter's prior assumptions about the text's meaning and their revision and refinement during the interpretative process (Gadamer, 2004, p. 267f). In other words: understanding the text as a whole is only possible with reference to its individual parts and vice versa. Although the concept's circularity can be criticised for its ambiguity as a metaphor (cf. Shklar, 2004), the hermeneutic circle established two basic principles that can still be regarded as key parameters of modern social science hermeneutics as well. First, the idea that the interpreter needs to be in constant doubt of his/her current state of interpretation, and must sceptically scrutinise every analytical strand. And, second, that the text cannot be simply understood from itself, but only with regard to its literary and socio-historical contexts. Put on its head, this parameter already indicates a characteristic that made the approach so attractive for the social sciences: at its core, social science hermeneutics is rather a context analysis based on texts than a mere text analysis.

From this common origin, a considerable number of hermeneutic approaches have emerged, for example *objective hermeneutics* (Lueger & Hoffmeyer-Zlotnik, 1994; Oevermann, Allert, Konau, & Krambeck, 1979; Reichertz, 2004), *sociology of knowledge hermeneutics* (Soeffner, 2004a, 2004b), *genre analysis* (Bergmann & Luckmann, 1995), *interpretive pattern analysis* (Lüders, 1991), *life-world analysis* (Honer, 1993, 2004) or the *documentary method* (Bohnsack, Pfaff, & Weller, 2010). Though owing a large debt to traditional hermeneutics and the hermeneutic circle, all of these approaches have moved away from its basic interpretative model. Instead of trying to understand a text by oscillating between the text as a whole and the various smaller parts it consists of, modern social hermeneutics approaches usually start with the deconstruction of the original material. This strategy aims at generating new insights and at reducing the risk of subsuming all new findings under some preliminary hypotheses.

The multitude of available approaches also indicates that they can be neither standardised nor applied to any research problem in the same way. In this regard, the hermeneutic methodology can rather be viewed as a common methodological framework that makes ideas and principles available of how to systematically approach the meaning dimension of social phenomena (Knassmüller & Vettori, 2009, p. 305). On the other hand, there are some key characteristics that are common to practically all approaches of modern social science hermeneutics. We introduce these before delving into the methodological aspects of the interpretation process in our next section:

- The focus on *extensity*, that is an attempt to reconstruct and consider as many interpretative alternatives as possible. As there are no rules on how a specific phenomenon is to be interpreted, and because the overlapping of different connotations and meaning layers signify there is no singular 'true' interpretation to a statement, putting the right questions to a text, and making sure not to exclude or overlook any potentially relevant meaning alternatives, are two key requirements of any hermeneutic interpretation process. Methodologically, this means to systematically search for the various latencies a manifest expression may carry, but also to sceptically assess them and explain under what circumstances they can actually be regarded as meaningful. For this, it is necessary to find a balanced dealing with the interpreters' previous or theoretical knowledge, and to disclose any prior assumptions, so they won't unduly influence the interpretation. This can only be achieved through constant critical reflection on the findings and the method itself. Relatedly, at its core, modern social science hermeneutics aims at creating new theses instead of subsuming observations under already existing ones: that is it is always reconstructive and not subsumptive (cf. Oevermann, 2002). This can also be regarded as one of the key differences between our ways of everyday understanding and hermeneutics as a scientific method of comprehension (understanding of the second order, cf. Soeffner, 2004b).
- The *deconstruction* of the original (text) material: that is breaking it up into small units and developing criteria of validity for every analytical strand against which the interpretations are constantly checked. In contrast to classic hermeneutics and the idea of the hermeneutic circle, the modern hermeneutic methods abstain from approaching the text as a whole, where each previous reading — in a process of oscillating between holism and particularism — provides the assumptions that are tested and developed during each subsequent reading. Following Oevermann's (2002) theoretical premise that the relevant meaning structures are at least latently represented in every component of the material, the texts are rather deconstructed and broken up into smaller units of meaning. Through this deconstruction, the text is stripped of its immediate context

which could otherwise dominate the interpretation process (cf. Vettori, 2012). In this regard, it is also advisable that the interpreters do not know the entire text before starting with their interpretation, in order to avoid the temptation to align every interpretation with their knowledge of what is still to come. Subsuming all interpretative strands under the interpreters' pre-knowledge would thus impede all text-immanent criteria for checking the interpretation's validity, and make it more difficult to gain new insights into the phenomenon.

- The principle of *sequentiality*: that is acknowledging a text's internal structure as a number of sequences whose specific chronological order is one of the most important clues on the underlying meaning structures. This principle is owed to the assumption that structures of meaning also follow a principle of sequentiality (cf. Oevermann, 2002, p. 6f): within any action or communication sequence, a preceding act opens certain possibilities for subsequent acts while precluding others. Following Lueger (2010), only an approach that is oriented at this sequentiality principle is able to understand the process through which actions and communications are structured. Practically, this means that, although it is possible to skip parts of the text (maybe because they are redundant or do not bear any obvious relation to the research questions), it is not recommendable to 'jump backwards': that is interpret earlier sequences after the later ones. It is very difficult to blend out any knowledge about how the case at hand will unfold, thus making it more likely to miss clues on its internal logic and relevant interpretative strands (see also Vettori, 2012).

THE INTERPRETATIVE PROCESS: A STEP BY STEP RECONSTRUCTION OF DIFFERENT LEVELS OF MEANING

As argued above, hermeneutics is first and foremost interested in the construction of realities within specific socio-historical contexts, and the ways in which they are constituted. The starting point is always a specific case, which is analysed and then contrasted to other cases with regard to the typical and case-transgressing patterns that are embedded within its case-specific logic. Consequently, the selection of the cases (and the respective material for analysis) is of utmost importance, demanding a strategy as envisioned in Glaser and Strauss's theoretical sampling principle (1967,

p. 45ff) as a foundation for the comparative analysis. Following Glaser and Strauss, the cases are selected based on their relevance for theory development, but the researcher should also find a balance between similar cases (in order to increase the theory's reliability) and between cases of maximal structural variation (in order to increase the theory's range and generalisability). The analysis is to be concluded, once a state of 'theoretical saturation' (*ibid.*, 67ff) is reached: that is when the researcher cannot expect new data or cases to make a relevant contribution to theory development.

Once a case is selected, the researcher has to collect/construct the data to be analysed. In order to analyse these systematically, the data have to be fixated: that is be brought to a form that can be repeatedly approached (e.g. as an interview transcript, a video or as a manifest artefact). As a result, data for hermeneutic analyses are never ephemeral (such as actors' situational observations of actions in the context of our every day understanding), but are rather put into the form of protocols, allowing for elaborate interpretation processes without any undue pressure of time. Such protocols can be texts, but also pictures or artefacts in which the researched constructions and practices manifest, and which have to be 'translated' into text. Consequently, the most frequently used materials are documents and interview protocols, but also photographs or films. Ideally, the materials are only marginally influenced manifestations of the examined life-world (e.g. 'natural' data that can already be found in the field). Yet in most cases, such data are not available, but have to be created as part of the research process. Interviews, for example, are a popular and often suitable means to create data for the interpretation – yet with the interviewer and the interview situation being very influential factors on the conduct of the interview itself, it is necessary to keep this influence at a minimum, for example by using narrative and open interview approaches instead of structured ones. Nevertheless, it is important to consider the ways the data were collected and/or constructed as a meaning context of its own, and include them in the interpretation process (cf. Hitzler & Honer, 1997). Last, but not least, the decision on what materials to use is largely dependent on the research question (which material can provide the necessary answers?), on the structure of the research field (who and what are the field's main players and the researcher's relationship to the field?) and the progress of the theory building: it is quite common to use different materials or focus on different aspects within the cyclical logic of a hermeneutic research process.

In order to ensure the quality of the interpretation, and corresponding to the sequentiality principle described above, the interpretation process itself always follows a step by step logic, varying the interpretative perspectives and foci. In this way, the interpretation of previously analysed units can be checked against later units and findings. Hence, after breaking the text material up according to the deconstruction principle, the material is then analysed unit by unit, with decisions on the next unit to be analysed always contingent on the state of the theory building. The size of the unit, however, can vary greatly, depending on the focus of the interpretation, and ranging from short particles and small phrases to entire paragraphs (cf. Froschauer & Lueger, 2003; Lueger, 2010).

Fig. 1 depicts a typical interpretation process (taken and adapted from Vettori, 2012, p. 99f). In practice, this interpretation model will always have to be adapted and adjusted to the specific research question and interpretative situation — the six steps described should thus be regarded as an

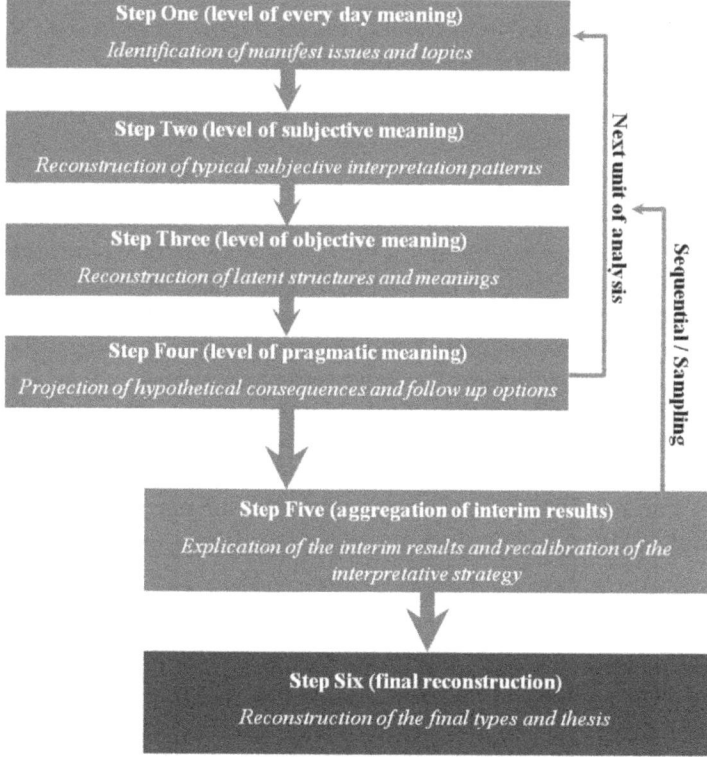

Fig. 1. Typical Interpretation Process (adapted from Vettori 2012, p. 107).

example for the general systematic of a hermeneutic analysis, but not be viewed as a guideline that needs to be followed in every aspect.

- *Step one: Identification of manifest issues and topics (level of every day meaning)*

The first step creates the basis for all subsequent steps, searching the text for its manifest content, in terms of its denotative (literal) meaning as well as with regard to an everyday understanding of the statements in the text. When analysing a rather small unit of meaning (usually a single expression or phrase), the main purpose is to paraphrase the expression in different ways in order to reconstruct how it might be typically understood (everyday speech perspective). When analysing longer units (e.g. paragraphs or even longer pieces of text), there is an additional need to reduce them by summarising the key content. Consequently, the paraphrase should not become too abstract and reduced – yet the collection of manifest themes and viewpoints this first step results in is an important basis for the subsequent approaching of the less obvious underlying meaning.

- *Step two: Reconstruction of typical subjective interpretative patterns (level of subjective meaning)*

In this second step, the interpreter deliberately shifts the perspective to the communicator by putting him/herself into the speaker's/writer's place. Here, the focus does not lie any longer on how a certain phrase might be usually understood, but on how it might have been intended to be understood. Yet, as the actual intentions of the text producers cannot be known, they can only be reconstructed as typical subjective meanings. By reconstructing the typified perspectives and sense-making patterns of the acting subjects, the interpreter gets valuable hints about the contextual structures of meaning in which those actors (and their own interpretations) are embedded. This leads to the question, under what contextual circumstances such an interpretation comes into existence – or, in a social-constructivist sense, holds truth for the actors in specific situations.

- *Step three: Reconstruction of latent structures and meanings (level of objective meaning)*

Consequently, the third step shifts the focus from the acting subjects to their enacted contexts. It is this reservoir of socially shared and mostly institutionalised (and in this sense 'objective') meaning structures which form the core of most hermeneutic approaches. The interpreter looks for the structural conditions that have to be presumed in order for a statement/text fragment to make sense. During this analytical step, the method is implementing the final transit from a text analysis to a context analysis. In other words, the interpreter tries to take a look 'behind the scenes' of the text, aiming to reconstruct the latent structures and patterns which have triggered/conditioned the actor's choice of expression, including the wording, grammar or the overall sequentiality (cf. Froschauer & Lueger, 2003, p. 151; Lueger, Sandner, Meyer, & Hammerschmid, 2005). Specific word choices, unusual expressions, disruptions, grammatical structures (e.g. active vs. passive, conditionals), repetitions, generalisations or banalities all can contain hints about the underlying socially shared rules, norms and structures. Whenever the interpreter identifies such valuable particularities (ignoring the temptation to simply read over them), they are subjected to the question of what they might tell – albeit not in a psychological but in a sociological sense. Under what circumstances or in which contexts are such linguistic choices and decisions socially meaningful? The result of this third step is a compilation of potentially relevant structural conditions – a sort of thesis fragments.

- *Step four: Hypothetical consequences and follow up options (level of pragmatic meaning)*

This step has two main purposes and acts as an important link between the various interpretative cycles. (1) In its conceptual function it concludes the immediate interpretative cycle by adding another element to the reconstructive process. This is the first (and only) step in which the interpreter is allowed to distance himself from the actual text by asking about the hypothetical structural effects that arise from the previous interpretations (e.g. logical consequences whether the respective conditions were in effect; influence on actions, perceptions, communications and interpretations of the field actors). (2) In its falsification function it provides the criteria against which the plausibility of the preliminary thesis fragments are checked in the subsequent cycles. Once the potential effects of a certain structural condition are defined, it becomes possible to check whether these effects are actualised in subsequent sequences or further material. Consequently, at the end of the fourth step, the interpreter specifies what future sequences and cases would need to look like/address if certain interpretative strands were actually relevant within the field. What would speak for/against a certain thesis fragment in the material still to be analysed?

With the description of the fourth step, the main analytical cycle is completed: after defining the potential consequences and 'touch-stones', the interpreter approaches another unit of meaning or text fragment and starts again with the paraphrasing – with one small extension. One of the first questions that are directed at the text asks about whether the expectations and indications, that were defined at the end of step four, are realised in the new passage. If not, it is not necessarily a sign that the whole strand should be discarded, but rather very carefully observed during the rest of the interpretation.

- *Step five: Aggregation of the interim results and recalibration of the interpretative strategy*

Following the premises of a cyclically organised hermeneutic research design, the interpretative results are gradually summarised, compared and critically scrutinised. Such an incremental integration is not only compatible with the sequential reconstructive logic, but should also impede the premature solidification of the interpreter's impressions and conclusions. The careful documentation of these interim aggregations is of particular importance, as hermeneutic interpretations – even though they often change and vary during the research process – eventually seem self-evident and appear as if they had always been present and thus invisibilise their own processual reconstruction and development (cf. Froschauer & Lueger, 2009, p. 118). After the analysis of several cases, the preliminary results have to be condensed to first tentative patterns by way of comparison. It is necessary to note that this step does not produce complete theses or types, but rather fragmentary accumulations of structural elements that potentially (in the sense of 'plausibly') belong together. Consequently, similar variants can provisionally exist in parallel as can contradictory ones. Finally, the gaps and open questions that emerged in the course of this aggregation guided the selection of the next cases and the additional questions for the next interpretative cycle, as the main purpose for each new cycle is to deepen the understanding of the field's main patterns by challenging the interim results. It is only after these results have achieved a level of structural stability and theoretical saturation that the final integrative step can be taken.

- *Step six: Reconstruction of the final types and/or thesis*

In general, the concluding analysis relies on an arrangement of second order constructions, which, following Schütz (1972), are based on the typifications of the actors themselves. At their core, the results of hermeneutic interpretations are structural generalisations that aim to depict a certain type in terms of its internal rules and patterns. It does not matter how often a certain type or its characteristics appear in the material – understanding its specifics (and the similarities and structural differences to other types) is much more important. Carried by the principles of constant comparative analysis (Glaser & Strauss, 1967) – that is looking for minimal and maximal contrasts – the structural elements identified in the previous steps either lead to the (re)construction of a new type (abduction) or are subsumed under an already existing type (qualitative induction). Although both approaches are closely intertwined, the starting phase usually is dominated by the abductive logic (justifying Oevermann's claim that hermeneutic analyses are in general reconstructive rather than subsumptive: cf. Oevermann, 2002), whereas in the later phases the types are rather 'fleshed out' than renewed. Subtypes or new types are constructed when the coherence of a previously defined type becomes increasingly brittle or shows irresolvable internal inconsistencies and contradictions. The preliminary results are condensed to the clearest types with regard to their most fundamental characteristics.

Overall, the quality of hermeneutic interpretations is strongly dependent on the critical reflexivity of the researchers and a variety of quality assurance mechanisms, such as the deconstruction of the material, the sequential but circular interpretative approach, a thorough and effective sampling strategy and the critical examination of previous interpretative threads against later ones. Most of these elements have already been described as part of the interpretative model above, but a few additional techniques and principles are well worth mentioning (cf. Froschauer & Lueger, 2009, p. 199f; Knassmüller & Vettori, 2009, p. 310f):

- Separation of data collection and interpretation: for example by excluding the interviewers from the interpretation of the interviews which they have conducted, as they have knowledge of the full text and might not be able to distance themselves from it (they could have a consulting function).
- Team interpretation: a team of about three to four different interpreters can increase the range of different interpretative strands, as well as the necessity for effective arguments. The team members should also be able to handle conflicts and could take different roles within the team (e.g. the role of an 'advocatus diaboli' who systematically challenges the others). It is also advisable to take at least one more experienced interpreter on board, as the various methodological pitfalls can be very challenging for an inexperienced team.
- No time pressure: specific goals and the ambition to interpret as quickly as possible can be counterproductive, because valuable interpretations could be prematurely discarded.

- Reflexive phases after every full interpretative cycle: this can also be supported by supervision from other researchers or relevant actors from the
  research field, who help to untangle thematic, methodic or emotional
  knots.
- The systematic variation of data, methods, perspective and interpreters
  in order to reduce one-sided influences and to create new insights.

These recommendations should not be read as research norms, but are
intended to enrich the research experience and increase the significance and
explanatory power of the results. In this regard, it is not the singular standards but their interplay and integration in a sensible overall design which
ensures their comprehensibility and acceptance (particularly as not every
recommendation might be observable, depending on the specifics of a
research situation).

FINDING MEANING IN HIGHER EDUCATION: AN OVERLOOKED POTENTIAL?

In our introduction we argued the potential of hermeneutic approaches for
several research areas, considering the relevance of the meaning dimension
within all educational fields, processes, structures and interactions. On the
other hand, we have also stated that modern social hermeneutics still plays
a very minor role in the range of higher education research methods, particularly outside of the German-speaking community. Vettori's (2012) examination of conflicting, coalescing and co-existing interpretive patterns in
Austrian higher education (and how these underlying meaning structures
shape − and even subvert − the discourse and daily actions in often
unintended directions) is one of the few higher education studies currently
available in English. For educational research in general, Scheid and
Twardella (2012) provide an excellent overview of current research strands
on educational institutions and educational processes. Further insights can
be gained by Ohlhaver's (2011) study on professionalisation and pedagogical case orientation in teacher education, and Sutter's (2009) inquiry of the
communicative construction of communication rationales in educational
contexts. In general, however, the potential of this methodological tradition
in higher education research is still something to be developed, particularly
with regard to its strong links to theoretical paradigms, such as new institutionalism, phenomenology and systems theory. There is still a lot of sense
to be made of and meaning to be found in today's higher education.

REFERENCES

Berger, P. L., & Luckmann, T. (1966). *The social construction of reality: A treatise in the sociology of knowledge.* Garden City, NY: Anchor Books.

Bergmann, J. R., & Luckmann, T. (1995). Reconstructive genres of everyday communication. In U. M. Quasthoff (Ed.), *Aspects of oral communication* (pp. 289–304). Berlin: de Gruyter.

Blumer, H. (1969). *Symbolic interactionism. Perspective and method.* Berkeley, CA: University of California Press.

Bohnsack, R., Pfaff, N., Weller, W. (Eds.). (2010). *Qualitative analysis and documentary method in international educational research.* Opladen: Barbara Budrich.

Bourdieu, P. (1995). *The logic of practice.* Stanford: Stanford University Press.

Dilthey, W. (1990 [1910]). *Der Aufbau der geschichtlichen Welt in den Geisteswissenschaften.* Suhrkamp: Frankfurt.

Froschauer, U., & Lueger, M. (2003). *Das qualitative Interview. Zur Praxis interpretativer Analyse sozialer Systeme.* Wien: WUV.

Froschauer, U., & Lueger, M. (2009). *Interpretative Sozialforschung: Der Prozess.* Wien: Facultas.

Gadamer, H.-G. (2004 [1975]). *Truth and method.* London: Continuum.

Garz, D., & Kraimer, K. (1991). *Qualitativ-empirische Sozialforschung. Konzepte, Methoden, Analysen.* Opladen: Westdeutscher Verlag.

Glaser, B. G., & Strauss, A. L. (1967). *The discovery of grounded theory: Strategies for qualitative research.* New York, NY: Aldine de Gruyter.

Grondin, J. (1994). *Introduction to philosophical hermeneutics.* Yale: Yale University.

Hitzler, R., & Honer, A. (1997). *Sozialwissenschaftliche Hermeneutik.* Opladen: Leske + Budrich.

Hitzler, R., Reichertz, J., & Schröer, N. (1999). *Hermeneutische Wissenssoziologie. Standpunkte zur Theorie der Interpretation.* Konstanz: UVK.

Honer, A. (1993). *Lebensweltliche Ethnographie. Ein explorativ-interpretativer Forschungsansatz am Beispiel von Heimwerker-Wissen.* Wiesbaden: Deutscher Universitätsverlag.

Honer, A. (2004). Life-world analysis in ethnography. In U. Flick, E. V. Kardorff, & I. Steinke (Eds.), *A companion to qualitative research* (pp. 113–118). London: Sage.

Hufnagel, E. (2000). *Einführung in die Hermeneutik.* St. Augustin: Gardez!.

Husserl, E. (1999 [1929]). *Cartesian meditations. An introduction to phenomenology.* Dordrecht: Kluwer.

Joisten, K. (2009). *Philosophische Hermeneutik.* Berlin: Akademie Verlag.

Jung, T., & Müller-Doohm, S. (1993). *"Wirklichkeit" im Deutungsprozess. Verstehen und Methoden in den Kultur- und Sozialwissenschaften.* Frankfurt/M: Suhrkamp.

Knassmüller, M., & Vettori, O. (2009). Hermeneutische Verfahren. Verstehen als Forschungsansatz. In R. Buber & H. Holzmüller (Eds.), *Qualitative Marktforschung. Konzepte – Methoden – Analysen* (pp. 299–317). Wiesbaden: Gabler.

Kurt, R. (2004). *Hermeneutik. Eine sozialwissenschaftliche Einführung.* Konstanz: UVK.

Lincoln, Y. S., & Guba, E. G. (1985). *Naturalistic inquiry.* Beverly Hills, CA: Sage.

Lüders, C. (1991). Deutungsmusteranalyse. Annäherungen an ein risikoreiches Konzept. In D. Garz & K. Kraimer (Eds.), *Qualitativ-empirische Sozialforschung, Konzepte, Methoden, Analysen* (pp. 277–408). Westdeutscher Verlag: Opladen.

Lüders, C., & Meuser, M. (1997). Deutungsmusteranalyse. In R. Hitzler & A. Honer (Eds.), *Sozialwissenschaftliche Hermeneutik* (pp. 57–79). Opladen: Leske + Budrich.

Lueger, M. (2010). *Interpretative Sozialforschung: Die Methoden.* Wien: Facultas.

Lueger, M., & Hoffmeyer-Zlotnik, J. H. P. (1994). Hermeneutic interpretation in qualitative research: Between art and rules. In I. Borg & P. Ph. Mohler (Eds.), *Trends and perspectives in empirical social research* (pp. 294–307). Berlin: de Gruyter.

Lueger, M., Sandner, K., Meyer, R., & Hammerschmid, G. (2005). Contextualizing influence activities. An objective hermeneutical approach. *Organization Studies, 26*(8), 1145–1168.

Luhmann, N. (2013). *Introduction to systems theory*. Cambridge: Polity Press.

Oevermann, U. (1993). Die objektive Hermeneutik als unverzichtbare Grundlage für die Analyse von Subjektivität. Zugleich eine Kritik der Tiefenhermeneutik. In T. Jung & S. Müller-Doohm (Eds.), *"Wirklichkeit" im Deutungsprozess, Verstehen und Methoden in den Kultur- und Sozialwissenschaften* (pp. 106–189). Frankfurt/M: Suhrkamp.

Oevermann, U. (2001). Die Struktur sozialer Deutungsmuster – Versuch einer Aktualisierung. *In Sozialer Sinn, 1*, 35–81.

Oevermann, U. (2002). *Klinische Soziologie auf der Basis der Methodologie der objektiven Hermeneutik – Manifest der objektiv hermeneutischen Sozialforschung*. Retrieved from http://publikationen.ub.uni-frankfurt.de/volltexte/2005/540/pdf/ManifestWord. pdf. Accessed on 21 November 2012.

Oevermann, U., Allert, T., Konau, E., & Krambeck, J. (1979). Die Methodologie einer "objektiven Hermeneutik" und ihre allgemeine forschungslogische Bedeutung in den Sozialwissenschaften. In *Soeffner Hans-Georg (Hrsg.): Interpretative Verfahren in den Sozial- und Textwissenschaften* (pp. 352–434). Metzler: Stuttgart.

Ohlhaver, F. (2011). Fallanalyse, Professionalisierung und pädagogische Kasuistik in der Lehrerbildung. *Sozialer Sinn, 2*, 279–304.

Reichertz, J. (2004). Objective hermeneutics and hermeneutic sociology of knowledge. In U. Flick, E. V. Kardorff, & I. Steinke (Eds.), A companion to qualitative research (pp. 290–296). London: Sage.

Scheid, C., & Twardella, J. (2012). Tagungsbericht: Die Objektive Hermeneutik in der Bildungs- und Unterrichtsforschung. *Forum Qualitative Sozialforschung, 13*(1), Art. 27. Retrieved from http://nbn-resolving.de/urn:nbn:de:0114-fqs1201271

Schein, E. H. (2004). *Organizational culture and leadership* (3rd ed.). San Francisco, CA: Jossey-Bass.

Schleiermacher, F. (1995 [1838]). *Hermeneutik und Kritik. Herausgegeben von Manfred Frank*. Frankfurt: Suhrkamp.

Schütz, A. (1972). *The phenomenology of the social world*. Evanstone: Northwestern University Press.

Schütz, A. (1982). *Das Problem der Relevanz*. Frankfurt: Suhrkamp.

Shklar, J. N. (2004). Squaring the hermeneutic circle. *Social Research, 71*(3), 657–658.

Soeffner, H.-G. (2004a). *Auslegung des Alltags – Der Alltag der Auslegung. Zur wissenssoziologischen Konzeption einer sozialwissenschaftlichen Hermeneutik*. Konstanz: UVK.

Soeffner, H.-G. (2004b). Objective hermeneutics and hermeneutic sociology of knowledge. In U. Flick, E. V. Kardorff, & I. Steinke (Eds.), *A companion to qualitative research* (pp. 95–100). London: Sage.

Sutter, H. (2009). Pädagogische Interaktion. Eine hermeneutisch-rekonstruktive Fallstudie zur kommunikativen Konstruktion der Verständigungsverhältnisse in institutionellen Kontexten der Erziehung. *Sozialersinn, 1*, 99–152.

Thiselton, A. C. (2009). *Hermeneutics. An introduction*. Grand Rapids, MI: Eerdmans Pub.

Vettori, O. (2012). *A clash of quality cultures – Conflicting and coalescing interpretive patterns in Austrian higher education*. Vienna: Phil. Diss.

Weber, M. (1978 [1922]). *Economy and society. An outline of interpretative sociology*. Berkeley, CA: University of California Press.

NARRATIVES AND ACCOUNTS: THEIR COLLECTION AND ANALYSIS

Sara Delamont and Paul Atkinson

ABSTRACT

A great deal of contemporary research in education, and in the social sciences more generally, is conducted through interviews. Interview-derived accounts and narratives have been used as data for many decades. We argue that, despite their popularity and their long history, such data are not always subjected to rigorous analysis. Researchers too often treat interviews as sources of insight about informants' experiences and feelings, but pay insufficient attention to the forms and functions of such accounts. We argue that they need to be approached through the analytic lens of accounting devices and narrative structures. We exemplify this approach through 'academic' narratives: scientists' discovery accounts and accounts of doctoral supervision. We emphasise how such accounts need to be examined in terms of the discursive construction of reality. Such an approach is an important corrective to the selective reporting of 'atrocity stories' about postgraduate education.

Theory and Method in Higher Education Research II
International Perspectives on Higher Education Research, Volume 10, 43–61
Copyright © 2014 by Emerald Group Publishing Limited
All rights of reproduction in any form reserved
ISSN: 1479-3628/doi:10.1108/S1479-3628(2014)0000010008

INTRODUCTION

'I felt it was like sweeping water trying to get them to work'.

That comment from a doctoral supervisor, an anthropologist we called pseudonymously Dr Drummock, is typical of the vivid, evocative speech that can be captured when collecting narratives, in this case about his career as a supervisor (Delamont, Atkinson, & Parry, 2000). When informants are encouraged to tell their stories in their own words, colourful metaphors, cries of pain, torrents of praise and tales of triumph and tragedy are produced along with apparently 'factual' accounts of people and events. Interviews, of individuals or of small groups, whether conducted face-to-face, on the telephone or in cyberspace, are one of the commonest methods used in social and educational research. They are pervasive in higher education research. In the course of this chapter we consider the appropriate use and analysis of data derived from interviews.

We focus specifically on interview materials as narratives and accounts. We outline some traditions of narrative scholarship, highlight some key higher education studies based on narrative from the Anglophone world (e.g. Middleton, 2001), and, most importantly, argue that narratives must be analysed, and not just celebrated in a naïve way, as if they reported some transparently authentic experience − or, even worse, provided relatively unproblematic evidence of reported events. Our main argument concerns the inadequacy of too many interview-based studies that do not pay sufficient attention to the intrinsic organisation of accounts and narratives themselves. It is important to realise that characteristic narrative forms, story types and rhetorical devices provide speakers with significant cultural resources to enact a wide range of phenomena: memories, identities, complaints, justifications, comparisons and so on. We argue, therefore, that we need to analyse interview materials in terms of the speech-acts they include, the genres of narrative they reflect and the cultural resources that informants bring to bear.

Social scientists have collected narratives, such as the life history, the *testimonio* (a distinctive genre of personal accounts of suffering associated with Central and South American informants), the atrocity story, oral reminiscences and accounts of educational, criminal or illness experiences for over 80 years. The pioneer qualitative social scientists in Chicago from 1920 to 1940 used the collection of narratives, orally or in documentary form, as one of their core ways to understand social life. Shaw's (1930) life history of an American mugger − *The Jackroller* − being among the famous early social science narratives (see also Snodgrass, 1982). In educational research life histories, curriculum histories, atrocity stories and teachers' teaching stories have been popular for the past 30 years. We have written about the collection and analysis of narrative data elsewhere (Atkinson & Delamont, 2006a, 2006b). Our general position is that rich narratives are a popular form of social science data, but they have to be understood as data of a particular type.

We concentrate on the narratives provided by university research scientists (Batchelor, Parsons, & Atkinson, 1997), by postgraduate students and their supervisors (Delamont et al., 2000) and by social science academics (Delamont, 2003), because that is where our own higher education research has taken place. However, because educational research of any kind, including higher education research, is always enriched by deploying systematic strategies to compare and contrast educational settings and participants with non-educational settings and participants (Delamont, Atkinson, & Pugsley, 2010), we draw upon debates about narrative research in other *milieux*. In the specific case of narrative research one of the vigorous areas of debate is in the sociology of health and illness, where there is a controversy about the appropriate use of illness narratives (Atkinson, 1997, 2009, 2010). Similarly we rehearse Gilbert and Mulkay's (1984) critique of the ways in which scientists' interview talk had been used by sociologists, which is not routinely recognised as foundational in higher education research. It could, of course, be argued that higher education research in general ought to take more explicit account of research on scientists' accounts, and those of other knowledge producers (cf. Sampson & Atkinson, 2011, 2013). In the course of this chapter, therefore, we discuss narrative research in general, and discuss some of the key scholars who have worked with narrative materials. We then illustrate selectively the key points with reference to our own work on doctoral supervision.

Narrative Research

The 'narrative turn' in the social sciences, including educational research, has been a major feature of the past 30 years, and shows no sign of abating. The collection of narratives is an important part of research on and in higher education. For example, most of the research in Becher, Henkel, and Kogan (1994), Burgess (1994), Clark (1993), Mullins and Kiley (2002) and Pole (2000) on postgraduate researchers and their supervisors is taken

from staff and student narratives. The research on the British doctoral *viva
voce* examination by Morley et al. (2002) and Tinkler and Jackson (2000) is
dominated by examining narratives collected from students.

The commonest types of narrative collected include oral history, life history, illness narratives, *testimonio*, teaching and supervising memories, and
atrocity stories. Narratives are *social* phenomena. They are produced and
performed according to shared social conventions. Social organisations are
constituted by the oral work which produces and reproduces individual,
collective and organisational identities. Narratives are also crucially part of
many ceremonial and ritual occasions, and are a way to display skills and
expertise.

The original Chicago School sociologists collected written and oral narratives from the first three decades of the twentieth century (Plummer, 2001)
onwards, including Hughes's (1961) *The Fantastic Lodge*, a life history of a
jazz groupie and heroin addict, and Heyl's (1979) life history of a brothel
owner. In anthropology the collection of personal narratives has a long history (Faubion, 2001) that continues into recent work by, for example Abu-
Lughod (1993) and Behar (1996, 2007). In education teacher narratives,
including life history and atrocity stories, have been published by, for example Witherill and Noddings (1997), Cortazzi (1991), Chase (1995) and
Goodson (1995). Cortazzi (1993), in particular, demonstrated the value of
applying narrative analysis to teachers' accounts. His approach was
notable for its sustained application of formal narrative analysis, as well as a
methodological commentary advocating such analytic procedures (Cortazzi,
1991, 2001). In the 1980s the research potential of the Latin American *testimonio*, an oral and life history produced by a member of a subaltern group,
became a subject of educational research debate. Menchù's (1984) *testimonio*
was attacked by Stoll (1999), who argued that the events described were not
'true', which produced two special issues of the journal *Qualitative Studies of
Education* (2000, 2003) in which educational researchers reflected on the use
(s) of personal testimony for potential action, healing victims and for understanding educational institutions and processes.

The two most important things that need to be understood about
narrative data are that what separates research from journalism (such as
the work of Studs Terkel) is the social scientific analysis done on the narratives, and their relation to 'reality'. Firstly, we argue that informants'
accounts have structure. They have characteristic forms. Narratives reflect
cultural conventions in terms of their intrinsic, indigenous organisation.
Labov and Waletsky (1967) provided an early, classic statement of
how narrative forms structure personal experience. Recurrent structural

elements construct plausible, well-formed accounts that conform to cultural expectations concerning stories and reminiscences. Narratives, in other words, have their own 'grammar', and analysis needs to be attentive to those organisational features. For a much more recent version of the approach, see Labov (2013). This is not a matter of empty formalism: narrative forms encapsulate powerful cultural assumptions about *what* is worth telling, and *how* it is appropriate to tell it. As Hymes (1981) documented, story-telling is based on cultural conventions of *ethnopoetics*, and narratives can display complex structures. Narratives that 'work' in any particular national, religious or workplace culture have to obey the story-telling conventions of that culture. Heath's (1982, 1983) contrast between the story telling conventions of an African-American and a working class white American community in the Carolinas is the most famous example of that. Every feature of an appropriate story in the white neighbourhood seemed dull and flat in the African-American neighbourhood, where fantasies and 'embroidery' were valued.

The analysis of genre is also important. Even the most apparently 'private' of experiences are demonstrably recounted in accordance with generic cultural conventions. This is the message of Plummer's (1995) analysis of sex-related stories: notwithstanding the fact that these stories relate extremely personal and private events, they conform to shared conventions of telling. In this sense, therefore, personal stories share properties with folk tales (cf. Propp, 1968), urban legends (Tucker, 2005) and myths (Leach, 1969). Each individual telling embeds recurrent themes and structures. In other words, such data are simultaneously personal and collective, and are based on shared cultural conventions.

Genres of narrative, therefore, include varieties of accounts that have distinctive *moral* force. They construct events and actors with a particular evaluative orientation, for instance. Dingwall (1977), drawing on work among health professions, calls attention to the importance of one particular genre of occupational narrative he categorises as 'atrocity stories'. Such stories, by no means confined to the health field, but especially piquant among doctors, nurses and others, have a variety of functions, not least as vehicles for the transmission to novices of occupational values, shared assumptions about success and failure, and general precepts as to conduct and comportment. They are an important feature of occupational culture and its oral transmission. Occupational rhetoric provides members of the occupation with the means of organising and evaluating their own work and that of others.

Equally, and often closely related to atrocity stories, there are genres of narrative that position the narrator as a victim of circumstances, or as a complainant about the actions of others. Consequently, they embed speech acts that formulate 'problems' or 'complaints', that have pervasive conventions, and are found in many social contexts. Complaints often are couched in terms of what have been called 'extreme formulations' (ordinarily, exaggerations). They also embed the attribution of motives to others in apportioning 'blame'. Equally, there are, of course, narratives that position the teller as the 'hero' of her or his own story. But it should be noted that there are many social contexts in which there are clear cultural preferences. 'Heroes' are often expected to display modesty, and to construct their accounts of success accordingly. Mulkay's analysis of Nobel laureates' acceptance speeches is a prime example (Mulkay, 1985). Modesty in this context is clearly a rhetorical device, as Mulkay cleverly demonstrates by making us think about the consequences of taking prize-winners' acceptance speeches literally (in short, the prizes would have to be returned if the recipients really deserved so little of the credit).

Scientists' narratives of scientific discoveries have also been analysed to yield discursive resources used to construct stories of particular significance. The pioneering work of Gilbert and Mulkay (1984) showed that scientists used alternating repertoires to account for their scientific work. Local, personal and *contingent* effects alternate with *empiricist* accounts based on the logic of scientific inquiry. The two are reconciled, discursively speaking, by the device that 'the truth will out', justifying faith in the inexorable revelation of scientific truth. Similar accounts of scientific work have displayed the rhetorical construction of chance and skill in narratives of a genetic discovery (Batchelor et al., 1997), while Sampson and Atkinson (2013) add an analysis of biomedical scientists' repertoires of emotional discourse in their narratives of genetic discovery. Again, we should note that there are culturally preferred modes of expression: accounts of 'chance' mitigate accounts that might otherwise seem self-congratulatory, for instance. Discursive resources can also be used to construct accounts of what 'counts' as real work, what 'we' do, as opposed to what 'they' do. Hargreaves's (1984) analysis of teachers' 'contrastive rhetoric' documents key aspects of occupational talk and oral culture among school teachers. Hargreaves shows how teachers construct their everyday accounts – particularly *evaluative* accounts of their work and circumstances – through the use of contrastive, comparative devices.

In other words, narratives and accounts, including those derived from research interviews, are not unmediated representations. They have their intrinsic forms of organisation. They reflect socially shared conventions. They are themselves socially constructed, composed out of recurrent genres and rhetorical devices. Interviews, it may be argued, are even more than that. As Atkinson and Silverman (1997) argued, we live in an 'interview society' that values personal reflection and revelation, the confessional and the emotional response. The popularity of interviewing in contemporary social science is in turn a reflection of this cultural preoccupation. Too much social science – notably 'qualitative' research – depends on interview-derived data. Moreover, too much of it fails to pay adequate analytic attention to the formal properties of narratives and accounts. Too often, informants' narratives are reproduced as if they spoke for themselves, and as if they conveyed informants' experiences. Moreover, the enthusiasm for extended interviews in the social sciences, as in everyday life, seems to reflect an essentially romantic view of the social actor, an individual whose interior, private experience can be revealed through confessional talk. Narrative analysis itself also reflects different analytic traditions. There are disciplinary and even national traditions that furnish their own intellectual styles and subject matter (Atkinson, Seweryn, & Tirini, 2011).

It is possible to derive a radical critique of interview data in social research on the basis of these elementary observations. One can extend a critique of methodologically naïve approaches to reject the use of interviews altogether. That is not our shared view. It is not necessary to deny interviews any referential value altogether. It *is* the case that interview accounts should not be used unproblematically as proxies for the observation and recording of social encounters and activities. To that extent, conventional distinctions between 'what people do' and 'what people say they do' (or did) remain valid. On the other hand, we also recognise that what people say are themselves forms of social action, and speech-acts have their own cultural force. But, equally, what people say, and how they say it, is composed from shared, conventional resources. So memories of the past, reports of events, complaints, boasts and so on are actively constructed by and through discursive means. Consequently, we need to address interview-derived accounts from three complementary perspectives: for information, for perspective and for form. In other words, the interview may – with suitable caution – be used to discover aspects of what is described. It may also be analysed with reference to the social position of the speaker: that is, with a view to his or her interests and frames of reference. Thirdly, one may attend to *how* the referential and perspectival functions are realised: one may analyse interview talk with a view to its rhetorical devices and its narrative structure.

What we should *not* do is simply to celebrate and reproduce informants' accounts. We should not treat them as privileged or 'authentic' expressions of personal experience, or to incorporate the 'voices' of informants in an unmediated fashion. Debates concerning these perspectives have been expressed most forcibly among sociologists and anthropologists of medicine, surrounding the proper treatment of 'illness narratives'. While some commentators treat illness narratives, and narratives more generally, as special kinds of materials, others strike a methodologically more cautious note, suggesting that we should treat these narratives as social actions, like any others. Advocates of the illness narrative as 'special' include Kleinman (1988), Mishler (1984) and Frank (1995, 2006). The best known critiques are by Atkinson (1997) and Atkinson and Silverman (1997). The overview by Thomas (2010) and responses to it (Atkinson, 2010; Bochner, 2010; Frank, 2010) encapsulate many key issues in this particular debate.

The relevance of this particular controversy goes beyond the specific issues of health and illness. It provides a microcosm of methodological differences that can and should inform the proper use of interview materials. As we have already suggested, the widespread advocacy of qualitative research methods, and the consequent reliance on extended interviews as methods of data collection, mean that these issues need to be addressed across a broad range of traditions in social and educational research. This is not, of course, a comprehensive account of narrative research and its analytic techniques. Equally, we are not alone in making these kinds of observations about interviews, accounts and narratives. A broader range of topics and strategies, and a perspective congruent with our own, are to be found in the collection edited by Holstein and Gubrium (2012), while Bamberg (2007) provides a state-of-the-art survey of the field.

All of the issues that we have already identified have, as we shall demonstrate, direct relevance for higher education studies. Informants in the academy couch their accounts of academic work in terms of identifiable genres of narrative. Those genres include styles of autobiographical work that reflect distinctive disciplinary cultures or subcultures. Indeed, the symbolic boundaries that define academic disciplines are, to an extent, discursively produced through accounting devices. Accounts of experiences and practices deploy contrastive rhetoric in juxtaposing the present and the past, though the values attributed to each may vary: the past may be represented in terms of a utopian golden age, or in terms of outmoded bad practice. Doctoral students' accounts of their own research, the supervision they received and the experience of being examined (such as Middleton, 2001) can all be couched in terms of story types (atrocity stories, troubles nobly born, success against all odds). Such accounts draw on socially shared devices. That does not make them any more or less 'true'. We do not imply that they are invented out of whole cloth. But equally, we must beware of treating them at face value, as unvarnished representations of personhood, actions or states of affairs.

ACADEMIC NARRATIVES

We now illustrate just some of the issues we have outlined in the first half of this chapter. Each aspect deserves a more extended treatment, and we can only provide exemplification rather than extended analysis. We do so by revisiting a number of our own interview studies. We look back at our study of supervisors of doctoral students and of candidates conducted in the 1990s, and published in Delamont et al. (2000). We do the same with a series of extended interviews with genetic scientists, and published by Batchelor, Parsons, and Atkinson (1996) and Batchelor et al. (1997). All names and places are pseudonyms, and some details have been changed to preserve informants' anonymity.

We recognise that our academics' accounts are situated, but there is no reason to believe that they are entirely context-specific, either in form or content. We are not constrained to believe that our informants generated accounts that were totally dependent on the research interview, and that their narratives or descriptions were constructed entirely de novo. We may not be able to extrapolate from interview discourse directly to social action, but we may be entitled to assume (in the absence of evidence to the contrary) a close family resemblance between interview accounts and accounts more widely circulated among colleagues. Interview talk may provide reasonable evidence as to the oral culture of the occupational group. It is, therefore, in that spirit that we have undertaken a preliminary analysis of academics' accounts of supervisory experience.

Scientists' accounts of scientific work display a number of key accounting devices. Moreover, their accounts of scientific discovery are, of course, accounts delivered from a particular standpoint. Discovery accounts are not unvarnished chronicles of events. Scientists position themselves and their research groups in relation to discovery claims, priority claims and credit for discovery. Our own research in Cardiff on the discovery of the Myotonic Dystrophy gene, for instance, clearly identified different 'stories' about the same scientific work of collaboration and discovery among different research groups. These accounts are also couched in terms of recurrent discursive devices. The following extract is taken from an interview with a university scientist who played a central role in the discovery of the gene for Myotonic Dystrophy. He was interviewed shortly after the discovery was announced by three different research groups in a series of papers in *Nature*. Here he describes a particular juncture in the discovery process — a search for the location and nature of the genetic anomaly responsible for this wasting disease. The extract displays a very characteristic feature of scientists' discourse.

> D. Well, we always knew that it was very close. The job that I have now, I actually was appointed a year before I took it up, but I asked to stall as long as I possibly could, because I knew we were very close, the problem was that we had been very close for a long time, and sometimes with hindsight it was obvious that's how it works, but, for example, Huntingdon's disease, they are very very close in a similar position to what we were two years ago, I would say, and they could find that gene anywhere from tomorrow to two years on, or even longer depending on the nature of the mutation.
>
> I. Was that the same with the Myotonic [Dystrophy] gene? It could have been found any time?
>
> D. It was entirely chance, although there was a lot of hard work and we can now look back and say, OK it's obvious that we were about to jump over the edge, and we were going to find it, but at the same time when you were busy working away there it didn't seem that obvious, so the reason everything evolved as quickly as it did was because of the nature of the of the mutation, now had it been a point mutation, like say just a single base pair change, we would probably still be looking.
>
> I. Because it was triplets, the triplet repeat.
>
> D. Because it was a piece of DNA which amplifies and was obvious from a Southern blot, that is why it was so easy when it was identified.

Here we see more or less precisely the sort of accounting that Gilbert and Mulkay (1984) described. We see the close juxtaposition of an explanation of the discovery based on 'chance', a version of what Gilbert and Mulkay describe in terms of a *contingent* accounting repertoire. At the same time, the scientist accounts for the discovery in terms of the inevitable revelation of science, guaranteed through hard work. The constellation of hard, purposeful scientific work corresponds to what Gilbert and Mulkay refer to as the empiricist repertoire. The two alternating modes of accounting, that are expressed simultaneously, are reconciled through what Gilbert and Mulkay call 'the Truth Will Out Device' (TWOD) that asserts the ultimate inexorability of a given scientific discovery. The alternating accounting repertoires provide scientists with the means to maintain the standard view of scientific truth while inserting their own and others' biography into the scientific process.

By the same token, when scientists claim some credit for a scientific discovery, it is often mitigated, in order to acknowledge the convention of modesty. This is apparent in the following extract of an interview with a different scientist telling us about the same genetic discovery — the location of the Myotonic Dystrophy gene:

> R. Interesting question. In hindsight it would have been nice to follow the whole 59a through. At the time it didn't really bother me that I was channelled into the other jobs as well because I was still working up the 59a stuff in a way, and getting mileage out of that, I could see that sort of coming, and also it was a group effort, so you can't just have everything to yourself. There were four of us working on it and the rationale was Shelley had already had learned the sequencing and was doing sequencing on other things, so she would take over that.

> I. What do you feel, staying with 59a, the significance of that is?

> R. Well, I am very much afraid of blowing my own trumpet but I suppose it was a very significant step, it did very much narrow our concentration on a particular region. It did narrow our concentration, and the data didn't seem to conflict with anything previous, which made us more sure about it.

This feature is not, of course, confined to scientists' accounts. But it is a recurrent feature of them, and the significance of discovery and personal credit means that it reflects a key aspect of the epistemic culture of science. In addition, scientists' accounts also position the informant and the work of scientific discovery in terms of highly personal, even emotional, expression. For instance, the same scientist, discussing the same genetic discovery, told us:

> I. Did you feel, I know you were central on 59a and various other sequences, but did you feel that you were central to that, in the final days or whatever?

> R. No, I didn't. Am I allowed to say all this?

> I. I will be discreet the way it is used don't worry about that.

> R. In the final days I did feel, I definitely felt part of it and it was great to be part of the whole thing. I felt a bit aside from it as well, I mean in a way obviously Helen and Duncan and Dave Brook and people like that, they had been working on it much longer that I had so it's right that they got most of the limelight and it was nice to be there on the sidelines. Basking in the glory.

> I. You felt that you were on the sidelines?

> R. A little bit.

In a rather different vein, we also note that the nature of disciplines and their relationships are also organised through discursive devices. As we have already noted, varieties of contrastive rhetoric are used to construct disciplinary boundaries. For instance, in a discussion of interdisciplinary environmental science, a senior academic said:

> It's just that certain problems, in order to address them and to solve them, you need skills which come from compartments which are separated from the conventions of teaching in universities. And the particularly obvious case is where physical geography and physical geology allow. [In] many universities the geography is in the Arts Faculty and certainly in [Cambridge] none of the geology undergraduates would take geography courses, not vice versa. A certain amount of interchange between the Faculties and they'd talk to one another, but not very much. And recently I've been examining at [St. Andrews] University where the geology department was effectively closed down, or at least required to merge with the geographers as a result of the Earth Sciences Review three years ago. And seeing those students come through having taken modules in geography and geology. The geography modules are very much book learning, even if they're on very similar subjects. They have to read a lot, whereas the geologists do a lot of practical work, and the conventions of how the subject is taught is quite different.

The point here is not that the arrangements for teaching at the two universities are described inaccurately, or that this is a matter of invention. Rather, the cumulative effect of this brief account − and it continues in this vein in the original interview − is to deploy some recurrent rhetorical features in constructing this disciplinary distinction. The contrast between 'book-learning' and practical work is a recurrent trope in the discursive construction of disciplinary types and boundaries. In other words, a stock formula glosses the more straightforward description of university arrangements.

At the risk of repeating ourselves, therefore, we reiterate our basic analytic point: in collecting and reporting interview data, we must be aware of the discursive constructions of reality that interview-derived accounts embody. That does not mean that they are fantasies, or that interview informants are untruthful. We need to recognise that the interview-derived accounts are not a transparent medium, but are based on collective models of representation, common tropes and conventions. This is especially true of accounts that deal with intense, personal or even private 'experiences'. These too are never unmediated. Interviews do not grant us access to such experience independently of styles and genres of narrative reconstruction. Consequently, studies in higher education need to be especially careful of reporting the genre of 'atrocity stories' as if they represented a self-evident state of affairs.

In our study of doctoral students and their supervisors, there were several genres of narrative that recurred. Obviously they are 'true' in substance, but they also conform to a broader type of stories, rather than being a series of unique happenings. The following extract from a scientist who identifies himself as an engineer, and works in an interdisciplinary research environment, is a typical form of account:

> Well, I think, you see, I did take on a student – if I go back through my recent PhD students – I took on an [international] student who was an absolute pain in the proverbial! He was hard-working but he caused me so much hassle because, the whole department so much hassle, and I was spending my time just trying to sort out social problems as much as anything ... I kept warning him that he would fail his exam, his oral exam. He would not listen and sure enough he failed quite abysmally. He's in a re-sit situation so I can't say more. The second person I had was one of our own graduates who was multi-disciplinary, pretty good two-one [degree class] and he was a person who came through the system when I was abroad, and he came and talked to me. He seemed to be very knowledgeable on what he'd done. I saw his undergraduate project, and apart from one criticism I said 'Yes', you know. And I thought, you know, that I was onto something good, working on the area of energy. It soon seemed to me that although he had perhaps a good social science background and he had done a course in computing, I found that when it came to it he could not do even the simplest modelling. And then when it came to it I saw some things and I said, 'Look, statistically, what are these saying?' And he hadn't even grasped the basics of, the basic statistics, even though he'd come through our own course. And I thought 'Well that is strange. Okay, he may not be so hot on the maths, but surely you should have seen a flaw in your reasoning, because just looking at the data there seems to be a problem statistically in what you've done'.

We note, to begin with, that this account embeds a contrastive device, between the international student, whose shortcomings are not specified, beyond personal problems, an unwillingness to listen and in general being 'a pain in the proverbial'. In contrast, the problems of the home-grown student are specified, and identified in terms of training prior to doctoral work. There is an implicit difference between what needs to be narrated as between an international and a home-grown student, it would seem. Equally, however, both episodes in the narrative can also be heard as forms of complaint about the students in question. In this and similar accounts by academics there is also a sense of 'betrayal', in that initial hopes for the doctoral candidate are disappointed. Note too that the story of disappointment for the second student contains story elements that are reminiscent of the sort of structural features identified by Labov (2013). Here the action-complication elements hinge on the disappointment and disillusionment, expressed through the contrast between the student's prior accomplishment and qualification, on the one hand, and his failure to cope with the statistics of the doctoral project. It is, moreover, characteristic that such a failing is expressed graphically and vividly: here it is all the more vivid for being expressed through reported direct speech. Such a story follows a very common style, in which there is a process of 'revelation', through which the true shortcomings of the student are progressively displayed. That these are recurrent and graphic kinds of account should also, of course, remind us of the danger inherent in interview studies: seizing on the most graphic accounts and giving them undue prominence. If we recognise that atrocity stories or disappointment stories are one among several genres, we should also acknowledge that it is too easy for researchers to reproduce and to amplify accounts of this kind. Atrocity stories and dramatic contrasts can too readily be used to construct exaggerated impressions of social events. This is doubly dangerous when they are taken at face value, rather than being treated as examples of rhetorical formulations.

The following extract is from an interview with a doctoral student working at the borders between anthropology and sociology. It exemplifies a recognisable kind of story about supervision and its vicissitudes.

My supervisor changed when Sam went to Canada. Then there was a bit of a gap, and Fergus is my supervisor. So because I'd met him before anyway, socially, I did see him in between but it was just social. But he was always there. I didn't have to report to him, but it was made clear that if there was any problem I could contact him.

I: How did you manage to carry on with the same topic in a different discipline?

Well I changed rather. Part of it was the dissatisfaction with the sociology department as well, because what I'd wanted to do − I'd gone there wanting to do a PhD, registered for an MA because of the upgrading thing. I had a supervisor who was very difficult about what I wanted to do and, initially, what I wanted to do was to find a group of women and begin by talking to them. And he wasn't interested in that, he wouldn't let me do it. Then suggested narrowing it down, and he said 'No'. And this went on till Christmas when he suggested looking into journalism reports, the way things are constructed in the press, which wasn't what I really wanted to do. He had a lot of journalistic contacts, so he offered me all this and said I could do participant observation with journalists. Then, maybe, I was very naïve, over-trusting, but anything I said I'd do to contact the press, it was 'oh well, every little helps', and he was looking up his contacts and got more insistent that he did it. And before Easter he said he'd contacted them and there was nothing he could do to help me. And the next day I found out the ESRC wouldn't renew my grant. Then he said he was off on sabbatical, all within the course of two days. So I felt that after six months of work I'd achieved nothing. And the other thing was he didn't see that I had a problem. So when I went to him and said 'What shall I do? This idea has collapsed', his response was that that's how things went. Which was when I hit the roof. Anyway, I came back then with the proposal that I'd originally had right at the beginning, so it was a complete waste of a year, and most of my writing had to be based on what I'd read, a lot of theoretical stuff.

At the time of the interview, this student was conducting fieldwork, so to some extent this story of neglect and betrayal turned out also to be one of survival and at least a partial overcoming of troubles. It is, however, a not uncommon example of the broad genre of 'trouble' stories.

The following extract from an interview with a social scientist exemplifies the use of extreme formulations in the construction of an autobiographical account. There is no need to deny this academic's personal feelings in order to recognise simultaneously the rhetorical force of these formulations. If authors treat these and similar formulations unduly literally, however, they can easily be used to create an over-dramatized and unduly pessimistic picture of academic life.

I examined a PhD thesis a couple of weeks ago, and I was thinking about it afterwards – thinking how nice we were to that person, myself and the internal person. And I had the most horrible viva anybody could ever have, I think. I did the most deplorable thing, I got upset and burst into tears, so I have a very bad memory of my viva. Looking back at the one I assisted with, I realised that with mine it was a question of human rights. It was appallingly badly examined. It was probably partly my fault, because you're not meant to know who your external is going to be, but usually there's an unofficial discussion about it. And I was not entirely happy about my external, but Laotian studies are not very general in this country and short of having someone from France, which didn't seem to be in question, or America, I was examined by a historian from Reddingdale. There were things – like he didn't know the conventions for the bibliography in anthropology. We have a convention where you don't capitalise every single word in a book title, and I had a twenty-five page bibliography and he went through and put a circle through every single letter he thought should have been capitalised. There were a lot of typing errors, but I got the cheapest typist I could, who typed a lot of things wrong, so that he said things like 'This sentence hasn't got a verb in it'. And the examiner missed the train, so I was waiting for two hours with the other examiner and the supervisor, so in terms of nervous stress it was awful. At the end of it I didn't know if I'd passed, and at Kingsford normally you're told. And they didn't say 'Well done' or anything. It was just 'We want the typing mistakes corrected in three weeks'.

This account displays features common to complaints and atrocity stories. Notably, extreme formulations are used. A stressful viva examination (and some of the problems are, the informant admits, of her own making), and having to wait for the examiner, are described in terms of 'human rights' violations. But it would be easy to treat the extreme formulations at face value and to present this story as prima facie evidence of extremely difficult vivas, and pointing to all sorts of problems inherent in the system. Such formulations are, of course, more obviously reportable than the sort of account we present below, where nothing ghastly is reported, and hence there is apparently little that is newsworthy.

> Mine was really nice, which seemed quite unusual, because a lot of people have had horrible vivas. I had an internal examiner who I actually knew, and who was very interested in the development side of things I was talking about, and was the more critical of the two. The external examiner was interested in other aspects of the theory and was in fact very supportive of what I'd done. So all the days preparing for it, thinking there were masses of holes they could pick in it, and in fact they didn't. My external liked what I'd done, and didn't really have an awful lot to say. There were certain questions about slants of interpretation, why I'd done something a certain way, which I think I satisfied them ... The internal was much more the critical of the two and actually had some major quibbles with my conclusion, though he felt there were things that could be put right in a publication, it didn't affect the value of the thesis as a thesis.

It is, of course, noticeable that, far from displaying extreme formulations, accounts like this one tend to downplay any problems: the internal examiner's criticisms are reduced to 'quibbles', for instance.

This is clearly not an exhaustive analysis of all the possibly relevant discursive features of such interview materials. We present them here for illustrative purposes, in order to demonstrate the relevance of our general contention to current and future research in higher education.

THE FUTURE OF NARRATIVE RESEARCH IN HIGHER EDUCATION

To some extent, the foregoing discussion must be counted an auto-critique on our part. When we first reported our own study of doctoral students and their supervisors, we did not subject the analysis to this sort of formal analysis. But as we have illustrated, analyses that go beyond the thematic analysis of content can demonstrably develop our understanding of academics' and students' standpoints. As we hope to have demonstrated, there is a valuable role for narrative research in studies of higher education. We are not advocating a complete moratorium on the collection of narratives and accounts. In common with others, we are advocating a methodical and disciplined approach to their analysis. Accounts of academic life in higher education, including the conduct of research, are replete with stories and speech acts. Academics are, indeed, adept at constructing such narratives. They are part of their stock-in-trade, and they help to construct their professional identities.

Narratives of all kinds are a valuable source of insight. However, they must be recognised for what they are — rhetorical performances — and they need to be collected with that understanding at the forefront of the researcher's thinking. They needed to be collected with a greater attention paid to social context and researcher reflexivity; but above all they must be analysed.

There is no point at all in carrying forward the naïve idea that narratives are a transparent source of 'facts' about higher education, or a direct route to an interior authentic self. The narrative self should not be valorised, especially as a unique, suffering self. The latter is an especially prevalent danger in some contemporary fields: a form of pathetic fallacy that conflates the social sciences with a preoccupation with persons' feelings and emotions. In other words, the main point of our discussion here is a call for more sophisticated treatments of narratives and other data from interviews. There are, to put it bluntly, too many lazy publications that are underanalysed, identifying and reproducing raw chunks of interview transcript as if they spoke for themselves, or adopting credulous attitudes towards informants' accounts.

REFERENCES

Abu-Lughod, L. (1993). *Writing women's worlds: Bedouin stories.* Berkeley, CA: University of California Press.

Atkinson, P. A. (1997). Narrative turn or blind alley? *Qualitative Health Research, 7*(3), 325–344.

Atkinson, P. A. (2009). Illness narratives revisited: The failure of narrative reductionism. *Sociological Research Online, 14*, p. 5. Retrieved from www.socresonline.org.uk/14/5/16.html

Atkinson, P. A. (2010). Negotiating the contested terrain of illness narratives − An appreciative response. *Sociology of Health and Illness, 32*(4), 661–662.

Atkinson, P. A., & Delamont, S. (2006a). Rescuing narrative from qualitative research. *Narrative Inquiry, 16*(1), 164–172.

Atkinson, P. A., & Delamont, S. (Eds.) (2006b). *Narrative methods. Four volumes.* London: Sage.

Atkinson, P. A., Seweryn, A., & Tirini, S. (2011). Knowing selves: Biographical research in Europe. *International Review of Qualitative Research, 4*(4), 461–486.

Atkinson, P. A., & Silverman, D. (1997). Kundera's immortality: The interview society and the invention of the self. *Qualitative Inquiry, 3*, 304–325.

Bamberg, M. (Ed.). (2007). *Narrative − State of the art.* Amsterdam: John Benjamins.

Batchelor, C., Parsons, E., & Atkinson, P. (1996). The career of a medical discovery. *Qualitative Health Research, 6*(2), 224–255.

Batchelor, C., Parsons, E., & Atkinson, P. (1997). The rhetoric of prediction, skill and chance in the research to clone a disease gene. In M. A. Elston (Ed.), *The sociology of medical science and technology* (pp. 101–125). Oxford: Blackwell.

Becher, T., Henkel, M., & Kogan, M. (1994). *Graduate education in Britain.* London: Jessica Kingsley.

Behar, R. (1996). *The vulnerable observer: Anthropology that breaks your heart.* Boston, MA: Beacon.

Behar, R. (2007). *An island called home: Returning to Jewish Cuba.* New Brunswick, NJ: Rutgers University Press.

Bochner, A. (2010). Resisting the mystification of narrative inquiry. *Sociology of Health and Illness, 32*(4), 662–665.

Burgess, R. G. (Ed.). (1994). *Postgraduate education and training in the social sciences.* London: Jessica Kingsley.

Chase, S. E. (1995). *Ambiguous empowerment.* Amherst, MA: University of Massachusetts Press.

Clark, B. R. (Ed.). (1993). *The research foundations of graduate education.* Berkeley, CA: California University Press.

Cortazzi, M. (1991). *Narrative analysis.* London: Falmer.

Cortazzi, M. (1993). *Primary teaching: How it is: A narrative account.* London: David Fulton.

Cortazzi, M. (2001). Narrative analysis in ethnography. In P. Atkinson, A. Coffey, S. Delamont, J. Lofland, & L. Lofland (Eds.), *Handbook of ethnography* (pp. 384–394). London: Sage.

Delamont, S. (2003). *Feminist sociology.* London: Sage.

Delamont, S., Atkinson, P. A., & Parry, O. (2000). *The doctoral experience.* London: Falmer.

Delamont, S., Atkinson, P. A., & Pugsley, L. (2010). The concept smacks of magic: Fighting familiarity today. *Teaching and Teacher Education, 26*(1), 3–10.

Dingwall, R. (1977). Atrocity stories. *Work and Occupations, 4*(4), 371–396.

Faubion, J. (2001). Currents of cultural fieldwork. In P. Atkinson, A. Coffey, S. Delamont, J. Lofland, & L. Lofland (Eds.), *Handbook of ethnography* (pp. 39–59). London: Sage.

Frank, A. W. (1995). *The wounded storyteller.* Chicago, IL: The University of Chicago Press.

Frank, A. W. (2006). Health stories as connectors and subjectifiers. *Health: An Interdisciplinary Journal, 10*(4), 421–440.

Frank, A. W. (2010). In defence of narrative exceptionalism. *Sociology of Health and Illness, 32*(4), 665–667.

Gilbert, G. N., & Mulkay, M. (1984). *Opening Pandora's box.* Cambridge: Cambridge University Press.

Goodson, I. (1995). The story so far: Personal knowledge and the political. *International Journal of Qualitative Studies of Education, 8*(1), 89–98.

Hargreaves, A. (1984). Contrastive rhetoric and extremist talk. In A. Hargreaves & P. Woods (Eds.), *Classrooms and staffrooms.* Milton Keynes: Open University Press.

Heath, S. B. (1982). Questioning ant home and at school. In G. Spindler (Ed.), *Doing the ethnography of schooling.* New York, NY: Holt, Rinehart and Winston.

Heath, S. B. (1983). *Ways with words.* Cambridge: Cambridge University Press.

Heyl, B. S. (1979). *The madam as entrepreneur.* New Brunswick, NJ: Transaction Books.

Holstein, J. A., & Gubrium, J. F. (Eds.). (2012). *Varieties of narrative analysis.* Thousand Oaks, CA: Sage.

Hughes, M. L. (1961). *The fantastic lodge.* Greenwich, CO: Fawcett.

Hymes, D. (1981). *In vain I tried to tell you: Essays in native American ethnopoetics.* Philadelphia, PA: University of Pennsylvania Press.

Kleinman, A. (1988). *The illness narratives.* New York, NY: Basic Books.

Labov, W. (2013). *The language of life and death: The transformation of experience in oral narrative.* Cambridge: Cambridge University Press.

Labov, W., & Waletsky, J. (1967). Narrative analysis: Oral versions of personal experience. In J. Holm (Ed.), *Essays on the verbal and visual arts.* Seattle, WA: University of Washington Press.

Leach, E. R. (1969). *Genesis as myth and other essays.* London: Cape.

Menchù, R. (1984). *I, Rigoberta Menchù.* London: Verso.

Middleton, S. (2001). *Educating researchers: New Zealand education PhDs 1948–1998.* Palmerston North: New Zealand Association for Research in Education.

Mishler, E. (1984). *The discourse of medicine.* Norwood, NJ: Ablex.

Morley, L., Leonard, D., & David, M. (2002). Variations in vivas. *Studies in Higher Education, 27*(3), 263–274.

Mulkay, M. (1985). Noblesse oblige: An analytical parody. In M. Mulkay (Ed.), *The word and the world* (pp. 237–256). London: Allen and Unwin.

Mullins, G., & Kiley, M. (2002). It's a PhD not a Nobel Prize. *Studies in Higher Education, 27*(4), 369–386.

Plummer, K. (1995). *Telling sexual stories: Power, change and social worlds.* London: Routledge.

Plummer, K. (2001). *Documents of life 2: An invitation to critical humanism.* London: Sage.

Pole, C. (2000). Technicians and scholars in pursuit of the PhD. *Research Papers in Education, 15*(1), 95–111.

Propp, V. (1968). *Morphology of the folk tale.* Austin, TX: University of Texas Press.

Sampson, C., & Atkinson, P. (2011). Accounting for discovery. *Narrative Inquiry, 21*(1), 88–108.

Sampson, C., & Atkinson, P. (2013). The golden star: Emotion, legacy and scientific discovery. *Sociological Review, 61*(3), 573–590.

Shaw, C. (1930). *The jackroller: A delinquent boy's own story.* Chicago, IL: University of Chicago Press.

Snodgrass, J. (1982). *The jackroller at seventy.* Lexington, MA: D.C. Heath.

Stoll, D. (1999). *Rigoberta Menchu and the story of all poor Guatemalans.* Boulder, CO: Westview.

Thomas, C. (2010). Negotiating the contested terrain of narrative methods in illness contexts. *Sociology of Health and Illness, 32*(4), 647–660.

Tinkler, P., & Jackson, C. (2000). Examining the doctorate. *Studies in Higher Education, 25*(2), 167–180.

Tucker, E. (Ed.). (2005). *Campus legends: A handbook.* Westport, CT: Greenwood.

Witherill, C., & Noddings, N. (Eds.). (1997). *Stories lives tell: Narrative and dialogue in education.* New York, NY: Teachers College Press.

METHODOLOGICAL MEDITATIONS ON PRODUCING RICH NARRATIVE DATA

Cecilia Jacobs

ABSTRACT

This chapter focuses on the methodological implications of producing rich narrative data about higher education at the meso-level. While micro- and macro-level higher education studies often miss out on the nuances of the practices that happen in between, meso-level research straddles these levels, often bringing both 'structuralist' and 'agentic' tensions into interplay. The chapter highlights the importance of the academic 'workgroup' as a unit of analysis in understanding the interplay between the micro-level of individuals in academia and the macro-levels of the university and the higher education sector. The study investigated the practices of a 'workgroup' of academics who engaged in a common project over a period of three years. Researching how academics make meaning of their practices requires the use of alternative methodologies which are relatively under-utilised in higher education. The methodologies and iterative data production strategies used in the study are discussed in the chapter, including the processes of grounded open coding and segmentation of the data, as well as the levels of discourse analysis.

Theory and Method in Higher Education Research II
International Perspectives on Higher Education Research, Volume 10, 63–81
Copyright © 2014 by Emerald Group Publishing Limited
All rights of reproduction in any form reserved
ISSN: 1479-3628/doi:10.1108/S1479-3628(2014)0000010009

*Finally the chapter provides some reflections on the data analysis pro-
cess, highlighting the challenges for data production when conducting a
meso-level analysis.*

INTRODUCTION

This chapter engages the question of which methodologies produce rich
data about higher education at the meso-level. Trowler (2005a, p. 16) refers
to the meso-level as 'the missing level of analysis', and describes it as 'the
point of social interaction by small groups such as exist in the classroom, in
the university department, in the curriculum-planning team or in a hundred
other task-based teams within the higher educational system'. Researching
at the meso-level raises interesting methodological issues, according to
Trowler and Cooper (2002), since conflict and lack of consensus tend to
characterise what happens at this level. Qualitative research provides a key
means of developing knowledge about the rapidly changing nature of
higher education, and the use of 'fine-grained' research methods (Trowler,
2012) produces the kind of data needed for a fresh look at the complexities
in the field of higher education.

The study referred to in this chapter, fully explicated elsewhere (Jacobs,
2007), was situated at the meso-level of higher education, and attempted
to understand the academic literacy practices of a 'workgroup' of 20 academics who engaged in a common project over a period of three years. The
meso-level research conducted in the study highlighted the importance of
what Trowler refers to as the academic 'workgroup' as a unit of analysis in
understanding the interplay between the micro-level of individuals in academia, and the macro-levels of institution and higher education. It thus starts
to address the gap in meso-level educational analysis and theory development that Trowler raises. The study examined how the 20 academics, who
worked collaboratively in 10 partnerships between academic literacy and
disciplinary specialists, constructed their understandings of a collaborative
approach to the teaching of academic literacies. The primary focus of the
research was on how these 10 pairs of collaborating academics negotiated
understandings of their academic literacy teaching practices, and how
this process influenced their conceptualisations of academic literacies.
Researching how academics understand and make meaning of their practices
requires the use of alternative methodologies which are relatively under-
utilised in higher education. Researchers such as Clegg (2007) challenge

higher education researchers to ask difficult questions about what mechanisms are at work in higher education. This has implications for the methodological approaches most suited to answer difficult questions. The research questions underpinning the study referred to in this chapter were of the 'meaning-making' kind, attempting to explore lecturers' understandings of their academic literacy teaching practices, and the methodological approaches most suited to answering these questions were of the 'fine-grained' kind.

This chapter focuses broadly on the methodological implications of producing rich narrative data retrospectively; in this case, when research participants reflect on processes and practices which have taken place in the past. After an initial focus on issues of theory and method, the chapter covers the iterative stages in the data production phase, and outlines the processes of grounded open coding and segmentation of the data, which preceded the discourse analysis. The focus then shifts to an explication of the two levels of discourse analysis that were applied to the data, namely, representational and presentational. Finally, I will offer some of my reflections as a researcher about the significance of meso-level analysis and its ability to mediate between the micro- and the macro-levels of higher education, often bringing both 'structuralist' and 'agentic' tensions into interplay.

THEORY AND METHOD

The study was situated both theoretically and methodologically within an academic literacies framing. Lillis and Scott (2007) argue that 'academic literacies' as a field of inquiry constitutes a particular epistemology, that of literacy-as-social-practice, and a specific ideology, that of transformation. They also characterise 'academic literacies' as an approach through which *practice* is privileged above *text*. This has both theoretical and methodological implications. The privileging of *practice*, together with understandings of literacy-as-social-practice, calls for particular methodologies. Lillis and Scott (2007, p. 11) argue that the principal empirical methodology inherent in such an ideological model of literacy is that of ethnography, which involves both the observation of practices, as well as participants' perspectives on their practices. The emphasis is thus on what they term 'dialogic methodologies' and 'a commitment to staying rooted in people's lived experiences', in 'an attempt to explore what may be at stake for them in specific contexts' (Lillis & Scott, 2007, p. 13). The methodological challenge for the study referred to in this chapter was that it retrospectively explored the participants' perspectives on their practices. In looking back on a lived experience, as it were, understandings of these practices could not be explored through traditional ethnographic methodologies, such as the observation of practices in real time. Instead the study engaged participants in a process of reflection on three years of collaborative academic literacy teaching practices. Towards this end narrative methodology and life history approaches were used to explore retrospectively the processes that occurred among the 20 academics as they negotiated understandings of their academic literacy teaching practices.

METHODOLOGICAL CONSIDERATIONS

The study immersed itself in what Lather (1991, 2006) refers to as the pro-liferation of paradigms. Rather than aligning the study with a particular paradigm and adopting 'the kind of methodolatry where the tail of metho-dology wags the dog of inquiry' (Lather, 2006, p. 47), I examined what was methodologically appropriate at each phase of the data production process and flexibly pursued an iterative process of data collection, where each layer of the data production process became a springboard for a deeper probing into the participants' understandings of academic literacies. As the focus of the study was on the process underpinning a collaborative approach to the teaching of academic literacies, as well as on how the parti-cipants understood this process, it was appropriate to use 'ex post facto' or existing data rather than real time data, and then design a data production plan that enabled participants to recall and reflect on past experiences, as well as explore their own understandings.

Although the overarching approach to data production was through nar-rative methodology, I drew on life history research methods (Goodson & Numan, 2003; Goodson & Sikes, 2001) to collect data about participants' experiences of their three-year, collaborative academic literacy teaching practices. Towards this end the study included photographs and various other artefacts from the three-year period as visual stimuli, displayed in the data production space, in an effort to stimulate participants' recall of their experiences and provide an environment for in-depth reflections. The space in which the data was produced thus became a methodological tool in the study and enabled research participants to reflect on their past experiences.

The study also drew on grounded theory approaches (Glaser, 2002), where the emphasis was not on how accurately the data described reality, but rather on the abstractions or concepts emerging from the data, what Maxwell (1992) refers to as theoretical validity. Trowler (2012, p. 276) makes the point that in such fine-grained qualitative research 'knowledge-ability and sense-making are foregrounded because explanation is sought more than correlation'. The onus is, therefore, on the researcher, to carefully compare data from many different participants. In my study the data was internally validated by looking at 20 cases of the same phenomenon (a collaborative approach to the teaching of academic literacies), when jointly collecting and coding the data. Such 'close-up' research presents particular problems in terms of the theory–data relationship, as Trowler points out. As an 'insider', conducting emic or bottom-up research, I was influenced not only by my own tacit theories, but also by those held by the participants.

The purpose of employing narrative and life history methods in the study was to enable the research participants to reflect on their experiences in a way that would better produce rich data. According to Labov (1997), it is when participants 'change mode', such as from answering predetermined interview questions to telling their stories in an informal and relaxed mode, that those who are good story-tellers produce elaborated narratives containing important insights. Thus, the interviewing process in the study was largely a passive listening on the part of the researcher. In the grounded theory approach however, while the initial purpose of interviews is to elicit data without interrupting the narrator, later data production (such as the focus group sessions in the study) involved focussed questions based on emergent categories.

Ethnographers such as Lather (1991), Widdershoven (1993), St Pierre & Pillow (2000) and Tierney (2002) point out that the narratives produced by research participants are not unproblematic. Data produced in this way is a result of a negotiated relationship between the researcher and narrator. As the researcher determines who narrates, and provides the topic around which the story is to be told, the relationship between researcher and narrator is asymmetrical. The researcher needs to be constantly aware of this asymmetry as the descriptive data analysis proceeds, to avoid sanitising the quality of the data produced (Reissman, 1993). In grounded theory however, 'all is data' (Glaser, 2001), and researcher influence is not seen as impacting on the quality of the data. According to Glaser (2002, p. 12), grounded theory sees 'researcher impact on data as just one more variable to consider whenever it emerges as relevant. It is like all grounded theory categories and properties; it must earn its relevance'. Researcher bias is thus seen as part of the research, not something to be covered up, and a vital variable to weave into the constant comparative analysis. The research site provided a research environment in which constant comparative analysis could take place, as the collaborative practices being studied took place within 10 different partnerships, across 10 different disciplines of study. This was an important factor in ensuring theoretical validity.

Qualitative research is seldom concerned with generalisability as a way of ensuring external validity. What is of more general concern in qualitative studies, in an effort to validate such studies, is what Lincoln and Guba (1985) refer to as 'transferability'. Transferability is about 'thick description', where the onus is on the researcher to provide rich, contextual detail that would enable the reader to determine how transferable, or not, the researcher's insights and interpretations are within their own context. Maxwell (1992, p. 115) raises an interesting methodological perspective when he says that 'the value of a qualitative study may depend on its lack of external generalizability in a statistical sense; it may provide an account of a setting or population that is illuminating as an extreme case or "ideal type"'. I regarded my study as something of an 'ideal type', because the practices being studied were not typical. A more typical scenario would be isolated and fragmented practices, often by individuals working without institutional co-ordination. The context for this study was a common set of collaborative practices that were happening simultaneously in many different institutional sites, yet all connected through an institutional project. This can be seen as an extreme set of cases or 'ideal types'. Its research value is, then, in illuminating the processes underpinning this unusual case, which in turn could address similar possibilities at other higher education sites. It also has research value in providing a more compelling argument for how the teaching of academic literacies might be done differently than would a study of more typical practices. The unit of analysis in the study was, therefore, a co-ordinated collaborative approach to the teaching of academic literacies, and the focus of the study was on both the process underpinning this approach, as well as on how the participants understood this process and constructed themselves within it.

Sampling was not applied in the first round of data production, in an effort to achieve theoretical validity, which required that the researcher compared data from many different participants. This also builds the credibility of the data, what Lincoln and Guba (1985) refer to as 'referential adequacy' or a well-developed data corpus. Towards these ends all participants involved in the institutionally co-ordinated project were invited into the research study. In the second round of data production, which was based on emergent categories from the first round of data, some theoretical sampling (Strauss, 1987) was used for the final focus group sessions. The goals of this type of sampling are to make sure that the researcher has 'adequately understood the variation in the phenomena of interest in the setting, and to test developing ideas about that setting by selecting phenomena that are crucial to the validity of those ideas' (Maxwell, 1992, p. 293). These developing ideas, emerging from the first round of data, were then distributed to all participants as a preliminary analysis of the data and formed the basis for two of the focus group sessions. Lincoln and Guba (1985) refer to this process as member checks, which further build the credibility of the data.

The technique of 'purposive' (Cohen & Manion, 1994), or 'purposeful' (Patton, 1990) sampling was also applied to the final focus group session, where the developed categories and their developing relationships were tested with a group of participants. The criteria for selection were equal numbers of academic literacy and disciplinary specialists, a range of disciplines, the ability to articulate conceptualisations, as well as the typicality of emerging constructs. These criteria were regarded as important because, in testing the developing theoretical constructs, the participants needed to be typical sources of these constructs and needed to have the ability to articulate their thinking in order to engage with the constructs. Theoretical sampling, such as this, requires that the participants sampled provide the researcher with the maximum opportunity to discover variations among concepts and to densify categories in terms of their properties and dimensions (Strauss & Corbin, 1998).

DISCUSSION OF DATA PRODUCTION STRATEGIES

When research interrogates higher education practices, and the focus is on the processes underpinning such practices, it is often appropriate to use 'ex post facto' (Freeman, 1996b) data rather than real time data. This was the case in this study, as there was a focus on how the participants understood the process underpinning their practices, and also how they constructed themselves within their practices. This type of data requires a data production plan that enables participants to recall and reflect on past experiences. My strategies included different methods of stimulated recall, such as a 'memory room' and personalised portfolios, and reflective freewriting, visual representations, in-depth narrative interviews and focus group sessions. The data production techniques explored three different modalities of communicative expression: oral, written and visual. The oral mode was explored through the narrative interviews and the focus group sessions, while the written mode was explored through the freewriting and the portfolios, and the visual mode was explored through the visual representations created by the participants, as well as the memory rooms prepared by the researcher. Each of these data production strategies was iterative. I employed participant observation and the analysis of documentation as an initial strategy in setting the scene for the narrative interviews, as well as directed focus group sessions as a follow-up to the narrative interviews.

Participant Observation

My 'insider' position had allowed me to observe first-hand many of the processes reflected on by the participants in the study. My observations were recorded through observation notes, e-mails, photographs and video footage, as well as personal reflective statements. This documentation provided a secondary data set against which I was able to verify many of the processes reflected by participants in their freewriting, narrative interviews and focus groups, which comprised the primary data set.

Survey of Documentation

The purpose of the survey of documentation was to create a 'memory room' and to develop a personalised portfolio for each participant. These strategies were in preparation for the stimulated recall sessions which were a crucial part of the process towards producing the deep, rich data required to answer the research questions.

The Memory Rooms

The memory rooms were created using various project resources surveyed in the documentation survey process, in an effort to stimulate participants' recall of their experiences and provide an environment for in-depth reflections. The memory rooms were used as a methodological space in two ways in the data production process. In the first instance they were created as a space to house all research participants for a collaborative freewriting exercise, and in the second instance as a space within which to conduct the individual narrative interviews. The memory rooms were a large part of the stimulated recall strategy; therefore a familiar space was chosen. The choice of venue was an important part of the data collection process as the space itself was charged with memories for the participants, a factor which many of them noted. The effect of the space as a methodological tool, in creating memories for the participants, was very evident in the interviews. A number of participants commented on this during the narrative interviews, and some even incorporated the visual displays of project memorabilia into their reflective narratives.

The Freewriting Exercise

All research participants were invited to participate in a freewriting exercise reflecting their lived experience of the collaborative approach to the teaching of academic literacies. They were invited to focus on any aspects of their experience and to write about those aspects that first came to mind or which stood out for them when they thought about their experiences. No further guidelines were given as to content or length, and no time limit was set for the exercise. Most participants wrote for between 20 and 30 minutes. This writing formed part of the personalised portfolios prepared for each participant by the researcher, and they became the 'interview schedule' for the latter parts of each narrative interview.

Personalised Portfolios

The researcher compiled a personalised portfolio as an historical account to trigger the reflections of each participant. The portfolios contained various pieces of documentation, such as photographs, planning documents, joint lesson plans, integrated assessment tasks and so on. The purpose of the portfolio was twofold, to stimulate participants' recall of their experiences in preparation for the narrative interviews, and to serve as a reflective tool to aid participants in their creation of a visual representation of their lived experiences of the collaborative approach to the teaching of academic literacies.

Visual Representations

Each of the participants was requested to create a visual representation of their lived experiences of the collaborative approach to the teaching of academic literacies. They were given the freedom to focus on any aspects of their experiences, particularly those aspects that first came to mind and those issues which stood out for them. They were also asked to reflect both the good and the bad experiences in the visual, by focussing on moments, feelings, people, activities, processes, places or events that were significant to them. The form of the visual representation was left entirely up to the individual participant and a range of forms emerged, such as mindmaps, drawings, collages, a comic strip and even an unfolding board game. These visual representations were collected before the narrative interviews took place and became the 'interview schedule' for the first half of each narrative interview.

The Narrative Interviews

All the research participants were interviewed over a period of two months. The planning of the interviews over this short period of time was an important part of the iterative data production process. Although this was a very intensive period for the researcher, the timeframe allowed for ideas and emerging constructs from each interview to shape the exploration and probing for the interviews which followed. This is an important consideration for researchers following a grounded theory approach, where the nature of the emerging constructs is undefined and often articulated and understood in different ways by different participants. The interviews were unstructured and individually conducted. There was no common interview schedule, with each interview constructed around data produced by the individual participants themselves.

Each interview had roughly the same structure. The first part of the interview was the narrative section, where the respondent was encouraged to deconstruct the visual representation they had created, uninterrupted by the researcher. A similar methodology was employed by Prior and Shipka (2003, p. 185) in their attempts to generate 'a thick description of literate activity' in their narrative interviews with academic writers. The second part of the interview tended to be a question and answer session, where the researcher probed more deeply into areas of the visual representation and explored some of the issues raised by the respondent in the earlier deconstruction of the visual. The third part of the interview focused on the freewriting, and was also a question and answer session, where the researcher explored in more detail the issues raised by the respondent in the freewriting.

The visual representation and the freewriting therefore became the 'interview schedules' which generated the narrative accounts of the participants' experiences. The visual representation and the freewriting also provided the researcher with data in two different modes, visual and written, which enabled the participants to engage with the complexities of their experiences in complementary ways. This clearly contributed to the production of rich data, a factor which was evident in the interview with the participant who had declined to prepare the visual representation. In this interview, which was one of the shortest, the participant seemed unable to tap into some of the complexities of her experience, often remarking that she did not understand why certain processes had taken place in the way that they had. Similarly, in two other short interviews where there had been no freewriting, and where the visual representations had amounted to a list of headings with some key words listed underneath, there was also superficial engagement with experiences and an apparent difficulty in explaining some processes underpinning their experiences. On the other hand, those participants who produced freewriting, as well as complex visual representations which attempted to show the inter-relatedness of their experiences, yielded rich interview data which tapped into a range of complexities and often ran into a full two hours of interviewing.

The Focus Group Sessions

Three focus group sessions took place after all the narrative interviews had been transcribed and a preliminary analysis had taken place. This preliminary analysis was distributed to all participants for reading and comment before the focus group sessions took place. Each focus group session was with a different grouping of participants. The first session was with the academic literacies specialists only, the second session was with the disciplinary specialists only and the final session was with a mix of both groups. The focus group sessions were set up in this way so that the developing ideas, emerging from across participants' interviews in the first round of data production, could be further explored. It was clear, from a preliminary analysis of the first round of data production that a number of the emerging issues were around differences between academic literacies and disciplinary specialists. Trowler (2012) raises the contested nature and status of fine-grained data as a 'wicked' issue. In my study it was clear in the early stages of analysis that this contestation required further exploration. In an effort to further explore these differences openly, the researcher chose to engage with academic literacies and disciplinary specialists separately, so that they would feel free to speak candidly about these differences.

The first two focus group sessions were set up in the same way. All of the academic literacies specialists were invited to participate in the first focus group session, and all of the disciplinary specialists were invited to participate in the second focus group session. In both focus group sessions, fragments of transcriptions from the narrative interviews were selected and used to stimulate discussion. Both focus groups were given the same transcribed fragments, which were selected because they illustrated the developing ideas emerging from across participants' interviews in the first round of data production. Participants were given an opportunity to peruse the fragments at the start of the session, after which they were asked to respond to what was being raised in them.

The third focus group session sought to bring together the two groups. As the total number of participants was too unwieldy for a focus group session, it was decided to select from the group using theoretical sampling. Four academic literacies and four disciplinary specialists were invited to participate in this final focus group session. This session was planned drawing on a method referred to in the activity theory literature as a 'boundary crossing laboratory' (Engeström, 2001). This method aims to confront various 'actors' involved in a particular 'activity' with the internal tensions and dynamics in their respective institutional contexts. These dynamics, according to Engeström, can, by their own inner contradictions, energise a serious learning effort on the parts of such actors. While the context of my study was quite different to that of Engeström's, I felt that there were enough synergies for the method to be adapted for my final focus group session. The transformative agenda inherent in the method was in synergy with the theoretical framing within which my study was located. The boundary crossing laboratory focus on tensions was also synergistic with the preliminary data analysis of my study, in which a number of the emerging issues were around the dynamics resulting from differences between academic literacies and disciplinary specialists. Although the context of my study was higher education and Engeström's context was health care, they are very similar in that the 'communities of practice' being investigated in both contexts were not well-bounded functional systems or centres of co-ordination. In the case of my study, the 'community of practice' was bounded by its co-ordination as an institutional project with a limited life-span, rather than a more stable locus of control embedded in existing institutional systems.

The boundary crossing laboratory method was adapted for the final focus group session in that it was applied to only a single session, a factor which limits the transformative agenda somewhat, in that the learning challenge is dealt with in a once-off way, rather than through a series of learning events occurring 'in a changing mosaic of interconnected activity systems' (Engeström, 2001, p. 140). Another adaptation was that, in recreating the activity systems between the academic literacies and the disciplinary specialists, for the boundary crossing laboratory, I was bound by ethical considerations and issues relating to the theoretical validity of the study. In the ethical interests of participant confidentiality and anonymity, and in the theoretical validity interests of abstraction, I was obliged to use the theoretical abstractions arising from the data analysis process as the 'case' to be discussed, rather than an actual case involving collaboration between academic literacies and disciplinary specialists. This adaptation favoured the research agenda above the transformative agenda.

REFLECTIONS ON THE DATA ANALYSIS

The choice of data analysis strategies is as crucial to the quality of 'fine-grained research methods' as the data production techniques. A range of options are available to the researcher. Freeman (1996b) presents us with a continuum of categories ranging from a priori analysis, through guided analysis and negotiated analysis, to grounded analysis. A priori analysis refers to categories of data analysis that are determined before the process of data production commences. Guided analysis refers to categories of data analysis that are determined a priori and which guide the analysis, but which are modified through interaction with the data as the process of analysis unfolds. In a negotiated analysis, both the categories and the process of analysis is developed by the researcher in conjunction with input from the research participants. In grounded analysis, both the categories and the analysis emerge from the data, with a priori expectation on the part of the researcher at a minimum. It can be argued that the grounded analysis end of the continuum is never completely grounded, as the researcher is never innocent in the data production process, having designed the research process in a particular way.

Although I would argue that the first round of data analysis in my study was closer to the grounded analysis end of the continuum than to any of the other points on the continuum, it has to be acknowledged that certain choices in the data production phase, such as how the memory rooms were set up and how the personalised project portfolios were compiled, were not untainted by the researcher's position. The second round of data analysis in my study, however, was closer to the negotiated analysis point on the continuum. Having established the categories and completed a preliminary data analysis in a more grounded way, the second round of data analysis sought to refine and sharpen the categories and preliminary analysis through a process of negotiation with the research participants.

Discourse Analysis

The narrated data (in the form of transcribed narrative interviews and focus groups) were analysed using discourse analysis at the level of 'meaning beyond the clause' (Martin & Rose, 2003, p. 1). There are different ways of analysing narrated data. Structural analysis, which involves analysis at the whole 'text' level, looks at the interview transcript as a whole and analyses the rhetorical moves at the text level. Then there is linguistic analysis, also known as 'micro-analysis', which operates at the micro-level of words and sentences. I was looking at a level somewhere between these two. I was interested in analysing what the research participants were mobilising, through what they said (or didn't say) and how they said it. This required me to look at a level of meaning beyond the isolated word or clause, but also at meanings located within smaller chunks of text than a whole interview. Discourse analysis was well suited to this purpose, and I employed two levels of discourse analysis, referred to as representational analysis and presentational analysis (Freeman, 1996a).

According to Freeman, representational analysis treats language data as information, by studying what is said and not necessarily how it is said. Presentational analysis studies the relationships embodied in language data, by studying how the language is conveying meaning through the use of words. So, language itself becomes the locus of study. These approaches are, in Freeman's opinion, complementary and largely inseparable, and should be integrated to enhance and deepen data analysis and interpretation of findings. Such integration of representational and presentational analysis strengthens the validity of the study, in that the researcher is now able to show evidence of the processes of learning, self-definition and change underpinning what participants are saying. The integration of these two levels of analysis in this study revealed both *what* participants had learned from their practices, and what had changed for them, as well as *how* it had been learned and how the change occurred.

Grounded Analysis

The primary data used in the first-level analysis comprised the verbatim transcripts of the narrative interviews, as well as the freewriting produced by the participants. Following a grounded analysis, this data was systematically analysed using a bottom-up strategy which aimed to develop conceptual categories from the patterns emerging from the data, and ultimately to produce theory. As soon as the first batch of transcripts became available, a process of open coding commenced. Open coding (Strauss & Corbin, 1998) is an analytic task involving three processes, naming concepts, defining categories and developing categories in terms of their properties and dimensions.

Open coding is an attempt by the researcher to open up the text to explore thoughts, ideas and meaning within it. By breaking the data down into discrete parts, the researcher is able to examine it closely and compare data across sources for similarities and differences. From an open coding of the first transcripts and freewriting, a number of concepts emerged across the data. These concepts were named and loosely defined as five broad categories, which were each developed with four sub-categories as the interviewing was completed. A first-level analysis was then circulated to all participants, and the properties and dimensions of these categories were further developed. The initial five broad categories were then refined into four broad categories as a result of the three focus group sessions, which were also recorded and transcribed, adding to the primary data set for further analysis.

The second level of analysis was representational, in that I was closely examining what was being said in order to refine the grounded categories emerging from the first level of analysis. In the second level of analysis, therefore, the developed categories from the level one analysis were further refined. The third level of analysis was presentational, in that I was analysing how the language was conveying meaning through the use of words. This level of analysis complemented the representational analysis and enabled me to gain insight into the thinking of the participants in a way that a representational analysis alone was not able to do. The presentational level of analysis was layered onto the representational level of analysis for each new sub-category, for each of the four broad conceptual categories generated by the first-level grounded analysis.

In an attempt to foreground the voices of the participants, I chose to intersperse the representational analysis with chunks of transcript from the narrative interviews, freewriting and focus groups. This was in an attempt to avoid extensive 'thick descriptions', typical in ethnographic studies, which sometimes overwhelm the meaning intended by the participant. Harrison (2003) cautions against researchers becoming the authority for the knowledge gained, and speaking for the participants, leading to a situation where the meaning of the quote is overwhelmed by the researcher's writing, and the quote is understood only through what the researcher has said, rather than through the words of the participant. Rather than narrating the story of their lived experiences as research participants in my words, I chose to thematically weave their words into a narrative interspersed with representational and presentational analyses. In this way I drew the data into the analysis.

METHODOLOGICAL MEDITATIONS

While most research into higher education focuses on either the macro-level, such as the many higher education policy studies, or the micro-level, such as the many studies focussing on lecturers or students, there is a lack of integration between macro- and micro-level analyses at the meso-level (Trowler, 2012), where the focus is on interaction by small teams or 'work-groups' in higher education. Trowler (2005b) situates workgroups at a level just below the academic department, and defines them as groups of academics who engage in some common project over a period of time. He claims that it is at the level of workgroups that higher education studies are best able to understand the interplay between subjectivities and socio-cultural practices.

Trowler problematises both micro- and macro-level higher education studies, which he claims miss out on much of the practices that happen in between. He asserts that micro-level studies, which tend to focus on the individual, often stress agency over structure and psychological over socio-cultural factors, while macro-level studies tend to emphasise structure and essentialise the epistemological. Trowler critiques 'methodological individualism', which he sees as the dominant approach to educational research, for failing to capture social processes, and proposes alternative approaches, such as ethnography, focus groups, discourse analysis, naturally occurring data, observant participation, secondary data, triangulated interviews, insider research and narrativity for meso-level analyses.

This study attempted to move beyond what Trowler refers to as 'agentic' (micro) and 'structuralist' (macro) levels of analysis, towards a 'socio-cultural' approach to analysis which took into account departmental cultures and the discourses through which they were expressed. The methodological implications of this choice are evident in the data production strategies discussed in the chapter. According to Trowler, some of the challenges for data production when conducting a meso-level analysis are surfacing what is implicit, capturing macro influences that might not be apparent to the research participants, and balancing 'emic' (insider or bottom-up) and 'etic' (outsider or top-down) approaches. These challenges were confronted in a variety of ways in the study reported here.

In balancing 'emic' and 'etic' approaches, I used a grounded 'emic' approach which I applied to the data in order to elicit the emerging conceptual categories, which in turn became the 'etic' lens for analysing the data. In surfacing the implicit, I followed an iterative data production process, where each stage of the process was a precursor to, and prepared the space for, deeper reflection in the phase of data production that followed. In capturing macro influences that might not be apparent to the research participants, I applied three different levels of analysis to the data. The first grounded level of analysis sought to systematically analyse the data using a bottom-up strategy that aimed to develop conceptual categories from the patterns emerging across the data set. The second level of analysis was representational, where attention was paid to *what* was being said in order to refine the grounded categories emerging from the first-level analysis. The third level of analysis was presentational, where attention was focused on *how* the language of participants was conveying meaning through the use of words.

The significance of meso-level analysis is that it mediates between the micro- and the macro-levels, often bringing both 'structuralist' and 'agentic' tensions into interplay. This is especially true of academic literacies work, where practitioners have to juggle multiple roles often held in tension. This leads to new ways of understanding higher education that take into account issues of power and identity that permeate all three of these levels. However, such fine-grained analysis at the meso-level is not unproblematic. The iterative nature of the data production process and the layered analysis result in time-consuming and often laborious work for the researcher, which can significantly slow down the research process.

As mentioned at the start of the chapter, the meso-level research conducted in this study highlighted the importance of the academic 'work-group' as a unit of analysis in understanding the interplay between the micro-level of individuals in academia, and the macro-levels of the university and the higher education sector. The layered analysis, which sought to locate the analysis of discourse within its basis in the social structure of the university specifically and the higher education sector generally, suggests that systemic change in academic literacy teaching practices requires the infusion of academic literacy work into the existing systems of the university. This has implications for how academic literacies specialists understand their work in higher education, and for how the university and the higher education sector understand the work of academic literacies specialists.

REFERENCES

Clegg, S. (2007). *Extending the boundaries of research into higher education.* Inaugural lecture. Leeds Metropolitan University. Carnegie Faculty of Sport and Education.

Cohen, L., & Manion, L. (1994). *Research methods in education* (4th ed.). London: Routledge.

Engeström, Y. (2001). Expansive learning at work: Toward an activity theoretical reconceptualisation. *Journal of Education and Work, 14*(1), 133−156.

Freeman, D. (1996a). "To take them at their word": Language data in the study of teachers' knowledge. *Harvard Educational Review, 66*(4), 732−761.

Freeman, D. (1996b). The 'unstudied problem': Research on teacher learning in language teaching. In D. Freeman & J. C. Richards (Eds.), *Teacher learning in language teaching.* Cambridge: Cambridge University Press.

Glaser, B. G. (2001). *The grounded theory perspective: Conceptualization contrasted with description.* Mill Valley, CA: Sociology Press.

Glaser, B. G. (2002). Constructivist grounded theory. *Forum: Qualitative Social Research, 3*(3). Retrieved from http://www.qualitative-research.net/fqs-texte/3-02/3-02glaser-e.htm

Goodson, I., & Numan, U. (Eds.). (2003). *Life history and professional development: Stories of teachers' life and work.* Lund: Studentlitteratur.

Goodson, I., & Sikes, P. (2001). *Life history research in educational settings: Learning from lives.* Buckingham: Open University Press.

Harrison, N. (2003). Grounded theory or grounded data? The production of power and knowledge in ethnographic research. *The Australian Journal of Indigenous Education, 32,* 101−106.

Jacobs, C. (2007). Towards a critical understanding of the teaching of discipline-specific academic literacies: Making the tacit explicit. *Journal of Education, 41,* 59−82.

Labov, W. (1997). Some further steps in narrative analysis. Retrieved from http://www.ling.upenn.edu/~labov/sfs.html

Lather, P. (1991). *Getting smart: Feminist research and pedagogy within the postmodern.* New York, NY: Routledge.

Lather, P. (2006). Paradigm proliferation as a good thing to think with: Teaching research in education as a wild profusion. *International Journal of Qualitative Studies in Education, 19*(1), 35–57.

Lillis, T., & Scott, M. (2007). Defining academic literacies research: Issues of epistemology, ideology and strategy. *Journal of Applied Linguistics, 4*(1), 5–32.

Lincoln, Y. S., & Guba, E. G. (1985). *Naturalistic inquiry.* Beverly Hills, CA: Sage.

Martin, J. R., & Rose, D. (2003). *Working with discourse: Meaning beyond the clause.* London: Continuum.

Maxwell, J. A. (1992). Understanding and validity in qualitative research. *Harvard Educational Review, 62*(3), 279–300.

Patton, M. Q. (1990). *Qualitative research and evaluation methods* (2nd ed.). Newbury Park, CA: Sage.

Prior, P., & Shipka, J. (2003). Chronotopic lamination: Tracing the contours of literate activity. In C. Bazerman & D. Russell (Eds.), *Writing selves/writing societies: Research from activity perspectives.* Fort Collins, CO: The WAC Clearinghouse.

Reissman, C. K. (1993). *Narrative analysis.* London: Sage.

St Pierre, E. A., & Pillow, W. S. (2000). *Working the ruins: Feminist poststructuralist theory and methods in education.* New York, NY: Routledge.

Strauss, A. (1987). *Qualitative analysis for social scientists.* Cambridge: Cambridge University Press.

Strauss, A., & Corbin, J. (1998). *Basics of qualitative research: Techniques and procedures for developing grounded theory.* Thousand Oaks, CA: Sage.

Tierney, W. G. (2002). Get real: Representing reality. *International Journal of Qualitative Studies in Education, 15*(4), 385–398.

Trowler, P. (2005a). A sociology of teaching, learning and enhancement: Improving practices in higher education. *Revista de Sociologia, 76*, 13–32.

Trowler, P. (2005b). *Rethinking teaching and learning regimes in higher education: Lessons from South Africa.* Invited talk to the Centre for Higher Education Development, University of Cape Town, South Africa.

Trowler, P. (2012). Wicked issues in situating theory in close-up research. *Higher Education Research & Development, 31*(3), 273–284.

Trowler, P., & Cooper, A. (2002). Teaching and learning regimes: Implicit theories and recurrent practices in the enhancement of teaching and learning through educational development programmes. *Higher Education Research and Development, 21*(3), 221–240.

Widdershoven, G. A. M. (1993). The story of life: Hermeneutic perspectives on the relationship between narrative and life history. In R. Josselson & A. Lieblich (Eds.), *The narrative study of lives* (Vol. 1). London: Sage.

MORE-THAN-HUMAN THEORISING – *INCLUSIVE* COMMUNITIES OF PRACTICE IN STUDENT PRACTICE-BASED LEARNING

Paul Hodge, Sarah Wright and Fee Mozeley

ABSTRACT

How might deeply embodied student experiences and nonhuman agency change the way we think about learning theory? Pushing the conceptual boundaries of practice-based learning and communities of practice, this chapter draws on student experiential fieldwork 'on Country' with Indigenous people in the Northern Territory (NT), Australia, to explore the peculiar silence when it comes to more-than-human[1] features of situated learning models. As students engage with, and learn from, Indigenous epistemologies and ontologies, they become open to the ways their learning is co-produced in and with place. The chapter builds a case for an inclusive conceptualisation of communities of practice, one that takes seriously the material performativity of nonhuman actors – rock art, animals, plants and emotions in the 'situatedness' of socio-cultural

Theory and Method in Higher Education Research II
International Perspectives on Higher Education Research, Volume 10, 83–102
Copyright © 2014 by Emerald Group Publishing Limited
All rights of reproduction in any form reserved
ISSN: 1479-3628/doi:10.1108/S1479-3628(2014)0000010010

contexts. As a co-participant in the students' community of practice, the more-than-human forms part of the process of identity formation and actively helps students learn. To shed light on the student experiences we employ Leximancer, a software tool that provides visual representations of the qualitative data drawn from focus groups with students and field diaries.

INTRODUCTION

How do we begin to explain the learning that takes place when students invoke inanimate objects as exuding agency? How might we better understand the way searing heat promotes reflection? What theoretical tools do we have to comprehend deeply embodied experiential learning? This chapter attempts to address these questions by considering the learning that takes place beyond formal academic settings (Wenger, 1998) and 'acquisitional' (Sfard, 1998) models. To begin our exploration we turn to two key figures that recognise the importance of context and participation in learning.

Lave and Wenger's (1991) seminal work on the 'situated' aspects of learning has become a lynchpin of educational theory and practice in higher education. In theorising the processes through which 'newcomers' (apprentices in their research) participate in socio-cultural communities of practice, Lave and Wenger foreground the role of participation in a learner's trajectory and emergent identity (see Wenger, 1998). Their emphases on relationships and the formative role of 'situated knowledges' and identify formation (Wenger, 1998), as part of participation in practice, has been taken up by others particularly in the literature on practice-based learning (Andrew, 2011; Andrew & Kearney, 2007; Hodge et al., 2011; Reid et al., 2008). In this chapter, we seek to contribute to theorising communities of practice drawing on research in an intercultural, experiential setting. More to the point, we want to push notions of inclusivity to incorporate many diverse 'others' that, to date, have been peripheral to, or entirely excluded from, the communities of practice literature. In particular, while authors have sought to develop Lave and Wenger's (1991) work, there remains a peculiar silence when it comes to more-than-human features of situated learning theories.

Our contribution to this gap in higher education research is two-fold. First, we provide a conceptually *inclusive* theorisation of communities of practice, one that considers the co-constitutive elements of nonhuman agency (Barad, 2008; Bennett, 2010; Stengers, 2010; Tuana, 2008). Here we look to Indigenous epistemologies encountered by students as they learn on and with 'Country'[2] as part of an experiential learning experience. Exploring students' engagement with the dynamism of Indigenous epistemologies and ontologies (Battiste, 2000; Louis, 2007), we unveil an expansive and transformative experience. Students acted with, and learnt from, nonhumans, rocks, animals, stories, overhangs, caves and temperature, in diverse ways. Drawing on this inter-cultural research, we problematise the way discussions on socio-cultural practices, identity formation and 'situatedness' have ignored other forms of agency — the nonhuman in a process of learning. We suggest that situated learning theories, and the communities of practice literature in particular, would benefit from an engagement with an interactionist ontology (Tuana, 2008) that foregrounds the agency of the material, in this case, things such as storms, heat and Country, as co-constitutive in the process of identity formation for students undertaking experiential learning. This 'co-becoming', to use Isabelle Stengers' term (2010; see also Bawaka et al., 2013; Wright & Hodge, 2012), refers to the power of nonhumans 'to make [human] practitioners think, feel, hesitate' (2010, p. 15). Material agency in our example is embedded in the situatedness and sociality of being on Country. In these theorisations, the latter is a 'co-participant' within necessarily *inclusive* communities of practice.

The second contribution is methodological. In formulating these theorisations we employ Leximancer, a software programme that provides visual accounts of qualitative data by generating key themes and connecting pathways tracing student experiences. The software reveals the interwoven and multifaceted dimensions of learning in place, that is, learning through the physicality of the landscape and its agency as students find themselves immersed in experience. The data is drawn from focus groups with students and field diaries as part of empirical research carried out during an eight-day intercultural student field trip to the NT, Australia. The field trip involves students meeting and working with Larrakia, Bininj, Koongurrukun, Limilngan-Wulna, Wagiman and Jawoyn, Indigenous traditional owners (TOs) of Darwin, Adelaide River, Litchfield, Kakadu and Southwest Arnhem Land, as they collaboratively design and complete a work-integrated project to enhance the business activities of the TOs.

The chapter opens with a discussion on the work of Lave and Wenger (1991) and Wenger (1998) focusing particularly on the situatedness that characterizes the way learners participate among others in communities of practice. Having stressed the centrality of identity formation in this participatory trajectory and given several examples of how their work has been used in student learning, we ponder the deeper implications of Lave and Wenger's (1991) situatedness and the limitations of their conceptualisations. The following section highlights a range of theorisations on the more-than-human including the vitality and agency of the nonhuman world. Here the concept of interactionist ontology (Tuana, 2008) is introduced along with the 'things' that fall outside human-centric notions of agency. The discussion on the more-than-human foregrounds Indigenous epistemologies and Country as co-constitutive of one's becoming. The next section introduces the research that forms the basis of our theorising and describes Leximancer, the software used to generate the themes and concepts used in the analysis. The empirical discussion elaborates on the Leximancer findings revealing the agency of more-than-human elements in student practice-based learning. The data drawn from the focus groups and field diaries uncovers a rich array of experiential learning filled with more-than-human moments as the latter impresses its materiality and agency. In the conclusion we consider the implications of the expansive ontology we adopt in arguing for a deeper engagement with more-than-human communities of practice.

COMMUNITIES OF PRACTICE – SITUATED LEARNING

Lave and Wenger (1991) and Wenger's (1998) work on conceptualising communities of practice as a contextual and situated learning practice has had a formative effect across the social sciences. Their work emphasises the learning that takes place as a result of co-participation among others within communities of practice. Lave and Wenger (1991) use the term *legitimate peripheral participation* (LPP) to explain how new learners participate in the socio-cultural practices of communities of practitioners and that their participatory trajectory leads to full participation in that community. In this developing participatory schema, 'newcomers' and 'old-timers' co-participate as new identities, activities, and communities of knowledge and practice transform the former as they are absorbed into the 'culture' of the community of practice.

A key element of this 'absorption' is language or learning how to talk in the manner of a full participant through 'story telling'. It is the relaying of 'situated stories', of difficult cases or shared predicament, that serve a vital part of diagnosing and reinterpreting shared practices while fashioning forms of memory and reflection. As Lave and Wenger (1991) put it, the purpose of language as story telling is not '... to learn *from* talk [but] to learn *to* talk as a key to legitimate peripheral participation' (1991, p. 109; emphasis in original).

Wenger (1998) elaborates on these earlier conceptualisations to focus on the construction of identities in the process of co-participation in communities of practice. He considers four components of this theory of social learning describing each as necessary characteristics of social participation and processes of learning and of knowing. These include: *meaning* (a way of talking about our individual and collective ability to experience our life and the world as meaningful); *practice* (a way of talking about the shared historical and social resources, frameworks and perspectives that sustain mutual engagement in action); *community* (a way of talking about the social configurations in which our enterprises are defined as worth pursing and our participation is recognisable) and *identity* (a way of talking about how learning changes who we are and creates personal histories of becoming in the context of our communities) (Wenger, 1998, p. 5).

Instrumental to Wenger's (1998) process of identify formation as social participation is that people do not just participate in certain activities with certain people as part of this mutual engagement, but that they become 'active' participants in the '*practices* of social communities and constructing *identities* in relation to these communities' (Wenger, 1998, p. 4; emphasis in original). Part of this process of active participation, for Wenger (1998), is the construction and development in these communities of practice of various 'routines, rituals, artifacts, symbols, conventions, stories and histories' (1998, p. 6). Communities of practice, then, for Lave and Wenger (1991) and Wenger (1998), are created through relationships between people built on shared socio-cultural practices. Within this learning trajectory co-participation produces changed identities within a community of practitioners.

The work of Lave and Wenger (1991) and Wenger (1998) has had a major influence on how we understand the contextual dynamics and diverse practices that make up the participatory elements of communities of practice. This is particularly the case when explaining the situated knowledges that characterise a range of educational settings involving student learning (Andrew, 2011; Andrew & Kearney, 2007; Hodge et al., 2011; Reid et al., 2008). Reid et al. (2008), for example, emphasise the situated nature of identity formation in student career development as the latter engage professional communities of practice *through* social practices, histories, skills and discourses. For psychology students, the experiences of co-participation in communities of practice are central to the shaping and reinforcing of contextualised identity formation. Similarly, Andrew and Kearney (2007) and Andrew's (2011) research draws on communities of practice literature to better understand migrant student experiences as part of community placements, particularly as a site of sociocultural and socio-linguistic learning. In each case, the authors highlight participation and 'immersive experience' (2007, p. 32) as students develop emergent identities through the sociocultural and situated encountering of 'cultures' and discursive practices of placement communities.

The themes of immersion and of context, the 'immersive experience' and the development of *contextualised* identities clearly continue to be central to theorising communities of practice. But what really does this immersion and contextualisation imply? The ways that immersion and contextualisation occur with and through the more-than-human world has, we argue, largely been left unexamined. Within the literature, the acknowledged members of communities of practice are human. Humans are agents that act on or in context. Yet such an implication sits uneasily with Lave and Wenger's attention to the practices, symbols, artifacts and other deeply contextualised practices through which communities of practice are formed. What might it mean for the literature to attend more deeply to those artifacts, to the situated nature of learning, 'in the context of our lived experience of participation in the world?' (Wenger, 1998, p. 3). Can nonhumans promote reflection? Does the 'context' have some level of agency in a community of practice beyond a backdrop to [human] action? How might we start thinking about an inclusive conceptualisation of communities of practice, one that takes into account the more-than-human as an active agent of learning as participation in the world?

MORE-THAN-HUMAN AGENCY

To grapple with the way that nonhumans − things, emotions, processes and affects − might actively constitute communities of practice, we turn to recent work in post-humanism and more-than-human materiality (Alaimo & Hekman, 2008; Bennett, 2010; Braun & Whatmore, 2010; Coole & Frost, 2010). This work seeks to understand nonhumans as vital players in the world. Nonhumans, whether animal, vegetable, mineral, process, thought, feeling or dream, are not inert or passive, but are active players in public life. For Bennett (2010), while humans may not attend to it, we are surrounded by vital materiality. Vital materiality constitutes our worlds, our actions, our selves. The ethical task is to attend, to 'cultivate the ability to discern nonhuman vitality, to become perceptually open to it' (Bennett, 2010, p. 14).

Such assertions are not meant to be abstract or rhetorical. The ways that things and processes create more-than-human publics are tangible, material; hurricanes may bring down a president (Tuana, 2008), worms may create agricultural land (Bennett, 2010), a wind may call a turtle in to shore providing food for a community (Bawaka et al., 2013), while a goal in a football match must be considered the product of the kicker, her dynamic relationships with the team, the wind direction, the ball moving through space, the goal (Massumi, 2002). Indeed, the very meaning of a human cannot be untangled from matter, from nonhumans (Bawaka et al., 2013; Barad, 2008; Kirby, 2008; Haraway, 2008; Tuana, 2008) so that plastics are absorbed through the lining of our stomachs, spectacles empower vision, air pollutants invade our lungs and our cells, bacteria in our gut keep us healthy and absorb nutrients and minerals make our bones. This is what Tuana refers to as an 'interactionist ontology', which refutes separations between the natural and the social instead maintaining that we live 'in the thick of things' (Pickering, 2001, cited in Tuana, 2008), existing in and through our interactions with each other and with the more-than-human. Such an ontological perspective has interesting implications for the notion of identity within communities of practice literature. While identity formation may indeed be usefully understood as developing from mutual engagement in relational ways (as Wenger elucidates), the engagement here must be understood within a more-than-human world where clear-cut distinctions between what is human and what is not are impossible. Relationality becomes an ontological statement.

One way of conceptualising the diverse relationalities of a more-than-human world is through the notion of assemblage. Assemblages are more-than-human amalgams of bodies, places, theories, social strategies, practices, trajectories and things that engage with each other to different extents, for differing amounts of time and that themselves exceed the assemblage (Bennett, 2010; Delanda, 2006; Deleuze & Guattari, 1987; Featherstone, 2011; Wright, 2013). Like Lave and Wenger's communities of practice, assemblages are emergent and contingent, the products of relational processes rather than constituted 'things'. While the social world is indeed complex, it is complex in real, material, emerging and more-than-human ways. The sociality of a community of practice, then, can be extended to incorporate a more-than-human sociality if we understand a community of practice as constituted through more-than-human assemblages.

As Tuana (2008, p. 209) points out, however, 'it is easier to posit an ontology than to practice it'. To deeply attend to the role of nonhumans in learning requires a major ontological shift. In order to help us make this shift, and to 'take epistemic responsibility for the distinctions we employ' (*ibid.*, p. 192), we turn to Indigenous mentors and their allies in academia. Here, we draw inspiration from Indigenous ontologies that have long recognised the world as vital, relational and interactionist (Christie, 2006; Howitt & Suchet-Pearson, 2003; Louis, 2007; Rose, 2005). Many Indigenous people understand their relationship with the world as one of co-becoming within which the agency of the nonhuman world is taken for granted, *normal*. Within Indigenous Australia, this is encapsulated in the concept of Country. Country refers not only to the land, to a territorially bounded area, but to the people, animals, winds, spirits, songs, law, knowledges and diverse myriad more-than-humans that co-constitute it. Country, is always in a state of co-becoming with its diverse tangible and non-tangible beings, all of whom are acknowledged as sentient and sapient (Bawaka et al., 2013). As Rose explains, 'Country is a place that gives and receives life. Not just imagined or represented, it is lived in and lived with … [C]ountry is a living entity with a yesterday, today and tomorrow, with a consciousness, and a will toward life. Because of this richness, [C]ountry is home, and peace; nourishment for body, mind and spirit; heart's ease; (Rose 1996, p. 7).

Indigenous ontologies, then, tend not to acknowledge a hierarchy privileging human knowledge, law or action. Rather, all beings may know and may act. As Burarrwanga et al. (2012, p. 22−23) state:

> They are not voiceless, you know. Animals, that is. But then neither are rocks or winds, tides or plants. They all speak. They all have language and knowledge and Law. They send messages to us; talk to us and to each other. All we have to do is listen; listen and then act … To listen closely, to hear, requires relating to the world in a different way, understanding ourselves in a different way. And once you do that, you have to act in a different way, with a different kind of ethics.

If nonhumans can know, have knowledge, then they can teach. It is a matter of attending, relating, as Burarrwanga et al. (2012), suggest, to the more-than-human in a different way and acting differently. What, then, does this mean for our efforts to broaden Lave and Wenger's conceptualisation of communities of practice to incorporate more-than-human agencies? If, as Isabelle Stengers (2010, p. 15) suggests, nonhumans have the power 'to make [human] practitioners think, feel, hesitate', do they have the power to help us learn? On the other hand, can we truly understand the processes of learning if we ignore the role of things, feelings, thoughts, relations, weather, animals, technology? In order to grapple more deeply with the role of nonhumans in learning, we turn now to a specific instance of student learning in the context of an intercultural field trip.

INTERCULTURAL RESEARCH AND METHODOLOGY

The research we draw on in this chapter involved working with students while undertaking an eight-day field trip to the NT as part of the final year development studies course, Rethinking Development. During the eight days students worked with Indigenous tour operators to collaboratively design and complete a work-integrated project that could be used by operators to enhance their business activities. In addition to the work-integrated projects, students participated in daily activities with TOs of Darwin, Adelaide River, Kakadu and Southwest Arnhem Land. The research was designed to explore the myriad of educative scenarios[3] that students encountered while participating in collaborative work-integrated projects with Indigenous tour operators.

Our research methodology draws on Leximancer, which is a software programme that provides qualitative analysis of textual data by extracting semantic meaning and relationships between concepts (see Smith & Humphreys, 2006). Semantic meaning is created through a conceptual analysis that considers the presence and frequency of words and phrases and the co-occurrence of words that make up a concept. Explicit and implicit concepts are identified and relationships are created through recognition of a concept's co-occurrence. The terms around a word indicate its meaning. In Leximancer maps, themes are collections of related concepts in close proximity on the map and the theme name is the most prominent concept. The theme circles are intended to capture high-level ideas or trends that involve multiple concepts. The size of the theme circles can be set by the user and the themes are colour-coded using a heat scale. Red is the hottest, with the highest level of concept occurrence, through to indigo, which is the coolest and has the lowest level of occurrence. The dot size of each concept is indicative of frequency of occurrence and the lines between concepts indicate the relationality. This data is represented visually as concept maps. The software also provides various quantitative analyses represented as datasets and can be exported into tables and reports.

Our empirical data includes transcripts from two focus group interviews and 12 student field diaries. Within the settings concepts that were used interchangeably were merged, such as Indigenous and Aboriginal, as were concepts of considerable similarity such as learn, learning and learnt. With the theme parameters set at 55%, six overarching themes with nested concepts emerged. The themed map is shown in Fig. 1 and the concept map in Fig. 2. For our analysis we extracted the concepts within each theme on the basis of likelihood of co-occurrence, noting the top five percentage bands. The exported data is shown in Table 1 and shows the number of co-occurrences between the concepts within a theme and the calculated likelihood of a concept being used in relation to the themed concept.

While Leximancer has been used to explore communities of practice in other fields such as health services (Braithwaite & Westbrook et al., 2009; Cretchley et al., 2010), government (McKenna & Waddell, 2007) and the corporate sector (Campbell et al., 2011; Dann, 2010), there is little research

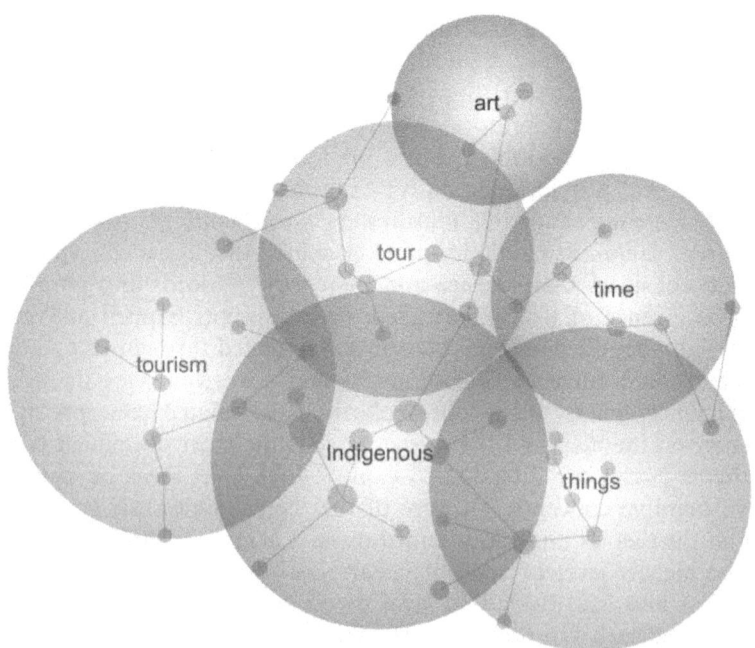

Fig. 1.   Leximancer Map of Themes.

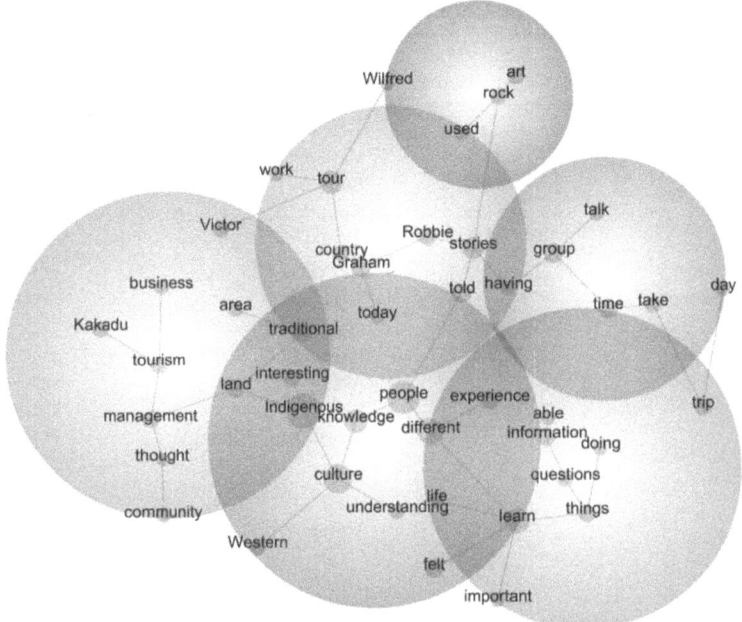

Fig. 2. Leximancer Map of Concepts.

that uses Leximancer in educational settings and fewer still in the area of student learning. By emphasising the methodological innovations of this software to highlight the relational stories of the embodied experience of learning on Country, we seek to fill this gap. Leximancer provides an innovative platform to give voice to the interwoven and multifaceted dimensions of learning in place such as learning through the physicality of the landscape and its agency as students find themselves immersed in experience. As a methodology, Leximancer makes visible a multitude of more-than-human elements that shape student learning.

INCLUSIVE COMMUNITIES OF PRACTICE – STORIES FROM STUDENT PRACTICE-BASED LEARNING ON COUNTRY

Without doubt, the role of people, of humans and their stories, play an important part of the community of practice experienced by students. The

Table 1. Leximancer Concept Co-Occurrence.

Theme/Concept	Likelihood of Co-occurrence	Theme/Concept	Likelihood of Co-occurrence
1. Indigenous		2. Tour	
Culture	26%	Victor	24%
People	26%	Business	23%
Interesting	21%	Robbie	15%
Land	21%	Area	12%
Area	19%	Group	12%
3. Management		4. Things	
Business	23%	Doing	12%
Victor	14%	Important	9%
Culture	9%	Able	8%
Area	8%	Life	8%
Kakadu	7%	Learn, trip, different[a]	7%
5. Time		6. Art	
Able	14%	Rock	88%
Take	13%	Stories	10%
Told	10%	Used	8%
Doing	10%	Told	7%
Graham	9%	Wilfred, talk, having[a]	6%

[a]Indicates multiple concepts with the same likelihood of co-occurrence percentage.

Indigenous tour operators, Robbie, Graham, Victor and Wilfred, in particular featured strongly in the student diaries and interviews. It is telling that both individual people and human constructs feature prominently in the Leximancer map (Fig. 2). The three concepts with the highest count in the data were *Indigenous, culture* and *people*. There were also strong links between these three concepts. When using the word *Indigenous*, for example, it was most likely that the students would link the concept *Indigenous* to either *culture* or *people* (a likelihood of 26% in each case, see Table 1). This is reflected in the students' words. For example, one student commented:

> It was astounding. We heard stories of art, dreaming, death, nature, tradition and history and I loved every minute. His representations to us highlighted how little I know and how different we are culturally, through our ideologies, knowledges, discourses and society. Fundamentally separated, I began to realise why there is so much fragmentation with 'Western' Australian culture and Traditional Indigenous culture.

As Lave and Wenger acknowledge, the stories are strongly situated. They are utterly bound up with place and the experience of place as well as the particular configuration of people, stories, knowledges, practices, conventions and histories of the group. In this intercultural setting, the students are fully aware that they can never talk in the manner of a full participant, talk as Wilfred talks, but they can develop shared practices with Wilfred, with each other and with other community development workers they meet along the way. Yet, to frame this event as a solely human one, to limit the social interaction here to people, is to ignore the wider scope of the event or educative scenario. The stories occurred in a place, 'on Country', as was acknowledged in many ways by the students. While the likelihood of the word Indigenous being linked to *people* or *culture* was 26%, the likelihood of it being linked to *land* (21%) or to *area* (19%) were also very high (see Table 1). Indeed, if we understand the concept of Indigenous as an assemblage of concepts, we see an amalgam of the human and more-than-human, of individual, community, place, affect and process. Meaning was co-constructed, yes, but not just with the Indigenous tour guide, lecturers and other students, but with the art, dreaming, death, nature, tradition and history (for a discussion of storytelling as a more-than-human event see Wright et al., 2012). The students' descriptions evoke this powerfully. The following quote, while generated through a search on *Indigenous*, with *Wilfred* as a prominent linking concept, nonetheless powerfully evokes Country in important ways. The overhangs and caves illustrate the point of Indigenous continuity on the land, abundant rock art tells stories and temperature differences speak of Indigenous ecological knowledge. These are specific, tangible learnings that the students traced directly from their interactions with the nonhuman world.

> [Wilfred, the Indigenous tour operator] told many stories while interpreting the essence of his country, guiding us between sheer rock walls and through wash-out and chasms. At every turn there was abundant rock art which had been layered over time as each generation came and went from the hill. The darkened underface of the overhangs and caves were testament to groups which sought shelter from the wet, siting their fires generation upon generation. It was apparent that even on such a hot day those special places we were taken to were cool and dry.

Indeed, the Leximancer maps themselves are far from human-dominated. Three of the major concepts, *art*, *time* and *things*, highlighted in Fig. 1, speak directly to events, processes and objects beyond a human focus. The concept *art*, for example, was identified as the sixth most prominent theme (see Fig. 1). *Art* was most related to *rock* (88%) and then to *stories* (10%) (Table 1). Rocks, then, tell stories. While such a statement may stretch credibility within a Western ontology, it is not so within Indigenous frameworks which readily acknowledge the agency of Country in all its materiality. Porr and Bell (2011), for example, grapple with the materiality of rock art through discussion of the world-view of the Indigenous Ngarunyin from the Kimberley region of Northwest Australia. Porr and Bell (2011) point out that art sites, like other objects deemed inanimate in Western frameworks, are acknowledged as important actors that can and do participate in social interactions (see also Bird-David, 1999; Cruikshank, 2005; Ingold, 2006; Povinelli, 1995). Indeed, even within the reflections of the students themselves, clear links between things (*rock*, *art*) and learning emerged. There was a mutual engagement in these moments; a more-than-human community was developed through practice albeit in ephemeral ways. The temperature difference in the caves was not a static thing, it was not a long-standing member of the community of practice in the same way that a work-supervisor might be, but it nevertheless formed part of the shared predicament. This, then, is a tangible example of co-participation among others within communities of practice but the 'others' are more 'other' than Lave and Wenger acknowledge. 'Others' like rocks, art, views, stories, overhangs, caves and temperature variations participated in central ways. Here, then, the vitality and agency of the nonhuman world emerges in ways directly applicable to student learning.

Another student captured beautifully the way that place, the view, the lookout, her feelings, the sun, were able to contribute to a transformative experience:

> This afternoon we went to Ubirr where we listened to talks given by Gary at a number of sites including a painting of the Rainbow Serpent and the main art gallery. This was amazing and the detail and history of the site was amazing. However I was equally astounded by the views at Nadab Lookout, it seemed no matter how many photos I took or words I wrote I was never going to capture the sheer beauty and feelings evoked by the magnitude of the surrounding landscape and sun setting.

It becomes clear that attempts to label some concepts as human and others as nonhuman are misguided. Culture, as anthropologists would remind us, is constituted in part through material things (Bird-David, 1992). Country is constituted not only by animals and plants, rocks and winds, spirits and dreams, but also by human beings (Bawaka et al., 2013). It is simply not possible to separate people from the place, the stories from the art, the feelings from the learning. This, then, reflects Tuana's interactionist ontology where learning takes place in the thick of things, through relationships with people, place and myriad nonhumans. Indeed the identities that are constructed through the student field-trip are identities of co-becoming (Bawaka et al., 2013; Stengers, 2010). They are neither static nor individualistic. Rather they come about through entangled engagements with each other and with the more-than-human world. Identities are indeed, as Wenger states, constructed in relation to communities; they are produced relationally through diverse more-than-human communities of practice.

The processual, emerging and contingent nature of the communities of practice, is also clear. The more-than-human, inclusive communities of practice experienced by the students were the product of diverse relational processes, uneven trajectories that met and engaged for periods of time. The practices of the communities continued to evolve as particular connections emerged and faded:

> I think one big difference that I've found between learning in a lecture hall or being here is the range of emotions that you probably go through whilst being here. For example, it was sort of hot today and we've walked all this way and you're hot and you're sweaty and you're tired and then you get there and you know when you stop for one of those breaks and hear one of the Indigenous people talking about their art work, it's like a massive release that's been taken off you and you're even more in awe because you've done the hard work to get there ... Here we've felt the connection and we've been here for days, we hear different interpretations of things and you are getting your own opinion out there about stuff.

While students grappled with the place of the more-than-human in their learning, and to attend to Country around them, they were very much guided by the Indigenous ontologies and epistemologies communicated by the Indigenous hosts. *Indigenous* was not only the most used concept (Fig. 2), but also the concept most connected to other major concepts. A focus on the vitality of the world was also explicit in many of the stories the students heard and discussed, and the operators actively encouraged them to listen deeply. As one student explained:

> When we were looking at a rock painting with Victor I walked into a tree branch because I was too busy looking at the painting and not where I was going. Victor remarked 'Careful, so the tree doesn't hate you'. When at Wollombi[4] I accidentally stepped on a ground rock carving and Uncle Paul remarked, 'Careful that the bird doesn't bite you'. In both cases I found it very interesting the way that the environment was depicted as a living being that has the ability to move and feel. I thought that these two events nicely sum up how Aboriginal people are part of the [C]ountry and the different way in which they view the environment compared to non-Indigenous people.

Nonhumans were real teachers here but to see them the students needed to attend carefully. The Indigenous hosts prompted them to acknowledge the role of Country as a teacher, as an active participant in their learning. As a student reported of one of the operators, 'He believes that working on Country is the best way for people to gain an understanding'. Country, work, practice, the sweat, the listening, the birds, carvings and trees helped constitute the community of practice. More-than-human agencies abound in these accounts. The learning experienced by students, their moments of realisation and of transformation, the development of their practice and their identities are all empowered by myriad beings and becomings.

CONCLUSION

Lave and Wenger (1991) and Wenger's (1998) situated learning theory foregrounds the richly contextualised socio-cultural practices that constitute communities of practice. Their contribution, and that of others who have drawn on this work, lie in the centrality given to participation as a medium through which practices become meaningful in a certain learning trajectory. It is the situatedness and sociality of this participation that brings into being emergent identities formed through various 'routines, rituals, artifacts, symbols, conventions, stories and histories' (Wenger, 1998, p. 6). Indeed, the practices and things that make up 'the context of our lived experience of participation in the world' (Wenger, 1998, p. 3) are constitutive of 'a profound connection between identity and practice' (Wenger, 1998, p. 149; emphasis added). Developing this practice then 'requires the formation of a community whose members can emerge with one another and thus acknowledge each other as participants' (Wenger, 1998, p. 149).

We argue that the communities of practice literature would be considerably deepened by also acknowledging the more-than-human as LPP (Lave & Wenger, 1991). While Lave and Wenger name other than human things as partly making up the socio-cultural practices of communities of practice, the participating identities are that of people. Yet, as we have discussed in the learning of student's during fieldwork in the NT, Country too plays a formative role in co-emergence and identity formation in practice-based learning. The examples given illustrate vividly the vitality, materiality and agency of rocks, art, views, stories, overhangs, caves and temperature. Along with interactions with Indigenous tour operators and others, these more-than-human elements were central to the 'mutual engagement in action' (Wenger, 1998, p. 5) of students transformative experiences.

Co-participation in these embodied moments of co-becoming or co-emergence can be traced directly to interactions with the nonhuman world. In other words, it is the contingent assemblages of the human and more-than-human – the situatedness and diverse sociality of these communities of practice – that constitute a student's learning trajectory and emergent identity. The latter's 'absorption' into the culture of more-than-human communities of practice as part of this learning trajectory involves deeply relational dialogues but not of the kind envisaged by Lave and Wenger (1991). Rather than just learn how to *talk* (as a participant) students in the educative scenarios described here learn how to *listen* as a participant. Participation with and on Country involves dialogues of a silent kind.

What we propose in this chapter requires a fundamental shift in the ontological orientation of current theorising on communities of practice, particularly as it relates to student practice-based learning. To further enrich our understandings of the contextualised and situated participation that Lave and Wenger (1991) and Wenger (1998) and others have in mind involves positing a more inclusive conceptualisation of the participating 'who' in communities of practice. In the case of student practice-based learning in the NT, a more inclusive theoretical lens is necessary to suitably incorporate the sociality of more-than-human communities of practice. By embracing an expansive ontology, one that refutes separations between the natural and the social worlds (Pickering, 2001, cited in Tuana, 2008), the vital materiality and agency of nonhumans come into view. 'They all speak', as Burarrwanga et al. (2012, p. 22) tell us. But to be able to hear requires us to relate differently, and as Burarrwanga et al. (2012) suggest, this means understanding ourselves in different ways. By attending to the agency of the nonhuman (as well as the human), the rocks, art, views, stories, overhangs, caves, temperature and seeing these as 'not voiceless' (Burarrwanga et al., 2012) there is a strong case to be made to include the more-than-human in communities of practice theorising.

Drawing on this intercultural research, we problematise the way existing literature discusses the socio-cultural practices, identity formation and 'situatedness' of communities of practice. To embrace the material vitality of nonhumans in the process of becoming – in the formation of student identities as part of more-than-human communities of practice is to acknowledge and respect those knowledges often marginal within higher education learning theories. By contributing an inclusive and deeply relational conceptualisation of communities of practice, one that embraces an Indigenous epistemologies, we remain committed to the legitimation of such knowledges within largely humanist-dominated educational traditions.

NOTES

1. Our use of the term more-than-human aims to highlight the knowledge and agency of human and nonhuman elements such as animals, places, emotions and stories.

2. Country is a term used in Aboriginal English to describe land as a living, sentient, richly diverse and multidimensional 'nourishing terrain' (Rose, 1996). Country is viewed as an intertwining of Indigenous kinship, ancestry and responsibility and is reflected in terms such as 'speaking to country', 'listening to country' and 'making country safe' (Bradley, 2001). Notably, 'country' can also refer to these same entwined links to the sea (Langton, 1996).

3. We adopt the term 'educative scenarios' as we have used elsewhere (Hodge et al., 2011) to capture the expansive range of learning experiences indicative of student fieldwork. 'Educative' in the sense used here includes unintended or unexpected experiences. Interpreted in this way, educative scenarios need not require, for instance, an instructional setting and student–teacher interaction but may involve a relational connection with a certain environment, in this case, Country.

4. Wollombi is located 80 kilometers west of Newcastle and is the traditional land of the Darkinjung peoples. The student is commenting on their experience during another fieldtrip undertaken as part of the Rethinking Development course.

ACKNOWLEDGEMENTS

We would like to thank the Indigenous tour operators and their families for welcoming the students and inviting them and us onto their Country – we appreciate the warm generosity and value the knowledge shared. We would also like to thank the students who participated in the research during the 2011 field trip to the NT. Finally, we acknowledge support from the Office of External Relations at The University of Newcastle for their financial assistance toward the research.

REFERENCES

Alaimo, S., & Hekman, S. (2008). *Material feminisms*. Bloomington, IN: Indiana University Press.

Andrews, M., & Kearney, C. (2007). Practicing in and learning from community placements. *New Zealand Studies in Applied Linguistics*, *13*(2), 31–45.

Andrews, M. (2011). "The real world": Lived literacy practices and cultural learning from community placement. *Australian Journal of Language and Literacy*, *34*(2), 219–235.

Barad, K. (2008). Posthuman performativity: Toward an understanding of how matter comes to matter. In S. Alaimo & S. Hekman (Eds.), *Material feminisms* (pp. 120–155). Bloomington, IN: Indiana University Press.

Battiste, M. (2000). *Reclaiming indigenous voice and vision.* Vancouver: UBC Press.
Bawaka Country, Suchet-Pearson, S., Wright, S., Lloyd, K., & Burarrwanga, L. (2013). Caring as Country: Towards an ontology of co-becoming in natural resource management. *Asia Pacific Viewpoint, 54*(2), 185–197.
Bennett, J. (2010). *Vibrant matter: A political ecology of things.* London: Duke University Press.
Bird-David, N. (1992). Beyond "the original affluent society": A culturalist reformulation. *Current Anthropology, 33*(1), 25–47.
Bird-David, N. (1999). Animism revisited. Personhood, environment and relational epistemology. *Current Anthropology, 40*(supplement), 67–91.
Bradley, J. J. (2001). Landscapes of the mind, landscapes of the spirit: Negotiating a sentient landscape. In R. Baker, J. Davies, & E. Young (Eds.), *Working on country: Contemporary indigenous management of Australia's lands and coastal regions* (pp. 295–307). Melbourne: Oxford University Press.
Braithwaite, J., Westbrook, J. I., Ranmuthugala, G., Cunningham, F., Plumb, J., Wiley, J., & Debono, D. (2009). The development, design, testing, refinement, simulation and application of an evaluation framework for communities of practice and social-professional networks. *BMC Health Services Research, 9*(1), 162.
Braun, B., & Whatmore, S. (2010). *Political matter.* Minneapolis, MN: University of Minnesota Press.
Burarrwanga, L., Ganambarr, R., Ganambarr-Stubbs, M., Ganambarr, B., Maymuru, D., Wright, S., … Bawaka Country. (2012). They are not voiceless (pp. 22–39). *2013 Voiceless Anthology.* Crows Nest: Allen and Unwin.
Campbell, C., Pitt, L., Parent, M., & Berthon, P. (2011). Understanding consumer conversations around ads in a Web 2.0 world. *Journal of Advertising, 40*(1), 87–102.
Christie, M. (2006). Transdisciplinary research and aboriginal knowledge. *The Australian Journal of Indigenous Education, 35*, 78–89.
Coole, D., & Frost, S. (2010). *New materialisms: ontology, agency, and politics.* London: Duke University Press.
Cretchley, J., Gallois, C., Chenery, H., & Smith, A. (2010). Conversations between carers and people with schizophrenia: A qualitative analysis using Leximancer. *Qualitative Health Research, 20*(12), 1611–1628.
Cruikshank, J. (2005). *Do glaciers listen?: Local knowledge, colonial encounters, and social imagination.* Vancouver: UBC Press.
Dann, S. (2010). Redefining social marketing with contemporary commercial marketing definitions. *Journal of Business Research, 63*(2), 147–153.
Delanda, M. (2006). *A new philosophy of society: Assemblage theory and social complexity.* New York, NY: Continuum.
Deleuze, G., & Guattari, F. (1987). In B. Massumi (Trans.), A thousand plateaus: Capitalism and schizophrenia. Minneapolis, MN: University of Minnesota Press.
Featherstone, D. (2011). On assemblage and articulation. *Area, 43*(2), 139–142.
Haraway, D. (2008). *When species meet.* Minneapolis, MN: University of Minnesota Press.
Hodge, P., Wright, S., Barraket, J., Scott, M., Melville, R., & Richardson, S. (2011). Revisiting 'how we learn' in academia: Practice-based learning exchanges in three Australian universities. *Studies in Higher Education, 36*(2), 167–183.
Howitt, R., & Suchet-Pearson, S. (2003). Ontological pluralism in contested cultural landscapes. In K. Anderson, M. Domosh, S. Pile, & N. Thrift (Eds.), *Handbook of cultural geography* (pp. 557–569). London: Sage Publications.

Ingold, T. (2006). Rethinking the animate, re-animating thought. *Ethnos, 71*(1), 9–20.

Kirby, V. (2008). Natural convers(at)ions: Or, what if culture was really nature all along? In S. Alaimo & S. Hekman (Eds.), *Material feminisms* (pp. 214–236). Bloomington, IN: Indiana University Press.

Langton, M. (1996). Art, wilderness and *Terra Nullius*. In R. Sultan & P. Josif (Eds.), *Perspectives on indigenous people's management of environment resources* (pp. 11–24). Darwin: Northern Land Council.

Lave, J., & Wenger, E. (1991). *Situated learning: Legitimate peripheral participation.* Cambridge: Cambridge University Press.

Louis, R. P. (2007). Can you hear us now? Voices from the margin: Using Indigenous methodologies in geographic research. *Geographical Research, 45*, 130–139.

Massumi, B. (2002). *Parables for the virtual.* Durham, NC: Duke University Press.

McKenna, B., & Waddell, N. (2007). Media-ted political oratory following terrorist events. *Journal of Language and Politics, 6*(3), 377–399.

Pickering, A. (2001). In the thick of things. Keynote address for Taking Nature Seriously conference, University of Oregon, February, 2001.

Porr, M., & Bell, H. R. (2011). "Rock-art", "animism" and two way thinking: towards a complementary epistemology in the understanding of material culture and "rock-art" of hunting and gathering people. *Journal of Archaeological Method and Theory, 19*(1), 161–205.

Povinelli, E. (1995). Do rocks listen: The cultural politics of apprehending Australian Aboriginal labour. *American Anthropologist, 97*(3), 505–518.

Reid, A., Dahlgren, L. O., Petocz, P., & Dahlgren, M. A. (2008). Identity and engagement for professional formation. *Studies in Higher Education, 33*(6), 726–742.

Rose, D. B. (1996). *Nourishing Terrains.* Canberra: Australian Heritage Commission.

Rose, D. B. (2005). An Indigenous philosophical ecology: Situating the human. *The Australian Journal of Anthropology, 16*(3), 294–305.

Sfard, A. (1998). On two metaphors for learning and the dangers of choosing just one. *Educational Researcher, 27*(2), 4–13.

Smith, A. E., & Humphreys, M. S. (2006). Evaluation of unsupervised semantic mapping of natural language with leximancer concept mapping. *Behavior Research Methods, 38*(2), 262–279.

Stengers, I. (2010). Including nonhumans in political theory: opening Pandora's box? In B. Braun & S. Whatmore (Eds.), *Political matter: Technoscience, democracy, and public life* (pp. 3–34). Minneapolis, MN: University of Minnesota Press.

Tuana, N. (2008). Viscous porosity: Witnessing Katrina. In S. Alaimo & S. Hekman (Eds.), *Material feminisms* (pp. 188–213). Bloomington, IN: Indiana University Press.

Wenger, E. (1998). *Communities of practice: Learning meaning and identity.* Cambridge: Cambridge University Press.

Wright, S. (2013). *Resistance. Handbook of human geography.* Thousand Oaks, CA: Sage.

Wright, S., & Hodge, P. (2012). To be transformed: Emotions in cross-cultural, field-based learning in northern Australia. *Journal of Geography in Higher Education, 36*(3), 355–368.

Wright, S., Lloyd, K., Suchet-Pearson, S., Burarrwanga, L., Tofa, M., & Bawaka Country. (2012). Telling stories in, through and with Country: Engaging with Indigenous and more-than-human methodologies at Bawaka, NE Australia. Special Issue 'Placing Indigenous Geographies: Implications for Geographical Thought and Practice. *Journal for Cultural Geography, 29*(1), 39–60.

RESEARCHING ACADEMIC WRITING: WHAT TEXTOGRAPHY AFFORDS

Sue Starfield, Brian Paltridge and Louise Ravelli

ABSTRACT

This chapter discusses textography as a strategy for researching academic writing in higher education. Textography is an approach to the analysis of written texts which combines text analysis with ethnographic techniques, such as surveys, interviews and other data sources, in order to examine what texts are like, and why. It aims to provide a more contextualized basis for understanding students' writing in the social, cultural and institutional settings in which it takes place than might be obtained by looking solely at students' texts. Through discussion of the outcomes of a textography, which examined the written texts submitted by visual and performing arts doctoral students at a number of Australian universities, we reflect on what we learnt from the study that we could not have known by looking at the texts alone. If we had looked at the texts without the ethnographic data not only are there many things we would not have known, but many of the things we might have said would likely have been right off the mark. Equally, had we just had the ethnographic data without the text analysis, we would have missed the

Theory and Method in Higher Education Research II
International Perspectives on Higher Education Research, Volume 10, 103–120
Copyright © 2014 by Emerald Group Publishing Limited
All rights of reproduction in any form reserved
ISSN: 1479-3628/doi:10.1108/S1479-3628(2014)0000010011

insights provided by the explicit text analysis. The textography enabled us to see the diversity of practices across fields of study and institutions as well as gain an understanding of why this might be the case, all of which is of benefit to student writers and their supervisors.

INTRODUCTION

Students and disciplinary teachers are often challenged by the essentially tacit nature of 'the rules' of academic writing (Elton, 2010). Indeed, as Aitchison and Lee (2006) argue in their discussion of doctoral education, while writing is frequently identified as a problem for many students, ways of thinking and talking about the central role of writing in knowledge production remain largely absent from debate. Further, writing is often viewed as a set of generic skills that can be taught separately from content, a view which can be seen as still dominant in the academy. In this chapter we explore an approach to researching academic writing within disciplinary contexts that we argue can help us better understand the tacit knowledge that is so commonly identified as problematic. This may help shift disciplinary teachers and teachers of writing from generic skills approaches to more contextually sensitive approaches to teaching writing (Hyland, 2013).

Approaches to understanding the nature of academic writing in higher education and the challenges writing pedagogy presents to both students and academics have, until recently, tended to adopt quite distinct methodologies. Academic literacies researchers, for example, have argued that writing in academic settings involves the command of a repertoire of linguistic practices which are based on complex sets of values, viewpoints, beliefs, purposes, rules and ways of using language. Different types of writing, further, involve different approaches to the construction and presentation of knowledge (Lea, 2008; Street, 2010). Research in the academic literacies tradition has been based mostly on case studies and ethnographies (Lillis & Scott, 2007). These studies have pointed to what some of these 'ways of writing' are and what students need to do, and understand, in order to succeed in their particular academic setting. English for academic purposes research (see Hyland, 2006; Jordan, 1997) has also focussed on the writing practices of specific disciplines. It has, however, been much more textual in its orientation and has focussed, in particular, on the language and discourse conventions of academic texts in specific, disciplinary settings (see e.g. Hyland, 2000, 2008). Wingate and Tribble (2012) have recently argued for drawing these approaches together in ways that combine the best of both of these traditions. This chapter discusses the use of textographies as a research approach which we believe has the potential to do just this in ways that will assist teachers of academic writing, disciplinary specialists and those who study academic writing.

As an illustration of the potential of textographic approaches for understanding academic writing within the complex contexts in which it takes place, the chapter will discuss a study which examined the written texts submitted by visual and performing arts doctoral students for examination at a number of Australian universities (Paltridge, Starfield, Ravelli, & Nicholson, 2011; Paltridge, Starfield, Ravelli, Nicholson, & Tuckwell, 2012a; Paltridge, Starfield, Ravelli, & Tuckwell, 2012b; Ravelli, Paltridge, & Starfield, 2013; Starfield, Paltridge, & Ravelli, 2012). In the chapter, particular attention will be given to a discussion of what textography affords as a research strategy and what this could mean for the researching and teaching of academic writing.

WHAT IS A TEXTOGRAPHY?

The term 'textography' was first coined by Swales (1998a, 1998b) and Swales and Luebs (1995) to describe a methodology that aims to get an inside view of the worlds in which texts are written, why texts are written as they are, and the values that underlie the texts that have been written (Katz, 1999). A particular goal of a textography is to examine the 'situatedness' of written texts (Swales, 1998a). A textography, thus, aims to explore the context in which a text is produced in order to gain an understanding of why the text is written as it is. This examination of context includes consideration of the role and purpose of the text, the audience for the text, expectations of the particular discourse community and the text's relationship with other similar texts. It also considers texts that surround the text in terms of the chain of genres and networks (Devitt, 2004; Swales, 2004; Tardy, 2003) of which it is a part. A textography, then, is more than a traditional text analysis yet less than a full-blown ethnography. Its prime focus of interest is the text and it aims to develop 'ethnographically sensitive text analytic tools which enable researchers to bring the text back into frame' (Lillis & Scott, 2007, p. 22). It does not, necessarily, involve the sustained engagement over a period of time with the research site that one would expect of ethnography. Rather, it draws on a range of ethnographic techniques and combines these with text analysis, with the aim of understanding both the form and formation of the texts that people write.

A TEXTOGRAPHY OF DOCTORAL WRITING IN THE VISUAL AND PERFORMING ARTS

Doctoral degrees in the visual and performing arts are a fairly recent entrant to the research higher degree landscape in the United Kingdom, the United States and Australia. The number of universities offering these degrees has increased in the last decade or so as a result of art schools and colleges being merged with universities. These new communities and their members have had to conform to 'the scholarly expectations of the university as a whole' (Johns & Swales, 2002, p. 17). Original research and scholarship in the visual and performing arts has now become a major concern for the institutions and for people working in these areas (Evans, Macauley, Pearson, & Tregenza, 2003). One of the ways in which this has been addressed is through the introduction of doctoral degrees in these areas of study.

The common denominator in these doctorates is the production by the student of both a creative work of some kind and a written text. Both pieces of work are evaluated as part of the doctoral examination process, and the term 'thesis', in the visual and performing arts, is typically used to refer to the combined work. The kinds of texts that students write for these degrees are, at times, different from the texts that students write in the conventional thesis-only degree and challenge, in some ways, the expectations of what a doctoral thesis should look like and what it 'does' in these areas of study. Conventional doctoral theses, of course, also vary in their format, conventions and expectations. The addition of a visual or performance component to the thesis, however, further complicates matters and extends the notion of 'text' in this particular context (see Ravelli et al., 2013 for further discussion of this). These doctorates, thus, require us to re-think doctoral writing and the extent to which the doctoral thesis that has for some time been 'stabilised for now' (Schryer, 1994, p. 108) is now changing in response to the new and developing situation in which it is now located.

Visual and performing arts doctorates also differ from the conventional thesis-only degree in their examination. Kiley (2009, pp. 889–890) writes that the 'doctoral examination in Australia is based on the written dissertation, usually a maximum of 100,000 words, as the single item of examination'. However, this is not typically the case for doctoral degrees in the visual and performing arts, we learnt. Here, the creative component is typically examined in situ; that is, in person in an exhibition space or a theatre with all of the examiners present. The written component, however, is most typically examined at a different time, after the exhibition or performance back in the examiners' office or wherever they choose to do their reading of the student's text. The two-part structure of the doctorate and the particular nature of the examination process can pose a challenge to the student, who has to make a number of decisions about the relationship between the two components of their work and how to represent this relationship in their written text. As the literature on practice-based doctorates indicates, writing is considered difficult for many whose primary self-identity is that of artist or performer (Collinson, 2005; Hockey & Allen-Collinson, 2005), with some questioning the need to provide contextualisation of the research via a written component at all (e.g. Candlin, 2000).

The practice-based doctorate in the visual and performing arts is also distinctive in that 'significant aspects of the claim for the doctoral characteristics of originality, mastery and contribution to the field are held to be demonstrated through the original creative work' (United Kingdom Council for Graduate Education, 1997, p. 18). This could include judgement of the submission as a contribution to knowledge in the field, or showing doctoral level powers of analysis and mastery of existing contextual knowledge in a form which is accessible to and auditable by knowledgeable peers (Evans et al., 2003).

The various attempts to codify and reach consensus on the nature of the practice-based doctorate, as shown in the debate over the terms 'practice-based' versus 'practice-led' research (see e.g. Candy, 2006; Durling & Friedman, 2000; Haseman, 2006; Haseman & Mafe, 2009; Smith & Dean, 2009), are a further indication that the doctoral thesis in the visual and performing arts is still in the process of development. The terminology used to define this field is much debated and definitions sometimes overlap one another, or are contested, with terms such as 'practice-based research', 'practice as research', 'practice-led research', 'performance as research', 'research through practice' and 'creative practice as research' seeking legitimation (see Paltridge et al., 2011; Phillips, Stock, & Vincs, 2008). In this chapter we adopt 'practice-based' as our default term, while, at the same time, acknowledging that it is contested, reflecting the relatively unstable nature of the field.

Dally, Holbrook, and Graham (2004) and Baker, Buckley, and Kett (2009) further point to considerable variation between universities regarding the form that the written component accompanying the creative component of these degrees should take, and how the two components submitted for the degree should be evaluated. Others such as Barrett (2007) provide advice for doctoral writers in the visual arts but do not accompany this advice with examples from sample texts which illustrate the points that they make. Elkins's (2009) book contains extracts from studio art doctorates, but does not discuss, in any great length, these works in terms of the particular contribution that writing makes to the overall projects.

Prior to our embarking on our study of the practice-based doctorate in the visual and performing arts in Australia, little work had investigated the actual nature of the written component of practice-based doctorates in the visual and performing arts, and the goals, assumptions, values and understandings that underlay the work written and submitted for examination in these areas of study. As MacLeod and Holdridge (2004, p. 156) pointed out in the UK context, 'there is a remarkable dearth of material which provides substantial evidence of the "form" and structure of doctorates [in the visual arts]'. Our goal, then, was to explore both the form and function of these texts through both a close textual analysis and through the use of ethnographic research techniques in order to gain insights into the worlds in which the texts were written.

Our choice of textography as a framework for our study was motivated by the way in which it enabled us to draw on existing research methods (in this case, discourse analysis, surveys, interviews, document analysis, observations etc.) within the context of a single overarching design for the study. We were especially interested in exploring the forces that shape the production of the students' texts. That is, we wanted to learn not only what were typical features of the texts but also why the texts were written in the way that they were. While there are other studies that use ethnographic data to explore the motivations of texts (see e.g. Harwood, 2006; Hyland, 2003a; Nickerson, 2000), very few of these studies adopt the level of methodological complexity that ours does.

Design of the Study

The study was carried out in a number of stages. The first stage of the study established a database of institutions, their doctoral programs, assessment regimes and numbers of recent graduates to determine the extent of practice-based doctoral submissions taking place in Australia in the visual and performing arts. Our aim in doing this was to understand the range, extent and nature of these doctoral theses so that the findings of our study would be able to contribute to discussions of present practices as much as possible. At the time we collected the data for the study (2008), 29 institutions offered these degrees and there were 1,779 students undertaking them.

An online survey with a specific focus on doctoral supervision of practice-based theses was then completed by 32 supervisors. Questions covered in the survey included the participants' experience of doctoral supervision, the fields of study covered and characteristics of the examination process. Subsequent questions focused on the written component and asked specifically about the relationship between the written and creative components, the typical length of the written component, its typical organisational patterns, the characteristics of high quality doctoral work in the specific area of study, the nature of university guidelines in relation to practice-based submissions, how a significant contribution to knowledge could be demonstrated in the specific field of study and finally, what students typically found most straightforward and most challenging about their doctoral writing.

The next stage of the project involved the collection of doctoral texts selected on the advice of supervisors working in the schools and faculties identified through the survey. Supervisors, as expert members of the community, were asked for recommendations of 'high quality' theses, which most desirably represented the kinds of doctoral submissions in their areas of study. We thus collected 36 doctoral texts which became the focus of our analysis. In all cases this involved obtaining copies of the written component of the submissions with, where possible, accompanying DVD and CD ROMs which had been produced as records of the visual/performance component of the degree. It was, thus, only through the ethnographic components of the study that we were able to identify what the 'complete' texts actually were, as library copies of these particular theses did not necessarily contain all the constituent parts. Indeed, some parts of the examinable outputs may have been ephemeral, such as being at an exhibition or a performance which can only be captured, in part, on a DVD or CD.

The areas of study we examined and numbers of texts in each of these areas are shown in Table 1.

Fifteen of the student authors of these texts and 15 supervisors were interviewed, as much as possible paired around the students' doctoral work. A number of the interviews included site visits to the universities where the theses had been produced. Some of these supervisors had been examiners of some of the doctoral works that were collected, adding a

Table 1.   Areas of Study in the Sample Texts.

Visual Arts		Performing Arts	
Painting	7	Dance	6
Mixed media	5	Theatre	1
Drawing	2	Music	3
Digital media	8		
Photography	2		
Sculpture	2		

further dimension to the data. The interviews were particularly important in helping us understand how students and supervisors felt about their place in the academy, and the role and nature of their doctoral theses. This not only added to the extant literature about these phenomena, but drew our attention to key points to focus upon in our analysis.

As part of our contextual analysis, we also looked at university handbooks and prospectuses, as well as information given to students in relation to their candidature; that is, 'texts that surround the texts'. We read published research into visual arts PhD examination, as well as books and journals that discussed visual and performing arts research more generally. We read in-house art school publications and discussion papers on doctoral studies in the visual and performing arts. We attended roundtable discussions on the topic, as well as doctoral students' exhibition openings. At these openings we were able to get a sense of how the students saw their doctoral projects in relation to the texts that they were writing, and which of these had the most prominence for them, most typically the creative work itself.

The Thesis in Visual and Performing Arts Doctorates

One of the study's key overall findings involves the notion of what constitutes a 'text', or more precisely, a 'thesis', in these areas of study. Much of this knowledge was gained through the ethnographic component of our methodology; that is, through the survey and interview data we collected rather than by looking at the texts alone. We also found very strong local institutional factors shaping what is considered an acceptable piece of writing for this degree, what it should do and what issues it should address, showing how the community in which we were working is far from homogeneous in terms of its requirements and expectations. There was some disagreement between institutions as to how an examination should proceed and what the 'thesis' should contain. We found, further, at a broader level, a certain unease about the place of doctoral study (and to some extent research) in the life of practicing artists and those that had taken up employment in the academy.

For the majority of our informants, though, 'the thesis' was not simply the written component of the submission but included the visual and/or performance component of the doctoral project. We found, however, a certain amount of variation in how these theses (that is, both the written and creative components) are encountered and assessed. Examiners may, for example, view the creative work with or, on occasion, without the written component. The written component may be the fully developed piece of writing or it may, in some cases, be a 'framing document' with the more extended piece of writing being submitted some time (in some cases, months) after attending the exhibition or performance. The broader audience for the creative work is likely to see the visual or performance component without the written text, although they may know (or not) of the student's larger project. Later, readers may read the written component in hard copy, online, either with or without access to the original creative material, which, if it is available, is in the form of an 'appropriate durable record' (Duxbery & Grierson, 2008), which provides a comprehensive visual documentation of the research in the form of a workbook, or a DVD, CD or material placed on the web. These findings, from the ethnographic data that we collected, helped us to understand the textual component of the study. The textography, thus, helped us to draw these parts of the study together in a way that revealed the inter-connectedness of each of these components, rather than just one or the other, in helping us to understand the texts that students in these areas of study need to write for their doctoral degrees.

While there has been some research into the overall organizational structures of more traditional doctoral theses in the research literature (see e.g. Paltridge, 2002; Paltridge & Starfield, 2007), very little attention has been given to the texts that doctoral students write in the visual and performing arts. One of the foci of the study, then, was the overall organization or *macrostructures* (Gardner & Holmes, 2009; Paltridge et al., 2012b; van Dijk, 1980) of the texts that the students submitted as part of their examination in these areas of study. We were also interested in how these patterns of organization are related to those found in more established examples of the doctoral thesis in other areas of study. We then considered the discourse analytic side of the study in the light of the other data that was collected. We, thus, aimed to provide an explicit textual account of the students' texts that we would not have gained, had we relied on ethnographic data alone.

In many of the visual and performing arts doctoral texts that we examined we found components that match those of a conventional doctoral dissertation, and in approximately the same order; but the components were typically much less discretely divided or specifically named, so there may be three 'review of art' chapters that have 'topic-based' headings (headings which reflect the general content, or topic, of the chapter), and across these three chapters we might see elements corresponding to both a review of literature and to methodology. Similarly there may be one or more chapters that describe and/or critique and theorise the student's own work, where the conventional elements of 'results' and 'discussion' are intermingled.

What we saw in our study, especially, is that there is a range of possibilities for the written text that is part of a doctoral submission in the visual and performing arts. Specifically, the text and the creative component may be seen as separate products and processes in which parallel 'codes' or 'voices' are presented; that is, the artist and the academic as in Haley's (2005) *Mirror as Metasign: Contemporary Culture as Mirror World.* Or these two may be more closely combined where one code or voice recontextualises the other, as in Fenton's (2007) *Unstable Acts: A Practitioner's Case Study of the Poetics of Postdramatic Theatre and Intermediality* (see Paltridge et al., 2012a, 2012b for further discussion of these projects).

Our study also highlighted how texts change (Berkenkotter, 2007; Devitt, 2004), and resist change, within institutions. The main centripetal force for stability (Bakhtin, 1981) in this context is the underlying functions of a doctoral thesis, such as the need to contextualize the research, the need to engage with theory, the need to place the research within a broader field and the need to demonstrate the way/s in which the doctoral project moves the field forward. We found that, while there was considerable variation in how the doctoral texts we examined were organized, they were still influenced by these expected requirements of doctoral dissertations. Some students achieved this by drawing on a conventional dissertation structure of introduction, review of the literature, methods, results, discussion and conclusion. Often, however, they took these categories and re-conceptualized them in a way that better fitted their area of study and particular project, and that might not be immediately recognizable as examples of the typical elements that make up the macrostructure of a more conventional doctoral dissertation. For example, the review of the literature may be a review of a particular artist's work, or a review of particular ways of conceptualizing art practice. The written text might also be a parallel discussion to the visual project which provides an intellectual accompaniment to the work rather than an explanation of the work.

We also learnt, through the ethnographic data, about the influence of key figures and institutions in terms of how students might present their text which, in a number of cases, was extremely strong; that is, the centrifugal forces (Bakhtin, 1981) for change that influenced the students' texts. For example, one text we examined seemed like an 'outlier' in relation to the other texts. The doctorate was supervised by a key person in the institution where it was submitted who was, at that time, the Associate Dean for Research and the author of the text is now a faculty member at that institution. It is, thus, very likely that texts of this kind, which at one point might be considered an 'exception', will continue to be produced at that institution. We also found, through the interviews, that one of the institutions strongly favoured practice-led research (vs. practice-based research), as the professor in that department had published widely on this topic and was seen as one of the leading figures working with this approach.

What We Learnt from the Textography

So, what did we learn from the study that we could not have known by looking at the texts alone? First, more generally, we learnt about the (at times contested) place of the visual and performing arts in the academy and the impact that this may have on both students and their supervisors and their writing practices. As Fairskye (1993, pp. 2–3) has argued:

> artists in the academy have felt like 'gate crashers' at the University's dinner party... asked to show their I.D. before they're allowed to sit down at the table with everyone else.

We also learnt about the history of doctoral degrees in the visual and performing arts. They are, for example, increasing in popularity in the United Kingdom and Australia but are strongly resisted in some US universities (see Jones, 2006, 2009 for a discussion of this). We saw ways in which the practice-based doctorate in the visual and performing arts is reflective of more 'traditional' doctoral dissertations, as well as new and emerging discursive strategies and conventions in doctoral writing in the academy. The study, thus, helped us gain a degree of insider knowledge that prevented us from making our own (uninformed) judgements about what was a 'successful' or 'less successful' piece of writing in the particular context.

We learnt, further, about the challenges these texts present for student writers. At one of the presentations we gave on this project a student said, 'I am a successful artist. Why do we have to write?' (see Starfield et al., 2012 for further discussion of this). In the survey we asked supervisors: 'What do students find most straightforward in this kind of writing?' A common response was 'nothing'. When we asked them 'What do students find difficult in this kind of writing?', they typically said 'everything'. Writing is, however, a key way in which knowledge is accredited in the academy and, notwithstanding the place of creative work in all of this, it is something that students, at least at the present time, need to master.

Our study, then, demystified doctoral writing in the visual and performing arts in a way, we believe, that is useful to both students and their supervisors. If we had looked at texts alone (without the ethnographic data) not only are there many things we could not say regarding attitudes and institutional practices, but many of the things we might have said could have well been off the mark. For example, Haley's thesis, with its parallel relation between written and creative components, sets up a kind of relationship which on the surface looks unsuccessful, because there are few explicit connections between the two components of the work. In context, however, not only were these connections obvious, the thesis itself was also highly successful. Equally, if we had just the ethnographic data without the text analysis, then we would have missed the insights provided by the explicit analysis of the texts and the range of macrostructures that characterized these successful texts.

So, in sum, the textography was able to show us the diversity of practices across fields of study and across institutions, as well as provide us with some kind of understanding for why this might be the case, all of which is of immense benefit to both students and their supervisors. More broadly, our study argues for the importance of contextualizing academic writing studies in line with the case put by other researchers (see e.g. Flowerdew, 2011; Lillis, 2008; Perales-Escudero & Swales, 2011; Swales & Rogers, 1995), so that we not only produce *descriptions* of academic texts, but also *explanations* that can increase our *understanding* of the texts that students need to write.

Implications for Teaching

The study described in this chapter aimed to gain insiders' perspectives on the texts that were produced as well as to uncover some of the 'dynamic and complex situated meanings and practices that are constituted in and by the writing' (Lillis, 2008, p. 355). The study suggests, further, that teachers of academic writing need to be cautious about adopting approaches to writing pedagogy that rely on generic or prescriptive models of what particular texts should look like. Teachers need to be aware of the specific conditions of production and reception of the students' texts within their own institutional context.

MacLeod and Holdridge (2004) point to the importance of students looking at previous students' texts as a guide to how they might present their own work. The examples they look at will become both 'the history and the precedent' (2004, p. 166) which will inform what they, themselves, will do in their written work. We suggest that writing teachers (and students' supervisors) collect a corpus of successful texts from their own institutional context that they can make available to their students with appropriate indication as to why these texts might be considered successful. This type of 'rhetorical consciousness-raising' has been found to be extremely helpful in the teaching of academic writing (Johns, 1993; Paltridge et al., 2009; Swales, 1995). While we acknowledge that local contexts may constrain the choices students make as to the shape and form of their texts, our research, we hope, begins to provide an understanding of the options and choices available to students in specific domains of academic writing.

Our textographic project, we hope, will help to provide a research-informed basis for the development of teaching and learning initiatives which target the specific writing and textual production needs of students in specific areas of study. A better understanding of what counts as successful writing in specific areas of study and disciplinary communities is essential for this. This is especially important in areas such as those discussed in this chapter where, at present, there is very little information available which can be drawn on for providing writing guidance and support. We also hope that, in some way, the perspective we propose helps to address the issue raised at the beginning of this chapter about the lack of focus in academic writing research on the role of writing in knowledge construction and production and the very specificity of this writing (and knowledge production) in particular disciplinary contexts.

A textography (and our study), of course, has many of the same limitations as ethnographic approaches in general. One of these is the size of the sample on which our claims are based. Our aim, however, is not to provide a generalised statement about doctoral writing in the visual and performing arts but, rather, observations that further research might build on, and add to. Hopefully, in our fuller descriptions of this project (Paltridge et al.,

2011, 2012a, 2012b, Ravelli et al., 2013; Starfield et al., 2012), we have provided sufficient details on the nature and source of our sample texts and
our analyses of them, so that readers can consider the extent to which our
findings can be transferred or compared to what might be found in
another, similar set of texts in similar academic settings. By doing this, we
hope we have been able to provide credibility, dependability and transferability (Lincoln & Guba, 1985) to our study via the 'audit trail' we have
left, so that other people reading our research can see what we did and how
we reached the conclusions that we did.

The multi-method approach we propose in this chapter is, of course, evident in other literacy research (see Barton, 2013 for a review of this work),
where ethnographic approaches are sometimes juxtaposed with discourse
analysis in order to increase the credibility and dependability of the
research. Our goal, however, has been rather different. It has been to use
each approach to inform the findings of the other in a way that is interconnected and that aims to bridge the gap between text and context, yet still
maintains a focus on the text. The textual data, thus, does not sit alongside
the ethnographic data. Rather, the textual analysis is informed by it (Lillis,
2008).

CONCLUSION

In the project described in this chapter, the analysis goes 'beyond the text'
(Freedman, 1999) to investigate the ways in which language is used in specific writing contexts and the reasons for it. It is essential, then, for students
to explore these kinds of contextual factors before they begin reading for
and writing their texts (Johns, 2008). As Macbeth (2006, p. 182) has
argued:

> all of us enter the university as novices ... Even so, those of us who arrive without
> familiarity of the kinds of writing that will be expected of us usually struggle the most.
> This seems to be as true of those of us who are native speakers of English as well as
> those of us who are learning English as another language.

The key, then, is 'how a newcomer to the academic community goes
about learning its sociocultural practices' (Macbeth, 2006, p. 181) and how
we might help students to do this. The use of textographies, we would
suggest, is one way in which this might be done. Projects of this kind can
examine 'the forces outside the individual which help guide purposes, establish relationships, and ultimately shape [student's] writing' (Hyland, 2003b,

p. 18). In particular, they can uncover 'what can and cannot be said and done' (Johns et al., 2006, p. 244) in particular texts; as well as the goals, assumptions and values that are presupposed by expert readers of the texts. That is, they can make visible to students the choices and constraints (Devitt, 2004) available in the writing they are doing so that they 'can locate themselves and begin to participate within these genres more meaningfully' (Johns et al., 2006, p. 245) and, hopefully, more successfully.

REFERENCES

Aitchison, C., & Lee, A. (2006). Research writing: Problems and pedagogies. *Teaching in Higher Education, 11*, 265–278.

Baker, S., Buckley, B., & Kett, G. (2009). *Creative arts PhD: Future-proofing the quality in creative arts doctoral programs.* Australian Learning and Teaching Council, Strawberry Hills, NSW, Australia.

Bakhtin, M. M. (1981). *The dialogic imagination: Four essays* (M. Holquist, Trans.). Austin, TX: University of Texas Press.

Barrett, E. (2007). Developing and writing creative arts practice research: A guide. In E. Barrett & B. Bolt (Eds.), *Practice as research: Approaches to creative arts enquiry* (pp. 185–205). London: I.B. Tauris.

Barton, D. (2013). Ethnographic approaches to literacy research. In C. A. Chapelle (Ed.), *The encyclopaedia of applied linguistics.* Oxford: Blackwell. doi:10.1002/9781405198431. wbeal0398

Berkenkotter, C. (2007). Genre evolution? The case for a diachronic perspective. In V. K. Bhatia, J. Flowerdew, & R. H. Jones (Eds.), *Advances in discourse studies* (pp. 178–191). London: Routledge.

Candlin, F. (2000). Practice-based doctorates and questions of academic legitimacy. *International Journal of Art and Design Education, 19*, 96–101.

Candy, L. (2006). *Differences between practice-based and practice-led research.* Retrieved from http://www.creativityandcognition.com/research/practice-based-research/differences-between-practice-based-and-practice-led-research/. Accessed on 26 October 2012.

Collinson, J. A. (2005). Artistry and analysis: Student experiences of UK practice-based doctorates in art and design. *International Journal of Qualitative Studies in Education, 18*, 713–728.

Dally, K., Holbrook, A., & Graham, A. (2004). The processes and parameters of fine art PhD examination. *International Journal of Educational Research, 41*, 136–162.

Devitt, A. (2004). *Writing genres.* Carbondale, IL: Southern Illinois Press.

Durling, D., & Friedman, K. (Eds.). (2000). *Doctoral education in design: Foundations for the future.* Stoke-on-Trent, UK: Staffordshire University Press.

Duxbery, L., & Grierson, E. M. (2008). Thinking in a creative field. In L. Duxbury, E. M. Grierson, & D. Waite (Eds.), *Thinking through practice: Art as research in the academy* (pp. 7–17). Melbourne: RMIT Publishing.

Elkins, J. (Ed.). (2009). *Artists with PhDs: On the new doctoral degree in studio art.* Washington, DC: New Academia Publishing.

Elton, L. (2010). Academic writing and tacit knowledge. *Teaching in Higher Education*, *15*, 151–160.

Evans, T., Macauley, P., Pearson, M., & Tregenza, K. (2003). *A brief review of PhDs in the creative and performing arts in Australia*. Retrieved from http://dro.deakin.edu.au/view/ DU:30004959. Accessed on 9 August 2012.

Fairskye, M. (1993). Frankly, I may be a genius, but don't call me Dale, I'll call you. Ornithology and art? *A bird's eye view of conceptual rigour in contemporary art practice*. Queensland Art Gallery, Brisbane.

Fenton, D. (2007). *Unstable acts: A practitioner's case study of the poetics of postdramatic theatre and intermediality*. PhD thesis, Queensland University of Technology, Brisbane, Australia.

Flowerdew, J. (2011). Reconciling contrasting approaches to genre analysis: The whole can equal more than the sum of the parts. In D. Belcher, A. M. Johns, & B. Paltridge (Eds.), *New directions in English for specific purposes research* (pp. 119–144). Ann Arbor, MI: University of Michigan Press.

Freedman, A. (1999). Beyond the text: Towards understanding the teaching and learning of genres. *TESOL Quarterly*, *33*, 764–768.

Gardner, S., & Holmes, J. (2009). Can I use headings in my essay? Section headings, macro-structures and genre families in the BAWE corpus of student writing. In M. Charles, S. Hunston, & D. Pecorari (Eds.), *Academic writing: At the interface of corpus and discourse* (pp. 251–271). London: Continuum.

Haley, S. (2005). *Mirror as metasign: Contemporary culture as mirror world*. PhD thesis, University of Melbourne, Australia.

Harwood, N. (2006). (In)appropriate personal pronoun use in political science: A qualitative study and a proposed heuristic for future research. *Written Communication*, *23*, 424–450.

Haseman, B. (2006). A manifesto for performative research. *Media International Australia incorporating Culture and Policy*, *118*, 98–106.

Haseman, B., & Mafe, D. (2009). Acquiring know-how: Research training for practice-led researchers. In H. Smith & R. T. Dean (Eds.), *Practice-led research, research-led practice in the creative arts* (pp. 211–228). Edinburgh: Edinburgh University Press.

Hockey, J., & Allen-Collinson, J. (2005). Identity change: Doctoral students in art and design. *Arts and Humanities in Higher Education*, *4*, 77–93.

Hyland, K. (2000). *Disciplinary discourses: Social interactions in academic writing*. Harlow, UK: Longman.

Hyland, K. (2003a). Dissertation acknowledgements: The anatomy of a Cinderella genre. *Written Communication*, *20*, 242–268.

Hyland, K. (2003b). Genre-based pedagogies: A social response to process. *Journal of Second Language Writing*, *12*, 17–29.

Hyland, K. (2006). *English for academic purposes: An advanced resource book*. London: Routledge.

Hyland, K. (2008). Genre and academic writing in the disciplines. *Language Teaching*, *41*, 543–562.

Hyland, K. (2013). Writing in the university: Education, knowledge and reputation. *Language Teaching*, *46*, 53–70.

Johns, A. M. (1993). Written argumentation for real audiences: Suggestions for teacher research and classroom practice. *TESOL Quarterly*, *27*, 75–90.

Johns, A. M. (2008). Genre awareness for the novice academic student: An on-going quest. *Language Teaching, 41,* 237–252.

Johns, A. M., & Swales, J. M. (2002). Literacy and disciplinary practices: Opening and closing perspectives. *Journal of English for Academic Purposes, 1,* 13–28.

Johns, A. M., Bawarshi, A., Coe, R. M., Hyland, K., Paltridge, B., Reiff, M.-J., & Tardy, C. M. (2006). Crossing the boundaries of genre studies: Commentaries by experts. *Journal of Second Language Writing, 15,* 234–249.

Jones, T. E. (2006). A method of research for reality: Research and research degrees in art and design. In K. MacLeod & L. Holdridge (Eds.), *Thinking through art: Reflections on art as research* (pp. 226–240). London: Routledge.

Jones, T. E. (2009). The studio art doctorate in America. In J. Elkins (Ed.), *Artists with PhDs: On the new doctoral degree in studio art* (pp. 81–85). Washington, DC: New Academia Publishing.

Jordan, R. R. (1997). *English for academic purposes: A guide and resource book for teachers.* Cambridge: Cambridge University Press.

Katz, S. M. (1999). Review: Other floors, other voices: A textography of a small university building. *The Journal of Business Communication, 36,* 422.

Kiley, M. (2009). 'You don't want a smart Alec': Selecting examiners to assess doctoral dissertations. *Studies in Higher Education, 34,* 889–903.

Lea, M. R. (2008). Academic literacies in theory and practice. In N. Hornberger (Ed.), *Encyclopedia of language and education* (pp. 634–645). New York, NY: Springer.

Lillis, T. (2008). Ethnography as method, methodology, and "deep theorizing". *Written Communication, 25,* 353–388.

Lillis, T., & Scott, M. (2007). Defining academic literacies research: Issues of epistemology, ideology and strategy. *Journal of Applied Linguistics, 4,* 5–32.

Lincoln, Y., & Guba, E. (1985). *Naturalistic inquiry.* Beverly Hills, CA: Sage.

Macbeth, K. (2006). Diverse, unforeseen and quaint difficulties: The sensible responses of novices in learning to follow instructions in academic writing. *Research in the Teaching of English, 42,* 180–207.

MacLeod, K., & Holdridge, L. (2004). The doctorate in fine art: The importance of exemplars to the research culture. *International Journal of Art and Design Education, 23,* 155–168.

Nickerson, C. (2000). *Playing the corporate game: An investigation of the genres and discourse strategies in English used by Dutch writers working in multinational corporations.* Amsterdam: Adophi.

Paltridge, B. (2002). Thesis and dissertation writing: An examination of published advice and actual practice. *English for Specific Purposes, 21,* 125–143.

Paltridge, B., & Starfield, S. (2007). *Thesis and dissertation writing in a second language.* London: Routledge.

Paltridge, B., Harbon, L., Hirsh, D., Phakiti, A., Shen, H., Stevenson, M., & Woodrow, L. (2009). *Teaching academic writing: An introduction for teachers of second language writers.* Ann Arbor, MI: University of Michigan Press.

Paltridge, B., Starfield, S., Ravelli, L., & Nicholson, S. (2011). Doctoral writing in the visual and performing arts: Issues and debates. *The International Journal of Art and Design Education, 30,* 242–255.

Paltridge, B., Starfield, S., Ravelli, L., Nicholson, S., & Tuckwell, K. (2012a). Doctoral writing in the visual and performing arts: Two ends of a continuum. *Studies in Higher Education, 37,* 989–1003.

Paltridge, B., Starfield, S., Ravelli, L., & Tuckwell, K. (2012b). Change and stability: Examining the marcostructures of doctoral theses in the visual and performing arts. *Journal of English for Academic Purposes, 11*, 332–334.

Perales-Escudero, M., & Swales, J. M. (2011). Tracing convergence and divergence in pairs of Spanish and English research article abstracts: The case of Ibérica. *Iberica, 21*, 49–70. Retrieved from http://www.doaj.org/doaj?func = abstract&id = 775200. Accessed on 26 November 2012.

Phillips, M., Stock, C., & Vincs, K. (2008). *Dancing between diversity and consistency: Refining assessment in postgraduate degrees in dance.* Western Australian Academy of Performing Arts at Edith Cowan University, Perth. Retrieved from http://eprints.qut.edu.au/27955/. Accessed on 9 August 2012.

Ravelli, L., Paltridge, B., & Starfield, S. (2013). Extending the notion of text: The creative arts doctoral thesis. *Visual Communication, 12*(4), 395–422.

Schryer, C. (1994). The lab vs. the clinic: Sites of competing genres. In A. Freedman & P. Medway (Eds.), *Genre and the new rhetoric* (pp. 105–124). London: Taylor and Francis.

Smith, H., & Dean, R. T. (2009). Introduction: Practice-led research, research-led practice – Towards the iterative cyclic web. In H. Smith & R. T. Dean (Eds.), *Practice-led research, research-led practice in the creative arts* (pp. 1–3). Edinburgh: Edinburgh University Press.

Starfield, S., Paltridge, B., & Ravelli, L. (2012). Why do we have to write?: Practice-based theses in the visual and performing arts and the place of writing. In V. K. Bhatia, C. Berkenkotter, & M. Gotti (Eds.), *Insights into academic genres* (pp. 169–190). Bern: Peter Lang.

Street, B. V. (2010). Academic literacies: New directions in theory and practice. In J. Maybin & J. Swann (Eds.), *The Routledge companion to English language studies* (pp. 232–242). London: Routledge.

Swales, J. M. (1995). The role of the textbook in EAP writing research. *English for Specific Purposes, 14*, 3–18.

Swales, J. M. (1998a). Textography: Toward a contextualization of written academic discourse. *Research on Language and Social Interaction, 31*, 109–121.

Swales, J. M. (1998b). *Other floors, other voices: A textography of a small university building.* Mahwah, NJ: Laurence Erlbaum.

Swales, J. M. (2004). *Research genres: Explorations and applications.* Cambridge: Cambridge University Press.

Swales, J. M., & Luebs, M. (1995). Towards textography. In B.-L. Gunnarson & I. Backlund (Eds.), *Writing in academic contexts* (pp. 12–29). Unit for advanced Studies in modern Swedish (FUMS). Uppsala, Sweden: Uppsala University.

Swales, J. M., & Rogers, P. (1995). Discourse and the projection of corporate culture: The mission statement. *Discourse and Society, 6*, 223–242.

Tardy, C. M. (2003). A genre system view of the funding of academic research. *Written Communication, 20*, 7–36.

United Kingdom Council for Graduate Education. (1997). *Practice-based doctorates in the creative and performing arts and design.* Coventry, UK: UKCGE.

van Dijk, T. A. (1980). *Macrostructures: An interdisciplinary study of global structures in discourse, interaction and cognition.* Mahwah, NJ: Lawrence Erlbaum.

Wingate, U., & Tribble, C. (2012). The best of both worlds? Towards an English for academic purposes/academic literacies writing pedagogy. *Studies in Higher Education, 37*, 481–495.

LEARNING ARCHITECTURES AND COMMUNITIES OF PRACTICE IN HIGHER EDUCATION

Jonathan Tummons

ABSTRACT

There is considerable variety in the use and citation of Wenger's framework of communities of practice in educational research. In some cases, citations and references to Wenger's work are superficial and lack meaningful theoretical application. In others, citations and use of Wenger's work are critical and insightful, thoughtfully applying Wenger's framework to a range of educational settings. The effect of these variable uses is a conceptual slippage that leads to the framework being misapplied, misunderstood and over-simplified. In this chapter I foreground the under-used idea of learning architectures. A learning architecture consists of an assemblage of components that may allow learning to take place. Such an assemblage might consist of a place (rooms, workshops, facilities), tools and equipment (textbooks, materials, handbooks, reading lists) and activities that require and encourage mutual engagement (seminars, tutorials, group presentations). In this chapter, drawing on previously published ethnographic research, one teacher-training course is used to model a learning architecture approach. At the same time, the

Theory and Method in Higher Education Research II
International Perspectives on Higher Education Research, Volume 10, 121–139
ISSN: 1479-3628/doi:10.1108/S1479-3628(2014)0000010012

chapter introduces and resolves one of the more contested aspects of Wenger's framework, namely the position of pedagogy and assessment within a community of practice.

INTRODUCTION

Much current and recent research and writing relating to learning, teaching and assessment in UK higher education (and, indeed, in other education sectors and national contexts as well) rests on theoretical perspectives that can be conveniently summarised as drawing on theories of learning as social practice, on those theoretical approaches to learning that focus not on what might happen within the head or mind of the individual student, but on the social and cultural spaces in which students work and learn. Models such as communities of practice, activity systems and expansive apprenticeships occupy a prominent position in contemporary research writing (Ashwin, 2009; Trowler, 2008). This prominence is in stark contrast to UK higher education teacher training literature (Biggs & Tang, 2011; Fry, Ketteridge, & Marshall, 2008), which still predominantly employs theoretical frameworks that draw on individual cognition models of learning, on acquisition rather than participation metaphors (Sfard, 1998).

The argument that I am going to put forward is an attempt to foreground the use of social practice theories of learning in higher education. It derives in the first instance from perceived problems with the ways in which social practice theories are expounded and applied. I am going to argue that, if social practice theories were used more critically and more thoroughly, they would be able to contribute to conversations about learning, teaching and assessment in higher education in a more immediately pragmatic, coherent and convincing manner than is currently the case. I am going to draw on *communities of practice* theory (Lave & Wenger, 1991; Wenger, 1998). More specifically, I am going to draw on an element of this theory, *learning architecture*, that can provide a theoretically convincing account of learning, teaching and assessment within higher education.

THE USES AND MISUSES OF THEORY

What is theory? Tight has argued that theories are suppositions that explain something, or seek to explain it, and posits theory as the ability to explain or understand the findings of research within a conceptual framework (2004, p. 399). Ashwin, similarly, positions theory as informing the conceptualisation of research: the framing of research questions, the analysis of the data that is created, and understanding the significance of the findings that are drawn. At the same time, he warns against using theory to structure research in such a way that the research simply consists of a tautological restatement of the theory in question (2009, p. 133). But the very variable uses of theory by educational researchers would seem to suggest that the positions occupied by Tight and Ashwin are not widely shared (see also Hammersley, 2012; Trowler, 2012). In particular, Thomas has argued that the use of theory has been superseded by an excess of *theory talk*, erroneously used to claim 'epistemological legitimacy and explanatory commentary' (2007, p. 85), positioning himself within a broader cultural turn that highlights the fragility rather than utility of theory (McArthur, 2012). Clearly, then, as a community of education researchers we do ourselves few favours if our use of theory is flawed or damaged. Not only does this impact on the quality or generalisability of our own research (Gobo, 2008), or on the epistemological foundations of the theory or theories themselves (Thomas, 2007), but also on the broader acceptance of the practical possibilities afforded by the research – such as the use of communities of practice theory to inform learning and teaching practices in higher education.

I shall return to the broader problem that surrounds theory use and theory talk in education research later on. For now, I want to turn to communities of practice theory (Wenger, 1998). If I am going to argue – and I am – that communities of practice theory can contribute constructively to conversations about learning, teaching and assessment in higher education, then I first need to establish a critical and thorough understanding of what communities of practice actually are.

DEFINING COMMUNITIES OF PRACTICE

Learning is a consequence of engagement in social practice (Lave & Wenger, 1991; Wenger, 1998). Learning is 'the same' whether or not any kind of educational structure has been established to provide a context for it: there are no contrasts between 'formal' and 'informal' learning, for example (Lave & Wenger, 1991, p. 40). As people engage in social practices of different kinds, their engagement 'entails learning as an internal constituent' (*ibid.*, p. 35), a process that Lave and Wenger refer to as *legitimate peripheral participation*. Indeed, such engagement is described as a *condition* for effective learning (*ibid.*, p. 93). That is to say, learning happens when people participate in practice. According to this theory, learning is not a phenomenon that occurs solely 'in the head'. Rather, it is a social and cultural process that involves and entails changes to the whole person, and how s/he acts and moves within the social world. Learning changes how people think, act and speak: it changes people's identities (*ibid.*, p. 151).

Learning through legitimate peripheral participation takes place within social and cultural spaces which are referred to as communities of practice (Lave & Wenger, 1991). Communities of practice are everywhere. We are all members of multiple communities of practice, some of which overlap with others. Sometimes, we are not even aware that we are members of a particular community, not least because only a very few have been subject to methodical, critical scrutiny (invariably by academic writers in books and book chapters, journal articles, conference papers or theses). As people in a social world, we engage in all kinds of activities − *practices* − as part of our 'everyday' lives, interacting with other people, sometimes in close proximity and sometimes at a distance or by proxy: at work, at play, with families or with friends. In order to take part in these various practices people come together in *communities* so that they can talk about their practices, share them and learn more about them. These *communities of practice* can be found in both formal and informal settings (remembering that the learning that occurs in these is the same at an epistemological and ontological level). Examples include tailors, amateur radio operators, butchers, recovering alcoholics and office-based computer users (Lave & Wenger, 1991; Wenger, 1998). Other examples include adult learners in a basic skills class (Harris & Shelswell, 2005), teachers of mathematics (Cobb & McClain, 2006) and education researchers (Hodkinson, 2004). In some communities, members will meet and talk on a regular basis; in others, they will meet only infrequently. Some communities have existed for a long time; others are relatively new. Some communities establish and sustain close relations with others, sharing aspects of their practice, while others are relatively self-sufficient. None, however, are isolated. All communities of practice share specific structural qualities. There are three attributes that are posited as maintaining the coherence of practice within a community: *mutual engagement, joint enterprise* and *shared repertoire* (Wenger, 1998, pp. 73–85).

Mutual engagement is the term used by Wenger to refer to the ways in which members of a community of practice interact with each other and do whatever they do. Members of a community might engage with others in a complementary manner or an overlapping manner, depending on the relative competence and positions that they occupy. Because working together creates differences as well as similarities, mutual engagement is never homogenous. Things can be done, argued over or spoken about in various ways so long as these are reconcilable to the *joint enterprise* of the community of practice. *Joint enterprise* refers to the shared work or endeavour of the community of practice. In order to engage in practice, members draw on the *shared repertoire* of the community, the habits, discourses, routines, ways of talking, tools, structures and other artefacts that over time have been created or adopted by a community of practice. Such artefacts serve a number of functions. They allow the members of a community to make statements about their practice, to express their identities within the community, and they represent the history of mutual engagement within the community. The repertoire can be seen as *reifying* aspects of the practices of a community (to reify something means to turn a concept or mental construct into a physical thing — for example, abstract notions of justice can be reified into statutes). And, reflecting the different ways in which members engage in practice, so members draw on the repertoire of the community in differential ways as they learn.

MOVING COMMUNITIES OF PRACTICE INTO HIGHER EDUCATION

The problem with communities of practice theory, when considering how it might be used to explain or inform higher education practice, is that it rests on a particular theory of learning — situated learning — that rejects discourses and modes of formal instruction:

> In a community of practice, there are no special forms of discourse aimed at apprentices or crucial to their ... movement toward full participation that correspond to ... the lecturing of college professors. (Lave & Wenger, 1991, p. 108)

But if there is no such thing as formal instruction within a community of practice, then using communities of practice theory to explicate learning, teaching and assessment within higher education contexts is immediately rendered problematic. How can a theory that explicitly denies the existence of formal modes of instruction be taken seriously as a way of explicating learning and teaching interactions in higher education? In this context, it is all the more surprising that within current and recent literature that draws on communities of practice theory, there have been relatively few serious attempts to solve this theoretical problem, even though the theoretical tools to do so are available.

Let me provide four examples of uses of communities of practice theory that are inadequate or incomplete, that embody the kinds of partial or insufficient use of theory that I addressed at the start of this chapter. (I draw here on my own wider research into learning, teaching and assessment in higher education (Tummons, 2012).) For example, in an article that proposes a model of assessment practice in higher education wherein criteria are negotiated between students and tutors in an attempt to generate greater understanding of the assessment process amongst students, Rust, O'Donovan and Price state that 'a social constructivist view of learning ... argues that knowledge is shaped and evolves through increasing participation within different communities of practice' (2005, p. 232). And yet the article makes no attempt to consider where these communities of practice might be, how they might be defined or how their different practices may be understood.

A similarly cursory use of the term 'community of practice' is found in an article by Elwood and Klenowski (2002), in reporting their research into assessment practices on a masters-level education module. In the article, two terms are employed: 'community of shared practice' (a rather tautological expression: by definition, the practices of a community are always, necessarily, shared) and 'community of assessment practice', sometimes interchangeably. And yet the model of learning that the article rests on as a whole draws more on individual cognition and acquisition models of deep and surface learning, and 'learning to learn'. Once again, the fundamental characteristics (the shared repertoire, the joint enterprise, the mutual engagement) of the community or communities of practice that the paper refers to are left unexplored.

In reporting research that explores the reliability of portfolio-based assessment within a masters-level course for teachers in higher education, Baume and Yorke (2002) propose that one of the ways by which portfolio-based assessment can be defined as *reliable* is through the development of shared understandings of what the assessment process entails between course participants, course tutors and the course team (the academic staff who create the course in question). They go on to propose that the ways in which these three sets of actors interact and work together 'come close to constituting a "community of practice"' (Baume & Yorke, 2002, p. 23). But there is no further discussion about how this community might be understood. Nor is there any discussion about what it is about this group of actors and their shared endeavours within the course that means that they only 'come close' to being a community of practice: what is stopping a 'community of practice' from emerging, and why?

And finally, through her research into assessment practices across two different academic departments within one university, Shay (2005, 2008) posits assessment as a socially situated interpretive act, and highlights the tensions and ambiguities that surround emergent definitions of assessment validity and reliability, and the emergent definition of assessment criteria, within what she terms academic communities of practice, although these are never explicitly defined (a point also noted by Trowler, 2008, pp. 95–97).

This is not to deny the important arguments and ideas that these four – and other – articles and chapters put forward. All of the works cited in the preceding four paragraphs are scholarly, well written, useful (and not just to me) and, rightly, widely cited. But I am not so sure that the uses of communities of practice theory in these works satisfy the use of theory positions outlined by Ashwin (2009), Hammersley (2012) and Tight (2004), amongst others. Specifically, none of these works addressed the fundamental problem of how to reconcile the position of formal instruction within a theoretical framework that rejects it. The argument that I am presenting here is that if communities of practice theory is used more critically, more thoroughly and more carefully, then it would be capable of more immediately practical and recognisable contributions to the scholarship of learning and teaching. But before this can be done, we have to solve the pedagogy problem.

THE PEDAGOGY PROBLEM IN COMMUNITIES OF PRACTICE: FOREGROUNDING LEARNING ARCHITECTURES

Much of the research that has been done with communities of practice theory has understandably, and quite correctly, focused on what has been termed 'informal learning' (Boud & Middleton, 2003; Rock, 2005; Viskovic, 2005). This is emphatically not because communities of practice theory posits a distinction between 'formal' and 'informal' learning, however. Rather, this is a reflection of communities of practice theory rejecting the notion of pedagogy as a discrete form of instructional discourse. I have already indicated that the theoretical elements that we need in order to solve the pedagogy problem are already to be found within communities of practice theory. It is to these elements that I shall now turn.

I propose that through the use of Wenger's (1998) concept of *learning architecture*, the position of pedagogy – of teaching – within a community of practice can be explained in a theoretically coherent and consistent manner. This is a concept that has, perhaps surprisingly, only very seldom been drawn on by researchers and writers (Brosnan & Burgess, 2003; McLoughlin & Lee, 2008; Sorensen & Ó Murchú, 2004). Learning architecture allows the researcher to put pedagogy, assessment, curriculum and other elements of formal educational provision into an account of learning that rests on a socially situated paradigm. It also in effect forces the researcher to take the time and space to define and describe the communities of practice where this learning is located. In this way, the researcher is required to provide the kind of rich, ethnographic descriptions of the communities of practice being explored that hark back to the ethnographic and anthropological roots of Lave and Wenger's (1991) and Wenger's (1998) original works, in order to provide similarly rich, authoritative and convincing descriptions of the learning architectures that are being explored.

Learning architecture is, simply put, a design for learning that emphasises the need for the design (the curriculum, the environment, the people and so forth) to afford the learners with opportunities to participate in the practice of a community – and hence opportunities to learn – that are defined in alignment to Wenger's (1998) wider communities of practice theory. Learning architecture needs to provide affordances for mutual engagement, joint enterprise and shared repertoire (as described above). Or, to put it another way, the establishment of a learning architecture in a higher education setting is a necessary precursor to the establishment of a community of practice in that setting.

A learning architecture consists of an assemblage of components or resources that can allow learning to take place. Such an assemblage of resources might consist of a place (laboratories, seminar rooms, workshops, libraries, information technology suites), tools and equipment (tools, textbooks, materials, handbooks, reading lists), people (lecturers, teachers, technicians, students, support workers) and activities (experiments, seminars, tutorials, practical tasks, assignment tasks), all designed to create a context within which learning takes place. One of these resources – the one which has historically been so problematic in applying communities of practice theories to formal educational contexts – is teaching, which is understood here as being part of the learning architecture, rather than a separate process that stands outside it. Teaching becomes part of the repertoire of the community of practice. As such, and in common with other elements of the repertoire of any community of practice, it is a cultural tool that can be employed by those members of the community who have the appropriate expertise to access it: the teachers.

However, as has already been discussed, the introduction of teachers, and by extension of teaching, into a communities of practice framework raises profound theoretical problems when Lave and Wenger's rejection of a language of formal instruction is recalled. According to this earlier perspective, it is the emergent and improvised quality of learning that precludes a discourse of formal instruction. Learning is simply too fluid, characterised by subjectivities and ambiguities, to be reconciled with the kinds of formal curricula that are to be found within universities. But Wenger later finds an elegant solution to this problem:

> ... teaching does not cause learning: what ends up being taught may or may not be what was taught, or more generally what the institutional organisation of instruction intended. Learning is an emergent, ongoing process, which may use teaching as *one of its many structuring resources*. (Wenger, 1998, p. 267, emphasis added).

Learning architectures always need to be carefully planned and designed, therefore, but these processes are not to be conflated with the actual learning that might happen. Through positioning teaching as just one component amongst many others within a learning architecture, Wenger argues that the practice of teaching is no more able to straightforwardly shape, predict or control learning than are textbooks able to be read and understood in only one way (an issue that I shall return to below).

A LEARNING ARCHITECTURE FOR INITIAL TEACHER EDUCATION

In order to provide a worked example of learning architecture, I shall draw on my own prior research: a multi-sited ethnography of one initial teacher education course for the UK learning and skills sector (the term used to describe the provision of vocational and technical education and training in further education colleges). I conducted my fieldwork, which consisted of documentary research, interviews and observations, over a three-year period. The course that I researched is, in common with other teacher education courses for the learning and skills sector, delivered predominantly on a part-time in-service basis within further education colleges which franchise their teacher education provision as a form of *higher education in further education* from a nearby university. The course that I researched was, during my fieldwork, being delivered across a large network of almost thirty colleges: I conducted my research at four of these colleges. Although my research represents just one curriculum within UK higher education, I argue that my findings are generalisable across other higher education curricula that share similar delivery modes and patterns of assessment (Tummons, 2010a, 2010b, 2011, 2012).

According to Wenger, a learning architecture must always be built around four key theoretical elements of communities of practice theory. More accurately, these elements are referred to as *dualities*, and are so called because each element consists in turn of two inter-related theoretical aspects. The four dualities are: reification and participation; designed and emergent; local and global; and identification and negotiability (Wenger, 1998, p. 271ff; see also Brosnan & Burgess, 2003, p. 26–7; Sorensen & Ó Murchú, 2004, pp. 190–197), and these will now be discussed, and examples given, in turn:

(i) Reification and participation

For members to learn the practices of a community, they need to be afforded opportunities to both take part in the work of the community (i.e. to participate), and also to create the kinds of objects or artefacts that capture and make solid the work of the community (i.e. to reify). This duality focuses attention, therefore, on the balance that has to be found to allow learners firstly to come to know about, use or otherwise draw on the existing tools, objects and artefacts of a community, and secondly to amend, add to, edit or reconfigure these same tools and objects. According to communities of practice theory, it is through both acts – participation *and* reification-that people learn. Examples of the kinds of objects that are found within the *community of teacher education practice* that was the focus of my research include *reading lists* and *module guides* (which are reified within this community of practice) and teacher education *textbooks* and *academic journal articles* (which are reified outside this particular community of practice – an issue that I shall return to shortly). Objects such as these are typical of just about any course within a higher education context. Examples of the kinds of objects that students can add to, interact with or reify include firstly *written assignments*, in common with many other curricula, and *schemes of work* and *lesson plans*, which are created by the students during their teaching placements before being compiled in a portfolio for assessment, and are more specific to teacher education programmes.

(ii) Designed and emergent

Because, as has already been noted, learning is a fluid, complex and somewhat unpredictable phenomenon, it is important to recognise that no learning architecture can ever predict the kinds of learning that will take place within the community of practice. Consequently, the design of the architecture has to be mindful of the different ways in which learners will talk about and work with the resources that have been afforded to them, the ways in which different teachers will interact with their students, the ways in which the use of tools or materials might change over time, and so forth. So, a learning architecture has to be *designed* (e.g. curricula have to be written, staff have to be employed, resources have to be purchased, workshops or laboratories have to be equipped and so forth), but the learning that will happen within these spaces will always be *emergent* (that is to say, unpredictable, capable of leading to surprising or unexpected outcomes and so forth). This relationship between design and emergence can be seen clearly at work in the design of assignment tasks such as *individual learning plans*, which are written in such a way as to allow different genres or levels of response from learners, all of whom may choose to respond to the plan in slightly different ways, or 'standard' academic *essays* that allow students some latitude in negotiating the precise topics or themes that are to be covered.

(iii) Local and global

Communities of practice do not exist in isolation: they are all connected to greater or lesser degrees in networks that Wenger (1998) refers to as *constellations*. These constellations allow for the movement of both people and objects between different communities of practice that are more-or-less closely related. No community of practice is isolated and entirely indigenous in its culture, but the extent to which the practices of one community are shared with or borrowed from another community will of course vary. In this way, every community of practice consists of elements that are both *local* (i.e. native or indigenous) and *global* (i.e. borrowed or shared from elsewhere in the constellation). Sometimes communities of practice might have close relationships with their neighbours, allowing members and materials to cross the boundaries between them. Examples of shared artefacts within the community of initial teacher education practice include the *handbooks* and

module guides. These are produced at the central university and distributed to all of the colleges where the course is delivered. An example of
a shared practice within the community is the cross-college *internal
moderation* of student work, which involves the movement of both people (teachers) and objects (students' portfolios of assessment) across
community boundaries. Communities of practice are also connected to
more distant neighbours, perhaps through the local appropriation of a
resource, procedure or tool from an outside community of practice. An
example of a procedure is the *Integrated Quality and Enhancement
Review*, the audit of higher education in further education provision
carried out according to regulations set down by the Quality Assurance
Agency for Higher Education. The use of academic *journal articles* by
teachers and students as a learning and teaching resource is an example
of a practice that relies on the sharing of global resources.

(iv) Identification and negotiability

If a community of practice is going to thrive, then it needs to allow
members to strike a balance between matching up to the requirements
or standards of the community, and being able to act independently
within it. If a learner feels powerless or ignored within a community of
practice, then s/he will become alienated from it and consequently will
not feel able or willing to participate and as a result will not be able to
learn. If, however, learners are able to make some kind of choice or
informed input regarding aspects of their practice, then their participation within the community of practice, and hence their learning, will
be deeper and more meaningful. A balance needs to be struck, therefore, regarding the extent to which members *identify* with the practices,
goals or aspirations of a community, and the extent to which members
can *negotiate* aspects of their practice. Examples of activities that allow
such a balance (although not at the expense of the coherence of the
curriculum which must of course be carefully sustained) within the
community of teacher education practice include *negotiated assignment
tasks* (such as allowing students to focus on particular theories when
writing essays on curriculum), and the dialogue and feedback that
occurs around *observations of teaching practice* (the times and details
of which can be negotiated between the student and the teacher, in
stark contrast to the 'drop-in' observations that are characteristic of
quality assurance and inspection regimes).

So what is the learning architecture for initial teacher education that was
the focus of my research and is the focus of this chapter? Put simply, this

learning architecture consists of things and people, an assemblage of the material and the spatial that once gathered together constitute a community of practice where some learning will happen. It consists of tools and artefacts (handouts, reading lists, smartboards and course planners), processes and procedures (moderation meetings, tutorials, induction sessions and diagnostic assessments), spaces and places (timetables, seminar rooms, libraries and computer suites) and activities (writing, debating, reading and teaching). It cannot predict what exactly will be learned by the people who move within and across it, but it can establish an environment, a space (institutional, geographic, temporal) in which some kinds of learning about some kinds of things – in this case, becoming a teacher – can be afforded to the learners who choose to be there.

LEARNING ARCHITECTURES AND COMMUNITIES OF PRACTICE IN HIGHER EDUCATION: CONCLUSIONS

At the start of this chapter, I proposed that there were two strands to the argument that I am presenting here. The first related to the need for a more coherent and critical use of Wenger's communities of practice theory, in order to answer those critiques of education research that position theory use as inconsistent, tautological or lacking cumulative application. The second related to the benefits that a communities of practice perspective – necessarily drawing on learning architecture – would offer to current discourses around learning, teaching and assessment in higher education, which continue to be dominated by individual cognition models of learning and quality assurance discourses that assume that learning is predictable, auditable and prone to 'scientific' evaluation. I now offer conclusions relating to each of these in turn.

Conclusions (i): We Need to Talk about Learning

A lot of journal articles and books rest on a very narrow reading and/or understanding of Wenger's (1998) communities of practice framework. The term 'community of practice' gets used indiscriminately, often with little recourse to any detailed or critical exposition of the theory: as evidenced by the four examples of communities of practice research that were discussed earlier in this chapter. Much of this literature fails to take account that communities of practice theory is a theory of learning where learning is understood as being a social practice. As such, any claims within such literature to have anything serious to say about learning teaching and assessment are highly problematic. The term 'community of practice' is used indiscriminately by researchers who then do not go on to define or describe where these communities are, what their practises are, how their repertoires are constituted and so on. And while other examples drawn from extant literature makes better use of Wenger's work, this is also, often, partial. Although other accounts have addressed formal educational contexts that would assume some kind of pedagogic discourse to be present, such accounts have not satisfactorily theorised the position of such a discourse of instruction within communities of practice (Harris & Shelswell, 2005; James, 2007; Malcolm & Zukas, 2000; McArdle & Ackland, 2007).

The first point that I wish to make here is to foreground the necessity of using Wenger's communities of practice theory in a more coherent manner. I am not arguing that specific components from Wenger's work should not be drawn on in isolation in order to explore or unpack particular issues of themes. Wenger's concept of the *double edge of reification* provides an excellent example of a discrete component of his work that has wider applicability across other theoretical perspectives that share the same assumptions about learning that communities of practice theory occupies (1998, p. 62ff). In its exposition of the inability of artefacts to contain a single fixed meaning but instead to be prone to multiple interpretations mediated by the biography and experience of the user, it is in clear alignment to a number of other theoretical perspectives. Social practice accounts of literacy also stress the different meanings that people bring to the texts that they use in *literacy events*, in which the meanings taken from texts are mediated by the social practices that enfold them (Barton, 2007; Lillis, 2001). This in turn is closely aligned to the *text-reader conversation*, a concept found in *institutional ethnography* (Campbell & Gregor, 2004; Smith, 2005), which describes reading a text as a conversation in which the reader plays both parts, firstly activating the text – by reading it – and then responding to it or acting on it, although probably not quite in the way intended by the author. Any one of these three concepts is perfectly capable of being compared or contrasted with another as part of a rigorous theoretical debate about the meanings ascribed to a text by the person who is reading it.

However, the broader concept of the *community of practice* is not so straightforwardly discrete. The three concepts referred to in the previous paragraph all contain what might be termed a straightforward and easily understood central thesis: that different people will take different meanings, for different reasons, from the same text. Our everyday experiences of trips to the cinema or joining book clubs lead to the same phenomenon: that a few of us might watch the same film or read the same book, and take different meanings from them. But if we are going to describe something as *a community of practice*, then we cannot simply stop there. We need to describe the mutual engagement of the community; we need to describe the joint enterprise of the community; and we need to unpack the shared repertoire of the community. Only by doing all of this are we able to state satisfactorily what the practice of the community actually is, and therefore what kinds of things its members are learning. All of these are theoretical necessities, not optional extras. In essence, therefore, when we talk or write about communities of practice, we are talking about learning. And, therefore, when we talk or write about communities of practice, we need to be prepared to talk about all of these other elements as well.

Conclusions (ii): Communities of Practice, Pedagogy and Learning Architecture

Having established that communities of practice theory both requires and deserves comprehensive as well as critical treatment, the use of learning architecture allows us to solve the problem of how to position pedagogy — a discourse of instruction — within a community of practice. Once teaching is established as part of the architecture, the presence within a community of practice of pedagogy no longer contradicts the broader point that learning is improvised and emergent. Or, to put it another way, it is only through using Wenger's learning architecture framework that it becomes possible for us to use communities of practice theory to describe formal educational provision such as higher education. However, the argument that I have presented here is not solely concerned with establishing robust theoretical foundations for educational research. Communities of practice theory, as a subset of the sociocultural turn that is increasingly foregrounded in pedagogic research in higher education, also provides us with ways of investigating a number of issues that are of wider pedagogical and political importance.

The specific issues that I wish to raise here are concerned with audit, inspection and the dominant discourses of quality assurance that shape so many aspects of professional practice in higher education (Dill, 1999; Shore & Wright, 2000). The expansion of UK higher education after 1992 has been characterised by the growth of performativity cultures that have interposed themselves into many aspects of academics' lives: audit and inspection (the Quality Assurance Agency and Ofsted); documentism; the steady increase in the bureaucratic and management duties of the academic; planning and documenting regimes for both teaching (specifically, the growth of outcomes-based models of teaching in higher education based on behaviourist theories of learning (Illeris, 2007) and research (the Research Excellence Framework)). Technologies such as these – and it is the dominant outcomes-based approach to learning (and by extension, to teaching and assessment as well) that are of greatest importance and relevance here – rest on notions of manageable accountability that in turn rest on the idea that what people learn, and the way that other people teach it, can be straightforwardly measured and evaluated.

But there is a fundamental problem with this account. Communities of practice theory tells us that learning is emergent, fluid, and difficult to predict or to control. Learning architectures theory allows us to understand that the structures that are created within formal educational institutions will undoubtedly support or provoke or sustain learning, but that what kind of learning it will be, when exactly it will happen or exactly which elements of the architecture will be most efficacious in creating a context for learning, are more problematic and difficult to quantify. Put simply, even with the most rigorous and comprehensive architectures – planning, curriculum, resources, staffing, procedures, meetings and so forth – it is at a fundamental level impossible to state exactly what will be learned, how it will be learned, and when.

So what are the implications of this for learning and teaching in higher education? I am not arguing for the complete dismantling of the management and bureaucratic structures that envelop pedagogic practices within UK higher education. However I am arguing that their purview needs to be revised. Helping to ensure that appropriate architectures are established and sustained is a complex task, and it needs to be managed carefully and systematically within and across institutions. The presence of appropriate teaching accommodation, sufficient library and online resources and appropriately expert and qualified teaching staff are all facets of a learning architecture that can and must be accounted for. But the learning that happens within, around and through these architectures is nebulous, slippery at best. Learning, and its relationship to the activity that we refer to as teaching, cannot be measured and audited in the same way as can the provision of up-to-date equipment, legible and understandable course documentation or sufficient copies of core books.

This argument has consequences for audit and quality assurance systems that are both simple and profound. They are simple because I am not suggesting that the actual processes that are currently to be found in the UK higher education sector need to be altered or revised in terms of the actual activities that are carried out (such as inspection, programme appraisal, external examination and the like). They are profound because I am suggesting that the focus of such quality assurance processes needs to be altered, to concentrate on those things which can be audited or measured, such as the tangible aspects of a learning architecture, and away from those intangible things, such as learning, that cannot be so audited due to their richness, their unpredictability and their complexity.

REFERENCES

Ashwin, P. (2009). *Analysing teaching-learning interactions in higher education: Accounting for structure and agency.* London: Continuum.

Barton, D. (2007). *Literacy: An introduction to the ecology of written language* (2nd ed.). Oxford: Blackwell.

Baume, D., & Yorke, M. (2002). The reliability of assessment by portfolio on a course to develop and accredit teachers in higher education. *Studies in Higher Education, 27*(1), 7–25.

Biggs, J., & Tang, C. (2011). *Teaching for quality learning at university* (4th ed.). Maidenhead: Open University Press.

Boud, D., & Middleton, H. (2003). Learning from others at work: Communities of practice and informal learning. *Journal of Workplace Learning, 15*(5), 194–202.

Brosnan, K., & Burgess, R. (2003). Web based continuing professional development – A learning architecture approach. *Journal of Workplace Learning, 15*(1), 24–33.

Campbell, M., & Gregor, F. (2004). *Mapping social relations: A primer in doing institutional ethnography.* Lanham, MD: AltaMira.

Cobb, P., & McClain, K. (2006). The collective mediation of a high-stakes accountability programme: Communities and networks of practice. *Mind, Culture and Activity, 13*(2), 80–100.

Dill, D. (1999). Academic accountability and university adaption: The architecture of an academic learning organisation. *Higher Education, 38,* 127–194.

Elwood, J., & Klenowski, V. (2002). Creating communities of shared practice: The challenges of assessment use in learning and teaching. *Assessment and Evaluation in Higher Education, 27*(3), 243–256.

Fry, H., Ketteridge, S., & Marshall, S. (Eds.) (2008). *A handbook for teaching and learning in higher education.* London: Routledge.

Gobo, G. (2008). Reconceptualising generalisation: Old issues in a new frame. In A. Alasuutari, L. Bickman, & J. Brannen (Eds.), *The Sage handbook of social research methods.* London: Sage.

Hammersley, M. (2012). Troubling theory in case study research. *Higher Education Research and Development, 31*(3), 393–406.

Harris, S. R., & Shelswell, N. (2005). Moving beyond communities of practice in adult basic education. In D. Barton & K. Tusting (Eds.), *Beyond communities of practice: Language, power and social context*. Cambridge: Cambridge University Press.

Hodkinson, P. (2004). Research as a form of work: Expertise, community and methodological objectivity. *British Educational Research Journal, 30*(1), 9–26.

Illeris, K. (2007). *How we learn. Learning and non-learning in school and beyond*. London: Routledge.

James, N. (2007). The learning trajectory of 'old-timers': Academic identities and communities of practice in higher education. In J. Hughes, N. Jewson, & L. Unwin (Eds.), *Communities of practice: Critical perspectives*. London: Routledge.

Lave, J., & Wenger, E. (1991). *Situated learning: Legitimate peripheral participation*. Cambridge: Cambridge University Press.

Lillis, T. (2001). *Student writing: Access, regulation, desire*. London: Routledge.

Malcolm, J., & Zukas, M. (2000). Becoming an educator: Communities of practice in higher education. In I. McNay (Ed.), *Higher education and its communities*. Buckingham: Open University Press.

McArdle, K., & Ackland, A. (2007). The demands of the double shift: Communities of practice in continuing professional development. *Journal of Vocational Education and Training, 59*(1), 107–120.

McArthur, J. (2012). Virtuous mess and wicked clarity: Struggle in higher education research. *Higher Education Research and Development, 31*(3), 419–430.

McLoughlin, M., & Lee, M. (2008). A learning architecture framework (LAF) for developing community, engagement and professional identity for pre-service teachers. In I. Olney, G. Lefoe, J. Mantei, & J. Herrington (Eds.), *Proceedings of the second emerging technologies conference 2008*. University of Wollongong, Wollongong.

Rock, F. (2005). 'I've picked some up from a colleague': Language, sharing and communities of practice in an institutional setting. In D. Barton & K. Tusting (Eds.), *Beyond communities of practice: Language, power and social context*. Cambridge: Cambridge University Press.

Rust, C., O'Donovan, B., & Price, M. (2005). A social constructivist assessment process model: How the research literature shows us this could be best practice. *Assessment and Evaluation in Higher Education, 30*(3), 231–240.

Sfard, A. (1998). On two metaphors for learning and the dangers of choosing just one. *Educational Researcher, 27*(2), 4–13.

Shay, S. (2005). The assessment of complex tasks: A double reading. *Studies in Higher Education, 30*(6), 663–679.

Shay, S. (2008). Researching assessment as social practice: Implications for research methodology. *International Journal of Educational Research, 47*(3), 159–164.

Shore, C., & Wright, S. (2000). Coercive accountability – The rise of audit culture in higher education. In M. Strathern (Ed.), *Audit cultures: Anthropological studies in accountability, ethics and the academy*. London: Routledge.

Smith, D. (2005). *Institutional ethnography: A sociology for people*. Lanham, MD: Altamira Press.

Sorensen, E., & Ó Murchú, D. (2004). Designing online learning communities of practice: A democratic perspective. *Journal of Educational Media, 29*(3), 189–200.

Thomas, G. (2007). *Education and theory: Strangers in paradigms*. Maidenhead: Open University Press.

Tight, M. (2004). Research into higher education: An a-theoretical community of practice? *Higher Education Research and Development, 23*(4), 395–411.

Trowler, P. (2008). *Cultures and change in higher education: Theories and practice.* Basingstoke: Palgrave Macmillan.

Trowler, P. (2012). Wicked issues in situating theory on close-up research. *Higher Education Research and Development, 31*(3), 273–284.

Tummons, J. (2010a). The assessment of lesson plans in teacher education: A case study in assessment validity and reliability. *Assessment and Evaluation in Higher Education, 35*(7), 847–857.

Tummons, J. (2010b). Institutional ethnography and actor-network theory: A framework for researching the assessment of trainee teachers. *Ethnography and Education, 5*(3), 345–357.

Tummons, J. (2011). 'It sort of feels uncomfortable': Problematising the assessment of reflective practice. *Studies in Higher Education, 45*(3), 471–483.

Tummons, J. (2012). Theoretical trajectories within communities of practice in higher education research. *Higher Education Research and Development, 31*(3), 299–310.

Viskovic, A. (2005). 'Community of Practice' as a framework for supporting tertiary teachers' informal workplace learning. *Journal of Vocational Education and Training, 57*(3), 389–410.

Wenger, E. (1998). *Communities of practice: Learning, meaning and identity.* Cambridge: Cambridge University Press.

A TEMPORAL APPROACH TO HIGHER EDUCATION RESEARCH

Oili-Helena Ylijoki

ABSTRACT

This chapter presents some basic concepts on time studies and discusses what a temporal approach can offer for higher education research. Being an invariable constituent of life, time structures and organizes activities and processes in higher education, covering all of its levels and functions. Furthermore, the current policy agenda that emphasizes the need for higher education to accelerate innovation flows, and to speed up the production of new knowledge and workers, accentuates the importance of the temporal perspective. The chapter examines the dominant, taken-for-granted conception of time — clock time — which involves a linear, quantitative, cumulative, homogenized, abstract and decontextualized conception of time. The core features of clock time are described by the four Cs put forward by Barbara Adam: creation, commodification, colonization and control of time. It is argued that, in the current digital, post-modern era, social acceleration reshapes and transforms the nature of clock time, which results in compression of time, shrinking future and extended present, all manifest in the overall speeding-up of life. In addition, a temporal lens for analysing higher education is presented, with

Theory and Method in Higher Education Research II
International Perspectives on Higher Education Research, Volume 10, 141–160
Copyright © 2014 by Emerald Group Publishing Limited
ISSN: 1479-3628/doi:10.1108/S1479-3628(2014)0000010013

examples from empirical studies on time and temporalities in academic work and identity building.

INTRODUCTION

Time is usually taken for granted in higher education research. It tends to be an unquestioned and implicit undercurrent when investigating different levels and aspects of higher education, seldom put under close scrutiny. Moreover, when time is incorporated in study design, for instance by including time series or before-and-after measurements, it is in most cases embedded in a specific and simplistic notion of time, that is, clock time. Time studies, which have seen a growing interest in social sciences in recent years (e.g. Adam, 1995, 2004; Hassan & Purser, 2007; Nowotny, 1994; Rosa & Scheuerman, 2009), emphasize the complexity and multi-layered nature of time; clock time being just one – yet hegemonic – conception of time, interlinked with industrialization and the rise of modernity. Although clock time has come to be seen as a self-evident fact of life, like time itself, it is a social and cultural construction. By making visible the overwhelming grip of clock time which prevails in the collectively sustained natural attitude, time studies can offer new perspectives for gaining a deeper understanding of the temporal underpinnings of higher education.

The starting point in time studies is that time, interwoven with space and matter, is the fundamental constituent of all spheres of life. Adam (1990, 1995, 1998, 2004), one of the most influential authors in time studies, stresses that all cultures across history have created collective ways to relate with the past and future, to come to terms with the finitude of human existence and to synchronize activities in social life. Although these core temporal challenges of humankind seem to be universal, the ways in which they are responded to vary significantly in different contexts. According to Adam, '*how* we extend ourselves into the past and future, *how* we pursue immortality and *how* we temporally manage, organize and regulate our social affairs has been culturally, historically and contextually distinct' (2004, p. 123). These different manners to relate with time, in turn, deeply affect how life is lived and made sense of, including in institutional life.

In this chapter I will present some of the key conceptions and arguments of time studies, and discuss what this theoretical approach could mean in the context of higher education research. First I will examine in more detail the nature of clock time, and thereafter introduce the notion of social acceleration. According to it, the current digital, post-modern era is dominated by compression of time, resulting in an overall speeding-up of life. Next, I will outline a temporal lens for analysing higher education, captured by four key concepts: timeframe, timing, temporality and tempo. Then I will present two empirical studies on academic work which draw upon a temporal approach. Finally, at the end of the chapter I will reflect on the core points and the potential in this kind of theoretical framework for higher education research.

CLOCK TIME: THE FOUR CS

Clock time, involving a linear, quantitative, cumulative, homogenized, abstract and decontextualized conception of time, has become a normalized and self-evident temporal frame to make sense of and understand the functioning of higher education, as well as other spheres of social life. The core features of clock time have been conceptualized by the four Cs: creation, commodification, colonization and control of time (Adam, Whipp, & Sabelis, 2002). I will introduce each of these concepts, drawing principally on the work of Adam, but references to other time theorists are also included.

Creation of Clock Time

When somebody asks what time it is, the normal response is to look at a watch — or recently a mobile phone. Yet, clock time is not in any way a natural time, that is, time embedded in nature. Adam (1990, 1995, 1998, 2004) highlights that events and processes in nature — both environmental and bodily — are variable, context dependent and inherent in things and processes, such as the time for a plant to grow and wither, the variation between daylight and darkness, or the duration of winter. Clock time, by contrast, is invariable and precise. One hour is one hour, and any variation means that the clock is going wrong (Adam, 2004, p. 101). Furthermore, clock time is external, abstract and independent from context and content (irrespective of what is happening and under which conditions, whether it is day or night, summer or winter). It follows that clock time is a socially constructed time, a time created to human design, as Adam (2004) calls it.

Unlike the variable rhythms of nature, the invariant and precise measurement by a clock is a human invention.

The roots of clock time stem from the Benedictine monasteries of medieval Europe where the mechanical clock was introduced. Through the use of clocks, it was possible to transform the traditional seasonally based 'hours' into uniform durations, which, in turn, established a regular and rigid daily rhythm in monastic life (Zerubavel, 1981, p. 38). From the beginning, clock time was thus related to time discipline and moral obligation: it guided monks to avoid wasting time and to spend time punctually and effectively according to a strict timetable in the service of God. Gradually, clock time spread from monasteries to other spheres of society, and, finally, with the rise of industrialization, gained its dominant position. Other notions of time faded into the background, and the abstract and quantitative clock time, counting hours, minutes and seconds, turned into the self-evident and unquestioned understanding of time, 'time *per se*' (Adam, 1995, p. 25).

In the context of higher education, the triumph of clock time is manifest at all levels. Academic life is thoroughly structured by clock time rhythms, organizing and ordering activities, among other things, into classes, terms, funding periods and assessment cycles. Internalization of the norms of clock time belongs to the hidden curriculum of education, as at lower levels schoolchildren learn to adapt to externally formulated timetables with regular and fixed slots for arrival, lessons, breaks, eating and other school-day activities (Adam, 1995, pp. 59–64).

Commodification of Time

Commodification of time is encapsulated in the slogan 'time is money', characterizing the key feature of industrialization. The original attachment of clock time with the religious pursuit for salvation turned into a quest for money and profit. The abstract, decontextualized clock time was a perfect partner for abstract, decontextualized money, as Adam (2004, p. 126) points out. Clock time became the medium by which the values of labour, tasks, products and services were measured and evaluated. Yielding to an abstract exchange value, clock time could be utilized as a necessary tool for translating work into money, irrespective of what use value the outputs may have. In this way, time became commodified, inherently and intimately linked with money, and, at the same time, an integral component of production. The inherent link between clock time and money is apparent also in what Adam (2004, pp. 126–7) calls the built-in clock of capital: 'When "time is money" then time costs money and time makes money because the economic practice of charging interest means that capital has a built-in clock that is constantly ticking away'.

The commodification of time does not concern only capitalist production but permeates other spheres of life as an underlying assumption. In everyday life time is understood as a scarce resource, which, like money, can be saved, spent, borrowed, invested, allocated, stolen, and so on. Yet, there is a difference. Whereas accumulation of money means a growth of wealth that can continue indefinitely, the accumulation of days and years in human existence means growing older and getting closer to death (Adam, 2003b).

Time as commodity is interrelated with power relations: 'whose time is valuable to whom and whether or not the value involved can and should be translated into money' (Adam, 2004, p. 127). For instance, there are time-rich-money-poor and time-poor-money-rich persons. In practice, the latter are able to exchange money for time by buying time-saving services and devices, which transforms money into time, whereas the other way round tends to be no option (Adam, 2004, p. 127). In this way, time as commodity is embedded in time politics, creating and sustaining hierarchies in temporal relations. In higher education, time politics is especially evident in academic capitalism (Slaughter & Leslie, 1997), in which one party is able to buy the time of the other and exchange it for money, such as in temporal hierarchies between academic researchers and funding agencies, or among departments, university management and the ministry.

Control of Time

Since time is money, it needs to be controlled in order to guarantee its utilization effectively with maximum profitability. This has been done by increasing the activity within the same unit of time (more effective machines and intensification of labour), reorganizing the sequence and ordering of activities (Taylorism and Fordism) and through flexibilization and the elimination of unproductive times from the process (just-in-time production) (Adam, 2004, p. 128).

Time control, aiming at economic profit, is interwoven with the compression of time (Adam, 2004). The faster the product moves through the system, the higher profit it gains. Therefore, speed becomes crucially important: maximizing the pace and tempo of activities is a high priority in time control. In the current higher education context, the valorization of speed is exceptionally apparent in the policy demand to speed up knowledge transfer from university to society, in order to promote economic growth and competitiveness.

Rooted in industrial production, time control has extended into other areas of social activity. Moreover, as an unquestioned part of a shared understanding of time, it tends to be transformed from managerial control into internalized time discipline, not in need of external steering and surveillance (e.g. Walker, 2009). In the context of higher education too, time control can be either external or self-controlled. It can refer, for instance, to external time management systems in which academics are required to report on which tasks, and for how long, they have allocated their working time, but also to internalized time control in the form of being continuously aware of the need to use time as productively and efficiently as possible.

Colonization With and Of Time

Clock time has also acted as a tool for colonizing. Adam (2004, pp. 136–143) differentiates two aspects of this: colonization with time and colonization of time. Colonization with time refers to the global imposition of clock time in the form of time zones, world time and standard time, all of which have contributed to the dominance of abstract clock time worldwide. Irrespective of space or cultural context, western clock time has been normalized and absorbed as a taken-for-granted norm, with all other times being neglected and repressed as backward or uncivilized.

Colonization of time means the penetration of clock time into all levels and forms of activities. It involves conquering darkness, engaging in economic activities at night, through, for instance, in night work, shift work and non-stop consumption. Moreover, the past and the future become colonized. Both are understood according to the logic of clock time; that is, in terms of what threats, costs or benefits they hold for the present. The present therefore gains an overwhelming position, becoming extended both towards the past and the future. The future is anticipated and calculated on the basis of the past, for maximizing benefits for the present. Adam (2004, p. 142) calls this the 'what's-in-it-for-us-now' approach, which means that the future becomes subordinated and colonized by the present.

As a consequence, clock time can be seen to break through into all spheres of living, including one's most personal and intimate life. This makes it difficult to protect or enjoy other temporalities untouched by the logic of clock time. In higher education, this kind of temporal colonization is manifest, for instance, in a long-hours working culture, which entails a normative expectation to use as much time as possible to work in order to qualify as 'a true academic' (Ylijoki, 2013), resulting in fewer and fewer spaces for alternative temporalities.

NETWORK TIME AND SOCIAL ACCELERATION

The four Cs of clock time are integrally intertwined with industrialization and modernity. However, they do not capture the specific emergent features of temporality in the current societal context, as defined by globalization and fast and instantaneous communication networks. Although clock time still forms an unquestioned and self-evident understanding of time, its nature has transformed in a significant way. Instead of linearity, predictability and control, time is increasingly characterized by instantaneity, simultaneity, immediacy, volatility, and non-sequential and non-linear processes. As a logical extension of the modernist project, in the current 24/7 society electronically constituted instantaneity and simultaneity are key temporal features, enabling real-time communication globally (Adam, 1995, 2004; Bauman, 2000; Held & Nutzinger, 1998; Leccardi, 2007).

Hassan and Purser (2007) argue that neoliberal globalization linked with the revolution in information and communication technologies have produced a new relationship with time. According to them, it is a question of a change from 'an economic and social system based on Fordism to one based on flexible accumulation' (p. 9). They describe this new temporal relationship through the concept of network time (see also Hassan, 2003). While clock time was an integral part of modernity, network time is an integral part of the present era. Network time is based on clock time, but it is a clock time which has been massively compressed and does not have the predictability afforded by clock time. Therefore, Hassan (2003, p. 236) argues, it is 'even more dictatorial than the clock, because unlike the clock, the network is unpredictable, volatile and chaotic'.

Associated with the concept of network time, Rosa (2010, p. 8) claims that we 'are tightly regulated, dominated and suppressed by a largely invisible, de-politized, undiscussed, under-theorized and unarticulated time regime', which is governed by the logic of social acceleration. This logic is based on the imperatives of clock time, especially the compression of time embedded in time control. However, in the current societal context, time compression reaches a new pitch, becoming increasingly intensified, coercive and all-encompassing. Rosa (2009, 2010) distinguishes three forms of social acceleration. Technological acceleration means the speeding up of transportation, communication and production. Acceleration of social change refers to the decline of the stability of social institutions and practices. For instance, the change rate in family and work relations have accelerated from an inter-generational pace in early modern society to generational pace in modernity, to an intra-generational pace in the current late modern context. Finally, acceleration of the pace of life points to peoples' experiences of time going faster and faster, accompanied by such phenomena as fast food, speed-dating and drive-through funerals. Also, some measurements suggest that there is a clear tendency, among other things, to eat faster, sleep less and do more within a given period of time by reducing the pauses or carrying out more things simultaneously.

The reasons behind the acceleration processes are manifold. Rosa (2009) mentions first the economic reason, stemming from the bedrock of clock time: the more you can produce in a certain period of time, the more profit you get. Secondly, there is a cultural impulse. Instead of waiting for the fulfilment of living in the life hereafter, secularized collective western thinking emphasizes the need to live as full lives as possible in this world and to gather maximum experience, leading to hectic living. Thirdly, Rosa distinguishes a structural reason. Society is differentiating structurally and functionally into smaller and smaller fragments, resulting in increasing complexity which requires more and more time for attempts to gain integration and control.

The different dimensions of acceleration deeply affect how time is understood and experienced: the 'high-speed society' (Rosa & Scheuerman, 2009) is characterized by time pressure, time scarcity, time famine and hurry, since people and organizations are captured by 'fast time' (Eriksen, 2001). Furthermore, acceleration is accompanied by changes in the interrelations between the past, present and future. On the one hand, the past loses its importance. In a rapidly changing environment, previous achievements have little or no weight, but individuals, groups and organizations have to prove their worth constantly (Sennett, 1998). On the other hand, the future is shrinking, because in hectic living there is no time for careful planning and democratic debates; besides, there is not much point in doing so, while amidst constant change the future becomes highly unpredictable. Adam (2009) clarifies the historically changing stance toward the future with the concepts of 'fate', 'fortune' and 'fiction'. In early modern society, the future was understood as fate in the hands of God, which cannot be influenced by human intervention. In modern society, the future became a fortune, a site to be conquered and made profit of by rational planning and effective measures; while, in late modern society, the future has turned out a fiction, something that is uncertain, volatile, chaotic and beyond human control. This kind of new relationship with the future fosters a 'culture of short-termism' (Hassard, 2002), 'the state of emergency' (Virilio, 2009) and 'the tyranny of the moment' (Eriksen, 2001).

However, acceleration is not an all-embracing process. Rosa (2010) emphasizes that there are natural speed limits, as many physical processes cannot be accelerated. There are also counter-trends, such as special movements dedicated to different kinds of slow living. Moreover, neither all social groups nor all parts of the world are equally colonized by temporal acceleration. Besides, as Rosa and Scheuerman (2009, p. 13) state, 'even if most spheres of social life are now speeding up, it seems unlikely that they are all doing so at the same pace'.

What is particularly important is that acceleration tends to create paradoxical consequences. Adam (2004) stresses that, when the complex, simultaneous, instantaneous and volatile network time is combined with the linear, sequential, invariable and predictable clock time, conflicts and paradoxes emerge. In the context of globally networked communication and faster and faster connections, time control and predictability become difficult if not altogether impossible. Thus, control of time through increasing compression leads to loss of control, because speed exceeds all possibilities for temporal synchronization and integration. Thus paradoxically, 'the rationalization of time, taken to its limits, becomes irrational' (Adam, 2003a, p. 73).

In a similar manner, time-saving devices afforded by the development of information technology can end up increasing time pressure. E-mailing and the internet save time enormously when compared with earlier ways to communicate and gather information, but, then again, they also immensely increase the amount of available information and communication, so that people tend to become ever more overloaded with less time at their disposal (Eriksen, 2001; Held & Nutzinger, 1998). Hence, time-saving technology increases the lack of time.

Higher education makes no exception to the general notion of social acceleration and speed valorization. For instance, higher education policy, increasingly subordinated under innovation policy, emphasizes the need to speed up the transfer of new knowledge and skills from academia to industry in order to accelerate innovation flows, and so promote the economic growth and competitiveness of firms, regions, nations and the European Union in global markets. At the level of institutions, universities need to react quickly to the changes in the turbulent environment and compete for resources, world-class staff, top students and standings in the rankings, often leading to reforms, mergers and restructuring (Harman & Meek, 2002; McKelvey & Holmén, 2009). Similarly, at the level of work practices, academics are faced with increasing competition and stronger pressures to produce more and better outcomes in shorter periods of time, such as providing fast supervision, intensifying degree production and publishing more in higher-class forums. These are all manifestations of acceleration processes taking place in the present-day university.

TIMESCAPE AND THE FOUR TS

Although based on clock time and shaped by acceleration processes, our relationship with time always involves a plurality, co-existence and mutual implication of different times. In spite of the dominance of clock time, there are other culturally constituted social relations of time, which Adam calls 'shadow times'. She says 'Not all time is money. Not all human relations are exclusively governed by the rationalized time of the clock. Not all times are equal' (Adam, 1995, p. 94). Instead, there are times that are lived and generated in the shadow of the clock time. As one example, she gives the time of caring which does not follow timetables, schedules and deadlines; neither is its value defined in monetary terms. Likewise, it could be argued that in higher education there are shadow times behind official schedules and time discipline, such as time for personal development and ripening of ideas. These are not regulated by the clock but by the logic of 'event time' (Levine, 2005): they take the time that a given task or event requires, irrespective of the institutional time order. However, Adam reminds us that there is power hierarchy involved, so that 'time that cannot be accorded a money value is consequently suspect and held in low esteem' (1995, p. 99).

Adam (1998) describes the complexity, multi-layeredness, interdependency and mutually implicating nature of time using the concept of *timescape*. She emphasizes that the notion of 'scape' is important, because it indicates that time is inseparable from space and matter, and that context matters (2004, p. 143). The key point is that there is no single time, only a multitude of times which interpenetrate and permeate our daily lives. Timescape encompasses natural time (birth/death, day/night, sleep/being awake, growth/decay), involving some invariable temporal forms such as the unidirectionality of the life cycle (we get older, not younger), which forms the basis of the human condition. Likewise, timescape entails biographical time and generational time, embedded in the historical flux of time and creating a specific relationship with our contemporaries, predecessors and successors (Schutz, 1976). Through the notion of timescape, Adam also reminds us of the crucial importance of subjective time experiences. The context dependent, embodied time is lived and experienced, allowing also access into the past through memories and into the future through plans, dreams and fantasies. Hassan (2003, p. 233) makes the point by saying that, 'We breathe in time, we dream in it, we imagine in it, we remember in it, we anticipate it and we approach death in it. Time is fundamentally embodied in everything we do'.

According to Adam (1995), the complexity, multi-dimensionality and mutual interdependence of timescape can be analysed through the lens of the four Ts: timeframe, timing, temporality and tempo. Timeframe and timing are 'when times', whereas temporality and tempo are 'process times'. All the four Ts are mutually implicated, internally interwoven and interrelated.

Timeframe means the setting within which something happens. Since the emergence of clock time, timeframes tend to be provided by the clock and calendar. For instance, the university term and the research assessment period have a certain beginning and ending, which provide a specific cyclicality and rhythmical structure for university life that has to be taken into account while planning, organizing and monitoring activities. However, Adam points out that timeframes are not entirely determined by the clock and calendar – there is room for alternative, contextual, qualitative and variable time in the social and organic rhythms of everyday life. The timeframe for a university reform, for example, tends to be attached to different interpretations by official timetables, actual practices at the grass-roots level and the lived experiences of individuals – creating competing and conflicting versions of the frame within which the reform is and should be taking place.

Timing is a 'when time' too, differentiating good and right time from bad and wrong time. Timing implies that clock time in itself is not enough for understanding human time. For the abstract time of the clock and calendar all time is equal, for which reason it is irrelevant and meaningless to talk about good and bad time. From the angle of clock time, one hour and one week are always one hour and one week, but in social life it makes a big difference which hour and week are in question. In addition, timing encompasses synchronization of activities as well as making priorities. In academic work, for instance, one often needs to negotiate proper timing among colleagues to reach smooth collaboration. Likewise, academic work involves making decisions about priorities: which tasks are the most important, and which can be put on a waiting list. This creates time orders, defining the sequences according to which different tasks are carried out. In this way, timing is intimately related with power and hierarchical structures, since it is crucial who defines temporal sequences and priorities, and what room there is for individual choice. Similarly, power relations have an important role in defining what counts as good and right timing: for instance, through what kinds of timings a successful academic career path has to be constructed.

Temporality is a 'process time', concerning how things and events are evolving in time. It refers to continuity and change in social activity, covering both cyclical and linear changes which, according to Adam (1995), mutually implicate each other. Temporality includes cycles in which plants grow, produce seeds and die, people and animals are born, live and die, and so on. Within these cycles, there are unidirectional changes so that there is no un-aging, un-dying or un-birth — the temporality is rooted in an irreversible, linear direction from birth to death (Adam, 1995, p. 22). Academic life also entails cyclical processes returning annually, weekly and daily, and linear processes evolving from a beginning to an end. On the one hand, new students enter university, study and graduate in continuous cycles; on the other hand, studying proceeds from the beginning to the end and cannot undo what is once learnt. In addition, both continuity and change are crucial features of temporality in a higher education context. For instance, disciplinary cultures and academic values have long roots, which are to some extent resistant to change. In spite of all the radical transformations, many characteristics of the medieval university are hence still recognizable in the current entrepreneurial mass university (Walker, 2009).

Finally, tempo concerns the pace and rhythm of social activity. This aspect of time is at the core of the acceleration thesis, which emphasizes the speeding-up of the pace of social activity. However, all of the four Ts are internally interwoven. The acceleration of tempo is intimately intermingled with a narrower, short-term timeframe, increasingly tight and fixed timings and a growing amount of change processes, all taking place simultaneously and creating experiences of hurriedness and time pressure. Yet, the acceleration thesis recognizes also social deceleration (Rosa, 2010). The tempo can also slow down, like in traffic jams on increasingly faster motorways. Like traffic jams, some changes in academia, such as the introduction of several electronic systems, aimed at intensifying and increasing the tempo of work processes, have actually produced deceleration and a slowing of the pace of work. Furthermore, tempo also entails a context-dependent subjective dimension. Time may fly or it can drag, it may pass slowly or too quickly, depending on the context. This cannot be measured by the clock, since all it can capture is the standard, quantitative, repetitive and decontextualized time, not subjective experiences of time.

EMPIRICAL STUDIES ON TIME IN HIGHER EDUCATION

In my own work I have drawn upon a temporal approach while exploring academic work and identity building among Finnish academics. Originally my interest in time studies grew when I and my colleague Hans Mäntylä read through interviews on work experiences gathered with 52 academics working in different positions and different fields. It was striking and astonishing how much and how strongly the interviewees talked about time, especially a lack of it. This raised an interest to look more deeply at the role of time in academic work. Aiming to capture the core dimensions of the timescape embedded in our interview material, we (Ylijoki & Mäntylä, 2003) discerned four conflicting time perspectives, which we called scheduled time, timeless time, contracted time and personal time.

Scheduled time refers to externally imposed timetables such as lecturing hours, meetings and deadlines for articles, projects, applications, assessments and so on. Analysed in the light of the four Ts, it could be said that the timeframe of scheduled time is narrow and fragmented into unconnected events and episodes, as academics are rushing from one duty and deadline to the next. The timing is fixed and mostly out of one's control. Temporality involves cyclical and linear processes as well as both continuity and change. For instance, in project research the same 'rat race' keeps going on, but then again each project has its own timetable with specific requirements. Finally, the tempo is hectic since the grip of schedules has become tighter. Altogether, scheduled time represents a clear manifestation of social acceleration taking place in higher education. It was by far the most general and prominent – yet not the only – time perspective upon which the academics interviewed relied while talking about their work experiences.

The opposite of scheduled time is what we called timeless time. While scheduled time is externally imposed and strictly regulated by the clock, timeless time means temporal freedom to define the timeframe, timing, temporality and pace of work. In timeless time academics entirely immerse in their work, research work in particular, concentrating on it in peace and quiet. In a way they transcend time as they forget the passing of time and constant time awareness. It follows that work is not structured by the logic of the clock but by the logic of the task one is doing — it takes all the time needed for its accomplishment. Timeless time is the time perspective academics strive for even if only very few are able enjoy this luxury time. For the rest, it is time they remember once having or time which they pursue to gain in the future. In any case, timeless time gives personal sense and meaning to work.

Contracted time, in turn, refers to the special time perspective of those academics who work on short-term employment. This category of staff was the vast majority among our interviewees, representing the situation in Finnish higher education. Contracted time is oriented towards the end of the present contract (how much time do I have left?), accompanied with a worry about the future (how/when/where can I get the next contract?). The timeframe is thus regulated by the length of the current contract. Timing is something where one must be always on guard, since a right timing is often the condition for getting the next contract. Temporality is experienced as a series of periods following one contract after another, with or without continuity in the work content. The tempo is fast, since the end of the contract tends to come all too soon, and there is a need to accomplish all the tasks required in the current employment and simultaneously to seek the next contract. Taken together, contracted time also speaks for acceleration in academic work.

Finally, personal time comes to the fore when academics reflect on the role of work in their lives as a whole. It is based on an awareness of the finitude of human existence, which raises such existential questions as how to use your limited lifetime, what eventually is important, what the relationship between work and life should be, and, ultimately, how to live a good life. In personal time the whole lifetime forms the timeframe within which academics reflect proper timings, changes and continuities, and the pace of their work and career. Especially, they ponder over what sacrifices working hard — often including weekends and holidays — has produced or may cause for their health and the well-being of their families. Thus, personal time concerns a balance between time devoted to academic work and to other commitments in life.

Altogether, the timescape of academic work discerned in our study is crystallized by intermingling, mutual implication, competition and conflict between the four time perspectives. The basic temporal problem is that externally imposed scheduled time, often combined with the pressure of contracted time, tends to colonize timeless time and personal time. In this sense, it is a question of power relations: who has power over academics' time, and to what extent do academics have temporal autonomy at their disposal. Yet, this is not the whole story, as the timescape is much more complex. Scheduled time also includes positive elements, enabling organizing one's work and its coordination and synchronization with the work of others. The problem, rooted in social acceleration, is that the grip of scheduled time has become tighter and tighter, overtaking other times. In addition, it is crucial to note the allure and attraction of timeless time for academics. The sacrifices in personal time are not only due to the intensification of scheduled time, but also stem from academics' own readiness and enthusiasm to use as much time as possible for their research.

These kinds of temporal conflicts have been found in other studies too. What we called the conflict between scheduled and personal time is commonly conceptualized as a distortion in work-life balance (see also Ylijoki, 2013). The temporal problems in combining academic work and private life, especially family responsibilities for female academics, have been reported, for instance, in another Finnish study (Nikunen, 2012), and among academics in the United Kingdom (e.g. Gornall & Salisbury, 2012), in Canada (e.g. Acker & Armenti, 2004) and in Australia (e.g. Currie, Harris & Thiele, 2000). Likewise, the conflict between scheduled and timeless time has resonance in other empirical studies. For example, Brown (2005, p. 463), while exploring the temporal landscape of academia, states that research tends to require 'a different kind of time' than is currently available. Menzies and Newson (2007), for their part, point to disconcerting consequences of increasing time pressure in academic work, as the globally wired university tends to be a place where there is 'no time to think'.

A special aspect of time conflicts in academic work concerns the role of e-mailing, a paradigmatic example of technological acceleration. Based on focus-group discussions among junior Finnish academics, our study (Ylijoki, Henriksson, Kallioniemi-Chambers, & Hokka, 2013) points to a temporal paradox: e-mailing both increases and decreases temporal autonomy in academic work. On the one hand, e-mails can be read and responded to almost anywhere at any time, allowing academics to choose the time and place that best suits them, and to flexibly combine work and non-work commitments. On the other hand, the threshold for communication via e-mail is low, resulting in a remarkable increase in the overall amount of communication. Linked with this, academics tend to feel that there is an external expectation to be always available and plugged in, which decreases temporal autonomy. In addition, e-mailing also allures and captivates academics by creating and sustaining meaningful interpersonal relationships, experiences of being connected and a sense of belonging. Sometimes academics even end up in an e-mail trap, being caught in an all-embracing, obsessive online checking. Thus, 'the fast time' (Eriksen, 2001) produced by e-mailing has paradoxical effects on academic work, a result which is found in other empirical studies (e.g. Currie & Eveline, 2011; Gornall & Salisbury, 2012; Menzies & Newson, 2008; Sabelis, 2007).

Contracted time, for its part, involves a special relation with the future, full of insecurity and uncertainty due to the precarious employment conditions. In another study (Ylijoki, 2010), I have explored how academics working on short-term contracts relate to their professional future. Based on interviews with Finnish academics, I distinguished three ideal typical future orientations. In instant living the future is bracketed – academics do not think about it. They do not have plans or goals, because amid constant change they are regarded as pointless. Instead they focus entirely on the tasks here and now, meaning the present gains a pervasive role. Correspondingly, the future remains open, vague, unpredictable and beyond one's control, as academics wait to see where the next contract, if one manages to get it, will take them.

Multiple futures, in contrast, mean speculating, imagining and constructing various professional futures, including career options outside academia, in case there will be no next contract in the university. Sometimes academics merely play with ideas of alternative futures; sometimes they seriously qualify themselves for optional career paths. Since the future is seen to be partly determined by one's own activity, academics worry about how to make the right choices. Due to constant pondering over future options, this orientation is only loosely embedded in the present, resulting in a certain kind of restlessness and inability to settle down.

Lastly, scheduled future involves a careful assessment of employment prospects, well-defined target setting and planning on how to reach goals and targets. Grounded on a socially shared timetable for proper career advancement, the future is divided into phases, forming a progressive career ladder. Thus, in scheduled future, risks and doubts inherent in the future are bracketed, and instead it is believed that, by working hard and avoiding time wasting, it is possible to control the future and achieve one's goal.

These future orientations show that contracted time includes radically different relations with the present and the future, indicating the diversity and complexity of the timescape. Scheduled future is embedded in a notion of the future as predictable and controllable, which is characteristic of the modern era. It co-exists with instant living and multiple futures in which the future is viewed as less in control or totally out of control, characteristic of the current nonstop, 24/7 society. In this way, the older layers of time notions do not displace the newer layers, but they co-exist and intermingle, often in conflictual and paradoxical ways (Adam, 2003a, p. 74; Walker, 2009, p. 505).

CONCLUSIONS

This chapter offers a few glimpses of what a temporal approach into higher education could offer. The empirical examples, based on some of my own research interests, have touched only on time in academic work. Since time is an integral and inseparable element in all of life, it is clear that a temporal approach entails a much wider scope of application, covering all levels and functions of higher education. Higher education can be seen as a contested terrain of temporal diversity, competition and conflicts, both in terms of its internal life and its manifold relations with society at large.

What is more, higher education as an institution, closely linked with the science system, has an important role in shaping the timescapes of present day society. Social acceleration, affecting our temporal relations and experiences, has several roots in scientific developments that have made speeding up processes possible. Therefore, higher education is not only affected by social acceleration but is also one of its producers. Furthermore, as Adam (1998) emphasizes, several technologies, such as synthetic chemicals, nuclear power and gene technology – all manifestations of the triumph of academic science – have effects, intended and unintended, for the distant future of successive generations of humans and other species. This raises moral and ethical questions concerning the temporal responsibility of higher education and the nature of knowledge that is created and disseminated in academic research, teaching and the service function.

In the social sciences, the interest in time arose when time-related problems started to grow and 'the logic of clock began to become dysfunctional for the socio-economic system of its creation' (Adam, 2003a, p. 60). It could be suggested that the same happens in higher education research. When and if such notions as 'no time to think' (Menzies & Newson, 2007), 'sleepless in academia' (Acker & Armenti, 2004) and 'abbreviated thinking'

(Hassan, 2003) begin to characterize the shared understanding of higher education, the paradoxical and dysfunctional outcomes of social acceleration and time compression become increasingly evident, requiring us to take time seriously in higher education research.

The aim of a temporal approach is to make the invisible, taken-for-granted temporal underpinnings of higher education visible, and to uncover the hidden rhythms of academia – both the dominant ones rooted in clock time, and the shadow times at the margins of hegemonic temporal orders. Unveiling how time orders and organizes higher education, and how the actors in higher education order and organize their activities with time, allows for a better understanding of the current functioning, tensions and challenges of higher education. Apart from this, faced with temporal traps and dysfunctions, time studies also strive for promoting change, creating alternatives and 'imagining otherwise' (Clegg, 2010). Since clock time is a social construction, it can be deconstructed and reconstructed. Adam and her co-authors (2002, p. 19) highlight this by stating that 'social scientists have an important role to play here, elaborating the time connections, showing how the control of time can lead to loss of control, and identifying access points for alternative action'.

REFERENCES

Acker, S., & Armenti, C. (2004). Sleepless in academia. *Gender and Education, 16*(1), 3–24.
Adam, B. (1990). *Time and social theory*. Cambridge: Polity Press.
Adam, B. (1995). *Timewatch: The social analysis of time*. Cambridge: Polity Press.
Adam, B. (1998). *Timescapes of modernity: The environmental & invisible hazards*. London: Routledge.
Adam, B. (2003a). Reflexive modernization temporalized. *Theory, Culture & Society, 20*(2), 59–78.
Adam, B. (2003b). When time is money: Contested rationalities of time in the theory and practice of work. *Theoria, 102*, 94–125.
Adam, B. (2004). *Time*. Cambridge: Polity Press.
Adam, B. (2009). *Changing times: Fate, fortune and fiction*. Time and Higher Education Workshop, 18–19 February 2009, Hendon Hall, UK.
Adam, B., Whipp, R., & Sabelis, I. (2002). Choreographing time and management: Traditions, developments, and opportunities. In R. Whipp, B. Adam, & I. Sabelis (Eds.), *Making time. Time and management in modern organizations* (pp. 1–28). New York, NY: Oxford University Press.
Bauman, Z. (2000). Time and space reunited. *Time & Society, 9*(2/3), 171–185.
Brown, R. B. (2005). Mapping the temporal landscape. *Management Learning, 36*(4), 451–470.

Clegg, S. (2010). Time future – The dominant discourse of higher education. *Time & Society*, *19*(3), 345–364.

Currie, J., & Eveline, J. (2011). E-technology and work/life balance for academics with young children. *Higher Education*, *62*(4), 533–550.

Currie, J., Harris, P., & Thiele, B. (2000). Sacrifices in greedy universities: Are they gendered? *Gender and Education*, *12*(3), 269–291.

Eriksen, T. H. (2001). *Tyranny of the moment. Fast and slow time in the information age*. London: Pluto Press.

Gornall, L., & Salisbury, J. (2012). Compulsive working, 'hyperprofessionality' and the unseen pleasures of academic work. *Higher Education Quarterly*, *66*(2), 135–154.

Harman, K., & Meek, L. (2002). Introduction to special issue: "Merger revisited": International perspectives on mergers in higher education. *Higher Education*, *44*(1), 1–4.

Hassan, R. (2003). Network time and the new knowledge epoch. *Time & Society*, *12*(2/3), 225–241.

Hassan, R., & Purser, R. E. (2007). Introduction. In R. Hassan & R. E. Purser (Eds.), *24/7: Time and temporality in the network society* (pp. 1–21). Stanford, CA: Stanford Business Books.

Hassard, J. (2002). Organizational time: Modern, symbolic and postmodern reflections. *Organization Studies*, *23*(6), 885–892.

Held, M., & Nutzinger, H. G. (1998). Nonstop acceleration. The economic logic of development towards the nonstop society. *Time & Society*, *7*(2), 209–221.

Leccardi, C. (2007). New temporal perspectives in the "High-speed Society". In R. Hassan & R. E. Purser (Eds.), *24/7: Time and temporality in the network society* (pp. 25–36). Stanford, CA: Stanford Business Books.

Levine, R. (2005). A geography of business. *Social Research*, *72*(2), 355–370.

McKelvey, M., & Holmén, M. (2009). Introduction. In M. McKelvey & M. Holmén (Eds.), *Learning to compete in european universities* (pp. 1–18). Cheltenham: Edward Elgar.

Menzies, H., & Newson, J. (2007). No time to think: Academics' life in the globally wired university. *Time & Society*, *16*(1), 83–98.

Menzies, H., & Newson, J. (2008). Time, stress and intellectual engagement in academic work: Exploring gender differences. *Gender, Work and Organization*, *15*(5), 504–522.

Nikunen, M. (2012). Changing university work, freedom, flexibility and family. *Studies in Higher Education*, *37*(6), 713–729.

Nowotny, H. (1994). *Time: The modern and postmodern experience*. Cambridge: Polity Press.

Rosa, H. (2009). Social acceleration: Ethical and political consequences of a desynchronized high-speed society. In H. Rosa & W. E. Scheuerman (Eds.), *High-speed Society: Social acceleration, power and modernity* (pp. 77–111). Philadelphia, PA: Pennsylvania State University Press.

Rosa, H. (2010). *Alienation and acceleration: Towards a critical theory of late-modern temporality*. Malmö: NSU Press.

Rosa, H., & Scheuerman, W. E. (Eds.) (2009). *High-speed Society: Social acceleration, power and modernity*. Philadelphia, PA: Pennsylvania State University Press.

Sabelis, I. H. J. (2007). The clock-time paradox: Time regimes in the network society. In R. Hassan & R. E. Purser (Eds.), *24/7: Time and temporality in the network society* (pp. 255–277). Stanford, CA: Stanford Business Books.

Schutz, A. (1976). *Collected papers II. Studies in social theory*. The Hague: Martinus Nijhoff.

Sennett, R. (1998). *The corrosion of character*. New York, NY: W.W. Norton.

Slaughter, S., & Leslie, L. L. (1997). *Academic capitalism*. Baltimore, MD: The Johns Hopkins University Press.

Virilio, P. (2009). The state of emergency. In H. Rosa & W. E. Scheuerman (Eds.), *High-speed society: Social acceleration, power and modernity* (pp. 201–214). Philadelphia, PA: Pennsylvania State University Press.

Walker, J. (2009). Time as the fourth dimension in the globalization of higher education. *The Journal of Higher Education, 80*(5), 483–509.

Ylijoki, O.-H. (2010). Future orientations in episodic labour: Short-term academics as a case in point. *Time & Society, 19*(3), 365–386.

Ylijoki, O.-H. (2013). Boundary work between work and life in the high-speed university. *Studies in Higher Education, 38*(2), 242–255.

Ylijoki, O.-H., Henriksson, L., Kallioniemi-Chambers, V., & Hokka, J. (2013). Balancing working time and academic work in Finland. In L. Gornall, C. Cook, L. Daunton, J. Salisbury, & B. Thomas (Eds.), *Academic working lives: Experience, practice and change* (207–214). London: Bloomsbury.

Ylijoki, O.-H., & Mäntylä, H. (2003). Conflicting time perspectives in academic work. *Time & Society, 12*(1), 55–78.

Zerubavel, E. (1981). *Hidden rhythms: Schedules and calendars in social life*. Chicago, IL: University of Chicago Press.

USING CRISP AND FUZZY SET-THEORETIC ANALYSES FOR MIDDLE-RANGE THEORISING: A CONFIGURATIONAL COMPARATIVE APPROACH TO CASE-BASED RESEARCH

Farshid Shams

ABSTRACT

The aim of this chapter is to introduce a methodology that enables researchers to employ a set of systematic comparative tools and techniques in their multiple case study research that allow them to move from drawing loose comparisons towards a more formalised type of analysis, while simultaneously paying attention to within-case complexities. This methodology stands between the qualitative and the quantitative methods and helps researchers to build middle-range theories (Mjoset, 2001) from small to intermediate numbers of cases. This methodology encompasses a number of techniques including crisp and fuzzy set-theoretic qualitative comparative analyses, which have been used in a wide range

Theory and Method in Higher Education Research II
International Perspectives on Higher Education Research, Volume 10, 161–182
Copyright © 2014 by Emerald Group Publishing Limited
All rights of reproduction in any form reserved
ISSN: 1479-3628/doi:10.1108/S1479-3628(2014)0000010014

of social science disciplines. However, these techniques have not received
sufficient attention from higher education scholars.

INTRODUCTION

Despite being relatively new, set-theoretic methods have been adopted by
many social scientists in various disciplines, such as organisational studies
(e.g. Fiss, 2007), comparative political studies (e.g. Avdagic, 2010), strategic
management (e.g. Kogut et al., 2004), public health (e.g. Warren et al.,
2013), legal studies (e.g. Arvind & Stirton, 2010) and sociology (e.g. Giugni &
Nai, 2013). Application of this method in the field of higher education,
however, is very limited (see for exception Schneider & Sadowski, 2010).
Considering that higher education research is an interdisciplinary field
(Teichler, 2005), there seems to be a great potential for employing configurational set-theoretic methods. More specifically, using this methodology
in higher education research can be very helpful for, firstly, the body of
research in this field is lacking sufficient robust theories and, secondly, the
implications of mostly qualitative research (particularly in Europe, less so
in the United States) that have been conducted in this field are hardly generalisable. This weakness arises from the fact that many multiple case study
designs aim at producing thick explanations of within-case complexities,
and then comparing them in a somewhat unstructured and descriptive way.
It is of paramount importance to note that many case-oriented studies are
limited by nature, and thus impose limitations on their findings. For example, conducting system-comparative research on the Bologna process in
continental Europe at the national or supra-national levels is limited to the
number of European countries, and therefore it is almost impossible to utilise conventional statistical methods. This is why a majority of scholars
choose either a single or multiple cases. Despite some of these studies being
very insightful, they do not provide sufficient ground for further generalisation of their implications.

Configurational set-theoretic analysis, however, is a method that
enables researchers to overcome some of these barriers and obstacles, by
offering a systematic approach to the case study method. Configurational
comparative methods (CCM) suggest a range of techniques for conducting
qualitative comparative analysis (QCA), such as crisp set QCA (csQCA),
multivariate QCA (mvQCA) and MSDO/MDSO (most similar different
outcome/most different similar outcome), which all share the same logic

(Rihoux & Ragin, 2009). The underlying assumption in all of these QCA techniques is that each case consists of several configurations. Each configuration is a unique combination of multiple factors that lead to a certain outcome (*ibid*). The basic mechanism of all QCA techniques involves reducing complexities by converting cases into a set of configurations.

In this chapter, I will try to explain the essence of this methodology with respect to research in higher education. It is not a full guideline for learning and applying this method in the higher education context, but it demonstrates the applicability of this method and suggests some areas where adopting this method can add significantly. Amongst the QCA techniques, the crisp set and the fuzzy set analyses have been selected for description.

ONTOLOGICAL VIEW OF QCA TECHNIQUES

The qualitative comparative analysis method emerged in the late 1980s in political science, with the purpose of synthesising the best aspects of variable-oriented and case-oriented approaches (Rihoux, 2003). QCA is a case-based method of analysis that introduces a number of techniques that include formal tools for comparing cases in a systematic/configurational way. That is, each case is known as a 'complex configurations of events and structures' (Ragin, 2004, p. 125). Identifying each case's micro-level characteristics helps researchers to better categorise the selected cases and compare them, while maintaining a holistic view of cases as larger complex entities (Breg-Schlosser, De Meur, Rihoux, & Ragin, 2009, p. 6).

A noteworthy characteristic of QCA that differentiates it from traditional case study methods is its semi-positivistic ontological basis. Unlike many comparative case studies that start with contrasting some raw case materials and lead to theory building, QCA, as well as helping with theory building, intends to test some theoretically informed statements. However, it can neither be categorised under positivism nor social constructivism, as Easton (2010) contends that case studies — in general — cannot serve the purpose of positivism. This is because they are not great in numbers, hence unable to discover generalisable social rules, nor can they fully address the goals of interpretivism, for they are 'largely epistemological in their objectives' (*ibid*, p. 127). QCA is a methodology that seems to have been developed by taking a critical realist stance on the social epistemology (Byrne, 2009, p. 103); thus cases are treated somewhat differently compared to the conventional case study methods.

In QCA an iterative dialogue between the researcher and the selected cases takes place. Therefore, it supports both inductive and deductive approaches. It is inductive because it enables the analyst to probe into different aspects of cases, and discover additional data from the data set (as opposed to the indicator-selection approach in a deductive statistical approach), but at the same time it suggests that testable variables must be theoretically informed (Rihoux & Lobe, 2009, p. 225). As mentioned earlier, all cases are inherently complex, and thus the primary role of QCA is introducing some techniques to help reduce these complexities and reach some level of parsimony. Then, the ultimate parsimonious solution, which is a solution with a minimum amount of complexity, will be taken as an anchor point to call upon further studies for moving from a middle-range theoretical statement towards a full-blown theory.

The purposeful selection of cases is a key point in the QCA method, as the aim is to corroborate or falsify a theoretical statement (Mahoney & Goertz, 2004). Therefore, cases are selected based on their sets of similarities and differences that would 'permit treating them as comparable instances of the same general phenomenon' (Ragin, 1992, p. 1). The purposeful selection of cases in QCA is, therefore, not an opportunistic action, for the reasons of selecting cases are very transparent.

BASICS OF QCA

A key point to understand the logic of QCA techniques is to comprehend the meaning of the set-theoretic approach and its asymmetrical nature. In social science, the number of sets to which individual cases belong are almost infinite. A higher education institution (HEI), for example, can simultaneously belong to the sets of: British universities, European universities and prestigious universities. All QCA techniques suggest identifying the key sets and zooming in on the causal relationships between them. For instance, let us assume that a hypothesis states that governmental intervention in national higher education policies, through keeping separate sectors within the higher education system, leads to maintaining a certain level of diversity. In order to test this hypothesis, one needs a number of cases (countries) in which the government has tried to keep separate sectors within the national higher education system. Having enough historical data and measurement tools to identify which countries have maintained their level of diversity in regard to their national higher education systems is also required.

In the QCA language, this hypothesis can be true if the set of countries with intervening governments constitute a sub-set of the set of countries with stable level of diversity over a period of time. When a set becomes a sub-set of another set, the existence of the hypothetical relationship can be proved for almost all of the cases in that set. In this example, the set of countries with intervening governments can be a subset of countries with an almost constant level of diversity, if almost all of the cases that have been recognised as countries with intervening governments have also been recognised as countries in which the higher education systems have remained diverse. If we arrive at this finding, it means that governmental intervention by keeping separate sectors is *sufficient* for maintaining diversity within the national higher education system. However, it is still unclear to us whether or not this is the only influential factor, or whether there might be other separate factors that lead to maintaining the diversity of a higher education system. Providing an answer to this question addresses the *necessity* of governmental intervention for maintaining diversity. It is important to note that if I find some countries with relatively stable diversity but without governmental intervention, this does not contradict my earlier finding. In other words, the sufficient condition that I have found will still be valid, but I will learn that there are other paths leading to the same outcome. Moreover, it is possible that one or more combinations of some conditions lead to the same outcome. This notion argues that various constellations of independent variables (conditions in the QCA language) can lead to the same dependent variable(s) (outcomes in the QCA language), and is called *multiple conjunctural causation* (Breg-Schlosser et al., 2009, p. 8). This concept includes two arguments: (a) different paths can generate the same outcome (also known as *equifinality*), and (b) some of the paths are built by a combination of conditions.

Multiple conjunctural causation runs against the basic assumption in all the conventional statistical models, in which an independent variable has the same impact on the dependent variable across all cases without being affected by the values of other causal conditions (Breg-Schlosser et al., 2009, p. 8). In other words, whereas in most statistical methods the purpose is finding a model that best fits the data, in QCA the researcher is looking for various combinations of conditions amongst a set of complex cases that would lead to the same outcome. Therefore, a set-theoretic relation is not of a correlational type. That is, unlike in statistical methods, in QCA the presence or absence of an outcome may be caused by different sets of conditions. In other words, set-relations are asymmetrical.

CRISP SET QCA

csQCA was the first QCA technique that was developed in the late 1980s. Based on general QCA principles, the aim of this technique is to reduce complexities towards reaching a parsimonious solution. Here, I will demonstrate how csQCA can be performed.

Imagine that I want to study the key determinants of market orientation of higher education institutions and I use the framework that is suggested by Hemsley-Brown and Oplatka (2010). Accordingly, the market orientation of a university has three components: student orientation (SO), competitor orientation (CO) and inter-functional co-ordination (IFC). In order to put this framework to the test, I hypothesise that if these three conditions are satisfied, the institution is a market-oriented institution. However, the set-theoretic examination of these causal relations will go beyond this and look at various combinations of those conditions. It is important to note that this example is completely different from what Hemsley-Brown and Oplatka (2010) present in their article. I have borrowed their analytical framework; what is demonstrated here is just an example with a made-up data set. Fig. 1 shows the hypothetical connections between the three conditions and the outcome.

The first step in testing the model is measuring the conditions (independent variables) and the outcome (dependent variable). Imagine that we have nine cases (higher education institutions) and a number of identified indicators for each concept to test the above model. An online survey was administered to academics in two higher education institutions. At this stage, for the indicators of each condition and the outcome, the selected variables will be combined so that they demonstrate a reliable scale at the

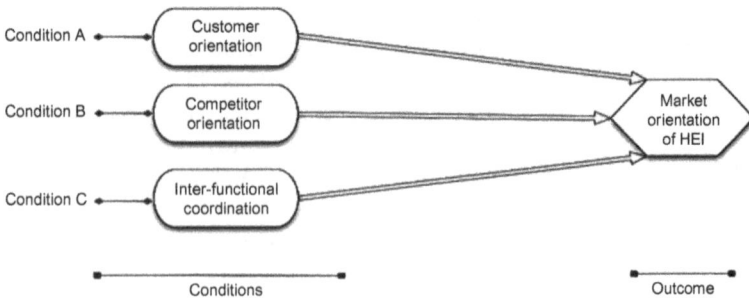

Fig. 1. Research Model.

end, which means that a minimum of Cronbach's $\alpha = 0.80$ is expected. Summative and mean scores will then be calculated. Although in csQCA, the crossover point, which is where the maximum ambiguity occurs (e.g. on a scale from 0 to 1, 0.5 is exactly at the same distance from 0 and 1) can be set anywhere providing that it can be justified, here, for the sake of simplicity, we take the mean of each scale as the cutting point. This is in line with the principles of csQCA that suggest dichotomisation of values. Therefore, for each of the conditions and the outcome, if the score is smaller than the mean, the ultimate value for that case for that particular condition will be set to zero; and if greater than the mean it will be set to 1. Therefore, we will have a set of binary data that can be presented in a table, which is called the truth table. Table 1 includes some hypothetical dichotomised data for this model.

Table 1. Truth Table for csQCA.

Cases	SO (Condition A)	CO (Condition B)	IFC (Condition C)	Market oriented (Outcome)
Case 1 (HEI1)	1	0	0	0
Case 2 (HEI2)	0	0	0	0
Case 3 (HEI3)	1	1	1	1
Case 4 (HEI4)	0	1	0	0
Case 5 (HEI5)	0	1	1	0
Case 6 (HEI6)	1	0	1	0
Case 7 (HEI7)	1	1	0	1
Case 8 (HEI8)	0	0	1	0
Case 9 (HEI9)	1	1	0	1

In Table 1, the conditions and the outcomes of each case have been shown. For example, for case 1, the only present condition is A and the outcome is absent, whereas for case 3 all conditions as well as the outcome are present. It can be seen that cases 7 and 9 have exactly identical conditions and outcome and, therefore, in a refined truth table they should be put together in a row. This data can also be illustrated in a Venn diagram (see Fig. 2).

Fig. 2, which has been created by the visualiser tool of the software Tosmana (Cronqvist, 2007), demonstrates the positions of the nine institutions vis-à-vis the identified conditions. The vertical line in the middle divides the large box into two areas based on the first condition (SO), and the horizontal line divides it into two different areas based on the second condition (CO). The third condition has been illustrated by a smaller box,

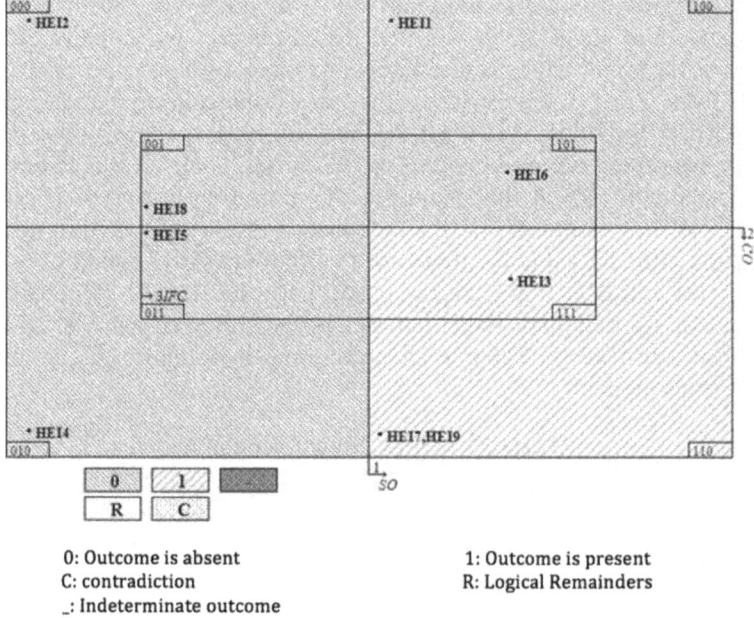

0: Outcome is absent   1: Outcome is present
C: contradiction   R: Logical Remainders
_: Indeterminate outcome

Fig. 2. Venn Diagram.

which is located in the middle. All cases that meet the first condition fall into the right side of the vertical line, and all of those that meet the second condition fall below the horizontal line. Cases that score one on the third condition are located inside the smaller box. For example, case 2 has scored zero on all of the three conditions. This has been shown in the small box at the top left corner of the diagram that contains three zeros. The outcome is apparently outside the acceptable area and thus is equal to zero. However case 3 is located where the outcome is equal to 1 since it has met all three conditions (look at the legend and the right-to-left hatched area).

In case there are configurations with contradictory outcomes (i.e. similar configurations producing a 1 and a 0 for different cases), these will be highlighted by a dotted box with a contradiction sign. In this example, however, there is no contradiction (C). Resolving that contradiction requires employing some more advanced techniques (see for description Rihoux & De Meur, 2009). The letter R represents logical remainders that are a number of combinations that logically exist, but have not been observed in the data set.

Using Boolean notation, each area in the Venn diagram can be described. For instance, the hatched area that includes cases 3, 7 and 9 can be formulated as follows:

$$SO^*CO^*IFC + SO^*CO^*IFC + SO^*CO^* \sim IFC \rightarrow Outcome$$

According to the Boolean notion, the logical AND is represented by * and + demonstrates logical OR. In the above formula, the plus signs divide the set of conditions for each case in the hatched area. It is clear that the conditions for cases 7 and 9 are exactly identical and, therefore, one can be omitted. Therefore, a more simplified version of this formula looks like:

$$SO^*CO^*IFC + SO^*CO^* \sim IFC \rightarrow Outcome$$

It can be read as: *the outcome is present for a situation with presence of condition SO AND presence of the condition CO AND presence of the condition IFC OR for a situation with presence of condition SO AND presence of condition CO AND absence of condition IFC.*

This statement and the formula clarifies that the outcome is achieved regardless of the presence or the absence of condition IFC. Thus, condition C is superfluous. Therefore, the formula can be further simplified as:

$$SO^*CO \rightarrow Outcome$$

This means that the presence of condition SO together with (logical AND) the presence of condition CO is sufficient for the presence of the outcome. In other words, being student oriented AND competitor oriented is a sufficient condition for a higher education institution to be market oriented.

A sufficient condition is a condition that exists (scores 1) and also generates score 1 for the outcome. Inherent in this statement is that, because of the asymmetrical causality of set relations, there should be no case with a present condition that leads to the absence of the outcome (Schneider & Wagemann, 2012, pp. 57–58).

It is important to note that our goal is not to identify those cases that meet all the conditions and lead to the outcome, but what we need to do is identify what conditions are *sufficient* and what conditions are *necessary* to produce the outcome. Despite being a useful tool, we do not always need to (or cannot) visualise cases in a Venn diagram. Here, I proceed with the csQCA algorithm and show, at the end, that the results are similar.

In Table 1 (and also in Fig. 2), cases 1, 3, 6, 7 and 9 score 1 on condition A. Amongst those, cases 3, 7 and 9 seem to be addressing the condition of sufficiency. However, the existence of cases 1 and 6 that lead to the absence of the outcome makes us argue that condition A is not sufficient for generating the outcome. Running the same test for conditions B and C leads to the same result. Therefore, none of the suggested conditions are sufficient to produce the outcome. However, it does not mean that the model is disproved. As mentioned earlier, unlike statistical methods, in QCA techniques the conditions that lead to the presence of an outcome can be completely different from those that lead to its absence. Thus, we should calculate ~A, ~B and ~C, which are the negations of the conditions in Table 1. We should then test the sufficiency of these negations for leading to the outcome. Furthermore, we should include all possible combinations of those conditions.

Table 2 includes additional columns that show the values for the negation of the three conditions. Negation of a condition with value of 1 is equal to 0 and vice versa. Similar to the sufficiency test for conditions A, B and C, the sufficiency of their negations for generating the outcome should be tested. As the result, neither of ~A, ~B and ~C are sufficient. In order to test if there are alternative routes to the outcome, additional columns have been added to Table 2 to calculate the value of some conjunctions. To keep it relatively simple, only six conjunctional properties have been presented in the table. The minimum value rule for logical AND and the maximum value rule for logical OR have been applied to calculate these values. That is, the value of multiple conditions with a logical AND between them is 1 only when the value for all of those conditions is 1; and the value of

Table 2. Truth Table of the Boolean Configurations.

Cases	A	B	C	~A	~B	~C	A*B	A*C	B*C	~A*B	C*~B	A+B	Outcome
HEI1	1	0	0	0	1	1	0	0	0	0	0	1	0
HEI2	0	0	0	1	1	1	0	0	0	0	0	0	0
HEI3	1	1	1	0	0	0	1	1	1	0	0	1	1
HEI4	0	1	0	1	0	1	0	0	0	1	0	1	0
HEI5	0	1	1	1	0	0	0	0	1	1	0	1	0
HEI6	1	0	1	0	1	0	0	1	0	0	1	1	0
HEI7, HEI9	1	1	0	0	0	1	1	0	0	0	0	1	1
HEI8	0	0	1	1	1	0	0	0	0	1	0	1	0

multiple conditions with logical OR is equal to 1 when at least one of the conditions in that combination is present. Running the sufficiency test for the conjunctional conditions leads to the conclusion that only A*B is a sufficient condition. This result is the same as the result from the analysis on the Venn diagram (A represents SO and B represents CO).

Testing necessity, however, requires employing different cases. In order to identify the necessary conditions for an outcome, all cases for which the outcome is present should be selected. A necessary condition is a condition that is present whenever the outcome is present. In this example, the outcomes for cases 3, 7 and 9 are present. Conditions A and B are also present for these cases, and there is no case for which either of the conditions of A and B are absent while the outcome is present. Therefore, condition A and condition B are necessary conditions for the outcome. It must be noted that, for performing a necessity test, conjunctional conditions with logical AND cannot be tested. This is because the minimal value rule has been applied to compute those values, and thus they are less likely to pass the test. However, combinations of conditions with logical OR can be put to test, given that the maximum value rule has been applied to them (see for detailed explanation Schneider & Wagemann, 2012). In this case, the configuration A + B is also a necessary condition, for wherever the outcome is present, A + B is also present.

FUZZY SET QCA

An obvious limitation of csQCA, which was explained in the previous section, is that it suggests force-fitting cases into two categories. A more advanced technique called multi-value QCA (mvQCA) was developed to allow for more categories (Herrmann & Cronqvist, 2009). However, in general, neither the dichotomisation in csQCA, nor the multichotomisation in mvQCA is capable of fully grasping the details of set relations. These techniques work well with ordinal data, whereby cases can be naturally separated. For example, a university is either a member of the set of European universities or not. However, with continuous variables, identifying such set memberships can be controversial. The suggested methods for dichotomisation and multichotomisation of continuous data can be used as shown in the previous example, but there is a likelihood that a lot of useful information gets lost in the process of transformation.

Therefore, by drawing on the fuzzy-set theory (Zadeh, 1965), Ragin (2000) developed an algorithm for analysing configuration of fuzzy set memberships in order to bypass the limitations of csQCA and mvQCA. The fundamental argument in fsQCA is that a case can simultaneously have memberships in multiple sets in varying degrees. Therefore, a case can be either fully inside a set (score 1), fully outside a set (score 0), more in than out (e.g. 0.8, 0.9) or more out than in (e.g. 0.2, 0.1). The crossover point is 0.5, which signifies a maximum amount of ambiguity regarding the membership of the case. A key point is that the thresholds must be set qualitatively, based on the researcher's substantive knowledge of the cases or theory. Therefore, the highest score is not necessarily equal to full membership in a set, and the lower score is not necessarily equal to non-membership. Furthermore, it is not necessary to have equal gaps between the intervals.

This method of qualitative calibration, therefore, is very different from a mechanical ranking of categories as in conventional quantitative methods. In order to further clarify this meaning, I will give an example. Imagine that we are studying the impacts of secondary students' financial status (mostly the student family's financial status) on their decisions about entering higher education or not. A widely used indicator of financial status is the level of income. Therefore, in our sample, we collect the income level of students' families and also information about their choices about entering higher education. Having this data set, a quantitative researcher would run some statistical tests to find out whether or not the variation in the income levels can explain the likelihood of students entering higher education. In this treatment, all the cases are ranked relative to each other. That is, a family with £20,000 income per year is richer than a family with £15,000 per year and thus, probably more likely to be able to afford higher education. Similarly, a family with the income of £155,000 is richer than a family that earns £150,000 per annum. The net amount of difference between these pairs is £5000, and a conventional quantitative technique treats them in the same way. However, thinking qualitatively, there is a big difference between the £5000 discrepancy in income in the low-income group and that in the high-income group. From a fuzzy set perspective, the variation in the high-level income group is irrelevant in the context of this study, because this variation is less likely to cause a case appear outside the set of students who enter higher education (i.e. both of the families in the higher income level are rich enough to afford higher education and the £5000 does not make any difference). However, the same variation in the other group can potentially separate the two cases: one becomes a member of the set and the other stays out. Therefore, a fuzzy set researcher would look for a theory or a framework that distinguishes the poor from the rich in that specific country. Using that theory or his/her substantial knowledge of cases, the researcher defines a number of meaningful cut-off points. These qualitative anchors identify the boundaries of sets; however, it must be reiterated that, unlike in quantitative studies, in fuzzy sets the intervals are not necessarily equal. Furthermore, each case that is a member in a set can simultaneously be a member in another set with a different degree of membership. This example shows how fuzzy set analysis cuts out the irrelevant variations in the light of context-related factors.

The number of thresholds is unlimited. A very simple form is the three value fuzzy set where full membership is equal to 1, full non-membership is equal to 0 and 0.5 is the crossover point. However, there are other value frames for fuzzy sets such as four values and continuous values (Ragin, 2009). Calibration of values and translating them to fuzzy sets is a key element in fsQCA technique. Ragin (2008, pp. 85–105) introduces two techniques for transforming interval-scale values to fuzzy set scores. Explaining the details of these methods is beyond the scope of this chapter, so I will just present the results of applying one of those methods to the data from the Hemsley-Brown and Oplatka (2010) example used previously. Here, I use the actual summative values for each variable (based on the imaginary data) and, by using one of the methods suggested by Ragin (2008), convert them to fuzzy numbers that are presented in Table 3.

Table 3.   Fuzzy-Set Membership of Cases in Causal Combinations.

	A	B	C	~A	~B	~C	A*B	A*C	B*C	~A*B	C*~B	A+B	Outcome
HEI1	0.8	0.3	0.3	0.2	0.7	0.7	0.3	0.3	0.3	0.2	0.3	0.8	0.4
HEI2	0.4	0.2	0.3	0.6	0.8	0.7	0.2	0.3	0.2	0.2	0.3	0.4	0.4
HEI3	0.7	0.8	0.9	0.3	0.2	0.1	0.7	0.7	0.8	0.3	0.2	0.8	0.7
HEI4	0.1	0.7	0.3	0.9	0.3	0.7	0.1	0.1	0.3	0.7	0.3	0.7	0.2
HEI5	0.2	0.9	0.8	0.8	0.1	0.2	0.2	0.2	0.8	0.8	0.1	0.9	0.3
HEI6	0.6	0.1	0.7	0.4	0.9	0.3	0.1	0.6	0.1	0.1	0.7	0.6	0.2
HEI7	0.8	0.7	0.3	0.2	0.3	0.7	0.7	0.3	0.3	0.2	0.3	0.8	1
HEI8	0.3	0.3	0.8	0.7	0.7	0.2	0.3	0.3	0.3	0.3	0.7	0.3	0.3
HEI9	0.9	0.9	0.2	0.1	0.1	0.8	0.9	0.9	0.2	0.1	0.1	0.9	0.9

In Table 3, the degrees of membership for ~A, ~B, ~C and six combinational configurations have also been calculated. In fuzzy algebra:

$$\sim A = [1] - A$$
$$\text{Logical AND}: X*Y = \text{Min}\ (X,\ Y)$$
$$\text{Logical OR}: X + Y = \text{Max}\ (X,\ Y)$$

Unlike in csQCA, which posits that cases could be separated and sorted in a truth table, in fsQCA, due to the partial set memberships, this separation is not possible.

In fuzzy sets, a causal relationship between a condition and an outcome is valid when the condition is a sub-set of the outcome. To be a subset, the membership score of the condition must be consistently either smaller than or equal to the membership scores of the outcome. In this example, at first glance, the only configuration that passes this rule is A*B, of which all the instances are smaller than or equal to the instances of the outcome, and the condition A + B is disqualified to be considered as a sufficient condition. Therefore, an early conclusion is that the only sufficient condition is A*B. However, in fuzzy set-theoretical terms, because of the partial memberships of cases in different sets, assessing subset relations requires more effort. Fig. 3 illustrates this subset relationship between the condition under which

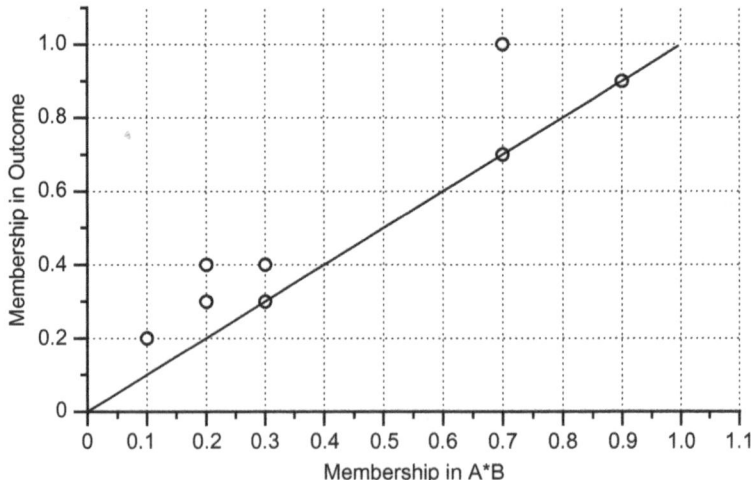

Fig. 3. Plot of Degree of Membership in Combination A*B against Degree of Membership in Outcome.

both SO (A) and CO (B) conditions are present and the outcome is also present.

In Fig. 3, eight dots that represent all nine cases (cases 4 and 6 have identical membership in A*B and in the outcome) are presented. The diagonal line is not a linear fit to the data, but it is a fixed line that is drawn from (0,0) to (1,1), dividing the space into two separate areas. All of the dots are located either in the area above or on the diagonal line. In theory, when a set is a subset of another set (the way of testing sufficiency), there should be no case in the area below the diagonal line $(X_i > Y_i)$ in the XY plot; and all cases must fall into the area where $X_i \leq Y_i$. However, in fuzzy set-theoretic analysis it is hard to find an almost perfect subset relationship like the relationship that we found in the above example. There are often a number of cases falling into the lower area, with some of them close to the diagonal line and some other far from it. Therefore, another tool is needed for testing sufficiency. That tool is measuring the *consistency* of the empirical data with the identified causal set relationship. Ragin (2008) introduced a formula for measuring set-theoretic consistency of sufficiency:

$$\text{Consistency of sufficiency } (X_i \leq Y_i) = \frac{\sum(\min(X_i, Y_i))}{\sum(X_i)}$$

This formula generates score 1 for the maximum amount of consistency. If a few cases drop below the diagonal line, the degree of consistency decreases. If that number goes below 0.5 it means that there are a considerable number of cases in the 'no-case' area at considerable distances from the borderline, and therefore the set relationship is inconsistent.

Testing necessary conditions in fuzzy sets is also more complicated than in crisp sets. However, similar to the definition of necessity in crisp sets, a necessary condition is a condition that is present whenever the outcome is present; but its presence does not guarantee the presence of the outcome. Therefore, to pass the necessity test, the instances of the outcome should build a set that is a subset of the instances of the condition. This means that all fuzzy set membership scores of cases in the condition must be greater than or equal to their membership scores in the outcome. Therefore, in an XY plot, if a condition is consistently necessary for the outcome, all cases fall in the area below the diagonal line.

In Fig. 4, the necessity of condition A + B for generating the outcome has been tested.

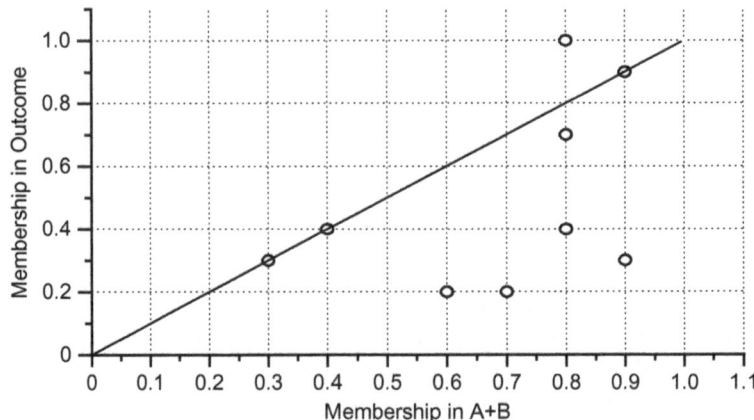

Fig. 4. Plot of Degree of Membership in Combination A + B against Degree of Membership in Outcome.

The plot shows that all cases except for one fall below the diagonal line. As mentioned earlier, in fuzzy set-theoretic analysis, it is not easy to conclude that a cause like A + B is not a necessary condition for the outcome by referring to the observed outstanding case. This is because that case has partial memberships in other sets. Therefore, the concept of consistency should be brought on board, but this time for testing necessary conditions. The following formula helps measuring the consistency of a necessary condition (Ragin, 2008):

$$\text{Consistency of necessity } (Y_i \leq X_i) = \frac{\sum(\min(X_i, Y_i))}{\sum(Y_i)}$$

Along with consistency for sufficient and necessary conditions, their *coverage* should also be calculated. Coverage evaluates the strength and the importance of a set-theoretic relationship. Given that, in the set-theoretic analysis, it is possible to have more than one path to the outcome, the importance of each path is relative to the existence of alternative paths. Therefore, it is possible to have a highly consistent set relation that has a low coverage. A key point in calculating coverage is that it should only be calculated for those sets that have been proven to establish a consistent subset of the outcome. Similar to consistency, coverage can be calculated for both sufficiency and necessity. The following formulas show how these concepts are measured (Ragin, 2008):

$$\text{Coverage of sufficiency } (X_i \le Y_i) = \frac{\sum(\min(X_i, Y_i))}{\sum(Y_i)}$$

$$\text{Coverage of necessity } (Y_i \le X_i) = \frac{\sum(\min(X_i, Y_i))}{\sum(X_i)}$$

For our example, I have calculated the consistency and the coverage for the three conditions and for a number of their combinations. Table 4 includes the results for the test of sufficiency and Table 5 presents the results for the necessity test.

Some scores in Tables 4 and 5 are high and thus highly likely to pass the tests, and some others clearly fail. For instance, for the sufficiency test, in Table 4, the consistency score for A*B is 1.00, which is the maximum, and the coverage is 0.79, which means that this configuration accounts for 79% of the instances in the outcome. However, we need to have some clear thresholds to identify the acceptable levels of consistency and coverage for both sufficiency and necessity conditions. Creating a truth table helps us to accomplish this task. To this end, quite similar to the procedure in crisp set analysis, I should find out the number of cases that correspond to each corner of the vector space. Vector space refers to a multi-dimensional area, which is created by combinations of conditions. When having only two conditions, the vector space is a square (4 corners), when the number of conditions is 3, the shape of the vector space is cubical (8 corners) and when the number of conditions increases it is not possible to draw the

Table 4. Results for Sufficiency Test.

Condition	Consistency	Coverage
A	0.83	0.90
B	0.75	0.84
C	0.65	0.59
A*B	1.00	0.79
A*C	0.92	0.54
B*C	0.77	0.54
A + B	0.67	0.95
A*B*C	1.00	0.50

Table 5.   Results for Necessity Test.

Condition	Consistency	Coverage
A	0.90	0.83
B	0.84	0.75
C	0.59	0.65
A*B	0.79	1.00
A*C	0.54	0.92
B*C	0.54	0.77
A + B	0.95	0.67
~A*B	0.56	0.45

shape, but we can calculate the number of corners and identify them. The number of corners is equal to 2^k, whereby K represents the number of conditions. With three conditions in this example, there are 8 corners based on which I can create a truth table.

The algorithm for creating a truth table from fuzzy numbers (Schneider & Wagemann, 2012, pp. 96–104) is lengthy and beyond the scope of this chapter. Therefore, instead of that, I use fsQCA 2.0 (Ragin, 2007), which is a free software that is developed for crisp and fuzzy set analyses. Table 6 is the truth table that I have created by using this software.

This truth table shows 8 corners, the number of cases that correspond to each corner and the consistency score for each corner. Allocating cases to corners is based on the rule that each case is located at a corner in which it has higher than 0.5 membership score. Now, it is time for the researcher to fill out the outcome column by setting a frequency cut-off point. When the number of cases is small, the cut-off is often 1 or 2, but with large numbers, finding a threshold requires looking at distributions and finding major gaps. Here, I choose number 2 as the cutting point, which means that only the rows with 2 or more cases are considered as a subset of the outcome, hence sufficient. Therefore, all of the corners with fewer than two cases will be eliminated. The next step is setting a threshold for consistency to be able to identify those causal relations that are subsets of the outcome. Ragin (2008, p. 114) suggests 0.75 as a general acceptable threshold. Therefore, in the truth table, from the remaining couple of rows, I manually give score 1 to the outcome of the first corner that has a raw consistency score equal to 1.00; and I give 0 to the outcome of the corner with the raw consistent score of 0.74 or lower, which is below the threshold (0.75).

Running a standard analysis with the assumption that all three conditions should contribute to outcome when present (according to the theoretical model presented in Fig. 1), the result in Table 7 is achieved.

Table 6. Truth Table for fsQCA.

A	B	C	Number	Outcome	Raw Consistent
1	1	0	2		1.00
1	0	0	2		0.74
1	1	1	1		1.00
0	1	1	1		0.76
0	1	0	1		0.76
0	0	0	1		0.72
0	0	1	1		0.78
1	0	1	0		N/A

Table 7. Results.

frequency cut-off: 2.00
consistency cut-off: 1.00
Assumptions: c (present), b (present), a (present)

	Raw Coverage	Unique Coverage	Consistency
B*A	0.79	0.79	1.00

Solution coverage: 0.795
Solution consistency: 1.00

According to these results, A*B is the only path that leads to the outcome. It means that being student oriented AND being competition oriented is a sufficient condition for a higher education institution to be market oriented. In Table 7, the raw coverage explains how much of the outcome is covered by each of the existing paths, and the unique coverage shows how much of the outcome is covered by a specific path. The solution coverage represents the amount of the outcome that is covered by the entire solution, particularly when a solution is complex. In this very simple example, however, these three are overlapping.

It must be noted that the software allows for running analyses that leads to the generation of three different results: complex, intermediate and parsimonious. Here, we only performed the standard analysis. Moreover, adding potential counterfactuals/logical remainders often generate different results (see Ragin & Sonnett, 2004). This is called counterfactual analysis, which is the process of evaluating the plausibility of remainders (i.e. cases that potentially exist, but have not been observed in the collected data set).

There are two types of counterfactuals: easy and difficult. If the researcher adds a remainder to a configuration that he/she − based on existing knowledge − is already confident leads to the outcome, it is called an easy counterfactual. A difficult counterfactual, however, is when the researcher wants to test a hypothesis that is not supported by substantive knowledge or theory, and there is no case that represents that configuration. For example, if I add some easy counterfactuals above, the result will be A*B*~C. Choosing between this more complex path and the more parsimonious solution that was found earlier depends on different factors; such as the substantive knowledge of the researcher or his/her preference for the level of parsimony. Furthermore, in a full analysis, the researcher should look for conditions or configurations that lead to the presence of the negation of the outcome, for set relations are asymmetrical.

The figures presented in Table 5 tells us the story of necessary conditions. Accordingly, condition A and condition B are the necessary conditions for the outcome. Condition A + B, which I had previously nominated for the necessity condition, is rejected due to its low coverage.

A highly important remaining issue is the concept of limited diversity. That is, with small to medium-sized N, it is highly likely that there will be a number of rows in the truth table with limited number of cases, or even no cases, but with the logical expectation of more cases in that row. As mentioned in the crisp set section, these rows are called logical remainders. Given that in fuzzy truth tables cases do not have full memberships in rows, but are more in than out when presented in a row, the logical remainders are those rows that lack enough cases with membership scores above 0.5. To learn about logical remainders and a standard procedure of dealing with these, I refer to Schneider and Wagemann (2012, pp. 160–177).

SUMMARY AND CONCLUSION

To sum up, the key learning points of this chapter are: (a) set-theoretic relations are completely different from correlational connections. One of the significant differences is that set-theoretic relations are asymmetrical; (b) in fsQCA, we calibrate values as opposed to measurement. To calibrate interval scales the researcher sets a number of qualitative threshold anchors, based on his/her substantive knowledge of the cases and/or a theory. Therefore, cases will not be ranked relative to each other, but rather classified in a number of sets that are created by meaningful cut-offs;

(c) conditions and configurations of conditions are used instead of independent variables. This enables researchers to take the interplay between the conditions into account; (d) the counterfactual analysis together with the Boolean minimisation algorithm allows for reducing complexities towards a parsimonious solution; (e) given the formal structure that this method puts in place, building middle-range theories from small to intermediate *N* has become possible.

The field of higher education can greatly benefit from this method. It can be performed in various types of studies that are carried out at both micro and macro levels. In particular, in studies with small N, using either crisp or fuzzy set-theoretic analysis can help in reaching a satisfactory level of generalisation.

REFERENCES

Arvind, T. T., & Stirton, L. (2010). Explaining the reception of the Code Napoleon in Germany: a fuzzy-set qualitative comparative analysis. *Legal Studies, 30*(1), 1–29.

Avdagic, S. (2010). When are concerted reforms feasible? Explaining the emergence of social pacts in Western Europe. *Comparative Political Studies, 43*(5), 628–657.

Breg-Schlosser, D., De Meur, G., Rihoux, B., & Ragin, C. C. (2009). Qualitative comparative analysis (QCA) as an approach. In B. Rihoux & C. C. Ragin (Eds.), *Configurational comparative methods: Qualitative comparative analysis (QCA) and related techniques*. Los Angeles, CA: Sage.

Byrne, D. (2009). Complex realist and configurational approaches to cases: A radical synthesis. In D. Byrne & C. Ragin (Eds.), *The Sage handbook of case-based methods* (pp. 101–111). Los Angeles, CA: Sage.

Cronqvist, L. (2007). *Tosmana – Tool for Small-N Analysis*, 1.3 ed. Marburg. Retrieved from http://www.tosmana.net/

Easton, G. (2010). Critical realism in case study research. *Industrial Marketing Management, 39*(1), 118–128.

Fiss, P. C. (2007). A set-theoretic approach to organizational configurations. *Academy of Management Review, 32*(4), 1180–1198.

Giugni, M., & Nai, A. (2013). Paths towards consensus: Explaining decision making within the Swiss global justice movement. *Swiss Political Science Review, 19*(1), 26–40.

Hemsley-Brown, J., & Oplatka, I. (2010). Market orientation in universities: A comparative study of two national higher education systems. *International Journal of Educational Management, 24*(3), 204–220.

Herrmann, A. M., & Cronqvist, L. (2009). When dichotomisation becomes a problem for the analysis of middle-sized datasets. *International Journal of Social Research Methodology, 12*(1), 33–50.

Kogut, B., MacDuffie, J. P., & Ragin, C. C. (2004). Prototypes and strategy: Assigning causal credit using fuzzy sets. *European Management Review, 1*, 114–131.

Mahoney, J., & Goertz, G. (2004). The possibility principle: Choosing negative cases in comparative research. *The American Political Science Review, 98*(4), 653–669.

Mjoset, L. (2001). Theory: conceptions in the social sciences. *International Encyclopedia of the Social and Behavioral Sciences, 23*, 15641–15647. Amsterdam: Elsevier.

Ragin, C. C. (1992). Introduction: Cases of "what is a case?". In C. Ragin & H. Becker (Eds.), *What is the case? Exploring the foundations of social inquiry*. Cambridge: Cambridge University Press.

Ragin, C. C. (2000). *Fuzzy-set social science*. Chicago, IL: University of Chicago Press.

Ragin, C. C. (2004). Turning the tables: How case-oriented research challenges variable-oriented research. In H. E. Brady & D. Collier (Eds.), *Rethinking social inquiry*. Lanham, MD: Rowman and Littlefield.

Ragin, C. C. (2007). *User's Guide to Fuzzy-Set/Qualitative Comparative Analysis 2.0*. Department of Sociology, University of Arizona, Tucson, AZ. Retrieved from www.u.arizona.edu/~cragin/fsQCA

Ragin, C. C. (2008). *Redesigning social inquiry: Fuzzy sets and beyond*. Chicago, IL: University of Chicago Press.

Ragin, C. C. (2009). Qualitative comparative analysis using fuzzy sets (fsQCA). In B. Rihoux & C. C. Ragin (Eds.), *Configurational comparative methods: Qualitative comparative analysis (QCA) and related techniques*. LA, London: Sage.

Ragin, C. C., & Sonnett, J. (2004). Between complexity and parsimony: Limited diversity, counterfactual cases, and comparative analysis. *Theory and Research in Comparative Social Analysis* (pp. 1–25). Department of Sociology, University of California, Los Angeles, CA. Retrieved from http://www.sscnet.ucla.edu/soc/soc237/papers/ragin.pdf

Rihoux, B. (2003). Bridging the gap between the qualitative and quantitative worlds? A retrospective and prospective view on qualitative comparative analysis. *Field Methods, 15*(4), 351–365.

Rihoux, B., & De Meur, G. (2009). Crisp-set qualitative comparative analysis (csQCA). In B. Rihoux & C. C. Ragin (Eds.), *Configurational comparative methods: Qualitative comparative analysis (QCA) and related techniques* (Vol. 51, pp. 33–68). California: Sage.

Rihoux, B., & Lobe, B. (2009). The case for qualitative comparative analysis (QCA): Adding leverage for thick cross-case comparison. In D. Byrne & C. C. Ragin (Eds.), *The Sage handbook of case-based methods*. London: Sage.

Rihoux, B., & Ragin, C. C. (2009). *Configurational comparative methods: Qualitative comparative analysis (QCA) and related techniques*. CA: Sage.

Schneider, C. Q., & Wagemann, G. (2012). *Set-theoretic methods for the social sciences: A guide to qualitative comparative analysis*. Cambridge: Cambridge University Press.

Schneider, P., & Sadowski, D. (2010). The impact of new public management instruments on PhD education. *Higher Education, 59*(5), 543–565.

Teichler, U. (2005). Research on higher education in Europe. *European Journal of Education, 40*(4), 447–469.

Warren, J., Wistow, J., & Bambra, C. (2013). Applying qualitative comparative analysis (QCA) in public health: A case study of a health improvement service for long-term incapacity benefit recipients. *Journal of Public Health*, 1–8 (first published online on May 3, 2013). Retrieved from http://jpubhealth.oxfordjournals.org/content/early/2013/05/02/pubmed.fdt047.full.pdf

Zadeh, L. A. (1965). Fuzzy sets. *Information and Control, 8*(3), 338–353.

ANALYTIC AUTOETHNOGRAPHY: ONE STORY OF THE METHOD

John Struthers

ABSTRACT

All researchers have a self, but how many understand how their self informs their identity and world view? The use of self is vital in relationships, especially where helping others to learn is central to the role. Many occupations, such as teaching and health care, require the individual to engage in reflective practices to inform how individuals give of themselves in professional practice. Despite the potential power of analytic autoethnography, there is an absence of clear examples which clarify how the theory and method are linked. From my background as a lecturer and mental health nurse I argue the value of analytic autoethnography as research-based self-study to assist self-development. This chapter has two main aims: (i) to provide an example as to how the theory and method within analytic autoethnography articulate into a research design; and (ii) to forewarn researchers as to the areas which require early consideration when constructing an analytic autoethnography to safeguard the researcher's psychological wellbeing. My experiences draw parallels between the cognitive reflective skills required within the research methods to review values and beliefs held within memories and

Theory and Method in Higher Education Research II
International Perspectives on Higher Education Research, Volume 10, 183–202
Copyright © 2014 by Emerald Group Publishing Limited
All rights of reproduction in any form reserved
ISSN: 1479-3628/doi:10.1108/S1479-3628(2014)0000010015

mental health cognitive therapies. The potential for cathartic insights increases the researcher's empathy to shape appropriate responses to assist others to learn.

INTRODUCTION

You know how sometimes you wished you knew something before you started, but it only becomes apparent when you are nearly finished? Analytic autoethnography is a unique methodology where the researcher turns the lens of inquiry on to their own personal accounts of events that concern them. Participating in the reflective data collection exercises within the methodology prompts self-study, which challenges previously held thoughts. Knowledge from existing social science theories are then used to create new learning to change attributions which underpin thoughts and behaviour. The insights gained from the self-study are then used by the researcher to inform more constructive ways of responding to the original area of concern.

I argue that, due to the personal emotional nature of memories being used as data, analytic autoethnography has to be lived through to fully appreciate the feelings associated with change prompted through reflective methodologies. Venturing into the unknown of self-study can be intimidating, especially when no guide provides an overview of how the methodological processes interrelate. This chapter offers a diagrammatical representation which I developed by merging the available methodological literature to plot my research design. The diagram has proved helpful in sharing ideas about analytic autoethnography with interested others. The diagram also offers a visual representation of how the abstract process of reflexivity interlinks with the methodological steps. Analytic autoethnography theory and method needs to be embodied by the researcher to bring about purposeful insights and outcomes. The content of this chapter provides the reader with what I now see as prerequisites, which allay some of the anxieties associated with the reflective disclosure within the research methods of analytic autoethnography.

I lived with the analytic autoethnography methodological process for two years, 2010−2012, during my thesis as part of a PhD in Educational Research at Lancaster University UK (Struthers, 2013). The aim of the thesis was to conduct an experiential analysis of the methodology and methods used within analytic autoethnography to explore how they may inform the lecturer's use of self-awareness when teaching mental health nursing. The research questions arose from the political and practice concerns relating to the use of reflective practices in mental health nursing. The research questions were:

1. What influences on self emerge from an analytic autoethnographic account of a lecturer in mental health nursing with a career spanning over 30 years?
2. What are the possible concerns for lecturers who wish to engage in doing an analytic autoethnography?
3. What relationships become apparent between self-awareness gained through analytic autoethnography and the changes in a lecturer's use of self when teaching mental health nursing?
4. In what way does the researcher/subject make sense of the different identities relating to self while doing and following an analytic autoethnography to enable their integrity to be maintained?

Reflective research methodologies such as analytic autoethnography require the text and the author to remain coupled, rather than separated, as if they both have an external reality (Alvesson & Skoldberg, 2012). To confirm the coupling between the text and myself I developed a critical interpretative narrative style of writing my story. All good stories have a beginning, middle and end, therefore I use these three headings to share the learning I experienced doing an analytic autoethnography. I continue to use a narrative writing style that foregrounds the use of 'I' within this chapter as testimony to how the combination of doing analytic autoethnography while being a PhD student assisted the development of my own identity and voice.

BEGINNING

In the beginning before I conducted an analytic autoethnography there was me. What I did not fully appreciate was the number of influences which had already shaped my self-identity, revealed as data for the analytic autoethnography through completing the 'culture gram exercise' (Chang, 2008). The culture gram required me as subject to map out all my cultural influences under specific headings provided. Be prepared as to what reflexive exercises can reveal through your disclosure. My decision to base the thesis on a methodology that could be creatively adapted to meet the unique features of personal situations was liberating, while simultaneously, for me, high risk. My engagement with reflexivity through the data collection exercises far exceeded any requirement I had previously faced in mental health nursing or teaching preparation and practice. Having been in health care and education for over 30 years, I now realised I had claimed to understand the effects of institutionalisation on clients with mental health issues (Goffman, 1963), but had not turned the reflective lens of institutionalisation on myself in any detail.

Two main approaches of autoethnography are evident within the literature: 'evocative' and 'analytic'. Both styles utilise ethnographic and narrative inquiry approaches to seek cultural understanding of autobiographical experiences, where the researcher is also the subject (Austin & Hickey, 2007; Starr, 2010). Evocative autoethnography leaves the narrative to resonate with the reader, emphasising the uniqueness of how each individual learns from sources such as stories, poetry and movies (Holquist, 2002). Whereas analytic autoethnography does not stop with the reader coming to their own personal understanding, but makes visible how the researcher's memories combine with social science theories to construct interpretations of particular events (Ellis, 2004). For whatever reason, autoethnographers seldom specify the evocative or analytic genre of their research design. This evasion in clarifying the type of autoethnographic methodology leads to a difficulty in conceptualising a distinct methodological approach for analytic autoethnography. The lack of a documented guide to analytic autoethnography results in the diversity of data types, analysis and presentation styles within autoethnographic research, appearing as unwieldy and unmanageable. My anxiety towards adopting analytic autoethnography was hampered by the lack of clear examples in the literature of how to bring together research methods within an analytic autoethnography design. Having critiqued over 30 autoethnographies within the literature review of the thesis, I could not locate any consistent methodological framework or definitive example for analytic autoethnography.

It is insufficient just to acknowledge the premise that each individual's world is constructed through their internal cognitive frames of reference (Anderson, 2006; Muncey, 2010). To embrace analytic autoethnography I had to shift from accepting dominant validity and reliability research arguments to accepting the epistemological basis of social constructivism. Analytic autoethnography's transformative potential rests on the social constructivist premise that self is not a stable construct and is therefore amenable to change (Starr, 2010). Embodying analytic autoethnography can be unnerving as it requires the researcher to deconstruct their previous world views that may have defended particular mind sets and courses of action.

The acceptance that self is not a stable construct is a double edged sword within analytic autoethnography. The self may develop from the reflexivity within analytic autoethnography; however, paradoxically the non-stability of self can also contest the value of memories as reliable data. De Freitas and Paton (2008) doubt that self can actually be accessed through self-study. I argue that memories are only a starting point from which the reflexivity and analysis is conducted. Kristeva (1991) has explored how aspects of what a person's self holds as 'strange' about themselves can inform relationships. Likewise, Winnicott's (2006) 'real self and false self' questions the source from which memories are accessed, whereas Lacan's (2005) 'mirror stage of self-development' relies on the psychological maturity of the individual to be able to reflect on their own behaviour.

What is helpful to manage the notion of instability of self is the concept of 'crystallisation', which offers a postmodern form of validity (Ellingson, 2011). Crystallisation enables contrasting perceptions to be included within the analysis of an event during analytic autoethnography. An event may have many interpretations depending from which lens of the crystal the individual's view is taken. The beliefs and values associated with a person's cognitive processes have the potential to customise their recalling of events in line with their world view. The use of multiple reflective lenses within the methodological approach guards against the limitations of self-enquiry. As definitions of reliability or validity relating to absolute truths no longer apply to analytic autoethnography, Guba and Lincoln's (1989) four factors of 'fairness', ontological authenticity, educative authenticity and catalytic authenticity offer an alternative framework to establish trustworthiness within the research design.

Definitions that exist for autoethnography such as Ellis, Adams, & Blocher (2011) reinforce how an individual's personal experience can be used for a wider social context.

> Autoethnography is an approach to research and writing that seeks to describe and systematically analyse (graphy) personal experiences (auto) in order to understand cultural experiences (ethno). This approach challenges canonical ways of doing research and representing others and treats research as a political, socially just and socially conscious act. The researcher uses tenets of autobiography and ethnography to do and write autoethnography. Thus, as a method autoethnography is both process and product. (Ellis, Adams, & Bochner, 2011, p. 1)

Fig. 1 summarises my research design, which merged Chang's (2008) step-by-step design and Muncey's (2010) four methods of journey,

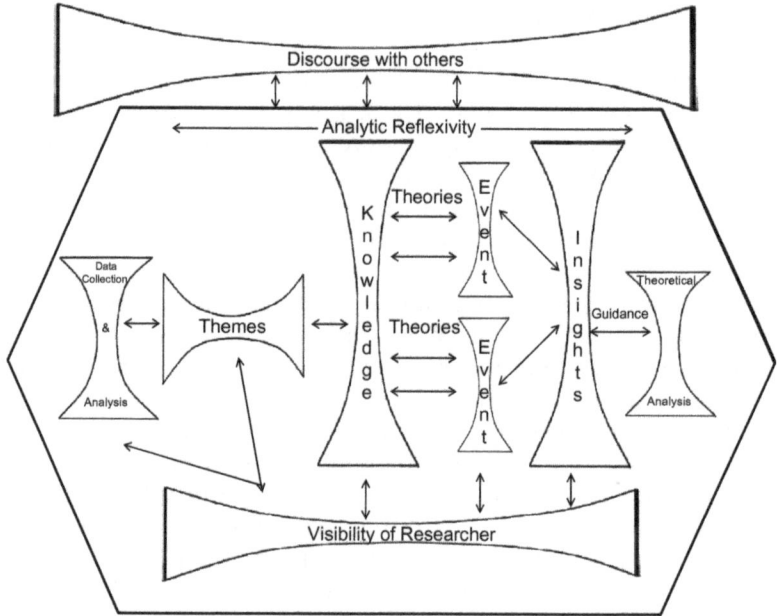

Fig. 1.   Analytic Autoethnography Diagram.

metaphors, snapshots and artefacts for autoethnography. The figure bridges
the text and methods between the three sources to establish and emphasise
the analytic component which create an analytic autoethnography.

Anderson's (2006) five key features of analytic autoethnography offer
the main structure to the diagram. The first key feature 'complete member
research status' is represented within the hexagon which sets the boundaries
of the function of the remaining four features. The remaining four features
– analytic reflexivity, visibility of the researcher, discourse with others and
theoretical analysis – are all informed by what the person brings in relation
to their complete membership research status. Although an analytic autoethnography may be developed by one individual, including dialogue with
other relevant informants increases the trustworthiness of analysis. In my
case, as a qualified mental health nurse and lecturer, male and over 50 years
of age, I included the voice of other mental health lecturers and males
within the 'Venn diagram' exercise when seeking comparisons with other
authors of autoethnographies. The creativity afforded within analytic autoethnography gave me the opportunity to arrange for an interviewer to

conduct a 360 degree feedback analysis interview. The interviews collated data on my teaching and managerial roles, from the perspective of three students, a mental health lecturer, line manager and my clinical supervisor.

The double headed arrows within the diagram indicate the two-way process of emotional and intellectual involvement when living through reflexive research methods. Although the methodology progresses from left to right of the diagram through the lenses, the double headed arrows also indicate how the developing analysis and creation of narratives stimulates further reflexivity. Challenges to personal memories are not restricted to the theme of the research, but can question many other personal life events too. The analysis of memories combines with other textual data, such as previous publications, reports or documents, often stimulating further data to come to mind. Recording the data on a 'data log' enables the sources and types of data to be reviewed prior to searching for themes (Chang, 2008). The themes within the data are identified in a manner similar to content analysis. Once the themes are established, the researcher critically applies their knowledge of different theories to develop alternative interpretations of events. Viewing a persistent concern from a different knowledge perspective can create new insights. Insights resulting from the continual process of analytic reflexivity within the data collection and analysis are the desired outcome for self-development. Applying social science theories to offer alternative explanation of one's behaviour of memorised events can be transformative in reframing how others were perceived at the time of the event. Rather than analytic autoethnography being focused on the researcher as subject it becomes inclusive of the relational interplay between others and organisations. The insights become new ways of knowing or 'mental products' (Collyer, 2011) that shape future thinking. Within analytic autoethnography the insights are repositioned back into current discourse through theoretical analysis, to inform the practices of others and contribute to future organisational and policy development. The visibility of the researcher is maintained in the narrative to capture the perspective transformations as they unfold throughout the reflexive process within analytic reflexivity.

Being able to visualise the methodological approach in a diagrammatical form, prior to commencing an analytic autoethnography, acts as guide to the sequence of methodological steps. The diagram also assists in indicating where specific skills are required. The researcher can then consider if they feel sufficiently skilled to engage purposefully and safely with reflection, cognitive challenges or creative writing. Otherwise the skills may have to be developed during the research period, interrupting the data collection and analysis activities.

MIDDLE

The diagram assisted the development of my analytic autoethnography data collection and analysis plan for my thesis. This is presented in Table 1 to clarify the different methods and stages within the methodology. The data collection and analysis plan details how various research methods can be brought together to explore the research questions.

Of course, epistemological caution remains:

> It is not possible to have direct and unmediated access to the social world and therefore it cannot be known directly. Rather, the world can only be known through our constructs of it. (Ashwin, 2012, p. 17)

Table 1. Data Collection and Analysis Plan.

Data Source	Data Collection and Reflexivity Exercises of a Themed Analytical Autoethnography	Analysis of Data to Create Autoethnography
1. Personal memory (Chang, 2008)	1. Timeline of life events. 2. Time cycle of monthly routines. 3. Proverbs used frequently. 4. Social rituals and celebrations. 5. Mentors impacting on life. 6. Artefacts from life. 7. Kinship diagram of family. 8. Drawing of place that assisted self-understanding.	Identification of themes across the data sources. Identification of particular themes that may be omitted across the data sources. The themes identified from the reflective account of completing each exercise are crafted into an autoethnography using a social critique analytical–interpretative style.
2. Self-observational/ self-reflective (Chang, 2008)	1. Systematic self-observation record of teaching activities. 2. Interactive self-observation record with colleagues, comparing approaches to teaching. 3. Personal values and preference associated with teaching. 4. Cultural identity and cultural membership as a teacher. 5. Discovering self through others writings.	Different creative writing styles are used to emphasise emotive elements, such as metaphor, poetry and detailing the nature of the journey related to the event (Ellis, 2004; Muncey, 2010).
3. External data (Chang, 2008)	1. Data from dialogical exchange with other colleagues in practice field. 2. Documentary and other artefacts, e.g. photographs,	The parts of the autoethnographic narrative relating to the research questions are considered in relation to current social science knowledge.

Table 1. (*Continued*)

Data Source	Data Collection and Reflexivity Exercises of a Themed Analytical Autoethnography	Analysis of Data to Create Autoethnography
	evaluations of teaching, publications. 3. 360 degree feedback analysis. 4. Social science literature to frame exploration and context.	Insights are then developed from the autoethnographic narrative in relation to broader implications for social structure that shape
4. Reflexive journal	Collate self-reflective field notes from experiences of doing an analytic autoethnography, PhD and self-development relating to teaching. Hand written journal. Capture thoughts on the practicality and value of analytic autoethnography as a means of developing a lecturer's self-awareness in teaching when teaching mental health nursing. The theoretical structure within analytic autoethnography is analysed in relation to the experiences of undertaking the methodological processes in accordance with Anderson's (2006) five key features of analytic autoethnography and Guba and Lincoln's (1989) qualitative research criteria.	identity and practice. Findings are produced for the methodological analysis based on the processes within the methodology.
5. Clinical supervision	Clinical supervision facilitated by the clinical supervisor every six weeks to reflect on my responses to the views of others from on-going dialogue. Supervision notes from my supervisor summarising the key issues discussed in each session.	

Therefore specific reflection and cognitive skills are required within analytic autoethnography to reveal our psychological constructs similar to cognitive therapeutic approaches. Reflective skills require the researcher to detail the constituents of an event, while drawing on cognitive skills relating to how they attribute power to other individuals. The availability of a 'listener' is essential to provide psychological support when revisiting previous traumatic life events. I recommend a listener entrusted to offer counsel and ensure that the researcher ethically maintains their own integrity, as it may be difficult to withdraw consent to your own personal enquiry.

Being forewarned about the emotional risks of using memories as data ensured that I included psychological support through my employer's clinical supervision system. Clinical supervision is an organisational arrangement to enable practitioners to safely explore with a trusted facilitator how they engage with personal and practice issues to encourage person centred development (Jasper, 2006; Sloan, White, & Colt, 2000). The range of data sources from my self and others avoids accusations of solipsism, when self is seen as the only reality. It is vital to log other sources of data such as reports, publications, novels and clinical supervision notes. These were collated in a spread sheet format, as a data log, to enable comparison of primary and secondary characteristics of each data item (Chang, 2008). Logging all the data provided a reference point to audit where data referred to within the analytic autoethnography had emerged. The comparison of the data also assisted the identification of where further data required to be collated.

To compensate for not being taught how to do an analytic autoethnography, I recommend reading Ellis's (2004) account of her experiences of teaching and conducting tutorials as she supported students through the dilemmas of undertaking an autoethnography. For me, it was like becoming a student in her fictional composite cohort. The learning I shared with the fictitious students assisted in unshackling me from my previous socialisation within dominant discourse. I was sufficiently liberated to develop a more creative writing style and use 'I' to write from the soul. I became more confident and convinced that learning could be evidenced through writing poetry, analysing photographs and using metaphors, and about the significance of my own accounts of my life events as learning worthy of sharing.

One of the themes that became evident to me through subjecting the data to content analysis, as within grounded theory, I named 'uniting selves'. Uniting selves collated the examples from the data that illustrated where I had concerns about sustaining my teaching practices and other responsibilities, while deconstructing aspects of my different identities within the process of analytic autoethnography.

Examples of the data that confirmed 'uniting selves' as a theme included the 'mentors impacting on life' exercise, which accessed my personal memory to recall how I had utilised Barbeau's conversational techniques within my own repertoire as a teacher and nurse. I watched the DVD of Barbeau with students in teaching sessions on several occasions, admiring how he (1987) offered cognitive challenges to others in a creative manner. I adopted a similar conversational approach in my practices as manager with colleagues, educationalist with students, nurse with clients and in my domestic settings. I felt Barbeau's style assisted me to facilitate my use of self when I possessed self-doubt associated with not being a qualified therapist or qualified group worker, as detailed in another theme in the research, 'knowing and doing'.

Data from my 360 degree feedback analysis illustrated how sometimes my mental defence mechanisms prompted my use of humour to avoid personal disclosure when teaching. Other comments from those interviewed by the facilitator for the 360 degree feedback reported warmth from those who knew me well, whereas others, if only meeting me briefly, could feel intimidated. Knowledge of these two different perceptions illustrates the importance of non-verbal and verbal messages. Being aware of such nuances can assist in distinguishing between when to be welcoming to students, as opposed to upholding organisational and professional regulations as a manager. However, the context of the feedback from within the 360 degree feedback analysis indicated that I could be misconstrued occasionally as intimidating within class. I could have chosen to ignore this data, or argue the others' perspective as their 'projection'. To support ontological authenticity I required revealing insider 'emic' aspects of my self as subject, whilst maintaining an outsider 'etic' perspective of researcher. Therefore I consciously focused the research enquiry on to an area which had been a concern to me, the occasions when others perceived me as intimidating.

A further example clarifying 'uniting selves' as a theme was the freehand drawing exercise of 'the place that assisted self-understanding'. I sketched a farmhouse where I and a colleague had facilitated a self-development residential. The drawing signified the importance of a fire in the hearth. I was keen to tend to the fire to display caring through providing warmth through the heat from the fire, rather than emotional warmth in a verbal or non-verbal manner with cohort members.

'Uniting selves' was also revealed through the 'culture gram' exercise identifying how my practices as teacher, manager, nurse and family man all competed with and informed each other. I recognised how many of my other roles had become dependent on my identity linked to my employment as a manager and lecturer.

To support a creative narrative writing style I used photography to create a metaphor for my thoughts on teaching. The metaphor was labelled 'log and axe' and acted as a central focus to develop an autoethnographic narrative, which drew on existing social science theoretical knowledge to explore my current use of self in teaching. An excerpt from my analytic autoethnography narrative is now presented (in italics) that incorporates Anderson's (2006) key characteristics of 'discourse with others', 'analytic reflexivity' and 'visibility of researcher'. The excerpt clarifies how the range of methods in the methodological design synthesises to create a narrative based on the initial data.

LOG AND AXE TEACHING METAPHOR

I explained my hand represented myself as a teacher, holding an axe, which represented the words and practices I use in teaching, while the log represented the student. When the axe splits the log, it is the first time the inside of the log has seen daylight becoming 'enlightened'. Therefore my communication skills are not only the words I use but the manner in which I use them. The thinking behind the intent of the words selected and delivered may be considered as hidden practices, when a teacher uses their self to inform

communication. Knowing the pressure to apply behind the axe, in relation to the type of axe or size of log, how to hold the axe and where and when to strike the log, are similar to technical skills linking the human to the axe as a tool. My words striking home to create a cognitive challenge, prompting adaptive cognitive reframing, like a 'whack on the side of the head' to stimulate more creative thinking (von Oech, 1998). *How the individual responds will influence my next communication.*

One of my colleagues with a cognitive behavioural mental health background challenged my metaphorical interpretation, indicating the student did not seem central to my metaphor. My colleague's pedagogical interpretation would have placed the axe in the hand of the student. From sharing this metaphor with my colleague I could see how I was in a position of power and authority deciding when the 'cutting remark' would be made. Our discussion considered handing over the power to the student, positioning myself as the piece of wood. The student could then decide how much they wished to 'axecess' me as an educational resource. The repositioning of the symbolic links within the metaphor challenged my thoughts about being defensive, to being more vulnerable, taking the 'blows' for the benefit of the student's development. The discourse with my colleagues enabled me to challenge my own perspective of giving of self in teaching. For the students' learning I require to be able to unite all aspects of myself to shape a meaningful response. I could see how my colleague's cognitive behaviour background had centred the power with the student to develop lifelong learning skills.

Further critical reviewing of the metaphorical interpretation of the wood cutting photograph with my clinical supervisor, who is a social worker with experience in the drug and alcohol field, questioned the representation of the shadow of the wood, axe and hand on the concrete slabs. An exchange of ideas led to considering the shadow representing the student emerging from the shadows, from a guided concrete pedagogical approach earlier in their three year programme, to a more student centred position as their identity as a mental health nurse and autonomous critical thinker emerged. This interpretation took a more long-term view of the effects of teaching and implied a longer term approach for people with substance dependency.

Sharing this alternative analysis when presenting my reflections to a group of teaching colleagues, the comment was made as to the difference in the size of the gap between the wood and the axe from the object and the shadow. This further perspective cautioned me about thinking I had to replace one behaviour with another, student centredness replacing teacher-led practices. To replace one behaviour with another may lead to further problems for the learning styles of other students. Now I have raised my conscious awareness of the different teaching approaches, I can take a more considered approach, depending on the circumstances that a student presents before deciding if I am the axe or log. Alternatively I can offer a safe liminal space, being the gap created as the axe is suspended above the log, as the student ventures between the threshold of different concepts (Land, Meyer, & Smith, 2008).

When showing the picture to another teaching colleague whose professional background was school nursing, her first reaction was that the picture was 'not convincing', as the angle of my hand holding the axe was not the way you cut wood with an axe'. I explained the picture was staged for the purposes of a pictorial metaphor but, as the teacher had a rural background, she was disconcerted that the picture was not accurate in its positional composition. As an example of how reflexivity does not stop, it further reinforced to me the need to ensure that my practice examples of mental health nursing reflected accurately the cultural context of contemporary practice. I contemplated how the school nurse's perception may have ensured educational material to young students had to engage them convincingly rather than be left to chance.

Within the analysis, my use of the log and axe metaphor reveals my thinking about teaching practices from different perspectives. The thinking illustrates different power and identity positions associated with being a student, teacher or practitioner. The metaphor makes visible to me my thoughts and actions within my teaching style, and how they are culturally specific (Lakoff & Johnson, 1980). I can detect the traces of how my actions as a teacher mirror the metaphorical interpretations based on my early psychological and cultural experiences. Using self in teaching appears to require re-scripting of the metaphorical conceptualisation from early socialisation. An axe can appear a brutal object if left only in the teacher's hand, as if teaching is tough work. I feel that the self-study makes visible my metaphorical conceptualisations, to enable being available for others to approach me as a resource, signifying a maturity in adjusting my use of self as a teacher. I have transferred such reactions to my parenting role, accepting that adolescents have to learn for themselves, no matter what worldly wisdom I may have accrued or wish to share (Winnicott, 2006).

The assumption that my use of words has the power to create a difference in how students may see the world, or that a student needs to rely on the teacher to bring light to a subject area, reflects a more authoritative stance rather than student centeredness. Other colleagues who processed the 'log and axe' metaphor and proposed alternative interpretations revealed their own neural conceptual systems in relation to their professional, cultural and cognitive processes (Cameron & Low, 1999).

Changing my educational philosophy from the self-awareness developed through the 'log and axe' metaphor illustrates the catalytic authenticity (Guba & Lincoln, 1989) resulting from the methodology, where action stems from self-development within the autoethnography. Further examples of insights are given in Table 2.

Unlike emotive autoethnography, the analytic autoethnography methodological process does not cease with the production of the autoethnographic narrative. Whereas emotive autoethnography leaves the narrative to resonate with the reader, analytic autoethnography accesses social science theories to offer alternative perspectives to understand recounted life events as data. The researcher then is faced with a decision as to what theories and how many theories to draw on to provide alternative explanations. I drew on psychodynamic and transactional analysis theories to consider how my earlier scripted behaviour still informed my relationships with others. Due to my mental health background, I was able to challenge previously held assumptions and recognise that I had done the best I could have at the time in question. I could now apply a more adaptable response to reflect the students' progression during their programme.

It could be argued that self-study can be limited if I only use what I currently know to offer alternative theoretical options. Developing discourse with others and exploring theories previously unknown to me illustrates how learning continues to restructure how I perceive myself. Being open to others' views and responses to early drafts of the narratives reinforces how my self-identity is informed through interaction with others. Linking back into dominant discourse to defend insights generated from analytic

Table 2. Examples of Insights Relating to Uniting Selves.

1.	Recognise the value of having others to trust when listening and responding to my reflective accounts. This avoids self-absorption and offers alternative interpretations.
2.	Reviewing attributions to memories in light of new perspectives and theories supports my use of self in teaching and provides examples of the value of reflexivity.
3.	To create the most advantageous educational response, the necessary skills have to be developed by the lecturer, to decide how, why and when to use reflexive methods most appropriately.
4.	Teaching is a further way of engaging in dialogue which continually informs my self, in relation to the skills required to enhance learning.

autoethnography may be criticised for weakening the creative elements of emotive autoethnography, which were developed to overcome the crisis of representation. However, leaving a narrative to resonate with others can also be criticised as just being story telling.

ENDING

Completing the theoretical analysis stage by repositioning the insights back into current theories and practice can have an immediate effect. As analytic autoethnography develops appreciation of how our values and beliefs shape our responses, it assists the strategic drive to promote compassionate communication to others who deliver health care (Department of Health, 2013). The need to be able to trust others to share perspectives and consider other people's world views can be implemented forthwith in collegiate settings. Being able to consider other professionals and the service users' world views is now central in a multi-professional, service user based model (Stickley & Basset, 2008).

The theoretical analysis step in my research suggests that if lecturers undertook an analytic autoethnography it would be one way to prepare them to educate others about identity, reflection and the use of self. For lecturers who teach mental health nurses, this would assist them to fulfil the Nursing and Midwifery Council (2010) standard to develop reflective practitioners for the future. Lecturers who have undertaken an analytic autoethnography would be able to role model appropriate self-disclosure. I have also implemented my new insights by selecting some of Chang's reflective exercises as teaching tools to assist students to consider how their own self-study informs caring relationships with others. Self-understanding is essential when self is used therapeutically within relationships within mental health care (Department of Health, 2009) and teaching (Palmer, 1998). Appreciating the mutuality of learning and how self-identity is a composite of stories from others and stories we hold about our self, assists in cautioning how data can inform decisions.

Finally, I adjust the methodological overview provided by the analytic autoethnography diagram to present specific details relevant to my thesis findings (Fig. 2). The changes detail the four themes from the data analysis. I list the theories which are accessible to me as knowledge as I review the events within 'teaching self-awareness' through the 'log and axe metaphor'. I refer to the use of defence mechanisms and adapting self to the learner's

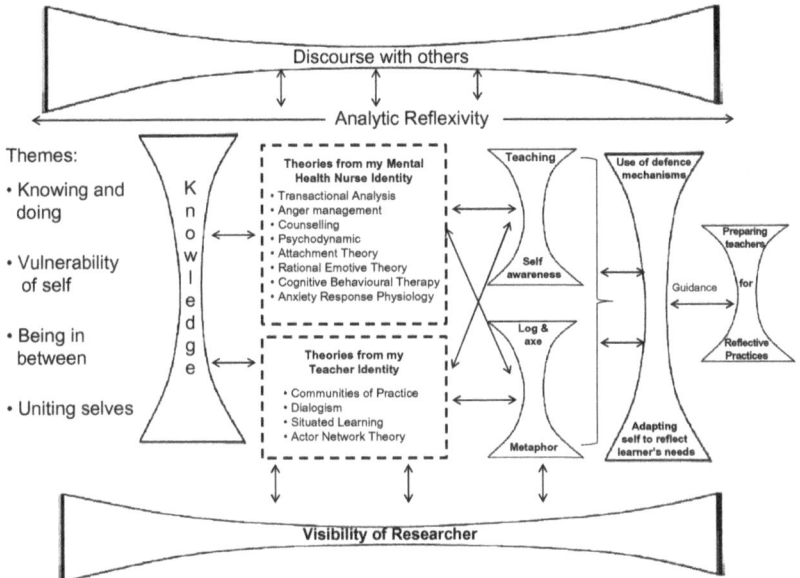

Fig. 2. Analytic Autoethnography Overview of Thesis.

needs as insights which resulted for me from the analytic reflexivity. These insights are then used to support theoretical analysis by suggesting that they could be incorporated into the preparation of teachers to teach others reflective practices and skills.

From my perception of being a lecturer and mental health nurse, there is a parallel process which emerges when doing analytic autoethnography that is similar to my perception of what a mental health service user may experience. The self-study leads to the review of life events and previous cognitive processes that may have resulted in over reliance on particular mental defence mechanisms. The theoretically analysed reflective narratives, based on completion of the reflective exercises, provide opportunities for cognitive reframing. Revised ideas can then shape alternative responses to others in future situations such as teaching. However, what is disclosed remains under the researcher's discretion. Ethical concerns are raised as to who is identified or implicated within stories of past events, and how tacit feelings become translated into text (Barthes, 1980). Tolich (2010) suggests the researcher should view their own autoethnography as an inked tattoo, cautious against over-disclosure. The disconcerting feelings of no longer being sure as to who you are, in the middle of an analytic autoethnography, may create similar levels of anxiety as a person attempting to regain their identity following a disruption to their mental health and social roles. Although I would have appreciated knowing many aspects of this chapter before I started my analytic autoethnography, one methodological aspect that could be developed further is the 'scatter gun' approach of what theories the researcher draws upon to offer alternative explanations of the memories of events. I suggest analytic autoethnography methodology may be enhanced by having at least one theoretical framework identified at the beginning to offer an internal consistency to alternative perspectives. I incorporated actor network theory (Latour, 2005) within the theoretical analysis to review how the insights in my analytic autoethnography may develop current practice and theory. If I had built actor network theory into the methodological design at the beginning, I would have purposely scrutinised the data regarding how non-human technology and my own human contributions link to sustaining my identity.

Having completed my analytic autoethnography I am left with the skills of reflexivity and crystallisation which have changed my world view. I am no longer the same person when I set out on the analytic autoethnography. I feel I now have a much clearer acceptance of my self to be more relaxed within teaching situations. This enables me to have less reliance on particular defence mechanisms and to be more empathetic in responses to others' situations. Most importantly, I am aware of the significance of my relationships with others, and how I can disclose appropriately to share stories about learning through life. More recent student evaluations of my teaching and feedback from conference presentations support my own subjective reappraisal. I attribute such changes in my use of self to the manner in which the skills required to conduct an analytic autoethnography reflect the therapeutic skills used with mental health. I suggest that because of my experiential knowledge of having worked through the emotional concerns raised through self-study, I am more understanding of service users' difficulty in engaging with relationship issues. I cannot 'unknow' what I know, unless I have a psychogenic fugue, cerebral trauma, dementia or get intoxicated inducing false memory. I do not know what alternative interpretations of my data I may have generated if I had used different theories for analysis. By drawing on my 30 years of being a mental health nurse and lecturer I illustrate how my professional socialisation and knowledge has been used by me to define myself and others. There may be some unanswered questions for the future as to why I was satisfied with the alternative perceptions developed from the analytic autoethnography. Perhaps one analytic autoethnography is insufficient to view self through all the possible lenses.

REFERENCES

Alvesson, M., & Skoldberg, K. (2012). *Reflexive methodology: New vistas for qualitative research* (2nd ed.). London: Sage.

Anderson, L. (2006). Analytic autoethnography. *Journal of Contemporary Ethnography, 35*(4), 373–395.

Ashwin, P. (2012). *Analysing teaching-learning interactions in higher education: Accounting for structure and agency.* London: Continuum.

Austin, J., & Hickey, A. (2007). Autoethnography and teacher development. *The International Journal of Interdisciplinary Social Sciences, 2,* 1833–1882.

Barbeau, C. (1987). *Coping with self: Coping with others. DVD.* San Jose, CA: IKon Press.

Barthes, R. (1980). *The pleasure of the text.* New York, NY: Hill and Wang.

Cameron, L., & Low, G. (1999). *Researching and applying metaphor.* Cambridge: Cambridge University Press.

Chang, H. (2008). *Autoethnography as method.* Walnut Creek, CA: Left Coast Press.

Collyer, F. (2011). Reflexivity and the sociology of science technology: The invention of "Eryc" the antibiotic. *The Qualitative Report, 16*(2), 316–340.

de Freitas, E., & Paton, J. (2008). (De) facing the self: Postcultural disruptions of the autoethnographic text. *Qualitative Inquiry, 15*(3), 483–498.

Department of Health. (2009). *New horizons: A shared vision for mental health.* London: Department of Health.

Department of Health. (2013). *Delivering high quality, effective, compassionate care: Developing the right people with the right skills and the right values.* London: Department of Health.

Ellingson, L. L. (2011). Analysis and representation across the continuum. In K. N. Denzin & Y. S. Lincoln (Eds.), *The Sage handbook of qualitative research* (4th ed.). Los Angeles, CA: Sage.

Ellis, C. (2004). *The ethnographic I: A methodological novel about autoethnography.* Walnut Creek, CA: Altamira Press.

Ellis, C., Adams, T. E., & Bochner, A. P. (2011). Autoethnography: An overview. Article 10. *Qualitative Research, 12.* Retrieved from http://www.qualitative-research.net/index.php/fqs/article/view/1589. Accessed on 6 October, 2011.

Goffman, E. (1963). *Stigma: Notes on the management of spoiled identity.* London: Penguin.

Guba, E. G., & Lincoln, Y. S. (1989). *Fourth generation evaluation.* Thousand Oaks, CA: Sage.

Holquist, M. (2002). *Dialogism: Bakhtin and his world.* New York, NY: Routledge.

Jasper, M. (2006). *Professional development, reflection and decision-making.* Oxford: Blackwell.

Kristeva, J. (1991). *Strangers to ourselves.* New York, NY: Columbia University Press.

Lacan, J. (2005). *Ecrits: A selection.* London: Tavistock.

Lakoff, G., & Johnson, M. (1980). *Metaphors we live by.* Chicago, IL: Chicago Press.

Land, R., Meyer, H. F., & Smith, J. (2008). *Threshold concepts within the disciplines.* Rotterdam: Sense.

Latour, B. (2005). *Reassembling the social: An introduction to actor-network-theory.* New York, NY: Oxford University Press.

Muncey, T. (2010). *Creating autoethnographies.* Los Angeles, CA: Sage.

Nursing and Midwifery Council. (2010). *Standards for pre-registration nursing education.* London: NMC.

Palmer, J. P. (1998). *The courage to teach: Exploring the inner landscapes of a teacher's life.* San Francisco, CA: Jossey-Bass.

Sloan, G., White, C. A., & Colt, F. (2000). Cognitive therapy supervision as a framework for clinical supervision in nursing: Using structure to guide discovery. *Journal of Advanced Nursing, 32*(3), 515–524.

Starr, L. J. (2010). The use of autoethnography in educational research: Locating who we are in what we do. *Canadian Journal for New Scholars in Education, 3*(1), 1–9.

Stickley, T., & Basset, T. (2008). *Learning about mental health practice.* Chichester: Wiley.

Struthers, J. (2013). *Analytic autoethnography: A tool to inform the lecturer's use of self when teaching mental health nursing?* Lancaster: Lancaster University.

Tolich, M. (2010). A critique of current practice: Ten foundational guidelines for autoethnographers. *Qualitative Health Research, 20*(12), 1599–1610.

von Oech, R. (1998). *A whack on the side of the head: How you can be more creative* (3rd ed.). New York, NY: Warner Books.

Winnicott, D. W. (2006). *The family and individual development.* London: Routledge.

THE DILEMMA OF METHODOLOGICAL IDOLATRY IN HIGHER EDUCATION RESEARCH: THE CASE OF PHENOMENOGRAPHY

Fiona Hallett

ABSTRACT

The premise of this chapter is that methodological 'tribes' in higher education create 'territories' of research practice that do little to encourage those new to research to reconceptualise methodology. This premise is based upon the perceived absence of dialogic space, beyond an expert academic community, that would allow open critique of the degree to which research methodologies make sense for those 'on the ground'. As such, it is argued that practices of this nature signify methodological process over genuine debate around methodological theory, which can serve to encourage methodological idolatry. Phenomenography has been selected, and analysed, in this chapter as an example of a research methodology used in higher education, in order to reveal both the encoded messages of phenomenography and the layering of meaning that such

Theory and Method in Higher Education Research II
International Perspectives on Higher Education Research, Volume 10, 203–225
ISSN: 1479-3628/doi:10.1108/S1479-3628(2014)0000010016

messages convey. The chapter concludes by arguing for a repositioning of research methodologies as ontologically coherent heuristic devices that enable us to generate and test theory, rather than as processes of discovery that may lead us to unsubstantiated claims of knowledge generation.

INTRODUCTION

This chapter aims to explore the social activity that surrounds educational research by attempting to conceptualise the sociology of a particular educational research methodology commonly used in higher education research. A central thesis of this chapter is that the methodological 'tribes and territories' (Becher & Trowler, 2001; Tight, 2008) that seek to defend and develop particular methodological traditions create something akin to methodological idolatry. This term has been selected to represent the ways in which academic communities debate, and utilise, methodological processes at the expense of broader theoretical engagement; potentially overrating the mechanics of research and underrating new ways of thinking. The problems with this are twofold. First, methodological 'tribes' can create 'territories' of practice that do little to encourage those new to research to reconceptualise methodology, creating space for conceptual stagnation. Second, if research methodologies are to impact upon a field of practice it is important that the academic community values the perspectives of those working in the field. In this instance, academics researching the field of higher education must create dialogic space beyond an expert academic community that critiques the usefulness of educational research methodologies, and the degree to which they make sense for those 'on the ground'.

A structuralist analysis of a chosen methodological paradigm, phenomenography, will be used to tease out the ways in which this methodological tribe functions and creates meaning. Phenomenography has not been selected as a prime example of the ways in which methodological tribes serve to mythologise research; rather it has been selected in order to give a concrete example of my argument. By drawing upon the work of Lévi-Strauss and Barthes it is possible to examine the ways in which experts can *mythologize* research processes leading to the aforementioned methodological idolatry.

Following the structuralist analysis, activity theory will be employed, as a heuristic device, to test this notion of a methodological myth by applying it to three research communities: experienced academics associated with a particular methodological tradition, early career academics working within the same tradition (using my own work as an example of this) and practitioner researchers in the field of higher education.

METHOD: STRUCTURALISM AND ACTIVITY THEORY

In *Structural Anthropology* (1963), Lévi-Strauss argues that the sociological purpose of a myth is to function as 'a kind of logical tool that helps a society to handle problems where experience and theory contradict each other' (p. 216). It seems logical to argue that educational research methodologies could achieve the same purpose if they were to be explicitly positioned as a means by which contradictions between theory and experience could be explored.

One process employed by Lévi-Strauss involved the examination of *mythemes*; segments of the myth that happen to portray an underlying structural meaning. Lévi-Strauss argued that the same mythemes 'rear throughout the myth' (1963, p. 211), and, as such, conceived the unfolding of a myth as conceptual repetition rather than as the detail of a narrative. Furthermore, Lévi-Strauss' work also demands an acknowledgement that structural meaning is positional in nature, and can only be available to us by reference to what we know about the way of life and social organisation of the societies whose myths we want to analyse.

Barthes (1967) extended the two primary components of linguistic structural analysis – the *system* (i.e. the parts of speech; the paradigmatic elements) and the *syntagm* (the arrangement of these elements in a syntactic sequence) – to illustrate how one might apply structural analysis. To exemplify this notion he described the components of the *system* of architecture as the possible variations in style of a single element in a building – the types of roof, wall, doorway – and the *syntagm* as the sequence and arrangement of these parts within an edifice. It would seem reasonable to argue that, likewise, the system of educational research, the methods and processes employed, are dictated by the syntagm of particular research paradigms and the theories that inform them. Such analogies are useful in this context as they allow us to analyse the components and arrangement of particular methodologies in order to reveal dichotomies that might exist at the epistemological or ontological level.

Therefore, this study aims to employ both of the structuralist methods discussed here. In the first instance mythemes will be identified within the chosen methodology. From this, the system and syntagm of each mytheme will be analysed in order to examine any constituent dichotomies that, if ignored, result in the acceptance of methodological processes that do little to move theory on; an outcome of which I am calling methodological idolatry.

Then, activity theory will be used to analyse the ways in which such mythemes might be enacted in practice. Activity theory is a useful tool for this purpose as it aims to explain how social artefacts and social organisations mediate social action (Engeström, 1987), as illustrated in Fig. 1.

Engeström describes this structure in the following way:

> The 'subject' refers to the individual whose agency is chosen as the point of view in the analysis, the object refers to the 'problem space' at which the activity is directed and which is moulded and transformed into outcomes with the help of physical and symbolic, external and internal mediating instruments. The community comprises multiple individuals who share the same general object and who construct themselves as distinct from other communities. The division of labour refers to both the horizontal division of tasks between the members of the community and to the vertical division of power and status. Finally the rules refer to the explicit and implicit regulations, norms and conventions that constrain actions and interactions within the activity system. (1987, p. 78)

In this instance, I aim to analyse the experience of phenomenographic outputs (objects) as articulated by researchers (subjects) from a range of backgrounds (communities). The power relations within, and between, the groups of researchers are defined by a series of 'rules' and by 'divisions of

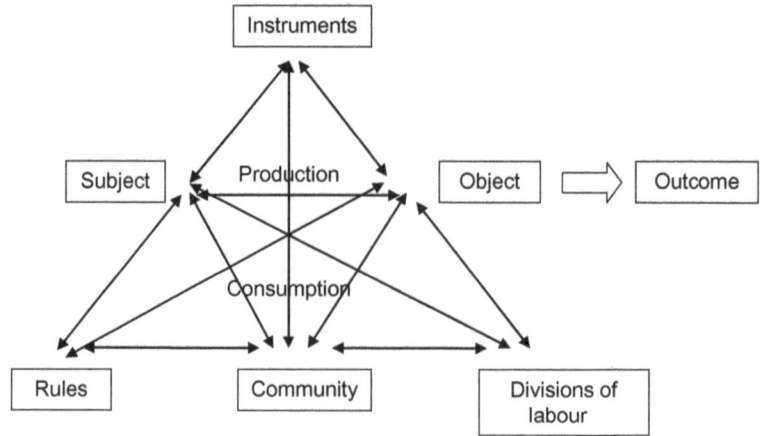

Fig 1. The Structure of Human Activity (Engeström, 1987, p. 78).

labour'. A further facet of activity theory relates to the belief that individuals do not have a direct and uninterpreted access to their environment, and that the relation between individuals and environment is considered mediated, established and developed through physical and intellectual tools, described here as mediating artefacts (Bakhurst, 1997; Díaz-Kommonen, 2004). The mythemes uncovered in the structuralist analysis can be further understood via analysis of these elements.

In addition, activity theory recognises that in any complex social system there will be competing goals, limited resources, differing values and a variety of desired outcomes; as such, actions are not fully predictable or rational, and the most well-planned and streamlined actions involve failures, disruptions and unexpected innovations. Such conflicting forces within activities have been termed 'contradictions' (Engeström, 1999, p. 32).

Internal Contradictions

Engeström (1987) maintains that a conceptual model of an activity system is particularly useful when one wants to make sense of systemic factors behind seemingly individual and accidental disturbances, or inner contradictions, occurring in daily practice. For the purpose of this chapter, research practices will be critiqued in order to ascertain the degree to which my proposition of methodological idolatry can be evidenced. Contradictions can be identified by examining what Roth and Tobin (2002, p. 116) describe as an 'ethnography of trouble', which, in this instance, will be interpreted from the real and imagined activities of three research communities.

Quaternary Contradictions

Quaternary contradictions are those that emerge from interactions between the changing central activity of one system and any neighbouring activity systems. It has been argued (Engeström, 2001) that, when considering multiple, interrelated activity systems, one is able to identify quaternary contradictions by acknowledging boundary crossings and contradictions between systems as challenging, but at the same time driving, factors of activity. Indeed, the primary motivation for looking at quaternary contradictions stems from a desire to develop concepts and tools to account for 'dialogue, multiple perspectives and networks of these intersecting systems' (Engeström, 2001, p. 135).

This study addresses three research activity systems; the first is an activity system of experienced researchers, identified via the literature, the second is exemplified by the work of an early career researcher, myself and the third comprises a theoretical research community based upon my own work with practitioner researchers in higher education. It is acknowledged that the evidence base for each of these activity systems varies considerably. Evidence from a broad body of literature has greater credibility than the evidence base of a single researcher, which itself is more credible than a perceived activity system based upon little more than anecdotal evidence. Therefore, in the activity theory analysis I intend to extend the structural analysis gleaned from the strongest evidence base, in order to examining possible internal contradictions within each activity system and then analyse how these socio-cultural factors might impact upon interactions between differing research activity systems. It is via these examinations that I intend to present evidence of methodological tribes creating territories that can result in unhelpful methodological idolatry.

THE EXAMPLE OF PHENOMENOGRAPHY

Phenomenography is a methodology designed to make variation of experience visible, to present alternative views (Åkerlind, 2005) and is identified as a process more of discovery than of verification (Säljö, 1997). As a research approach, phenomenography has emerged from an empirical base (Åkerlind, 2002) and holds that, irrespective of the nature of the phenomenon, there are always a limited number of ways in which the phenomenon is experienced (Dall'Alba & Walsh, 1989; Marton, 1994).

The range of ways people experience these phenomena are presented as 'categories of description' (Marton, 1981; Sandberg, 1997). These categories form the basis for the development of a hierarchy of understandings, known as the 'outcome space' (Marton, 1994). As such, the outcome space of a phenomenographic study contains a set of hierarchically structured categories of description concerning the phenomenon under examination (Järvinen, 2004). Every category in the outcome space can then be described in terms of structural and referential components. The structural component represents the internal and external horizons of the phenomenon, whereas the referential component involves the meaning given to the experience (Pang, 2003).

Whilst Harris (2008, p. 61) expresses concern that 'many theoretical aspects of phenomenography need clarification as most reported studies do not mention the ontological and epistemological assumptions that underpin them', there are a number of authors, notably Marton, Booth and Åkerlind, who do address issues of ontology. These authors describe phenomenography as having a non-dualist ontology, with Marton & Booth (1997, p. 122) explaining that the focus on the world as experienced gives phenomenography a non-dualist ontology in that it takes 'neither a positivist/objective approach, independent of human interpretation, nor does it take a subjectivist approach, focusing on internal constructions by the subject'. This position is cited as a reaction against representational epistemology and dualist ontology (Marton, 1982, p. 2).

In order to identify the bundles of relations that might be termed the mythemes of phenomenography, it is useful to examine the structure, commitments and assumptions evident in the work of experienced phenomenographic researchers.

Conceptions, Experiences and Understandings

The range of ways that people experience phenomena have been described, in the literature, as 'experiences' (Harris, 2008), 'conceptions' (Marton, 1981) or 'understandings' (Sandberg, 2000), with Marton & Pong acknowledging that:

> A conception ... has been called various names, such as 'ways of conceptualising', 'ways of experiencing', ways of seeing', 'ways of apprehending', 'ways of understanding and so on. (2005, p. 336)

Whilst Marton & Pong acknowledge, in the same paper, that conceptualising is not identical with experiencing, they justify this conflation of terms by stating that the 'reason for using so many different synonyms is that although none of them corresponds completely to what we have in mind, they all do to a certain extent' (*ibid.*). This point poses some difficulty as it has been argued that 'experience of a phenomenon may be crucially different from understanding of a phenomenon' (Dahlin, 2007, p. 332), as experiences 'consist mainly of perceptual judgements' whereas descriptions of understanding 'also involve conceptual judgements and theoretical propositions' (*ibid.*).

The Object and Outcomes of Phenomenographic Research

As mentioned earlier, the outcome space of a phenomenographic study contains a set of hierarchically structured categories of description concerning the phenomenon under examination (Järvinen, 2004). Marton and Booth (1997, p. 111) suggest that categories of description should meet three criteria:

- Each category should describe a different component of the phenomenon;
- Each category should be logically related and represented hierarchically and
- The outcome space should be made up of the minimum number of different categories that describe variation across the sample.

Whilst rules of this nature are not limited to phenomenographic methods, they do direct our attention to methodological systems and traditions rather than towards any underlying theoretical debate.

Referential and Structural Features of Categories of Description

The next stage of phenomenography involves redefining each category in the outcome space in terms of structural and referential components. In truth, at least as many phenomenographic studies omit this stage as include it. However, as the structural aspects of a category refer to 'the combination of features discerned and focussed upon by the subject' (Marton & Pong, 2005, p. 336), and the referential aspects of a category to 'the particular meaning of an individual object; anything delimited and attended to by subjects' (*ibid.*), when phenomenographic researchers intend to examine the historical, social and material factors that influence experiences, it could be argued that some notion of what is foregrounded in each experience and the assumptions implied by experiences are crucial.

Assumptions Inherent to Phenomenography

The literature around phenomenography discusses the following methodological assumptions that are worthy of consideration here:

- That the interview participants think about their experiences and that the way that an individual recalls an experience is a combined product of the individual, the experience and the surrounding environment; none of these factors can be viewed in isolation of the others (Åkerlind, 2002; Bowden & Green, 2005; Marton, 1982).

- That what someone has experienced is accessible, either through language or other methods (Säljö, 1997).
- That there is a limited number of ways a group of people can experience a given phenomenon (Bowden & Green, 2005; Marton, 1982; Marton & Booth, 1997).
- That it is possible to 'bracket' when analysing data (Ashworth & Lucas, 1998; Marton, 1994).

Any researcher undertaking phenomenographic research would be both committed to and potentially challenged by such assumptions.

The first assumption – that interview participants think about their experiences and that such conceptions are a combined product of the individual, the experience and the surrounding environment – is thought provoking. On the one hand, having adopted a non-dualist ontology, it would be difficult to see conceptions as anything but a combined product of the individual, the experience and the surrounding environment. However, the assumption that interview participants think about their experiences presents a greater challenge. First it requires some understanding of what it is to think about an experience, and whether thinking about a past experience, in any detail, alters the memory of that experience. In this way, such an assumption requires some recognition of what it is that we capture when we ask individuals to recall experiences, and whether the authenticity of the experience is lost in articulation. Thus, I would argue that it is essential for researchers to realise that the phenomenographic interview will not only capture variation in experience of a phenomenon, but also variation in intuition, insight and ways of thinking.

Similarly, it could be said that the second assumption – that a person's experiences are accessible, either through language or other methods – compels us to realise that the data set will demonstrate variability in capacity to articulate experience as much as it demonstrates variation of experience itself. Yet, if it can be argued that communicative action is the process through which people form their identities (Habermas, 1981), then one might also reasonably assume that a person's view of their 'lifeworld' can be mediated through language. This poses an interesting dilemma that, arguably, goes beyond the concerns expressed by Säljö (1997). As phenomenography is almost always conducted via semi-structured interviews, it excludes those members of society that are unable to articulate experience, for example those with additional learning needs. This may indicate that phenomenography has a limited ability to capture experience according to group and context.

The third assumption — that there is a limited number of ways in which a given phenomenon can be experienced — appears to be fairly plausible. Nevertheless, the growing practice of creating outcome spaces that represent between four and eight conceptions (Åkerlind, 2002, 2005; Bowden & Green, 2005; Marton, 1982; Marton & Booth, 1997) could serve to undermine the authenticity of the outcome space as the true representation of the limited ways in which a particular phenomenon is experienced. I wonder whether some consideration of what is meant by the term 'limited', and why, is necessary if phenomenography is to retain methodological credibility beyond the territorial bounds of the phenomenographic tribe.

The fourth assumption — that it is possible to 'bracket' earlier research findings, other evidence from apparently authoritative sources, the prior construction of hypotheses or questions of 'cause' (Ashworth & Lucas, 1998) when analysing data — can be seen as problematic by those beyond the phenomenographic community. Nevertheless, it is argued, by phenomenographers, that the bracketing process does not require the researcher to deny prior knowledge, but that it is designed to ensure that such knowledge, or, indeed, any previously constructed hypotheses, should not influence the creation of categories of description (Ashworth & Lucas, 1998). Despite such claims, Uljens (1996) argues that this aim might not be possible because an empirical study is framed by the guiding role of prior theory and the knowledge interest of a specific researcher. Nonetheless, and more usefully in my opinion, Uljens also argues that this should not be taken to mean that prior theory determines what interpretation will be reached, just that 'bracketing' is a contested concept. Indeed, as it has been argued that we 'possess the ability to consciously suspend our personal understanding of a subject matter in order to understand somebody else's perspective' (Uljens, 1996, p. 143), the concept of 'bracketing' can be translated as a willingness to attempt to avoid prejudging data; arguably the aim of many researchers.

THE STRUCTURAL ANALYSIS: PHENOMENOGRAPHIC MYTHEMES

From the elements of phenomenography described above, it could be claimed that the systems of meaning that 'rear throughout' this particular research methodology relate to the three constituent mythemes identified below. By using Barthes's theory of myth, we can examine the ways in which the system and syntagm of each mytheme can be created by phenomenographic tribes.

- Mytheme 1 – phenomenography, as practiced, can claim non-dualist ontology

The system (constituent parts) of this mytheme stems from a rejection of solely objectivist or subjectivist research approaches. However, the confusion around the use of 'conception' as an overarching term for experience, understanding, seeing, apprehending etc., allows for ontological creep into the world of subjectivism so strongly rejected in the claim for non-dualism. If the community of expert phenomenographers minimise debate around such theoretical dilemmas, it could be argued that they are seeking methodological justification over theoretical engagement. It is my argument that this leads to the overrating, and ultimately idolatry, of methodological process.

Likewise, the syntagm (arrangement of constituent parts) of this mytheme reveals that, whilst the claim to non-dualist ontology is somewhat upheld by a focus upon 'experience', the practice of using interview as a primary phenomenographic method leaves space for subjectivism and misinterpretation of the notion of an experience. It could be argued that it would be naïve to assume that recalled experiences, gathered at interview, represent the lifeworld of an interviewee, as intended by the non-dualist ontological arguments presented by phenomenographers. This concern leads to the second mytheme.

- Mytheme 2 – phenomenography has the potential to 'discover' experience as articulated by another

In some sections of the literature, the system of this mytheme relies upon an acceptance that the categories of description that form an outcome space fully represent the lived experiences of the researched. This claim relies upon the notion of 'interjudge reliability', described by Sandberg (1997, p. 205) as a process where reliability is determined by the extent to which other researchers are able to recognise the conceptions and categories determined by the first researcher. Indeed, Säljö (1997) asserts that an 80–90% agreement on categories of description between researchers is an appropriate level. Therefore, it could be argued that phenomenographic research conducted by a lone researcher is, in this respect, open to criticism. Alternatively, other authors (Åkerlind, 2005; Ashwin, 2006, Trigwell, 2006) argue that the purpose of sharing categories and evidence with others is to ensure that they appear reasonable to another researcher, not that they would come up with the same categories; to check communicative validity rather than interjudge reliability. This difference between recognition of categories and whether, or not, they appear to be a reasonable interpretation of the interview data offers slightly contradictory systems of the mytheme that may serve to cement, rather than challenge, ontological assumptions.

The syntagm of this mytheme rests upon two things; the use of interviews as a primary research method and the ability of the researcher to 'bracket' earlier research findings, other evidence from apparently authoritative sources and the prior construction of hypotheses or questions of 'cause'. As discussed, it could be seen as doubtful whether interview data captures variation in experience rather than variation in ability to articulate experience, and, where understandings are sought, variation in intuition, insight and ways of thinking. Likewise, it could be argued that the claim that a researcher can bracket other research findings and avoid prior construction of hypothesis ignores the arguments that an empirical study is framed by the guiding role of prior theory, the knowledge interest of a specific study and the 'interviewer's monopoly of interpretation' (Brinkmann & Kvale, 2005, p. 165).

This is not to ignore that phenomenographers would claim that the bracketing process does not require the researcher to deny prior knowledge. What is questionable is the degree to which phenomenographic researchers focus on such issues when conducting, and writing up, their work. Unchallenged assumptions can, in my view, lead to a primary focus on the mechanics of any research methodology.

• Mytheme 3 – phenomenographic outcome spaces can reveal structural and referential aspects of experience

The system and syntagm of the third potential mytheme is, perhaps, the most complex. Whilst Marton (1994) has described the structural components of categories of description as the internal and external horizons of the subject's boundaries of awareness, Andretta (2007, p. 156) interprets awareness as 'the person's total experience of the world at a given point in time rather than as a dichotomy of conscious and subconscious state', invoking a relationship of constant variation between things in the foreground of awareness and those in the background. The search for structural components of categories of description in phenomenographic research, therefore, might serve to question the aforementioned non-dualist ontology, moving this type of research closer to the subjectivism resisted by most phenomenographers as they seek to probe human interpretation in order to discern the subject's boundaries of awareness. Similarly, as the referential components of outcome spaces seek to disclose 'the particular meaning of an individual object; anything delimited and attended to by subjects' (Marton & Pong, 2005, p. 336), it is easy to see why ontological confusion may occur.

The next section of this chapter seeks to employ activity theory, as a heuristic device, in order to test this notion of a methodological myth by applying it to three researcher communities: experienced phenomenographic researchers, early career academics working in the same tradition and practitioner researchers in the field of higher education.

THE ACTIVITY THEORY ANALYSIS: INTERNAL CONTRADICTIONS

Experienced Phenomenographic Researchers

In terms of the 'structure of human activity', what we know about the claims made by experienced phenomenographic researchers can be used to analyse the ways in which they perceive, and create, each node of the activity system in order to identify internal contradictions. Therefore, whilst examining the aforementioned debates and tensions across the phenomenographic research community, it is possible to understand phenomenographic research as depicted in Fig. 2.

The model in Fig. 2 indicates the potential for an internal contradiction within the experienced phenomenographic researcher activity system, represented by a grey flash, illustrating tension created when different members of a methodological tribe create markedly differing mediating artefacts with a focus upon process rather than philosophical perspective.

Contradiction (Community vs. Mediating Artefacts)

One example of a contradiction between community and mediating artefact can be discerned via closer examination of divisions within the field of phenomenography.

Developmental phenomenographers (Bowden, 1995; Bowden & Green, 2005) have argued for phenomenography to be undertaken 'with the

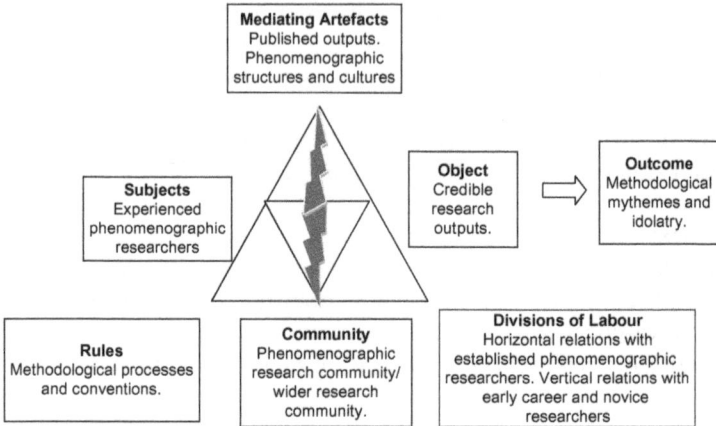

Fig. 2. Experienced Phenomenographic Researchers (After Engeström, 1987).

purpose of using the outcomes to help the subjects of the research, usually
students or others like them, to learn' (Bowden, 2000, p. 2). However,
whilst this aim is not necessarily incommensurate with what might be called
pure phenomenography, many studies that follow a developmental phenomenographic paradigm (e.g. those cited in Bowden & Green, 2005) have
used phenomenographic results, alone, to analyse organisational and social
infrastructures. As mentioned earlier, phenomenography was initially
designed to represent, or describe, qualitative variation of the ways in
which a phenomenon is experienced; ergo, in order to relate variation of
experience to the historical, social and cultural factors that create it, it
could be argued that the researcher must employ additional methodological
or theoretical approaches.

As such, differences in assumptions about what phenomenography can
realistically claim to achieve can be said to exist across the experienced phenomenographic research community. The degree to which such theoretical
dilemmas are ever explored in published outcomes, whatever the methodological approach adopted, is variable across methodological tribes and
worthy of deeper analysis elsewhere.

The Early Career Academic Working with Phenomenography

As with the outputs generated by experienced phenomenographic researchers, articles published by early career academics, working within

phenomenography, can be used to model an 'early career academic' activity system, and, once again, it is possible to make tentative suggestions regarding contradictions between nodes.

The model in Fig. 3 indicates two internal contradictions within the early career academic activity system, again represented by grey flashes. Both of these contradictions have been interpreted as having a focus on the object of research activity; the first in relation to tensions created when methodological rules are perceived as barriers to achievement of the object aims, and the second in relation to tensions between divisions of labour and object aims.

Contradiction No. 1 (Object vs. Rules)

The first contradiction is exemplified by two of the most commonly stated 'rules' of phenomenography: that there is a limited number of ways a group of people can experience a given phenomenon (Bowden & Green, 2005; Marton, 1982; Marton & Booth, 1997), and that it is possible to 'bracket' when analysing data (Ashworth & Lucas, 1998; Marton, 1994). The attention focused on these rules highlights the aforementioned concerns raised by Harris (2008) relating to the lack of clarification and debate around many theoretical aspects of phenomenography.

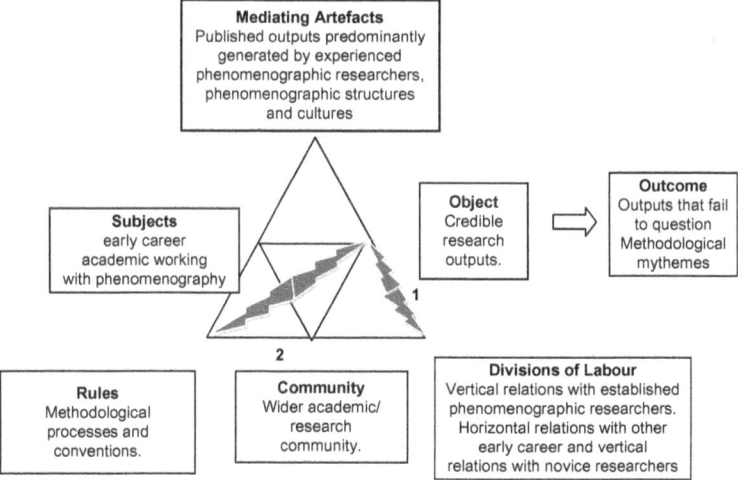

Fig. 3. Early Career Academics Working with Phenomenography (After Engeström, 1987).

If we take the example of an article produced by an early career academic, publishing a phenomenographic article for the first time (Hallett, 2010), the author fails to critique what might be meant by a 'limited number of ways' that a group of people can experience a given phenomenon, despite the diversity of the participants under study. Likewise, in relation to the second 'rule' identified here, it is notable that the author makes no reference to the process of bracketing, despite numerous references to the essential use of this process in phenomenographic texts. This is not unusual in phenomenographic outputs, and raises questions about the degree to which established methodological practices become entrenched and mythologised by repetition or omission.

Contradiction No. 2 (Object vs. Divisions of Labour)

The second contradiction, within this particular research community, questions the degree to which researchers new to a discipline are enabled and encouraged to dispute the claims of experienced researchers in the same field of study. For instance, the argument that 'understanding' has been used interchangeably with 'experience' and 'conceptualising', because 'although none of them corresponds completely to what we have in mind, they all do to a certain extent' (Marton & Pong, 2005, p. 336), presents a dilemma. Given the potential for vertical power relations between established phenomenographic researchers and early career academics, it is, perhaps, unsurprising that tensions might arise between the aim for credible research outputs and questions that researchers new to phenomenography might have around this conflation of terms.

The Practitioner Researcher in the Field of Education

The third activity system is purely theoretical in nature, and attempts to model the features of activity that would be faced by practitioner researchers in the field of higher education. Nonetheless, it is possible to make tentative suggestions regarding contradictions between nodes as modelled in Fig. 4.

The model in Fig. 4 indicates two potential internal contradictions within the practitioner researcher activity system. Specifically, tensions between the ways in which practitioner researchers might discern and describe the object of phenomenographic research and the mediating

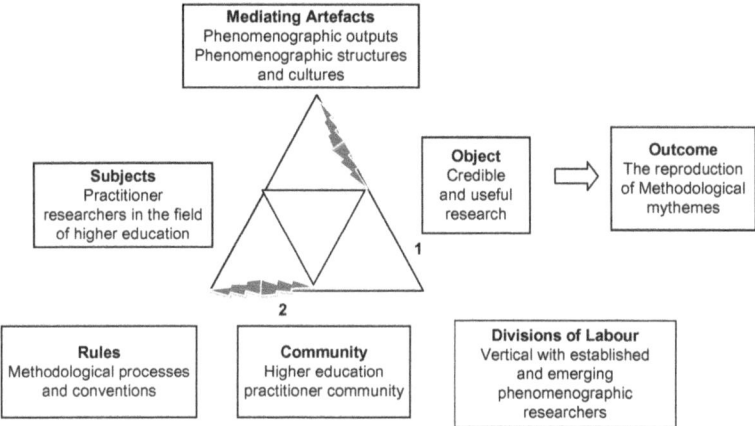

Fig. 4. Practitioner Researchers in the Field of Higher Education (After Engeström, 1987).

artefacts that are designed to enable such activity, allows the first contradiction to be identified. Likewise, examination of the interplay between the rules of phenomenographic research activity and a more diverse practitioner research community highlights a second potential contradiction.

Contradiction No. 1 (Object vs. Artefact)

It would be reasonable to assume that credible and useful research is the primary motivation for practitioner researchers to engage with any research methodology, including phenomenography. Whether such motivation stems from the desire to improve practice or from a need to attain academic credit is moot; the motivation to achieve credible and useful research outcomes can be reasonably assumed. However, this object motivation interacts with a number of mediating artefacts that shape the outcome of their activity, and have the potential to create internal contradictions within the practitioner researcher activity system. Mediating artefacts are articulated in the outputs created by phenomenographic researchers in two distinct ways; these can be conceptualised as community wide artefacts and individually created artefacts.

In terms of community wide mediating artefacts, phenomenographic outputs appear to acknowledge the non-negotiable nature of non-dualist ontology. However, it would be easy to see why, given the conflation of terms used in phenomenographic research, practitioner researchers might produce subjectivist research in the name of phenomenography. This concern is not limited to phenomenographic research, rather the lack of theoretical engagement with such issues can lead researchers to privilege process over independent theoretical challenge. Any tribe that creates immunity from theoretical interrogation, albeit unconsciously done, must own the risk of creating unhelpful process idolatry.

Furthermore, mediating artefacts designed by individual academic researchers, such as the use of 'experiences' or 'understandings' as the phenomena under study, whilst deriving from the aforementioned structures, could be seen as being interpreted differently by different researchers. This variation could produce significant tensions, with practitioners potentially misunderstanding the exact nature of what they are researching. As their research is likely to be used to inform practice, this presents a real dilemma to those who advocate phenomenography as a means to understand lived experience. In effect, this contradiction raises questions about differing discourses and the micro-politics of individual research methodologies.

As such tensions may exist whatever methodology is used, it is hoped that the exploration of phenomenography presented here might encourage others to extend this analysis to other research paradigms.

Contradiction No. 2 (Rules vs. Community)

It would be easy to imagine that, on reading a number of phenomenographic outputs, practitioner researchers would conform to a set of perceived rules within a short period of time. In addition, whilst some practitioner researchers might identify with a wider phenomenographic research community, it could be expected that they would retain a significant, and in most cases exclusive, focus on a community of fellow practitioners.

Indeed, it is difficult to imagine practitioner researchers viewing experienced researchers as part of their community, or themselves entering the experienced researcher community. As experienced researchers are well positioned to increase accessibility, this narrow, and arguably insular, community view leaves practitioner researchers little opportunity to engage more fruitfully in wider debates, and raises questions about the research identities produced by tensions between practitioners and a body of knowledge constructed by academics.

INTERACTING ACTIVITY SYSTEMS: QUATERNARY CONTRADICTIONS

The predominant tensions identified across all three systems relate to three activity system nodes: rules, object and divisions of labour. Further examination of these allows us to conceptualise potential power differentials across communities that may lead to methodological idolatry as conceived here.

Tension No. 1 (Rules)

In this example all three participant groups acknowledge a methodological system that is recognised, by each group, to potentially be unequal to the needs of the wider research community. However, these tensions only becomes contradictions, or conflicting forces (Engeström, 1999, p. 32), when the participant group feels unable to regain a sense of power by interpreting, or adapting, the rules of phenomenography to more closely meet their aims.

It could be speculated that power differentials appear to be hierarchical, with experienced phenomenographic researchers possessing the highest degree of power, followed by early career academics who demonstrate a degree of autonomy in their academic outputs, and practitioner researchers who may perceive a methodology defined by non-negotiable rules.

Tension No. 2 (Object)

Tensions between systems in relation to the object aim of activity appear to stem from a conflict between the functional nature of objects described by the majority of early career academics, and potentially discerned by practitioner researchers, and the processes debated by experienced researchers. However, it must be noted that even the most experienced phenomenographic researchers often fail to probe the theoretical basis of their chosen field. That the opinions expressed by experienced researchers diverge in this respect could be seen as a route to the under theorisation of research.

In contrast to the previous examination of tensions around the rules of phenomenography, tensions around the object of phenomenography might point to levels of power and autonomy that privilege both the experienced researcher and early career academic. These differentials appear to have the potential to benefit early career academics who have the opportunity, if they feel enabled to take it, to critique research methodologies which could result in a reactive, and by extrapolation less powerful, response from experienced researchers. At other times, these differentials appear to benefit experienced researchers who have established authority within their field. As such, both experienced and early career academic researchers demonstrate power levels that could be seen to contrast with the lack of power held by practitioner researchers. This contradiction raises questions about the identity of educational researchers and the discourses that result from conflicting identities. That such concerns are not peculiar to phenomenography is self-evident.

Tension No. 3 (Division of Labour)

In this example, perceived tensions could be seen to be an inevitable consequence of confused expectations of phenomenographic research. That such disparate views are acknowledged and accepted in the literature indicates a degree of autonomy with respect to role definition for experienced researchers. Whilst unsurprising, at face value, this could be of some concern to those engaging in educational research as an early career academic or practitioner researcher.

In contrast to tension no. 2, the early career academics, in this circumstance, could feel somewhat disempowered. Nevertheless, perceptions of power for early career academics, albeit limited, contrast with the perceived absence of power for practitioner researchers, who would appear to have little control over the development of methodological paradigms. The obvious lack of communication between these research groups could serve to entrench these potential power differentials, producing the kinds of hierarchical activity that leads to expert tribes creating non-negotiable territories that entrench levels of conformity that can lead to process idolatry.

In all, tension no. 3 demonstrates quaternary contradictions around divisions of labour, and further examination of these contradictions, once again, points to power differentials between experienced researchers, early career academics and practitioner researchers. From this evidence it would seem that flexibility in interpretation of divisions of labour serves to enforce a narrow, and disempowering, interpretation for early career academics, and, to a greater degree, practitioner researchers. As such, this contradiction raises questions about power, autonomy and participation.

CONCLUSION

This analysis of phenomenographic research, as an example of a research methodology used in higher education rather than a particular example of methodological idolatry, attempts to reveal both the encoded messages of this methodology and the layerings of meaning that derive from such messages. Whilst the ontological representation of the research oscillates between non-dualism and subjectivism, the aim to make valid claims for phenomenography to discover the variation in experience of others is signified throughout. Thus, in relation to the conflation of experience with understanding, the theoretical integrity of phenomengraphic research is challenged by representing these terms as interchangeable under the broader heading of conceptions. Practices of this nature signify the processes of phenomenography over genuine debate around methodological theory; this signification can serve to *mythologize* methodology thus encouraging methodological idolatry at the expense of broader theoretical engagement.

As a result, if we are to question theory—method relations in educational research (Ashwin & Case, 2012), we might seek to reposition methodologies as ontologically coherent heuristic devices that enable us to generate and test theory, rather than as processes of discovery that may lead us to unsubstantiated claims of knowledge generation. Indeed, it could be argued that the reproduction of methodological tribes that serve to establish uncontested methodological rules, learning objects and divisions of labour cannot fail to overrate methodological processes at the cost of genuine debate and theoretical engagement.

REFERENCES

Åkerlind, G. S. (2002). Principles and practice in phenomenographic research. *Proceedings of the international symposium on Current Issues in Phenomenography*, Canberra.

Åkerlind, G. S. (2005). Variation and commonality in phenomenographic research methods. *Higher Education Research and Development*, 24(2), 321–334.

Andretta, S. (2007). Phenomenography: A conceptual framework for information literacy education. *New Information Perspectives*, 59(2), 152–168.

Ashwin, P. (2006). Variation in academics' accounts of tutorials. *Studies in Higher Education*, 31(6), 651–665.

Ashwin, P., & Case, J. (2012). Questioning theory—method relations in higher education research. *Higher Education Research and Development*, 31(3), 271–272.

Ashworth, P., & Lucas, U. (1998). What is the 'world' of phenomenography? *Scandinavian Journal of Educational Research*, 42, 417–433.

Bakhurst, D. (1997). Activity, consciousness, and communication. In M. Cole, Y. Engeström, & O. Vasquez (Eds.), *Mind, culture, and activity: Seminal papers from the laboratory of comparative human cognition* (pp. 147–163). Cambridge: Cambridge University Press.

Barthes, R. ([1964] 1967). *Elements of semiology* (A. Lavers & C. Smith, Trans.). London: Jonathan Cape.

Becher, T., & Trowler, P. R. (2001). *Academic tribes and territories: Intellectual inquiry and the culture of disciplines* (2nd ed.), Buckingham: Open University Press.

Bowden, J. A. (1995). Phenomenographic research: Some methodological issues. *Nordisk Pedagogik, 15*(3), 144–155.

Bowden, J. A. (2000). The nature of phenomenographic research. In J. Bowden & E. Walsh (Eds.), *Phenomenography*. Melbourne: RMIT University Press.

Bowden, J. A., & Green, P. (2005). *Doing developmental phenomenography*. Melbourne: RMIT University Press.

Brinkmann, S., & Kvale, S. (2005). Confronting the ethics of qualitative research. *Journal of Constructivist Psychology, 18*, 157–181.

Dahlin, B. (2007). Enriching the theoretical horizons of phenomenography, variation theory and learning studies. *Scandinavian Journal of Educational Research, 51*(4), 327–346.

Dall'Alba, G., & Walsh, E. (1989). Assessing and understanding: A phenomenographic approach. *Research in Science Education, 19*, 1–17.

Díaz-Kommonen, L. (2004). *Expressive artifacts and artifacts of expression*. Working Papers in Art and Design, *3*, 138–141.

Engeström, Y. (1987). *Learning by expanding: An activity-theoretical approach to developmental research*. Helsinki: Orienta-Konsultit.

Engeström, Y. (1999). Activity theory and individual and social transformation. In Y. Engeström, R. Miettinen, & R.-L. Punamaki (Eds.), *Perspectives on activity theory* (pp. 19–38). Cambridge, UK: Cambridge University Press.

Engeström, Y. (2001). Engeström, Y 2001, 'Expansive learning at work. Toward an activity-theoretical reconceptualization'. *Journal of Education and Work, 14*(1), 133–156.

Habermas, J. (1981). Modernity versus postmodernity. *New German Critique, 22*, 3–8.

Hallett, F. (2010). The postgraduate student experience of study support: A phenomenographic analysis. *Studies in Higher Education, 35*(2), 225–238.

Harris, L. R. (2008). A phenomenographic investigation of teacher conceptions of student engagement in learning. *Australian Educational Researcher, 35*(1), 57–79.

Järvinen, P. (2004). *On research methods*. Tampere: Opinpaja Oy.

Lévi-Strauss, C. (1963). *Structural anthropology* (C. Jacobson & B. Grundfest Schoepf, Trans.) New York, NY: Doubleday Anchor Books.

Marton, F. (1981). Phenomenography: Describing conceptions of the world around us. *Instructional Science, 10*, 177–192.

Marton, F. (1982). *Towards phenomenography of learning: Integratial experiments aspects*. Göteborg: University of Göteborg, Department of Education.

Marton, F. (1994). Phenomenogrpahy. In T. Husen & T. Postlethwaite (Eds.), *International encyclopaedia of education* (Vol. 8), Oxford: Pergamon.

Marton, F., & Booth, S. (1997). *Learning and awareness*. Mahwah, NJ: Lawrence Erlbaum Associates.

Marton, F., & Pong, W. Y. (2005). On the unit of description on phenomenography. *Higher Education Research and Development, 24*(4), 335–348.

Pang, M. F. (2003). Two faces of variation – On continuity in the phenomenographic movement. *Scandinavian Journal of Educational Research, 47*(2), 145–156.

Roth, W. M., & Tobin, K. G. (2002). *At the elbow of another: Learning to teach by co-teaching.* New York, NY: Peter Lang.

Säljö, R. (1997). Talk as data and practice – A critical look at phenomenographic inquiry and the appeal to experience. *Higher Education Research and Development, 16*(2), 173–1890.

Sandberg, J. (1997). Are phenomenographic results reliable? *Higher Education Research and Development, 16*, 203–212.

Sandberg, J. (2000). Understanding human competence at work: An interpretive approach. *Academy of Management Journal, 43*(1), 925–943.

Tight, M. (2008). Higher education research as tribe, territory and/or community: A co-citation analysis. *Higher Education, 55*, 593–605.

Trigwell, K. (2006). Phenomenography: An approach to research into geography education. *Journal of Geography in Higher Education, 30*(2), 367–372.

Uljens, M. (1996). On the philosophical foundation of phenomenography. In G. Dall'Alba & B. Hasselgren (Eds.), *Reflections on phenomenography: Toward a methodology?* Gothenburg: Acta Universitatis Gothenburgensis.

THE POTENTIAL OF COMBINING PHENOMENOGRAPHY, VARIATION THEORY AND THRESHOLD CONCEPTS TO INFORM CURRICULUM DESIGN IN HIGHER EDUCATION

Gerlese Åkerlind, Jo McKenzie and Mandy Lupton

ABSTRACT

This chapter describes an innovative method of curriculum design that is based on combining phenomenographic research, and the associated variation theory of learning, with the notion of disciplinary threshold concepts to focus specialised design attention on the most significant and difficult parts of the curriculum. The method involves three primary stages: (i) identification of disciplinary concepts worthy of intensive curriculum design attention, using the criteria for threshold concepts; (ii) action research into variation in students' understandings/misunderstandings of those concepts, using phenomenography as the research approach; (iii) design of learning activities to address the poorer understandings identified in the second stage, using variation theory as a

Theory and Method in Higher Education Research II
International Perspectives on Higher Education Research, Volume 10, 227–247
Copyright © 2014 by Emerald Group Publishing Limited
All rights of reproduction in any form reserved
ISSN: 1479-3628/doi:10.1108/S1479-3628(2014)0000010017

guiding framework. The curriculum design method is inherently theory and evidence based. It was developed and trialed during a two-year project funded by the Australian Learning and Teaching Council, using physics and law disciplines as case studies. Disciplinary teachers' perceptions of the impact of the method on their teaching and understanding of student learning were profound. Attempts to measure the impact on student learning were less conclusive; teachers often unintentionally deviated from the design when putting it into practice for the first time. Suggestions for improved implementation of the method are discussed.

INTRODUCTION

This chapter presents a theory-informed and evidence-based method of curriculum design that involves combining phenomenography, the associated variation theory of learning and the theoretical notion of disciplinary threshold concepts. The method aims to focus teacher attention on and enhance student learning of particularly difficult but foundational concepts in the curriculum, where:

- threshold concepts are used to determine areas of the curriculum that require focused design attention;
- phenomenographic action research is used to identify what it is about these concepts that students find difficult to understand and
- variation theory is used to guide the design of teaching and learning activities to address these difficulties.

The pedagogical potential of phenomenography as a research approach for investigating variation in the ways in which students can understand (or misunderstand) the same disciplinary concept has long been recognised. Bowden (1994) first coined the term, 'developmental phenomenography', to describe phenomenographic research conducted with the aim of informing curriculum design, through its ability to identify what students with a sophisticated understanding of a disciplinary concept are noticing about the concept that students with a poor understanding do not notice.

The value of phenomenographic research for informing the 'what' of curriculum design is complemented by variation theory's focus on the 'how' – how teachers can best design learning activities to draw students' attention to those aspects of a disciplinary concept that they commonly miss noticing, but that need to be noticed in order to achieve a good understanding of the concept (Marton & Tsui, 2004).

In principle, phenomenography and variation theory could be applied to the teaching and learning of any concept, but this would be too resource-intensive to be practical. Only concepts that teachers recognise as being particularly problematic for students, but also as central to disciplinary knowledge, would justify the focused curriculum design attention involved. Consequently, the notion of threshold concepts (Meyer & Land, 2003) has also been incorporated into the method, to guide the selection of appropriate disciplinary concepts.

The curriculum design method thus has two principle aims:

1. to focus extra design attention on the most significant and difficult parts of the curriculum, using the notion of threshold concepts; and
2. to enhance teaching and learning of these particularly difficult concepts, using phenomenographic action research and the variation theory of learning.

The method was developed and trialed during a two-year project funded by the Australian Learning and Teaching Council (Åkerlind, McKenzie, & Lupton, 2010). To ensure broad applicability of the model across different higher education disciplines and contexts, teachers from two contrasting disciplines (physics and law) and four different universities (two research-intensive and two universities of technology) were invited to participate in the project trial. Examples from the trial will be drawn on throughout the chapter to illustrate the method, but the chapter is not a report of the trial as such. For a full report, see Åkerlind et al. (2010).

THRESHOLD CONCEPTS

The idea of threshold concepts (Land, Smith, & Meyer, 2008; Land, Meyer, & Baillie, 2010; Meyer & Land, 2003, 2005, 2006) was first elaborated in response to research that identified disciplinary ways of thinking and practicing in undergraduate teaching and learning. The proposition is that there are a limited number of concepts within each discipline that are 'threshold' in nature, in that they act as 'conceptual gateways' to disciplinary ways of thinking about a subject area. Once understood, they transform students' views of the subject area, because they enable students to coherently integrate what were previously seen as unrelated aspects of the subject, providing a new way of thinking about it.

Threshold concepts are thus seen as vital for students' learning in a discipline, because they provide 'a transformed internal view of subject matter, subject landscape, or even world view' (Meyer & Land, 2005, p. 373). This leads not only to new ways of understanding a subject area, but a shift in the learner's sense of professional or disciplinary identity. Threshold concepts have been referred to as the 'jewels in the curriculum' because they can be used to identify transformative points in students' learning. They also help explain why many students 'get stuck' at common points in the curriculum.

The proposition is that it is only through coming to understand the threshold concepts in a discipline that students can come to think like a subject specialist, and adopt a disciplinary way of thinking about the world. However, the transformative and integrative nature of these concepts makes them commonly troublesome for students to learn, and so they are often not fully understood by students. Meanwhile, due to the threshold nature of these concepts, such misunderstandings have long-lasting implications for students' learning in the subject area, and their ability to apply that learning in professional practice.

A focus on threshold concepts in curriculum design highlights for teachers areas of the curriculum that deserve special attention, not only because they represent transformative learning points for students, but because they are areas where students are most likely to experience difficulties. In addition, the integrative nature of threshold concepts means that a good understanding of these foundational concepts facilitates understanding of a host of related concepts, leading to an impact on student learning far beyond the individual concept in isolation.

While the potential power of a curriculum focus on threshold concepts is becoming increasingly recognised, ways of identifying and teaching threshold concepts are not yet clear. The method of curriculum design presented in this chapter addresses that gap by describing how phenomenography and the associated variation theory of learning can be used to inform the teaching and learning of threshold concepts.

Throughout their work, Meyer and Land describe a 'liminal' state of ontological and epistemological uncertainty that students enter as they start to grapple with the troublesome nature of a threshold concept (see Fig. 1).

Phenomenography and variation theory provide a coherent theoretical basis for understanding the posited stages in coming to understand a threshold concept, in terms of:

- identifying what it is that students find troublesome about the concept;
- describing the theoretical nature of the epistemic shift required to achieve a sophisticated understanding of the concept; and
- explaining why the shift is transformative and irreversible.

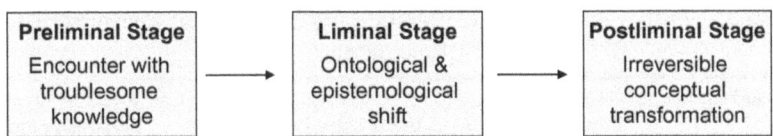

Fig. 1. Stages in Coming to Understand a Threshold Concept (adapted from Land et al., 2010, p. xii).

PHENOMENOGRAPHY

Since its inception in the late 1970s, phenomenography has become well known as an educational research approach for investigating variation in the ways in which people understand the same concept or phenomenon (Bowden & Green, 2005; Bowden & Marton, 1998; Bowden & Walsh, 2000; Marton, 1981, 1986, 1994; Marton & Booth, 1997). This includes student understanding of disciplinary concepts. However, phenomenography is less well-known for its theoretical basis, in terms of the epistemological and ontological claims underlying the approach (Bowden & Green, 2005; Bowden & Marton, 1998; Marton & Booth, 1997).

Phenomenography argues that individuals experience the world differently because experience is always partial. At any one point in time and context, people discern and experience different aspects of any concept or phenomenon to different degrees. This applies as much in the classroom as in the larger world. Thus, student understandings and misunderstandings of a disciplinary concept may be understood in terms of which aspects or features of the concept are discerned, and *not* discerned, in students' awareness of it.

Awareness of an aspect is indicated by the perception of the *potential for variation* in that aspect; lack of awareness is indicated by an implicit, taken-for-granted assumption of uniformity in that feature of the concept. Marton often uses the concept of colour to illustrate the point. If everything in the world were purple, that is if there were no variation, then the concept of colour (and indeed, purple) could not be experienced. It can only be experienced and understood at the point that a potential for variation is discerned.

A more complex example comes from the threshold concept of 'legal reasoning' in law (from the project trial). Students' understanding of 'the nature of legal rules' was identified as a critical feature or aspect of their overall understanding of legal reasoning (see Table 1). The least

Table 1. Different Ways of Understanding and Critical Features of Legal
Reasoning.

Critical Features	Category 1: A Formulaic Process for Predicting a Legal Outcome	Category 2: An Interpretive Process of Arguing for an Outcome that Benefits Your Client	Category 3: A Dynamic, Responsive and Innovative Process for Developing the Law to Reflect Changing Society
Purpose of legal reasoning	To accurately predict the outcome for your client (Adjudicate)	To produce the best outcome for your client (Advocate)	To produce the best outcome for society (Change agent)
Nature of legal rules (law) in legal reasoning	Rigid; completely clear	Ambiguous; manipulable; interpretable	Changeable – dissents; exceptions
Role of the HIRAC/ISAAC 'formulae'	It is legal reasoning	It is a tool for aiding legal reasoning	It is implicit/evident in legal reasoning

sophisticated way of understanding legal reasoning, as 'a formulaic process
for predicting a legal outcome', involves an understanding of legal rules as
rigid, unchangeable and completely clear (i.e. an implicit assumption of
uniformity in interpretation of a legal rule). In contrast, a more sophisticated understanding of legal reasoning, as 'an interpretive process of
arguing for an outcome that serves your client', includes awareness of legal
rules as manipulable, interpretable and ambiguous.

Phenomenographically, different ways of understandings the same concept may be understood as part of a larger whole, the *collective sum* of
ways of understanding. Given our common physiology and socio-cultural
backgrounds, it is assumed that different understandings of the same concept would typically be related, in a part-whole manner, through shared dis-
cernment of some of the same critical features of the concept. Analytically,
different understandings may commonly be ordered in terms of inclusivity
of awareness, producing a nested hierarchy of expanding awareness of
the different features. More inclusive understandings inherently represent
more sophisticated or complete understandings of the concept, because
an increasing number of aspects of the concept are being discerned.

For example, with the threshold concept of 'measurement uncertainty' in
physics (from the project trial), the phenomenographic action research

identified poor student understandings that derived from: (1) an awareness of the importance of searching for patterns in measurement data, but *without* awareness of the importance of applying error calculation formulae; and (2) an awareness of the importance of applying error calculation formulae, but *without* an awareness of the importance of thinking through the real-world implications of measurement error. What is needed for a sophisticated understanding is for students to be aware of and integrate *all three* aspects of uncertainty: data patterns, error calculations *and* real-world implications.

On this basis, conceptual development is *not* seen as requiring the rejection of students' existing understanding of a concept, but to expand their current awareness through helping them to discern additional aspects of the concept that they currently do not discern. This has led to the variation theory of learning, based on the argument that attempts to facilitate students' conceptual development should focus on optimising opportunities for them to experience variation in aspects of disciplinary concepts that they currently take for granted.

In brief, the relationship between phenomenography and variation theory is that phenomenographic research serves to *identify the critical features* that need to be highlighted for students when teaching and learning a concept, whilst variation theory provides guidance as to the most effective *ways of highlighting these features* for students, thus helping students to discern the critical features required to achieve a sophisticated understanding of the concept.

VARIATION THEORY OF LEARNING

Variation theory developed out of phenomenography in the early 2000s, with a shared epistemology but a particular focus on pedagogical implications and applications. Shifting from the phenomenographic focus on identifying variation in understanding of concepts, researchers started to investigate variation in the way concepts are presented in the classroom, and how this relates to the understandings students develop (Marton & Tsui, 2004; Rovio-Johannson, 1999a, 1999b; Runesson, 1999; Runesson & Marton, 2002).

According to variation theory, student learning of a concept is best facilitated in any teaching and learning activity by introducing variation in each of the critical features of the concept. This draws students' attention to different aspects of the concept by varying some aspects whilst keeping others constant. For example, continuing the physics illustration above, what is needed to draw students' attention to the real-world implications of measurement uncertainty is to expose them to situations in which data scatter and the error calculations are both held constant, whilst the real-world implications are varied. A resulting curriculum design example from the project trial was development of a tutorial exercise where students considered the same data and error calculation (i.e. data and error where held constant), but in the different contexts of measuring a bolt hole for a bridge versus the mass of a subatomic particle (i.e. real-world consequences varied).

Whilst it is common for teachers to vary different features of disciplinary concepts in an intuitive manner when teaching, this is typically done implicitly rather than explicitly. As a consequence, multiple features of a concept are commonly varied simultaneously, and in an ad hoc rather than a structured way. This creates confusing patterns of variation for students, in which it is much easier to miss noticing variation in some of the critical features than if each is varied separately while the others are held constant. Variation theory highlights the need for 'separation' of critical features, where teachers vary only one feature of a concept at a time, whilst holding the other features constant.

Variation theory also highlights the need for subsequent 'fusion' of the different features, by varying *all* of the critical features simultaneously. This is required to draw students' attention to the ways in which the different features can interact, and encourage an integrated understanding of the whole. However, doing this before students have discerned each of the critical features separately may impede rather than help their conceptual development. For example, it will be more difficult for students to notice the real-world implications of measurement uncertainty when teachers vary data, error calculations and real-world context simultaneously, than when only the real-world implications are varied, whilst data and error calculations are held constant.

The potential value of variation theory to curriculum design has been well documented at primary and secondary levels of education, through a series of government-funded educational initiatives in Hong Kong (Lo, Marton, Pang, & Pong, 2004; Pang & Marton, 2003, 2005). Although these initiatives are focused on pre-tertiary education, there are obvious implications for higher education and we drew on this work in developing the method.

THE CURRICULUM DESIGN METHOD

The curriculum design method involves three primary stages:

1. identification of disciplinary concepts worthy of intensive curriculum design attention, using the criteria for threshold concepts;
2. action research into variation in students' understandings/misunderstandings of those concepts, using phenomenography as a research approach;
3. design of learning activities to address the misunderstandings identified in stage 2, using variation theory as a guiding framework.

As with any curriculum design method, ongoing revisions to teaching and learning activities based on a review of the learning outcomes for students is also recommended. However, this stage is not specific to this method, so is not elaborated here.

A key challenge of implementing the method is introducing disciplinary teachers to three unfamiliar educational theories (for stages 1–3), an unfamiliar research approach (for stage 2) and an unfamiliar approach to curriculum design (for stage 3). The theoretical and evidence-based foundations of the method require involvement of an educational developer/researcher in the process, familiar with the theories and research approach, to guide disciplinary teachers through the process. However, the method does not require teachers to come to a sophisticated understanding of each theory or the analysis of student data; a minimal understanding and analysis is all that is required.

Resource-wise, active involvement of an educational developer in all stages of the process is only feasible on the assumption that there is a limited number of concepts of such foundational disciplinary value, and a commitment to dissemination of the outcomes. As identification of threshold concepts and investigation into student (mis)understandings of these concepts accumulates within a discipline, it would be possible for teachers to use these as a foundation for curriculum design and move straight to stage 3 of the method.

As with the Hong Kong initiatives, teacher peer groups were created to work together on curriculum design. This is important for reducing the individual workload associated with implementing the action research stage of the method in particular, and also provides enhanced professional development benefits for teachers, through sharing of ideas and practice. Another way in which academic workloads were catered for during the trial was to stagger the three stages of the method over an

18-month period. The aim was to identify an appropriate threshold concept before the start of the academic year, collect phenomenographic
research data from students in semester 1, analyse the data in semester 2,
design curriculum interventions over the academic break, then implement
these in semester 1 of the next academic year. The last semester of the
funded project focused on analysing and reflecting on the outcomes of
the implementations, followed by planning of revisions to the curriculum
design for the next year.

Stage 1 – Identification of an Appropriate Threshold Concept

The two disciplinary peer groups were supported in identifying an appropriate threshold concept for the project through provision of selected readings,
followed by a face-to-face workshop consisting of expert presentations, discussion, exercises and questions. During the workshop, participants were
introduced to the following criteria to help them in identifying threshold
concepts:

1. *Troublesome* – threshold concepts are often difficult to understand
   because a disciplinary understanding is alien or counter-intuitive to
   novices.
2. *Transformative* – understanding the concept results in a qualitative shift
   in individuals' perspective on the subject, and possibly their sense of
   identity and world view.
3. *Integrative* – full understanding of the concept exposes hidden inter-
   relatedness in the subject/discipline.
4. *Irreversible* – threshold concepts are unlikely to be forgotten, indeed
   students may 'forget' what it was like not to understand.

These are a simplified subset of the full range of characteristics associated with threshold concepts, but are adequate for the purposes of the
method.

To help make the criteria more meaningful to participants, the workshop included a group exercise in applying the criteria to the concept of
'ethics', plus a case study exercise based on potential threshold concepts
in health. Participants were then separated into disciplinary groups and
asked to brainstorm key concepts for first-year students in their discipline.
From this set of key concepts, they were then asked to identify potential
threshold concepts to be addressed in the project using the criteria specified
above.

Amongst those newly introduced to the notion of threshold concepts, there is often confusion between the idea of a 'threshold' versus a 'key' concept. It was hoped that asking participants to first identify key concepts, from which a subset of threshold concepts is then identified, would help reduce this confusion. Threshold concepts will inevitably be key concepts in a discipline, but not all key concepts will be threshold in nature.

After identifying a small set of potential threshold concepts, each disciplinary group was then asked to write a brief description of how each of these concepts met the four criteria. This exercise was an additional step to help them distinguish key from threshold concepts.

By the end of the workshop, each disciplinary group had agreed on a common threshold concept for the trial: 'legal reasoning' in law and 'measurement uncertainty' in physics. Interestingly, in identifying these concepts as threshold in nature, both disciplinary groups also concluded (with some surprise) that the concepts were typically *not* explicitly taught in their first-year curriculum. The foundational nature of these concepts had somehow led to the practice of leaving the learning of these concepts implicit, as something that would be picked up along the way of acquiring a degree without being explicitly addressed. This demonstrates the potential of a threshold concepts focus to curriculum design in providing a different way of thinking about curriculum.

Stage 2 – Action Research into Student (mis)understandings of the Concept

The purpose of the action research component of the method is to identify what it is about the threshold concept selected that students experience particular difficulty in understanding. To introduce participants to the complexity of phenomenographic research methods in a way that would be as manageable as possible for them, this stage of the project was addressed as three separate steps: interview design, conduct of interviews and interview analysis.

Interview design: participants were briefly introduced to phenomenography at the end of the workshop on threshold concepts. Two follow-up video-conference meetings were then organised for each disciplinary group over the semester to help them design an appropriate interview schedule for investigating student understandings of the selected threshold concept. Readings and interview design guidelines were provided and discussed during the video-conference meetings.

Both the physics and law interview schedules used the approach of semi-structured questions oriented around a trigger scenario: a solicitor's memo of advice for law; and two sets of data for physics. The intention was to give students a disciplinary-relevant scenario in which they needed to apply the threshold concept, then interview them about their thinking. The semi-structured interview questions explored how students came to their conclusions about the scenario, and in particular *why* they thought and said what they did. The aim was to enable different understandings of the concept to emerge.

Conduct of interviews: guidance in phenomenographic interviewing was provided through readings and written guidelines, conducting mock interviews during the video-conferencing meetings, and conducting pilot interviews, transcripts of which were shared and discussed. Each teacher was then asked to interview six of their first-year students, aiming for a total of 24 interviews for each discipline across the four institutions as a whole. The aim was to conduct a minimum number of interviews that might be expected to capture the range of key variation in students' understanding of the threshold concept. Final numbers were 21 interviews for law and 23 for physics.

Interview analysis: interviews were transcribed verbatim and analysed in two steps:

1. a preliminary analysis of the five to six interviews by each teacher; followed by
2. a final analysis of the total set of 21−23 interviews for each discipline.

The preliminary analysis involved a face-to-face meeting between an educational developer/researcher and each disciplinary teacher individually. Each teacher was provided with some readings on phenomenographic analysis and a brief guide to help them get started. During the analysis, participants were encouraged to compare and contrast student interviews in an iterative manner, looking for key similarities and differences in their responses. This process helps to highlight different aspects of the concept that some students may be aware of and others not. Teachers were then asked to group transcripts into categories, using a constant comparative method to maximise similarities within and differences between the categories. The groupings were seen as representing different ways of under-standing the concept, each way marked by different awareness of key features of the concept.

A whole group workshop was then held, with the aim of combining the interviews across institutions and progressing the interview analysis to a stage that would be adequate to inform curriculum design. The workshop started with further guidance to participants on how to analyse interviews phenomenographically. Participants then broke into disciplinary groups, each accompanied by an educational developer/researcher who worked with the groups to develop their analyses as far as possible within the time available. A fully fledged phenomenographic analysis was not possible nor anticipated within the timelines of the trial.

The law group identified three qualitatively distinct ways of understanding legal reasoning, as:

1. a formulaic process for predicting a legal outcome;
2. an interpretive process of arguing for an outcome that benefits your client;
3. a dynamic, responsive and innovative process for developing the law to reflect changing society.

Each understanding was marked by varying awareness of three critical features of the concept:

1. the purpose of legal reasoning;
2. the nature of the legal rule (law) in legal reasoning;
3. the role of the HIRAC/ISAAC (acronyms routinely taught to students to guide their presentation of a legal argument) 'formulae' in legal reasoning.

Other features of legal reasoning also emerged, such as the logical and structured nature of the legal reasoning process, but these three features were the ones regarded as *critical* in distinguishing one way of understanding legal reasoning from another. That legal reasoning is a structured process, for example, was a feature perceived in all of the understandings that emerged, so was not critical in distinguishing between them. As this feature was noticed by all students in the interview sample, the evidence is that they do not experience difficulty in noticing this aspect of legal reasoning, and so it does not require specialised curriculum design attention.

Whilst the outcomes of the phenomenographic research made sense to teachers in terms of their experience with students, this kind of distinction between what is critical and not critical to students' understanding was not predictable in advance. In the trial, teachers were asked to predict outcomes in advance of the action research to demonstrate this point.

The most critical feature determining the different understandings that emerged appeared to be varying perceptions of the nature of legal rules.

We use the term 'perceptions' here because, phenomenographically, the different understandings that emerged are seen as due to varying *awareness* of this aspect of legal reasoning. Many students were not aware that legal rules are open to different interpretations; they perceived legal rules as clear and rigid. The consequence of this is that it limited their understanding of legal reasoning to being an argument about the facts of a case (category 1 understanding). The purpose of legal reasoning is then experienced as primarily predictive – solicitors look at the facts of a case, compare them to the rule, and can then predict for their clients the likely legal outcome.

Students who are aware that rules are ambiguous and interpretable are able to experience a more sophisticated understanding of legal reasoning, where both the facts *and* the rule become open to argument. This allows legal reasoning to be understood as arguing for an interpretation of the rule that would produce the best legal outcome for the client (category 2 understanding) – solicitors look at the facts of a case, search for ambiguous elements of the rule that allow for interpretations that suit the facts, and can then argue for an interpretation that is most favourable to their client.

In category 3, the rules themselves are seen as changeable through changes in legislation. However, the group agreed that they were aiming only for a category 2 understanding for their first-year students. Consequently, the curriculum design was aimed at achieving this understanding, not a category 3 understanding.

Stage 3 – Design of Curriculum Interventions

The aim of the curriculum design stage is to improve students' understandings of the threshold concept by applying variation theory and the findings from the student interviews to the design of teaching and learning activities in the curriculum.

In the trial, the focus was on designing learning activities as interventions within the usual curriculum. The teachers were introduced to variation theory at the end of the second workshop and some readings were made available. Preliminary discussion of curriculum interventions commenced at the workshop, and continued through two subsequent video-conference meetings, as well as e-mail interchanges between teachers.

Teachers could not be expected to come to terms with the full complexity of variation theory within such a short period of time, nor is a full understanding essential for improved curriculum design. The main elements of variation theory that were emphasised for teachers were:

- what is *not* varied in design of teaching and learning activities is as significant for student learning as what *is* varied;
- students' attention needs to be drawn to each critical aspect of the concept in turn, by varying one aspect at a time whilst holding other aspects constant (separation of parts);
- students' attention also needs to be drawn to the ways in which the critical aspects relate to each other and integrate into a whole, by varying all aspects simultaneously (fusion of parts into a whole);
- separation needs to precede fusion.

Again, potential outcomes for stage 3 of the method will be illustrated through the law group design. As described above, students' understanding of 'the nature of legal rules' was identified as a critical feature of their overall understanding of legal reasoning. A category 1 way of understanding legal reasoning, as 'a formulaic process for predicting a legal outcome', involved a perception of legal rules as rigid, unchangeable and completely clear. From the teachers' perspective, this represented a misunderstanding of the nature and treatment of legal rules during legal reasoning. In contrast, a category 2 understanding of legal reasoning, as 'an interpretive process of arguing for an outcome that serves your client', includes awareness of legal rules as manipulable, interpretable and ambiguous. This was the understanding that the law teachers desired for their students.

According to variation theory, moving past a category 1 understanding to a category 2 understanding requires noticing the potential for variation in interpretation of legal rules. However, common law curriculum design practices involve the study of legal cases where multiple aspects of the legal scenario vary simultaneously, reducing students' chances of noticing variation in interpretation of rules in particular. Using variation theory, the law teachers prepared a design for a tutorial or workshop activity that involved students and teachers working through a series of four legal scenarios built around the potential offence of speeding in a vehicle:

Section 20 of the *Road Rules 2008* (NSW) states that: 'It is an offence for a driver to drive a vehicle at a speed over the speed limit applying to the driver for the length of road where the driver is driving'.

In each scenario, the legal rule was held constant, while application of the rule (and thus potential outcomes for the client) varied. This was first varied by introducing different contextual circumstances that could lead to different interpretations of the facts of the case. For example, 'Fred is driving a car. He passes a speed camera which records his speed at 60 kph in a 40 kph school zone'. This scenario raises the possibility of questioning the accuracy of the speed camera.

Then the potential for varying interpretations of terms in the rule itself were highlighted by a scenario in which Fred is sitting in the passenger seat of a parked car. He accidentally bumps the handbrake, releasing the brake, and the car begins to roll down a steep hill. Before the car rolls to a stop it is recorded by a speed camera doing 50 kph in a 40 kph school zone. This scenario raises the issue of the definition of a 'driver' and 'driving'.

It should be noted, however, that these scenarios illustrate separation without fusion. Instances of fusion occurred spontaneously during the class in response to questions and issues raised by students.

VALUE OF THE METHOD TO IMPROVING CURRICULUM DESIGN

The value of the curriculum design method was measured in two ways: (1) impact on student learning; and (2) impact on the professional development of the teachers involved in the trial implementation.

The impact on student learning was supportive of the method, but inconclusive. Nevertheless, teacher perceptions of the impact of the trial on their teaching and understanding of student learning were profound. Teachers' views were gathered through a confidential interview conducted by an independent evaluator. They reported benefits, sometimes of a transformational nature, in the following three areas:

1. Improved understanding of what it is that students find difficult when learning the concept.
   Physics: A lot of rather simplistic ideas about your students and their misconceptions that have to be confronted ... and you realise that in fact it's a little bit more complicated, what's going on in the students' minds than that.
   Law: So it really brings home to you the diversity of understanding, and that students can hear the same thing but experience it very differently.
2. Improved understanding of how best to teach the concept, as well as other disciplinary concepts.

Physics: Certainly it was informative ... and changes how I think about what I'll do in my own physics teaching.
Law: The way that we worked out the methodology will certainly be effective and will definitely be used in all future introductory law subjects.
3. An expansion in participants' *own* understanding of the concept.
Physics: It's certainly triggered a new cycle of thinking about it [measurement uncertainty] and possibly a different order of thinking about it.
Law: I think I have a more sophisticated understanding of what legal reasoning is than before I started the project ... So I think it's expanded, I guess, my view of what legal reasoning is.

Given that project participants were disciplinary academics with many years' experience, this last benefit is particularly pleasing and exceeds the anticipated outcomes of the method.

DISCUSSION

This chapter describes a method of curriculum design that is based on combining threshold concepts, phenonemographic action research and the variation theory of learning. The method is inherently theory and evidence based.

A trial of the method indicated that the threshold concepts focus provides a different way of thinking about curriculum for disciplinary teachers, with the teachers involved in the trial noticing that the threshold concepts they identified for the project were commonly left implicit in disciplinary curricula rather than addressed explicitly.

Similarly, the phenomenographic focus of the action research provided teachers with unexpected insights into what it is that students often fail to 'get' about the concept, and thus what needs to be emphasised in the design of teaching and learning activities. The action research part of the model was often described by the teachers as the most valuable part, providing unexpected insights into the student experience.

Applying variation theory to design of teaching and learning activities was the most difficult aspect of the model for teachers to implement. Whilst it is intuitive for teachers to spontaneously vary illustrations and applications of a concept when teaching, the simultaneous focus on invariance that variation theory provides is counter-intuitive for most teachers. Indeed, the lesson designs were often implemented in a less than ideal fashion, with spontaneous deviations from the plan. Observation or recording of initial implementations, with feedback on how the design was actually implemented in practice, would be a valuable part of the review process for teachers when first implementing this model.

Variation theory may also help explain how some typical approaches to teaching threshold concepts may unintentionally contribute to difficulties in student understanding. For example, in law, legal reasoning was often taught as an invariant process applied to varying cases. Variation theory would predict that this would encourage students to notice the details of the cases, but not the underlying common reasoning.

On the surface, the focus of the method on curriculum design around individual disciplinary concepts may seem inherently unintegrative across the range of concepts in a subject or course. However, integration lies in the level of complexity or breadth of the concept. For example, 'legal reasoning' and 'measurement uncertainty' are inherently broad and integrative concepts that run throughout many aspects of law and physics. The inherently integrative nature of threshold concepts means that a good understanding of these concepts facilitates understanding of a host of related concepts, leading to an impact on student learning far beyond the individual concept in isolation.

Participating teachers' perceptions of the potential for disciplinary uptake of the method was explicitly sought through confidential interviews conducted by an independent evaluator towards the end of the trial. The interviews sought teachers' views on:

- aspects of the method that they would continue to use in the future,
- whether there were any aspects that they would avoid using or processes that they would use differently, and
- whether they would recommend the method to colleagues in their own discipline and other disciplines.

Overall, the teachers were keen to continue using the method and happy to recommend it to colleagues. The greatest concern, in both their own continuing use and in recommending it to colleagues, was around the resource-intensive nature of the approach. However, when less time-intensive options were discussed, the general reaction was that there would be a substantial reduction in the learning and teaching gains from any abbreviations. The action research stage was regarded as the most time-consuming, but also the most insightful and rewarding aspect of the process, along with the experience of working in disciplinary peer groups.

Given the workload and other resources required, we suggest that the method would be most effectively used at a system-wide level, in discipline-level reviews or national projects such as those funded by the Office for Learning and Teaching in Australia. This would allow systematic identification of threshold concepts in a discipline and critical variation in student understandings of these concepts. Varied designs for teaching and learning of the concepts could then be tested and shared.

Further details of the method and the project trial are available from the project website at: http://www.thresholdvariation.edu.au. The website was created to provide a long-lasting resource to support ongoing dissemination of the method, including detailed materials from the physics and law case studies.

ACKNOWLEDGEMENTS

Funding for the trial project was provided by the Australian Learning and Teaching Council, an initiative of the Australian Government Department of Education, Employment and Workplace Relations.

We would like to thank Keith Trigwell from the University of Sydney, who worked with the authors as an educational researcher/developer in the project, and Camille McMahon, who conducted the independent evaluation of the project.

Particular thanks go to the law and physics academics who participated in the project trial, and whose involvement in the interview design, interview analysis, curriculum design and implementation led to the illustrations of potential outcomes provided in this chapter: Judith Jones and Paul Francis, Australian National University; Susan Carr-Gregg, Leanne Houston and Les Kirkup, University of Technology, Sydney; Rachael Field, Darren Pearce and Cheryl Treloar, Queensland University of Technology; and Manjula Sharma, University of Sydney.

REFERENCES

Åkerlind, G., McKenzie, J., & Lupton, M. (2010). *A threshold concepts approach to curriculum design: Supporting student learning through application of variation theory.* Australian Learning and Teaching Council Final Project Report, Creative Commons Australia

Licence. Retrieved from http://www.thresholdvariation.edu.au http://www.thresholdvariation.edu.au http://www.thresholdvariation.edu.au

Bowden, J. (1994). The nature of phenomenographic research. In J. Bowden & E. Walsh (Eds.), *Phenomenographic research: Variations in method* (pp. 1–16). Melbourne: EQARD, RMIT.

Bowden, J., & Green, P. (Eds.) (2005). *Doing developmental phenomenography*. Melbourne: RMIT Press.

Bowden, J., & Marton, F. (1998). *The university of learning*. London: Kogan Page.

Bowden, J., & Walsh, E. (Eds.) (2000). *Phenomenography*. Melbourne: RMIT University Press.

Land, R., Meyer, J. H. F., & Baillie, C. (2010). Editors' preface: Threshold concepts and transformational learning. In J. H. F. Meyer, R. Land, & C. Baillie (Eds.), *Threshold concepts and transformational learning* (pp. ix–xlii). Rotterdam: Sense Publishers.

Land, R., Smith, J., & Meyer, J. (Eds.) (2008). *Threshold concepts within the disciplines*. Rotterdam: Sense Publishers.

Lo, M., Marton, F., Pang, M., & Pong, W. (2004). Toward a pedagogy of learning. In F. Marton & A. Tsui (Eds.), *Classroom discourse and the space of learning*. Hillsdale, NJ: Lawrence Erlbaum.

Marton, F. (1981). Phenomenography – Describing conceptions of the world around us. *Instructional Science, 10*, 177–200.

Marton, F. (1986). Phenomenography – A research approach to investigating different understandings of reality. *Journal of Thought, 21*, 28–49.

Marton, F. (1994). On the structure of awareness. In J. Bowden & E. Walsh (Eds.), *Phenomenographic research: Variations in method* (pp. 89–100). Melbourne: EQARD, RMIT.

Marton, F., & Booth, S. (1997). *Learning and awareness*. Hillsdale, NJ: Lawrence Erlbaum.

Marton, F., & Tsui, A. (Eds.) (2004). *Classroom discourse and the space of learning*. Hillsdale, NJ: Lawrence Erlbaum.

Meyer, E., & Land, R. (2003). Threshold concepts and troublesome knowledge: Linkages to ways of thinking and practicing within the disciplines. In C. Rust (Ed.), *Improving student learning theory and practice – 10 years on*. Oxford: Oxford Centre for Staff and Learning Development.

Meyer, E., & Land, R. (2005). Threshold concepts and troublesome knowledge (2): Epistemological considerations and a conceptual framework for teaching and learning. *Higher Education, 49*, 373–388.

Meyer, E., & Land, R. (Eds.) (2006). *Threshold concepts and troublesome knowledge*. London: Routledge.

Pang, M., & Marton, F. (2003). Beyond "lesson study": Comparing two ways of facilitating the grasp of some economic concepts. *Instructional Science, 31*, 175–194.

Pang, M., & Marton, F. (2005). Learning theory as teaching resource: Enhancing students' understanding of economic concepts. *Instructional Science, 33*, 159–191.

Rovio-Johannson, A. (1999a). Constituting different meanings of the content of teaching and learning in higher education. Paper presented at the 8th European Association for Research in Learning and Instruction Conference, Gothenburg, Sweden.

Rovio-Johannson, A. (1999b). *Being good at teaching: Exploring different ways of handling the same subject in higher education*. Doctoral thesis, Gothenburg Studies in Educational Sciences 140, Acta Universitatis Gothoburgensis.

Runesson, U. (1999). Teaching as constituting a space of variation. Presented at the 8th European Association for Research in Learning and Instruction Conference, Gothenburg, Sweden.

Runesson, U., & Marton, F. (2002). The object of learning and the space of variation. In F. Marton & P. Morris (Eds.), *What matters? Discovering critical conditions of classroom learning* (pp. 19–38). Sweden: Acta Universitatis Gothoburgensis.

THEORY DEVELOPMENT AND APPLICATION IN HIGHER EDUCATION RESEARCH: THE CASE OF THRESHOLD CONCEPTS

Malcolm Tight

ABSTRACT

This chapter examines the case of threshold concepts, as an example of a theory being developed and applied within higher education research. It traces the origins and meaning of the term, reviews its application by higher education researchers and discusses the issues it raises and the critiques it has attracted. This case is of particular interest, as the idea of threshold concepts is little more than a decade old, yet in that time it has attracted considerable attention.

INTRODUCTION

Higher education is an inter-disciplinary field for research. With only a limited number of academic and other researchers devoting themselves full time and long term to researching higher education — at least outside of

Theory and Method in Higher Education Research II
International Perspectives on Higher Education Research, Volume 10, 249–267
ISSN: 1479-3628/doi:10.1108/S1479-3628(2014)0000010018

North America — most of those researching this field come from and remain based in other disciplines, departments or institutions, and their contributions are usually part time and/or short term.

This also, however, has a positive aspect, as it means that a diverse range of both methodologies and (more particularly for the present analysis) theoretical frameworks are applied to researching higher education. While the latter are often, therefore, introduced from other disciplines — by researchers with a background or interest in those disciplines — other theories are also developed within higher education research itself (Tight, 2012, 2013, 2014).

This chapter forms part of a larger research project, which is tracing the origins, spread and development of particular theories or theoretical frameworks of influence within higher education research. In addition to charting where they come from, how popular they are and how they change over time, the project will consider why and how these theories are being used, their relation to other frameworks, and the critiques of them that have been advanced.

In this chapter, the focus is on a theoretical framework developed within, rather than imported into, higher education research. This framework has been around for little more than a decade, but has proved to be both highly popular and widely applied to both research and teaching within different disciplines over that time. The framework or theory in question is that of threshold concepts (the idea that, within any discipline, there are particular concepts which are problematic to teach and learn, but which, once learned, enable the learner to cross a threshold to greater understanding).

The remainder of the chapter is organized in five main sections. First, the nature of theory and its relation to higher education research is briefly reviewed. The origins of the idea of threshold concepts are then discussed, and its meaning is considered. The application of the theory by other researchers is reviewed, and the issues and criticisms concerning it are examined. These findings are discussed further before, finally, some conclusions are reached.

THEORY

The idea of theory, or the ability to explain and understand the findings of research within a conceptual framework that makes 'sense' of the data, is the mark of a mature discipline whose aim is the systematic study of particular phenomena. (May, 2001, p. 29)

If the articulation and application of theory is a key characteristic of a mature discipline, it is an aspect that higher education researchers are steadily coming to terms with. Previous studies (Tight, 2004) indicated that much published higher education research showed little or no engagement with theory. The position, however, appears to be improving, particularly if we examine articles published more recently in the higher quality journals (Tight, 2012, 2014). The present chapter aims to contribute to a continuing improvement in engagement with theory by focusing on the application of a particular theoretical framework.

This apparent reluctance to engage with theory is partly due – as the quotation from May suggests – to the relative immaturity of higher education research as a field. A rather more important factor in this respect, however, has to do with the emphasis in much higher education research (and in educational research generally: e.g. Adams, Cochrane, & Dunne, 2012a, Pring, 2005) placed on the improvement of practice. Yet, theoretical development and practical improvement may go hand-in-hand; indeed, they can be mutually supportive.

In focusing on the place of theory in research, some looseness in language has to be accepted. A multiplicity of more or less analogous terms are in common usage alongside theory, including, for example, concept, idea, framework and model (thus, two of these terms are used by May in his quoted explanation of theory). This practice will also be followed in the remainder of this chapter.

Underlying this looseness of language, however, it has to be acknowledged that there is also a good deal of variability in the way the term 'theory' is used:

> Theory has a multitude of meanings, not all of which can be easily reconciled, making it a concept open to wide appropriation. For example, theory can simply mean an idea about a social configuration, or it can mean an intellectual formula that enables one to structure experience (or data, in terms of research); sometimes it is used broadly and is synonymous with philosophy, or it is used specifically as an interpretative description of experience. Theorizing can be an expansive business, in that it can be thought of as an act that generates new ways of thinking about the way the world is configured, and may be generalized and transferred to a multitude of new concepts in the expectation that it will throw light on them. (Adams, Cochrane, & Dunne, 2012b, p. 1)

In focusing here on the particular case of threshold concepts, therefore, one of the questions we may ask is what sort of theory threshold concepts is.

ORIGINS

Beaty (2006), in the foreword to one of a number of edited volumes on threshold concepts that have been produced in the last decade, traces the origins of this theory to a series of UK research and development projects undertaken in the 2000s. Meyer and Land (2003) are cited as the first published source, and they attribute the original idea to Meyer, who was drawing on Perkins' (1999) idea of troublesome knowledge.

Since then, Meyer and Land (2005, 2006a, 2006b, 2006c) together, as well as individually (Land, 2011, 2012) and with other authors (Baillie, Bowden, & Meyer, 2013; Land, Cousin, Meyer, & Davies, 2005; Land, Meyer, & Smith, 2008; Meyer, Ward, & Latreille, 2009; Shanahan, Foster, & Meyer, 2006), have produced a succession of publications on the topic. Clearly, it has been a productive way of thinking about particular aspects of higher education and its research and, as we shall see, not just for Land and Meyer.

Of course, neither Meyer nor Land were the first to match the words 'threshold' and 'concepts' together, though they certainly appear to be the first to have applied this term broadly in the context of researching teaching and learning in higher education. Researchers and practitioners in different disciplines have long recognized the existence of various kinds of concepts, some of which they have termed threshold concepts. Table 1 shows the results of a search in Google Scholar (undertaken on 31 May 2013) for the term 'threshold concepts'. It identifies the number of 'articles' (this includes books, book chapters, conference papers and online documents as well as journal articles) found using the term somewhere in the text, as well as the number including this term in their title.

The oldest use of the term found in this search dated to 1950, and was in an article on 'Auditory Masking and Fatigue' in the *Journal of the Acoustical Society of America* (Rosenblith, 1950). The earliest use found in a title dates to 1976, in an article on 'Dose-Response Relationship and Threshold Concepts' in the *Annals of the New York Academy of Sciences*. Clearly, as these titles indicate – and as the example journals, in which articles using the term were found, given in Table 1 also show – the term 'threshold concepts' has been used in specific ways in a wide variety of disciplinary contexts. These include, confining myself to just one letter of the alphabet, pathology, pest management, philosophy, physiology, politics and psychology.

Table 1 illustrates a steady growth in the use of the term 'threshold concepts' from the 1950s to the present day. In part this is, of course, a

Table 1. Articles[a] including the Exact Words 'Threshold Concepts' in Google Scholar by Date.

Date	Number of Articles	Number with Threshold Concepts in the Title	Example Journals
1950–1959	2	0	Journal of the Acoustical Society of America; Psychosomatic Medicine
1960–1969	18	0	International Journal of Pest Management; Journal of Invertebrate Pathology; Mind; Psychological Review
1970–1979	86	1	American Biology Teacher; Economic and Political Weekly; Philosophical Studies; School Science Review
1980–1989	252	2	American Chemical Society Symposium Series; Engineering Fracture Mechanics; New Forests; Scandinavian Political Studies
1990–1999	409	1	European Journal of Applied Physiology and Occupational Physiology; Geomorphology; Rough Sets and Current Trends in Computing
2000–2009	1050	73	Higher Education; Restoration Ecology; Sports Medicine; Studies in Higher Education
2010–	1440	109	British Journal of Occupational Therapy; Engineering Education; International Journal of Sports Physiology and Performance; International Studies Perspectives
Total	3257	186	

[a]The term 'articles' in Google Scholar include articles, books, book chapters, conference papers and online documents, but citations and patents have been excluded.

reflection of the growth of the academy over that period, and the multiplication of outlets for academic publication. To put it simply, over time more has been published on just about any topic you care to think of. Much of the most recent expansion shown in Table 1 is, however, down to the work of Meyer and Land, and its impact upon others.

Thus, 76% of the articles mentioning threshold concepts and 98% of the articles using this term in their titles date from 2000 or later. Most of these articles, particularly those using the term in their titles, are concerned with the application of threshold concepts as a theoretical framework to researching learning and teaching in higher education. The specialist usage of the terms in other disciplines has continued, but at a comparatively low level. Prior to 2003, when the first Meyer and Land publication on threshold concepts appeared, its application to thinking about higher education (or education more generally) does seem to have been confined to particular disciplinary contexts and meanings.

MEANING

Meyer and Land, in one of their earlier works on the topic, define threshold concepts in the following fashion:

> A threshold concept can be considered as akin to a portal, opening up a new and previously inaccessible way of thinking about something. (2006b, p. 3)

In other words, it is a concept that, once grasped and fully comprehended, enables the individual to move on significantly in their thinking. The same − or a similar but slightly varied − definition can be found in many of Meyer and Land's publications.

The idea of a threshold concept is usually immediately linked to that of troublesome knowledge:

> a threshold concept can of itself inherently represent ... *troublesome knowledge* − knowledge that is 'alien', or counter-intuitive or even intellectually absurd at face value. (*ibid.*, p. 4)

Indeed, this linkage is so close that 'Threshold Concepts and Troublesome Knowledge' has served as the title for several of Meyer and Land's joint publications, whether books, chapters or articles. In the case of the latter two forms of publication, a number is helpfully appended to the title to indicate both the ongoing development of their ideas and the stage that has been reached.

Meyer and Land give many examples in their publications of what may be considered as threshold concepts − for example *complex number* and *limit* in pure mathematics, *signification* and *deconstruction* in literary and cultural studies, and *opportunity cost* in economics − deliberately choosing them to illustrate the applicability of this idea across the diverse range of disciplines. Acknowledging that many types of concepts are recognized in the different disciplines, they distinguish threshold concepts from core concepts, which do 'not necessarily lead to a qualitatively different view of subject matter' (*ibid.*, p. 6).

A series of characteristics of, or criteria for distinguishing, threshold concepts have been mapped out:

> a threshold concept ... is likely to be: *Transformative*, in that, once understood, its potential effect on student learning and behavior is to occasion a significant shift in the perception of a subject, or part thereof ... Probably *irreversible*, in that the change of perception occasioned by acquisition of a threshold concept is unlikely to be forgotten, or will be unlearned only by considerable effort ... *Integrative*, that is it exposes the previously hidden interrelatedness of something ... Possibly often (though not necessarily always) *bounded* in that any conceptual space will have terminal frontiers, bordering with thresholds into new conceptual areas. Potentially (though not necessarily) *troublesome*. (*ibid.*, pp. 7–8)

Threshold concepts are also linked to the related idea of liminality, the condition of being between different states, in this case moving from a lack of understanding to an understanding of the concept in question:

> Central to the acquisition of threshold concepts is a consideration of what it might mean to be 'in the threshold'. The interest here is in variability in that state of being that may be thought of as *liminal*. (Meyer & Land, 2006c, p. 22)

Meyer, in particular, has also made considerable efforts to link the developing ideas around threshold concepts to other elements of learning theory, including metalearning activity (Meyer et al., 2009; Ward & Meyer, 2010), and capability and variation theory (Baillie et al., 2013).

APPLICATION

The idea of threshold concepts has undoubtedly had a significant impact upon the higher education research community over the last decade:

> There is now substantial evidence for threshold concepts in the disciplines, drawn from over 150 scholarly papers in 80 disciplinary or subject contexts from authors in the higher education sectors of many countries. (Land, 2011, p. 177)

Anyone wishing to check on or follow up these outputs would be well advised to visit Mick Flanagan's web site — www.ee.ucl.ac.uk/~mflanaga — where hundreds of articles, books, book chapters, conference papers and online sources dealing with threshold concepts are helpfully catalogued.

So far, four biennial international conferences have been held on the topic of threshold concepts, in 2006, 2008, 2010 and 2012. There have also been a number of special issues of pedagogical journals, including:

- ACCESS: *Critical Perspectives on Communication, Cultural and Policy Studies* (2011, 30, 2)
- *Journal of Faculty Development* (2012, 26, 3)
- *Planet* (2006, 17)

These journals contain series of shorter pieces, aimed at informing and updating the practitioner in a particular disciplinary field, and are not considered further in this chapter.

The analysis that follows in the remainder of this section has been largely limited to refereed journal articles, as arguably the most thoroughly reviewed and thus highest quality outputs. This has the benefit of simplifying the analysis, while also cutting out much of the duplication of outputs that occurs when conference papers are considered as well. The refereed journal articles were identified through searches on Google Scholar and on the Lancaster University Library online database.

Even with this restriction, it is clear that threshold concepts have been applied in a wide range of disciplines, including:

- accounting (Lucas & Mladenovic, 2007)
- biological sciences (Jordan, Tracy, & Johnstone, 2011; Ross et al., 2010)
- business/management (Coughlan & Graham, 2009; Wright & Gilmore, 2012; Yip & Raelin, 2011)
- computer science (Boustedt et al., 2007)
- dental education (Kinchin, Cabot, Kobus, & Woolford, 2011)
- economics (Davies & Mangan, 2007; Shanahan et al., 2006)
- engineering (Davey, 2012; Harlow, Scott, Peter, & Cowie, 2011; Holloway, Alpay, & Bull, 2010; Kabo & Baillie, 2009)
- geography (Fouberg, 2013; Srivastava, 2013)
- health care (Clouder, 2005; Tanner, 2011)
- history (Adler-Kassner, Majewski, & Koshnick, 2012)
- law (Wimshurst, 2011)
- literature (Abbott, 2013; Wisker, 2007)
- mathematics (Long, 2009; Scheja & Pettersson, 2010)
- nurse education (Stacey & Stickley, 2012)
- politics (Korosteleva, 2010)
- social work (Morgan, 2012)
- statistics (MacDougall, 2010)

As well as specific disciplinary applications, the idea of threshold concepts has also been applied to more generic higher education concerns, such as academic writing and literacies (Gourlay, 2009; Wallace, 2010; Wisker & Savin-Baden, 2009), doctoral research (Humphreys & Simpson, 2012; Kiley, 2009; Kiley & Wisker, 2009; Trafford & Leshem, 2009; Wisker & Robinson, 2009), information literacy and librarianship (Hofer, Townsend, & Brunetti, 2012; Townsend, Brunetti & Hofer, 2011) and sustainability (Sandri, 2013). It has also been applied in thinking about interdisciplinarity and cross-disciplinarity (Carmichael, 2012; Irvine & Carmichael, 2009; Land, 2012), and to other levels of education (Long, 2009).

Table 2 charts the refereed journal articles focusing on threshold concepts that I have been able to identify as having been published over the 11-year period 2003–2013. It is restricted to English language publications. It also lists a number of other publications by Land and/or Meyer to provide an idea of their continuing contribution to this field of research. It is, of course, possible that I may have missed some journal articles, but, if so, they are likely to have been fairly obscure.

Of the 53 refereed journal articles identified in the table, the majority, 28, of the first authors (where there were two or more authors, they typically came from the same country and institution, though there are quite a few examples of international collaborations) were based in the United Kingdom at the time of publication. The next largest first author contribution, 13, came from Australia, with 5 from the United States, 2 each from New Zealand and Sweden, and 1 each from Canada, Ireland and South Africa. The dominance of the United Kingdom, as the country where the idea originated is not surprising, but the spread through the Anglophone world is also evident.

The table shows a number of features commonly found when the dissemination or diffusion of successful ideas is studied (e.g. Rogers, 2003). Thus, few publications appear in the first few years after the development of the original idea, and these are largely confined to the idea's originators. Then the idea begins to spread and a few early adopters (e.g. Clouder, 2005) begin to add to the publications. Take-up then broadens out, with increasing numbers of researchers contributing to the debate. Thus, 5 articles were published in 2007, 12 (the maximum annually to date) in 2009 and 8 each in 2010, 2011 and 2012.

While these may seem relatively small numbers, in a field of research as diffuse and underdeveloped as higher education, they are more than respectable. And they would, of course, be significantly expanded if other forms of publication, particularly conference papers, had been included.

Table 2.   Refereed Journal Articles on Threshold Concepts, 2003–2013.

Year	Number of Articles	Authors
2003		*Meyer and Land*
2004		
2005	2	Clouder; *Land et al*; **Meyer and Land**
2006	1	*Meyer and Land*; **Shanahan, Foster, and Meyer**
2007	5	Boustedt et al.; Davies and Mangan; Lucas and Mladenovic; Rowbottom; Wisker
2008		*Land, Meyer, and Smith*
2009	12	Coughlan and Graham; Gourlay; Irvine and Carmichael; Kabo and Baillie; Kiley; Kiley and Wisker; Long; **Meyer, Ward, and Latreille**; Osmond, Bull, and Tovey; Trafford and Leshem; Wisker and Robinson; Wisker and Savin-Baden
2010	8	Cousin; Holloway, Alpay, and Bull; Korosteleva; MacDougall; Ross et al.; Scheja and Pettersson; Wallace; **Ward and Meyer**
2011	8	Harlow et al.; Jordan, Tracy, and Johnstone; Kinchin et al.; **Land**; Tanner; Townsend, Brunetti, and Hofer; Wimshurst; Yip and Raelin
2012	8	Adler-Kassner, Majewski, and Koshnick; Carmichael; Davey; Hofer, Townsend, and Brunetti; Humphrey and Simpson; **Land**; Morgan; Stacey and Stickley; Wright and Gilmore
2013	4	**Baillie, Bowden, and Meyer**; Barradell; Fouberg; Walker
2013[a]	5	Abbott; Quinlan et al.; Sandri; Srivastava; Zepke
Total	53	

[a]This includes articles which have been published online, and thus are available, and which will be published in print soon.

Notes: The table lists all identified refereed journal articles dealing with threshold concepts in learning and teaching in higher education. Selected other publications by Land and Meyer have been added for illustrative purposes: these are not included in the totals.

All publications by Land and/or Meyer are in bold. Those which are not refereed journal articles are in italics.

ISSUES AND CRITIQUES

Of course, as any new idea becomes more popular, and enters the mainstream of thinking in its area of research, it becomes the subject of increasing attention and thus critique: this is, after all, how the academy works. Issues and concerns associated with its usage and application are identified, applications to varied areas of practice raise further questions, and modifications or developments are suggested.

One of the earliest published critiques of threshold concepts theory was especially thorough and hard-hitting. It came within four years of the first publication of the idea in 2003 (Rowbottom, 2007), though it was actually responding to a book published in the previous year (Meyer & Land, 2006a). Rowbottom begins by questioning 'how can we empirically determine if there are such threshold concepts?' (2007, p. 264). He argues that:

> Meyer and Land not only fail to specify what is essential to a threshold concept, but also neglect to explain what they understand a concept to be. It is even more remarkable that a number of authors claim to have identified threshold concepts. (*ibid.*)

Rowbottom considers different views of the nature of concepts, and their relation to abilities, and concludes 'that so-called "threshold concepts" are not as easy to spot as anyone has previously thought, even if there are such things' (p. 268).

In a more recent analysis, Walker (2013) begins by noting that 'it appears that a Threshold Concept could be viewed as both a "product" (something developed in the mind of the learner) and a "process" (as a transformative journey with distinct stages)' (p. 248). He goes on to identify a number of issues or limitations:

> Despite their appeal, TCs have only a recent history, and there are several emerging issues. Firstly, and perhaps most importantly, is it a theory which explains empirical observations, or is it a concept incorporating and representing several abstract ideas? Secondly ... the relative paucity of empirical work would seem to grant considerable scope for innovation. Third, despite the intuitive nature of TCs how exactly are they defined? ... Fourth, and finally, despite some significant conceptual overlaps, none of the literature on TCs refers to Schema Theories of Learning. (pp. 250–251)

Walker argues that 'several powerful synergies exist between schema theories of learning and threshold concepts' (p. 252), which he then illustrates through an empirical study making use of the technique of semantic networks.

Barradell (2013) focuses on the problems in the identification of threshold concepts, and offers transactional curriculum inquiry, involving dialogue between teachers, students and educational designers, as a means of doing this. Quinlan et al. (2013), for their part, focus on problems with methodology. They conclude that 'It would be useful to bring together researchers who have been developing complimentary research methodologies, to compare and contrast these approaches and to develop more rigorous methodological protocols for the research' (p. 12).

DISCUSSION

These issues and critiques may be both extended and added to. To begin with, there is the issue, already identified, of what constitutes a threshold concept, and thus how we would identify one in practice. In this, the quotation from Meyer and Land (2006b, pp. 7–8) already used is revealing, but not in a particularly helpful way. Thus, in a few sentences, they make use of the qualifiers 'likely', 'probably', 'possibly often (though not necessarily always)' and 'potentially (though not necessarily)'.

Such imprecision in definition is unhelpful, if perhaps understandable in a new area of research. Set against this, however, we must place the impressive list of researchers − and those they have researched − who appear to have relatively little difficulty in identifying threshold concepts in their own disciplines. The question then becomes 'are they all identifying the same sort of thing?', or are these supposed threshold concepts just a ragbag of aspects of learning in disciplines in higher education that particular teachers have found difficult to get across?

The latter interpretation is supported when we consider the range of items that have been identified as threshold concepts. This is apparent even amongst the examples identified by Meyer and Land themselves, and referred to earlier. Thus, 'complex number' refers to a particular kind of number, 'opportunity cost' is a way of thinking about alternative options, and 'deconstruction' is a method of analysis.

If we look at the ways in which the idea of threshold concepts has been applied by those who have followed Meyer and Land's lead, their diversity becomes more confusing. To take just another three examples, Kinchin et al. (2011) identify the recording of a complete dental jaw registration (a process) as an example of a threshold concept in dental education, Sandri (2013) discusses systems thinking (recognizing and appreciating the inter-relatedness of many factors) in learning for sustainability, and Wisker and Savin-Baden (2009) consider the problems experienced by academics and research students in writing (a very generic process). Can a single theory, idea or framework usefully accommodate such variety?

This sense of threshold concepts theory being used by a range of researchers to explore a huge diversity of problems encountered in teaching and learning in higher education is further accentuated if we note the different terminologies being used to identify concepts. Meyer and Land, as we have seen, distinguish threshold concepts from core concepts, though, presumably, core concepts may be threshold concepts in some cases. Key concepts are also frequently identified and discussed in a variety of disciplines (e.g. Tight, 2002), though, again, they may not necessarily be threshold concepts.

Davies and Mangan (2007) take this discussion further, in considering conceptual change in economics. They distinguish between basic, discipline and procedural concepts, all of which can be threshold concepts. As examples, they list the distinction between price and cost as a basic threshold concept, opportunity cost reappears as an example of a discipline threshold concept, and elasticity is given as an example of a procedural threshold concept. The sense of an interesting idea being stretched too far gets stronger.

Another question we might ask here of threshold concepts is whether they are universal. In other words, if we continue with the example of opportunity cost in economics, is this always a problem for all students (presumably not), or is it a problem for a significant proportion? And, if the latter, how significant does the proportion have to be for it to qualify as a threshold concept? And is opportunity cost always a threshold concept in economics teaching, across institutions and systems, or is it more particular in its impact?

Finally, we might ask how the development of threshold concepts helps the practice of teaching and learning. Or, to put it another way, were teachers in higher education not already aware that particular ideas were causing their students problems in comprehension? And, if so, they probably had already worked out, more or less successful, strategies to help such students improve their understanding. If this is the case, how does labelling particular ideas or aspects of disciplines as threshold concepts assist those teaching or seeking to learn them?

CONCLUSION

Threshold concepts is an example of a theory or framework for thinking about particular issues that has achieved considerable popularity in the field of higher education research in a relatively short space of time. It has been taken up and applied by researchers to a wide diversity of disciplines and problems, and its usage has spread from the United Kingdom across the Anglophone world and beyond. Many have found it a useful theoretical framework, though a minority has critiqued it, while others have sought to develop it further. In short, Meyer and Land have had a significant impact with this idea: that much cannot be gainsaid.

Reservations and questions remain, however, and, in this concluding section, I will focus on two of them: what sort of theory is it? And where is threshold concepts theory going?

What Sort of a Theory Is Threshold Concepts?

As the brief discussion of theory earlier in this chapter indicated, the notion of theory is pretty broad in its application. Whether we choose to talk about theories, concepts (which is, of course, a word contained in threshold concepts itself), models, frameworks, combinations of these terms or whatever, we may characterize threshold concepts as one of these things; and, in this case, as a theory or theoretical framework. It clearly does offer, for many (though not all) people, a useful way for thinking about particular issues in learning and teaching in higher education.

So, what sort of theory is it? While it might not aspire to being thought of as high level or grand theory, of the order of quantum theory or Marxism, for example, it seems to fit one of the descriptions offered by Adams et al. (2012b, p. 1), and quoted earlier, quite well:

> Theorizing can be an expansive business, in that it can be thought of as an act that generates new ways of thinking about the way the world is configured, and may be generalized and transferred to a multitude of new concepts in the expectation that it will throw light on them.

In the case of threshold concepts, the 'world' being referred to is learning and teaching in higher education, a fairly contained context, and certainly not as far-reaching as the universe or global society. But, within the confines of that world, the evidence is that it has shown itself to be a useful theory.

Where Is Threshold Concepts Theory Going?

This second question is somewhat more difficult to answer, as it involves extrapolating from what has already taken place during the last decade forward into the future. An examination of Table 1, for example, might suggest that interest in threshold concepts will continue to expand, if not quite at an exponential rate. Reviewing Table 2, on the other hand – which focuses on the hard outcomes of threshold concepts research, in terms of journal articles – could lead one to suggest that interest, while still healthy, had already peaked.

The fifth biennial international conference on threshold concepts is being held in Durham (Land's current base and Meyer's former one) in 2014. Doubtless, this will generate a whole raft of new papers, some of which will see the light as refereed journal articles over the following years. And, as the discussion in this chapter indicates, there are still many aspects of threshold concepts theory which need more thought and research.

While it does not seem to have yet made a great impact in some parts of the (even English-speaking) world, most notably the United States, it could be argued that threshold concepts has become an established part of ways of thinking about learning and teaching in higher education. In so doing, it lines up alongside a whole range of other theoretical frameworks – such as approaches to learning, academic literacies, communities of practice and activity systems – that have been applied to this field.

The success of threshold concepts as a theory may, therefore, be judged in terms of how well it performs in comparison to, or in combination with, these other frameworks. The difficulty, of course, lies in assessing its performance. But simply identifying, and agreeing upon, more and more threshold concepts in more and more disciplines and sub-disciplines will not, in itself, be enough. Theory has to work to earn its keep.

REFERENCES

Abbott, R. (2013). Crossing thresholds in academic reading. *Innovations in Education and Teaching International* (p.11). doi:10.1080/14703297.2012.760865

Adams, J., Cochrane, M., & Dunne, L. (Eds.) (2012a). *Applying theory to educational research: An introductory approach with case studies.* Chichester: Wiley-Blackwell.

Adams, J., Cochrane, M., & Dunne, L. (2012b). Introduction. In J. Adams, M. Cochrane, & L. Dunne (Eds.), *Applying theory to educational research: An introductory approach with case studies* (pp. 1–10). Chichester: Wiley-Blackwell.

Adler-Kassner, L., Majewski, J., & Koshnick, D. (2012). The value of troublesome knowledge: Transfer and threshold concepts in writing and history. *Composition Forum, 26,* p.17.

Baillie, C., Bowden, J., & Meyer, J. (2013). Threshold capabilities: Threshold concepts and knowledge capability linked through variation theory. *Higher Education, 65*(2), 227–246.

Barradell, S. (2013). The identification of threshold concepts: A review of theoretical complexities and methodological challenges. *Higher Education, 65*(2), 265–276.

Beaty, L. (2006). Foreword. In J. Meyer & R. Land (Eds.), *Overcoming barriers to student understanding: Threshold concepts and troublesome knowledge* (pp. xi–xii). London: Routledge.

Boustedt, J., Eckerdal, A., McCartney, R., Mostrom, J., Ratcliffe, M., Sanders, K., & Zander, C. (2007). Threshold concepts in computer science: Do they exist and are they useful? *ACM SIGSE Bulletin, 39*(1), 504–508.

Carmichael, P. (2012). Tribes, territories and threshold concepts: Educational materialisms at work in higher education. *Educational Philosophy and Theory, 44*(S1), 31–42.

Clouder, L. (2005). Caring as a 'threshold concept': Transforming students in higher education into health(care) professionals. *Teaching in Higher Education, 10*(4), 505–517.

Coughlan, P., & Graham, A. (2009). Embedding a threshold concept in teaching and learning of product development management. *Creativity and Innovation Management, 18*(3), 190–198.

Cousin, G. (2010). Neither teacher-centred nor student-centred: Threshold concepts and research partnerships. *Journal of Learning Development in Higher Education, 2*, p.9.

Davey, K. (2012). Results from a study with threshold concepts in two chemical engineering undergraduate courses. *Education for Chemical Engineers, 7*, e139–e152.

Davies, P., & Mangan, J. (2007). Threshold concepts and the integration of understanding in economics. *Studies in Higher Education, 32*(6), 711–726.

Fouberg, E. (2013). "The World is no Longer Flat to me": Student perceptions of threshold concepts in world regional geography. *Journal of Geography in Higher Education, 37*(1), 65–75.

Gourlay, L. (2009). Threshold practices: Becoming a student through academic literacies. *London Review of Education, 7*(2), 181–192.

Harlow, A., Scott, J., Peter, M., & Cowie, B. (2011). 'Getting Stuck' in analogue electronics: Threshold concepts as an explanatory model. *European Journal of Engineering Education, 36*(5), 435–447.

Hofer, A., Townsend, R., & Brunetti, K. (2012). Troublesome concepts and information literacy: Investigating threshold concepts for IL instruction. *Portal: Libraries and the Academy, 12*(4), 387–405.

Holloway, M., Alpay, E., & Bull, A. (2010). A quantitative approach to identifying threshold concepts in engineering education. *Engineering Education*, p.11.

Humphrey, R., & Simpson, B. (2012). Writes of passage: Writing up qualitative data as a threshold concept in doctoral research. *Teaching in Higher Education, 17*(6), 735–746.

Irvine, N., & Carmichael, P. (2009). Threshold concepts: A point of focus for practitioner research. *Active Learning in Higher Education, 10*(2), 103–119.

Jordan, K., Tracy, F., & Johnstone, K. (2011). Threshold concepts as focal points for supporting student learning. *Bioscience Education, 18*, p.7.

Kabo, J., & Baillie, C. (2009). Seeing through the lens of social justice: A threshold for engineering. *European Journal of Engineering Education, 34*(4), 317–325.

Kiley, M. (2009). Identifying threshold concepts and proposing strategies to support doctoral candidates. *Innovations in Education and Teaching International, 46*(3), 293–304.

Kiley, M., & Wisker, G. (2009). Threshold concepts in research education and evidence of threshold crossing. *Higher Education Research and Development, 28*(4), 431–441.

Kinchin, I., Cabot, L., Kobus, M., & Woolford (2011). Threshold concepts in dental education. *European Journal of Dental Education, 15*, 210–215.

Korosteleva, E. (2010). Threshold concepts through enactive learning: How effective are they in the study of European politics? *International Studies Perspectives, 11*, 37–50.

Land, R. (2011). There could be trouble ahead: Using threshold concepts as a tool of analysis. *International Journal for Academic Development, 16*(2), 175–178.

Land, R. (2012). Crossing tribal boundaries: Interdisciplinarity as a threshold concept. In P. Trowler, M. Saunders, & V. Bamber (Eds.), *Tribes and territories in the 21st century: Rethinking the significance of disciplines in higher education* (pp. 175–185). London: Routledge.

Land, R., Cousin, G., Meyer, J., & Davies, P. (2005). Threshold concepts and troublesome knowledge (3): Implications for course design and evaluation. In C. Rust (Ed.), *Improving student learning: Diversity and inclusivity*. Oxford: Oxford Centre for Staff and Learning Development.

Land, R., Meyer, J., & Smith, J. (Eds.) (2008). *Threshold concepts within the disciplines*. Rotterdam: Sense.

Long, C. (2009). From whole number to real number: Applying rasch measurement to investigate threshold concepts. *Pythagoras, 70*, 32–42.

Lucas, U., & Mladenovic, R. (2007). The potential of threshold concepts: An emerging framework for educational research and practice. *London Review of Education, 5*(3), 237–248.

MacDougall, M. (2010). Threshold concepts in statistics and online discussion as a basis for curriculum innovation in undergraduate medicine. *MSOR Connections, 10*(3), 21–24, 41.

May, T. (2001). *Social research: Issues, methods and process* (3rd Ed.), Buckingham: Open University Press.

Meyer, J., & Land, R. (2003). *Threshold concepts and troublesome knowledge: Linkages to ways of thinking and practising within the disciplines.* Enhancing Teaching-Learning Environments in Undergraduate Courses, Occasional Report 4, (p. 14). School of Education, University of Edinburgh, Edinburgh.

Meyer, J., & Land, R. (2005). Threshold concepts and troublesome knowledge (2): Epistemological considerations and a conceptual framework for teaching and learning. *Higher Education, 49*(3), 373–388.

Meyer, J., & Land, R. (Eds.) (2006a). *Overcoming barriers to student understanding: Threshold concepts and troublesome knowledge*. London: Routledge.

Meyer, J., & Land, R. (2006b). Threshold concepts and troublesome knowledge: An introduction. In J. Meyer & R. Land (Eds.), *Overcoming barriers to student understanding: Threshold concepts and troublesome knowledge* (pp. 3–18). London: Routledge.

Meyer, J., & Land, R. (2006c). Threshold concepts and troublesome knowledge: Issues of liminality. In J. Meyer & R. Land (Eds.), *Overcoming barriers to student understanding: Threshold concepts and troublesome knowledge* (pp. 19–32). London: Routledge.

Meyer, J., Ward, S., & Latreille, P. (2009). Threshold concepts and metalearning capacity. *International Review of Economics Education, 8*(1), 132–154.

Morgan, H. (2012). The social model of disability as a threshold concept: Troublesome knowledge and liminal spaces in social work education. *Social Work Education, 31*(2), 215–226.

Osmond, J., Bull, K., & Tovey, M. (2009). Threshold concepts and the transport and product design curriculum: Reports of research in progress. *Art, Design and Communication in Higher Education, 8*(2), 169–175.

Perkins, D. (1999). The many faces of constructivism. *Educational Leadership, 57*(3), 6–11.

Pring, R. (2005). *Philosophy of educational research* (2nd ed.), London: Continuum.

Quinlan, K., Male, S., Baillie, C., Stamboulis, A., Fill, J., & Jaffer, Z. (2013). Methodological challenges in researching threshold concepts: A comparative analysis of three projects. *Higher Education* (p. 17). doi:10.1007/s10734-013-9623-y

Rogers, E. (2003). *Diffusion of innovations* (5th Ed.), New York, NY: Free Press.

Rosenblith, W. (1950). Auditory masking and fatigue. *Journal of the Acoustical Society of America*, *22*(6), 792–800.

Ross, P., Taylor, C., Hughes, C., Whitaker, N., Lutze-Mann, L., Kofod, M., & Tzioumis, V. (2010). Threshold concepts in learning biology and evolution. *Biology International*, *47*, 47–54.

Rowbottom, D. (2007). Demystifying threshold concepts. *Journal of Philosophy of Education*, *41*(2), 263–270.

Sandri, O. (2013). Threshold concepts, systems and learning for sustainability. *Environmental Education Research* (p.13). doi:10.1080/13504622.2012.753413

Scheja, M., & Pettersson, K. (2010). Transformation and contextualisation: Conceptualising students' conceptual understanding of threshold concepts in calculus. *Higher Education*, *59*(2), 221–241.

Shanahan, M., Foster, G., & Meyer, J. (2006). Operationalising a threshold concept in economics: A pilot study using multiple choice questions on opportunity cost. *International Review of Economics Education*, *5*(2), 29–57.

Srivastava, S. (2013). Threshold concepts in geographical information systems: A step towards conceptual understanding. *Journal of Geography in Higher Education* (p.18). doi:10.1080/03098265.2013.775569

Stacey, G., & Stickley, T. (2012). Recovery as a threshold concept in mental health nurse education. *Nurse Education Today*, *32*, 534–539.

Tanner, B. (2011). Threshold concepts in practice education: Perceptions of practice educators. *British Journal of Occupational Therapy*, *74*(9), 427–434.

Tight, M. (2002). *Key concepts in adult education and training* (2nd ed.), London: Routledge.

Tight, M. (2004). Higher education research: An atheoretical community of practice? *Higher Education Research and Development*, *23*(4), 395–411.

Tight, M. (2012). *Researching higher education* (2nd ed.), Maidenhead: Open University Press.

Tight, M. (2013). Discipline and methodology in higher education research. *Higher Education Research and Development*, *32*(1), 136–151.

Tight, M. (2014). Discipline and theory in higher education research. *Research Papers in Education*, *29*(1), 93–110

Townsend, L., Brunetti, K., & Hofer, A. (2011). Threshold concepts and information literacy. *Portal: Libraries and the academy*, *11*(3), 853–869.

Trafford, V., & Leshem, S. (2009). Doctorateness as a threshold concept. *Innovations in Education and Teaching International*, *46*(3), 305–316.

Walker, G. (2013). A cognitive approach to threshold concepts. *Higher Education*, *65*(2), 247–263.

Wallace, D. (2010). The grit in the oyster: Does an appreciation of threshold concepts in an adult literacies teaching qualification result in pearls of practice. *Literacy and Numeracy Studies*, *18*(1), 3–18.

Ward, S., & Meyer, J. (2010). Metalearning capacity and threshold concept engagement. *Innovations in Education and Teaching International*, *47*(4), 369–378.

Wimshurst, K. (2011). Applying threshold concepts theory to an unsettled field: An exploratory study in criminal justice education. *Studies in Higher Education*, *36*(3), 301–314.

Wisker, G. (2007). Crossing liminal spaces: Teaching the postcolonial gothic. *Pedagogy: Critical approaches to teaching literature, language, composition and culture*, *7*(3), 401–425.

Wisker, G., & Robinson, G. (2009). Encouraging postgraduate students of literature and art to cross conceptual thresholds. *Innovations in Education and Teaching International, 46*(3), 317–330.

Wisker, G., & Savin-Baden, M. (2009). Priceless conceptual thresholds: Beyond the 'stuck place' in writing. *London Review of Education, 7*(3), 235–247.

Wright, A., & Gilmore, A. (2012). Threshold concepts and conceptions: Student learning in introductory management courses. *Journal of Management Education, 36*(5), 614–635.

Yip, J., & Raelin, J. (2011). Threshold concepts and modalities for teaching leadership practice. *Management Learning, 43*(3), 333–354.

Zepke, N. (2013). Threshold concepts and student engagement: Revisiting pedagogical content knowledge. *Active Learning in Higher Education* (p.11). doi:10.1177/1469787413481127